# Frommer's®

# Cuba
## 3rd Edition

### by Eliot Greenspan

### with Neil E. Schlecht

Here's what the critics say about Frommer's:

"Amazingly easy to use. Very portable, very complete."
—*Booklist*

"Detailed, accurate, and easy-to-read information for all price ranges."
—*Glamour Magazine*

"Hotel information is close to encyclopedic."
—*Des Moines Sunday Register*

"Frommer's Guides have a way of giving you a real feel for a place."
—*Knight Ridder Newspapers*

Wiley Publishing, Inc.

Published by:

## Wiley Publishing, Inc.

111 River St.
Hoboken, NJ 07030-5774

ISBN: 978-0-471-94559-8

Editor: Billy Fox
Production Editor: Eric T. Schroeder
Cartographer: Guy Ruggiero
Photo Editor: Richard Fox
Anniversary Logo Design: Richard Pacifico
Production by Wiley Indianapolis Composition Services

Front cover photo: A bass player in Trinidad
Back cover photo: A family holiday at Varadero

For information on our other products and services or to obtain technical support, please contact our Customer Care Department within the U.S. at 800/762-2974, outside the U.S. at 317/572-3993 or fax 317/572-4002.

Wiley also publishes its books in a variety of electronic formats. Some content that appears in print may not be available in electronic formats.

Manufactured in the United States of America

5   4   3   2   1

# Contents

# List of Maps

## Acknowledgements

Big thanks to Billy Fox, who not only has a deft editorial hand, but is also a composer of and expert on Cuban music. Much of his experience and expertise made its way into this edition.

## An Invitation to the Reader

In researching this book, we discovered many wonderful places—hotels, restaurants, shops, and more. We're sure you'll find others. Please tell us about them, so we can share the information with your fellow travelers in upcoming editions. If you were disappointed with a recommendation, we'd love to know that, too. Please write to:

*Frommer's Cuba,* 3rd Edition
Wiley Publishing, Inc. • 111 River St. • Hoboken, NJ 07030-5774

## An Additional Note

Please be advised that travel information is subject to change at any time—and this is especially true of prices. We therefore suggest that you write or call ahead for confirmation when making your travel plans. The authors, editors, and publisher cannot be held responsible for the experiences of readers while traveling. Your safety is important to us, however, so we encourage you to stay alert and be aware of your surroundings. Keep a close eye on cameras, purses, and wallets, all favorite targets of thieves and pickpockets.

## About the Authors

**Eliot Greenspan** is a poet, journalist, and travel writer who took his backpack and typewriter the length of Mesoamerica before settling in Costa Rica in 1992. Since then, he has worked steadily for the *Tico Times* and other local media. He is also the author of *Frommer's Belize,* *Frommer's Costa Rica,* and *Frommer's Guatemala,* as well as *Costa Rica For Dummies,* and the chapter on Venezuela in *Frommer's South America.*

**Neil E. Schlecht** is the author and co-author of a dozen travel guides (including *Spain For Dummies,* *Frommer's South America,* and *Frommer's Peru*), as well as articles on art and culture and art catalogue essays, and is also a photographer. He now resides in northwestern Connecticut.

## Other Great Guides for Your Trip:

*Frommer's Belize*
*Frommer's Caribbean*
*Frommer's Costa Rica*
*Frommer's Mexico*
*Frommer's Portable Dominican Republic*
*Frommer's South America*

## Frommer's Star Ratings, Icons & Abbreviations

Every hotel, restaurant, and attraction listing in this guide has been ranked for quality, value, service, amenities, and special features using a **star-rating system.** In country, state, and regional guides, we also rate towns and regions to help you narrow down your choices and budget your time accordingly. Hotels and restaurants are rated on a scale of zero (recommended) to three stars (exceptional). Attractions, shopping, nightlife, towns, and regions are rated according to the following scale: zero stars (recommended), one star (highly recommended), two stars (very highly recommended), and three stars (must-see).

In addition to the star-rating system, we also use **seven feature icons** that point you to the great deals, in-the-know advice, and unique experiences that separate travelers from tourists. Throughout the book, look for:

| | |
|---|---|
| *Finds* | Special finds—those places only insiders know about |
| *Fun Fact* | Fun facts—details that make travelers more informed and their trips more fun |
| *Kids* | Best bets for kids and advice for the whole family |
| *Moments* | Special moments—those experiences that memories are made of |
| *Overrated* | Places or experiences not worth your time or money |
| *Tips* | Insider tips—great ways to save time and money |
| *Value* | Great values—where to get the best deals |

The following **abbreviations** are used for credit cards:

| | | | | | |
|---|---|---|---|---|---|
| AE | American Express | DISC | Discover | V | Visa |
| DC | Diners Club | MC | MasterCard | | |

## Frommers.com

Now that you have the guidebook to a great trip, visit our website at **www.frommers.com** for additional travel information on more than 3,500 destinations. We update features regularly to give you instant access to the most current trip-planning information available. At Frommers.com, you'll find scoops on the best airfares, lodging rates, and car rental bargains. You can even book your travel online through our travel booking partners. Other popular features include:

- Online updates to our most popular guidebooks
- Vacation sweepstakes and contest giveaways
- Newsletter highlighting the hottest travel trends
- Online travel message boards with featured travel discussions

# What's New in Cuba

Cuba seems to defy Benjamin Disraeli's famous maxim that "Change is constant." Some things never change in Cuba, including the government, architecture, and the fleet of old American cars. Other things, including the hotel and restaurant scene, change at a dizzying pace. The most important changes and new developments in the tourism field are listed here. For greater detail, see the individual destination chapters.

## CASTRO UPDATE

In July of 2006, Fidel Castro handed off the reins of government for the first time in 47 years. The reins were not passed far. In fact, Fidel turned over the day-to-day chores of governing to his younger brother Raúl, who was already the head of the Cuban armed forces and the head of Cuba's Communist party. As this book goes to press, rumors and conjecture continue to swirl. Castro, who turned 80 on August 13, 2006, underwent surgery for an undisclosed abdominal condition on July 31. Some say he is in the late terminal stages of stomach or intestinal cancer. In recent years, there have been news reports that the charismatic leader had Parkinson's disease, a terminal brain tumor, and any number of other illnesses and ailments. The Cuban government says he is doing fine and will live a long and fruitful life. As of mid-October, 2006, he has not resumed his duties as Cuba's president, and he has been seen very little in public.

News of Castro's illness led to celebrations in the Cuban-exile community of Miami. There literally was dancing in the streets. However, these celebrations have proven to be a bit premature. As exiles, politicians, and pundits discuss the changes that will occur in a post-Castro Cuba, there is little indication of any immediate or imminent changes. While common wisdom states that Raúl Castro lacks the charm, charisma, and love of the people that his older brother commands, the fact is that over the past 47 years, the Castro brothers and the Cuban Communist party have built a massive and enduring system that is unlikely to simply crumble as soon as Fidel Castro dies.

## PLANNING YOUR TRIP

The Cuban government has sought to discourage the use of U.S. dollars in Cuba by placing a 10% surcharge on any official exchange of U.S. dollars to the Cuban convertible peso, or CUC. To avoid this surcharge, it is best to travel with euros or British pounds.

## HAVANA

The **Hotel Saratoga** (© 7/868-1000; www.hotel-saratoga.com) is a stunning and wonderfully executed new luxury hotel in the heart of Habana Vieja.

The **NH Parque Central** (© 7/860-6627; www.nh-hoteles.es) is building an annex of 149 new rooms. The annex adjoins the current structure and will blend in architecturally. Construction of these new rooms is expected to be finished by late 2007.

Although it's by no means new, I just recently discovered the increasingly poorly kept secret dining spot **Los Nardos** (© 7/863-2985), located up a rickety flight of stairs entered through an almost unmarked doorway just across the street from El Capitolio.

## VIÑALES & WESTERN CUBA

Downtown Pinar del Rio finally has a reasonable hotel option. The new **Hotel Vuelta Abajo** (© 82/75-9381; www. islazul.cu) is housed in a wonderfully restored colonial building in the heart of the city's bustling downtown.

There's a new zip-line and harness **Canopy Tour** at the **Las Terrazas** (© 7/204-3739; www.lasterrazas.cu) tourism project.

## VARADERO & MATANZAS PROVINCE

The new luxury resort **Sandals Princesa del Mar** (© 45/66-7200; www.sandals princesadelmar.com) has finally gotten into a groove, after struggling for a couple of years to find a management team.

The venerable **Meliá Las Américas** (© 45/66-7600; www.solmeliacuba. com) has been reserved for adults-only, and converted to an all-inclusive regime. They also have a new sushi restaurant and separate new steakhouse and grill.

The former Maritim Varadero Beach Resort has been taken over by the Cuban Gaviota group and rechristened the **Playa Alameda Varadero** (© 45/66-8822; www.gaviota-grupo.com). It remains one of the most luxurious options in Varadero.

The **Beaches Varadero** was closed for an indefinite period and major remodeling in 2006. It is rumored that the Sandals hotel chain may give up its management contract over this property.

## TRINIDAD & CENTRAL CUBA

In Cienfuegos, the new **Hostal Palacio Azul** (© 432/55-5828; www.hoteles cubanacan.com) is an excellent new budget option overlooking the city's harbor in the desirable Punta Gorda section of town.

Next door to the Palacio Azul, and following an extensive remodeling, the **Club Cienfuegos** (© 432/51-2891) is a wonderful complex featuring a couple of restaurants, a bar, and a small marina.

In the heart of colonial Trinidad, the new **Gran Hotel Iberostar Trinidad** (© 419/6073; www.iberostar.com) has significantly upped the bar for accommodations in this historic old city.

Things are heating up out on the Cayería del Norte, where the new **Occidental Royal Hideaway Ensenachos** (© 7/204-3584; www.occidental-hoteles.com) has opened up with over 500 luxury rooms set just steps away from two of the most beautiful beaches in the country.

A little farther out on the cays, construction is still underway on the **Meliá Las Dunas** (© 42/35-0100; www. solmeliacuba.com), which will add another 900 or so rooms to the region. All three of the Meliá properties share the delightful and luxurious new **Aguas Claras Spa.**

## CAMAGÜEY & THE NORTHEASTERN COAST

In Morón, the former Carrusel Morón hotel is now **Hotel Morón** (© 33/5-2230; www.islazul.cu), having been transferred from the Cubanacán Chain to the Islazul chain.

Out on Cayo Coco, the former El Senador resort has been taken over by the NH hotel group and rechristened **NH Krystal Laguna Villas & Resort** (© 33/30-1470; www.nh-hotels.com). The massive resort is also in the midst of an $8-million makeover.

Also, on Cayo Coco, the new **Acuavida Talasoterapia** (© 33/30-2157) is a large spa facility offering a wide range of spa treatments and services.

## EL ORIENTE

The former Martim Costa Verde Beach Resort is now under management by the Spanish Blau chain, and aside from the minor name change to the **Blau Costa Verde Beach Resort** (© 24/3-0510; www.blau-hotels.com), little else has changed dramatically here.

## SANTIAGO DE CUBA

Right in the heart of downtown Santiago, the **Hostal Basilio** (© 22/65-1702) is an excellent new midrange hotel option.

Just down the road from the Hostal Basilio, the elegant, yet inexpensive, **Santiago 1900** (© 22/62-3507) is a great restaurant choice, with a variety of different rooms, patios, and balcony dining areas to choose from.

While it's been closed for over a year, it's worth checking to see if the **Bello Bar** is open again on the 15th floor of the Meliá Santiago hotel.

# 1

# The Best of Cuba

*by Eliot Greenspan & Neil E. Schlecht*

Cuba is unlike any other place on earth. What draws people to this fascinating Caribbean island is much more than beaches, sun, and cheap drinks, though there are plenty of all three for those who want them. One of the last Communist-bloc nations left, it doesn't suffer from the drab and desultory demeanor of its disappeared peers. Cuba's rich culture, unique political history, and continued survival through ongoing economic hardship make it one of the most eye-opening countries that experienced travelers can still discover. Seeing the best of Cuba means grooving to its intoxicating music, marveling at how Cubans improvise on a daily basis to make ends meet, and visiting a land in which the past 50 years seem to have passed by in some odd sort of state of frozen animation.

## 1 The Best Cuban Travel Experiences

- **Patronizing *Paladares* and *Casas Particulares:*** The best way to appreciate Cubans, as well as to have the opportunity to exchange ideas about Cuba and the outside world, is by stepping inside a *paladar* restaurant or a *casa particular,* the Cuban version of a simple bed-and-breakfast. These private initiatives, heavily taxed by the state, are one of the only ways Cubans have to earn badly needed hard currency, and they offer travelers a rewarding chance to see the country beyond the state-run hotels and restaurants.
- **Exploring la Habana Vieja (Old Havana):** No trip to Cuba is complete without at least a day (or more) spent in Habana Vieja. The streets and alleys of this colonial-era city center have been immaculately restored. You'll feel sucked back in time as you visit the plazas, churches, and forts here. Be sure to take a break from sightseeing and museum hopping to

stock up on souvenirs at the Calle Tacón market, your best one-stop shop in the country for this sort of stuff. See "What to See & Do" in chapter 4.
- **Spending an Afternoon at the Callejón de Hammel:** This short alley is lined with Salvador González's colorful murals and punctuated with scrap sculptures and shrines to Afro-Cuban deities. If you can make it on a Sunday afternoon, you'll be treated to a popular Afro-Cuban dance and music celebration. See "What to See & Do" in chapter 4.
- **Walking along Havana's Malecón:** Your best bet is to start in Habana Vieja and work your way toward the Hotel Nacional in Vedado. Take your time to stop and sit on the sea wall for a spell, and be sure to talk to some of the locals on your way. If you time it right, you will reach the Hotel Nacional in the late afternoon—a good time to grab a cool drink and

enjoy the setting sun from their "Compass Card" outdoor terrace. See "What to See & Do" in chapter 4.

- **Celebrating Las Parrandas:** As the end of the year rolls around, the little colonial town of Remedios gears up to host Las Parrandas, one of Cuba's grandest street parties and religious carnivals. Everything culminates on Christmas Eve in an orgy of drums, floats, and fireworks. See "Santa Clara" in chapter 7.

- **Hopping a Steam Train to the Valley of the Sugar Mills:** The colonial mansions in Trinidad were built with the riches of a booming Cuban sugar trade of the 18th and 19th centuries. The best way to see the Valle de los Ingenios, an extraordinarily lush valley once home to 60 sugar mills, is aboard a vintage 1907 American steam train to one of the sugar estates, Manaca-Iznaga, where you can survey the valley's many shades of green from a fantastic tower. See "Trinidad" in chapter 7.

- **Following in Fidel's Footsteps:** Waging a guerrilla war against the Batista dictatorship, Fidel Castro and his young comrades hid out in the Sierra Maestra mountains in the late 1950s. Their small-scale rebel base camp was never discovered, but visitors today can hike a trail through remote cloud forest up to Comandancia de la Plata, the command post where Fidel turned a country on its head. It's a fascinating glimpse of history from up close. See "Bayamo & the Sierra Maestra" in chapter 9.

- **Joining a Carnival Conga Line:** In the intense heat of summer, Santiago de Cuba explodes with the island's best carnival, an evocative celebration of the city's Afro-Caribbean roots. Ripe with *rumba* music, conga processions, booming percussion, fanciful floats, and wild costumes, it's a participatory party that has nothing to do with those cheesy conga lines people tend to do on cruise ships. See "Carnival & Other Santiago Festivals" in chapter 10.

## 2 The Best Historical Sights

- **Catedral de San Cristóbal** and **Plaza de la Catedral,** Havana (© 7/861-7771): Havana's cathedral and the plaza it sits on are perhaps Old Havana's most distinctive historical sites. The twin towers and worn baroque facade of this ancient church are beautiful both by day and at night. The small plaza it fronts is an atmospheric cobblestone square surrounded by perfectly restored colonial-era buildings with shops, museums, galleries, and restaurants. See p. 107.

- **Museo de la Ciudad,** Havana (© 7/861-6130): Old Havana's preeminent museum displays colonial-era art and artifacts. It's worth the price of admission alone to stroll the rooms, outdoor courtyards, and interior veranda of the former Palacio de los Capitanes Generales (Palace of the Captains Generals), which houses the museum. See p. 107.

- **Parque Histórico Morro y Cabaña,** Havana (© 7/863-7063 for El Morro, and 7/862-0617 for La Cabaña): Across the harbor from Old Havana, the Morro & Cabaña Historic Park complex is comprised of two major forts charged with protecting Havana's narrow and strategic harbor entrance. There's a lighthouse, several museums, restored barracks, batteries of cannons, and a handful of restaurants to explore, and a nightly *cañonazo* (cannon blast) ceremony is held here. See p. 114.

- **Cementerio de Colón,** Havana (℡ **7/832-1050**): Columbus Cemetery is an impressive collection of mausoleums, crypts, family chapels and vaults, soaring sculptures, and ornate gravestones. All of the dead are laid to rest above ground, and you'll be awed by the surfeit of marble and sun-bleached alabaster. The whole thing is laid out in an orderly grid of streets. See p. 112.

- **Monumento Ernesto Che Guevara,** Santa Clara (℡ **42/20-5878**): Featuring a huge sculpture of the revolutionary hero overlooking a vast plaza, this place is deeply revered by Cubans. Underneath the statue is a museum with exhibits detailing the life and exploits of "El Che," as well as a mausoleum holding Guevara's remains and the tombstones of 37 other revolutionary fighters killed with Guevara in Bolivia. See "Santa Clara" in chapter 7.

- **Trinidad:** The entire town of Trinidad qualifies as a historical site. The impeccably preserved relic—several blocks square of perfect pastel-colored mansions, churches, and cobblestone streets—is one of the greatest collections of colonial architecture to be found anywhere in the Americas. The star among Trinidad's colonial set pieces is the **Museo Romántico** (℡ **419/4363**), in an 18th-century mansion right on the main square. See "Trinidad" in chapter 7.

- **Plaza San Juan de Dios,** Camagüey (℡ **32/29-1318**): This dignified square is the highlight of Camagüey's colonial quarter, one of the largest in Cuba with more than a dozen 16th-, 17th-, and 18th-century colonial churches. Marked by cobblestones and colonial houses with red-tile roofs and iron window grilles, the understated plaza is home to a 17th-century baroque church and hospital of the order of San Juan de Dios. See p. 220.

- **Museo El Chorro de Maíta,** Guardalavaca (℡ **24/3-0421**): Guardalavaca is in the midst of the most important archaeological zone of Native American groups in Cuba. This small museum site is a Taíno burial ground from the late 15th and early 16th centuries, the biggest and finest American Indian cemetery discovered in Cuba. The very well-preserved remains of more than 100 members of the community reveal important clues about native groups after the arrival of the Spanish conquistadors. The museum displays ceramics and objects found at the site. See "Guardalavaca" in chapter 9.

- **Casa Velázquez (Museo de Ambiente Colonial Cubano),** Santiago de Cuba (℡ **22/65-2652**): Diego Velázquez founded the original seven *villas* in Cuba, and his 1515 mansion in Santiago de Cuba, the oldest house in the country and one of the oldest in the Americas, is still standing. Today it's a museum of colonial furnishings from the 16th to the 19th century. Individual pieces are splendid, but none manages to upstage the historical impact of the restored house itself. See p. 263.

- **Castillo El Morro,** Santiago de Cuba (℡ **22/69-1569**): Although nowhere near as expansive as its sister fort in Havana, this massive fortress is nonetheless quite impressive. You can almost feel a part of the history while walking the maze-like alleyways here, and the views are wonderful as well. See p. 263.

## 3 The Best of Natural Cuba

- **The Viñales Valley:** This broad, flat valley is punctuated by a series of limestone karst hill formations, or *mogotes*. The views from the small mountains surrounding the valley are spectacular. The area offers great opportunities for hiking, mountain biking, bird-watching, and rock climbing, as well as caves to explore. See "Viñales" in chapter 5.

- **Las Terrazas:** This planned eco-tourism project is set amid the Sierra del Rosario Biosphere Reserve. There are a host of trails and attractions here, including lakes, swimming holes, a zip-line canopy tour, and even some sulfur springs. The bird-watching is excellent. See "Sierra del Rosario Biosphere Reserve & San Diego de los Baños" in chapter 5.

- **Parque Nacional Ciénaga de Zapata:** The Zapata Swamp National Park is a massive expanse of mangroves, swamp, and wetlands housing an abundant variety of flora and fauna. The area is a mecca for bird-watchers, naturalists, and anglers. Your best bet for exploring the park is Playa Larga, a simple beach resort area catering to scuba divers. See "The Zapata Peninsula & Playa Girón" in chapter 6.

- **Parque Nacional Topes de Collantes:** The dense pine-covered mountains of the Sierra del Escambray lurk on the outskirts of Trinidad, and the Topes de Collantes National Park is a lovely, cool refuge from the town's stone streets. It's great for hiking, with several well-established trails, the best of which culminate in refreshing waterfalls. See "Trinidad" in chapter 7.

- **Baracoa:** Cuba's first settlement, overlooking a beautiful oyster-shaped bay, remains a natural paradise, with thick tropical vegetation, 10 rivers, and a distinctive flat-topped mountain called El Yunque, a UNESCO Biosphere Reserve that beckons hikers. Travelers into rafting, beaches, and boating will also find ample opportunities to explore this isolated area. See "Baracoa" in chapter 9.

- **Sierra Maestra:** The highest and longest mountain range in Cuba, the Sierra Maestra is full of lore for Cubans—it's where Fidel Castro and his band of rebels hid out and waged guerilla warfare against the Batista government in the 1950s. Stretching across three provinces, its peaks are almost on top of the rocky southern coastline. The Gran Parque Nacional Sierra Maestra and Parque Nacional de Turquino are perfect for hikers and nature lovers. See "Bayamo & the Sierra Maestra" in chapter 9.

## 4 The Best Outdoor Adventures

- **Landing a Marlin or Sailfish:** If you really want to emulate Ernest Hemingway, you'll head out to sea to fish. The waters off Cuba's coast are excellent for sport fishing year-round. Big game fish are best sought off the northern coast, while bonefish and tarpon are better stalked off the southern coast. **Marinas Puertosol** (www.cubanacan.cu) runs a string of marinas with modern, well-equipped sport-fishing fleets all around Cuba's coastline.

- **Rock Climbing the *Mogotes* of the Viñales Valley:** Although in its infancy, this is a rapidly developing sport in Cuba, and this area is the place to come and climb. Over 60 routes and 100 pitches have been marked and climbed, and more climbs are constantly being uncovered. See "Viñales" in chapter 5.

- **Scuba Diving at María la Gorda:** Cuba has many excellent dive destinations, but María la Gorda probably edges out the rest by offering consistently excellent conditions, a variety of sites, an amazing setting, and an excellent dive operation. However, there's excellent diving off of much of Cuba's coast, and if you want to combine diving with other attractions you can do so from just about any destination on the island. See "María la Gorda" in chapter 5.

- **Bird-Watching in the Zapata Peninsula:** A dedicated (and lucky) bird-watcher might be able to spot 18 of Cuba's 24 endemic species in the swamps, mangroves, and wetlands of the Zapata Peninsula. In addition to the endemics, ornithologists and lay bird-watchers can spot over 100 other varieties of shore birds, transients, and waterfowl in this rich, wild region. See "The Zapata Peninsula & Playa Girón" in chapter 6. Other top bird-watching destinations include **La Güira National Park** (see chapter 5), as well as the areas around Cayo Coco and Cayo Guillermo (see chapter 8) and Baracoa (see chapter 9).

- **Hiking and Rafting in Baracoa:** Baracoa, long isolated by impenetrable tropical vegetation, steep mountains, and rushing rivers, is an adventurer's dream. El Yunque, a curiously flat-topped limestone mountain, is home to dozens of bird species, orchids, and unique tropical plants and forest; it's also great for climbing. The Río Toa, the widest river in Cuba, is one of the few spots in Cuba for white-water rafting. See "Baracoa" in chapter 9.

- **Hiking Pico Turquino:** Pico Turquino, tucked within the celebrated Sierra Maestra National Park, is the highest peak in Cuba at just under 2,000m (6,560 ft.). The trail to the summit is swathed in cloud forest and tropical flora. Mountaineers in good physical condition can do the 15km (9-mile) round-trip journey in a day, but most camp overnight below the summit. The panoramic views of the coast and Caribbean Sea are breathtaking. See "Bayamo & the Sierra Maestra" in chapter 9.

## 5 The Best Beaches

- **Playa Paraíso** and **Playa Sirena:** These two connected beaches are the most outstanding of the uniformly spectacular beaches that stretch the length of Cayo Largo del Sur. Located on the more protected western end of the island, these two beaches are broad expanses of glistening, fine white sand, bordering the clear Caribbean Sea. There's a simple beachside restaurant on Playa Paraíso, and not much else here—and that's a large part of their charm. See "Cayo Largo del Sur" in chapter 5.

- **Varadero:** This is Cuba's premier beach resort destination, and it ranks right up there with the best in the Caribbean. We personally prefer some of the island's less developed stretches of sand. But if you're looking for a well-run all-inclusive resort loaded with amenities and activity options, Varadero is a good choice. Oh yeah, the 21km (13 miles) of nearly uninterrupted beach here are fabulous. See "Varadero" in chapter 6.

- **Playa Ensenachos** and **Playa Megano:** Located on the tiny islet of

Cayo Ensenachos, which is part of la Cayería del Norte, these protected crescents of sand drop off very gently, allowing bathers to wade 90m (300 feet) or more out into the calm, crystal clear waters. You'll have to shell out big bucks to visit these beaches, either staying at the **Occidental Royal Hideaway Ensenachos** or paying their hefty day-use fee. Both of these beaches are jaw-droppingly beautiful, but we slightly prefer Playa Megano. See "Santa Clara" in chapter 7.

- **Playa Ancón:** A wonderful white-sand beach and close runner-up to the more spectacular beaches of Cuba, attractive Ancón has one huge advantage: It's just minutes from one of the country's true treasures, Trinidad, and perfectly positioned for those who'd like a bit of colonial culture with their sun and sand (or vice versa). With good diving and one very nice resort hotel, it's sure to be built up soon. See "Trinidad" in chapter 7.

- **Cayos Coco** and **Guillermo:** These tiny cays off the north coast, separated from the Cuban mainland by a long man-made causeway, are tantalizingly tucked into shallow waters that flow into the Atlantic. There's barely a sign of the "real Cuba," but what you do get is stunningly unspoiled beaches, excellent diving, and a full contingent of watersports. See "Cayo Coco & Cayo Guillermo" in chapter 8.

- **Cayo Sabinal:** If it's seclusion and pristine nature you're after, find your way to this small cay on the northeastern coast. It has brilliant beaches protected by stunning coral reefs and almost no facilities to speak of. With its rich flora and fauna, Cayo Sabinal is an eco-tourist's dreamland. See "Camagüey" in chapter 8.

- **Guardalavaca:** Probably Cuba's prettiest resort area, Guardalavaca is a hot spot, but not overheated like Varadero. The area, a prime archaeological zone of pre-Columbian Cuba, is one of lush tropical vegetation, brilliant white sands, and clear turquoise waters. Long stretches of coastline are interrupted by charming little cove beaches, and some of Cuba's finest resort hotels are here. See "Guardalavaca" in chapter 9.

## 6 The Best Resort Hotels

- **Paradisus Varadero,** Varadero (⟨℗ 45/66-8700)**: This is the Sol Meliá's fanciest resort hotel in Varadero, with expansive grounds, a huge free-form pool, and all the activities and amenities you could hope for. There's a variety of dining options, and overall, they manage to create the feel of an intimate, romantic getaway better than any of the other large resort hotels in Varadero. See p. 161.

- **Tryp Península Varadero,** Varadero (℗ 45/66-8800): This is my top choice for a family resort in Varadero and an excellent all-around resort in its own right. The setting, facilities, and service are all tops, and the rooms are quite spacious and well equipped. The children's pools and play area are the best in Cuba. See p. 163.

- **Meliá Cayo Santa María,** Cayo Santa María (℗ 42/35-0500): This new resort is yet another of the Sol Meliá's excellent all-inclusive properties. This one is located on a very beautiful and very isolated patch of beach in la Cayería del Norte. The facilities are certainly top-notch, and the setting is just spectacular. See p. 177.

- **Brisas Trinidad del Mar,** Península Ancón, Trinidad (℗ 419/6500): This resort hotel on Playa Ancón has excellent sea and mountain views and is only minutes from the most beautiful colonial city in Cuba. The well-conceived design echoes the handsome architecture of Trinidad. See p. 193.

- **Meliá Cayo Coco,** Cayo Coco (© **33/30-1180**): Of the several fine hotels on Cayo Coco, Sol Meliá's top property on the cays is the most sophisticated and stylish, with cool bungalows overlooking a natural lagoon, elegant decor throughout, good restaurants, a beautiful pool area, and a great stretch of beach on a natural cove. See p. 211.

- **Sol Cayo Guillermo,** Cayo Guillermo (© **33/30-1760**): Relaxed and unpretentious, this lively resort hotel is less staid and pre-packaged than many of the big hotels on the cays. The cheery

bungalow-style rooms are perfect for a younger crowd. See p. 212.

- **Paradisus Río de Oro,** Playa Esmeralda (© **24/3-0090**). Perhaps Cuba's most sybaritic all-inclusive resort hotel, this sprawling Sol Meliá property hugs a rocky cliff and is distinguished by some of the most luxuriously designed grounds you'll find anywhere. Rooms are large, refined, and private. Sunbathers will have a hard time deciding between the terrific main beach, the nearly private small cove beaches, and the extraordinary pool area. Not to mention the massage hut that hangs out from the cliff over the sea. See p. 233.

## 7 The Best Hotels

- **Hotel Florida,** Havana (© **7/862-4127**): This is probably my favorite of the Habaguanex properties in Old Havana. The building features a wonderful open-air central courtyard, checkerboard marble floors, and oodles of colonial-era charm. The whole operation is elegant and refined, and located right on the pulse of things on busy Calle Obispo. See p. 86.

- **Hotel Saratoga,** Havana (© **7/868-1000**): Set right on the Paseo del Prado, with stunning views of El Capitolio from many of its rooms, this new hotel has the most comfortable and luxurious rooms of any hotel in or near Habana Vieja. Add to that a wonderful rooftop pool and bar, and this hotel is clearly one of the top choices in the city. See p. 87.

- **Meliá Cohiba,** Havana (© **7/833-3636**): Towering over the Malecón, this modern high-rise hotel offers excellent comfort, service, and amenities. Most of the rooms have fantastic views of the sea. The hotel is close to all of the action and attractions

Havana has to offer, and has plenty of restaurants, bars, and clubs of its own, including the very popular Habana Café. See p. 91.

- **Hotel Los Jazmines,** Viñales (© **8/79-6205**): With a spectacular setting on a hillside overlooking the Viñales Valley, this is hands down the best option in town. If you land one of the third-floor rooms with a balcony, you'll forgive the somewhat smallish rooms and minimal amenities. Los Jazmines makes a great base for exploring this region. See p. 134.

- **Gran Hotel Iberostar Trinidad,** Trinidad (© **419/6073**): This new hotel has seriously upped the bar in terms of comfort and luxury in Trinidad. Set fronting a quiet little park in the heart of downtown, this is clearly the top high-end choice in Trinidad. See p. 191.

- **Hotel La Unión,** Cienfuegos (© **432/55-1020**): Housed in a marvelously restored colonial mansion right in the heart of downtown Cienfuegos, this is one of the nicest boutique hotels in the country. With a couple of interior courtyards, neo-classical furnishings, and architectural touches, La Unión captures the elegance and charm of Cuba's bygone era. It's worth the small splurge for one of the spacious junior suites. See p. 183.

- **Hostal del Rijo,** Sancti Spíritus (© 41/2-8588): The concept of small boutique hotels with historic character is catching on in Cuba, and this boutique hotel in unassuming Sancti Spíritus is among the best of its kind in the country. In a beautifully restored colonial mansion, it has massive rooms with restrained decor, and it just might rank as the best hotel bargain in Cuba. See p. 202.

- **Gran Hotel,** Camagüey (© 32/29-2093): In the heart of Camagüey's colonial quarter, this 1930s hotel has real old-world character, a selection of atmospheric bars, and a terrace pool. The Gran Hotel offers tons of style at a bargain price—especially if you get one of the spacious corner rooms. See p. 221.

- **Hotel Colón,** Camagüey (© 32/28-3346): A stylish 1920s midsize hotel with newly restored historical touches, the charming Colón has a beautiful antique dark-wood lobby bar, a pretty interior patio, and very nicely appointed rooms, all for little more than a *casa particular.* See p. 222.

- **Hotel El Castillo,** Baracoa (© 21/4-5195): This hotel has history, charm, and a location to die for. Inside the walls of one of the town's oldest fortresses, up on a hill where the pool comes with splendid panoramic views of Baracoa and the bay, this is the kind of place you won't want to leave. Relaxed and unpretentious, it suits Baracoa perfectly. See p. 252.

- **Hotel Casa Granda,** Santiago de Cuba (© 22/65-3021): It's not Santiago's biggest or most expensive hotel, but the Casa Granda, in an elegant landmark building on Parque Céspedes in the heart of the city, is the place to stay if you want to be in the heady mix that is the Oriente region's capital. Renovation has dramatically improved the rooms, and the terrific terrace bars are among the best people-watching places in the city. See p. 268.

## 8 The Best Casas Particulares

- **Casa Particular Sandelis** ✴, Havana (© 7/832-4422): Located just across from the Hotel Nacional, this is practically the most prestigious address in Vedado—at a fraction of the cost. The hosts are helpful and friendly, and you even get an ocean view from the apartment's sixth-floor terrace. See p. 94.

- **Casa Ana María,** Cienfuegos (© 432/51-3269): Located right on the water, you get bay views from each of the two rooms here, and there's also a wonderful shared courtyard which opens to the water. The home is a charming, colonial-era fixer-upper, but don't worry, you'll be pampered here and not pressed into service. See p. 184.

- **Hostal Casa Múñoz,** Trinidad (© 419/3673): Historic Trinidad is well-stocked with beautiful colonial houses renting out rooms, but this one is distinguished not only by its impressive rooms and ever-expanding facilities, but also its gregarious and informative host, a photographer who knows Trinidad like the back of his hand. See p. 193.

- **La Pantera,** Sancti Spíritus (© 41/2-5435): A handsome early-19th-century house with marble pillars and high ceilings, this breezy private homestay has large rooms, very friendly live-in owners, and good, filling meals. See p. 203.

- **Casa Xiomara & Rodolfo,** Camagüey (© **32/28-1948**): Like having your own house in Camagüey, this huge and very well-maintained apartment offers a full kitchen, dining room, TV room, and a backyard terrace—and total privacy. It's considerably bigger and better equipped than most hotel rooms in Cuba. See p. 221.

- **Casa La Colina,** Baracoa (© **21/4-3477**): One of the things that makes Baracoa so extraordinary is its spectacular natural setting, and this handsome house has a fantastic terrace with panoramic views of the entire town and the bay leading out to the sea. The rooms are large and comfortable, and your host is a charm. See p. 253.

- **Casa Hugo & Adela,** Santiago de Cuba (© **22/62-6359**): Most of Santiago's best casas are in the leafy outer neighborhoods, but if you want to be in the thick of Santiago, with a comfortable room and a huge private rooftop terrace overlooking the old city and harbor, grab this room. See p. 268.

- **Casa Asensio,** Santiago de Cuba (© **22/62-4600**): Facility-wise, this house may be unrivaled in Cuba. It's a very large apartment with its own kitchen and a massive, private rooftop terrace. It's perfect for anyone planning to stay a while to explore Santiago de Cuba and the surrounding area in depth. See p. 270.

## 9 The Best Restaurants & Paladares

- **Café del Oriente,** Havana (© **7/860-6686**): Arguably the most elegant restaurant and cafe in Habana Vieja, this place serves well-prepared and creative international fare in a beautiful room just off the Plaza San Francisco. When the weather is nice, you can even sit at an outdoor table right on the plaza. See p. 99.

- **La Bodeguita del Medio,** Havana (© **7/867-1374**): This classic joint is a must for any visitor to Cuba. The *criolla* cuisine is excellently prepared, and it's an understatement to say the ambience is lively. Go ahead and have a mojito, but get one made with *añejo* rum. See p. 99.

- **La Guarida,** Havana (© **7/862-4940**): Atmosphere, fame, good food, and good times all combine in equal measure at perhaps the most famous paladar in Cuba. The walk up the rickety steps to this third-floor private restaurant is an experience in itself. See p. 102.

- **Roof Garden Restaurant,** Havana (© **7/860-8560**): The creative French-inspired menu and stunning setting make this probably the best high-end dining option in Havana. Try for a window table on the elevated area ringing the restaurant. See p. 100.

- **La Cocina de Lilliam,** Havana (© **7/209-6514**): Lilliam Domínguez has raised the bar for paladares around Havana. Her delicious *criolla* cooking always makes the most of whatever ingredients are locally available, and her softly lit garden setting is stunning. See p. 104.

- **La Fonda de Mercedes,** Las Terrazas (© **8/77-8647**): Working out of her apartment's simple kitchen, Doña Mercedes Dache serves up wonderfully prepared *criolla* cuisine. Meals are served on large tables in an open-air terrace overlooking a mountain lake. If you come to Las Terrazas, don't leave without eating here. See p. 138.

- **Paladar Estela,** Trinidad (© **419/ 4329**): A colonial house with a pretty garden patio dining area, this private home restaurant in the heart of the historic quarter of Trinidad serves epic proportions of well-prepared Cuban specialties. The friendly owners also rent a room. See p. 194.

- **La Campana de Toledo,** Camagüey (© **32/29-5888**): Located on one of the most authentic and elegant colonial squares in Cuba, this handsome, rustic restaurant with a pretty patio is a great spot for a midday break from the heat or a relaxed dinner. Dishes are more imaginative than the basic Cuban fare at most state-run establishments. See p. 223.

- **La Colonial,** Baracoa (© **21/4-5391**): The government seems to support the competition of private restaurants only nominally, and this is the last surviving paladar in Baracoa. The nicely decorated colonial house easily outclasses the state-run options in town, and it has good

service and a changing menu with several fresh fish dishes. See p. 254.

- **Restaurant El Morro,** Santiago de Cuba (© **22/68-7151**): Perched along the cliff next to the El Morro fortress, with spectacular views of the Caribbean, this popular open-air restaurant is a good-value lunch spot. There are plenty of fish dishes and a fixed-price midday deal, all served under a canopy of hanging plants that helps patrons beat the heat. See p. 272.

- **ZunZún,** Santiago de Cuba (© **22/ 64-1528**): One of the few upscale dining experiences in eastern Cuba, this elegant restaurant has several small, private dining rooms scattered throughout a large 1940s house in one of Santiago de Cuba's most pleasant suburbs. Attention to detail and presentation—dining elements seldom given much thought in Cuba—are a welcome surprise. It's best known for its top-quality seafood. See p. 271.

## 10 The Best of Cuban Nightlife

- **Tropicana,** Havana (© **7/267-1010**): This is the original and still reigning cabaret show in Cuba. The Tropicana has been at it for over 60 years and it shows no signs of slowing down. The sea of lithe dancers, the exuberance of their costumes, and the sheer excess of it all is worth the trip. It all occurs under the stars in the shadow of tall overhanging trees. There's a second Tropicana in Matanzas for visitors to Varadero, and another in Santiago. See p. 123.

- **El Gato Tuerto,** Havana (© **7/55-2696**): The mood is dark and bohemian, although the decor mixes Art Deco and kitsch in equal measure. The nightly show usually features three or four distinct acts,

which can range from sultry boleros to up-tempo jazz. A storyteller, poet, or comedian might perform between sets. See p. 124.

- **La Zorra y El Cuervo,** Havana (© **7/833-2402**): This is Havana's best jazz club, and that's saying a lot. The vibe is mellow and unpretentious in this compact basement club, but the music and acts are usually culled from the best Cuba has to offer. See p. 124.

- **Habana Café,** Havana (© **7/833-3636,** ext 2630) and Varadero (© **45/ 66-8070**): Mix the Tropicana with a Hard Rock Cafe, and Habana Café is more or less what you'd get. The floor show is a mix of cabaret-style dance numbers and slightly burlesque comedic bits, all anchored by a top-notch big band. After the show, the dance floor swings and writhes for hours. See p. 123 and 165.

- **Discoteca Las Cuevas,** north of Viñales (© **8/79-6290**): With a good sound system and lights bouncing off the stalactites, this is by far the best party spot in the Viñales Valley. See "Viñales" in chapter 5.

- **Trinidad:** Trinidad's popularity has ensured a steady menu of live-music offerings. Cuban bands play under the stars on the steps of the **Casa de la Música** until more energetic dancing and music get underway inside. The local **Casa de la Trova** also has a nightly roster of traditional Cuban bands, and even small, relaxed spots like the patio bars **La Canchánchara** and **Ruinas de Segarte** feature live *son.* If that's too traditional, then check out **La Cueva,** a funky dance club in a cave. See "Trinidad" in chapter 7.

- **Casa de la Trova,** Camagüey and Santiago de Cuba: Perhaps the country's two best Casas de la Trova, the traditional Cuban live-music spots, are in Camagüey and Santiago de Cuba. Camagüey's Casa is agreeably low-key, while Santiago's is legendary, having given birth to dozens of Cuba's most respected musicians and bands. Both are great places to mix with locals, try out some dance moves, and sip a mojito. See "Camagüey" in chapter 8 and p. 224 in chapter 10.

- **Calle Antonio Maceo,** Baracoa: Tiny Baracoa rocks at night with its own little version of Bourbon Street. People spill out of a half-dozen cafes, bars, and live-music venues, shifting gears from traditional *trova* to *son* and dance music to full-throttle dance club. Amiable emcees entertain audiences with romantic poetry and humor. See "Baracoa" in chapter 9.

## 11 The Best of Cuba Online

- **http://lanic.utexas.edu/la/cb/cuba**: Hosted by the University of Texas Latin American Studies Department, this site houses a vast collection of information about Cuba. This is hands down the best one-stop shop for Web browsing.

- **www.cubanacan.cu**: Cubanacán is probably the largest state-run tourism company, with hotels, transportation, and receptive tourism arms. They also have the best developed website of the handful of state-run agencies, although that's not necessarily saying much.

- **www.cubasi.cu**: CubaSi is the best of the state-sponsored, all-purpose

information sites on Cuba. It's got an English-language mirror of the principal site, as well as a good search engine and easy links to an online version of the Cuban telephone book.

- **www.casaparticular.info**: We find this the best of the clearinghouse sites for casas particulares. It has lots of links to casas in the main tourist destinations around Cuba.

- **www.cubamania.com**: This site is a lively, sometimes conflictive and controversial, forum site for all things Cuba. But there's plenty of good information to be had here.

# 2

# Planning Your Trip to Cuba

*by Eliot Greenspan*

**C**uba is probably the most intensely diverse island destination in the Caribbean, offering everything from standard fun-in-the-sun beach resort getaways to colonial city circuits, myriad land and sea adventure opportunities, tobacco and classic-car theme tours, and a wide array of cultural and artistic opportunities. There's a lot to see and do in Cuba, and most travelers will have to carefully pick and choose. This chapter will provide you with the necessary information and guidance to help you plan your perfect trip to Cuba.

## 1 The Regions in Brief

Cuba is the westernmost and largest of the entire chain of Caribbean islands, located at the convergence of the Caribbean Sea, the Gulf of Mexico, and the Atlantic Ocean just 145km (90 miles) south of Florida. They say that Cuba—if you use your imagination—looks something like a crocodile: The head is in the east, a line of small islands form the ridges along its back, the Sierra Maestra national park forms the front legs, the Zapata Peninsula forms the rear legs, and Pinar del Río province is the tail. Cuba is in fact a closely linked string of archipelagos, made up of over 4,000 separate little islands and cays.

Cuba's two major cities, Havana and Santiago de Cuba, are port cities with large protected harbors. Most of the island's other principal cities lie along its centerline, either right on or just off the Autopista Nacional (National Hwy.), the country's principal trade and transportation route.

**HAVANA & PLAYAS DEL ESTE** **Havana** is Cuba's capital and the country's most important cultural, political, and economic hub. With a wealth of museums, antique buildings, old forts, the Malecón seaside promenade, and modern restaurants, clubs, and cabarets, Havana is one of the liveliest and most engaging cities in Latin America. Just east of the city center are some 15km (10 miles) of very respectable white-sand beach, the **Playas del Este.** While nowhere near as stunning as some of Cuba's more celebrated beach destinations, the Playas del Este are certainly a suitable alternative, either as a base for exploring Havana or as an easily accessible place for some sun, sand, and sea.

**VIÑALES & WESTERN CUBA** Comprising the province of Pinar del Río, western Cuba is a wonderfully rustic region of farms and forests, flanked by some beautiful and relatively underpopulated beaches. The only real city in the province, **Pinar del Río,** is of limited interest on its own, but it serves as a gateway to **Viñales** and the **Vuelta Abajo,** Cuba's premiere tobacco-growing and cigar-manufacturing region. Just north of Pinar del Río, Viñales is a pretty little hamlet in an even prettier valley, surrounded by stunning karst hill formations. Viñales is Cuba's prime

# The Regions in Brief

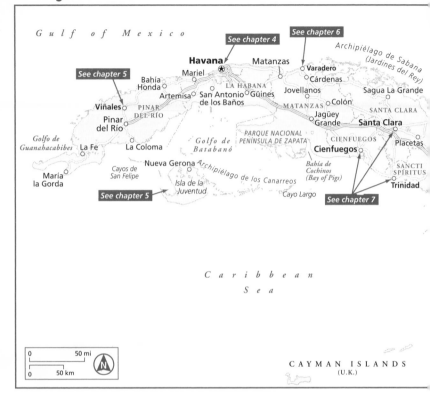

*Gulf of Mexico*

See chapter 4

See chapter 6

Archipiélago de Sabana (Jardines del Rey)

**Havana**    Matanzas    Varadero
Mariel                    Cárdenas
See chapter 5    Bahía    LA HABANA    Jovellanos    Sagua La Grande
Honda    Artemisa  San Antonio Güines    MATANZAS  Colón    SANTA CLARA
Viñales    PINAR    de los Baños    Jagüey    **Santa Clara**
Pinar    DEL RÍO    Grande
del Río            PARQUE NACIONAL    CIENFUEGOS    Placetas
*Golfo de*    *Golfo de*  PENÍNSULA DE ZAPATA
*Guanahacabibes*  La Fe    La Coloma    *Batabanó*    **Cienfuegos**
                                            SANCTI
                    Nueva Gerona            *Bahía de*    SPÍRITUS
María    Cayos de    Archipiélago de los Canarreos    *Cochinos*
la Gorda    San Felipe    Isla de la    *(Bay of Pigs)*    **Trinidad**
                    Juventud
See chapter 5            Cayo Largo    See chapter 7

*C a r i b b e a n*
*S e a*

0        50 mi
0      50 km    N

CAYMAN ISLANDS
(U.K.)

eco-tourist destination, with great opportunities for hiking, bird-watching, mountain biking, and cave exploration. On the far western tip of the island sits the tiny resort of **María la Gorda,** arguably home to the best of Cuba's overall excellent scuba diving. Lying off the southern coast of this region in the Caribbean Sea are the island destinations of **Isla de la Juventud,** yet another of Cuba's premiere scuba diving destinations, and **Cayo Largo del Sur,** another long stretch of dazzling and isolated white sand.

**VARADERO & MATANZAS PROVINCE**    Matanzas is Cuba's second-largest province and home to its most important beach destination, **Varadero.** Boasting some 21km (13 miles) of nearly uninterrupted white-sand beach, Varadero is Cuba's quintessential sun-and-fun destination, with a host of luxurious all-inclusive resorts strung along the length of this narrow peninsula. In addition to Varadero, Matanzas province is home to the beautiful colonial-era cities of **Matanzas** and **Cárdenas.**

In the southern section of the province is the **Ciénaga de Zapata,** a vast wetlands area of mangrove and swamp, renowned for its wildlife viewing, bird-watching, and fishing opportunities. This is also where you'll find the **Bahía de Cochinos (Bay of Pigs),** where the nascent Cuban

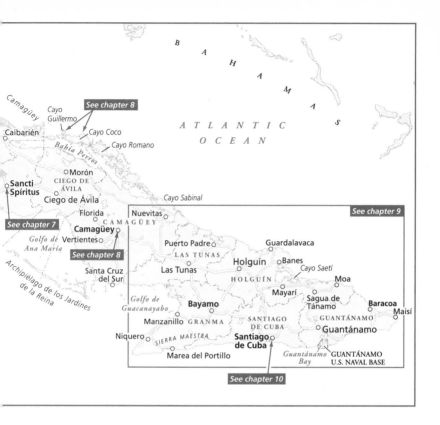

revolutionary state defeated an invasion force trained, supplied, and abetted by the United States. The beaches of **Playa Girón** and **Playa Larga** serve as a base for access to some of Cuba's best scuba diving.

**TRINIDAD & CENTRAL CUBA** Beginning with the provinces of Villa Clara and Cienfuegos, and including the neighboring province of Sancti Spíritus, central Cuba is the start of the country's rural heartland. Vast regions of sugar cane, tobacco, and cattle ranges spread out on either side of the Autopista Nacional, which more or less bisects this region as it heads east.

Trinidad is perhaps Cuba's quintessential colonial-era gem, with beautifully maintained and restored buildings set on winding cobblestone streets. The cities of **Santa Clara, Cienfuegos,** and **Sancti Spíritus** are considered lesser lights on the tourism circuit, but all offer ample charms in their own rights. Santa Clara is a lively university town, and is considered the "City of Che Guevara," with its massive memorial to the fallen revolutionary leader. To the north of Santa Clara lie the tiny colonial city of **Remedios** and the up-and-coming beach resorts of **la Cayería del Norte.** Cienfuegos is a charming port town with the country's second-longest seaside promenade. Sancti Spíritus is one of the original seven *villas* of Cuba, with some wonderful old historic churches and buildings, and a more natural feel than you'll find in other more touristy towns.

**CAMAGÜEY & NORTHEASTERN CUBA** This section of mainland Cuba is little more than a string of rural towns and small cities, anchored by two colonial-era cities. This is Cuba at its quietest, stuck in time and in no rush to break free. However, off the northern coast here lie a series of modern beach resorts built on long stretches of soft and silvery white sand, connected to the mainland by a long narrow causeway that seems to barely skirt the surface of the sea. The sister resort islands of **Cayo Coco** and **Cayo Guillermo** are two of the finest and most popular resort destinations in Cuba. Several lesser developed beach resorts stretch east along the coast on the string of islands making up the Archipiélago de Camagüey, better known as the Jardines del Rey (King's Gardens). The cities of **Ciego de Avila** and **Camagüey** are seldom explored colonial-era cities. The latter, in particular, has loads of charms and attractions, and is being restored to highlight much of its former glory.

**EL ORIENTE** For most of the country's history, the whole eastern end of Cuba was known as El Oriente. Today, it is comprised of four separate provinces: Holguín, Granma, Santiago de Cuba, and Guantánamo. This is a large region with a host of gorgeous natural attractions, highlighted by the mountains of the **Sierra Maestra,** a mecca for naturalists and adventure travelers as well as those looking to follow in the revolutionary footsteps of Fidel and Che, and the beautiful beaches of **Guardalavaca,** yet another of Cuba's premier beach resort destinations, with unimaginably fine white sand and calm turquoise waters. Of the cities here, only Santiago de Cuba is a tourist draw in its own right, although visitors to **Holguín, Bayamo,** or **Baracoa** will experience Cuba at its most authentic.

**SANTIAGO DE CUBA** This is Cuba's second city. Set between the Sierra Maestra mountains and the sea, Santiago is a beautiful and vibrant city with a rich artistic and cultural heritage. Santiago is considered the heart of Cuba's Afro-Cuban and Afro-Caribbean heritage, which is expressed in the music, dance, and religion you'll find here. Santiago's Carnival celebrations are by far the best in Cuba, and some of the best in the entire Caribbean.

The city itself has a beautiful colonial-era center and a host of interesting museums and attractions, including José Martí's tomb and mausoleum, the original Bacardí rum factory, and the impressive Castillo del Morro protecting the city's harbor. Nearby sites worth visiting include the El Cobre shrine to the island's patron saint, La Virgin de Caridad, and the Gran Piedra, a massive rock outcropping offering great hiking and views.

## 2 Visitor Information

Tourism is Cuba's number-one source of hard currency, and the government is actively involved in promoting tourism internationally. As a result, there's a fairly decent network of tourism boards and agencies in major cities around the world. Some offices are run by the Ministry of Tourism, others by one of the major state-run agencies like **Cubanacán,** **Havanatur,** or **Cubatur.** No matter the bureau, the focus is almost entirely on organized tours, but they can also give you some basic information. Agencies to contact include **Cuba Tourist Board Canada,** 1200 Bay St., Suite 305, Toronto M5R 2A5 (© **416/362-0700;** www.gocuba.ca), or 2075, rue University, Bureau 460, Montreal H3A 2L1

## Destination Cuba: Red Alert Checklist

- Cuba is one of the few remaining Communist nations in the world, and its international relations are often strained. Be sure to check with your local Cuban consulate or embassy about current visa and travel requirements.
- United States citizens are severely restricted in their ability to travel to Cuba. Check the information at the U.S. State Department website (http://travel.state.gov) regarding Cuba, as well as the more in-depth description of entry requirements listed below.
- Do you have the address and phone number of your country's embassy or consulate with you?
- Do any theater, restaurant, or travel reservations need to be booked in advance?
- Did you find out your daily ATM withdrawal limit? Did you check with your bank to see if your credit or debit card will work in Cuba?
- Do you have your credit card PINs?
- To check in at a kiosk with an e-ticket, do you have the credit card you bought your ticket with or a frequent-flier card?
- If you purchased traveler's checks, have you recorded the check numbers, and stored the documentation separately from the checks?
- Did you pack your camera, an extra set of camera batteries, and enough film?
- Do you have a safe, accessible place to store money?
- Did you bring emergency drug prescriptions and extra glasses and/or contact lenses?
- Did you leave a copy of your itinerary with someone at home?
- Did you stop the newspaper and mail delivery, and leave a set of keys with someone reliable?
- Do you have the measurements for those people you plan to buy clothes for on your trip?

(© 514/875-8004); **Cuba Tourist Board Great Britain,** 154 Shaftesbury Ave., 1st Floor, London WC2H 8HL (© 0207/ 240-6655; tourism@cubasi.info); and, in the United States, the **Cuban Interests Section** (© 202/797-8518; cubaseccion@ prodigy.net).

A host of other information is available online. The **Latin America Network Information Center** (http://lanic.utexas. edu/la/cb/cuba) is hands-down the best one-stop shop for helpful links to a wide range of travel and general information sites.

The Cuban government sponsors a number of websites, including **Cuba Travel** (www.cubatravel.cu), **CubaSi** (www.cubasi.cu), and **Directorio Turístico de Cuba** (www.dtcuba.com). All offer a fair quantity of travel-related information and links. State-run tourism agency websites—including **Cubanacán** (www.cubanacan.cu) and **Cubatur** (www. cubatur.cu)—are also good places to check for hotels, transportation, and package deals.

## 3 Entry Requirements & Customs

### ENTRY REQUIREMENTS

All travelers to Cuba must possess a valid passport, a return ticket, and a visa or tourist visa. Tourist visas are generally issued by the ticketing airline or travel agent. In a worst-case scenario, they can usually be bought on the spot upon clearing Customs. Tourist visas cost between CUC$25 and CUC$35, depending upon the issuing agent, and are good for up to 90 days, although Customs agents will sometimes issue them for just 30 days, or until the date of your return flight, unless you request otherwise. They can be extended for another 30 days once you arrive in Cuba for an additional CUC$25 fee. In order to extend your tourist visa, you must personally go to Havana's **Immigration Office,** Calle 20 between Avenidas 3 and 5, Miramar (℃ **7/58-5100**).

In the event you need a specific work visa, or if your travel agent or airline will not provide you with the tourist visa, you should contact the Cuban consulate or embassy in your home country.

### FOR RESIDENTS OF THE UNITED STATES

While it is not illegal for U.S. citizens to travel to Cuba, most are prohibited from spending any money in Cuba. This, in effect, is the "travel ban." The complicated prohibition, which allows for various exceptions, is governed by the U.S. Treasury Department and the Office of Foreign Assets Control (OFAC).

The Treasury Department grants certain licenses. Some of these licenses are implicit, such as those for full-time journalists and government officials on official business. Other licenses must be applied for on a case-by-case basis with the U.S. Treasury Department, including Cuban-American citizens making humanitarian visits to close family. Licenses granted for educational travel and certain humanitarian trips, particularly those organized by religious groups, used to be a major route for legal travel to Cuba, but these were severely curtailed by the Bush administration in 2004, with even tighter restrictions placed on licensed travel in 2005 and 2006.

Travel arrangements for licensed travelers can be made by an authorized Travel Service Provider, and travel can be made directly from U.S. gateway cities on regular charter flights. There are hundreds of authorized TSPs. A few of the most dependable are **ABC Charters** (℃ **305/263-6829;** www.abc-charters.com); **Marazul Tours** (℃ **800/223-5334** or 201/319-3900; www.marazultours.com); and **Tico Travel** (℃ **800/493-8426** in the U.S. or Canada, or 954/493-8426; www.destinationcuba.com).

Be careful about signing on for a "fully hosted" trip. According to the regulations, a U.S. citizen can travel to Cuba without violating the Treasury ban provided he or she does not pay for any goods or services, including food and lodging, or provide any services to Cuba or a Cuban national while in the country. This provision had been widely used by U.S. citizens to buy packages from Canadian, Mexican, or Bahamian tour agencies. However, the Treasury Department has caught on to this tactic and has declared any "fully hosted" trip that is clearly for pleasure or tourism is in violation of the regulations.

Failure to comply with Department of Treasury regulations may result in civil penalties and criminal prosecution upon return to the United States. For more information, contact the **Office of Foreign Assets Control,** U.S. Department of the Treasury, 1500 Pennsylvania Ave. NW, Treasury Annex, Washington, DC 20220 (℃ **800/540-6322,** or 202/622-2480; www.treas.gov/ofac). The OFAC also runs a Cuba Sanctions telephone hot

> *Tips* **Pick Your Poison**
>
> Some operators and guidebooks recommend lying if asked whether or not you were in Cuba. However, you then place yourself at risk for perjury charges, which in the end are easier for the United States government to prosecute, and potentially more serious. I recommend you say little or nothing about your travel to Cuba, but I don't recommend that you lie. Remember, under U.S. law you have the right to refuse to incriminate yourself.

line out of their Miami office (© **786/ 845-2829**).

As far as Cuba goes, U.S. travelers are welcomed with open arms. In fact, as an aid to those seeking to circumvent the Treasury ban, in most cases, Cuban immigration does not actually stamp U.S. passports (but you should ask the officer to be sure). For current information on Cuban entry and Customs requirements, you can contact the **Cuban Interests Section** (© **202/797-8518**).

**UNLICENSED TRAVEL** It is estimated that as many as 80,000 U.S. citizens travel to Cuba each year without a Treasury Department license. The vast majority of travelers use third-country gateway cities like Toronto, Montreal, Cancún, Nassau, or Kingston, and are never questioned or bothered by U.S. authorities upon return. However, the Bush administration has cracked down on unlicensed travelers, and reports of tourists being caught have increased dramatically.

**WHAT TO DO IF YOU GET BUSTED** Officially, U.S. citizens who violate the ban face up to 10 years in prison, $250,000 in criminal fines, and $55,000 in civil fines. If you are stopped upon returning from an unlicensed trip to Cuba and directly asked by the Customs and Immigration agents, you should give as little information as possible. United States citizens cannot be compelled to provide self-incriminating information. Furthermore you cannot be denied re-entry into the United States for traveling to Cuba. You will likely face a

long and uncomfortable search and questioning session, and be sent on your way. This will most likely be followed by the receipt of a pre-penalty notice from the OFAC. This letter will request specific information to prove or disprove your alleged travel to Cuba, and to threaten the various fines and penalties. At this point you should contact the **Center for Constitutional Rights** (© **212/614-6464;** www.ccr-ny.org), which runs the Cuba Travel Project and works in conjunction with the **National Lawyers Guild** (www.nlg.org/cuba) to provide legal assistance to U.S. citizens facing prosecution for traveling to Cuba. Typically, after the initial pre-penalty letter, the OFAC offers to settle the case for a reduced fine in the neighborhood of $1,500 to $2,500. Many travelers have opted to go this route. A very, very small number of cases have ever fully gone to trial. In late 2003, for the first time, three administrative judges were appointed to hear these cases. As of press time, only a handful of cases have been heard, with mixed results on behalf of the plaintiffs.

**FOR CUBAN NATIONALS**
The Cuban government doesn't recognize the dual nationality of citizens who are Cuban-born or the children of Cuban parents, particularly those who chose exile in the United States. The Cuban government requires some individuals whom it considers to be Cuban to enter and depart Cuba using a Cuban passport. Using a Cuban passport for this purpose does not jeopardize one's foreign citizenship; however, you

will probably have to use your home country's passport to exit and enter that country. Other Cuban nationals and exiles just need a visa, but acquiring this visa is more complicated than acquiring the simple tourist visa used by most other travelers.

If you are Cuban-born or the child of Cuban-born parents, you should check with the Cuban embassy or consulate in your country of residence, as well as your local immigration authorities. In Canada, contact the **Cuban Embassy,** 388 Main St., Ottawa, Ontario, K1S 1E3 (© **613/ 563-0141**); there are also consulates in Montreal and Toronto. In the U.K., contact the **Cuban Embassy,** 167 High Holborn, London, WC1 6PA (© **0207/240- 2488;** embacuba@cubaldn.com). In the U.S., contact the **Cuban Interests Section,** 2630 16th St. NW, Washington, DC 20009 (© **202/797-8518**).

## CUSTOMS
### WHAT YOU CAN BRING INTO CUBA
You may bring in all manner of effects meant for personal use, including video and still cameras, personal electronic devices, jewelry, and sports equipment. In addition, visitors may bring in up to 2 bottles of liquor, a carton of cigarettes, and up to 10 kilograms of medications, provided it is in its original packaging. Anything that might be deemed an import destined to be sold or given as a gift to a Cuban citizen will raise eyebrows and may be subject to stiff import duties and/or confiscation. This includes TVs, VCR or DVD players, telephones, fax machines, desktop computers, and most forms of appliances. In fact, by law you may only import up to CUC$250 worth of any merchandise, and there is a 100% duty on all but the first CUC$50 worth. In practice, most visitors can freely bring in reasonable quantities of basic goods, like dried foods, vitamins, pharmaceuticals, and household supplies, without it being taxed or confiscated.

*Note:* It is illegal to bring in any prerecorded videotapes or DVDs. Laptop computers are currently a gray area. Most travelers are permitted to enter with their laptop computers without any problem, although sometimes they are actually confiscated upon entry and returned just prior to your return flight.

## Gifts & Other Assistance

Cuba is greatly lacking in many consumer and health-related products, and many visitors make a point of bringing items that are hard to find or prohibitively expensive to give as gifts. However, some visitors may be concerned about paternalism or setting examples that influence Cubans to look upon all travelers as bearers of material goods (in some areas popular with tourists, begging has even become a minor issue). One possible solution is to take along gifts to offer to those who may welcome you into their homes or with whom you have some sort of meaningful interaction. Another is to seek out schools and local officials to ensure that gifts are properly distributed. Items greatly appreciated by all Cubans include toothpaste; aspirin and other medicines; sporting goods and equipment, especially baseballs, bats, and gloves; pens and colored pencils; makeup; clothing; and disposable diapers.

—Neil E. Schlecht

You may bring unlimited amounts of cash, but it is wise to declare quantities in excess of US$5,000, as you may have trouble re-exporting large quantities of cash, if discovered upon departure. For current and more detailed information, check out **www.aduana.islagrande.cu**.

## WHAT YOU CAN TAKE HOME

Travelers may export up to 23 cigars with no questions asked. Larger quantities—up to CUC$2,000 worth—can be exported, provided you show proof that they were bought in official Habanos S.A. outlets. There is no specified limit on the dollar value of arts and crafts items, or clothing you can take home with you. Travelers are officially limited to bringing home 2 bottles of rum or other spirits, although this limit is rarely enforced. Still, if the Customs officials deem your purchases to be of a commercial nature, you could face fines or confiscation.

To export some works of art you will need a permit from the **Registro Nacional de Bienes Culturales (National Register of Cultural Heritage).** Theoretically, any reputable gallery or shop will provide you with this permit along with your purchase. Handicrafts and artwork bought at street fairs is exempt from this requirement, although I have heard of cases of people being hassled upon departure for not having a permit for art that should be exempt.

*Note:* There's a CUC$25 departure tax. You must pay this in cash, so be sure to have it on hand.

For a clear summary of **Canadian** rules, write for the booklet *I Declare,* issued by the **Canada Border Services Agency** (© **800/461-9999** in Canada, or 204/983-3500; www.cbsa-asfc.gc.ca). Canada allows its citizens a C$750 exemption, and you're allowed to bring back duty-free one carton of cigarettes, 1 can of tobacco, 40 imperial ounces of liquor, and 50 cigars. In addition, you're allowed to mail gifts to Canada valued at less than C$60 a day, provided they're unsolicited and don't contain alcohol or tobacco (write on the package "Unsolicited gift, under $60 value"). All valuables should be declared on the Y-38 form before departure from Canada, including serial numbers of valuables you already own, such as expensive foreign cameras. *Note:* The $750 exemption can only be used once a year and only after an absence of 7 days.

U.K. citizens returning from **a non-E.U. country** have a customs allowance of: 200 cigarettes; or 50 cigars; or 250 grams of smoking tobacco; 2 liters of still table wine; 1 liter of spirits or strong liqueurs (over 22% volume); or 2 liters of fortified wine, sparkling wine, or other liqueurs; 60cc (ml) perfume; 250cc (ml) of toilet water; and £145 worth of all other goods, including gifts and souvenirs. People under 17 cannot have the tobacco or alcohol allowance. For more information, contact HM Customs & Excise at © **0845/010-9000** (from outside the U.K., 020/8929-0152), or consult their website at www.hmce.gov.uk.

The duty-free allowance in **Australia** is A$400 or, for those under 18, A$200. Citizens can bring in 250 cigarettes or 250 grams of loose tobacco, and 1,125 milliliters of alcohol. If you're returning with valuables you already own, such as foreign-made cameras, you should file form B263. A helpful brochure available from Australian consulates or Customs offices is *Know Before You Go.* For more information, call the **Australian Customs Service** at © **1300/363-263,** or log on to www.customs.gov.au.

The duty-free allowance for **New Zealand** is NZ$700. Citizens over 17 can bring in 200 cigarettes, 50 cigars, or 250 grams of tobacco (or a mixture of all three if their combined weight doesn't exceed 250g); plus 4.5 liters of wine and beer, or 1.125 liters of liquor. New Zealand currency does not carry import or export restrictions. Fill out a certificate of export, listing the valuables you are taking out of the country; that way, you can bring them back without paying duty. Most questions are answered in a free pamphlet available at New Zealand consulates and Customs offices: *New Zealand Customs Guide for Travellers, Notice no. 4.* For more information, contact **New Zealand Customs,** The Customhouse, 17–21 Whitmore St., Box 2218, Wellington (℗ **04/473-6099** or 0800/428-786; www.customs.govt.nz).

**SPECIAL RULES FOR U.S. CITIZENS**    Only licensed U.S. travelers can bring Cuban-bought goods back into the United States, and they are limited to US$100 in merchandise. It is highly recommended you have your receipts handy. All other travelers bringing back Cuban-made goods will be considered in violation of the Treasury embargo and their goods will be confiscated.

*Note:* It is illegal for U.S. citizens to import Cuban products even if they never stepped foot on the island. It does no good to try to convince the Customs agent confiscating your stogies that you bought them in a cigar shop in Canada or Mexico or Costa Rica.

## 4 Money

Cuba's state banking system is trying to keep up with the rise in international tourism and joint business ventures. Both the **Banco de Crédito y Comercio** and **Banco Financiero Internacional** have been opening up branches in most major business and tourist areas; most are open Monday through Saturday from 8am to 4pm. These banks are the place to go for cash withdrawals off of your non-U.S.-issued credit cards. They'll also work for cashing traveler's checks or changing currency, but your best bet for money-exchange transactions is the national chain of *casas de cambio* (money-exchange houses), **CADECA, S.A.** You'll find CADECA branches in most major cities and tourist destinations, as well as at all the international airports. Some of their more strategically located branches are open 24 hours. Don't be scared off by the long lines in front of most CADECA offices. These are invariably Cubans looking to buy dollars. Foreigners wanting to sell dollars for Cuban pesos can almost always jump to the head of the line and walk right in.

### CURRENCY

Although Castro has replaced the U.S. dollar with the Cuban convertible peso, or CUC, Cuba has always operated under a de facto dollarized economy. The CUC is an internationally unsupported currency, and it is, for all intents and purposes, pegged to the U.S. dollar. All of the CADECA branches and major banks will change U.S. dollars, euros, British pounds, and Canadian dollars.

There are, in fact, two distinct kinds of currency circulating in Cuba: the *moneda libremente convertible* ("convertible peso" or CUC), and the *moneda nacional* (Cuban peso or MN). Both the CUC and *moneda nacional* are divided up into units of 100 centavos. To complicate matters, the euro is also legal tender in many of the hotels, restaurants, and shops in several of the larger, isolated beach resort destinations.

The convertible peso functions on a near one-to-one parity with the dollar—at press time the official exchange rate was US$1=CUC$0.93. However, U.S. dollars are penalized by a 10% surcharge on all money exchange operations into convertible pesos. For this reason, it is best to carry any hard currency you plan on spending in Cuba as euros, British pounds, or Canadian dollars. All of these are freely exchanged at all CADECA branches and most banks around Cuba. Be sure to bring relatively fresh and new bills. Cuban banks will sometimes refuse to accept bills with even slight tears or markings. Also, it is wise to bring a calculator with you and carefully monitor the exchange process, as tellers have been known to deliberately shortchange unsuspecting and overly trustworthy tourists.

Convertible pesos come in 1, 3, 5, 10, 20, 50, and 100 peso bills. Convertible peso coins come in denominations of 5, 10, 25, and 50 centavos, and 1 peso. Although the government has long abandoned its official posture of a one-to-one parity between the Cuban peso (MN) and U.S. dollar, the habit of converting *moneda nacional* prices directly into dollars is still common in many situations.

Currently, Cuban pesos can be exchanged legally for U.S. dollars or CUC (and vice versa) at any CADECA money exchange office, most banks, and many hotels. The official exchange rate as of press time was around 26 pesos to the CUC. While opportunities for travelers to pay in Cuban pesos are few and far between, it is not a bad idea to exchange around CUC$5 for pesos soon after arrival. It may be possible to pay for some restaurants, taxis, local buses, movie theaters, and other goods or services in Cuban pesos, and the savings are substantial. If "MN" is displayed on the prices, you should theoretically be paying Cuban pesos. However, in most cases vendors will try to insist that any non-Cuban pay in convertible pesos, often at a one-to-one rate of exchange.

You can exchange any remaining convertible pesos for U.S. dollars or euros at the airport before leaving. Do so, as the convertible pesos will be useless outside of Cuba.

*Note:* Cubans still often use the term "peso" and "dollar" interchangeably. If you are quoted a price in pesos, it may not be the bargain you think it to be. To be clear, *"moneda nacional"* or "MN" always refers to Cuban pesos. Other terms for a U.S. dollar include *divisa, verde, guano,* and *fula.*

## CREDIT CARDS

**MasterCard** and **Visa** are widely accepted at hotels, car-rental agencies, and official restaurants and shops, with the caveat that they must not be issued by a United States bank or financial institution. **Diners Club** is also accepted, although to a much lesser extent. **American Express** cards are not accepted anywhere on the island. It is always best to check with your home bank before traveling to see if your card will work in Cuba.

Most *paladares* (private-home restaurants), *casas particulares* (private-home accommodations), and small businesses do not accept credit cards. In the more remote destinations, you should count on using cash for most transactions. Moreover, shaky phone connections and other logistical problems often get in the way of credit card usage. I actually saw some British travelers unable to use a card at a major hotel because the hotel was out of receipt tape, and they weren't sure when they would get more.

If your credit card is lost or stolen while you're in Cuba, you can contact **Fincimex** in the Tryp Havana Libre hotel on Calle 23 and M, Vedado, Havana (© **7/55-4466**). However, you're best off having written down in advance your issuing bank's telephone number and calling them directly. They will usually accept collect calls from anywhere in the world.

### ATMs

Cuba has a modestly expanding network of ATMs (automated teller machines) associated with a string of new banks, like the **Banco de Crédito y Comercio** and **Banco Financiero Internacional.** At present, the machines are still not universally compatible with international credit and debit cards. No credit or debit cards issued by U.S.-based companies will work at any of these machines. However, travelers from other countries have a decent

---

**Tips  Small Change**

When you change money, ask for some small bills or loose change. Petty cash will come in handy for tipping and public transportation. Consider keeping the change separate from your larger bills, so that it's readily accessible and you'll be less of a target for theft.

---

chance of being able to extract convertible pesos from ATMs at the international airport and most major tourist destinations. As with credit cards, it is always best to check with your home bank before traveling to see if your ATM card will work in Cuba.

*Note:* Remember that many banks impose a fee every time you use a card at another bank's ATM, and that fee can be higher for international transactions (up to $5 or more) than for domestic ones (where they're rarely more than $2).

You can use your credit card to receive cash advances at ATMs. Keep in mind that credit card companies protect themselves from theft by limiting maximum withdrawals outside their home country, so call your credit card company before you leave home. And keep in mind that you'll pay interest from the moment of your withdrawal, even if you pay your monthly bills on time.

## TRAVELER'S CHECKS

In Cuba, traveler's checks are accepted at most major hotels, government-run or chain restaurants, and major attractions, but far less readily than credit cards. The same prohibition against U.S. bank-issued tender applies for traveler's checks, although the Banco Financiero Internacional and some CADECA branches were cashing American Express and other U.S. bank–issued traveler's checks at press time. If you are a die-hard fan of traveler's checks, **Thomas Cook** (check www.thomascook.com to find your nearest branch) and **Visa** (© **800/227-6811,** or 0800/89-5078 in the U.K.) traveler's checks issued outside of the United States are still your best bet. Most banks, CADECA offices, hotels, and businesses charge commissions of between 1% and 5% for cashing traveler's checks.

## 5 When to Go

The tourist high season runs December through March, coinciding with the winter months in most northern countries. It also coincides with Cuba's dry season. Throughout this season, and especially around the Christmas and Easter holidays, the beaches and resorts are relatively full, prices are somewhat higher, and it may be harder to find an available rental car or room. Moreover, overbooking, a widespread problem in the Cuban tourism industry, is certainly much more of a problem during the high season. During the low season, you should be able to find discounts on rooms, car

rentals, and tour options. Moreover, resorts and attractions are much less crowded. However, temperatures are somewhat higher throughout low season, and periods of extended rainfall are not uncommon.

## CLIMATE

Cuba has two distinct seasons, rainy (May–Oct) and dry (Nov–Apr). The dry season is characterized by consistently sunny and temperate weather, with daytime temperatures averaging between 75° and 80°F (24°–27°C). However, temperature swings are greater during this period, and it can actually get somewhat chilly when cold fronts—or "northers"—creep down the eastern seaboard of the United States, particularly in the months of January and February. In contrast, the rainy season is overall a slightly warmer period in Cuba, with less dramatic same-day temperature swings. There's a small dry spell most years during August, which is also the hottest month to visit Cuba. The entire Caribbean basin is affected by an annual hurricane season (June–Oct), with September and October having the highest number of hurricanes.

## HOLIDAYS

Cuba has a very limited plate of official holidays, and aside from Christmas Day, no religious holidays are officially recognized by the state. The official holidays are **January 1** (Liberation Day), **May 1** (May Day, or Labor Day), **July 26** (Revolution Day), **October 10** (Anniversary of the beginning of the 1868 War of Independence), and **December 25** (Christmas Day). However, with the state having such total control, it's not uncommon for them to call mass rallies or entire national mobilizations as they see fit. Other important dates that sometimes bring Cuba to a de facto state of national holiday include: **January 28** (Birth of José Martí), **February 24** (Anniversary of the beginning of the 1895 War of Independence), **March 8** (International Women's Day), **April 19** (Anniversary of Bay of Pigs Victory), **July 30** (Day of the Martyrs of the Revolution), **October 8** (Anniversary of the Death of Che Guevara), **October 28** (Anniversary of the Death of Camilo Cienfuegos), and **December 7** (Anniversary of the Death of Antonio Maceo).

## CALENDAR OF EVENTS

Cuba has a packed schedule of festivals, congresses, and carnivals, and it seems like more are being offered each year. If no specific contact information is offered below, you can contact

**Paradiso** (© 7/832-9538; paradis@paradise.artex.com.cu), the tour agency arm of the national arts and cultural organization ARTex. Paradiso organizes theme tours and escorted trips based around most of the major festivals and cultural events occurring throughout the year. You can also find pretty good information at **www.cubatravel.cu**, **www.cult.cu**, and **www.loseventos.cu** (the last two are in Spanish only).

### February

**International Book Fair,** Havana. This large gathering of authors, publishers, and distributors is really only of interest to those who can read in Spanish. But if you can, this is an excellent Latin American book fair. Second week of February.

**Habanos Festival,** Havana. Cigar smokers won't want to miss this annual celebration of the Cuban stogie. Run by the official state cigar company, Habanos, S.A., events include lectures, factory visits, tastings, and a gala dinner with an auction of rare cigars. For more information, visit www.habanos.com. Late February.

### March

**International Festival of "La Trova" Pepe Sánchez,** Santiago de Cuba. If you like the sounds of traditional Cuban folk music, you'll want to hit this festival. Buena Vista Social Club member Eliades Ochoa was charged with organizing a recent version. Local Santiagueros are the heart of the festival, but singers and groups come from the entire island and throughout Latin America. Mid-March.

**Celebration of Classic Cars,** Havana. Recognizing the appeal of its huge fleet of classic American cars, Cuba has organized a weeklong celebration of these Detroit dinosaurs. Events include lectures, mechanical workshops, and parades. Owners from other countries are encouraged to bring their wheels to Cuba, and a caravan from Havana to another colonial city is usually orchestrated. Mid-March.

## April

**International Percussion Festival PERCUBA,** Havana. This large meeting of percussionists draws national and international scholars and players working in genres ranging from classical to fusion. Lectures, workshops, concerts, and colloquiums are all part of a dense bill. Call ✆ **7/203-8808** or visit www.cult.cu for more information. Mid-April.

## May

**May Day parades,** nationwide. If you're in Cuba for May Day, the traditional socialist celebration of Labor Day, you'll want to join (or at least watch) one of the many parades and public gatherings. The big daddy of them all takes place at the Plaza de la Revolución in Havana, where over 100,000 people usually gather to listen to Fidel's annual May Day speech. May 1.

## June

**International Festival "Boleros de Oro,"** Havana. You'll be crying in your mojito . . . and loving it. Theaters, clubs, and concert halls across Havana will be filled with the sweet and melancholy sounds of *bolero.* Concerts are also staged in Santiago and other major cities. Late June.

## July

**Fiesta del Fuego,** Santiago de Cuba. This event features lectures, concerts, parades, and street fairs celebrating Afro-Caribbean culture. Speakers, guests, and musical groups from around the Caribbean are usually invited. For more information, e-mail caribe@cult.stgo.cul.cu. July 3 to July 9.

**International "Old Man and the Sea" Billfish Tournament,** Playas del Este, Havana. Marina Tarará is the host to this annual big-game fishing

tournament. Call ✆ **7/897-1462** for more information. Mid- to late July.

**Carnival,** Santiago de Cuba. The most "African" city in Cuba throws an excellent annual carnival. Street parties and concerts are everywhere, and the colonial city is flooded with masked revelers and long conga lines. Second half of July.

## August

**Carnival,** Havana. Although not nearly as colorful or charismatic as Santiago's Carnival, there's still a good dose of public merriment, street parties, open-air music concerts, and the occasional parade. August 3 to August 15.

**Beny Moré International Festival of Popular Music,** Cienfuegos. Although he was actually born a few kilometers away in the little hamlet of Santa Isabel de las Lajas, he is celebrated here with a heavy schedule of concerts throughout most of the latter part of August, and sometimes into September.

**Carnival,** Matanzas. If you're looking for a good time, try to get to Matanzas during the third week of August. Although not as massive or elaborate as Carnival celebrations in Havana or Santiago, Matanzas still puts on a good party. The town has strong Afro-Cuban roots, and you'll experience this in body, flesh, food, and song throughout the week. Third week of August.

## September

**Fiesta de la Virgen del Cobre,** El Cobre, Santiago de Cuba. Cuba's national saint, the Virgin of Cobre, is revered by Roman Catholics and Santeras alike. There are pilgrimages to her altar in the small town of El Cobre, and celebrations in her honor nationwide. September 8.

**International Blue Marlin Tournament,** Havana. The Marina Hemingway is the fitting site for this annual big-game fishing tournament. For more information, call ✆ **7/204-6848** or check www.cubanacan.cu. Late September.

## October

**Days of Cuban Culture,** nationwide. In yet another show of Cuba's omnipresent anti-colonial spirit, the period traditionally marking Christopher Columbus's stumbling upon the New World are given over to celebrations of Cuban and Afro-Cuban culture. October 10 to October 20.

**International Festival "Matamoros Son,"** Santiago de Cuba. The silky sounds of Cuban *son* fill the streets and theaters of Santiago. Organized by the reigning champion of the genre, Adalberto Alvarez, this is a great chance to hear a solid week of some wonderful music. Visit www.cult.cu for more information. Mid-October.

**Havana International Ballet Festival,** Havana. Alicia Alonso, amazingly, is still going strong, and the Cuban National Ballet is still one of the most highly regarded troupes on the planet. Alicia uses this cachet to stage a wonderful annual international festival in the Gran Teatro de La Habana. For more information, call ✆ **7/855-3084** or visit www.balletcuba.cu. Late October.

## November

**Havana Biennale,** Havana. This is one of the premier Latin American art shows, bringing together and exhibiting a wide range of contemporary Latin

American artists working in a broad range of mediums and styles. Occurring in even-numbered years from mid-November to mid-December.

## December

**International Festival of New Latin American Film Festival,** Havana. This is one of the premier film festivals in Latin America. A packed schedule of films is shown in theaters over a period of 10 days throughout Havana, but predominantly in Vedado. For more information, check out www.habana filmfestival.com. Early December.

**International Jazz Festival,** Havana. This festival has had its ups and downs, and has struggled to find its annual slot. It seems to have found its groove, dovetailing with the film festival and organized for the past couple years by none other than Chucho Valdés. The festival usually draws a handful of top international bands and soloists to share the stage and billing with a strong stable of Cuba's best jazz talents. Mid-December.

**Las Parrandas, Remedios.** This extravagant public carnival features late night parades with ornate floats, costumed revelers, and a serious amount of fireworks. The big event occurs on December 24, but between the preparations, practice runs, and smaller imitations in neighboring towns, you'll be able to catch some of the excitement throughout most of late December.

## 6 Travel Insurance

### TRAVEL INSURANCE AT A GLANCE

Check your existing insurance policies and credit card coverage before you buy travel insurance. You may already be covered for lost luggage, canceled tickets, or medical expenses.

The cost of travel insurance varies widely, depending on the cost and length of your trip, your age and health, and the type of trip you're taking, but expect to pay between 5% and 8% of the vacation itself. You can get estimates from various providers through **InsureMyTrip.com.**

Enter your trip cost and dates, your age, and other information, for prices from more than a dozen companies.

Most tour operators and agencies who work in Cuba or book travel to Cuba offer a basic insurance package for around CUC$5 per day that includes in-country medical coverage with a zero-deductible of up to CUC$25,000; emergency evacuation and repatriation coverage of up to CUC$7,000; coverage for civil damages caused to third parties of up to CUC$25,000; and lost luggage coverage of up to CUC$400. Other coverage options also exist. These policies are invariably bought through **Asistur** (© 7/ **866-8527;** www.asistur.cu).

**TRIP-CANCELLATION INSUR-ANCE** Trip-cancellation insurance will help retrieve your money if you have to back out of a trip or depart early, or if your travel supplier goes bankrupt. Permissible reasons for trip cancellation can range from sickness to natural disasters. (Insurers usually won't cover vague fears, though, as many travelers discovered when they tried to cancel their trips in October 2001.) In this unstable world, trip-cancellation insurance is a good buy if you're purchasing tickets well in advance—who knows what the state of the world, or of your airline, will be in 9 months? Insurance policy details vary, so read the fine print—and make sure that your airline or cruise line is on the list of carriers covered in case of bankruptcy. A good resource is **"Travel Guard Alerts,"** a list of companies considered high-risk by Travel Guard International (see website below). Protect yourself further by paying for the insurance with a credit card—by law, consumers can get their money back on goods and services not received if they report the loss within 60 days after the charge is listed on their credit card statement.

*Note:* Many tour operators, particularly those offering trips to remote or high-risk areas, include insurance in the total trip cost or can arrange insurance policies through a partnering provider, which is a convenient and often cost-effective way for the traveler to obtain insurance. Make sure the tour company is a reputable one, however, and be aware that some experts suggest you avoid buying insurance from the tour or cruise company you're traveling with. They contend it's more secure to buy from a "third party" than to put all your money in one place.

For more information, contact one of the following recommended insurers (although given restrictions on travel to Cuba, U.S. citizens will need to confirm that trips to Cuba are insurable): **Access America** (© 866/807-3982; www.access america.com); **Travel Guard International** (© 800/826-4919; www.travel guard.com); **Travel Insured International** (© 800/243-3174; www.travel insured.com); and **Travelex Insurance Services** (© 888/457-4602; www.travelex-insurance.com).

**MEDICAL INSURANCE** For travel overseas, most health plans (including Medicare and Medicaid) do not provide coverage, and the ones that do often require you to pay for services upfront and reimburse you only after you return home. Even if your plan does cover overseas treatment, most out-of-country hospitals make you pay your bills upfront, and send you a refund only after you've returned home and filed the necessary paperwork with your insurance company. As a safety net, you may want to buy travel medical insurance, particularly if you're traveling to a remote or high-risk area where emergency evacuation is a possible scenario. If you require additional medical insurance, try **MEDEX Assistance** (© 410/453-6300; www.medex assist.com) or **Travel Assistance International** (© 800/821-2828; www.travel assistance.com; for general information on services, call the company's Worldwide Assistance Services, Inc., at ✆ **800/ 777-8710**).

**LOST-LUGGAGE INSURANCE** On domestic flights, checked baggage is covered up to $2,500 per ticketed passenger. On international flights (including U.S. portions of international trips), baggage coverage is limited to approximately $9.07 per pound, up to approximately $635 per checked bag. If you plan to check items more valuable than what's covered by the standard liability, see if your homeowner's policy covers your valuables, get baggage insurance as part of your comprehensive travel-insurance package, or buy Travel Guard's "BagTrak" product. Don't buy insurance at the airport, where it's usually overpriced. Be sure to take any valuables or irreplaceable items with you in your carry-on luggage, because many valuables (including books, money, and electronics) aren't covered by airline policies.

If your luggage is lost, immediately file a lost-luggage claim at the airport, detailing the luggage contents. Most airlines require that you report delayed, damaged, or lost baggage within 4 hours of arrival. The airlines are required to deliver luggage, once found, directly to your house or destination free of charge.

## 7 Health & Safety

### STAYING HEALTHY

Despite ongoing economic troubles and shortages, Cuba's healthcare system remains one of the best in Latin America. The country takes extremely proactive steps toward preventive public health, and common tropical diseases like cholera, malaria, and dengue fever are either uncommon or have been totally eradicated. You don't need any vaccinations to travel to Cuba, unless you are coming from a region with cholera or yellow fever, in which case the Cuban authorities will require proof of immunization.

Staying healthy on a trip to Cuba is predominantly a matter of common sense: **Know your physical limits** and don't overexert yourself in the ocean, on hikes, or in athletic activities. Cuba is a tropical country, so limit your **exposure to the sun,** especially during the first few days of your trip and, thereafter, from 11am to 2pm. Use a sunscreen with a high protection factor and apply it liberally. Remember that children need more protection than adults do.

There are no poisonous snakes in Cuba, which will put many minds at ease. In terms of **biting bugs,** your standard array of bees, wasps, mosquitoes, and sand fleas are present. Sand fleas are a slight nuisance at most beaches if there's no offshore breeze to clear them, particularly around sunrise and sunset. While there are also ticks and chiggers, so far, Lyme disease is not considered a problem. Bring repellent and wear light, long-sleeved clothing.

Overall, while **water** is potable throughout most of Cuba, I still recommend you stick primarily to bottled water, just to err on the side of safety. Virtually every hotel and restaurant catering to travelers will carry bottled water. Ask for *agua mineral sin gas.*

Contact the **International Association for Medical Assistance to Travelers (IAMAT)** (✆ **716/754-4883** or, in Canada, 416/652-0137; www.iamat.org) for tips on travel and health concerns in the countries you're visiting, and for lists of local, English-speaking doctors. The United States **Centers for Disease Control and Prevention** (✆ **800/311-3435;** www.cdc.gov) provides up-to-date information on health hazards by region or country and offers tips on food safety. The website **www.tripprep.com**, sponsored by a consortium of travel medicine practitioners, may also offer helpful advice on traveling abroad. You can find listings of reliable clinics overseas at the **International Society of Travel Medicine** (www.istm.org).

## WHAT TO DO IF YOU GET SICK AWAY FROM HOME

Cuba has an excellent nationwide system of hospitals and clinics and you should have no trouble finding prompt and competent medical care in the case of emergency. See the "Orientation" or "Fast Facts" sections of the individual destination chapters for specific recommendations. The system is entirely free for Cubans, but foreigners are charged for services. This is actually a significant means of income for the country; however, fees for private medical care are relatively inexpensive by most Western standards.

The country also has a strong network of pharmacies. However, it is always a good idea to carry a sufficient supply of any necessary prescription medicines you may need (packed in their original containers in your carry-on luggage), and a small first-aid kit with basic analgesic, antihistamine, and anti-diarrhea medications. You might also bring a copy of your prescriptions, with the generic name of the medication in case the pharmacist doesn't recognize the brand name. Don't forget an extra pair of contact lenses or prescription glasses.

If you suffer from a chronic illness, consult your doctor before your departure. For conditions like epilepsy, diabetes, or heart problems, wear a **MedicAlert identification tag** (© 888/633-4298; www.medicalert.org), which will immediately alert doctors to your condition and give them access to your records through MedicAlert's 24-hour hot line.

## THE SAFE TRAVELER

Cuba is an extremely safe country. Street crime is relatively rare. With the recent upsurge in tourism, there have been some reports of pickpocketing and muggings, but these are by far the exceptions to the rule. There's a strong security and police presence in most popular tourist destinations, and even outside the well-worn tourist routes theft and assaults are quite uncommon.

That said, you should be careful and use common sense. Given the nature of Cuba's socialist system, there exists a huge disparity in wealth between the average Cuban and any foreign visitor, even budget travelers. Don't flash ostentatious signs of wealth, and avoid getting too far off the beaten path, especially at night. Don't leave valuables unattended, and always use your hotel-room or front-desk safe.

## ECO-TOURISM

The **International Ecotourism Society** (TIES) defines eco-tourism as "responsible travel to natural areas that conserves the environment and improves the well-being of local people." You can find eco-friendly travel tips, statistics, and touring companies and associations—listed by destination under "Travel Choice"—at the TIES website, www.ecotourism.org. **Ecotravel.com** is part online magazine and part ecodirectory that lets you search for touring companies in several categories (water-based, land-based, spiritually oriented, and so on). Also check out **Conservation International** (www.conservation.org)—which, with *National Geographic Traveler,* annually presents **World Legacy Awards** (www.wlaward.org) to those travel tour operators, businesses, organizations, and places that have made a significant contribution to sustainable tourism.

There is a Cuban travel agency called **Ecotur** (© 7/649-1055), but I don't find them to have any specific expertise or orientation toward what I would consider true eco-tourism.

There are several swim-with-dolphin programs across Cuba, and I deal with each of these on an individual basis in the different destination chapters. For information about the ethics of swimming with dolphins and other outdoor activities, visit the **Whale and Dolphin Conservation Society** (www.wdcs.org) and **Tread Lightly** (www.treadlightly.org).

## 8 Specialized Travel Resources

### TRAVELERS WITH DISABILITIES

Most disabilities shouldn't stop anyone from traveling. There are more options and resources out there than ever before. And Cuba has been very forward-thinking in the recognition of the rights of persons with disabilities. Still, overall, Cuba is not an easy country for travelers with disabilities. While a few hotels are equipped to handle travelers with disabilities, they are far from the norm. Moreover, there's almost no private or public transportation service geared toward travelers with disabilities. The streets of Havana are rugged and crowded, and sidewalks, in particular, are often either totally absent or badly torn up. The Cuban people, however, are quite conscientious and embracing in their treatment of people with disabilities.

**Asociación Cubana de Limitados Físicos-Motores (The Cuban Disabled Association),** Calle 6 no. 106, between Avenidas 1 and 3, Miramar, Havana (© 7/204-9980; aclifim@infomed.sld.cu), is a Cuban organization charged with ensuring accessibility and lobbying for rights. The association is a member of the Disabled Peoples' International (DPI), and probably the best contact for travelers with disabilities in Cuba.

**The Society for Accessible Travel & Hospitality** (© 212/447-7284; www.sath.org) offers a wealth of travel resources for all types of disabilities and informed recommendations on destinations, access guides, travel agents, tour operators, vehicle rentals, and companion services. Annual membership costs $45 for adults, $30 for seniors and students.

### GAY & LESBIAN TRAVELERS

In general, Cuba has a poor record on gay and lesbian rights, and while the situation has improved somewhat, there are still high levels of homophobia and broad societal rejection of gays and lesbians. For decades following the Revolution, gays and lesbians were closeted and persecuted. The harsh measures they faced included forced labor and prison. The blockbuster movie *Fresa y chocolate (Strawberry and Chocolate)* certainly brought the issue to the forefront, yet little has changed in the prevailing views of this macho society. There are no openly accepted gay or lesbian establishments in Cuba, and none of the established gay and lesbian tour operators run trips to the island. While travelers are generally not hassled in Cuba and given somewhat further leeway in terms of social mores, same-sex signs of physical affection are rare and frowned upon across the country. Gay and lesbian couples and singles should take the prevailing social climate into account when traveling in Cuba.

The documentary film, *Gay Cuba,* by Sonja de Vries (Frameline Films; www.frameline.org), is an honest look at the treatment of gays and lesbians in modern Cuba. Despite its promising domain name, the website **www.gay-cuba.com** is somewhat out of date and light on truly helpful information.

**The International Gay and Lesbian Travel Association (IGLTA)** (© 800/448-8550 or 954/776-2626; www.iglta.org) is the trade association for the gay and lesbian travel industry, and offers an online directory of gay- and lesbian-friendly

## Race Relations in Cuba

Cuba is—very conservatively—estimated to be about one-third black and mulatto (in reality, the percentage is probably closer to two-thirds or more). Cuba officially declares itself to be colorblind, and, at least on the surface, the obvious mixed-race heritage and the strong presence of Afro-Cuban culture seem to support that notion. Though, as a society, Cuba is much less racist and male-dominated than it was before the Revolution, racism still exists, even if much of it is under the radar. Economic racism is widespread; relatively few black Cubans occupy positions of authority in the government, state enterprise, and tourism. Racist comments are as regrettably common as they are in other countries. Many Cubans assume blacks to be the majority of *jineteros* (male hustlers) and *jineteras* (female escorts), even though the reality is that hustling in Cuba is universal. Most Cubans also believe that the police harass blacks and mulattoes to a disproportionate degree, and travelers of African and Hispanic descent may experience the same. Spanish-speaking travelers accompanying Anglo-looking tourists are sometimes followed and questioned by police who ignorantly assume them to be Cuban hustlers working a beat.

In fact, one other disturbing aspect of this situation is that black tourists are sometimes mistaken for Cuban *jineteros* and given a hard time by security personnel upon entering hotels and restaurants.

—*Neil E. Schlecht*

travel businesses; go to their website and click on "Members."

## SENIOR TRAVEL

Cuba is a comfortable destination for senior travelers. Seniors are treated with deference and respect in Cuba. Moreover, it's a particularly safe country, with low levels of street crime, and the food and water are generally safe as well.

Mention the fact that you're a senior when you make your travel reservations—some of the hotel chains and package tour operators still offer discounts for seniors. However, don't expect to find specific senior discounts once you arrive in Cuba, where you will be lumped into the category of rich foreigner and gouged as much as possible, like all the rest.

**ElderTreks** ((C) **800/741-7956;** www.eldertreks.com) is a Canadian-based company that has, in the past, arranged small group adventure trips for those 50

and over, although Cuba is not on their current program.

## FAMILY TRAVEL

Cuba is an excellent destination for families, particularly if you want an all-inclusive beach vacation with a broad range of tours, activities, and entertainment options. Toward this end, Varadero would probably be your top choice, with a wealth of watersports activities and land-based adventures, including nearby caves to explore. The beach destinations of Cayo Coco, Cayo Guillermo, and Guardalavaca are also worth considering. If you do go the all-inclusive route, be sure the resort you choose has a well-run children's program, with a full plate of activities.

If your children are old enough, they should enjoy the colonial wonders of Habana Vieja (Old Havana), including its forts and castles. Hotels and attractions throughout Cuba often give discounts for children under 12 years old (and sometimes teens up to 16 or so often get away with admission at children's prices).

However, hotels offering regular, dependable babysitting service are few and far between. If you will need babysitting, make sure your hotel offers it before you leave home. To locate those accommodations, restaurants, and attractions that are particularly kid-friendly, refer to the "Kids" icon throughout this guide.

## SINGLE TRAVELERS

Cuba is a very safe country. Single travelers face no real specific threats or dangers. That said, don't throw common sense out the window. Single travelers—and women in particular—should still be careful when walking alone at night, both in Havana and in other more remote destinations. Cuba is also a somewhat typical "macho" Latin American nation, with an open and extroverted sense of sexuality. Single women can expect their fair share of catcalls, whistles, and propositions, especially in Havana. The best advice is to ignore the unwanted attention, rather than try to come up with a witty or antagonistic rejoinder. Women travelers should check out the award-winning website **Journeywoman** (www.journeywoman.com), a "real life" women's travel-information network where you can sign up for a free e-mail newsletter and get advice on everything from etiquette and dress to safety; or the travel guide *Safety and Security for Women Who Travel* by Sheila Swan and Peter Laufer (Travelers' Tales, Inc.), offering common-sense tips on safe travel.

Perhaps the biggest issue facing single travelers is that of *jineterismo,* which is a way of life in Cuba. In its most disturbing form, it has become synonymous with prostitution. Sex tourism and prostitution flourish in Cuba, and single travelers of both genders and any sexual persuasion will encounter constant offers for companionship, and usually more. In some cases, the terms are quite clear and a cash value is set. In others, the *jinetera* or *jinetero* is just looking for some restaurant meals, store-bought clothing, food, daily necessities, and sometimes even a good time. Many are looking to cement relationships with foreign tourists that could lead to marriage and a means of improving their standard of living on a longer-term basis, either on the island or abroad. See appendix A for more information on *jineterismo.*

## 9 Planning Your Trip Online

### SURFING FOR AIRFARES

The "big three" online travel agencies, **Expedia.com, Travelocity.com,** and **Orbitz.com** sell most of the air tickets bought on the Internet. (Canadian travelers should try expedia.ca and Travelocity.ca; U.K. residents can go for expedia.co.uk and opodo.co.uk.). **Kayak.com** is also gaining popularity and uses a sophisticated search engine (developed at MIT). Each has different business deals with the airlines and may offer different fares on the same flights, so it's wise to shop around. Expedia, Kayak, and Travelocity will also send you **e-mail notification** when a cheap fare becomes available to your favorite destination. Of the smaller travel-agency websites, **SideStep** (www.sidestep.com) has gotten the best reviews from Frommer's authors. The website (with optional browser add-on) purports to "search 140 sites at once," but in reality it only beats competitors' fares as often as other sites do.

Also remember to check **airline websites,** especially those for low-fare carriers such as JetBlue, AirTran, WestJet, or Ryanair, whose fares are often misreported or simply missing from travel agency websites. Even with major airlines, you can often shave a few bucks from a fare by booking directly through the airline and avoiding a travel agency's transaction fee. But you'll get these discounts only by **booking online:** Most airlines now offer online-only fares that even their phone agents know nothing about. For the websites of airlines that fly to and from your destination, go to "Getting There," p. 40.

Great **last-minute deals** are available through free weekly e-mail services provided directly by the airlines. Most of these are announced on Tuesday or Wednesday and must be purchased online. Most are only valid for travel that weekend, but some (such as Southwest's) can be booked weeks or months in advance. Sign up for weekly e-mail alerts at airline websites or check mega-sites that compile comprehensive lists of last-minute specials, such as **Smarter Travel** (smartertravel.com). For last-minute trips, **site59.com** and **lastminutetravel. com** in the U.S. and **lastminute.com** in Europe often have better air-and-hotel package deals than the major-label sites.

If you're willing to give up some control over your flight details, use what is called an **"opaque" fare service** such as **Priceline** (www.priceline.com; www.priceline. co.uk for Europeans) or its smaller competitor **Hotwire** (www.hotwire.com). Both offer rock-bottom prices in exchange for travel on a "mystery airline" at a mysterious time of day, often with a mysterious change of planes en route. The mystery airlines are all major, well-known carriers—and the possibility of being sent from Philadelphia to Chicago via Tampa is remote; the airlines' routing computers have gotten a lot better than they used to be. Your chances of getting a 6am or 11pm flight, however, are still pretty high. Hotwire tells you flight prices before you buy; Priceline usually has better deals than Hotwire, but you have to play their "name our price" game. If you're new at this, the helpful folks at **BiddingForTravel** (www. biddingfortravel.com) do a good job of demystifying Priceline's prices and strategies. Priceline and Hotwire are great for flights within North America and between the U.S. and Europe. But for flights to other parts of the world, consolidators will almost always beat their fares. *Note:* In 2004, Priceline added non-opaque service to its roster. You now have the option to pick exact flights, times, and airlines from a list of offers—or opt to bid on opaque fares as before.

## SURFING FOR HOTELS

Shopping online for hotels is generally done one of two ways: by booking through the hotel's own website or through an independent booking agency (or a fare-service agency like Priceline; see below). These Internet hotel agencies have multiplied in mind-boggling numbers of late, competing for the business of millions of consumers surfing for accommodations around the world. This competitiveness can be a boon to consumers who have the patience and time to shop and compare the online sites for good deals—but shop they must, for prices can vary considerably from site to site. And keep in mind that hotels at the top of a site's listing may be there for no other reason than that they paid money to get the placement.

Of the "big three" sites, **Expedia** offers a long list of special deals and "virtual tours" or photos of available rooms so you can see what you're paying for (a feature that helps counter the claims that the best rooms are often held back from bargain booking websites). **Travelocity** posts unvarnished customer reviews and ranks its properties according to the AAA rating system. (**Trip Advisor** [www.tripadvisor. com] is another excellent source of unbiased user reviews of hotels around the world. While even the finest hotels can inspire a misleadingly poor review from a picky or crabby travelers, the body of user opinions, when taken as a whole, is usually a reliable indicator.)

## Frommers.com: The Complete Travel Resource

For an excellent travel-planning resource, we highly recommend **Frommers.com** (www.frommers.com), voted Best Travel Site by *PC Magazine*. We're a little biased, of course, but we guarantee that you'll find the travel tips, reviews, monthly vacation giveaways, bookstore, and online-booking capabilities thoroughly indispensable. Among the special features are our popular **Destinations** section, where you'll get expert travel tips, hotel and dining recommendations, and advice on the sights to see for more than 3,500 destinations around the globe; the **Frommers.com Newsletter,** with the latest deals, travel trends, and money-saving secrets; and our **Travel Talk** area featuring **Message Boards,** where Frommer's readers post queries and share advice, and where our authors sometimes show up to answer questions. Once you finish your research, the **Book a Trip** area can lead you to Frommer's preferred online partners' websites, where you can book your vacation at affordable prices.

Other reliable online booking agencies include **Hotels.com** and **Quikbook.com**. An excellent free program, **TravelAxe** (www.travelaxe.net), can help you search multiple hotel sites at once, even ones you may never have heard of—and conveniently lists the total price of the room, including the taxes and service charges. Another booking site, **Travelweb** (www.travelweb.com), is partly owned by the hotels it represents (including the Hilton, Hyatt, and Starwood chains) and is therefore plugged directly into the hotels' reservations systems—unlike independent online agencies, which have to fax or e-mail reservation requests to the hotel, a good portion of which get misplaced in the shuffle. More than once, travelers have arrived at the hotel, only to be told that they have no reservation. To be fair, many of the major sites are undergoing improvements in service and ease of use, and Expedia will soon be able to plug directly into the reservations systems of many hotel chains—none of which can be bad news for consumers. In the meantime, it's a good idea to **get a confirmation number** and **make a printout** of any online booking transaction.

Be prepared for some pitfalls when booking directly through hotel websites in Cuba. Many of the state-run chains—**Gaviota, Habaguanex,** and **Cubanacán**—have primitive or poorly maintained websites, and their online booking mechanisms can be cumbersome and inconsistent. You'll definitely do better with the larger international chains like **Sol Meliá** (www.solmeliacuba.com), **Occidental** (www.occidental-hoteles.com), and **Barceló** (www.barcelo.com).

In the opaque website category, **Priceline** and **Hotwire** are even better for hotels than for airfares; through both, you're allowed to pick the neighborhood and quality level of your hotel before paying. Priceline's hotel product even covers Europe and Asia, though it's much better at getting five-star lodging for three-star prices than at finding anything at the bottom of the scale. On the downside, many hotels stick Priceline guests in their least desirable rooms. Be sure to go to the BiddingForTravel website (see above) before bidding on a hotel room on Priceline; it features a fairly up-to-date list of hotels that Priceline uses in major cities. For both Priceline and Hotwire, you pay upfront, and the fee is nonrefundable. *Note:* Some hotels do not provide loyalty program credits or points or other frequent-stay amenities when you book a room through opaque online services.

## SURFING FOR RENTAL CARS

For booking rental cars online, the best deals are usually found at rental-car company websites, although all the major online travel agencies also offer rental-car reservations services. The same caveat I mentioned above for booking rooms with the large state-run hotel chains applies to the state-run car-rental agencies.

## TRAVEL BLOGS & TRAVELOGUES

More and more travelers are using travel Web logs, or blogs, to chronicle their journeys online. To read travelogues about Cuba, try the forum section at www.cubamania.com. You can search for other blogs about Cuba at Travelblog. com or post your own travelogue at Travelblog.org. For blogs that cover general travel news and highlight various destinations, try Writtenroad.com or Gawker Media's snarky Gridskipper.com. For more literary travel essays, try Salon.com's travel section (http://salon.com/Wanderlust), and Worldhum.com, which also has an extensive list of other travel-related journals, blogs, online communities, newspaper coverage, and bookstores.

## 10 The 21st-Century Traveler

### INTERNET ACCESS AWAY FROM HOME

Travelers have any number of ways to check their e-mail and access the Internet on the road. Of course, using your own laptop—or even a PDA (personal digital assistant) or electronic organizer with a modem—gives you the most flexibility. But even if you don't have a computer, you can still access your e-mail and even your office computer from cybercafes.

### WITHOUT YOUR OWN COMPUTER

It's hard nowadays to find a city that *doesn't* have a few cybercafes. Although there's no definitive directory for cybercafes—these are independent businesses, after all—three places to start looking are at **www.cybercaptive.com** and **www.cybercafe.com**. In Cuba, you'll find cybercafes in most major tourist destinations. Most of the more upscale hotels and resorts also provide for guest connectivity in one form or another.

Most major airports, including the **José Martí International Airport** in Havana, now have **Internet kiosks** scattered throughout their gates. These kiosks, which you'll also see in shopping malls, hotel lobbies, and tourist information offices around the world, give you basic Web access for a per-minute fee that's usually higher than cybercafe prices. The kiosks' clunkiness and high price, however, mean you should avoid them whenever possible.

To retrieve your e-mail, ask your **Internet Service Provider (ISP)** if it has a Web-based interface tied to your existing e-mail account. If your ISP doesn't have such an interface, you can use the free **mail2web** service (www.mail2web.com) to view and reply to your home e-mail. For more flexibility, you may want to open a free, Web-based e-mail account with **Yahoo! Mail** (http://mail.yahoo.com). (Microsoft's Hotmail is another popular option, but Hotmail has severe spam problems.) Your home ISP may be able to forward your e-mail to the Web-based account automatically.

If you need to access files on your office computer, look into a service called

**GoToMyPC** (www.gotomypc.com). The service provides a Web-based interface for you to access and manipulate a distant PC from anywhere—even a cybercafe—provided your "target" PC is on and has an always-on connection to the Internet (as with Road Runner cable). The service offers top-quality security, but if you're worried about hackers, use your own laptop rather than a cybercafe computer to access the GoToMyPC system.

## WITH YOUR OWN COMPUTER

More and more hotels, cafes, and retailers are signing on as Wi-Fi (wireless fidelity) "hotspots," from where you can get high-speed connection without cable wires, networking hardware, or a phone line (see below). You can get a Wi-Fi connection one of several ways. Many laptops sold in the last year have built-in Wi-Fi capability (an 802.11b wireless Ethernet connection). Mac owners have their own networking technology, Apple AirPort. For those with older computers, you can plug in an 802.11b/**Wi-Fi card** (around $50). You sign up for wireless access service much as you do for cellphone service, through a plan offered by one of several commercial companies that have made wireless service available in airports, hotel lobbies, and coffee shops, primarily in the U.S. (followed by the U.K. and Japan). **T-Mobile Hotspot** (www.t-mobile.com/hotspot) serves up wireless connections at more than 1,000 Starbucks coffee shops nationwide. **Boingo** (www.boingo.com) and **Wayport** (www.wayport.com) have set up networks in airports and upscale hotel lobbies. **IPass** providers (see below) also give you access to a few hundred wireless hotel lobby setups. Best of all, you don't need to be staying at the Four Seasons to use the hotel's network; just set yourself up on a nice couch in the lobby. (Pricing policies can be byzantine, but in general you pay around $30 a month for unlimited access, and prices are dropping as Wi-Fi access becomes more common.)

To locate other hotspots that provide **free wireless networks** in cities around the world, go to **www.personaltelco.net/index.cgi/WirelessCommunities**.

For dial-up access, most business-class hotels throughout the world offer dataports for laptop modems, and a few thousand hotels in the U.S. and Europe now offer free high-speed Internet access using an Ethernet network cable. You can bring your own cables, but most hotels rent them for around $10. **Call your hotel in advance** to see what your options are.

In addition, major Internet Service Providers (ISPs) have **local access numbers** around the world, allowing you to go online by placing a local call. Check your ISP's website or call its toll-free number and ask how you can use your current account away from home, and how much it will cost.

The **iPass** network also has dial-up numbers around the world. You'll have to sign up with an iPass provider, who will then tell you how to set up your computer for your destination(s). For a list of iPass providers, go to www.ipass.com and click on "Individuals Buy Now." One solid provider is **i2roam** (www.i2roam.com; ℭ **866/811-6209** or 920/235-0475).

Wherever you go, bring a **connection kit** of the right power and phone adapters, a spare phone cord, and a spare Ethernet network cable—or find out whether your hotel supplies them to guests. Throughout Cuba, electricity is 110-volt AC, and most outlets are U.S.-style two- or three-prong. However, many of the large hotels and resorts that cater primarily to Canadian and European clientele are wired for 220 volts.

## USING A CELLPHONE

In Cuba, cellular service is controlled by **Cubacel** (ℭ **5/264-2266;** www.cubacel.cu). Cubacel has offices at the José Martí International Airport and in Havana and most major cities and tourist destinations. Cubacel offers cellphone rentals for

## Online Traveler's Toolbox

Veteran travelers usually carry some essential items to make their trips easier. Following is a selection of handy online tools to bookmark and use.

- **Airplane Seating and Food.** Find out which seats to reserve and which to avoid (and more) on all major domestic airlines at www.seatguru.com. And check out the type of meal (with photos) you'll likely be served on airlines around the world at www.airlinemeals.net.
- **Foreign Languages for Travelers** (www.travlang.com). Learn basic terms in more than 70 languages and click on any underlined phrase to hear what it sounds like.
- **Intellicast** (www.intellicast.com) and **Weather.com** (www.weather.com). Give weather forecasts for all 50 states and for cities around the world.
- **Mapquest** (www.mapquest.com). This best of the mapping sites lets you choose a specific address or destination, and in seconds returns a map and detailed directions.
- **Time and Date** (www.timeanddate.com). See what time (and day) it is anywhere in the world.
- **Travel Warnings** (http://travel.state.gov, www.fco.gov.uk/travel, www.voyage.gc.ca, www.dfat.gov.au/consular/advice). These sites report on places where health concerns or unrest might threaten American, British, Canadian, and Australian travelers. Generally, U.S. warnings are the most paranoid; Australian warnings are the most relaxed.
- **Universal Currency Converter** (www.xe.com/ucc). See what your dollar or pound is worth in more than 100 other countries.
- **Visa ATM Locator** (www.visa.com), for locations of PLUS ATMs worldwide, or **MasterCard ATM Locator** (www.mastercard.com), for locations of Cirrus ATMs worldwide.

CUC$6 per day, with a CUC$3 daily activation fee. You'll have to leave around a CUC$200 deposit and purchase a prepaid calling card. If you have your own phone, you will just have to pay the CUC$3 daily activation fee. Cubacel works with both TDMA phones and GSM systems. Prepaid calling cards are sold in denominations of CUC$10, CUC$20, and CUC$40. Rates inside Cuba run between CUC50¢ and CUC60¢ per minute, depending on the hour and destination called, and you are charged for both outgoing and incoming calls. Rates to the rest of the world run between CUC$1.50 and CUC$5 per minute.

## 11 Getting There

### BY PLANE

Cuba has 12 international airports. Havana is by far the principal gateway, although there are numerous regularly scheduled and charter flights to Varadero and Santiago de Cuba as well. To a lesser extent, international charter flights from Canada and Europe service Cayo Largo del Sur, Cienfuegos, Camagüey, Ciego de

Avila, Holguín, and Cayo Coco and Cayo Guillermo.

It's roughly a 70-minute flight from Miami to Havana; 3 hours and 30 minutes from New York to Havana; 4 hours and 30 minutes from Toronto or Montreal to Havana; and 10 hours from London to Havana. Most of the principal Caribbean basin gateway cities—Cancún, Gran Cayman, Kingston, Nassau, and Santo Domingo—are between 30 and 90 minutes to Havana by air.

Airfares vary widely, depending on the season, demand, and certain ticketing restrictions. But given the high number of charter flights and package tours to Cuba, combined with the stiff competition for vacation travel throughout the Caribbean, airfares are relatively cheap, and bargains abound. It really pays to shop around.

**Cubana** (ⓒ **7/834-4446;** www. cubana.cu) is Cuba's national airline and the principal carrier to the island, with regularly scheduled flights to a score of cities throughout the Americas, Europe, and Canada. Other carriers with regularly scheduled or charter service to Cuba include: **Air Jamaica** (ⓒ 800/523-5585 in North America, or 0207/962-9934 in the U.K.; www.airjamaica.com), **Air Canada** (ⓒ 888/247-2262 in North America, or 0871/220-1111 in the U.K.; www.aircanada.com), **Air Europa** (ⓒ 0870/777-7709; www.air-europa. com), **Air Transat** (ⓒ 866/847-1112; www.airtransat.com), **British Airways** (ⓒ 800/247-9297, or 0870/850-9850 in the U.K.; www.britishairways.com), **Condor Airways** (ⓒ 800/364-1667 in North America; www3.condor.com), **Grupo Taca** (ⓒ 800/722-8222 in the U.S. or Canada, or 0870/241-0340 in the U.K.; www.grupotaca.com), **Iberia** (ⓒ 0870/609-0500 in the U.K.; www. iberia.com), **Martinair** (ⓒ 416/364-3672 in Canada; www.martinair.com), **Mexicana** (ⓒ 800/531-3585 in North America; www.mexicana.com), and **Virgin Atlantic** (ⓒ 800/821-5438 in the U.S. or Canada, or 0870/574-7747 in the U.K.; www.virgin-atlantic.com).

There is no regularly scheduled service between the United States and Cuba, although there are numerous charter flights from Miami, and to a lesser extent from New York and Los Angeles. Licensed U.S. travelers are eligible to use these flights. For more information, see "Package Deals, Escorted Tours & Special-Interest Vacations," below.

## FLYING FOR LESS: TIPS FOR GETTING THE BEST AIRFARE
Passengers sharing the same airplane cabin rarely pay the same fare. Here are some ways to keep your airfare costs down.

- Passengers who can book their ticket either **long in advance or at the last minute,** or who **fly midweek** or **at less-trafficked hours** may pay a fraction of the full fare. If your schedule is flexible, say so, and ask if you can secure a cheaper fare by changing your flight plans.
- Search **the Internet** for cheap fares (see "Planning Your Trip Online," earlier in this chapter).
- Keep an eye on local newspapers for **promotional specials** or **fare wars,** when airlines lower prices on their most popular routes. You rarely see fare wars offered for peak travel times, but if you can travel in the off-months, you may snag a bargain.
- **Consolidators,** also known as bucket shops, are great sources for international tickets. Start by looking in Sunday newspaper travel sections. For less-developed destinations, small travel agents who cater to immigrant communities in large cities often have the best deals. *Beware:* Bucket shop tickets are usually nonrefundable or rigged with stiff cancellation penalties, often as high as 50% to 75% of

the ticket price, and some put you on charter airlines, which may leave at inconvenient times and experience delays. Several reliable consolidators are worldwide and available online. **STA Travel** has been the world's lead consolidator for students since purchasing Council Travel, but their fares are competitive for travelers of all ages. **ELTExpress (Flights.com)** (© **800/874-8800;** www.eltexpress. com) has excellent fares worldwide. They also have "local" websites in 12 countries. **Air Tickets Direct** (© **800/778-3447;** www.airtickets direct.com) is based in Montreal and leverages the currently weak Canadian dollar for low fares; they also book trips to places that U.S. travel agents won't touch, such as Cuba.

- Join **frequent-flier clubs.** Frequent-flier membership doesn't cost a cent, but it does entitle you to better seats, faster response to phone inquiries, and prompter service if your luggage is stolen or your flight is canceled or delayed, or if you want to change your seat. And you don't have to fly to earn points; **frequent-flier credit cards** can earn you thousands of miles for doing your everyday shopping. With more than 70 mileage awards programs on the market, consumers have never had more options, but the system has never been more complicated—with major airlines folding, new budget carriers emerging, and alliances forming (allowing you to earn points on partner airlines). Investigate the program details of your favorite airlines before you sink points into any one. Consider which airlines have hubs in the airport nearest you, and, of those carriers, which have the most advantageous alliances, given your most common routes. To play the frequent-flier game to your best advantage, consult Randy

Petersen's **Inside Flyer** (www.inside flyer.com). Petersen and friends review all the programs in detail and post regular updates on changes in policies and trends. Petersen will also field direct questions (via e-mail) if a partner airline refuses to redeem points, for instance, or if you're still not sure after researching the various programs which one is right for you. It's well worth the $12 online subscription fee, good for 1 year.

## LONG-HAUL FLIGHTS: HOW TO STAY COMFORTABLE

Long flights can be trying; stuffy air and cramped seats can make you feel as if you're being sent parcel post in a small box. But with a little advance planning, you can make an otherwise unpleasant experience almost bearable.

- Your choice of airline and airplane will definitely affect your leg room. Find more details at **www.seatguru. com**, which has extensive details about almost every seat on six major U.S. airlines. For international airlines, research firm Skytrax has posted a list of average seat pitches at **www.airlinequality.com**.
- Emergency exit seats and bulkhead seats typically have the most legroom. Emergency exit seats are usually left unassigned until the day of a flight (to ensure that someone able-bodied fills the seats); it's worth getting to the ticket counter early to snag one of these spots for a long flight. Many passengers find that bulkhead seating (the row facing the wall at the front of the cabin) offers more legroom, but keep in mind that bulkheads are where airlines often put baby bassinets, so you may be sitting next to an infant.
- To have two seats for yourself in a three-seat row, try for an aisle seat in a center section toward the back of

## Tips  Coping with Jet Lag

Jet lag is a pitfall of traveling across time zones. If you're flying north–south and you feel sluggish when you touch down, your symptoms will be the result of dehydration and the general stress of air travel. When you travel east–west or vice versa, however, your body becomes thoroughly confused about what time it is, and everything from your digestion to your brain is knocked for a loop. Traveling east, say from Chicago to Paris, is more difficult on your internal clock than traveling west, say from Atlanta to Hawaii, because most peoples' bodies are more inclined to stay up late than fall asleep early.

Here are some tips for combating jet lag:

- **Reset your watch** to your destination time before you board the plane.
- **Drink lots of water** before, during, and after your flight. Avoid alcohol.
- **Exercise and sleep well** for a few days before your trip.
- If you have trouble sleeping on planes, **fly eastward on morning flights.**
- **Daylight** is the key to resetting your body clock. At the website for **Outside In** (www.bodyclock.com), you can get a customized plan of when to seek and avoid light.
- If you need help getting to sleep earlier than you usually would, some doctors recommend taking either the hormone **melatonin** or the sleeping pill **Ambien**—but not together. Some recommend that you take 2 to 5 milligrams of melatonin about 2 hours before your planned bedtime—but again, always check with your doctor on the best course of action for you.

coach. If you're traveling with a companion, book an aisle and a window seat. Middle seats are usually booked last, so chances are good you'll end up with three seats to yourselves. In the event that a third passenger is assigned the middle seat, he or she will probably be more than happy to trade for a window or an aisle.

- Ask about entertainment options. Many airlines offer seatback video systems where you get to choose your movies or play video games—but only on some of their planes. (Boeing 777s are your best bet.)
- To sleep, avoid the last row of any section or the row in front of an emergency exit, as these seats are the least likely to recline. Avoid seats near highly trafficked toilet areas. Avoid seats in the back of many jets—these can be narrower than those in the rest of coach. You also may want to

reserve a window seat so you can rest your head and avoid being bumped in the aisle.

- Get up, walk around, and stretch every 60 to 90 minutes to keep your blood flowing. This helps avoid **deep vein thrombosis,** or "economy-class syndrome," a potentially deadly condition caused by sitting in cramped conditions for too long. Other preventive measures include drinking lots of water and avoiding alcohol (see next bullet).
- Drink water before, during, and after your flight to combat the lack of humidity in airplane cabins—which can be drier than the Sahara. Bring a bottle of water on board. Avoid alcohol, which will dehydrate you.
- If you're flying with kids, don't forget to carry on toys, books, pacifiers, and chewing gum to help them relieve ear pressure buildup during ascent and

descent. Let each child pack his or her own backpack with favorite toys.

## BY BOAT

When arriving by sea, contact the port authorities before entering Cuban waters 19km (12 miles) offshore on VHF channels 16, 19, or 68, or HF channel 2760. Skippers do not need to give advance notice or have a prior visa. If you plan on staying in the country for more than 72 hours, each crew member must apply for a tourist visa, which can be arranged by the harbormaster. All crew members must have current passports, and United States Treasury Department restrictions (see "Entry Requirements & Customs," earlier in this chapter) apply to all U.S. citizens. Skippers will also need to register their vessel upon arrival. A special permit, or *permiso especial de navigación,* is issued.

This permit costs around CUC$50 depending on the length of the vessel.

Cuba has a network of state-run, full-service marinas. Those that function as official points of entry and exit include their marinas in Jardines del Rey, María la Gorda, Cayo Largo del Sur, Cienfuegos, and Santiago de Cuba, as well as the Marina Hemingway in Havana and Marina Dársena in Varadero. For more information on the specific marinas, see the respective destination chapters.

Good resources for any sailor planning to visit Cuba are Simon Charles's *The Cruising Guide To Cuba* (Cruising Guide Publications, 1997) and Nigel Calder's *Cuba: A Cruising Guide* (Imray, Laurie, Norie & Wilson, 1999). While a little dated, both books are full of invaluable information, tips, and firsthand experiences aimed at cruising sailors.

## 12 Package Deals, Escorted Tours & Special-Interest Vacations

### PACKAGE DEALS & ESCORTED TOURS

Before you start your search for the lowest airfare, you may want to consider booking your flight as part of a travel package or an escorted tour. What you might lose in adventure, you'll gain in time and money saved when you book accommodations, and maybe even food and entertainment, along with your flight.

Packages are not the same thing as escorted tours. With a package, you travel independently but pay a group rate. Packages usually include airfare, a choice of hotels, and car rentals, and packagers often offer several options at different prices. In many cases, a package that includes airfare, hotel, and transportation to and from the airport will cost you less than just the hotel alone would have, had you booked it yourself. That's because packages are sold in bulk to tour operators—who resell them to the public at a cost that drastically undercuts standard rates.

Package tours can vary by leaps and bounds. Some offer a better class of hotels than others. Some offer the same hotels for lower prices. Some offer flights on scheduled airlines, while others book charters. Some limit your choice of accommodations and travel days. You are often required to make a large payment upfront. On the plus side, packages can save you money, offering group prices but allowing for independent travel. Some even let you add on a few guided excursions or escorted day trips (also at prices lower than if you booked them yourself) without booking an entirely escorted tour.

Escorted tours are structured group tours, with a group leader. The price usually includes everything from airfare to hotels, meals, tours, admission costs, and local transportation. This is a particularly popular option for U.S. citizens who don't want to deal with the bureaucracy of applying for an individual travel license. In most cases, escorted tours for

U.S. citizens will include the Treasury Department license.

Escorted tours—whether they're navigated by bus, motorcoach, train, or boat—let travelers sit back and enjoy the trip without having to drive or worry about details. They take you to the maximum number of sights in the minimum amount of time with the least amount of hassle. They're particularly convenient for people with limited mobility and they can be a great way to make new friends.

On the downside, you'll have little opportunity for serendipitous interactions with locals. The tours can be jam-packed with activities, leaving little room for individual sightseeing, whim, or adventure—plus they also often focus on the heavily touristed sites, so you miss out many a lesser-known gem.

Before you invest in an escorted tour, request a complete **schedule** of the trip to find out how much sightseeing is planned and whether you'll have enough time to relax or have an adventure of your own. Also ask about the **cancellation policy:** Is a deposit required? Can they cancel the trip if enough people don't sign up? Do you get a refund if they cancel? If *you* cancel? How late can you cancel if you are unable to go? When must you pay in full? If you choose an escorted tour, think strongly about purchasing trip-cancellation insurance, especially if the tour operator asks you to pay in advance. See the section on "Travel Insurance," p. 29. If you plan to travel alone, find out if they'll charge a **single supplement** or whether they can pair you with a roommate.

The **size** of the group is also important to know upfront. Generally, the smaller the group, the more flexible the itinerary, and the less time you'll spend waiting for people to get on and off the bus. Find out the **demographics** of the group as well. What is the age range? What is the gender breakdown? Is this mostly a trip for couples or singles?

Discuss what is included in the **price.** You may have to pay for transportation to and from the airport. A box lunch may be included in an excursion, but drinks might cost extra. Tips may not be included. Find out if you will be charged if you decide to opt out of certain activities or meals.

Before you invest in a package or escorted tour, get some answers. Ask about the **accommodations choices** and prices for each. Then look up the hotels' reviews in a Frommer's guide and check their rates online for your specific dates of travel. You'll also want to find out what **type of room** you get. If you need a certain type of room, ask for it; don't take whatever is thrown your way. Finally, look for **hidden expenses.** Ask whether airport departure fees and taxes, for example, are included in the total cost.

## RECOMMENDED PACKAGE & ESCORTED TOUR OPERATORS
### From the U.S.

There are over a hundred licensed travel service providers in the United States; almost all offer charter flights and packages. Some of the best and most reputable are:

- **ABC Charters** ☆ (© **305/263-6829;** www.abc-charters.com) is an excellent TSP and charter company based in Miami.
- **Marazul Tours** (© **800/223-5334** or 201/319-3900; www.marazultours. com) is a major operator for East Coast–based Cuban-Americans and their family members.
- **Tico Travel** ☆ (© **800/493-8426** in the U.S. or Canada, or 954/493-8426; www.destinationcuba.com) is a dependable company with operations throughout much of Latin America.

### From Canada

In addition to the agencies listed below, Canadian travelers, and others using Canada as a gateway, can check directly with **Air Transat Holidays** (© 866/322-6649 in the U.S. and Canada; www.air transatholidays.com), the tour agency arm of one of the principal charter flight companies to Cuba.

- **Sol Meliá Cuba** (© 416/533-8585; www.solmeliacuba.com) is the Canadian-based tour agency arm of the Sol Meliá company.
- **Signature Travel** ✦ (© 866/324-2883; www.signaturevacations.com) is the largest tour and package operator in Canada, with offices in Toronto, Montreal, Winnipeg, and Vancouver.

### From the U.K.

- **Cuba Welcome** ✦ (© 020/7731-6871; www.cubawelcome.com) is a good U.K.-based operator with a knowledgeable and dependable operation on the ground in Cuba.
- **Go Cuba Plus** (www.gocubaplus.com) is a well-established Web-based operator, with offices and representation throughout Europe and the British Virgin Islands.
- **Regent Holidays** ✦ (© 0870/499-1311; www.regent-cuba.com) is the specialized Cuba unit of this U.K. tour operator.
- **Journey Latin America** (© 020/8747-3108; www.journeylatin america.co.uk) is a large U.K.-based operator for trips throughout the hemisphere, with often very good deals on airfare.
- **Thomas Cook** ✦ (© 0870/750-5011; www.thomascook.com) is a major U.K.-based operator for trips around the world, with excellent operations in Cuba.

### From Australia & New Zealand

- **Caribbean Bound** (© 02/9267-2555; www.caribbean.com.au) is a specialist in travel throughout the Caribbean.
- **Caribbean Destinations** (© 03/9813-5258; www.caribbeanislands.com.au) is another Australian-based specialist in travel throughout the Caribbean.

### Cuba-Based Agencies

- **Cubalinda** (© 7/204-5584; www.cubalinda.com) is an excellent agency that provides hands-on service, and is especially adept at helping non-licensed U.S. travelers understand and work with the various options open to them.
- **Cuba Welcome** ✦ (© 020/7731-6871 in the U.K., or 7/863-3885 in Cuba; www.cubawelcome.com) is a U.K.-based operator that has an excellent operation on the ground in Cuba.

## SPECIAL-INTEREST VACATIONS

There are plenty of options for a special-interest or theme vacation to Cuba. Popular themes include cigars, Ernest Hemingway, classic cars, bird-watching, and Latin dance. In addition to the agencies and operators listed below, most of the package and escort tour operators listed above offer a selection of themed specialty tours.

- **GAP Adventures** ✦ (© 800/708-7761 in the U.S. and Canada, or 0870/999-0144 in the U.K.; www.gapadventures.com) is a major international adventure and educational tour operator with a full plate of theme tours to Cuba.
- **Global Exchange** ✦ (© 415/255-7296; www.globalexchange.org) is a nonprofit organization working to increase international understanding by conducting small-scale tours that emphasize educational or social aid themes.
- **Paradiso** ✦ (© 7/832-9538) is the tour agency arm of the Cuban arts and cultural organization ARTex.

Paradiso organizes theme tours and escorted trips, including tours based around most of the major festivals and cultural events, as well as participatory learning trips with instruction in a variety of arts.

## 13 The Active Vacation Planner

Active tourism is in its relative infancy in Cuba. Still, the island offers myriad opportunities to add a bit of adrenaline and adventure to your vacation. Watersports are the main draw here, and Cuba abounds with outstanding opportunities to fish, sail, snorkel, and scuba dive. For those looking for some dry-land adventure activities, there are great options for biking and rock climbing, and you might even be able to get on a diamond to play some baseball.

**BASEBALL**    Baseball is the national sport and, after salsa dancing and sex, Cuba's greatest national passion. Cuba's amateur players are considered some of the best in the world, and the premier players are aggressively scouted and courted by Major League Baseball. The regular season runs November through March, and playoffs and the final championship usually carry the season on into May. Most major towns and cities have a local team. Some of the consistently better teams include Pinar del Río, Sancti Spíritus, Santiago de Cuba, Santa Clara, and of course Havana's Industriales. It's usually easy to buy tickets at the box office for less than 5 Cuban pesos, or ask at your hotel and perhaps they can get you tickets in advance.

If you want to actually get out and play, you should be able to find a pickup game to join. Although they have temporarily suspended their organized trips, check out the website of **Baseball Adventures** (☏ 707/937-4478; www.baseball adventures.com), which used to offer fully-hosted trips geared toward serious players looking to play and train with local Cuban pros.

*Tip:* If you're planning on playing, bring some extra equipment—balls, bats, and gloves—to leave behind. It'll be greatly appreciated and is a great means of getting into a game.

**BIKING**    With a local reliance on bicycles for everyday transportation and a relatively well-maintained road network serving a small motor vehicular fleet, Cuba is a great country to tour by bicycle. There are very few operations renting decent bikes in Cuba, so it's best to bring your own. I also recommend organized trips, as the logistics of traveling through Cuba still make it a bit difficult for independent bike touring. One dependable operation offering regular bike tours and quality bike rentals in Cuba is **Wow Cuba** (☏ 800/969-2822 or 902/368-2453; www.wowcuba.com). Anyone thinking of bicycling in Cuba should pick up a copy of Wally and Barbara Smith's *Bicycling Cuba: Fifty Days of Detailed Rides from Havana to Pinar Del Río and the Oriente* (Backcountry Guides, 2002).

**BIRD-WATCHING**    Over 350 resident and migratory species of birds can be spotted in Cuba, including some 24 endemic species. True, experienced Cuban bird guides are still rare, and there are few established bird-watching tour operations in Cuba. A couple of organized tour options are offered by the British company **Cuba Welcome** (☏ 020/7731-6871 in the U.K.; www.cubawelcome.com) and the Canadian operation **Quest Nature Tours** (☏ 416/633-5666; www.quest naturetours.com). Some of the best places to go bird-watching in Cuba include **La Güira National Park,** the **Zapata Peninsula, Cayo Coco** and **Cayo Guillermo,** the **Sierra Maestra** mountain region, and **Baracoa.** Bird-watchers will want to bring a copy of *Birds of Cuba* (Comstock

Publishing, 2000), by Orlando Garrido, Arturo Kirkconnell, et al.

**FISHING** There's fabulous deep-sea sportfishing for marlin, sailfish, tuna, dorado, and more off of most of Cuba's extensive coastline, while the Zapata Peninsula and Cayo Largo del Sur may just be some of the best and least exploited bonefishing spots left in the hemisphere. The mountain lake and resort of Hanabanilla is getting good grades as a freshwater ground for widemouth and black bass. A half-day of fishing should cost between CUC$150 and CUC$400, while a full day can run between CUC$300 and CUC$1,400, including gear and lunch, depending on the size of the boat and number of fishermen. There's a broad network of state-run marinas all around Cuba; the greatest number are run by **Cubanacán** (© 7/208-6044; www.cubanacan.cu) and **Gaviota** (© 7/66-9668; www.gaviota-grupo.com). All offer sportfishing charters. For more information, see individual destination chapters.

**GOLF** The country's only regulation 18-hole golf course is the **Varadero Golf Club** (© 45/66-8442; www.varaderogolfclub.com). The course is a relatively flat resort course, with lots of water, plenty of sand, great views, and almost no rough. Greens fees run CUC$77 for a round, plus an extra CUC$33 for a cart. Club rental will cost you CUC$15. Golfers would probably want to stay at the adjacent **Meliá Las Américas** (© 45/66-7600; www.solmeliacuba.com), although you can make reservations and play here from any hotel in the area.

In Havana, there's the **Club de Golf Habana,** Carretera Vento Km 8, Capdevila, Rancho Boyeros (© 7/55-8746 or 7/649-8820), which has a decent little 9-hole course.

**MOUNTAIN & ROCK CLIMBING** These sports are in their infancy in Cuba, but excellent opportunities abound, especially around the Viñales Valley. **Cuba Climbing** (www.cubaclimbing.com) can point you to the right rocks and answer any questions you might have.

**SAILING** Whether you take a day sail, or decide to go cruising the coastline for a week or so, opportunities to sail the clear waters off Cuba abound. The state-run marinas in Varadero, Jardines del Rey, Camaguey, Santiago, Cienfuegos, and Cayo Largo del Sur all offer charter sailboats, as well as a variety of day sailing options. See the individual destination chapters for more information.

**SCUBA DIVING & SNORKELING** There are fabulous scuba diving and snorkeling opportunities on the coral reefs, ocean walls, and ancient wrecks that lie just off Cuba's coasts. **María la Gorda, Isla de la Juventud, Playa Larga, Playa Girón,** and **Los Jardines de la Reina** are widely considered the absolute top scuba-diving destinations, but in each case, the accommodations options are either rustic or decidedly geared toward hard-core dive enthusiasts and almost no one else. You will also find perfectly acceptable dive opportunities and operations in **Varadero, Cayo Coco, Cayo Guillermo, Guardalavaca,** and **Cayo Largo del Sur,** as well as far more comfortable and varied accommodations. For more information, see specific destination chapters.

**SURFING** Cuba is not considered a world-class surfing destination, and there are very few Cuban surfers or surf tourists. Still, this is part of the charm of surfing in Cuba, and there are waves and breaks all along the island's long coastline, including right off the Malecón in Havana. For good information and a primer, check out **www.havanasurf-cuba.com**. You will definitely have to bring your own board, and I would recommend bringing a board (or two) that you wouldn't mind leaving behind for some very appreciative Cuban grommet.

**TENNIS** Many of the large-scale beach resorts have tennis courts. Almost all are outdoor courts, and very few are lit. If you're set on playing tennis on your trip, be sure to check in advance if you hotel or resort has courts. Your options are much more limited in Havana, unless you're staying at one of the few city hotels with a court. Your best bet in Havana is to try to book a court at the **Occidental Miramar,** Avenida 5, between Calles 78 and 80, Miramar, Playa (✆ 7/204-3584), which has six courts, or head to the **Club Habana,** Avenida 5, between Calles 188 and 192, Reparto Flores, Playa (✆ 7/204-5700), or **Club de Golf Habana,** Carretera Vento Km 8, Capdevila, Rancho Boyeros (✆ 7/55-8746), which each have a few courts open to the general public. All charge around CUC$10 per hour.

## 14 Getting Around

### BY CAR

Driving a rental car is an excellent way to travel around Cuba. The roads are generally in pretty good condition, and there's very little traffic—although you'll have to keep a sharp eye out for horse-drawn carriages, slow-moving tractors, scores of bicyclists, and pedestrians taking over major roadways. There are a handful of state-run car-rental companies, with a large, modern fleet of rental cars to choose from. Prices and selection are rather standard, with an abundance of small, economy Japanese and Korean cars to choose from. A rental car should cost you between CUC$45 and CUC$75 per day, including insurance and unlimited mileage. Some agencies start you off with a full tank of gas that they charge you for—above the rental fee—then give no credit for any gas left in the tank upon returning the car. Discounts are available for multiday rentals. It's always a good idea to have a reservation in advance, especially during peak periods, when cars can get a little scarce. However, there's a Catch-22 here, in that many of the state-run agencies don't have a trustworthy international reservations system. As is the case with rampant overbooking of hotel rooms, when demand outstrips supply, the car-rental agencies will often not honor your seemingly confirmed reservation.

The main car-rental companies are **Cubacar** (✆ 7/273-2277; www.cubanacan.cu); **Havanautos** (✆ 7/835-3142; www.havanautos.cu); **Micar** (✆ 7/204-8888); **Transtur** (✆ 7/862-2686 or 7/861-5885; www.transtur.cu); and **Vía Rent A Car** (✆ 7/861-4465; www.gaviota-grupo.com). All have desks at the airport, and at a host of major hotels around Havana and the rest of the country.

All car-rental agencies in Cuba offer insurance coverage for between CUC$10 and CUC$20 per day. Coverage is sometimes obligatory. Most carry a CUC$200 to CUC$750 deductible. Some do not cover theft, but this is a very minor problem in Cuba. If you hold a private auto insurance policy, you may be covered abroad for loss or damage to the car, and liability in case a passenger is injured. The credit card you used to rent the car also may provide some coverage. However, be sure to check whether or not your insurance company or credit card coverage excludes rental cars in Cuba. Moreover, this type of coverage probably does not cover liability if you caused the accident. Check your own auto insurance policy, the rental company policy, and your credit card coverage for the extent of coverage.

Be very thorough when checking out your car, and make sure that all accouterments (like a spare tire, jack, and radio) are present and accounted for. Moreover, be sure to have the agent note every little nick and scratch, or you risk being charged for them upon your car's return.

Gasoline costs around CUC$1 per liter, or CUC$3.80 per gallon. Gone are the gas shortages of several years ago. Service stations are plentiful and conveniently located on the major highways and in most major towns and cities.

Every car-rental agency will provide you with a decent road map. Alternately you can try to get a copy of the **International Travel Map: Cuba** (ITMB Publishing; www.itmb.com) before arriving, or you can see what maps are available at the various hotel gift shops and tourist stores.

While driving is generally easy and stress-free, there are a couple of concerns for most foreign drivers here. First (and most annoying) is the fact that there are **very, very few road signs** and directional aids. The Ministry of Tourism is aware that this is a major problem, and I have been expecting them to address this for the past 5 years or so. As of yet, they've made very little progress. Secondly, there's the issue of **hitchhikers.** Cuba's public transportation network is grossly overburdened and hitchhiking is a way of life. The highways sometimes seem like one long line, with periodic swellings, of people asking for a lift, or *botella.* While cases of kidnappings and muggings of drivers offering lifts are rare, you should still take care in whom you pick up. However, the biggest hassle of offering rides is twofold: When you stop, you are likely to be swarmed by supplicants, who will want to stuff your car to the brink of its carrying capacity; and most hitchhikers are looking for relatively short hops, so once you pick up a load you might find yourself suddenly making constant stops to let your passengers off—at which point there will almost certainly be a new rider immediately vying to snag the just-emptied seat.

One final note: ***Stop at all railroad crossings!*** It's the law, and it's also an important safety measure. Cuba's railroad network crisscrosses its highway system at numerous points. Trains rarely slow down and even rarer still are protective crossbars or warning lights. Police often hang out at railroad crossings, both to warn drivers when a train is coming and to dole out tickets to those who don't come to a stop.

## BY PLANE

**Cubana** (© 7/834-4446; www.cubana. cu) is the principal national and international carrier for Cuba. The other principal commuter and charter carriers are **AeroCaribbean** (© 7/879-7524; www. aero-caribbean.com), **Aerogaviota** (© 7/ 203-0668), and **Aerotaxi** (© 7/836-4064). Among the four of them, there's a full schedule of commuter flights connecting Havana and Varadero with the destination cities of Baracoa, Bayamo, Camagüey, Ciego de Avila, Manzanillo, Nueva Gerona (Isla de la Juventud), Guantánamo, Holguín, Santiago de Cuba, Las Tunas, Cayo Largo, and Cayo Coco. Fares average around CUC$60 to CUC$120 one-way. The exception is Isla de la Juventud, which costs just CUC$25 to CUC$50 each way from Havana. If you know you'll need an internal flight, try to have your travel agent or tour operator book it in advance. If not, you can easily book flights from the tour desks at almost any hotel in Cuba.

## BY BUS

For all intents and purposes, the only buses a tourist will ride in Cuba are those run by **Víazul** (© 7/881-1413; www. viazul.com). In general, Víazul buses are modern and comfortable. Since the tickets must be paid in hard currency, which precludes most Cubans from using them, there is less demand and greater availability. While it is possible for tourists to travel on standard Cuban buses, it is often complex, impractical and problematic—and you will almost certainly be charged in CUC, at rates just slightly cheaper than Víazul.

Víazul travels to most major tourist destinations in Cuba. The main Víazul station is located in Nuevo Vedado, Havana, across from the metropolitan zoo. However, some of their routes, including the popular Viñales and Pinar del Río route, can be booked and boarded at the main bus terminal near the Plaza de la Revolución. For schedules and prices, see the regional chapters that follow.

## BY TRAIN

The state-run train agency, **Ferrocuba** (© 7/861-8540 or 7/862-8081), has offices in each train station. Havana is connected to Pinar del Río in the west, and Santiago de Cuba in the east by regular rail traffic. There are usually one or two trains a day heading west, and a half-dozen or so heading east. Intermediate cities with regular service include Matanzas, Santa Clara, Ciego de Avila, Camagüey, Las Tunas, and Holguín. The principal train station, or **Estación Central,** is located in Havana at Calle Egido and Calle Arsenal, Habana Vieja (© 7/862-1920 or 7/861-4259).

Unlike the state-run bus service, there are usually seats available on most trains. However, most trains are in rather bad shape, with uncomfortable seats and limited amenities. Be sure to bring along some food and something to drink. Even if there's a cafeteria car onboard, which isn't always the case, you might not find any of their offerings particularly appealing, and they might just run out somewhere along the line. Moreover, train travel in Cuba is notoriously erratic, with frequent schedule changes and delays. It is always best to check current schedules and conditions before buying a ticket and undertaking a train journey.

The most attractive rail option for travelers is the 12-hour express train to Santiago de Cuba leaving Havana each evening at 6:05pm; the fare is CUC$50 to CUC$62. This train only makes stops in Santa Clara and Camagüey, and is the most modern and comfortable train in the whole national system. For more information on traveling by train, see the regional chapters that follow.

## 15 Tips on Accommodations

Most hotel options in Cuba have been divvied up among a few large state-run chains: **Islazul, Gaviota, Cubanacán, Gran Caribe,** and **Habaguanex.** These chains generally stake out distinct territories. Habaguanex has near monopoly control over the hotel scene in Habana Vieja in Havana. Their properties tend to be in the midrange to upper end, and most are in beautifully restored colonial buildings. Gaviota, Cubanacán, and Gran Caribe divvy up the remainder of the midrange to upper-end offerings around the country. Islazul runs the most economical hotels, although they have begun refurbishing some real gems in the colonial heart of some of Cuba's more interesting cities.

In recent years, these large state-run companies have begun signing management contracts with international hotel chains, usually resulting in improved service and hospitality. While the international **Barceló, Corralia, Maritim,** and **Occidental** chains run a few hotels each, predominantly in Havana and Varadero, the major player is the Spanish **Sol Meliá** chain, which manages 25 midrange to high-end properties in Cuba. In general, the Sol Meliá hotels are some of the best run and most comfortable in the country.

At most of Cuba's principal beach resorts, the majority of hotels are large

## _Tips_  Snuggle Up

King- and queen-size beds are at a premium in Cuba. Very few of the midrange options offer beds big enough for two adults, and even some of the fancier hotels, including many of the Habaguanex properties, only offer rooms with two twins.

**all-inclusive resorts.** Most work with large groups of Canadian and European travelers on weeklong charter packages. These feature a steady diet of buffet meals, organized activities and entertainment, and late-night revelry. These are not the places to come if you want to explore and experience Cuba and its culture. Also, if you're staying at an all-inclusive, you should book the a la carte restaurant options as soon as possible during peak seasons, or you'll be eating all your meals at the crowded buffets.

Aside from official hotels and resorts, the other principal lodging option in Cuba is a *casa particular,* or private house. To meet demand and inject just a bit of economic relief (and nascent capitalism) into the system, the government has authorized certain households to rent out rooms. An official casa particular should display a small plaque or sticker declaring it to be a government sanctioned *casa.* The newest symbol appears to be a blue capital "H" set on its side, with slightly bent horizontal lines, and the top horizontal line longer than the bottom one. It should also say *arrendador divisa.* Alternately, you might see one of the older plaques or stickers with of one or two inverted blue or green "V"s. Following a recent policy change, casas particulares can have no more than two rooms for rent. Most are quite modest—you are basically living with a Cuban family. It's a crapshoot whether or not they'll have a private bathroom. On the upside, most casas particulares offer meals at very reasonable prices, and staying in one is a great way to meet and interact with Cubans (something much, much harder to do at "official" hotels and resorts).

Be aware that if you show up at a casa particular on the recommendation of a taxi driver or *jinetero,* they will expect a commission of between CUC$1 and CUC$5, which is invariably added on to your bill.

## 16  Tips on Dining

Do not come to Cuba for fine dining. While it's possible to minimize the pain, finding good food, service, and value is a challenge in Cuba. Most restaurants that cater to tourists are run by large state-owned corporations, and as a whole they are often overpriced and mediocre. Even the popular and highly touted restaurants here often suffer from inconsistency and indifferent service. *Note:* Be especially on the lookout for overcharging, either in the form of phantom charges or inflated prices.

In addition to hotel restaurants and official state-run tourist restaurants, the principal dining option in Cuba is the *paladar.* Like casas particulares, paladares are private homes that have been granted permission to serve foreign tourists. Paladares are small, with a seating limit of just 12, and subject to various limitations. They cannot serve shrimp or lobster for instance, and cannot accept credit cards. They are also heavily taxed by the state. However, Cubans are a creative lot and you will find paladares that have figured ways around many of these limitations.

Paladares tend to open and close, move, or change their name or menu with great frequency. They also often run out of menu items, or simply can't find the raw materials to begin the day with. However, there are some dependable and long-standing paladares. In fact, several of these are among the best restaurants in the country. At these, you'll almost certainly need a reservation, or be prepared to wait.

In general, you should tip between 10% and 15%, keeping in mind that this represents a huge amount of hard currency for most Cubans. Some restaurants add a 10% service charge to bills; whether or not it's actually given to the waitstaff is questionable. Also, if you show up at a paladar on the recommendation of a taxi driver or *jinetero,* they will expect a commission of between CUC$3 and CUC$5, which is often added to your bill.

Given the unique economic and social conditions of Cuba, there is little street food to speak of, aside from a few odd pizza and ice-cream vendors. Cuban street pizza features heavy dough, with a molten mess of sauce and gooey cheese topping, served as small individual discs on wax paper.

With a recent influx of foreign capital and a move toward modernization, fast-food chains have begun popping up around Cuba. The most prominent of these is **El Rápido,** which has numerous outlets serving fried chicken, burgers, hot dogs, microwave pizzas, and other fast-food staples. Another chain worth mentioning is **Pizza Nova,** which has several outlets in Havana and in various provincial cities. This chain specializes in thin-crust pizza and good pastas.

## LOCAL CUISINE

Cuban, or *criolla,* cuisine is a mix of European (predominantly Spanish) and Afro-Caribbean influences. The staples of the cuisine include roasted and fried pork, beef, and chicken, usually accompanied by rice, beans, plantains, and yucca. Oddly, Cubans do not eat large amounts of seafood, although fish and lobster dishes are on the menu at most tourist restaurants. In general, Cubans do not use aggressive amounts of spice or hot peppers, although onions, garlic, and, to a much lesser extent, cumin are used fairly liberally.

With the exception of breakfast, most meals come accompanied with some combination of white rice and beans. *Arroz moro,* or *moros y cristianos* (Moors and Christians), is the common name for black beans mixed with white rice. *Congrí* is a similar dish of red beans and white rice already mixed. Sometimes the rice and beans are served separately.

The national dish—which unfortunately you won't often find on restaurant menus, but it's worth sampling if you do—is *ajiaco,* a chunky meat and vegetable stew. *Ajiaco* comes from the Taíno word "aji" for chile pepper, although the dish is seldom prepared very spicy. You're much more likely to find *ropa vieja* (literally, "old clothes"), a sauté of shredded beef, onions, and peppers; or *picadillo,* a similar concoction made with ground beef and sometimes featuring olives and raisins in the mix.

If you're looking for a light bite, try a *bocadito,* literally a "little bite," which is what they call a simple sandwich, usually made of ham and/or cheese.

---

## Fun Fact La Bomba

If you want to order papaya, remember to call it *fruta bomba*. In Cuba, the word "papaya" is almost always used as pejorative slang referring to a woman's most private part.

Aside from the excellent Coppelia ice creams, you'll generally find rather slim pickings for dessert. Flan is popular, but seldom outstanding. I feel similarly about *natilla,* a simple sweet pudding that usually comes in either chocolate or coconut flavors. Many dessert menus will feature some sort of sweet marmalade, usually *guayaba,* papaya, or coconut, accompanied by cheese. Unfortunately, the cheeses used are generally bland and nondescript.

## WETTING YOUR WHISTLE

Most Cubans simply drink water or any number of popular soft drinks, including Sprite and Coca-Cola, whose locally produced equivalents are called Cachito and Tu Cola, respectively. While many hotels and restaurants serve freshly squeezed orange juice for breakfast, you'll have a harder time finding other fresh fruit juices than you'd expect in the Caribbean tropics. One of the more interesting nonalcoholic drinks you're likely to run across is *guarapo,* the sweet juice of freshly pressed sugar cane.

Cubans also drink plenty of coffee, and they like to brew it strong. Order *café*

*espresso* for a straight shot, or *café con leche* if you'd like it mixed with warm milk. Ask for *café americano* if you want a milder brew.

Cuba produces a small handful of pretty good lager beers. Cristal, Bucanero, and Mayabe are the most popular. If you want something slightly darker and stronger, try a Bucanero dark. Cuba has recently begun to produce a few wines, under the Sorao label. If you're a wine drinker, you'll want to avoid these and hope there are some Chilean, Italian, or Spanish bottles on the wine list.

Cuba does produce excellent rums. Most visitors soon have their fill of mojitos (light rum with lime juice, fresh mint, sugar, and club soda) and daiquiris (light rum, sugar, lemon juice, and shaved ice). Another popular cocktail is the *cuba libre* ("Free Cuba"), which is simply a rum and Coke with a squeeze of lime. If you want something beyond the endless mojitos and daiquiris, you might enjoy a well-aged *añejo* rum, either neat or on the rocks. Try a Havana Club or Santiago brand 7-year *añejo reserva,* and you may even give up single malt scotch!

## 17 Recommended Books, Film & Music

There's a wealth of books on Cuba's history and politics. For a good historical overview, try Jaime Suchlicki's latest edition of **Cuba: From Columbus to Castro and Beyond** (Brasseys, Inc., 2002), or Richard Gott's **Cuba: A New History** (Yale University Press, 2004). At over 1,800 pages, Hugh Thomas's *Cuba, Or The Pursuit of Freedom* (Da Capo Press, 1998) is far more comprehensive, but a duller read.

A unique account of post-revolutionary Cuba comes from a well-known Latin American journalist, Alma Guillermoprieto, who writes of the 6 months she spent in Cuba in the early '70s teaching dance. **Dancing with Cuba: A Memoir of the Revolution** (Pantheon, 2004) is a portrait

of the artistic world of Cuba in the '70s and a self-reflective memoir of the author's political awakening.

No reading list for Cuba would be complete without a biography or two of Fidel Castro and Che Guevara. The best are Lyeceseter Coltman's **The Real Fidel Castro** (Yale University Press, 2005), Tad Szulc's **Fidel: A Critical Portrait** (Avon Books, 2000), and Jon Lee Anderson's **Che Guevara: A Revolutionary Life** (Grove, 1997). Also worth a read are *Guerilla Prince: The Untold Story of Fidel Castro* by Georgie Anne Geyer (Little, Brown & Company, 2002), and *The Life and Death of Che Guevara* by Jorge Castañeda (Vintage Books, 1998). There are also several volumes of writings worth looking into by both Fidel and Che. Che's own *The Motorcycle Diaries: Notes On a Latin American Journey* (Ocean Press, 2003) provides an interesting glimpse into the social and psychological genesis of this great revolutionary figure, although it deals with the period in Che's life prior to meeting Fidel and going to Cuba. The book was made into a very successful film by director Walter Salles.

Another compelling perspective on the Revolution is offered by Enrique Oltuski, a former Shell Oil engineer and a leader in the 26th of July movement, in *Vida Clandestina: My Life in the Cuban Revolution* (Jossey-Bass, 2002).

Any exploration into Cuban literature should include the works of poets José Martí and Nicolás Guillén, as well as the novels and prose writings of Alejo Carpentier and José Lezama Lima. Prominent works that exist in English include Guillermo Cabrera Infante's *Three Trapped Tigers* (Marlow & Co., 1997), and several of Reinaldo Arenas's novels and his best-selling autobiography *Before Night Falls* (Penguin, 1994), made into a stunning film by Julian Schnabel.

Also worth reading is Cristina García's novel, *Dreaming in Cuban* (Ballantine Books, 1993), which chronicles the lives of three Cuban women after the Revolution. If you like García's book, you might also enjoy Ana Menéndez's *Loving Che* (Atlantic Monthly Press, 2003), the story of one woman's quest to uncover the mysteries and romance of her mother's past.

Of course, it goes without saying that you've already read Hemingway's *The Old Man and the Sea* (Scribner, 1999) and Graham Greene's *Our Man in Havana* (Penguin, 1991).

Uruguayan-born mystery writer Daniel Chavarría has lived in Havana since 1968. His *Adios Muchachos* (Akashic Books, 2001), whose protagonist is the city's prettiest prostitute, is a tight and entertaining novel that captures the frenetic feel and folly of modern Cuba.

There's a huge selection of travelogues. A good place to start in this genre is *The Reader's Companion to Cuba*, edited by Alan Ryan and Christa Malone (Harvest Books, 1997), which includes entries by Trollope, Anaïs Nin, Langston Hughes, Thomas Merton, Tommy Lasorda, and Amiri Baraka, among others; and *Traveler's Tales Cuba: True Stories*, edited by Tom Miller (Traveler's Tales Inc., 2001), which focuses on more modern writers like Cristina García, Pico Iyer, Andrei Codrescu, and the editor himself.

Special-interest reading highlights include *The Pride of Havana: A History of Cuban Baseball* by Roberto González Echevarría (Oxford University Press, 2001); *The Havana Cigar: Cuba's Finest* by Charles Del Todesco (Abbeville Press, Inc., 1997); *Cars of Cuba* by Cristina García (Harry N. Abrams, 1995); and *Memories of a Cuban Kitchen* by Mary Urrutia Randelmann (Wiley Publishing, Inc., 1996).

To prepare your ears for the variety of Cuban beats you will hear on your trip, there are several books you may want to check out on Cuban music. Ned Sublette has written an extensive history of the Mambo, *Cuba & Its Music: From the First Drums to the Mambo* (Chicago Review Press, 2004), that takes an in-depth look at the roots of the mambo. If jazz is more in tune with your interests, check out *Cubano Be, Cubano Bop: One Hundred Years of Jazz in Cuba* (Smithsonian Books, 2003) by Leonardo Acosta and Daniel S. Whitesell. Or, for books that cover a wider range of Cuban music, look into Ed Morales's *The Latin Beat: The Rhythms & Roots of Latin Music, from Bossa Nova to Salsa & Beyond* (DaCapo Press, 2003) or *Cuban Music From A to Z* (Duke University Press, 2004) by Helio Orovio.

In addition to the poignant *Before Night Falls* and the excellent *The Motorcycle Diaries,* mentioned above, there are a host of wonderful films that can be rented prior to any trip to Cuba. One true classic film available on DVD is **Soy Cuba (I Am Cuba)** by the great Russian director Mikhail Kalatozov, who shot this Communist-era piece of social-realist propaganda in Cuba shortly after the Revolution. The film features a screen-play by Russian poet Yevgeny Yev-tushenko and the Cuban writer and filmmaker Enrique Piñeda Barnet.

Cuba's own film industry has produced several fine films, including the cele-brated *Fresa y Chocolate (Strawberry and Chocolate), Memorias del Subdesarrollo (Memories of Underdevelopment),* and *Muerte de un Burócrata (Death of a Bureaucrat),* all by Tomás Gutiérrez Alea. One of my favorite Cuban films is the animated comedy *Vampiros de la Habana (Vampires of Havana).*

For a good look into the conflict between Cubans in Cuba and their rela-tives and friends in the United States, check out *Azucar Amarga (Bitter Sugar)* by Leon Ichaso, or *Quien Diablos es Juli-eta (Who The Hell Is Juliette?)* by Carlos Marcovich. The movie *Buena Vista Social Club* documents the rediscovery and new-found fame of some of Cuba's great traditional musicians.

The accompanying Grammy-award winning CD *Buena Vista Social Club* is as good a place as any to start listening to Cuban music. Music is quite possibly Cuba's greatest cultural treasure and export. I recommend just about anything by Cuba's two great singer-songwriters Sil-vio Rodriguez and Pablo Milanes. These two, along with Noel Nicola, are widely credited with creating the regional genre of Nueva Trova, or New Folk music. Celina Gonzalez is the reigning queen of traditional Cuban folk music. For classic salsa, pick up discs by Celia Cruz, Los Van Van, and NG La Banda. Cuban jazz is world renowned and you can get a good glimpse into its depth and complexity by listening to Chucho Valdes, Irakere, and Gonzalo Rubalcaba. For a more in-depth discussion of Cuban music, see "Cuban Culture" in appendix A.

## FAST FACTS: Cuba

**Area Codes** Cuba has a somewhat arcane system of area codes. Area codes around the country range from 1- to 4-digits. To make a call within Cuba, you do not need to dial the area code if you are a calling a number within the same area code. However, if dialing another area code, you must first dial "0" then the area code.

**Business Hours** There are no hard and fast rules, but most businesses and banks are open Monday through Friday from 9am to 5pm. Some businesses and banks close for an hour for lunch. Shops and department stores, especially those that cater to tourists, tend to have slightly more extended hours, and are usually open on Saturday and Sunday.

**Cameras & Film** Never pack film—exposed or unexposed—in checked bags, because the new, more powerful scanners in most airports can fog film. The film you carry with you can be damaged by scanners as well. X-ray damage is cumulative; the faster the film, and the more times you put it through a scan-ner, the more likely the damage. Film under 800 ASA is usually safe for up to five scans. If you're taking your film through additional scans, U.S. regulations permit you to demand hand inspections. In international airports, you're at the mercy of airport officials. On international flights, store your film in transparent baggies, so you can remove it easily before you go through scanners. Keep in mind that airports are not the only places where your camera may be scanned: Highly trafficked attractions are X-raying visitors' bags with increasing frequency.

Most photo supply stores sell protective pouches designed to block damaging X-rays. The pouches fit both film and loaded cameras. They should protect your film in checked baggage, but they also may raise alarms and result in a hand inspection.

You'll have little to worry about if you are traveling with **digital cameras.** Unlike film, which is sensitive to light, the digital camera and storage cards are not affected by airport X-rays, according to Nikon. Still, if you plan to travel extensively, you may want to play it safe and hand-carry your digital equipment or ask that it be inspected by hand.

Carry-on scanners will not damage **videotape** in video cameras, but the magnetic fields emitted by the walk-through security gateways and hand-held inspection wands will. Always place your loaded camcorder on the screening conveyor belt or have it hand-inspected. Be sure your batteries are charged as you may be required to turn the device on to ensure that it's what it appears to be.

*Car Rentals* See "Getting Around," p. 49.

*Currency* See "Money," p. 24.

*Driving Rules* See "Getting Around," p. 49.

*Drugstores* Called *farmacias* in Spanish, drugstores are relatively common throughout the country, although not necessarily well stocked. Those at hospitals and major clinics are often open 24 hours. Many hotels, particularly the larger ones, have either a small pharmacy or basic medical clinic on-site. There's a 24-hour pharmacy at the international terminal of the José Martí International Airport in Havana.

*Electricity* You will find a mix of electrical currents and plug types in use in Cuba. Around 90% of the hotels and casas particulares use 110 volts current with standard U.S.-style two- or three-prong outlets. However, some outlets I found are rated 220 volts, particularly in hotels that cater to European clientele. These are usually marked and sometimes accept only two-prong round plugs. For all intents and purposes you should have personal appliances rated for 110-volt current, with U.S.-style prongs, or the appropriate converters. It is also a good idea to carry a three-to-two prong adapter for any appliance you have that has a three-prong plug.

*Embassies & Consulates* All major consulates and embassies, where present, are in Havana. **Canada:** Calle 30 no. 518, at the corner of Avenida 7, Miramar (© 7/204-2517; fax 7/204-2044). **United Kingdom:** Calle 34 no. 702, Miramar (© 7/204-1771; fax 7/204-8104). Though neither an embassy nor consulate, the **United States Interests Section,** Calle Calzada between Calles L and M, Vedado (© 7/833-3551; fax 7/833-1084), is the official U.S. government representation on the island.

*Emergencies*  In most cases, you will want to dial ✆ **116** for any emergency. This is technically the number for the police, but it seems to be gaining acceptance as a national number for any type of emergency. Alternately, you can dial ✆ **114** for an ambulance, and ✆ **115** for the fire department. The three-digit emergency numbers are part of an ongoing effort to institute a national program for emergency response. However, in some areas of the country it is still not fully functional. At none of these numbers can you assume you will find an English-speaking person on the other end.

*Etiquette & Customs*  Cubans are a friendly, open, and physically expressive people. They strike up conversations easily and seldom use the formal terms of address in Spanish. However, be aware that as a foreigner, many Cubans who start a conversation with you are hoping in some way to get some economic gain out of the relationship. *Jineterismo,* or jockeying, is a way of life in Cuba. This may involve anything from offers to take you to a specific restaurant or hotel (for a commission) to direct appeals for money or goods. See appendix A for more on *jineterismo.*

Dress is generally very informal, in large part due to the tough economic times faced by the broad population. Suits are sometimes used in business and governmental meetings, although a simple light, short-sleeved cotton shirt with tie, or a *guayabera,* are more common. The guayabera is a loose-fitting shirt with two or four outer pockets on the front and usually a few vertical bands of pleats or embroidery. The guayabera is worn untucked, and is quite acceptable at even the most formal of occasions.

Perhaps the greatest etiquette concern is about what you say. Open criticism of the government or Fidel Castro is a major taboo. Don't do it—especially in open public places. Thought police, community revolutionary brigades, and reprisals for vocal dissent are an ongoing legacy of Cuba's political reality. One effect of this is that while Cubans you meet will often be very open and expressive with you, they tend to immediately clam up the minute another Cuban unknown to them enters the equation.

*Holidays*  See "Calendar of Events," earlier in this chapter.

*Information*  See "Visitor Information," earlier in this chapter.

*Internet Access*  Internet access is becoming more and more common and available in Cuba. However, it is still in the early stages and most of your options will be confined to the business centers of higher-end hotels, particularly in Havana, Varadero, and Santiago de Cuba. Rates at hotel business centers range from CUC\$5 to CUC\$10 per hour. An alternative to hotel business centers are certain **Etecsa** offices equipped with computers and Internet access. In order to use these, you must purchase a CUC\$6 card good for 1 hour of usage. A scratch-off login number and password on the back is good for use on any Etecsa computer around the country.

*Language*  Spanish is the official language of Cuba. English is spoken at most tourist hotels, restaurants, and attractions. Outside of the tourist orbit, English is not widely spoken, and some rudimentary Spanish will go a long way.

Indigenous and African languages have had a profound and lasting influence, and you will find many words—like cigar, barbacoa, and conga—tracing their origin to indigenous and African sources used widely across the island. Various African dialects are still widely used in the songs and ceremonies of Santería and other syncretic religions, although almost no one speaks them conversationally.

*Laundry*  Dry cleaners and laundromats—be they full-service or self-serve—are few and far between in Cuba. Hotel laundry services, which can sometimes be expensive, are far more common.

*Liquor Laws*  Cuba has no firm or clear liquor laws. Beer, wine, and liquor are served at most restaurants and are available at most gift shops and hard-currency stores.

*Mail*  A post office is called a *correo* in Spanish. You can get stamps at the post office and gift shops or the front desk in most hotels. The Cuban postal system is extremely slow and untrustworthy. You can count on every parcel and piece of mail being opened and inspected. The price is CUC50¢ for a postcard to anywhere in the world. For a letter, the cost is CUC80¢. A package of up to 1 kilogram (2.2 lb.) will cost CUC$10 to CUC$20 to ship depending upon your destination country.

However, it is best to send anything of any value via an established international courier service. **DHL,** Calle 26 and Avenida 1, Miramar, Havana (✆ 7/204-1578; www.dhl.com), provides broad coverage to most of Cuba. **EMS Cubapost,** Calle 21 no. 1009, between Calles 10 and 12, Vedado, Havana (✆ 7/831-3328), is Cuba's state-run express-mail service, with desks at most post offices. *Beware:* Despite what you may be told, packages sent overnight to U.S. addresses tend to take 3 to 4 days to reach their destination.

*Maps*  Most car-rental agencies and many hotels will give you a copy of basic nationwide and Havana road maps. The Cuban Geographic and Cartographic Institute publishes a couple of much more detailed maps; most tourist gift shops and Infotur kiosks carry these maps. If you're buying a map before your trip, try to get the **International Travel Map: Cuba** (ITMB Publishing; www.itmb. com). You'll also find good maps online at **www.cubaroutes.com** and **www. cubamapa.com**.

*Newspapers & Magazines*  The nationwide Spanish-language daily, *Granma,* is a thin paper with sparse coverage of local and international news, and a strong party-line editorial bias. The paper is not nearly as widely available as daily papers in most other countries, although there are some street vendors, and many hotels do get copies each morning. English digest versions of *Granma* come out every few days and are available at many hotels. A handful of other daily and weekly newspapers are published, and usually even harder to find than *Granma.* These include *Trabajadores, Juventud Rebelede,* and a host of regional rags.

Probably the most useful newspaper for travelers is the bilingual cultural publication *Cartelera,* which is available at the front desks of most hotels in Havana. There are also several periodic glossy magazines, some of which are bilingual; of these, *Prisma* and *Business Tips on Cuba* are of most interest to foreign visitors.

*Passports*  **For Residents of the United States:** Whether you're applying in person or by mail, you can download passport applications from the U.S. State

Department website at **http://travel.state.gov**. To find your regional passport office, either check the U.S. State Department website or call the **National Passport Information Center** toll-free number (© **877/487-2778**) for automated information.

**For Residents of Canada:** Passport applications are available at travel agencies throughout Canada or from the central **Passport Office,** Department of Foreign Affairs and International Trade, Ottawa, ON K1A 0G3 (© **800/567-6868**; www.ppt.gc.ca).

**For Residents of the United Kingdom:** To pick up an application for a standard 10-year passport (5-year passport for children under 16), visit your nearest passport office, major post office, or travel agency or contact the **United Kingdom Passport Service** at © **0870/521-0410** or search its website at www.ukpa.gov.uk.

**For Residents of Ireland:** You can apply for a 10-year passport at the **Passport Office,** Setanta Centre, Molesworth Street, Dublin 2 (© **01/671-1633**; http://foreignaffairs.gov.ie). Those under age 18 and over 65 must apply for a €12 3-year passport. You can also apply at 1A South Mall, Cork (© **021/272-525**) or at most main post offices.

**For Residents of Australia:** You can pick up an application from your local post office or any branch of Passports Australia, but you must schedule an interview at the passport office to present your application materials. Call the **Australian Passport Information Service** at © **131-232,** or visit the government website at www.passports.gov.au.

**For Residents of New Zealand:** You can pick up a passport application at any New Zealand Passports Office or download it from their website. Contact the **Passports Office** at © **0800/225-050** in New Zealand or 04/474-8100, or log on to www.passports.govt.nz.

*Pets* Pets can be brought into Cuba with proper documentation and vaccinations. Definitely contact your closest Cuban consulate or embassy before attempting to bring your pet with you.

*Police* Nationwide, you can dial © **116** for police, although you shouldn't expect to find an English-speaking person on the other end of the line. In general, the police are quite helpful and not to be feared. Bribery and graft are not an issue. In the event of robbery, the police are your best bet, but for physical emergencies or other threats of serious danger, you are probably best off contacting your embassy.

*Smoking* Although Fidel gave up smoking years ago, Cuba remains a major producer of tobacco and tobacco products. Many Cubans smoke. Antismoking campaigns are just beginning in Cuba. A few hotels and restaurants have created nonsmoking rooms and areas, although given the local environment and the fact that a majority of the tourism here is European, this remains the exception, not the rule.

*Taxes* There are no direct or specific taxes on goods or services in Cuba. However, tourist restaurants have begun adding a 10% service charge on to their bills, so be sure to check before calculating any tip—although it's doubtful that the 10% goes to your server. There is a CUC$25 departure tax that must be paid in cash upon leaving the country.

*Telephones* The phone numbering system inside Cuba is being modernized, but it remains quite confusing. City and area codes can range from 1 to 4 digits, and individual phone numbers can range from 4 to 7 digits. You do not need to use the city or area code for local calls, but you must dial 0 followed by the city or area code for any long-distance call within Cuba, or to a cellphone.

**To call Cuba:** If you're calling Cuba from the United States:

1. Dial the international access code: 011
2. Dial the country code: 53
3. Dial the area code and then the number. The whole number you'd dial for a number in Havana (area code 7) would be 011-53-7-000-0000.

**To make international calls:** To make international calls from Cuba, first dial 119 and then the country code (U.S. or Canada 1, U.K. 44, Ireland 353, Australia 61, New Zealand 64). Next you dial the area code and number. For example, if you wanted to call the British Embassy in Washington, D.C., you would dial 00-1-202-588-7800.

**For directory assistance:** Dial 113 if you're looking for a number inside Cuba, and dial 180 for numbers to all other countries.

**For operator assistance:** If you need operator assistance in making a call, dial 00 if you're trying to make an international call and 0 if you want to call a number in Cuba.

**Toll-free numbers:** Numbers beginning with 0800 within Cuba are toll-free, but calling a 1-800 number in the States from Cuba is not toll-free. In fact, it costs the same as an overseas call.

*Time Zone* Havana is 5 hours behind GMT, or on par with Eastern Standard Time in the United States and Canada. Daylight saving time is observed by setting clocks ahead 1 hour from the last Sunday in March to the last Sunday in October.

*Tipping* Most Cuban workers earn incredibly low salaries in dollar terms, so tips are an extremely important and coveted source of supplemental income. With the rise in tourism, all sorts of workers now expect and work for tips, including taxi drivers, porters, waiters, guides, and restaurant musicians. Taxi drivers in particular are loath to give any small change on a fare. So if the meter reads CUC$2.05, you are expected to pay CUC$3, although you are certainly within your rights to ask for CUC50¢ or so change. Porters should be tipped between CUC50¢ and CUC$1 per bag. Some restaurants include a 10% service charge, although you should probably tip the waiter an additional 5% to 10% depending upon the quality of service, or even more, as it's very doubtful they see much of that 10% service charge.

*Toilets* Public restrooms are hard to come by. You must usually count on the generosity of some hotel or restaurant, or duck into a museum or other attraction. Although it's rare that a tourist would be denied the use of the facilities, you should always ask first. In broad terms, the sanitary conditions of public restrooms in Cuba is much higher than those found throughout the developing world, although at gas stations and less affluent establishments, toilet seats are sometimes missing.

Many restrooms have an attendant, who is sometimes responsible for dispensing toilet paper. Upon exiting, you are expected to either leave a tip, or pay a specified fee, between CUC5¢ and CUC20¢.

*Water*   Water is generally safe to drink throughout the country. However, since many travelers have tender digestive tracts, I recommend playing it safe and sticking to bottled water, sold as *agua mineral sin gas.*

# 3

# Suggested Cuba Itineraries

Cuba is a big island—the largest in the Caribbean—and its attractions and charms run the gamut from the hustle and bustle of Havana, to the colonial grandeur of Trinidad and a host of other small and shockingly well-preserved old cities and towns, to the steamy, vibrant streets of Santiago, to the sparkling waters and white sands of a half-dozen or more top-notch beach destinations. So, you will need to plan well to make the most out of any trip here. The following itineraries should be used as rough outlines. Other options include specialized itineraries focused on a particular interest or activity. Bird-watchers could design an itinerary that visits a series of prime bird-watching sites. Latin dance or art enthusiasts could arrange a specialized trip to focus on these interests. And revolutionary history buffs could build a trip around visits to the Moncada barracks (Cuartel de Moncada) in Santiago, the Che Guevara Memorial (Monumento Ernesto Che Guevara) in Santa Clara, and the Bay of Pigs (Playa Girón). Feel free to pick and choose—you can combine a bit of one, with a smidgen of another, or come up with something entirely on your own.

## 1 Cuba in 1 Week

This is a tough one. Many visitors are content to spend an entire week soaking up the rays and lying in the sand at an all-inclusive beach resort. I sometimes devote an entire week to Havana. However, the following itinerary seeks to pack a handful of Cuba's top attractions into a concise, yet doable, week-long visit. You'll get a taste of the country's best big city and it's top colonial-era town, as well as a bit of time on the beach.

### Day ❶: Arrive & Settle In To Havana

Arrive and check-in to your hotel. Take an afternoon walk along the **Malecón** and have a sunset cocktail at the **Hotel Nacional de Cuba** ✹✹ (p. 91). For dinner, head to either **La Guarida** ✹✹ (p. 102) or **La Cocina de Lilliam** ✹✹ (p. 104), two of the city's best *paladares.* Be sure to make a reservation as soon as you get to your hotel, because these places book up fast. After dinner, catch some jazz at **La Zorra y el Cuervo** ✹✹ (p. 124).

### Day ❷: Step Back In Time

Start the morning off in **Habana Vieja** (see chapter 4). Visit the **Plaza de la Catedral,** the **Plaza de Armas, Plaza Vieja,** and **Plaza de San Francisco.** Be sure to tour the **Museo de la Ciudad** ✹✹ (p. 107), the **Castillo de la Real Fuerza** ✹ (p. 106), and any other attractions that catch your attention. Have lunch at **La Bodeguita del Medio** ✹✹ (p. 99). After lunch head toward Parque Central and visit **El Capitolio** ✹ (p. 111), the **Museo Nacional de las Bellas Artes** ✹✹ (p. 109), and the **Museo de la**

# Cuba in 1 Week / Cuba in 2 Weeks

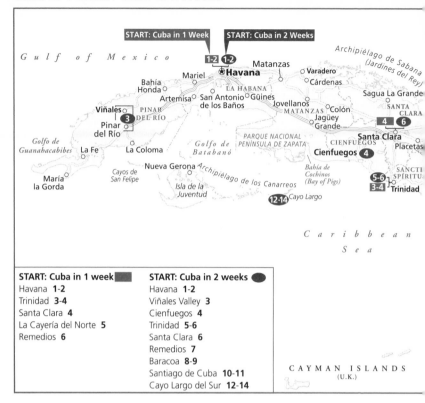

**Revolución** ⍟ (p. 108). Finish up your afternoon strolling along the outdoor art exhibit that is **Callejón de Hammel** ⍟⍟⍟ (p. 110). In the evening go to the **Tropicana** ⍟⍟⍟ (p. 123) for dinner and a show.

### Day ❸: Time for Trinidad

Head for Trinidad. Stay either in the new **Gran Hotel Iberostar Trinidad** ⍟⍟⍟ (p. 191) or one of the many *casas particulares* right in the colonial center of this classic little city. Spend the afternoon touring Trinidad's colonial era landmarks, including the **Plaza Mayor,** the **Plazuela El Jigüe,** the **Iglesia de la Santísima Trinidad,** and the **Museo Romántico** ⍟⍟ (p. 190). For dinner, make a reservation at **Paladar Estela** ⍟⍟ (p. 194). After dinner, stroll around the Plaza Mayor and listen

for where the action is. It might be a salsa or *son* band playing on the steps below the **Casa de la Música** ⍟ (p. 194), or it might be in any one of several clubs nearby.

### Day ❹: Checking In With Che

Spend the morning walking around Trinidad, and shopping at the various little street markets around town. From Trinidad, head north to **Santa Clara** ⍟, Che Guevara's city. Your first and most important stop here is the massive and impressive **Monumento Ernesto Che Guevara** ⍟ (p. 173), set on the Plaza de la Revolución Che Guevara. In the early evening, head to **Parque Vidal,** the downtown heart and soul of Santa Clara. Stop in to tour the **Teatro La Caridad,** and then head to **La Casa del Gobernador** (p. 176) for dinner. After dinner,

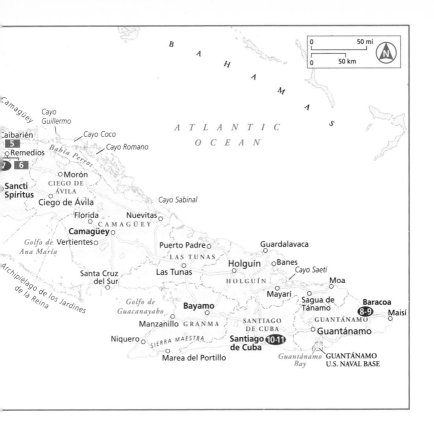

see if there's anything happening at **Club Mejunje** ✦✦ (p. 176).

### Days ⑤ & ⑥: Hit The Beach
From Santa Clara, head to **La Cayería del Norte** ✦✦✦ (p. 177), where you will find a handful of large, luxurious resorts on some of the finest beaches in Cuba. Be sure to stop for a bit in the tiny, colonial-era town of **Remedios** ✦✦✦ (p. 176) on your way. And then settle in for some

serious relaxation. There's excellent snorkeling and scuba diving, as well as numerous opportunities to indulge in other watersports. Or you can just chill.

### Day ⑦: Going Home
Return to Havana in time for your international connection. If you have extra time, head to the Calle Tacón street market ✦✦✦ (p. 121) to do some last-minute shopping before you go.

## 2 Cuba in 2 Weeks

If you've got 2 weeks, you'll be able to hit all the highlights mentioned above, as well as some others, including Cuba's second city Santiago, a side-trip to the gorgeous *mogotes* and tobacco farms of the Viñales valley, and visits to Cienfuegos and Baracoa, two underappreciated Cuban cities. And, you get to do all this at a slightly more relaxed pace to boot. This itinerary starts off very similar to the one-week version above, but soon diverges.

## Day ❶: Arrive & Settle In To Havana

Arrive and settle in to your hotel. Spend the afternoon walking along the **Malecón** ✪✪✪ and have a sunset cocktail at the **Hotel Nacional** ✪✪ (p. 91). After sunset, head over for dinner at **Los Doce Apóstoles** ✪ (p. 105) in the **Parque Histórico Morro y Cabaña** ✪✪ (p. 114). Stick around for the *cañonazo* ceremony.

## Day ❷: Step Back In Time

Start the morning off in **Habana Vieja** ✪✪✪. Visit the **Plaza de la Catedral,** the **Plaza de Armas, Plaza Vieja,** and **Plaza de San Francisco.** Be sure to tour the **Museo de la Ciudad** ✪✪ (p. 107), the **Castillo de la Real Fuerza** ✪ (p. 106), and any other attractions that catch your attention. Have lunch at **La Bodeguita del Medio** ✪✪ (p. 99). After lunch head toward Parque Central and visit **El Capitolio** ✪ (p. 111), the **Museo Nacional de las Bellas Artes** ✪✪ (p. 109), and the **Museo de la Revolución** ✪ (p. 108). Finish up your afternoon strolling along the outdoor art exhibit that is **Callejón de Hammel** ✪✪✪ (p. 110). In the evening head to the **Tropicana** ✪✪✪ (p. 123) for dinner and a show.

## Day ❸: The Viñales Valley By Day, Jazz At Night

Sign on for an organized day-tour of the **Viñales valley** ✪✪. You'll get to take in some of Cuba's best natural scenery, and also visit a tobacco farm and cigar-rolling facility. You'll probably also visit the Guayabitas liquor factory in **Pinar del Río** (p. 130), and take a quick tour through **La Cueva del Indio** (p. 132). This jam packed day-tour should still get you back to Havana in time for a dinner

at one of the city's standout paladares, followed by some hot jazz at **La Zorra y el Cuervo** ✪✪ (p. 124) or the **Jazz Café** ✪ (p. 124).

## Day ❹: Cienfuegos, la Perla del Sur

Pick up a rental car and head for **Cienfuegos** ✪, a bustling port city on the southern coast, with a compact, yet very attractive colonial-era core. Get to know the old center around **Parque José Martí,** visiting the **Catedral de la Purísima Concepción** and the **Teatro Tomás Terry** ✪ (p. 180). In the afternoon, head out to the Punta Gorda district and have a sunset drink at the **Cienfuegos Yacht Club** (p. 182). For dinner, try the historic old **Palacio del Valle** ✪ (p. 185).

## Day ❺: Time for Trinidad

From Cienfuegos, it's a short hop to **Trinidad** ✪✪✪, with some beautiful scenery along the coast. Stay either in the new **Gran Hotel Iberostar Trinidad** ✪✪✪ (p. 191) or one of the many casas particulares right in the colonial center of this classic little city. Spend the afternoon touring Trinidad's colonial era landmarks, including the **Plaza Mayor,** the **Plazuela El Jigüe,** the **Iglesia de la Santísima Trinidad,** and the **Museo Romántico** ✪✪ (p. 190). For dinner, make a reservation at **Paladar Estela** ✪✪ (p. 194). After dinner, stroll around the area around the Plaza Mayor and listen for where the action is. It might be a salsa or *son* band playing on the steps below the **Casa de la Música** ✪ (p. 196), or it might be in any one of several clubs nearby.

## Day ❻: Checking In With Che

Spend the morning walking around Trinidad, and shopping at the various little street markets around town. From

Trinidad, head north to **Santa Clara** ⍟, Che Guevara's city. You're first and most important stop here is the massive and impressive **Monumento Ernesto Che Guevara** ⍟ (p. 172), set on the Plaza de la Revolución Che Guevara. In the early evening, head to **Parque Vidal,** the downtown heart and soul of Santa Clara. Stop in to tour the **Teatro La Caridad,** and then head to **La Casa del Gobernador** (p. 176) for dinner. After dinner, see if there's anything happening at **Club Mejunje** ⍟⍟ (p. 176).

### Day ⑦: Remedios and Back To Havana

In the morning, drive to the nearby town of **Remedios** ⍟⍟⍟ (p. 176). This is one of Cuba's smallest and best-preserved old colonial-era towns. Tour the **Iglesia de San Juan Bautista** ⍟⍟ (p. 176), with its intricately carved and ornate baroque altar, and stop for a cool drink or light lunch at the open-air **Café El Louvre** ⍟ (p. 177) right on the town's central plaza. Allow yourself a little over 4 hours to drive from Remedios back to Havana, where you'll turn in your rental car, before taking flight for the rest of your trip.

### Days ⑧ & ⑨: Head East to Baracoa

From Havana, take a flight to **Baracoa** ⍟⍟⍟ (p. 248), the oldest, and arguably most beautiful city in Cuba. You'll definitely want to stay in the **Hotel El Castillo** ⍟⍟ (p. 252), with its commanding setting on a hillside over the city. Spend 1 day exploring the architecture

and old-world charms of the city, and another hiking the lush forests around **El Yunque** ⍟⍟ (p. 251). Despite its diminutive size, Baracoa is a bustling little burg with excellent art galleries, bars, and nightlife.

### Days ⑩ & ⑪: Sweltering Santiago

In Baracoa, you can arrange for a transfer or private taxi to **Santiago de Cuba** ⍟⍟⍟, the island's second-largest city. If you want to be in the heart of downtown, choose the **Hotel Casa Granda** ⍟⍟ (p. 268), while if you're looking for more comfort, amenities, and facilities, you should book a room in the **Meliá Santiago de Cuba** ⍟⍟ (p. 269). You'll need 2 days to fully explore this beautiful colonial-era port city, with its host of historical and architectural attractions. Be sure to schedule at least 1 night at Santiago's fabulous **Casa de la Trova** ⍟⍟⍟ (p. 276).

### Days ⑫, ⑬ & ⑭: Hot Sun, Cool Sands, Clear Water

Finish your trip off with some downtime at an all-inclusive resort on **Cayo Largo del Sur** ⍟⍟⍟ (p. 149). You'll have to fly here from Havana, and you're best off just buying a 3-day/2-night package from any of the tour desks in Havana or Santiago. You should easily be able to arrange a flight from Santiago to Havana that connects with a flight to Cayo Largo and to ensure that your flight from Cayo Largo gets you into Havana in time for your international connection and flight home.

## 3 Cuba for Families

Most of Cuba's principal attractions—its art, architecture, history, music, cigars, and so on—are geared toward adults. There are, in fact, few attractions or activities geared for the very young. This is why I recommend families base themselves out of a large all-inclusive resort with a well-developed children's program. For my money, Varadero is the best bet, although a case can be made for Guardalavaca, as well. Both have a host of excellent all-inclusive resorts. If your children are worldly and inquisitive, feel free to swap out some resort days for the more cultural side trips to cities, destinations, and attractions described in some of the other itineraries in this chapter.

### Day ❶: Arrive in Varadero

Fly directly into **Varadero.** I recommend the **Tryp Península Varadero** 🏶🏶🏶 (p. 163), which has an excellent children's program and tons of activity and tour options. After settling into your room, check out the **children's program** and any **activities** or **tours** scheduled for the coming days. Feel free to adapt the following days' suggestions accordingly. Spend some time on the beach or at the pool. After dinner, attend the hotel's nightly cabaret show.

### Day ❷: Take In An Attraction Or Two

Varadero is chock-full of attractions geared toward the whole family. You can head to the little **Parque de Diversiones** (p. 156), which is a bare-bones amusement park, or see the dolphin show at the local **Delfinario** (p. 156). If your family is adventurous, try the **Jungle Tour** 🏶, which is a fast and furious trip through the mangroves aboard sit-on-top motorized watercraft.

### Day ❸: A Trip To Trinidad

All of the hotel tour desks offer day trips to **Trinidad** 🏶🏶🏶. While some travel via bus, you should splurge and take a plane. Trinidad is an immaculately preserved colonial city, with a very compact central core that shouldn't tire or bore your children. In fact, they should get a kick out of the rough cobblestone streets, ancient architecture, vibrant street markets, and a real glimpse into everyday Cuban life.

### Day ❹: Parents' Day Off

Drop the kids off with the **children's program** for at least 1 full day and treat yourselves to some time alone. If you play golf, schedule a round at the **Varadero Golf Club** 🏶 (p. 156). Or, if you want to pamper yourself, take advantage of the excellent **spa services** right at the Tryp Peninsula Varadero. Pick up the kids and treat them to dinner off of the resort grounds. I recommend the **Mesón del Quijote** (p. 164), which is housed in a building with a medieval-style turret beside it.

### Day ❺: Head For The High Seas

Sign up for a day-cruise on one of the many sailboats operating out of Varadero. These cruises head out to nearby cays, and include some snorkeling time, as well as lunch either on the boat or on some private little island beach.

### Day ❻: Parents' Night Off

This is your last day, so take advantage of the resort's in-house facilities and activities, but be sure to reserve a babysitter for the evening and make reservations for dinner and a show at the **Tropicana Matanzas** 🏶🏶 (p. 152).

### Day ❼: Heading Home

Use any spare time you have before your flight out of **Varadero** to buy last-minute souvenirs and gifts, or just laze on the beach or by the pool.

## 4 Colonial Treasures Highlights Tour

Cuba's colonial cities are some of the best preserved and architecturally intact examples to be found anywhere in the hemisphere. From the remarkable restored grandeur of Old Havana to the rugged realism of Trinidad to tiny Baracoa—the oldest colonial city in the Americas—there's a wealth of history, beauty, and overall awe to be found touring the country's colonial treasures.

## Days ❶ & ❷: Havana

Follow the itinerary as laid out above in "Cuba In 2 Weeks."

## Day ❸: Cienfuegos

Pick up a rental car and head for **Cienfuegos** ✿, a bustling port city on the southern coast, with a compact, yet very attractive, colonial-era core. Get to know the old center around **Parque José Martí,** visiting the **Catedral de la Purísima Concepción** and the **Teatro Tomás Terry** ✿ (p. 180). In the afternoon, head out to the Punta Gorda district and have a sunset drink at the **Cienfuegos Yacht Club** (p. 182). For dinner head to the historic old **Palacio del Valle** ✿✿ (p. 185).

## Day ❹: Trinidad

From Cienfuegos, it's a short hop to **Trinidad** ✿✿✿, with some beautiful scenery along the coast. Stay either in the new **Gran Hotel Iberostar Trinidad** ✿✿✿ (p. 191), or one of the many casas particulares right in the colonial center of this classic little city. Spend the afternoon touring Trinidad's colonial-era landmarks, including the **Plaza Mayor,** the **Plazuela El Jigüe,** the **Iglesia de la Santísima Trinidad,** and the **Museo Romántico** ✿✿ (p. 190). For dinner, make a reservation at **Paladar Estela** ✿✿ (p. 194). After dinner, stroll around the Plaza Mayor and listen for where the action is. It might be a salsa or *son* band playing on the steps below the **Casa de la Música** ✿ (p. 186), or it might be in any one of several clubs nearby.

## Day ❺: Sancti Spíritus

While its colonial center is modest in size and level of restoration, **Sancti Spíritus** nonetheless retains a wonderful sense of its former glory and receives far less tourist traffic than any other city on this tour. You'll definitely want to walk along **Calle Llano** ✿, a narrow cobblestone alleyway of pastel-colored and tile-roof houses. You'll also want to have lunch or dinner at one of the outdoor patio tables overlooking the old stone **Puente Yayabo (Yayabo bridge),** which was built in 1825. Be sure to book a room at the **Hostal del Rijo** ✿✿, a very comfortable hotel in a restored old mansion set right on a quiet little plaza.

## Days ❻ & ❼: Camagüey

Although far less celebrated—or visited—than Trinidad, **Camagüey** ✿✿ just may be Cuba's richest colonial-era city, outside of Old Havana, in terms of art, architecture, and general ambience. The city's colonial core retains its highly irregular layout and an unequaled collection of impressive 16th-, 17th-, and 18th-century churches. The city's **Plaza del Carmen** ✿✿ (p. 220) and **Plaza San Juan de Dios** ✿✿✿ (p. 220) are two impeccable and evocative city squares. Sitting right near the center of all the ancient action, the wonderful old **Gran Hotel** ✿✿ (p. 221) should be your first choice.

## Day ❽: Bayamo

Even though most of this city was deliberately torched in 1869 as an act of civil disobedience, it still makes a wonderful stop on a route taking in Cuba's principal colonial cities. You'll definitely want to stay at the **Hotel Royalton** ✿ (p. 242), which sits right on the central **Parque Céspedes** ✿✿. You'll also want to visit the **Casa Natal de Céspedes** ✿ (p. 241), the birthplace of the "father of the Cuban nation," and the only house on the square that escaped destruction from the fire.

## Days ❾ & ❿: Santiago de Cuba

This is a colonial highlights tour, so you'll want to stay in the heart of downtown; choose either the **Hotel Casa Granda** ✿✿ (p. 268), the **Hostal Basilio** ✿ (p. 267), or the private **Casa Leonardo y Rosa** ✿ (p. 269). You'll need 2 days to fully explore this beautiful colonial-era port city, with

# Colonial Treasures

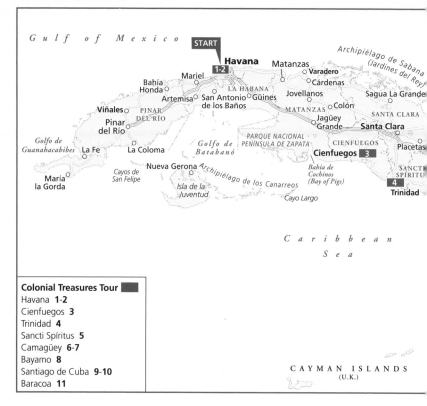

its host of historical and architectural attractions. Be sure to schedule at least 1 night at Santiago's fabulous **Casa de la Trova** ✦✦✦ (p. 276). Turn in your rental car here in Santiago.

## Day ⑪: Baracoa

From Santiago, take a Víazul bus, private taxi, or short commuter flight to **Baracoa** ✦✦✦ (p. 248), the oldest and arguably most beautiful city in Cuba. It's fitting to finish off this tour in the oldest city on the island. You'll definitely want to stay in the **Hotel El Castillo** ✦✦ (p. 252), with its commanding setting on

a hillside over the city. Spend your time here exploring the architecture and old-world charms of the city. Despite its diminutive size, Baracoa is also a bustling little city with excellent art galleries, bars, and nightlife.

## Day ⑫: Heading Home

From Baracoa, take a flight back to **Havana** in time for your international connection. If you have extra time, head to the **Calle Tacón** street market ✦✦✦ (p. 121) to do some last minute shopping before you go.

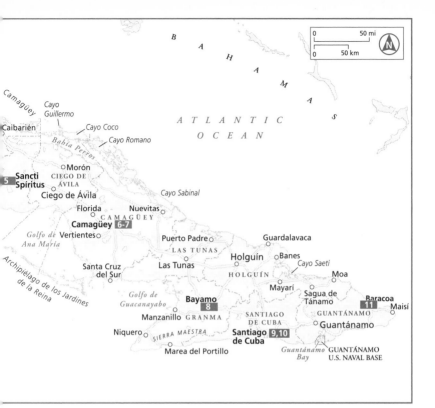

Camagüey
Cayo
Guillermo
Cayo Coco
Caibarién
Cayo Romano
Bahía Perros

ATLANTIC
OCEAN

Morón
**Sancti** CIEGO DE
**5 Spíritus** ÁVILA
Ciego de Ávila
Cayo Sabinal
Florida Nuevitas
CAMAGÜEY
**Camagüey 6-7**
Golfo de Vertientes
Ana María
Puerto Padre
Guardalavaca
LAS TUNAS
**Holguín** Banes
Santa Cruz Las Tunas
del Sur HOLGUÍN
Cayo Saetí
Moa
Archipiélago de los Jardines
Golfo de
Guacanayabo
**Bayamo**
Mayarí
Sagua de
Tánamo
**Baracoa**
**11** Maisí
de la Reina
Manzanillo GRANMA
SANTIAGO
DE CUBA
GUANTÁNAMO
Niquero SIERRA MAESTRA
**Santiago 9,10**
de Cuba
Guantánamo
Marea del Portillo
Guantánamo GUANTÁNAMO
Bay U.S. NAVAL BASE

0          50 mi
0          50 km

## 5 Havana in 3 Days

Havana is an amazing—at times, overwhelming—city, overflowing with history, art, architecture, culture, nightlife, and more. Three days will allow you to visit its most important attractions, and maybe even to discover some of its lesser known charms.

### Day ❶: Start In The Old City

Start your day in Habana Vieja. Visit the **Plaza de la Catedral,** the **Plaza de Armas, Plaza Vieja,** and **Plaza de San Francisco.** Be sure to tour the **Museo de la Ciudad** ✮✮ (p. 107), the **Castillo de la Real Fuerza** ✮ (p. 106), and any other attractions that catch your attention. Have lunch at **La Bodeguita del Medio** ✮✮ (p. 99). Spend the afternoon exploring the area around Parque Central, which includes **El Capitolio** ✮ (p. 111), the

**Museo Nacional de las Bellas Artes** ✮✮ (p. 109), and the **Museo de la Revolución** ✮ (p. 108). Make a reservation in advance and take the 2pm tour of the Partagas cigar factory (p. 111).

As the day cools down, take a stroll on the **Malecón** ✮✮✮ (p. 112). If you've got the energy, you should be able to make the 20-minute walk to the **Hotel Nacional** ✮✮ (p. 91) in time for a sunset mojito at their outdoor bar.

**LA GUARIDA** ✦✦✦
For dinner you'll want to climb the rickety, dimly-lit steps to La Guarida, the city's most celebrated paladar. Reservations here are essential. See p. 102.

## Day ❷: Vedado & Miramar

Start the morning strolling along the beautiful tombs and mausoleums of **Cementerio de Colón** ✦✦ (p. 112). From here, head over the outdoor art exhibit that is the **Callejón de Hammel** ✦✦✦ (p. 110). By now, you should have worked up enough of a sweat for a refreshing bowl of ice cream at **Coppelia** ✦ (p. 113).

From Vedado, take a Coco Taxi to Miramar and the Playa district. Be sure to visit the **Maqueta de la Habana** ✦ (p. 114), a rather impressive mock-up model of the entire city. Since you're out in this neck of the woods, have a late lunch at **La Cocina de Lilliam** ✦✦ (p. 104), on the one hand because it's an excellent restaurant, and on the other, because your dinner tonight will be pedestrian at best. After lunch, head to the **José Martí Memorial** (p. 113), and enjoy the panoramic view from the highest spot in Havana. See if it matches up well with what you saw and learned at the Maqueta de la Habana.

**TROPICANA** ✦✦✦
It's time to pull out all the stops and head to the **Tropicana** for dinner and a show. This place is the original and still best cabaret show in Cuba. Stick around after the show for some serious salsa dancing in the attached Salón Arcos de Cristal club. See p. 123.

## Day ❸: More Habana Vieja

On Day 3, give yourself another day in **Habana Vieja**—there's just no way you had a chance to see it all in 1 day. Be sure to visit some of the art galleries and to spend some time shopping at the **Calle Tacón** outdoor market ✦✦✦ (p. 121). Have lunch on one of the ancient plazas here. I recommend either the restaurant **Santo Angel** ✦ (p. 100) or the **Cafetería El Portal** (p. 101). In the late afternoon, head over to the **Parque Histórico Morro y Cabaña** ✦✦ (p. 114) and explore the two forts and the various museums at this complex.

**LOS DOCE APÓSTOLES** ✦
After touring the complex, grab an outdoor table near sunset at **Los Doce Apóstoles,** and enjoy the view of Havana across the harbor from this restaurant. Be sure to finish your dinner in time for the *cañonazo* ceremony. See p. 105.

After dinner and the *cañonazo*, head to **Zorra y el Cuervo** ✦✦ (p. 124) for a late night, jazz concert.

# 4

# Havana

*by Eliot Greenspan*

It's hard to convey the wonder, sensuality, and odd fallen beauty of Havana. Hard to imagine a city with such rhythm and verve. A city at once so tremendously vibrant and at the same time laid-back. Until you've taken a lazy stroll along the Malecón, gotten lost in the time warp of Habana Vieja's colonial cobblestone streets, ridden in a 1940 Dodge taxi through crumbling Centro Habana, danced salsa until dawn after catching the Tropicana floor show, or witnessed Afro-Cuban religious rituals on the street, anything I write will simply not suffice.

Originally established in 1514 on Cuba's southern coast, by November 1519, San Cristóbal de la Habana had been moved to and rechristened in its present-day location on the island's north coast, at the mouth of a deep and spacious harbor with a narrow and protected harbor channel. Before long, Havana had become the most important port in the Spanish colonial empire, a natural final gathering place for the resupply and embarkation of the Spanish fleet before returning to the Old Country laden with bounty. By 1607, Havana had been declared the capital of colonial Cuba, and by the early 1700s, it was the third-largest city in the Spanish empire, behind Mexico City and Lima.

Subsequent centuries saw Havana grow steadily in wealth, size, and prominence. Havana was luckily spared the bulk of the violence and fighting that occurred in Cuba's Wars of Independence, and later revolutionary war. Following the mysterious sinking of the USS *Maine* in Havana harbor in 1898, a long period of direct U.S. control and indirect U.S. influence followed. This period saw the first indications of suburban sprawl and the growing importance of the western neighborhoods of Vedado and Miramar. This era was also marked by a strong presence of mob activity, with the likes of Al Capone, Meyer Lanksy, and Lucky Luciano setting up shop in Havana.

Havana has been largely frozen in time in the wake of the 1959 Revolution. Decades of economic crisis and shortages have left much of Havana in severe decay and decomposition. The great exception to this rule is Habana Vieja, which has been meticulously restored to much of its colonial glory. Although this is beginning to change, with the recent boom in tourism and tourism-related growth, what new construction has occurred over the past 40 years has largely borne the drab architectural stamp of the former Soviet Union and its central state planning. Luckily, most of this has taken place largely outside the boundaries of the traditional city center. Today, Havana, with some 2.5 million inhabitants, is the largest city in the Caribbean and Cuba's undisputed political, business, and cultural center.

## 1 Orientation

## ARRIVING

### BY PLANE

Arriving international passengers clear Customs on the ground level of Terminal 3 at the **José Martí International Airport** (© 7/266-4133; airport code HAV). All of the major car-rental agencies have kiosks or booths just outside of Customs. There's also an **Infotur** kiosk (© 7/866-3333; www.infotur.cu), where you can buy a map and pick up some brochures, and they should even be able to help with reservations.

There's an ATM among all the booths and kiosks on the ground floor, and another on the second floor, where departing passengers check in. Etecsa, the national phone company, has booths with card-operated pay phones on this level, as well as on the second floor. You can either buy a card from them, if their booth is manned, or from one of the souvenir vendors on the second floor.

Taxis wait in a long line just outside the ground floor exit. Unfortunately, all the different taxi companies are thrust into the lineup and are assigned to clients in order. Thus it's luck of the draw if you get one of the more expensive cab companies, such as **Taxi OK,** or one of the more economical ones, such as **Panataxi** or **Havanautos.** If you're really trying to save a few bucks, you can try demanding a Panataxi or Havanautos taxi or you could try negotiating a flat rate. A good rate to any hotel in downtown Havana is CUC$10 to CUC$15, although it's not uncommon for the meter or arranged fee to top out at CUC$20 to CUC$25.

Some charter flights and all national flights arrive at either Terminal 1 or 2. Both terminals also have Infotur offices or kiosks, an ATM or two, telephones, and taxis.

If you're driving from the airport, the main artery into Havana is Avenida de Rancho Boyeros. This will bring you to the Plaza de la Revolución and the towering José Martí Memorial. In general terms, if you continue straight, or roughly north toward the sea, you will hit the University of Havana and Vedado. Miramar and Playa will be to the left (west) and are best reached via the Malecón, while Centro Habana and Habana Vieja will be to the right (east).

### BY CAR

Entering Havana by car is a confusing mess. Almost none of the major arteries into downtown are marked. This is especially true of the Autopista Nacional coming in from the east, which dumps you unceremoniously into the midst of an urban mess of some of the city's outer neighborhoods. Similarly, while there is ostensibly a beltway, or *Circunvalación,* around the downtown area, it and its various exits are virtually entirely unmarked.

One good tactic for navigating Havana is to somehow find your way to the Malecón; from there, the entire city is relatively easily accessible. The main thoroughfare through Miramar and Playa is Avenida 5.

### BY TRAIN

The principal train station, or **Estación Central,** is located in Habana Vieja at Calle Egido and Calle Arsenal (© 7/862-1920 or 7/861-4259). There are always plenty of taxis waiting at the station.

### BY BUS

The main **Víazul** bus station (© 7/881-1413; www.viazul.com) is located at Avenida 26 and Zoológico in Nuevo Vedado, on the outskirts of downtown. **Astro** buses

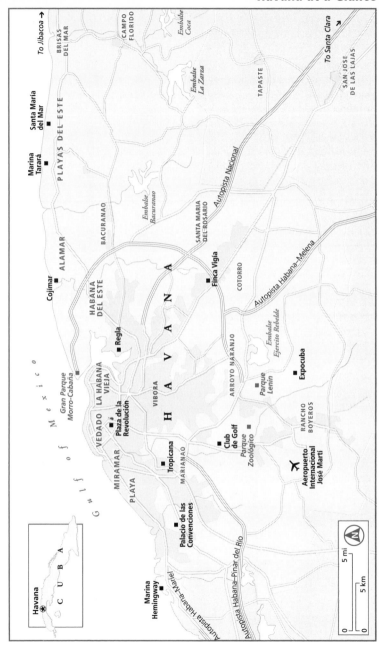

(© 7/879-2456) arrive at their main terminal at Avenida de la Independencia and Calle 19 de Mayo, near the Plaza de la Revolución. There are always taxis available at both stations.

## BY BOAT

Cubanacán's **Marina Hemingway,** Avenida 5 and Calle 248, Santa Fe, Playa (© 7/ 204-6848; www.cubanacan.cu), is the principal port of call and official point of entry for clearing Customs and Immigration. When arriving by sea, contact the marina before entering Cuban waters (19km/12 miles offshore) on VHF channels 16 or 19, or HF channel 2760.

Commercial cruise ships dock at the Sierra Maestra Terminal in Habana Vieja, just off the Plaza de San Francisco.

## VISITOR INFORMATION

**Infotur** (© 7/866-3333; www.infotur.cu) is the official state-run tourist information agency. They have offices or kiosks in several strategic spots around Havana, and in each of the three terminals at the airport. The latter are open 24 hours daily. They can provide you with some brochures and information, and they can usually help you make reservations. Most of the kiosks also have a selection of maps and various local tourist guides and books for sale.

There are a handful of large, state-run tour agencies that have desks at most hotels around town; these include **Havanatur** (© 7/204-8409; www.havanatur.cu), **Cubanacán** (© 7/208-6044; www.cubanacan.cu), and **Cubatur** (© 7/833-3142; www.cubatur.cu). These are your best bets for information and tour bookings around the country.

## CITY LAYOUT

Havana was a major city built around its ample and protected harbor. The oldest colonial-era buildings are closest to the harbor, and the bulk of the expansion heads out west from there. The city is bordered along its northern edge by the Caribbean Sea. The majority of Havana's denizens live in large, densely populated working-class neighborhoods to the south of the principal downtown business and tourist neighborhoods. While there are communities on the eastern side of the harbor, the most important neighborhoods and developments are all found on the western side. These communities are generally laid out in a series of abutting grids, although they often abut at odd angles.

While the streets in Vedado and Playa tend to be numbered or carry a letter designation, the neighborhoods of Habana Vieja and Centro Habana have only named streets. To make matters more confusing, most of the streets in Habana Vieja and Centro Habana have two or more names—those that appear on maps and street signs are often different from their common names. Wherever possible, I've tried to give the most common and popularly used name.

In Habana Vieja and Centro Habana, street names are generally displayed on little plaques or signs attached to the sides of corner buildings at street intersections. The plaques tend to be hung relatively high, at about 3m (10 ft.) or so. In Vedado and Playa, you'll want to look lower, as most intersections feature a half-meter-high (2-ft.) concrete block in a sort of pyramid shape, with the street name engraved on it.

Street addresses are usually given as follows: Prado no. 22, e/ Tejadillo y Empedrado, or 23 e/ L y M. In the case of the first example, the address is for building 22

# La Habana Vieja & Centro Habana

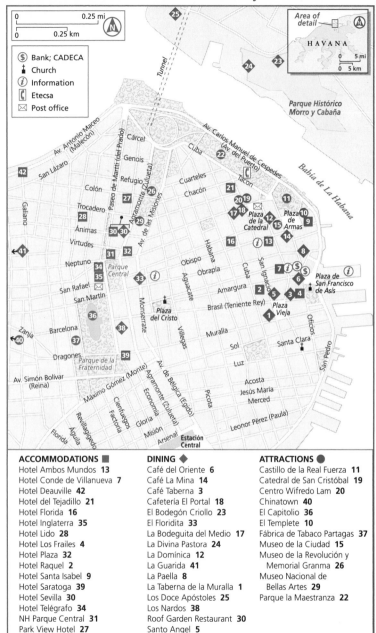

**ACCOMMODATIONS ■**

Hotel Ambos Mundos **13**
Hotel Conde de Villanueva **7**
Hotel Deauville **42**
Hotel del Tejadillo **21**
Hotel Florida **16**
Hotel Inglaterra **35**
Hotel Lido **28**
Hotel Los Frailes **4**
Hotel Plaza **32**
Hotel Raquel **2**
Hotel Santa Isabel **9**
Hotel Saratoga **39**
Hotel Sevilla **30**
Hotel Telégrafo **34**
NH Parque Central **31**
Park View Hotel **27**

**DINING ◆**

Café del Oriente **6**
Café La Mina **14**
Café Taberna **3**
Cafetería El Portal **18**
El Bodegón Criollo **23**
El Floridita **33**
La Bodeguita del Medio **17**
La Divina Pastora **24**
La Dominica **12**
La Guarida **41**
La Paella **8**
La Taberna de la Muralla **1**
Los Doce Apóstoles **25**
Los Nardos **38**
Roof Garden Restaurant **30**
Santo Angel **5**

**ATTRACTIONS ●**

Castillo de la Real Fuerza **11**
Catedral de San Cristóbal **19**
Centro Wifredo Lam **20**
Chinatown **40**
El Capitolio **36**
El Templete **10**
Fábrica de Tabaco Partagas **37**
Museo de la Ciudad **15**
Museo de la Revolución y
  Memorial Granma **26**
Museo Nacional de
  Bellas Artes **29**
Parque la Maestranza **22**

on Paseo del Prado, located between the cross-streets Calle Tejadillo and Calle Empedrado. In the second case, the address is for an unnumbered building on Calle 23 between Calles L and M. Note that Cuban addresses frequently omit the word "Calle" or "Avenida." Also, Cubans usually refer to Avenida 5 as "Quinta Avenida," "5ta Avenida," or—most commonly—simply "5ta."

## NEIGHBORHOODS IN BRIEF

**La Habana Vieja** La Habana Vieja (Old Havana) is the historic colonial heart of Havana. Located at the eastern edge of the city, in the area beginning around the Paseo del Prado, or Paseo de Martí, and the Parque Central, and extending to the Harbor Channel, it is a dense collection of colonial-era and neocolonial houses, mansions, churches, seminaries, and apartment buildings punctuated by a few picturesque plazas and parks. UNESCO declared Habana Vieja a World Heritage Site in 1982, and today it is one of the most beautiful restored colonial cities in the world. You will find the city's greatest collection of museums and attractions here, as well as a broad selection of restaurants and beautifully restored boutique hotels. This is an area best explored on foot.

**Centro Habana** In many ways, Central Havana is little more than the necessary and neglected area connecting Habana Vieja with Vedado. It is defined on its northern edge by the Malecón, the seaside pedestrian walkway that stretches from Habana Vieja to the end of Vedado. The stretch of the Malecón (and everything inland from it) between the Hotel Nacional and Habana Vieja is a study in decay and decomposition. Still, it is quite picturesque and charming in its own way. Centro Habana is primarily a residential area, although it does have a high concentration of *casas particulares* (private rooms for rent).

*Beware:* I cannot stress enough the level of decay and decomposition here. Balconies, crown molding, and other large chunks of brick, mortar, and stone regularly drop off of buildings here, sometimes injuring passersby below.

**Vedado & the Plaza de la Revolución** Beginning more or less at the Hotel Nacional and extending west to the Almendares River, and south to the Plaza de la Revolución, Vedado is a busy mix of middle- to upper-class houses and businesses. As the older sections of Habana Vieja and Centro Habana began to overflow, residential and business growth centered on Vedado. Calle 23, or La Rampa, is the principal avenue defining Vedado, and it's where you'll find Coppelia, the Tryp Habana Libre (former Havana Hilton), and the Hotel Nacional. The broad Plaza de la Revolución sits on high ground on the southern edge of Vedado and houses several government agencies, in addition to the towering José Martí Memorial, the National Theater, and the National Library.

**Playa** This upscale residential district is located just west of Vedado, past the Almendares River. The most important neighborhood here is **Miramar,** home to many prominent businesses and most of the resident foreign community in Cuba. Almost all of the various embassies and diplomatic missions have set up shop in the various Batista-era mansions that make up this neighborhood. There are several large and luxurious business-class hotels here, as well as many private rooms for rent in wonderfully maintained neocolonial mansions.

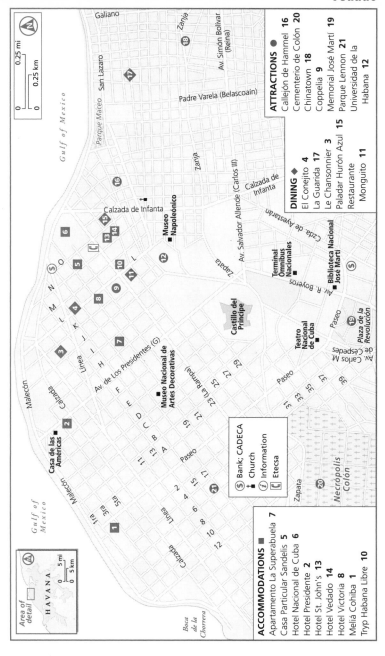

Galiano

Gulf of Mexico

Parque Maceo

San Lazaro

Av. Simón Bolívar (Reina)

Zanja

Padre Varela (Belascoaín)

Zanja

Calzada de Infanta

Calzada de Infanta

Museo Napoleónico

Cda. de Ayestarán

Av. Salvador Allende (Carlos III)

Calzada de Infanta

Zapata

Castillo del Príncipe

Terminal Omnibus Nacionales

Av. R. Boyeros

Biblioteca Nacional José Martí

Paseo

Teatro Nacional de Cuba

Av. Carlos M. de Céspedes

Plaza de la Revolución

Malecón

Calzada

Av. de Los Presidentes (G)

Línea

Museo Nacional de Artes Decorativas

23 (La Rampa)

25

27

29

Paseo

31

33

35

37

39

Casa de las Américas

Malecón

3ra

5ta

Línea

Calzada

Paseo

Zapata

Necrópolis Colón

Gulf of Mexico

Boca de la Chorrera

**Area of detail**

HAVANA

0   5 mi
0   5 km

0   0.25 mi
0   0.25 km

## ATTRACTIONS ●
Callejón de Hammel  **16**
Cementerio de Colón  **20**
Chinatown  **18**
Coppelia  **9**
Memorial José Martí  **19**
Parque Lennon  **21**
Universidad de la Habana  **12**

## DINING ◆
El Conejito  **4**
La Guarida  **17**
Le Chansonnier  **3**
Paladar Hurón Azul  **15**
Restaurante Monguito  **11**

## ACCOMMODATIONS ■
Apartamento La Superabuela  **7**
Casa Particular Sandelis  **5**
Hotel Nacional de Cuba  **6**
Hotel Presidente  **2**
Hotel St. John's  **13**
Hotel Vedado  **14**
Hotel Victoria  **8**
Meliá Cohiba  **1**
Tryp Habana Libre  **10**

Ⓢ Bank; CADECA
✝■ Church
ⓘ Information
🄲 Etecsa

**Habana del Este & Playas del Este**
On the eastern banks of the harbor is Habana del Este, and about 11km (6¾ miles) farther east along the coast are the Playas del Este, or eastern beaches, which stretch on for about 15km (10 miles) of their own. Habana del Este and Playas del Este are connected to the rest of Havana by a tunnel running between Habana Vieja and the area around the Morro Castle. There are also frequent little passenger ferries running between Habana Vieja and the neighborhoods of Regla and Casablanca. The towns that comprise Habana del Este, Alamar, Cojímar, and Ciudad Panamericana, are working-class and industrial.

The beaches of Playas del Este, on the other hand, are beautiful stretches of white sand fronting the Caribbean Sea. These beaches are popular with both Cubans and travelers alike.

**Near the Airport** The area near and around the airport is an industrial wasteland. There are no hotels or facilities for tourists in the area directly around the airport. Playa and Miramar, about a 15- to 20-minute drive away, are the closest neighborhoods for travelers looking for quick access to the airport; however, the extra time and distance to hotels in Vedado or Habana Vieja are rather negligible.

## 2 Getting Around

### BY TAXI

There are a host of different taxi companies with modern fleets geared toward the tourist trade. Almost all tourist taxis have meters. Rates vary somewhat, but most of the meters start at CUC$1.75 for the first kilometer and then charge between CUC50¢ and CUC85¢ for each additional kilometer. The most economical cabs are the **Panataxi** (✆ 7/55-5555), **Micar** (✆ 7/204-2719), **Habanataxi** (✆ 7/832-3232), and **Havanautos Taxis** (✆ 7/832-3232) lines. **Taxi OK** (✆ 7/204-0000) and **Fénix** (✆ 7/863-3149) are the most expensive companies. **Transtur** (✆ 7/208-6666) and **Transgaviota** (✆ 7/203-7000) seem to fall in the middle.

Other options include horse-drawn carriages; the so-called **Coco Taxis** (✆ 7/873-1411), round open-air two-seaters powered by a motorcycle; and antique cars that range from a Ford Model T to a 1957 Chevy. Both the horse-drawn carriages and Coco Taxis run around CUC$5 to CUC$10 per hour, with around a CUC$3 minimum. **Gran Car** (✆ 7/33-5647) is the most reputable agent for antique car rentals. Gran Car rates, with a driver, run CUC$15 per hour or CUC$100 per day, with discounts for multiday rentals.

Peso taxis and freelance taxis are lesser options for most tourists. Both are either outright illegal or marginally illegal for tourists, although it's the driver, not the rider, who is at risk. If you opt for either one of the options, be sure to fix your price beforehand, and don't be surprised if the driver is somewhat paranoid about the money transfer, and/or refuses to drop you off right at your hotel.

### BY FOOT

Havana is a great town to walk around. It's almost entirely flat and very safe. Early morning, late afternoon, and early evenings are the prime times to walk. High heat and heavy humidity can make long walks, particularly around midday, a little uncomfortable. La Habana Vieja is best explored by foot, and a walk along the Malecón is nearly obligatory. Attractions in Vedado and Miramar are a little spread out, making

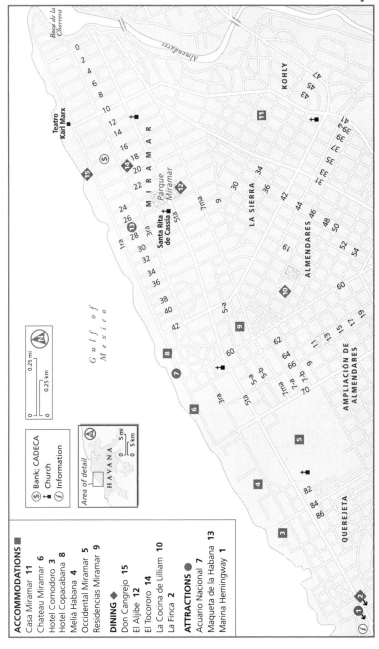

**ACCOMMODATIONS** ■
Casa Miramar **11**
Chateau Miramar **6**
Hotel Comodoro **3**
Hotel Copacabana **8**
Meliá Habana **4**
Occidental Miramar **5**
Residencias Miramar **9**

**DINING** ◆
Don Cangrejo **15**
El Aljibe **12**
El Tocororo **14**
La Cocina de Lilliam **10**
La Finca **2**

**ATTRACTIONS** ●
Acuario Nacional **7**
Maqueta de la Habana **13**
Marina Hemingway **1**

Ⓢ Bank; CADECA
✝■ Church
ⓘ Information

*Area of detail*

HAVANA

0        5 mi
0    5 km

*Gulf of*
*Mexico*

0        0.25 mi
0    0.25 km

them less desirable to explore by foot, although a walk along La Rampa in Vedado, or Quinta Avenida (Av. 5) in Miramar are both rewarding.

## BY CAR

There's really no reason for tourists to rent a car to explore Havana. Taxis are plentiful and relatively inexpensive. Moreover, streets are poorly marked and it's a confusing city to navigate.

One exception would be to rent an antique car from **Gran Car** (✆ 7/33-5647). Gran Car's fleet runs from restored 1930s open-air Ford cruisers to classic 1950s Chevys, Buicks, De Sotos, and Studebakers. Rates, with a driver, run around CUC$15 per hour or CUC$100 per day, with discounts for multiday rentals.

If you do want to rent a modern car while in Havana, there are a host of options, including **Cubacar** (✆ 7/273-2277; www.cubacar.info); **Havanautos** (✆ 7/835-3142; www.havanautos.cu); **Micar** (✆ 7/204-8888); **Transtur** (✆ 7/862-2686 or 7/861-5885; www.transtur.cu); and **Vía Rent A Car** (✆ 7/861-4465; www.gaviota-grupo.com). All of the above companies have desks at the airport, and at a host of major hotels around Havana. See "Getting Around" in chapter 2 for more information.

In general, traffic is much lighter than you'd find in most major urban areas. However, you do have to pay more attention to a wide range of obstacles ranging from pedestrians and bicyclists to horse-drawn carriages. While most roads in Havana are in pretty decent shape, it's not uncommon to come across huge potholes or torn-up sections of road with no markings or warnings. Moreover, street markings and signs are minimal, making navigation challenging.

## BY BUS

For all intents and purposes, Havana's woefully overburdened urban bus system is no longer a viable option for tourists. Routes and service are inconsistent, the buses are overcrowded, and there are no readily available route maps and schedules.

Truly hearty travelers and independent souls can give the local buses a try. Your best bet is to query locals about routes and hours and where to find the appropriate stop. A large number of metro buses either originate or have a stop at the Parque de la Fraternidad, a block south of the Capitolio. Most buses are entered from the front, although some are still entered from the rear and use an honor system of passing your coins forward. Some have separate lines for those wanting a seat *(sentado)* and those willing to stand *(parado)*. Fares run around 20 to 30 centavos in Cuban pesos *(moneda nacional)*.

One useful bus for tourists is the daily **Víazul** (✆ 7/881-1413; www.viazul.com) running from Havana to Playas del Este. This bus leaves from Havana daily at 8:40am and 2:20pm, returning from Playas del Este at 10:30am and 4:40pm. Pickups and drop-offs can be arranged at most hotels on each end of the trip. Fare is CUC$5.

## FAST FACTS: Havana

*Airport*  See "Arriving," earlier in this chapter.

*Babysitters*  Your hotel front desk is your best bet for finding a babysitter.

*Bookstores*  In Habana Vieja, check out **La Moderna Poesía,** Calle Obispo 527 (© **7/861-6640**), or **La Librería Internacional,** Calle Obispo 526 (© **7/861-3283**), which are directly across the street from each other. In Vedado, head to **Ateneo,** Calle Linea, between Calles 12 and 14 (© **7/833-9609**).

*Car Rentals*  See "Getting Around," above.

*Currency Exchange*  Currency exchange offices are ubiquitous around Havana. There are branches of the state-run *casa de cambio* **CADECA** (© **7/55-5701**) throughout Havana, as well as at the airport and in the lobbies of most major hotels. Most banks will also exchange money.

*Dentists*  **Hospital Cira García,** Calle 20 no. 4101, Playa (© **7/204-2811;** www. cirag.cu), and other major medical centers also provide dental care. If you want a specific recommendation, contact your embassy, or ask at your hotel's front desk. Alternately, you can contact **Asistur** (© **7/866-8527;** www.asistur.cu), which can help you with dental emergencies.

*Doctors*  Cuba has a surfeit of doctors and many hotels catering to tourists have one or two on staff. If not, your hotel is still probably your best bet for a recommendation. You can also try contacting your embassy or **Asistur** (© **7/866-4499;** www.asistur.cu), which specializes in emergency medical care and insurance for travelers.

*Drugstores*  Well-stocked drugstores are few and far between in Havana. There's a 24-hour pharmacy at the international terminal of the José Martí airport (© **7/266-4105**). The pharmacies at the **Hotel Plaza** (© **7/861-5703**) in Habana Vieja, and **Tryp Havana Libre** (© **7/834-6100**) in Vedado, usually have decent stocks. In Miramar, you can try the **Farmacia Internacional,** Avenida 41 and Calle 20 (© **7/204-2051**).

*Embassies & Consulates*  See "Fast Facts: Cuba," in chapter 2.

*Emergencies*  Cuba is attempting to implement a universal emergency phone response network. In most cases you will want to dial © **116** for any emergency. Alternately you can dial © **114** or 7/204-2811 for an **ambulance;** © **7/867-7777** for the **police;** and © **115** or 7/850-0105 for the **fire department.** At none of these numbers can you assume you will find an English-speaking person on the other end.

*Express Mail Services*  The main office of **DHL,** Calle 26 and Avenida 1, Miramar (© **7/204-1578;** www.dhl.com), will pick up and deliver anywhere in Havana. **EMS Cubapost,** Calle 21 no. 1009, between Calles 10 and 12, Vedado (© **7/831-3328**), is a Cuban-run express mail service with a desk at most post offices.

*Eyeglasses*  Look for the word *óptica.* **Optica Miramar,** Avenida 7 and Calle 24, Miramar (© **7/204-2269**), is one of the better *ópticas* catering to foreign residents and visitors. They have a branch in downtown Havana at Calle Neptuno 411, between San Nicolás and Manrique (© **7/863-2161**).

*Hospitals* Your best bet is **Hospital Cira García,** Calle 20 no. 4101, Playa (© 7/ 204-2811; www.cirag.cu), which provides emergency services and long-term care. Another possibility is the **Hospital Hermanos Almeijeiras,** Calles San Lázaro and Belascoaín, Centro Habana (© 7/877-6077).

*Internet Access* Internet access is becoming more and more common and available in Havana. However, it is still in the early stages and there are few real Internet cafes to speak of. The most popular Internet cafe in town is located at **El Capitolio** (p. 111). The rate here is CUC$5 per hour, and the 10 machines here are often booked solid. Aside from this, your best options are the various hotels with business centers and/or Internet cafes; most of these charge between CUC$5 and CUC$8 per hour, with even higher rates occasionally charged at the fancier hotels. Alternately, you can go to any **Etecsa** office. These offices sell disposable access cards at CUC$6 per hour that are good at any Internet-equipped Etecsa office in the country. There's one at Calles Tacón and Chacón in la Habana Vieja (© 7/860-7511).

*Maps* The various Infotur booths and kiosks around town sell a pretty decent map of Havana for CUC$1; sometimes they'll even give you a copy for free. Most rental-car agencies and hotels can also give you a copy of the same, or similar, map. The Cuban Geographic and Cartographic Institute publishes a couple of much more detailed maps of Havana, including the *Ciudad de la Habana Mapa Turistica,* which you can get at most tourist gift shops and Infotur kiosks. You'll also find good maps online at **www.cubaroutes.com** and **www.cubamapa.com**.

*Photographic Needs* Most of your photographic needs will be met by the rival chains of **Photoservice** and **Photoclub** shops. These offer 1-hour or overnight developing services and usually carry an assortment of film and some replacement batteries. Between the two chains there are numerous outlets across Havana. For any repairs or more complicated needs, try **Fotografía Luz Habana,** Calle Tacón 22, between Calles O'Reilly and Empedrado, la Habana Vieja (© 7/ 863-4263).

*Police* Dial © **116** or 7/867-7777. Although it's possible someone who speaks English can be rounded up, do not expect to find an English-speaking person on the other end. In the event of serious danger, you are probably better off contacting your embassy (non-licensed U.S. citizens should contact the U.S. Interests section only as a last resort).

*Post Office* Most major hotels either have small post office branches, or will sell you stamps and post letters. This is generally your best bet, as the *correos* (public post office branches) are often crowded and inefficient. In Habana Vieja, there's a *correo* on the west end of the Plaza de San Francisco. There's another on the side of the Gran Teatro toward the Capitolio. Both are open Monday through Saturday from 8am to 5pm. In Vedado, you should head to the **Tryp Habana Libre,** Calles L and 23 (© 7/834-6100).

*Safety* Havana is a very safe city. There's a strong police presence and street crime is uncommon, especially in tourist areas. But because streetlights are virtually nonexistent, it's wise to avoid the dark alleys and side streets of Havana after dark. Popular tourist spots are relatively safe at night. Still, given the vast economic gap between Cubans and tourists, you should be careful about where you walk and whom you engage. It is best not to wear much jewelry or make other showy signs of wealth.

*Taxis* See "Getting Around," earlier in this chapter.

## 3 Where to Stay

There's a wide range of hotel options and *casas particulares* (private rooms) for rent in Havana. Hotel options are divvied up among the large state-run chains. **Habaguanex** has monopoly control over the hotel scene in Habana Vieja, and **Gaviota, Cubanacán,** and **Gran Caribe** own the remainder of the midrange to upper-end offerings around Havana. Of the international hotel chains, the major player in town is the Spanish-owned **Sol Meliá,** which manages three large high-end properties in Havana. Given the fact that hotel chains control so much of the market, one major problem is a generalized lax attitude toward overbooking. Habaguanex and Gran Caribe are particularly notorious for this. Confirmed reservations at Gran Caribe's Hotel Nacional or Habaguanex's Santa Isabel are often shuttled off to one of their sister properties, usually with no compensation and little sympathy.

There are literally thousands of casas particulares in Havana. The neighborhoods of Centro Habana, Vedado, and Playa have the greatest concentration of casas particulares, although Habana Vieja is starting to catch up. In general, the rooms and homes are kept very clean, while the furnishings and amenities are quite simple. The rates average between CUC$7 and CUC$20 per person, and meals are often available at very reasonable prices. With the broad offering and rapid turnover in the market, it's impossible to list a representative selection of casas particulares. I've tried to include the most dependable and long-standing options in each neighborhood below. In addition, you can check out **www.casaparticular.info**.

Given the compact nature of Havana, the proximity of its major attractions, and the wide availability of relatively inexpensive taxis, the neighborhood you choose is not a limiting factor. In general, most visitors will want to spend most of their time exploring Habana Vieja, so the hotels there or nearby in Centro Habana are best for direct walking access. Large group and package tourists, as well as business travelers, are usually funneled toward hotels in Miramar and Playa, about a 10- to 15-minute ride away from most of the action, although the area is home to some of the better dining and nightlife options. Vedado is a sort of middle ground, with plenty of accommodations and dining options, easy access to the rest of the city's attractions, and quite a few natural charms of its own.

***Note:*** While 110-volt electricity with standard U.S.-style plugs are the national norm, the high percentage of European travelers has led many hotels to add on 220-volt outlets or to fully convert. The Meliá chain, for example, has mostly 220-volt outlets, although they usually include at least one 110-volt outlet in each bathroom.

### LA HABANA VIEJA

With few exceptions, all of the hotels in Old Havana are run by the Cuban chain Habaguanex. And all of these are intimate boutique hotels in beautifully refurbished old buildings. I've listed my favorite Habaguanex hotels below, but there are others that are nearly as nice; check **www.habaguanex.com** for the complete listing. One nice perk of staying at a Habaguanex hotel is that you get free admission to most of the museums in Old Havana.

## VERY EXPENSIVE

**Hotel Conde de Villanueva** ✦   This place is geared toward cigar freaks, and only true aficionados should stay here. The hotel features one of the better and most respected cigar shops in town, La Casa del Habano, which rents out private humidors so that regular clients can always have their own personal reserve. The rooms are large and soaked in old-world charm, not to mention the scent of tobacco—all are smoking rooms, of course. The better and more expensive rooms come with Jacuzzi jets in the tubs and views over the street. The building dates back to the end of the 18th century, and features a large portrait of its namesake count in the entryway. Sebastian, the pet peacock, roams the large central courtyard. The semiformal Vuelta Abajo restaurant serves good Cuban cuisine, and there's a wonderful, shady little park just across the street.

Calle Mercaderes 202 (between Calles Lamparilla and Amargura), la Habana Vieja. ✆ **7/862-9293.** Fax 7/862-9682. www.habaguanex.com. 9 units. CUC$160 double; CUC$220–CUC$242 suite. Rates include breakfast. Rates slightly lower during off season, higher during peak weeks. MC, V. Free valet parking. **Amenities:** 2 restaurants; 2 bars; concierge; limited room service; laundry service; dry cleaning. *In room:* A/C, TV, minibar, safe.

**Hotel Florida** ✦✦ *Finds*   This is my favorite of the converted old colonial mansions in Habana Vieja. Built in 1836 and turned into a hotel in 1885, the Florida is stately and elegant and I'd give it an unqualified nod over the Santa Isabel (see below), except for the fact that a couple of the rooms don't have any windows. However, if you do get one of the window rooms or one of the suites, you may find it hard to head out and explore the city. The rooms are decorated with a mix of imitation and real antique furnishings, wrought-iron beds, checkerboard marble floors, and tasteful framed prints. The entrance is located right on the busy Calle Obispo, and it's possible to miss it amid all the hustle and bustle. The tranquil central courtyard provides immediate relief, surrounded by soaring stone columns connected by high arches.

Calle Obispo (corner of Calle Cuba), la Habana Vieja. ✆ **7/862-4127.** Fax 7/862-4117. www.habaguanex.com. 25 units. CUC$150 double; CUC$200 suite. Rates include breakfast. Rates slightly lower during off season, higher during peak weeks. MC, V. Free valet parking. **Amenities:** Restaurant; 2 bars; concierge; tour desk; car-rental desk; 24-hr. room service; laundry service; dry cleaning. *In room:* A/C, TV, minibar, hair dryer, safe.

**Hotel Raquel** ✦   This is one of the newer additions to the Habaguanex chain, and yet another stunningly restored old building. The facade is a visual orgy of bas-relief work, while the centerpiece of the marble-tiled lobby here is a soaring stained-glass atrium ceiling. The third-floor rooms share a large rooftop terrace, with wonderful views over Old Havana. The rooms themselves are spacious and attractively decorated with lamp fixtures and headboards of artistically crafted iron. However, at these prices I'd expect more than a 13-inch television and two twin beds (only two of the standard rooms here have a queen-size bed, although the suites do come with a king-size bed). This is often called "the Jewish hotel." The restaurant features borscht and latkes, while various lobby displays pay homage to Cuba's small but active Jewish tradition. In fact, many of the staff members are drawn from the local Jewish community.

Calle Amargura, at the corner of San Ignacio, la Habana Vieja. ✆ **7/860-8280.** Fax 7/860-8275. www.habaguanex. com. 25 units. CUC$200 double; CUC$250 suite. Rates include breakfast. Rates slightly lower during off season, higher during peak weeks. MC, V. Free valet parking. **Amenities:** Restaurant; 2 bars; concierge; tour desk; 24-hr. room service; laundry service. *In room:* A/C, TV, minibar, hair dryer, safe.

**Hotel Santa Isabel** ★★   This is one of the most highly touted hotels of the Habaguanex chain, and it *is* a lovely little hotel, wonderfully located on the eastern end of the Plaza de Armas. Still, they're stretching things when they tout it as a top-tier luxury hotel. Sure, it's elegant and charming, and definitely a top choice in Old Havana, but the rooms and bathrooms are rather compact, and you won't find many of the amenities you'd expect at most luxury hotels. The rooms themselves are dark and understated, with high ceilings and iron bed frames. The junior suites have a small sitting room and extra television, as well as Jacuzzi jets in their standard-size tubs. However, the best rooms in the house, aside from the sumptuous Santovenia suite, are room nos. 304 through 314, which come with large rooftop terraces overlooking the plaza. The central open-air patio courtyard with a bubbling fountain is a great spot for breakfast or a quiet break from the midday heat.

Calle Baratillo 9 (between Calles Obispo and Narciso López), Plaza de Armas, la Habana Vieja. ✆ 7/860-8201. Fax 7/860-8391. www.habaguanex.com. 27 units. CUC$200 double; CUC$300 junior suite; CUC$400 Santovenia suite. Rates include breakfast. Rates slightly higher during peak weeks. MC, V. Free valet parking. **Amenities:** Restaurant; bar; secretarial services; 24-hr. room service; babysitting; laundry service; dry cleaning; nonsmoking rooms. *In room:* A/C, TV, minibar, hair dryer, safe.

**Hotel Saratoga** ★★★ *Finds*   This new hotel has the most luxurious rooms and appointments of any Habana Vieja property. Even the standard rooms are very spacious, with marble or tile floors, elegant furnishings, and all the modern amenities. Each comes with a tub and separate shower. Many have a private balcony and view over Havana's bustling streets. Several of the suites here are truly special. I like the Suite Capitolio, which is a corner unit with a fabulous view of the Capitol dome from the king-size bed. The Prado and Habana suites are also top-notch rooms. Despite having nearly 100 rooms, this place still feels like a boutique hotel. One of the best features here is the delightful rooftop pool. Perhaps the only criticism I have of this hotel is the fact that its lobby and mezzanine bar areas are a bit on the small side.

Paseo del Prado 603, la Habana Vieja. ✆ 7/868-1000. Fax 7/868-1002. www.hotel-saratoga.com. 96 units. CUC$240–CUC$290 double; CUC$385–CUC$650 suite. Rates include breakfast. MC, V. Free parking. **Amenities:** Restaurant; 2 bars; rooftop pool; small gym; concierge; tour desk; 24-hr. room service; laundry service; dry cleaning; nonsmoking rooms. *In room:* A/C, TV, dataport; minibar, hair dryer, safe.

**Hotel Sevilla** ★★   This is the best of the three grand old hotels (Sevilla, Inglaterra, and Plaza) near the Parque Central. Plus it's got a pool and well-equipped little health club, which the other old dames lack. Still, all three are easily eclipsed by the new Hotel Saratoga (see above). Some of the standard rooms are a bit small, and it's definitely worth the splurge for a superior or junior suite—you'll get a lot more space. The hotel was actually built in two stages, and all of the current rooms are in the newer Biltmore addition, which dates from the 1920s. The original 1908 Grand Sevilla operates as a hotel training school, although the original ornate Moorish-influenced lobby area is still working and quite impressive. The ninth-floor **Roof Garden Restaurant** (p. 100) is one of the top dining options in town.

Calle Trocadero 55 (corner of Calle Prado), la Habana Vieja. ✆ 7/860-8560. Fax 7/860-8582. www.sofitel.com. 178 units. CUC$150–CUC$280 standard; CUC$230–CUC$320 superior or junior suite. MC, V. Free valet parking. **Amenities:** 2 restaurants; 2 bars; outdoor pool; health club; concierge; tour desk; car-rental desk; 24-hr. room service; massage; babysitting; laundry service; dry cleaning. *In room:* A/C, TV, minibar, hair dryer, safe.

**NH Parque Central** ★★   This modern, upscale hotel dominates the northern end of Havana's small Central Park. Behind a wall of glass doors fronting the park sits the large atrium lobby area. The rooms are new and spacious, with dark colors, thick fabrics, and fresh carpeting. The marble bathrooms even have a separate bathtub and shower. These are probably the most comfortable luxury rooms in Habana Vieja, and the hotel offers a broad array of amenities and services—although it lacks the old-world charm and sense of time travel offered by other hotels in this part of town. The suites are huge, and some have private balconies with nice views over the park and toward El Capitolio. Service is relatively efficient and attentive, something that cannot always be said about most other hotels in Habana Vieja.

Calle Neptuno (between Calles Prado and Zulueta), la Habana Vieja. ⓒ 7/860-6627. Fax 7/860-6630. www. nh-hoteles.es. 227 units. CUC$270 double; CUC$336 suite. MC, V. Free valet parking. **Amenities:** 2 restaurants; 2 bars; 2 lounges; small rooftop pool; health club; Jacuzzi; concierge; tour desk; car-rental desk; well-equipped business center; 24-hr. room service; massage; babysitting; laundry service; dry cleaning; nonsmoking rooms. *In room:* A/C, TV, minibar, hair dryer, safe.

## EXPENSIVE
**Hotel Ambos Mundos** 🟡 Hemingway claimed this was "a good place to write," and the room (no. 511) where he wrote parts of *For Whom The Bell Tolls* is a shrine to the late author, featuring his typewriter and photocopies of some of his handwritten drafts and notes. The hotel is a popular stop on the tourist trail and a good base for exploring Habana Vieja. The rooms are simple and somewhat spartan, but they are clean and comfortable, and most have high French doors opening to some view of the bustling streets. A few even have small balconies. Most folks love the compact old iron-grated elevator running up the inside of the central staircase; however, it's woefully inadequate to meet demand, so if you're staying on an upper floor you might find waiting for it frustrating. Breakfast is served on the rooftop patio under shady arbors with a wonderful view of the harbor and Habana Vieja; this is also a great spot for a refreshing drink any time of day or night. The lobby bar is also quite popular, and features live music most of the day and much of the night.

Calle Obispo 153 (corner of Calle Mercaderes), la Habana Vieja. ⓒ **7/860-9530.** Fax 7/860-9532. www.habaguanex. com. 52 units. CUC$130 double; CUC$160 minisuite. Rates include breakfast. Rates slightly lower during off season, higher during peak weeks. MC, V. Street parking nearby. **Amenities:** 2 restaurants; 2 bars; tour desk; car-rental desk; in-room massage; babysitting; laundry service. *In room:* A/C, TV, fridge, safe.

**Hotel del Tejadillo** 🟡 It's hard to find a better located hotel in Habana Vieja. Just a half-block from the Plaza del Catedral and La Bodeguita del Medio, and about 2 blocks from the Malecón, this recently renovated old mansion provides decent value and ample colonial charm. The spacious rooms have high ceilings, comfortable new beds, and Oriental throw rugs. About half of them come with fully equipped kitchenettes. Most are arrayed around a typical central courtyard, with a central fountain surrounded by lush tropical plants and large sculptures. The biggest drawback here is the fact that quite a few rooms have no windows. Breakfast is served in a little dining room, or in a separate open-air courtyard. There's a lively little bar here that is far enough removed from the rooms as to not keep you up.

Calle Tejadillo 12 (corner of Calle San Ignacio), la Habana Vieja. ⓒ **7/863-7283.** Fax 7/863-8830. www.habaguanex. com. 32 units. CUC$120 double; CUC$150 suite. Rates include breakfast. Rates slightly lower during off season, higher during peak weeks. MC, V. Street parking nearby. **Amenities:** Bar; concierge; tour desk; laundry service; dry cleaning. *In room:* A/C, TV, kitchenette in some units, fridge, safe.

**Hotel Los Frailes** 🟡 *(Finds)* While I find the staff dressed in mock monk garb a little bit cheesy (not to mention how hot and uncomfortable it must be for them), this is still a lovely little hotel located in the heart of Habana Vieja. The rooms have high ceilings, smooth stucco walls, and heavy wooden beds. Unfortunately, most of the rooms here lack windows, and only two of the four minisuites come with queen-size beds (the rest come with two twins). The narrow central courtyard is engulfed in lush tropical foliage cascading down from the second floor hallways, and features a murmuring fountain, traveling art expositions, and a Plexiglas viewing port into the building's 19th-century water collection system.

Calle Teniente Rey 8 (between Calles Mercaderes and Oficios), la Habana Vieja. ✆ 7/862-9383. Fax 7/862-9718. www.habaguanex.com. 22 units. CUC$120 double; CUC$150 minisuite. Rates include breakfast. Rates slightly lower during off season, higher during peak weeks. MC, V. Street parking nearby. **Amenities:** Bar; concierge; tour desk; 24-hr. room service; laundry service; dry cleaning. *In room:* A/C, TV, minibar, safe.

**Hotel Plaza** 🏆   Built in 1909, this is one of the more historic hotels in Habana Vieja. Heck, suite no. 216 is still rented out, replete with bat and ball and other memorabilia from one of its more famous guests, the Sultan of Swat, Babe Ruth. Albert Einstein and Isadora Duncan were also guests here. However, historic charm is in greater supply than actual comfort or luxury; rooms feel a bit dated and spartan, and you'll find just as many famous ghosts haunting the nearby Hotel Sevilla (see above), while enjoying much more comfortable accommodations. Still, the rooms are spacious and clean, and quite a few have narrow private balconies. The lobby is worth checking out, whether you're staying here or not, for its intricate mosaic tile floor, bas-relief trim, and stained-glass atrium skylights. And, by all means, come by for an afternoon drink at the rooftop **Solarium Bar** 🏆🏆, with great views of Havana and the neighboring Bacardi building.

Calle Ignacio Agramonte 267, la Habana Vieja. ✆ 7/860-8583 or 7/867-1075. Fax 7/860-8869. www.hotelplaza cuba.com. 188 units. CUC$100–CUC$140 double; CUC$150–CUC$175 suite. Rates include breakfast. MC, V. Free valet parking. **Amenities:** 2 restaurants; 2 bars; concierge; tour desk; car-rental desk; 24-hr. room service; laundry service; dry cleaning. *In room:* A/C, TV, minibar, hair dryer, safe.

## MODERATE

**Park View Hotel** *Value*   This is one of the newer additions to the Habaguanex stable and one of its better values. This old hotel, originally opened in 1928, has been entirely restored and remodeled. Rooms, while by no means large, are comfortable and inviting. Their biggest drawbacks are the tiny 13-inch television sets and the smallish bathrooms, which have slightly cramped corner shower units. Three interior units on each floor have no window, while the end rooms are slightly larger and come with a small balcony overlooking the shady little park that gives this hotel its name. The seventh-floor restaurant offers standard Cuban and international fare, but serves it up with a wonderful view over the Morro Castle.

Calle Colón (corner of Calle Morro), la Habana Vieja. ✆ 7/861-3293. Fax 7/863-6036. www.habaguanex.com. 55 units. CUC$80 double. Rates include breakfast. Rates slightly lower during off season, higher during peak weeks. MC, V. Free valet parking. **Amenities:** Restaurant; 2 bars; concierge; tour desk; 24-hr. room service; laundry service; dry cleaning. *In room:* A/C, TV, minibar, safe.

## INEXPENSIVE

Due to Habaguanex's almost complete control of the area, there are no budget hotel options in Habana Vieja, and few standout casas particulares. Still, this is one of the best locations in Havana, and you can certainly try **Casa Ramón y Maritza,** Calle Luz 115, between Calles San Ignacio and Inquisidor (✆ 7/862-3303; maritzamirabal@ yahoo.es); **Casa Mari,** San Juan de Dios 60, between Calles Habana and Compostela (✆ 7/863-1298); **Chez Nous,** Calle Teniente Rey 115, between Calles Cuba and San

Ignacio(② **7/862-6287;** cheznous@ceniai.inf.cu); or **Casa Elvia Olivares,** Calle Aguacate 509, Apartment 402, between Calles Sol and Muralla (② **7/867-5974**).

## CENTRO HABANA

With the exception of the Deauville, all of the hotels listed here are either right on, or very close to, the dividing line between Habana Vieja and Centro Habana, and so quite convenient for exploring Old Havana.

### EXPENSIVE

**Hotel Telégrafo** 🌟🌟    This recently restored hotel is actually over a century old, yet features the boldest and most contemporary architecture and interior design in town. Instead of trying to recapture a sense of the past, this place offers a brash mix of Art Deco furnishings, playful light fixtures, and modern Cuban art and sculpture throughout the hotel. The rooms feature soaring high ceilings, and proportionately high painted headboards. A majority have views over the Parque Central, although a few let out onto the interior courtyard. Unfortunately, the hyper-hip interior design ends up leaving the rooms feeling a bit spartan and uninviting. All rooms come with a cellphone and personally assigned local number, a nice touch for business travelers. The hotel's snack bar is located in a first-floor courtyard under ancient brick-and-stone arches in ruin, which set off a massive and intricate mosaic wall, small pool and fountain, and modern track lighting. It's open 24 hours, has a few computers with Internet connections, and is one of the hotel's finest features. This is definitely a great spot for a coffee, drink, or light bite.

Calle Prado 408 (corner of Neptuno), Centro Havana. ② **7/861-1010.** Fax 7/861-4741. www.habaguanex.com. 63 units. CUC$150 double; CUC$200 suite. Rates include breakfast. Rates slightly lower during off season, higher during peak weeks. MC, V. Free valet parking. **Amenities:** 2 restaurants; bar; concierge; tour desk; car-rental desk; 24-hr. room service; laundry service; dry cleaning. *In room:* A/C, TV, minibar, hair dryer, safe.

### MODERATE

**Hotel Deauville**    This place doesn't look like much from the outside and things don't get significantly better inside. The entire structure suffers from significant wear and tear. But it is located right on the Malecón and most rooms have a private balcony overlooking the sea. The views from the rooms on the higher floors are wonderful, and the corner rooms—with windows on two sides—are particularly nice. The Deauville does a brisk business in package tours, and is often full with French and German groups. The rooftop pool here is a popular spot. Their advertised rates are a bit high for what you get, but if you're booked here as part of a package, or if you can get a lower rate, this is a pretty good option for a few days in Havana. The restaurants and included buffet breakfast are embarrassments.

Calle Galiano 1 (between the Malecón and San Lázaro), Centro Habana. ② **7/33-8812.** Fax 7/33-8148. 144 units. CUC$50–CUC$85 double. Rates include breakfast buffet. MC, V. Street parking nearby. **Amenities:** 2 restaurants; 2 bars; dance club; outdoor pool; tour desk; car-rental desk; laundry service; dry cleaning. *In room:* A/C, TV, safe.

**Hotel Inglaterra** 🌟    This is yet another of the more historic and better located hotels in Havana, although it's definitely showing its age—it's been in business since 1875. The ornate lobby, with its colorful Moorish mosaics, and the lively street-side cafe, are the best features here. Rooms are perennially desultory and dated, and most have small bathrooms. However, quite a few of the rooms do come with a small balcony overlooking the Parque Central, a nice perk. The rooftop bar is one of the few such perches to stay open relatively late, although the walls here are too high to enjoy the views while seated at your table.

Paseo del Prado 416 (in front of Parque Central), Centro Havana. ℂ 7/860-8595. Fax 7/860-8254. www.grancaribe. cu. 83 units. CUC$80–CUC$120 double. Rates include breakfast. MC, V. Free valet parking. **Amenities:** 3 restaurants; 2 bars; concierge; tour desk; car-rental desk; 24-hr. room service; laundry service; dry cleaning. *In room:* A/C, TV, minibar, hair dryer, safe.

### INEXPENSIVE

There are literally hundreds of official and unofficial rooms for rent in private homes throughout Centro Habana. Many are quite dilapidated and run down, but a few are well maintained and charming. One popular *casa* is that of **Jorge Díaz,** Calle Gervasio 209, between Calles Concordia and Virtudes (ℂ 7/870-0489; www.cubanasol. com), a large and lovely old home, which is also known as La Casona Colonial. Other popular options include **Casa Esther Cardosa,** Calle Aguila 367, between San Miguel and Neptuno (ℂ 7/862-0401; esthercardoso@hotmail.com); **Casa Vicky,** Calle Barcelona 60, between Aguila and Amistad (ℂ 7/863-8923; virtudes624@yahoo.es); and **Casa del Scientífico,** Paseo de Martí 212, at the corner of Calle Trocadero (ℂ 7/862-4511).

**Hotel Lido** *Value*    Although one block removed from the Prado, this is a much better bet than its nearby sister, the Hotel Caribbean. In general, the rooms are larger and more comfortable. Interior rooms lack windows and are a tad stuffy, but the end rooms have wonderful private balconies overlooking Calle Consulado. The fourth-floor rooftop restaurant serves uninspired budget fare but offers good views over Havana.

Calle Consulado 210 (between Calles Animas and Trocadero), Centro Habana. ℂ/fax 7/867-1102. www.islazul.cu. 64 units. CUC$31–CUC$38 double. Rates include breakfast. MC, V. Street parking nearby. **Amenities:** Restaurant; bar; tour desk; laundry service. *In room:* A/C, TV, safe.

## VEDADO & THE PLAZA DE LA REVOLUCION AREA
### VERY EXPENSIVE

**Hotel Nacional de Cuba** *★★*    Sitting on a high bluff overlooking the Malecón, this is Havana's signature hotel, and it's loaded with atmosphere. Two massive turrets loom overhead as you approach the entrance along its palm-lined driveway. The long, tiled lobby, with its high ceilings and heavy painted beams, is the heart and hub of this joint, and it's almost always bustling. The rooms themselves are large and well appointed, although somewhat drab and showing their age. Some of the standard rooms have quite small bathrooms, and no dresser with drawers. The suites and deluxe rooms are generally quite nice, however. Over half the rooms have ocean views, although only a rare few have private balconies. The hotel has a vast lawn area on its high bluff that opens out toward the sea. My favorite spot here is the "Compass Card," an outdoor terrace made of marble inlaid in the pattern of a nautical compass. This is a great place to grab a table for a sunset drink overlooking the Malecón, with giant cannons protecting you on either side.

Calle O (corner of Calle 21), Vedado. ℂ 7/873-3564, -3565, -3566, -3567. Fax 7/873-5171. www.grancaribe.cu. 457 units. CUC$115–CUC$180 double; CUC$200–CUC$400 suite; CUC$950 Presidential suite. Rates include breakfast buffet. MC, V. Free valet parking. **Amenities:** 4 restaurants; 3 bars; 2 lounges; cabaret; 2 outdoor pools; lit outdoor tennis court; concierge; tour desk; car-rental desk; business center; salon; 24-hr. room service; in-room massage; babysitting; laundry service; dry cleaning. *In room:* A/C, TV, minibar, hair dryer, safe.

**Meliá Cohiba** *★★★*    Sitting just off the Malecón, this high-rise hotel, with its sharp angles and alternating walls of stone and glass, is probably the most modern building in Havana. Moreover, the Meliá Cohiba, along with its sister hotel, the Meliá Habana (p. 94), provide all the services and amenities luxury travelers are looking for in a top-rated hotel. Rooms are large and comfortable, and most have excellent views, particularly those on the higher floors. The executive floors and services here make this by far the best choice for business travelers, and it's got a wonderful outdoor pool and the best-equipped health club I've found at any hotel in Havana. The Cohiba has a wide range of restaurants and shops, and even its buffet restaurant is a treat, with live cook stations and enough space and flow as to not feel like a cattle car. The **Habana Café** ✦ is one of the better club/restaurants in town, with a nightly floor show and live music. The executive floors and *Servicio Real* upgrade, which includes Internet and business-center privileges, as well as a constantly refreshed and extensive buffet in the executive lounge, make this by far the best choice for business travelers.

Av. Paseo (between Avs. 1 and 3), Vedado. ✆ **7/833-3636.** Fax 7/834-4555. www.solmeliacuba.com. 462 units. CUC$225 double; CUC$275 junior suite; CUC$325–CUC$500 suite. CUC$50–CUC$150 supplement for Servicio Real upgrade. MC, V. Valet parking CUC$8 per day. **Amenities:** 5 restaurants; 3 bars; 2 lounges; large outdoor pool; indoor squash court; well-equipped health club; Jacuzzi; sauna; concierge; tour desk; car-rental desk; business center; shopping arcade; salon; 24-hr. room service; in-room massage; babysitting; laundry service; dry cleaning; nonsmoking rooms. *In room:* A/C, TV, dataport, minibar, hair dryer, safe.

**Tryp Habana Libre** ✦✦    Formerly the Havana Hilton, this historic landmark is the place Fidel Castro first called home following the fall of Batista. Rising high above Havana from a spot on La Rampa, this hotel offers some of my favorite views of the city and sea from most of its rooms. The two-story open lobby area is striking, with its amoeba-shaped pool and massive modern sculpture surrounded by flowering plants and palms. The rooms themselves are large and comfortable, although they feel dated, despite the fact that most of the carpets and furniture are new. Of the dining and entertainment options, I find the famous Trader Vic's–style **Polinesio** an overpriced disappointment, although you might appreciate the 24-hour diner-style **La Rampa Cafetería**—I did. The 25th-floor **Turquino Cabaret** might not have the best floor show in town, but it does have the best view and regularly stages A-list concerts and performances.

Calles L and 23, Vedado. ✆ **7/834-6100.** Fax 7/834-6365. www.solmeliacuba.com. 572 units. CUC$200–CUC$220 double; CUC$300 junior suite; CUC$440–CUC$660 suite; CUC$1,500 Presidential suite. Rates include buffet breakfast. Children under 12 stay free. MC, V. Valet parking CUC$4 per day. **Amenities:** 5 restaurants; 3 bars; 2 lounges; dance club; outdoor pool; concierge; tour desk; car-rental desk; business center; shopping arcade; salon; 24-hr. room service; babysitting; laundry service; dry cleaning; nonsmoking rooms. *In room:* A/C, TV, dataport, minibar, hair dryer, safe.

### EXPENSIVE

**Hotel Presidente** ✦✦ *Finds*    This is the most elegant hotel in Vedado—even more so, I think, than the Hotel Nacional de Cuba (see above). The impeccable Victorian-style lobby features black-and-white marble floors, pink marble wainscoting, and real antiques. Some of the standard rooms are a bit compact, while others are quite spacious. About half (generally the even-numbered rooms) have good ocean views. On the 10th floor you'll find two large suites with wonderfully inviting oceanview terraces. There's a refreshing outdoor pool on the ground level, and a poolside bar and grill. While the hotel is just 2 blocks from the Malecón, it's not very close to much else.

Calle Calzada 110 (corner of Av. de los Presidentes), Vedado. ✆ **7/55-1801.** Fax 7/33-3753. www.hotelesc.com. 158 units. CUC$120–CUC$150 double; CUC$200–CUC$300 suite. Rates include buffet breakfast. MC, V. Free valet parking. **Amenities:** 2 restaurants; 2 bars; outdoor pool; tour desk; car-rental desk; laundry service; dry cleaning. *In room:* A/C, TV, minibar, hair dryer, safe.

**Hotel Victoria** ⓐ    This little business-class hotel is one of the few boutique-style hotel options in Vedado. Overall, in this category the Hotel Presidente is a much nicer hotel, although the Victoria is closer to the action in Vedado. The cozy carpeted rooms are a bit on the small side, but they do have high ceilings. For a business-class hotel, the business center is a bit small, but Internet use is free for guests. Be careful here: The neighboring FOCSA building funnels the sea breezes right at the Victoria's entrance. When the winds are up, they can almost knock you off your feet.

Calles 19 and M, Vedado. ⓒ **7/33-3510.** Fax 7/33-3109. www.hotelvictoriacuba.com. 31 units. CUC$80–CUC$140 double. MC, V. Free parking. **Amenities:** Restaurant; 2 bars; lounge; small outdoor pool; concierge; tour desk; car-rental desk; small business center; 24-hr. room service; babysitting; laundry service; dry cleaning. *In room:* A/C, TV, minibar, hair dryer, safe.

## MODERATE

**Hotel St. John's** ⓥ๏๏๏๏    This is a perennially popular choice for budget and midrange travelers. It definitely gets the nod over its nearby neighbor the Hotel Vedado (see below). Rooms are clean and simple. Most are pretty spacious and the furnishings are relatively modern. Rooms on the ninth floor and above have wonderful views. If you don't have a room on a higher floor, you can always spend time in the tiny rooftop pool or its adjoining restaurant. The hotel is right in the heart of Vedado, just a block off La Rampa.

Calle O (between Calles 23 and 25), Vedado. ⓒ **7/33-3740.** Fax 7/33-3561. 77 units. CUC$67–CUC$80 double. Rates include breakfast buffet. MC, V. Street parking nearby. **Amenities:** 2 restaurants; 2 bars; dance club; outdoor pool; tour desk; car-rental desk; laundry service; dry cleaning. *In room:* A/C, TV, safe.

**Hotel Vedado**    This popular Vedado hotel is somewhat nondescript. Sure it'll do in a pinch, but it's rather uninspired and uninspiring. Rooms are distributed in two neighboring towers, and there's a kidney-shaped pool on the ground floor between them. Opened in 1952, the lobby retains the original Art Deco feel, and apparently some of the original vinyl chairs and couches. The hotel has a tiny exercise room, where the best feature is a little sauna.

Calle O (between Calles 23 and 25), Vedado. ⓒ **7/33-4072.** Fax 7/33-4186. 203 units. CUC$67–CUC$80 double. Rates include breakfast buffet. MC, V. Street parking nearby. **Amenities:** 3 restaurants; 2 bars; cabaret; outdoor pool; exercise room; sauna; tour desk; car-rental desk; laundry service; dry cleaning. *In room:* A/C, TV, safe.

## INEXPENSIVE

Given that this was one of Havana's prime middle-class neighborhoods, there's a glut of casas particulares, many in wonderful old neoclassical and Art Deco homes and apartment buildings. In addition to the options listed below, you could also try **Casa Matilde Gómez,** Calle 15 no. 152, between Calles K and L, Apartment 127, 12th floor (ⓒ **7/832-5783**); **Casa María Elena,** Calle 13 no. 106, between Calles L and M, Apartment 5 (ⓒ **7/832-4346**); **Casa Sandra,** Calle G no. 301 (at the corner of Calle 13), 13th floor (ⓒ **7/863-5547;** www.accommodationhavana.com); or **Casa Iraida,** Calle 19 no. 376, between Calles G and H, Apartment 10-A (ⓒ **7/832-4084**).

**Apartamento La Superabuela**    The name of this popular casa particular translates as "the Super Grandma," and that's how you'll be thinking of your host María Esther in no time. The air-conditioned rooms are simple, located on the second floor of this well-situated 1920s-era home. Breakfast is served for between CUC$3 and CUC$5 per person, and they even have a late-model mountain bike you can rent.

Calle I no. 355 (between Calles 17 and 19), Vedado. ☎ 7/832-3033. la_superabuela@hotmail.com. 2 units. CUC$25–CUC$35 double. No credit cards. Street parking. **Amenities:** Bike rental; laundry service. *In room:* A/C, no phone.

**Casa Particular Sandelis** 🙊   Located on the sixth floor of a corner building just across from the Hotel Nacional, this clean and well-run casa particular is a great choice in Vedado. The classic Art Deco building is entered by climbing one of two mirror-image curving staircases. The rooms are comfy, and your hosts, Lenin and Carolina, are a delight. The apartment has a couple of inviting common areas, including a living room and a terrace area, the latter with good views toward the Malecón and Caribbean Sea. They'll cook for you or let you use the kitchen facilities. Hard-core animal rights activists might be put off by the various stuffed animal showpieces. Quite a few other folks rent rooms in this building, so if this place is full, they can usually refer you to another room.

Calle 21 no. 4 (between Calles N and O), Apto. 61, Vedado. ☎ 7/832-4422. www.sandelisroom.com. 2 units. CUC$35 double. No credit cards. Street parking. **Amenities:** Kitchen. *In room:* A/C, TV, fridge.

## PLAYA
### VERY EXPENSIVE

**Meliá Habana** 🙊🙊   This modern luxury hotel is set on a coral ledge on the edge of the Caribbean. Its rows of balconies are draped with flowing ferns, and the building gets wider as it gets higher, giving it an inverted pyramid effect. Most of the rooms here have excellent ocean views from their good-size private balconies. The rooms are large and comfortable, with high ceilings and big bathrooms. The most striking feature here is the ground-level lagoon surrounded by lush tropical gardens and filled by man-made waterfalls set under soaring columns. The lagoon almost seems to blend into the free-form pool, which is billed as the largest in Cuba. As at the Meliá Cohiba, the executive floors and services are top-notch here, making it a good choice for business travelers. The hotel is the unofficial default hub of the business scene in Miramar.

Av. 3 (between Calles 76 and 80), Miramar, Playa. ☎ 7/204-8500. Fax 7/204-8505. www.solmeliacuba.com. 409 units. CUC$225–CUC$275 double; CUC$275–CUC$375 junior suite; CUC$500 suite. MC, V. Valet parking CUC$4 per day. **Amenities:** 4 restaurants; 3 bars; 2 lounges; coffee shop; large outdoor pool; 2 outdoor tennis courts; small, well-equipped exercise room; sauna; concierge; tour desk; car-rental desk; business center; shopping arcade; salon; 24-hr. room service; babysitting; laundry service; dry cleaning; nonsmoking rooms. *In room:* A/C, TV, dataport, minibar, hair dryer, safe.

**Occidental Miramar** 🙊🙊   This modern and massive luxury hotel is an impressive and imposing presence in the heart of Miramar's business district. It has nicer rooms than the Meliá Habana (see above), but it's 2 blocks from the sea and has fewer dining and entertainment options. The rooms are all at least junior suites, with one queen-size bed and a comfortable sitting area. The beds are some of the firmest I've found in Havana. The bathrooms are just a tad on the small size in proportion to everything else here. Only the eight end-unit suites here have balconies, although these balconies are large. This place does a brisk business in group and conference travel.

Av. 5 (between Calles 78 and 80), Miramar, Playa. ☎ 7/204-3584. Fax 7/204-3583. www.occidental-hoteles.com. 427 units. CUC$140–CUC$220 double; CUC$250–CUC$300 suite. MC, V. Free valet parking. **Amenities:** 3 restaurants; 2 bars; lounge; large outdoor pool; 6 outdoor tennis courts (2 lit); indoor squash court; well-equipped exercise room; sauna; children's center; concierge; tour desk; car-rental desk; business center; shopping arcade; salon; 24-hr. room service; babysitting; laundry service; dry cleaning; nonsmoking rooms. *In room:* A/C, TV, dataport, minibar, hair dryer, safe.

## EXPENSIVE

**Hotel Chateau Miramar** ☆  This place is attempting to stake out the boutique business-class market. For lack of any competition, it is doing just that, although I don't think it has the warmth, charm, or personality I expect in a high-end boutique hotel, and for any business person I'd recommend any of the large business-class hotels in town over this option. The standard rooms here are on the small side, while the junior suites and suites are more than ample. The decor is rather nondescript and impersonal, although the marble bathrooms are spacious. Most rooms come with a private balcony, and some of these are quite roomy. Suite no. 416 is the best room and view in the house, while any room with a number ending in 09 through 16 will have an ocean view. One of the more unique and appealing features here is the fact that each room comes with a 21-inch flatscreen television, equipped with Internet, fax, and e-mail, all activated by a wireless keyboard. The hotel is right on the waterfront, just behind the National Aquarium.

Av. 1 (between Calles 60 and 62), Miramar, Playa. ☎ 7/204-1952. Fax 7/204-0224. www.hotelescubanacan.com. 50 units. CUC$125 double; CUC$150–CUC$170 suite. MC, V. Free valet parking. **Amenities:** Restaurant; snack bar; 2 bars; lounge; outdoor pool; concierge; tour desk; car-rental desk; business center; 24-hr. room service; massage; laundry service; dry cleaning. *In room:* A/C, TV, dataport, minibar, hair dryer, safe.

**Hotel Comodoro** ☆  Located next to the Meliá Habana (see above), this complex has the feel of a South Florida condo community. The hotel rooms in the main building are acceptable, although I'd definitely opt for one of the one- or two-bedroom bungalows, which are housed in a series of two-story blocks spread around a maze of free-form pools. The bungalows all come with kitchenettes or full kitchens, making them a good option for longer stays. All of the rooms here have a balcony or patio. The Comodoro has a tiny patch of beach, which has been dump-trucked in and set next to a natural pool created by a break wall just off the coast here.

Av. 3 and Calle 84, Miramar, Playa. ☎ 7/204-5551. Fax 7/204-2089. www.hotelescubanacan.com. 119 units, 324 bungalows. CUC$90–CUC$110 double; CUC$135–CUC$155 suite; CUC$118–CUC$248 bungalow. MC, V. Free parking. **Amenities:** 2 restaurants; snack bar; 2 bars; dance club; natural saltwater pool and a series of free-form freshwater pools; watersports equipment/rentals; concierge; tour desk; car-rental desk; shopping arcade; salon; 24-hr. room service; massage; laundry service; dry cleaning. *In room:* A/C, TV, safe.

**Hotel Copacabana** ☆  Once you get beyond the noisy caged parrots in the lobby, this seaside hotel is a good option in Miramar. The average-size rooms are bright, cheery, and in good shape, although the bathrooms are on the small side. While not all come with a private balcony, most do—and most of these have excellent ocean views. A few even have suspended woven rattan chairs on the balconies, which make them great places to sit with a good book, swinging in the breeze overlooking the Caribbean. There's a large, free-form freshwater pool with an interesting abstract fountain in the center, and an even larger saltwater "pool" formed by a breakwater enclosing an area off the coral coastline. A Brazilian theme runs throughout, from the Ipanema lobby bar to the Itapoa steakhouse. Catering to European tour groups, this is a lively hotel.

Av. 1 (between Calles 44 and 46), Miramar, Playa. ☎ 7/204-1037. Fax 7/204-2846 www.hotelescubanacan.com. 168 units. CUC$80–CUC$110 double; CUC$140–CUC$180 suite. Rates include breakfast buffet. MC, V. Free parking. **Amenities:** 4 restaurants; 2 bars; lounge; dance club; saltwater pool and freshwater pool; 2 lit outdoor tennis courts; small exercise room; sauna; limited watersports equipment/rentals; concierge; tour desk; car-rental desk; salon; 24-hr. room service; babysitting; laundry service; dry cleaning. *In room:* A/C, TV, minibar, hair dryer, safe.

## INEXPENSIVE

As in Vedado and Centro Habana, there are scores of casas particulares and private rooms for rent in Playa. Given the fact that this was a popular upper-class residential neighborhood prior to the Revolution, most are housed in large, comfortable homes and apartments. In addition to the casas listed below, you could try **Casa Gina,** Calle 86 no. 526, between Avenidas 5 and 7 (✆ **7/203-4034**). Alternately, you could see if there's space at the Ministry of Education's **Hostal Icemar,** Calle 16 no. 104, between Avenidas 1 and 3 (✆/fax **7/203-7735**), a dependable budget option popular with students and backpackers.

**Casa Miramar**    You'll feel like you stepped back in time at this impeccably restored Spanish-colonial residence. The white stucco exterior and red roof-tile accents give this home a distinctive look. The rooms, named after Columbus's ships, are all comfortable and clean, and each comes with a private balcony, although that of La Nina is quite small. The biggest drawback here is that the three rooms share a common bathroom, although it's bright, spacious, and immaculately kept.

Calle 30 no. 3502 (between Calles 35 and 37), Miramar, Playa. ✆ **7/209-5679.** 3 units. CUC$35–CUC$50 double. V. Free parking. **Amenities:** Restaurant; laundry service. *In room:* A/C, no phone.

**Residencias Miramar**    This is an excellent casa particular with wonderful hosts. The rooms are clean and modern, and each comes with its own phone and a small fridge. Common areas include a comfortable living room, and a shady patio area amid well-tended gardens. Meals are available throughout the day for very reasonable prices, and Ernesto and Eva can help arrange tours and activities, as well as arrange homestays with friends in Habana Vieja and Vedado.

Av. 7 no. 4403 (between Calles 44 and 46), Miramar, Playa. ✆ **7/202-1075.** www.habanasol.com. 2 units. CUC$30 double. No credit cards. Free parking. **Amenities:** Restaurant; laundry service. *In room:* A/C, minifridge.

## NEAR THE AIRPORT

There are no hotels at or truly near the airport. Luckily, the bulk of Havana hotels are just a 15- to 30-minute car ride away. The closest hotels to the airport are those in Playa. Of these, Cubanacán's **Hotel Bello Caribe** (✆ **7/273-9906;** www.hoteles cubanacan.com) is probably the closest, at just 10km (6¼ miles) from the airport. This is a decent option, although it's only a few minutes closer to the airport than the other Playa and Miramar options listed above.

## HABANA DEL ESTE & PLAYAS DEL ESTE

The beaches of Playas del Este are quite beautiful. Moreover, the four long, consecutive beaches here are just a 15- to 25-minute taxi or car ride from Habana Vieja, making it a good choice for combining your fun in the sun with some city pleasures. However, the hotel choices here are limited and rather desultory. While there are several all-inclusive resorts, offering a whole range of entertainment and activities options, they are far less polished and attractive than similar options in Varadero or other prime all-inclusive destinations. In fact, if you want a beautiful beach resort just a little bit farther east of Playas del Este, head to **Breezes Jibacoa** (see below).

## EXPENSIVE

**Blau Club Arenal** ⚑    Sandwiched between the Itabo lagoon and Playa Santa María, this is the best of the former Horizontes all-inclusives in this area, and it's gotten even better after having been taken over by the Spanish Blau chain. The rooms are of good size and have plenty of windows or big sliding glass doors opening on to private balconies or terraces. I think it's worth the slight splurge for one of the superior rooms or junior suites. The hotel does a brisk business in European group travel.

Laguna Itabo, between Santa María del Mar and Boca Ciega. ℂ **7/97-1272**. Fax 7/97-1287. www.blau-hotels.com. 169 units. CUC$130–CUC$150 double; CUC$150–CUC$190 suite. Rates are all-inclusive. MC, V. Free parking. **Amenities:** 2 restaurants; 3 bars; dance club; large outdoor pool; small gym; 2 tennis courts; free watersports equipment; tour desk; car-rental desk; babysitting; laundry service. In room: A/C, TV, fridge, safe.

**Club Atlántico**    Not to be confused with the Apartotel Atlántico, this is a comfortable and relatively modern all-inclusive option. The rooms are standard-issue affairs, with two twin beds and a little balcony or terrace. The buffet meals here are nothing to write home about or look forward to, but on the upside, the all-inclusive rates do include all your drinks and the use of nonmotorized watersports equipment. There's an inviting and refreshing kidney-shaped pool that overlooks and lets out onto the beautiful beach here. Try for an oceanview third-floor room.

Av. Las Terrazas, Santa María del Mar, Playas del Este. ℂ **7/97-1085.** Fax 7/96-1532. www.grancaribe.cu. 92 units. CUC$78–CUC$120 double. Rates are all-inclusive. MC, V. Free parking. **Amenities:** Restaurant; snack bar; 2 bars; outdoor pool; outdoor tennis court; free watersports equipment; tour desk; car-rental desk; in-room massage; babysitting; laundry service. In room: A/C, TV, minibar, safe.

**Villas Los Pinos** ✦    These independent villas are probably the plushest accommodations in Playas del Este and well-suited to longer stays. The villas are a mix of two-, three-, and four-bedroom units, in a series of two- and three-story buildings. Most villas come with their own swimming pool. The entire complex, moreover, borders a beautiful section of beach. The rooms vary considerably, but most are quite spacious, with rattan furnishings and well-equipped kitchenettes. Some have wonderful raised decks with ocean views. I like unit nos. 44 and 45 for their views, while unit no. 34 has its own squash court. For CUC$25 per day, you can hire your own cook and personal housekeeper.

Av. Las Terrazas 21 (between Calles 4 and 5), Santa María del Mar, Playas del Este. ℂ **7/97-1361.** Fax 7/97-1524. www.grancaribe.com. 70 units. CUC$100–CUC$130 double; CUC$150–CUC$200 2-bedroom villa; CUC$200–CUC$250 3-bedroom villa; CUC$250–CUC$300 4-bedroom villa. MC, V. Free parking. **Amenities:** 3 restaurants; 2 bars; 20 outdoor pools; 2 outdoor tennis courts; small exercise room; sauna; watersports equipment/rentals; tour desk; car-rental desk; in-room massage; babysitting; laundry service. In room: A/C, TV, kitchenette, fridge, safe.

### INEXPENSIVE

In addition to the hotel listed below, the Playas del Este beach town of Guanabo has a high concentration of casas particulares. Try **Casa Trullijo,** Av. Quebec 55, between Calles 478 and 482, Guanabo (ℂ **7/96-3325;** www.cubanasol.com); or **Casa Oliva,** Calle 468 no. 714, Guanabo (ℂ **7/96-2819**). The latter even has a small swimming pool.

**Hotel Tropicoco** 🄥𝘢𝘭𝘶𝘦    This imposing five-story hotel stretches on for a hundred yards or so in each direction from its blocky concrete lobby. This place hosts many group and package tours, and it's usually pretty lively. Still, it's hard not to find the Soviet-style architecture of this resort a little depressing, particularly the rectangular pool, wedged in to a shady area in an alcove of the building. The whole complex has been remodeled and the rooms and facilities are in decent shape. Most of the rooms face the sea, although only a few have balconies, and overall they are unspectacular and on the small side. The best feature here is the fact that a beautiful and extremely popular section of beach is located just across the street.

Avs. Sur and Las Terrazas, Santa María del Mar. (✆) **7/97-1371.** Fax 7/97-1389. www.hotelescubanacan.com. 188 units. CUC$95–CUC$120 double. Rates are all-inclusive. MC, V. Free parking. **Amenities:** 2 restaurants; 3 bars; large outdoor pool; small exercise room; sauna; watersports equipment/rentals; tour desk; car-rental desk; salon; in-room massage; babysitting; laundry service. *In room:* A/C, TV, kitchenette, fridge, safe.

## A LITTLE FARTHER EAST

**Breezes Jibacoa** 🐾🐾   This plush, all-inclusive resort is set on a beautiful patch of beach, located about halfway between Havana and Varadero. The hotel is less than an hour's drive from downtown Havana, making daytrips, and even evening outings to the capital, convenient. The rooms are large, comfortable, and modern and many come with just one king-size bed. This resort is geared toward single adults and couples, and no children under 14 are allowed. The suites have a separate sitting area, fridge, CD player, and the best beach views in the house. All rooms come with a private balcony. A huge swimming pool is set in the center of the resort, and a wide range of activities are offered.

Playa Jibacoa. (✆) 47/29-5122. Fax 47/29-5150. www.superclubscuba.com. 250 units. CUC$226–CUC$428 double. Rates are all inclusive. MC, V. No children under 14. **Amenities:** 4 restaurants; 6 bars; cabaret; large outdoor pool; small, well-equipped gym; 2 tennis courts; free watersports equipment; free bicycles; tour desk; car-rental desk; in-room massage; laundry service. *In room:* A/C, TV, coffeemaker, hair dryer, safe.

## 4 Where to Dine

It's been said before, and it's worth repeating: Do not come to Cuba for fine dining. In addition to mediocre food and service, overcharging is attempted with disheartening frequency, including at many of Havana's best and most popular restaurants.

*Paladares* (private restaurants) are common in Havana. They are officially limited to no more than 12 seats, and cannot serve lobster or shrimp. While as a whole they tend to lack stability and suffer the whims of governmental intervention, quite a few have established themselves as some of the better, long-standing restaurant options in Havana. In fact, the best of these often outshine most of the official government-run options.

Aside from the restaurants listed below, fast-food chains are starting to pop up around Havana. The most prominent of these is **El Rápido,** which has numerous outlets serving fried chicken, burgers, hot dogs, microwave pizzas, and other fast-food staples. Another chain worth mentioning is **Pizza Nova,** Calle 17 and Calle 10, Vedado ((✆) 7/55-1339), which also has outlets in Marina Hemingway and several provincial cities. This place has good thin-crust pizza and respectable pastas. Finally, for breakfast or a quick bite, look out for **Pain de Paris** storefronts, featuring a wide range of fresh-baked breads, croissants, and pastries, as well as simple sandwiches.

## LA HABANA VIEJA

In addition to the places mentioned below, budget travelers swear by the **Restaurante Hanoi,** Calles Teniente Rey and Oficios ((✆) 7/867-1029), although I was rather disappointed to find virtually no Vietnamese influence on the decidedly mediocre *criolla* and Chinese cuisine here.

### VERY EXPENSIVE

**El Floridita** 🐾 CRIOLLA/INTERNATIONAL   This is by far the classiest of the many Hemingway hangouts in Habana. In fact, El Floridita is so upscale, I have a hard time imagining the rugged writer really enjoying this place. It'll cost you CUC$6 for a daiquiri in "The Cradle of the Daiquiri"—be sure to get it shaken, not blended.

The bartenders' deep-red jackets blend perfectly with the plush decor. The long bar takes up a good portion of the front room. There's quieter and more formal seating in the back, although even if you land a table just off the bar, this place is never rowdy. The food here is acceptable but can't justify the hefty price tags. If you do stick around for a meal, stick to the seafood. The sautéed shrimp, which is prepared tableside, is a good bet. I recommend El Floridita mostly as a cool and refreshing place to stop for a drink in the middle of a hot afternoon walking around Old Havana.

Calle Obispo 557 (corner of Calle Monserrate). ☎ **7/863-1301.** Reservations recommended. Main courses CUC$12–CUC$42. MC, V. Daily 11am–midnight.

## EXPENSIVE

### Café del Oriente ★★ *Finds* INTERNATIONAL    This elegant little restaurant sits just off the Plaza San Francisco and, when the weather permits, features a few outdoor tables. Inside you'll find a cool, large room, with a beautiful patterned marble floor, high ceilings, and dark wainscoting on the walls. In the center of the restaurant is a large U-shaped bar. The menu here is one of the more extravagant in Havana, with entrees that include fried frogs' legs and steamed mussels with truffle sauce. For the main course, I like the stewed rabbit with figs and truffles, or the fresh sole in an anchovy sauce. Even if you don't take a full meal here, this is a great place to stop for a drink or cup of coffee while touring Old Havana. In fact, it's open daily 24 hours for a very late night or early morning pick-me-up.

Calle Officios 112 (corner of Calle Armargura). ☎ **7/860-6686.** Reservations recommended. Main courses CUC$12–CUC$30. MC, V. Daily 24 hr.

### La Bodeguita del Medio ★★ CRIOLLA    The "B del M," as it's also known, oozes history and suffers from overcrowding. Still, it is pretty much a must-visit for any first-time trip to Havana. The collage of famous photos and signatures that crowd the walls here are legend. You'll definitely want a reservation, although even with a reservation, you'll probably end up waiting for a table—this place is just that popular. Tradition would have you start things off with a mojito, although the mojitos here are notoriously weak. Definitely order one with 3- or 5-year-old *añejo* rum if you plan on enjoying it. The food—simple and well-prepared Cuban dishes—is pretty good. The slow-roasted pork is my favorite, although the *ropa vieja* (shredded beef) gives it a run for its money. No matter what you order, make sure you have it served with plenty of yuca with *mojo* (gravy) and the *arroz morro,* black beans with rice. This place is crowded and rowdy, so don't come expecting anything less.

Calle Empedrado 207 (between Calles San Ignacio and Cuba). ☎ **7/867-1374.** Reservations recommended. Main courses CUC$8–CUC$28. MC, V. Daily 10:30am–midnight.

### La Domínica ★★ ITALIAN    This is the best Italian restaurant in town. Skip the formal and stuffy seating inside and grab one of the outdoor tables under a canvas umbrella on the old brick streets. If the band were playing "'O Sole Mio" instead of "Guantanamera," you might almost forget you're in Havana and think you were dining at a sidewalk trattoria in Rome. There's a wood-burning oven turning out excellent thin-crust pizzas. The pastas are cooked al dente and served in big portions. My favorite is the *penne alla pulcinella,* which comes in a tomato cream sauce seasoned with anchovies and caviar. For main dishes I'd recommend the *saltimbocca alla Romana* or the *veal alla pizzaiola.* Finish everything off with some *cassata siciliana* and an espresso.

Calles O'Reilly and Mercaderes. ☎ **7/860-2918.** Reservations recommended. Pizzas and pastas CUC$6–CUC$12; main courses CUC$10–CUC$26. MC, V. Daily noon–midnight.

**Roof Garden Restaurant** ☆☆ *Finds* FRENCH/INTERNATIONAL    Located on the top floor of the Hotel Sevilla, this is one of the finer restaurants in Havana, with arguably the finest setting. The large dining room has a massively high ceiling with intricate bas-relief work and moldings. The room is ringed by floor-to-almost-ceiling windows that are left open in all but the most inclement weather. Marble floors and huge chandeliers complete the ambience. The menu is one of the more adventurous in town, with such entrees as monkfish in a basil-curry sauce, lobster stewed in rum, and leg of lamb with fresh thyme and a coffee-infused sauce. For starters, I recommend the rabbit turrine with a fresh-herb-and-wine jelly. And to finish off the night decadently, go for the profiteroles with ice cream and chocolate sauce. This place is also known as the "Torre del Oro."

Calle Trocadero 55 (corner of Calle Prado). ℂ **7/860-8560**. Reservations recommended. Main courses CUC$9–CUC$32. MC, V. Daily 7–10:30pm.

**Santo Angel** ☆ *Finds* INTERNATIONAL    With a handful of outdoor tables right on the Plaza Vieja, as well as others on the broad covered veranda facing the plaza, this is arguably one of the most atmospheric restaurants in Old Havana. You'll definitely want to choose one of the aforementioned tables over those in the indoor dining rooms. The adventurous menu attempts to match the grandeur of the ambience, with mixed results. You can start things off with a cold asparagus soup or some seafood bisque. For a main dish, I like the lobster rings in cherry sauce. The chefs here are inconsistent, and at times, I've left very pleased, while on other occasions I've been sorely disappointed.

Calle Teniente Rey 60, at the corner of Calle San Ignacio. ℂ **7/861-1626**. Reservations recommended. Main courses CUC$8–CUC$28. MC, V. Daily 11:30am–11pm.

## MODERATE

**Café La Mina** CRIOLLA    This popular place has a privileged location right on the Plaza de Armas. There's covered seating in three separate patios, with ferns and arbors and caged parakeets providing additional atmosphere, as well as several dining rooms spread through the interior of a couple of connected buildings. The food is standard and acceptable tourist fare. The combo *Caribeña La Mina* is a sauté of chunks of chicken, pork, and shrimp in a tasty sauce with a hint of rum. The Traditional Cuban Combo comes with a mojito, black beans and rice, some grilled pork in *mojo*, and dessert. There's an attached ice-cream parlor and informal cafe. This is a good place to while away a few hours midday, or to take a break while walking around Habana Vieja.

Calles Obispo and Oficios, Plaza de Armas. ℂ **7/862-0216**. Reservations not required. Main courses CUC$7–CUC$28. MC, V. Daily 24 hr.

**La Paella** ☆ SPANISH    This is the premier paella place in Havana. The paellas are well prepared—in fact, they have won a few international prizes. Stick to a traditional paella with chicken and sausage, or splurge on a lobster and seafood special. This place used to be a real bargain, but prices have basically doubled in the past year. They also have a host of meat, poultry, and seafood items, but go with the house specialty. The atmosphere is warm and lively, with heavy wooden tables and colorful ceramic accents everywhere.

In the Hostal Valencia at Calle Oficios 53 (between Calles Lamparilla and Obrapía). ℂ **7/867-1037**. Reservations recommended. Main courses CUC$8–CUC$24. MC, V. Daily noon–midnight.

## INEXPENSIVE

**Café Taberna** *(Value)* CRIOLLA/INTERNATIONAL    This lively joint is housed in a beautifully restored 18th-century building with high ceilings, just off the Plaza Vieja. Photos of Beny Moré and other popular mambo acts adorn the walls, and there's a long bar with an impressive wall of booze stacked behind it. The food is standard and uninspired fare, but this is one of the few places in Habana Vieja that won't break your bank for a simple meal. The outdoor seating seems like an afterthought, and feels a little too far removed from the action and ambience.

Calles Mercaderes and Teniente Rey, Plaza Vieja. ℂ **7/861-1637.** Reservations not required. Main courses CUC$4–CUC$9. MC, V. Daily noon–midnight.

**Cafetería El Portal** CRIOLLA    The El Patio restaurant complex has a handful of dining options, and this is the only one really worth a visit. With seating on the large covered patio, and a couple dozen small tables set right on the Plaza de la Catedral, it's hard to find a spot with more character in Habana Vieja. The menu is small, but this place is big on atmosphere. The only real splurge here is the lobster and shrimp medallions in a light vinaigrette, which, although small, is a decent deal at CUC$12. If you're hungrier, you can have a Cuban sandwich or a small steak, both of which will come with French fries and fill you up. The mojitos here are acceptable and will run you CUC$3. The outdoor tables start getting some shade around 2pm, and all night long they provide wonderful views of the Cathedral's lighted bell towers. This is a great spot for a drink and light meal day or night. If you do opt for one of the pricier tables inside, be sure to snag one of the few tables on the second floor balconies overlooking the plaza.

Calle San Ignacio 54 (corner of Calle Empedrado), Plaza de la Catedral. ℂ **7/867-1034.** Reservations not accepted. Main courses CUC$4–CUC$17. MC, V. Daily 24 hr.

**La Taberna de la Muralla** *(Finds)* GRILL    Havana's only brewpub is blessed with a beautiful setting on a corner overlooking Plaza Vieja. Grab a seat at one of the wrought-iron tables under a broad canvas umbrella on the edge of the plaza when the weather's right, or one of the heavy wooden tables on the covered patio or indoor dining room when it's not. The small and simple menu is made up almost entirely of grilled-to-order pork chops, chicken breasts, or fish filets, or kabobs of chicken, shrimp, lobster, or a mix of the three. Order a pint of the home-brewed amber or dark beer and admire the large copper brewing tanks just behind the bar. Large groups or heavy drinkers can order a *dispensa*, a tall, clear glass tube filled with beer, featuring a spout at the bottom and a thinner tube filled with ice running up its center.

Calle San Ignacio (corner of Calle Muralla), Plaza Vieja. ℂ **7/866-4453.** Reservations not accepted. Main courses CUC3–CUC$9. MC, V. Daily 11am–midnight.

**Los Nardos** *(Value)* INTERNATIONAL/SPANISH    When there's no line out front, it's easy to miss the entrance to this popular place. Once you climb the run-down stairs to this third-floor haunt, you find a cool and dark room with heavy wooden furniture packed tight in a midsize dining room. One wall is loaded with a large case brimming with soccer trophies and memorabilia from the Spanish cultural group that runs this place. The menu has a few Spanish staples, including gazpacho, paella, and sangria, but mostly it's made up of huge, reasonably priced portions of standard meat, chicken, and seafood dishes. Everything is good, although unspectacular.

The wine list is relatively large, and slightly overpriced, yet given the food prices it's worth the splurge for one of their better bottles.

Paseo del Prado 563 (between Teniente Rey and Dragones, across from El Capitolio). (© **7/863-2985.** Reservations not accepted. Main courses CUC$4–CUC$15. No credit cards. Daily 11:30am–11:30pm.

## CENTRO HABANA

I am decidedly unimpressed with the Asian food available in Cuba. This goes for the handful of Chinese restaurants in Havana's little Chinatown, too. However, if you do venture to the block-long Cuchillo de Zanja, or just crave a change from *criolla* cooking, your best bets are **Restaurante Pacífico,** Cuchillo de Zanja and Calle San Nicolás (*©* **7/863-3243**), and **Restaurante Tien-Tan,** Cuchillo de Zanja 17 (*©* **7/861-5478**).

### MODERATE

**La Guarida** ★★ CRIOLLA   The most famous paladar in Cuba owes its renown in equal parts to the wonderful ambience, excellent cuisine, and the starring role it played in several scenes in the Cuban blockbuster film *Fresa y chocolate.* The three small rooms of this converted apartment are reached by climbing three stories of steep, run-down, and poorly lit stairs. The signed celebrity headshots let you see the stars in whose steps you have just followed. Start things off with some ceviche, gazpacho, or their signature appetizer of eggplant caviar, a tasty vegetable paste that has the texture the name implies. *Caimanero* (fresh red snapper) might come in a white-wine or sweet-and-sour sauce—both are good, as are the honey-mustard chicken and pork medallions in mango sauce. There's an extensive selection of Spanish, French, Italian, and Chilean wines. The ornate facade and balcony balustrades make this place worth a peek during the daytime. (To locate this paladar, see the "Vedado" map on p. 79, or better yet, just tell its name to any taxi driver.)

Calle Concordia 418 (between Calles Gervasio and Escobar). (© **7/862-4940.** Reservations required. Main courses CUC$11–CUC$17. No credit cards. Daily 7pm–midnight.

## VEDADO & THE PLAZA DE LA REVOLUCION AREA

In addition to the places listed below, you might try **Sierra Maestra** (© **7/55-4011**), which serves nouvelle Cuban cuisine in an elegant setting on the 25th floor of the Tryp Habana Libre hotel.

### MODERATE

**El Conejito** INTERNATIONAL   The name means "little rabbit," but there's more than just a little bit of rabbit on the menu here: grilled, baked, *a la criolla,* or *ali oli* (in garlic *mojo,* or gravy) are just some of the treatments our furry friend gets. Not to mention rabbit sausage, rabbit terrine, and rabbit ham for starters. Almost all the rabbit dishes are reasonably priced at around CUC$7 to CUC$9. Avoid the house specialty, *conejo financiera,* which comes in a busy yet bland sauce, and stick to simpler preparations. There are also more traditional meat and seafood options, but I'd go with the bunny. The place is modeled on an English Tudor pub, with brick walls and heavy, dark interior beams. There's a small attached bar that is usually pretty quiet.

Calles M and 17. (© **7/832-4671.** Reservations not required. Main courses CUC$5–CUC$20. No credit cards. Daily noon–11pm.

**Le Chansonnier** ★★ CRIOLLA/FRENCH   This long-standing (although itinerant) paladar serves French-inspired *criolla* cuisine, in a homey setting. High ceilings, antique clocks, and a huge crystal chandelier give this place plenty of charm. Start things off with some of the homemade pâté or eggplant gratin. The chicken in mushroom sauce and Dijon pork chop are both good, but if you want something special, get the duck in a red-wine-and-olive sauce. There's a small selection of fairly priced French and Spanish wines. There are only five tables here in the somewhat new digs, but when I last visited, the owner was talking about moving to an even bigger house nearby, and maybe adding lunch.

Calle J no. 257 (between Linea and Calle 15). ✆ 7/832-1576. Reservations recommended. Main courses CUC$10–CUC$14. No credit cards. Daily 7pm–midnight.

**Paladar Hurón Azul** ✿ CRIOLLA/INTERNATIONAL    Tucked away on a lightly trafficked street, yet still close to the hustle and bustle of Vedado, this small restaurant is a calm and elegant joint popular with tourists and Cuban elite alike. The indoor dining rooms feature beautiful paintings by prominent local artists. While not as festive or popular as La Guarida (see above), the food and service here are excellent. Several house combo plates are offered, based around either a chicken or pork main dish. This place is not to be confused with the open-air patio bar of the same name run by the Union de Escritores y Artistas Cubanos (UNEAC).

Calle Humbolt 153 (corner of Calle P). ✆ 7/879-1691. Reservations recommended. Main courses CUC$8–CUC$14. No credit cards. Daily noon–midnight.

### INEXPENSIVE
**Restaurante Monguito** _Finds_ CRIOLLA    This little joint has just five plastic tables with plastic lawn chairs in a narrow room. Plastic flowers in cheap vases, a couple of squawking parrots in the back, and kitschy, semiholographic nature scenes on the main wall complete the ambience. The _bistec uruguayo,_ a kind of deep-fried pork _cordon bleu,_ is huge, and the _pollo a la cacerola,_ baked chicken in a tomato sauce, is excellent. Try to get a seat near one of the fans, because—despite the massive air-conditioning unit—this place can get a little stuffy, especially midday.

Calle L (between Calles 23 and 25, directly across from Tryp Habana Libre). ✆ 7/831-2615. Reservations not accepted. Main courses CUC$4–CUC$8. No credit cards. Daily noon–11pm.

## PLAYA
### VERY EXPENSIVE
**El Tocororo** ✿ CRIOLLA/INTERNATIONAL    Like its progeny, La Finca (see below), this is a place whose reputation precedes it, and whose actual performance can't quite justify the prices and renown. The food and service are fine, but they don't live up to the fanfare. There's no fixed menu, but if the waiter's suggestions don't hit the mark, ask and they may be able to accommodate you. Most main dishes run between CUC$25 and CUC$35, with lobster—which you choose from a tank—topping things off at around CUC$40 a pop. They sometimes have exotic game here, ranging from ostrich to crocodile. Almost anything can be prepared with whatever sauce or preparation you might desire. The restaurant is housed in an attractive old Miramar mansion; the decor is cluttered and eclectic, with Tiffany lamps, stained glass, assorted hanging plants, and carved parrots dominating the scene. There's also an attached little sushi bar and restaurant, **Sakura,** serving traditional and respectable Japanese cuisine.

Av. 3 and Calle 18. ✆ 7/204-2209. Reservations recommended. Main courses CUC$15–CUC$40. MC, V. Daily noon–midnight.

**La Finca** *(Overrated)* CRIOLLA/INTERNATIONAL    Touted as one of the finest restaurants in Havana and the favorite haunt of Gabriel García Márquez and top party brass, this elegant little place, run by one of the country's few "celebrity chefs," is a let-down. While the setting is gorgeous, the food is pedestrian and tired. The chef, Erasmo, earned his fame at El Tocororo (see above) before setting up shop here. The menu and ambience of the two restaurants are actually quite similar, down to the Tiffany lamps, signed pieces of wine crates, and plentiful hanging ferns. Definitely grab a seat on the back patio under the high Plexiglas roof, with ornamental wrought-iron work and wrought-iron tables and chairs. The *pechitos de camaron,* deep-fried shrimp shells, are a good opener. The safest bets are the straightforward steak and lobster dishes. Avoid the fried lobster with sweet-and-sour sauce. And watch out for extra and hidden charges here. **Rancho Palco** is a slightly more moderately priced restaurant next door that caters to groups and mass tourism.

Av. 19 and Calle 140. © 7/240-9346 or 7/823-5838. Reservations recommended. Main courses CUC$12–CUC$30. MC, V. Mon–Sat noon–midnight.

## EXPENSIVE

**Don Cangrejo** *(★)* SEAFOOD    This oceanfront restaurant is one of the better and most dependable options for seafood in Havana. The place is actually run by the Ministry of Fisheries and not one of the tourist restaurant chains, so the fish is fresh and generally well prepared. The menu is extensive, but your best bet is to stick to a piece of simply prepared fresh snapper or grouper. If you want something heavier, they do a lot of cheese and gratin sauces, often with shrimp, crab, or lobster thrown in. Weather permitting, the best seats are outdoors on the open-air patio right beside the water, and around the moatlike little courtyard pool. The indoor seating is semiformal and heavily air-conditioned. If you're going to dine indoors, try to snag one of the second-floor window tables just off the little bar. The place has a decent and reasonably priced wine list and a knowledgeable sommelier.

Av. 1 (between Calles 16 and 18). © 7/204-4169. Reservations recommended. Main courses CUC$8–CUC$30. MC, V. Daily noon–midnight.

## MODERATE

If you can't get a table at La Cocina de Lilliam (see below), **La Esperanza,** Calle 16 no. 105 between Avenidas 1 and 3 (© **7/202-4361**), is another excellent paladar set up in an old sprawling home in Miramar.

**El Aljibe** *(★)* CRIOLLA    This popular tourist restaurant is a pleasant surprise. The fixed-price *pollo asado El Aljibe* (CUC$15) is the way to go here. Served all-you-can-eat family-style with white rice, black beans, fried plantain, French fries, and salad, the slow-roasted chicken comes in a wonderful, slightly sweet-and-sour garlic *mojo* that goes well over the rice. This place serves busloads of people on a regular basis, and despite the assembly-line efficiency of the operation, you can still enjoy the pleasant open-air restaurant, with its tall, steeply pitched thatch roof and rustic red-tile floors. Sure there are a handful of meat and seafood options, but trust me, stick to the house specialty.

Av. 7 (between Calles 24 and 26). © 7/204-1583 or 7/204-4233. Reservations recommended. Main courses CUC$10–CUC$24. MC, V. Daily noon–midnight.

**La Cocina de Lilliam** *(★★)* *(Finds)* CRIOLLA    The elegant softly lit outdoor garden seating here would be enough to recommend this family-run paladar, but the food's excellent as well. Lilliam Domínguez has a deft touch. Try the garbanzo, ham, and onion appetizer, and then opt for a piece of fresh fish, usually grouper or snapper, simply grilled. The menu varies, but if they've got it, order the *ropa vieja,* made with lamb here instead of the traditional beef. This place is getting quite popular so reservations are essential, especially if you want one of the outdoor tables.

Calle 48 no. 1311 (between Calles 13 and 15). ℂ **7/209-6514.** Reservations highly recommended. Main courses CUC$7–CUC$14. No credit cards. Daily noon–3pm and 7–11pm.

## HABANA DEL ESTE & PLAYAS DEL ESTE
### EXPENSIVE

**La Divina Pastora** SEAFOOD/CRIOLLA    This place has a wonderful setting, just behind a battery of big cannons below the Fortaleza la Cabaña, near the water and overlooking Habana Vieja. However, you'll be paying extra for the setting, and most of the seating is indoors, with no view of the city. The food here, while acceptable, does nothing to justify the prices. You might as well order the lobster, as it's the only thing that costs more or less what you'd pay for it anywhere else—and you know they're fresh, since you get to pick your dinner from a large tank of live ones. If you're not especially hungry, check out the **El Mirador** bar next door, which has better views from its outdoor tables, and a small, simple menu of sandwiches and light meals.

Parque Histórico Morro y Cabaña, Carretera de La Cabaña. ℂ **7/860-9990.** Reservations recommended. Main courses CUC$14–CUC$30. MC, V. Daily noon–11pm.

### MODERATE

**El Bodegón Criollo** CRIOLLA    A couple of huge wine casks hanging over the door mark the entrance to this, the principal restaurant at the Fortaleza la Cabaña complex (see Parque Histórico Morro y Cabaña, p. 114). The dining room occupies a long, wide, former storage room in the old fortress, with arched ceilings and brick floors. A small bar dominates a much smaller adjacent room. The food is simple and filling. I recommend the *grillada criolla,* which is a mixed plate of grilled beef, chicken, and pork served with *moros y cristianos* (black beans and rice). The grilled lobster is a good choice as well. Make a reservation for around 7pm if you want to eat and be out in time to snag a good spot for the nightly *cañonazo* ceremony. The Fortaleza la Cabaña complex is popular with Cubans and actually has several restaurants—you might want to try the nearby **La Fortaleza,** a peso restaurant that serves similar and slightly less expensive food in a much less formal setting.

Fortaleza la Cabaña. ℂ **7/862-0617.** Reservations recommended. Main courses CUC$5–CUC$20. MC, V. Daily noon–11pm.

**La Terraza** ⚓ SEAFOOD/CRIOLLA    This place is de rigueur for any Hemingway tour of the island. The ghosts of Papa and his pal Gregorio Fuentes are omnipresent here—just saunter through the swinging saloon-style doors and look around. The small restaurant is actually somewhat unable to cope with its fame, but if you get here early or have a firm reservation, you'll enjoy the well-prepared seafood, cool sea breezes, and a great view across the small plaza in Cojímar to the sea without a wait. The seafood paella is pretty good, and the lobster is usually fresh.

Calle 152 no. 161, Cojímar. ℂ **7/93-9232.** Reservations recommended. Main courses CUC$8–CUC$28. MC, V. Daily 11am–11pm.

**Los Doce Apóstoles** ⚓ CRIOLLA    I prefer this place to the far more pretentious and nearby La Divina Pastora (see above). Set at the base of the Morro Castle, just behind a battery of 12 cannons—hence the name "The Twelve Apostles"—the setting is actually nicer than that at La Divina Pastora, with great views day or night at a collection of open-air patio tables. When it's raining or the sun's too strong, you can take a seat at one of the less picturesque indoor tables. Stick to the reasonably priced *criolla* fare and, if you've come for dinner, hang around after you finish, as this joint often gets jumping after the *cañonazo* ceremony.

Parque Histórico Morro y Cabaña, Carretera de La Cabaña. ℭ 7/860-9990. Reservations recommended. Main courses CUC$8–CUC$28. MC, V. Daily noon–11pm.

## 5 What to See & Do

Havana is a city with a rich historical and architectural legacy. There are scores of sights and attractions, ranging from museums to churches to city squares to colonial forts—and more. There's easily a week's worth of worthy attractions. I've tried to select and describe the most important sights below.

At many attractions a CUC$2 to CUC$5 fee is added on for the taking of photos, and as much as CUC$25 for shooting video. This policy seems to be applied somewhat erratically.

All of the major tour agencies offer **city tours.** These affairs generally take in as many attractions as can be fit into the allotted time period. The most common tours include stops at the José Martí Memorial, a ride along the Malecón, and a walk around Habana Vieja (including stops at a handful of churches and attractions, and of course La Bodeguita del Medio). Some include tours of any number of the attractions listed below, with perhaps a visit to El Morro or the Hemingway Museum thrown in, while others are theme-based—castles and forts, churches, tobacco, art, or Hemingway, for example. Different tour agencies mix-and-match the various attractions at their discretion. If you want to see something specific, be sure it's on the tour you sign up for. The tours can range from 4 to 8 hours in length and cost between CUC$15 and CUC$50 per person.

### THE TOP ATTRACTIONS
#### LA HABANA VIEJA

In addition to the places mentioned below, there are scores of other interesting little museums and attractions. Moreover, many of the hotels and restaurants mentioned above (including El Floridita, Hotel Santa Isabel, and Hotel Ambos Mundos, to name just a few) are practically attractions in their own right, and worth a quick visit on any walking tour.

One of the prime attractions in Habana Vieja is the expansive daily street market of arts and crafts ✵✵✵, open from 10am until around 6pm on Calle Tacón, facing the Harbor Channel. See "Shopping," later in this chapter, for more information.

**Castillo de la Real Fuerza** ✵    This well-preserved 16th-century fort sits within a broad cloverleaf moat. This is the oldest fort in Havana, and the oldest surviving fort in the hemisphere. It was actually pretty much a failure, built too small and too far from the harbor entrance to be of much use. Still, crossing over the old drawbridge and walking around the ancient stone battlements gives a great sense of history. The most distinctive feature of this compact fort is the weathervane, **La Giraldilla,** which has come to be the city's defining symbol. The original 1634 bronze sculpture is actually on display at the Museo de la Ciudad, but a copy still adorns the top of the fort's bell tower. Today, the fort also contains the **Artistic Ceramic Museum,** with ceramic works by Wifredo Lam, Amelia Peláez, and Mirta García Bus, among others.

Calle O'Reilly 2 (at Av. del Puerto). (*C*) **7/861-5010.** Admission CUC$2 adults, free for children under 12. Daily 8am–7pm.

## Catedral de San Cristóbal  ☆☆☆
This is Old Havana's classic cathedral. The plaza fronting the cathedral and the church's baroque facade, with its asymmetrical towers, are the most visited attractions in Habana Vieja. Inside, the cathedral is simple, almost to the point of austerity, thanks to a radical 19th-century neoclassical makeover. Still, the vaulted ceilings, massive stone pillars, and modest collection of art and antiquities certainly make it worth a visit. Of these, the 17th-century wooden sculpture of Saint Christopher is quite interesting—note the shortened legs, which were cut in order to get the piece into place. Despite the official visiting hours listed below, the church is frequently closed tight. If you're lucky, you might be able to attend Mass here at 8pm on Monday, Tuesday, Thursday, or Friday, or at 10:30am on Sunday.

Calle Empedrado 156, Plaza de la Catedral. (*C*) **7/861-7771.** Free admission. Mon–Sat 10:30am–12:30pm; Sun 9am–12:30pm.

## Centro Wifredo Lam  ☆
This little museum and gallery is dedicated to the memory of Cuba's most treasured modern artist. The museum houses a sizeable collection of Lam's lithographs and acrylic works, as well as works of art and sculpture from the artist's personal collection. There's usually an interesting traveling exhibit in a separate gallery space. If you want to take a break, there's a simple cafe in a cool central courtyard.

Calle San Ignacio (corner of Calle Empedrado). (*C*) **7/861-3419.** Admission CUC$2 adults, free for children under 12. Mon–Sat 10am–5pm.

## El Templete
A tall (and still growing) ceiba tree stands in front of this neoclassical Doric temple. The tree is the younger cousin of a fallen giant that stood here, on the site where local citizens celebrated the town's first Mass and town meetings in the early 1500s. Behind the tree stands the "little temple," which was built between 1754 and 1828. Inside, you'll find three large canvases by Jean-Baptiste Vermay depicting the inauguration of the Temple, as well as depictions of those town meetings and Masses. You'll also find a bust of the artist beside an urn containing his ashes.

Calles Baratillo and O'Reilly, Plaza de Armas. (*C*) **7/861-2876.** Admission CUC$1 adults, free for children under 12. Daily 9:30am–6:30pm.

## Museo de la Ciudad  ☆☆
The Museum of the City is housed in the Palacio de los Capitanes Generales (Palace of the Captain Generals), a beautiful example of 18th-century Cuban baroque, and one of the most important and well-preserved buildings

---

### *Moments* Strolling Calle Obispo

Calle Obispo is one of the most charming and distinctive streets in Habana Vieja. This bustling pedestrian-only boulevard conveniently connects Parque Central and the nearby Capitolio with the Plaza de Armas and its many surrounding attractions, making it a classic route for any walking tour of Habana Vieja.

---

## A Quick Key to Havana's Parks & Plazas

Any tour of Habana Vieja will be oriented around the several colonial plazas or squares, and the Parque Central (Central Park). Although relatively close together, each is almost a world of its own. The principal attractions of each are described in greater detail below, but here's a general overview.

The smallest, **Plaza de la Catedral,** is probably the most visited. Named for the cathedral that defines its northern boundary, this compact cobblestone square is surrounded by a series of stunning colonial-era buildings and former palaces. With the cathedral's bell towers lit up each night, this is a great plaza to visit after dark. Within a 1-block radius in any direction, you will find La Bodeguita del Medio, the Centro Wifredo Lam, the Museo de Arte Colonial, and the lively Calle Tacón street market.

The **Plaza de Armas** probably has the densest concentration of historical buildings and attractions. Surrounding the shady urban park that now takes up the plaza, you'll find the Palacio de los Capitanes Generales and Museo de la Ciudad, the Castillo de la Real Fuerza, El Templete, and the Hotel Santa Isabel, housed in the former palace of the Count of Santovenia. Most days, the square is lined with stands set up by scores of used-book sellers.

The oldest, **Plaza Vieja,** was first laid out in 1599 and was dubbed "Plaza Nueva" (New Square). It soon lost prominence to the better located Plaza de Armas and Plaza de la Catedral. In fact, for most of the last half of the 20th century, it served simply as a parking lot. However, it has recently been meticulously restored. At the center of the broad open square is a replica of an 18th-century fountain. Surrounding it are historic buildings representing 4 centuries of construction.

in Habana Vieja. The seat of Cuba's government for over a hundred years, the building now features a dozen or so rooms with polished marble floors and ornate architectural details holding displays of colonial-era relics and artifacts. It's worth the price of admission just to stroll along the broad second-floor interior veranda overlooking the lush central courtyard, with its white marble statue of Christopher Columbus. And don't miss the Throne Room, with its thick red-velvet draperies, an array of treasures, and plush throne built for use by Spain's visiting monarchs. Allow yourself at least an hour to tour the museum.

Calle Tacón (between Calles O'Reilly and Obispo), Plaza de Armas. © 7/861-6130 or 7/861-2876. Admission CUC$3 adults, free for children under 12. Daily 9am–6pm.

**Museo de la Revolución y Memorial *Granma*** ⟨⟨ Housed in the former Presidential Palace, the Museum of the Revolution and Granma Memorial outlines in copious detail Cuba's history, with an emphasis on its independence and revolutionary struggles. In addition to the history lessons, exhibits, and memorabilia, there are wonderful works of art and some stunning architectural details, including a replica of Versaille's Hall of Mirrors, ornate bas-relief work, and interior decorations by Tiffany. Outside you'll find several trucks, tanks, planes, and even a bit of a shot-down U2 spy plane, all surrounding the glass-enclosed *Granma,* the 59-foot motor launch that

Near the waterfront, you'll find the **Plaza de San Francisco.** Asymmetrical in shape, this is the most open and uncluttered plaza in Habana Vieja. Facing the Sierra Maestra ship terminal, it is anchored by the Fuente de los Leones (Lion's Fountain), which was carved in 1836 by Italian sculptor Giuseppe Gaggini, modeled after a sister fountain in the Alhambra in Granada, Spain. The area's former importance as a business center is quickly noted in the imposing facades of the Lonja de Comercio (Stock Exchange) and a couple of large banks and money exchange houses that dominate the northern side of the plaza. The southern edge is defined by the lovely 16th-century Basílica Menor de San Francisco de Asís. Be sure to climb the bell tower here, the tallest church tower in Havana, for a wonderful view of Habana Vieja and its harbor.

**Parque Central** marks the western boundary of Habana Vieja. This is a popular local gathering spot, particularly known for its heated conversations about baseball. It is bordered on the west by the Paseo de Martí, or Prado, featuring El Capitolio and the Gran Teatro de la Habana. On the eastern edge, you'll find the Palacio del Centro Asturiano, which now holds the international collection of the Museo de las Bellas Artes. Classic hotels that ring the park include the Hotel Inglaterra, Hotel Plaza, and the Hotel Telégrafo, as well as the modern Hotel Parque Central. A short stroll down the Prado will soon bring you to the Museo Nacional de las Bellas Artes, Museo de la Revolución, and the Memorial Granma. While just 1 block in the other direction, heading toward Habana Vieja on Calle Obispo, you'll hit El Floridita.

carried Fidel Castro, Che Guevara, and 80 other fighters to the island in 1956. Give yourself at least an hour to see it all.

Calle Refugio 1 (between Calles Monserrate and Zulueta). ✆ 7/862-4091. Admission CUC$4 adults, free for children under 12. Guided tours are given throughout the day and cost an additional CUC$2. Daily 10am–5pm.

**Museo Nacional de las Bellas Artes** ✰✰   The National Fine Arts Museum fills three floors of this square-city-block building, and the design—with a central courtyard and zigzagging ramped stairwell—can make navigating the upper floors confusing, so allow yourself plenty of time, and be prepared to get mildly lost inside. An extensive collection of Cuban art and sculpture is on display at the newly renovated main building here. Modern masters like Wifredo Lam, Raúl Martínez, Amelia Peláez, and Rene Portocarrero are well represented. The international collection is now housed in a recently restored early-20th-century gem of a building. This collection leans heavily on classical and neoclassical European works, although there are some American, Latin American, and Oriental works on display. Give yourself at least 2 hours to tour either museum, or more if you want to get a good feel for the extensive Cuban art collection.

Cuban Art Collection: Calle Trocadero (between Calles Zulueta and Monserrate). International Collection: Calle San Rafael (between Calles Zulueta and Monserrate). ✆ 7/861-3858. www.bellasartes.cult.cu. Admission CUC$5 adults, free for children under 12. Tues–Sat 10am–4pm; Sun 10am–2pm.

## Luis Posada Carriles

On October 6, 1976 Cubana Aviations flight 455 was blown up by plastic explosives, killing all 73 people aboard. The victims included Cuba's entire Olympic fencing team. The man implicated in the bombing, Luis Posada Carriles, is emblematic of the confusing and contradictory nature of U.S.-Cuban relations, and relevant in terms of the current "War On Terror."

A former CIA operative and U.S. Army officer, the 78-year-old Posada Carriles took part in the failed Bay of Pigs invasion and later worked with the Nicaraguan Contras to destabilize the Sandinista government. He has bragged, and later denied, being responsible for the Cubana airplane bombing, as well as a string of bombings at hotels and tourism facilities in Cuba in which several civilians and tourists were killed. Along with Orlando Bosch, he is implicated in the 1976 bombing in Washington, D.C., which killed Chilean ambassador Orlando Letelier.

Posada Carriles has been jailed in both Venezuela and Panama. He broke out of jail in Venezuela in the mid-1980s, but was later arrested on charges of attempting to assassinate Fidel Castro at a 2000 regional summit in Panama. In July 2005, Posada Carriles was pardoned by outgoing President Mireya Moscoso. He is currently being held in an immigration detention center as the result of his illegally entering the United States, after his requests for political asylum were denied.

Posada Carilles represents an embarrassment to the United States. A self-proclaimed and proud "terrorist," he is seen as being coddled by the Bush Administration, which has so far refused to prosecute him under any terrorist statutes or grant extradition officially requested by both Cuba and Venezuela.

**Parque La Maestranza** *Kids*   Located right in Habana Vieja, this 2-block stretch of city park is dedicated to the little ones. There are pony rides and a little train ride, as well as jungle gyms and inflatable rooms for romping around in. There are usually some clowns or mimes on hand, and balloons, popcorn, and soft drinks are for sale. This place is decidedly low-key and low-tech by Western standards, but the mix of mostly Cuban and some foreign kids never seems to mind.

Calle Cuarteles (between Calle Tacón and Av. del Puerto). Admission CUC$2. Daily 9am–5pm.

### CENTRO HABANA

**Callejón de Hammel** ★★★ *Finds*   Nearly every inch of this narrow 2-block-long alleyway is painted in bright colors, the work of painter Salvador González. Most are mural-size depictions of Afro-Cuban deities. There are also sculptures made from scrap and old bike parts, as well as an *Nganga,* a sacred place for the celebration of Palo Monte rituals centered on a giant cauldron. There are crafts and food for sale in this open-air bazaar, and González also has a small gallery here. At noon each Sunday, this is the site of a weekly Afro-Cuban music and dance show and celebration headed up by the renowned folkloric group Clavé y Guaguanco. (To locate this alleyway, see the "Vedado" map on p. 79.)

Callejón de Hammel, between Calles Espada and Aramburu. Free admission. Daily 24 hr.

**Chinatown** *Overrated*  You'll see Havana's Chinatown touted in local literature, tour offerings, and other guidebooks. Overall, it's quite a disappointment. Occupying a small section of Centro Habana, it has few distinguishing features, a very small population of residents of Chinese descent, and none of the vibrancy of Chinatowns in cities like New York, San Francisco, or Toronto. A block-long pedestrian-only street, **El Cuchillo de Zanja** is packed with nondescript and unimpressive Chinese restaurants and shops. The biggest attraction here is the large pagoda-style **Dragon's Gate** located at the corner of Calle Dragones and Calle Amistad. Perhaps the most interesting attraction is the **Iglesia de la Caridad,** which features a statue of a Virgin that some say has Asian features. (To locate this area, see the "Vedado" map on p. 79.)

In the area bordered by Calles Dragones, Zanja, Rayo, and San Nicolás. Free admission. Daily 24 hr.

**El Capitolio** *Modeled* after its U.S. cousin, the Cuban Capitol is a stunning architectural work of grand scale—it's actually a tiny bit taller and longer than the Washington version. There's not a whole lot to see here, but it's worth climbing the steep steps and taking a quick tour. I was impressed by its scale and the intricately inlaid marble floors. The entrance hall features a replica of a 25-carat diamond imbedded in the floor from which all highway distances radiating out from Havana are measured. There's also the Statue of the Republic, a 17m-tall (56-ft.), 49-ton Roman goddess covered in gold leaf, which some claim is Jupiter. You can walk around the old parliamentary hall and, if you're lucky, visit the library. Regular guided tours are offered for CUC$1 per person. There are some Arts-and-Crafts galleries inside the Capitolio, as well as a simple restaurant and a popular Internet cafe.

Calle Prado (between Calles San José and Dragones). ℂ 7/860-3411. Admission CUC$3 adults, free for children under 12. Mon–Sat 9am–7pm.

**El Malecón** *This* oceanside pedestrian walkway stretches all the way from the Castillo de San Salvador de la Punta in Habana Vieja to the Almendares River that separates Vedado from Miramar (about 7km/4¼ miles in total). No trip to Havana is complete without at least some time spent strolling and lingering along the Malecón, which is the social center for a wide range of Cubans. Throughout the day, you'll see children swimming and men fishing off the coral outcroppings that border the walkway, and at night you're sure to see lovers entwined on cozy perches and groups of revelers all along the seawall.

The section fronting Centro Habana is perhaps the most picturesque, with the crumbling facades and faded paint of neoclassical and neo-Moorish buildings and apartments lining the avenue that separates the Malecón from the city. If you've got the legs and time, a walk from the Hotel Nacional to Habana Vieja (or vice versa) is in order, and should only take you about 20 to 25 minutes. On rough days, you may have to time your steps—or cross the street—as waves break furiously over the seawall. Alternatively, you can hire a horse-drawn carriage or Coco Taxi for the trip.

Free admission. Daily 24 hr.

**Fábrica de Tabaco Partagas** *Founded* in 1845, this is Cuba's largest and perhaps most renowned cigar factory, producing around 5 million cigars a year. The off-yellow and rust-trimmed neoclassical facade is resplendent in the Havana morning sunlight. (You can take your best photos of it from the west-side windows of El Capitolio.) Official tours are offered only at 10am and 2pm daily, although you can sometimes work your way into one of the many tour groups that come through all day long. Throughout the day, you can stop in and buy cigars from their well-stocked shop, La Casa del Habano.

Alternately, or in conjunction, you can visit the nearby **Fábrica de Tabaco H. Upmann,** Calle Amistad 407, between Calles Barcelona and Dragones (© **7/862-0081**), or the **Fábrica de Tabaco La Corona,** Calle Zulueta 106, between Calles Colón and Refugio (© **7/862-6173**), which are similarly charged with producing some of the country's finest cigars.

Calle Industria 524 (behind the Capitolio). © **7/862-4604**. 20-min. guided tour CUC$10 (reservations recommended). Mon–Sat 9:30–11am and 12:30–3pm.

## VEDADO

**Cementerio de Colón** ⭑⭑  A miniature city of mausoleums, crypts, family chapels and vaults, soaring sculptures, and ornate gravestones, Columbus Cemetery covers 55 hectares (136 acres). Designed by Spanish architect Calixto de Loira in the mid-1800s, it is laid out in grids around a central chapel. The main entrance features a large sculpture of Faith, Hope, and Charity in Carrara marble. There's also a large monument to fallen soldiers of the Revolutionary Armed Forces, and an impressive stainless steel sculpture capping a memorial to the martyrs of the 1957 attack on Batista's Presidential Palace. One of the most popular graves is that of La Milagrosa (The Miraculous One). The story goes that when Amelia Goyri de la Hoz died in childbirth in 1901, she was buried with her stillborn daughter placed at her feet. When the tomb was opened a few years later, the baby was found in her arms. Amelia is now considered the protector of pregnant women and newborn children. Pilgrims

---

## Frommer's Favorite Havana Experiences

- Take a walk along the **Malecón,** and then, for a slight change of pace, grab a Coco Taxi or horse-drawn carriage for a different take on Havana's most popular promenade.
- Wander the streets of **Habana Vieja.** Allow yourself to get lost in time and the beautiful architecture of its colonial streets, buildings, and plazas.
- Have dinner at the delicious and atmospheric paladar **La Guarida,** housed in a crumbling old building used in the famous Cuban film *Fresa y chocolate.*
- Visit the **Plaza de la Catedral** ⭑⭑⭑ at night, stopping to grab an outdoor table at **Cafetería El Portal** to sip a drink and soak in the sight of the **Catedral de San Cristóbal's** lighted bell towers.
- Visit a **cigar factory** and enjoy the aromas of Cuba's top export being manufactured in timeless fashion before your very eyes.
- Head to the **Callejón de Hammel** to admire the street art and murals of this Centro Habana neighborhood. Try to come on a Sunday afternoon and you'll be able to enjoy the spectacle of an Afro-Cuban religious show and celebration.
- Pull out all the stops and treat yourself to dinner and a show at the **Tropicana.**

## (Finds) Imagine

Beatles fans will want to stop by the little **Parque Lennon (Lennon Park)** at Calles 17 and 6 in Vedado, where you'll find a life-size statue of John Lennon seated on a park bench. The "smart Beatle" is quite revered here, and there is an annual open-air concert in this park every December 8, featuring a wide-range of prominent Cuban musicians, singing his songs and commemorating his assassination.

paying homage must not turn their backs to the tomb upon leaving. Brief guided tours are available (free, but a tip is generally expected), or you can buy a little guide-book with a detailed map (CUC$5) at the entrance.

Calles Zapata and 12. (©) **7/832-1050.** Admission CUC$1 adults, free for children under 12. Daily 8am–5pm.

**Coppelia** (★ (Moments)   Made famous in Tomás Gutiérez Alea's hit film *Fresa y choco-late (Strawberries and Chocolate),* this is the main branch of the Cuban national ice-cream company. At the center of the block-long complex is a postmodern building of curving concrete and glass, surrounded by a series of open courtyards with wrought-iron tables, where customers are served bowls of the frozen nectar. There are actually a dozen or so small booths selling cones and bowls spread around the park. Still, Cop-pelia is yet another glaring case of tourist apartheid: Cubans form long lines to wait their turn at a table or stand while tourists, who are paying in dollars and not pesos, are always taken to the head of the line, or shown to a separate dollar stand. There are usually only two or three flavors available on any given day; if you're there on a rum raisin day, you're in for a treat.

Calles 23 and L. Daily 11am–midnight.

**Memorial José Martí**   The 109m (358-ft.) marble tower here is the highest point in Havana. At the base of the tower is a massive statue of the poet and national inde-pendence hero José Martí. Inside the base is a small museum dedicated to Martí fea-turing manuscripts, memorabilia, portraits, and other informative displays. An elevator takes visitors up to a series of lookout rooms atop the tower, offering far-reaching panoramic views of Havana. The lookout is by far the most interesting and popular attraction here, although there's also a little theater where concerts and poetry readings are sometimes held.

Plaza de la Revolución, Nuevo Vedado. (©) **7/884-0551** or 7/59-2347. Admission CUC$5 adults, free for children under 12. Mon–Sat 9am–5pm.

**Universidad de la Habana**   The compact campus of Havana's main university sits on some high ground in Vedado close to the former Havana Hilton. The broad stair-case leading up to the school, with its signature *Alma Mater* statue of a seated woman with outstretched arms, is a popular gathering spot for students, and you can some-times catch impromptu concerts here. There are a couple of unimpressive museums on campus—those of Natural Sciences and Montane Antropology—as well as the nearby and slightly more interesting **Museo Napoleónico,** Calle San Miguel 1159, at the corner of La Ronda ((©) **7/879-1412**), with its large collection of Napoleonic-era memorabilia.

Calles L and 27, La Ronda. (©) **7/879-3488.** Free admission. Mon–Sat 8am–6pm.

## PLAYA

**Acuario Nacional** ⭐ *Kids*   A few years ago, the National Aquarium got a major face-lift and improvements are ongoing. It's not SeaWorld or the Baltimore Aquarium, but this is a pretty spiffy attempt for Cuba. A variety of tanks and pools re-create all the major water habitats of Cuba, and sea lion and dolphin shows are presented throughout the day. There are a couple of simple cafeteria-style restaurants, and one pseudo-fancy option, the Gran Azul Restaurant, with a huge Plexiglas wall opening on to a large tank where two sad and claustrophobic dolphins swim. This place is very popular with Cuban families and school groups, so it's a great place to mingle.

Av. 3 and Calle 62, Miramar. 📞 7/202-5872 or 7/203-6401. www.acuarionacional.cu. Admission CUC$5 adults, CUC$3 students and children under 12. Tues–Sun 10am–6pm.

**Maqueta de la Habana** ⭐   I was prepared to dis this miniature display of Havana, but left oddly impressed—or maybe I just liked the way it helped me with my job. The realistic scale model of the city takes up almost 88 sq. m (947 sq. ft.). You can walk around it on the ground level, or climb a narrow interior balcony that rings three walls here. There's usually some traveling art exhibition on the walls that ring the model. A guide can be hired for CUC$20 for any size group. This is not to be confused with a similar (and much smaller) scale model of Old Havana, found in Old Havana, of course.

Calle 28 (between Avs. 1 and 3), Miramar. 📞 7/202-7303. Admission CUC$3 adults, CUC$1 students and children under 12. Tues–Sat 9:30am–5:30pm; Sun 9am–1pm.

## OUTSIDE DOWNTOWN

**Museo Ernest Hemingway**   I have mixed feelings as to the experience of visiting this place, since visitors are not allowed into the former home of the famous writer. Sure you get a bit of the feel for Hemingway, but you also end up feeling like a Peeping Tom. Circling the ground floor you can see the house more or less as it was when Hemingway was living and writing here. There's a copious collection of books, paintings, and stuffed animal heads. In addition to an old typewriter, artworks by Picasso, Miró, and Klee are some of the more prized possessions. There's a small tower separate from the main house that has a gift shop and some rooms with rudimentary exhibits, and you can even climb it for a better view all around. In the surrounding gardens, you can see Papa's pet cemetery and the author's dry-docked fishing boat, *Pilar*.

Finca la Vigía, San Francisco de Paula, Carretera Central Km 12.5. 📞 7/891-0809. Admission CUC$3 adults, free for children under 12. Mon–Sat 10am–4pm; Sun 9am–1pm.

**Parque Histórico Morro y Cabaña** ⭐⭐   Located across the Harbor Channel from Habana Vieja, this historic park of forts, battlements, and barracks was responsible for the protection of Havana for centuries. The complex is actually made up of two separate forts, or attractions: the **Castillo del Morro** and **La Fortaleza de San Carlos de la Cabaña.**

The Morro Castle, or "El Morro" as it is most commonly known, is the first fort you'll come to after crossing under the harbor channel tunnel. Sitting on the point overlooking Havana's narrow harbor channel, it was built between 1589 and 1630 and served as an important line of defense against pirate attack and naval invasion. In addition to its ramparts, barracks, and banks of cannons, El Morro has a series of exhibition rooms and mini-museums. You can walk the fort's ancient streets and even climb the still-functioning 19th-century lighthouse here. El Morro offers up excellent views

## Moments The *Cañonazo*

The *cañonazo* (cannon blast) ★ is a picturesque ritual that takes place at La Fortaleza de San Carlos de la Cabaña every night. An honor guard in 18th-century military garb emerges from the barracks at about 8:40pm and conducts a small parade to a bank of cannons overlooking Havana's harbor channel. With pomp and circumstance, the cannon is loaded and fired precisely at 9pm. About 1,000 people show up each night, the vast majority of them Cubans. Arrive early if you want a good vantage point. The blast itself is quite loud—you can hear it in most parts of Havana—so protect your ears. You can combine the ceremony with a meal at one of the nearby restaurants.

of Havana and the curve of the Malecón, and there are several restaurant and bar offerings here.

About a kilometer (½-mile) away, and separated by a deep ravine, is the larger La Fortaleza de San Carlos de la Cabaña, more popularly referred to as simply "la Cabaña." Built between 1764 and 1774, in response to the British invasion, the long fort is a miniature city, with a high perch overlooking the Harbor Channel and Habana Vieja. As at El Morro, there are several exhibition halls and a handful of restaurants, bars, and gift shops here. One of the more popular exhibition halls is the **Comandancia de Che Guevara,** a room where the revolutionary leader briefly set up a command post after storming the fort in January 1959. Be sure to stop in at the cigar shop, which features the longest cigar in the world, an 11m (36-ft.) stogie that hangs above your head and is duly registered in the Guinness Book of World Records.

There are separate entrance fees for each attraction. A taxi to the complex from Havana should cost between CUC$5 and CUC$7. You can walk between the two forts—it's about a 15-minute walk that's only moderately strenuous if you stick to the high ground—or you can take a taxi between the two for under CUC$2.

Carretera de La Cabaña, Habana del Este. ✆ 7/863-7063 for El Morro; ✆ 7/862-0617 for La Cabaña. Admission El Morro CUC$3 adults, free for children; La Cabaña CUC$3 adults before 6pm, CUC$5 adults after 6pm, free for children under 12. El Morro daily 8am–8pm; La Cabaña daily 10am–midnight.

## 6 Outdoor Pursuits

**BASEBALL** Baseball is the national sport and, after salsa dancing and sex, the greatest national passion. Cuba's amateur players are considered some of the best in the world, and the premier players are aggressively scouted and courted by the Major Leagues. Quite a few have defected and signed with major-league clubs, while other outstanding players are content to stay, turning down lucrative offers. The regular season runs November through March, and playoffs and the final championship usually carry the season on into May. Industriales, the main Havana team, plays at the **Estadio Latinoamericano,** Calle Zequeira 312, Cerro (✆ 7/870-6526). It's usually easy to buy tickets at the box office for less than 5 Cuban pesos, or ask at your hotel and perhaps they can get tickets for you in advance—although for these you'll probably end up paying CUC$1 to CUC$3.

**BIKING** Despite the fact that so much of Havana's transportation is conducted on bicycles, there are no rental agencies or outlets for tourists wishing to get around town by bike. Your best bet for bicycling in Cuba is to bring your own set of wheels and head outside of Havana.

**GOLF** While the only regulation 18-hole course in the country is located in Varadero (see chapter 6), the **Club de Golf Habana,** Carretera Vento Km 8, Capdevila, Rancho Boyeros (© 7/55-8746 or 7/649-8820), has a decent little 9-hole course for true golf junkies. A round of 9 holes will run you CUC$20. Each hole actually has two sets of tees, so you can actually play 18 holes, and fake the impression that it's a regulation course. A round of 18 holes costs CUC$30. Club rental is an extra CUC$10 and a caddy will cost you CUC$5.

**GYMS** There are no chains of modern gyms and spas in Havana. Visitors looking for a regular workout on modern gym equipment or an aerobics class should stick to the larger hotels with well-equipped facilities (see "Where to Stay," earlier in this chapter, for more details). If you're not staying at one of these hotels, you can use the facilities at the **Meliá Habana** or **Meliá Cohiba** for CUC$10.

**Club Habana,** Avenida 5, between Calles 188 and 192, Reparto Flores, Playa (© 7/204-5700; www.clubhabanacuba.com), has a decent gym and will let guests use the facilities for CUC$20 to CUC$30 per day.

**JOGGING** The **Malecón** is a fabulous place to jog. Early mornings and late afternoons, when the heat has somewhat abated, are best. You'll have to watch your step in certain sections where the sidewalk is torn up or deteriorated, but overall this is the choice route for jogging. Further afield, joggers could try **Parque Lenin,** Calle 100 and Carretera de la Presa (© 7/44-3026), which is open Tuesday through Sunday from 9am through 5:30pm. This massive park is a major recreational area for locals and has several trails and internal roadways good for jogging.

**SCUBA DIVING** While the diving is nowhere near as good as you'll find in more dedicated dive destinations in Cuba, it's certainly possible to do some underwater exploring out of Havana. Your best bet is to head over to Cubanacán's **Hotels y Villas Marina Hemingway,** Avenida 5 and Calle 248, Santa Fe, Playa (© 7/204-6848; www.cubanacan.cu), or **Marina Tarará,** Vía Blanca Km 18, Playa Tarará, Habana del Este (© 7/897-1462), located 18km (11 miles) east of the city. There's also a dive shop at the **Hotel Copacabana,** Avenida 1, between Calles 44 and 46, Miramar, Playa (© 7/204-1037). It should cost you between CUC$50 and CUC$85 for two tank dives, including equipment and lunch. You might also consider a day trip to Varadero or Playa Girón for generally better conditions, and not much more cost.

**SPORT FISHING** It's easy to follow in Hemingway's wake and try your luck at landing a big one. As with diving, your best bet is to head over to Cubanacán's **Hotel y Villas Marina Hemingway,** Avenida 5 and Calle 248, Santa Fe, Playa (© 7/204-6848; www.cubanacan.cu), or **Marina Tarará,** Vía Blanca Km 18, Playa Tarará, Habana del Este (© 7/897-1462). Depending on the size of the boat and number of fishermen, a half-day of sport fishing should cost between CUC$150 and CUC$500, while a full day will run you between CUC$400 and CUC$1,400, including gear and lunch.

**SWIMMING** If your hotel does not have a swimming pool, most of the larger hotels allow nonguests use of their pool facilities for a price. Rates generally range between CUC$5 and CUC$10 per person. The nicer options include the **Meliá Habana, Hotel Copacabana,** and **Club Habana** in Playa; the **Hotel Nacional** and

**Meliá Cohiba** in Vedado; and the **NH Parque Central** and **Hotel Sevilla** in Habana Vieja.

Although it's possible to use the small beach at the Club Habana, the nearby Playas del Este is your best bet for some beach time. Most tour agencies and hotel tour desks offer a day trip to Playa Santa María del Mar for CUC$25 to CUC$40, including round-trip transportation, lunch, and often free run of the facilities at one of the all-inclusive hotels out there.

*Note:* Do not be tempted to join the locals you see swimming off the coral outcroppings just below the Malecón. The coral is jagged and sharp, and the seas can get suddenly rough. Moreover, in recent years there have been complaints that the water is very polluted.

**TENNIS**  Unless you're staying at one of the few Havana hotels with a court, your options are limited. Your best bet is to try to book a court at the **Occidental Miramar,** Avenida 5, between Calles 78 and 80, Miramar, Playa (© 7/204-3584), which has six courts, or head to the **Club Habana,** Avenida 5, between Calles 188 and 192, Reparto Flores, Playa (© 7/204-5700), or **Club de Golf Habana,** Carretera Vento Km 8, Capdevila, Rancho Boyeros (© 7/55-8746), each of which has a few courts open to the general public. All charge around CUC$10 per hour.

## 7 Shopping

### THE SHOPPING SCENE

Havana is by no means a great shopping city (although it is the best in Cuba). Given the reality of the Cuban economy, all shops selling any goods above and beyond the basic necessities are by default geared entirely toward tourists, a small community of foreign diplomats and workers, and an even smaller community of Cubans earning enough hard currency to afford such luxuries. Hence, it's a challenge to find interesting shops offering unique local items at good prices. In general, stores throughout Havana are open from 9am through 5pm, 7 days a week. Some may open earlier and close later, particularly in heavily trafficked tourist areas. Virtually none close for lunch.

All shops selling to tourists operate exclusively with hard currency—U.S. dollars, euros, and Cuban Convertible Pesos. Most are run by big state-owned enterprises. The most common stores belong to the **Caracol** chain, which is geared primarily to tourists, while the **Tiendas Panamericanas** chain specializes in household and domestic items aimed at foreign residents. In recent years, modern malls have begun popping up. Everything stated above holds true for the offerings you'll find here.

**ARTex** ☆ (© 7/204-0813; www.soycubano.com) is the state-run company in charge of managing Cuba's artistic export products (hence the name "ARTex"). Their job runs the gamut from promoting Cuban musicians and artists abroad to marketing their goods and negotiating contracts. ARTex operates a series of storefronts around the country, either stand-alone affairs or placed in prominent hotels or tourist attractions. Depending on the size and location, these shops usually carry a good selection of Cuban music, tourist T-shirts, and kitschy arts and crafts. The better ones have decent quality drums and percussion instruments, as well as art prints and posters. In Miramar, head to ARTex's **Bazar Volveré,** Calle 3, between Calles 78 and 80 (© 7/204-8185); in Vedado check out their **Bazar La Habana Sí,** Calle 23 no. 301, at the corner of Calle L (© 7/832-0632), across from the Tryp Habana Libre.

## SHOPPING A TO Z
### ART GALLERIES
**Galería Acacia** This gallery is the place to go for high-end contemporary Cuban art, and a good place to see who the up-and-coming hot artists are. Calle San José 114 (between Calles Industria and Consulado), Centro Habana. (℡ 7/863-9364.

**Galería Víctor Manuel** This place has a pretty good selection of modern decorative paintings, crafts, and a few pieces that could qualify as real artwork. Given its prime location and popularity, don't expect anything to come cheap. Calles San Ignacio and Callejón del Chorro, Plaza Catedral, la Habana Vieja. (℡ 7/861-2965.

**La Casona** Located in a series of rooms over two floors of the Casa de los Condes de Jaruco on Plaza Vieja, this wonderful gallery has similar works to those found at Víctor Manuel, but the selection is better, and there's less of a cattle-car mass-market feel to the place. Calle Muralla 107 (corner of Calle San Ignacio), Plaza Vieja, la Habana Vieja. (℡ 7/861-8544.

### CERAMICS
**Terracota 4** This working studio-cum-gallery in Old Habana features the works of Amelia Carballo, Angel Nornirella, and José Ramón. The pieces show a wide-range of influences and utilize a wide-range of techniques. One or more of the artists is usually on hand, and sometimes you'll get a chance to see them working. Calle Mercaderes (between Calles Obrapía and Lamparilla), la Habana Vieja. (℡ 7/806-9417.

### CIGARS
Cigars are Cuba's most-prized product. The word "Cubans" is synonymous with the highest quality cigars on the planet. Locally, they are called *puros* or *habanos;* the latter is the name of the country's official cigar company. All of the various brands—Partagas, Cohiba, Romeo y Julieta, Punch, and so on—are marketed by Habanos S.A. Cigars not officially sold by Habanos fall into the various categories of black- and gray-market stogies. Habanos markets its product through a series of storefronts usually called something like La Casa de Tabaco or La Casa del Habano. Official sales are also offered at shops on location at most cigar factories, as well as at many higher-end hotels, restaurants, and attractions around town. **Beware:** Black- and gray-market cigars sold on the street or by *jineteros* (hustlers) are more often than not falsely marked lower-quality machine-made cigars.

Cuban cigars range widely in size and shape. Prices range from around CUC$30 to CUC$50 per box for the smallest, lowest quality *puros,* to over CUC$400 per box for the more coveted cigars. Most shops sell only complete boxes, although certain cigars are usually available individually, or in boxes of five.

The best **La Casa del Habano** shops are those in the Hostal Conde de Villanueva at Calle Mercaderes 222, Habana Vieja (℡ 7/862-9293); the Partagas cigar factory at Calle Industria 524, behind El Capitolio (℡ 7/862-4604); and in the Quinta y 16 shopping minicomplex at Avenida 5 and the corner of Calle 16, Miramar (℡ 7/204-1185). Another nice one in Habana Vieja is the **Casa del Ron y Tabaco Cubana,** Calle

---

**The Real Deal**

Authentic boxes of Cuban cigars should be sealed and have HECHO EN CUBA (Made in Cuba) burned into the bottom of the box.

Obispo and Calle Bernaza (© 7/33-8911), where you can combine two of Cuba's greater pleasures—smoking cigars and drinking rum.

## FASHION

In addition to the high-fashion shop mentioned below, perhaps the most distinctive clothing items a traveler can buy include T-shirts with the image of Che Guevara on the front, and the revolutionary's signature green *boina* (beret) with a little red star in front.

Men might want to pick up a guayabera or two. This cool, pleated, and embroidered tropical shirt comes in a variety of (mostly) solid colors, and in both long- and short-sleeve versions. As a rational alternative to heavy suits and ties in a tropical clime, guayaberas are appropriate for everything from informal occasions to high-level government and business meetings (in Cuba, at least). You'll find guayaberas for sale all over; some of the typically touristy gift shops even carry them. One good place to shop for a guayabera is **El Quitirín,** Calle Obispo and San Ignacio (© 7/862-0810). For a more upscale selection, head over to Miramar and shop at **La Maison** (see below); **Le Select,** Avenida 5 and Calle 28 (© 7/204-7410); or **Joyería Quinta y 16** (see "Jewelry," below).

**La Maison**    This minicomplex in an old Miramar mansion is the home of Cuban haute couture. Several stores spread around the rambling converted home feature a range of men's and women's fashion, jewelry, and accessories. There's a nightly runway fashion show (CUC$10), as well as a modest cabaret show, combined with the fashion show on weekends. Calle 16 no. 701 (corner of Av. 7), Miramar, Playa. © 7/204-1543.

## HANDICRAFTS

Cuba doesn't have a particularly strong tradition in producing handicrafts, but the rise in tourism has seen local artisans quickly making up for lost time. Tourist gift shops as well as the street markets discussed below are well stocked with locally produced handicrafts. The best buys are woodcarvings and statues, papier-mâché masks and religious figures, and simple jewelry made from shells and seeds. You'll also find a host of Afro-Cuban percussion instruments for sale. Drums you'll find include the two-headed hourglass-shaped *bata* drums, paired bongos, carved African-style religious drums, and congas, the modern salsa backbone. *Shekeres* (gourd shakers) and *claves* (two wooden sticks used to play the fundamental rhythm in various Cuban genres) are also available. The Calle Tacón street market (see below) is your best bet for any of the above.

## JEWELRY

There are few good jewelry shops in Cuba, which has no real history of producing fine jewelry. You'll find a plethora of simple, artisan-produced necklaces, bracelets, rings, and earrings at most tourist shops and street markets. If you look hard enough, you'll actually find some well-made and attractive pieces. Unfortunately, the nicest jewelry being produced in Cuba is usually made with tortoiseshell or black coral, both natural resources slow to replenish and easily endangered by over-harvesting.

The most common jewelry worn by Cubans are bracelets and necklaces of colored glass or plastic beads representing the various Afro-Cuban deities. You can pick these up at the street markets mentioned below. Be sure to ask about the significance of the pieces you are interested in and what deities they represent.

**Joyería Quinta y 16**    This is the trendiest jewelry shop in the trendiest little minimall in Havana's trendiest neighborhood. Come here if you want to drop a wad of cash for some strands of gold, silver, and diamonds, although the selection is far from inspiring. Av. 5 and Calle 16, Miramar. © 7/204-6963.

*Tips*  **Don't Run to Buy *Ron***

Your best bet for buying rum is the duty-free shop at the airport. The prices and selection are as good here as you'll find anywhere on the island, and you'll save yourself the hassle of hauling heavy bottles around with you on your travels.

## MUSIC

Music is one of Cuba's greatest exports. Many CDs available in Cuba are also widely available abroad or via the Internet. Most CDs in Cuba sell for between CUC$8 and CUC$15. However, be careful: Unless you are shopping at one of the official state-run stores, the CDs you buy may be low-quality bootlegs.

If you're looking for salsa, pick up a disc or two by Los Van Van or NG La Banda. Fans of Cuban folk music should definitely stock up on records by Silvio Rodriguez and Pablo Milanes. Jazz fans will want some Chucho Valdés with Irakere, and Gonzalo Rubalcaba, while those looking to groove to some Afro-Cuban sounds should check out Sintesis, Los Muñequitos de Matanzas, Yoruba Andabo, and Clavé y Guaguanco. For *son* and mambo pick up discs by Adalberto Alvarez y su Son, or the classic rereleases of Beny Moré and Peréz Prado. Finally, since you've probably already got a copy of *Buena Vista Social Club,* you might stock up on solo albums by its various members: Compay Segundo, Rubén Gonzales, Eliades Ochoa, and Omara Portuona.

**Egrem** (www.egrem.com.cu) is the national recording industry's signature label, the home of many prominent Cuban musicians. Egrem has a series of storefronts around the country called **Casa de la Música Egrem.** You can also buy discs at one of the many **ARTex** shops around Havana, or you can shop the ARTex catalog online at **www.discuba.com**.

**Casa de la Música Habana**    Housed in a classic old apartment building in Centro Habana, this is the nicest and best stocked of the Egrem storefronts. They also feature daily concerts at 4 and 10pm. Calle Galiano (between Calles Concordia and Neptuno), Centro Habana. ✆ 7/862-4165.

**Longina Música**    This ARTex shop has an excellent selection of CDs and cassettes, as well as sheet music, magazines, and one of the better stocks of Afro-Cuban drums, shakers, and claves you'll find. Calle Obispo 360, la Habana Vieja. ✆ 7/862-8371.

## PERFUME

**Habana 1791**    This attractive shop in Old Havana sells traditional perfumes and aromatherapy distillations in faux-vintage glass jars and vials. The place is sometimes marketed as a "perfume museum." Calle Mercaderes 156 (corner of Calle Obrapía), la Habana Vieja. ✆ 7/861-3525.

## RUM

After cigars, rum is one of Cuba's signature products. Cuba produces several fine rums. The most commonly sold brand, **Havana Club,** comes in white and dark varieties of various vintages and ages. The premier rum in Cuba is Havana Club's 15-year-old Gran Reserva. This sells for anywhere from CUC$75 to CUC$100 per bottle. It's good, but I don't think it's worth the price tag. However, their 7-year-old Añejo Reserva is a damn fine rum at around CUC$12 per bottle. Other good rums include **Ron Varadero, Matusalém, Ron Caney, Ron Santiago,** and **Ron Mulata.**

## STREET MARKETS

The biggest and best street market in Havana features three narrow rows of stalls stretching over a full city block. It's open daily from 10am to 6pm in Habana Vieja on **Calle Tacón** ✦✦✦, between Calles Empedrado and Chacón. In addition to the typical arts and crafts and souvenir T-shirts, you'll find scores of local painters selling their wares. Most are rather amateurish renderings of street scenes and famous landmarks. However, you'll find a few good painters and graphic artists here if you look hard enough.

A much **smaller street market** occurs daily in Vedado in a small open area on the south side of La Rampa, at Calle 23 between Calles M and N. The market, which is open daily from 9am to 5pm, features less artwork than the market on Calle Tacón, but it has plenty of woodcarvings and simple jewelry on offer.

*Note:* Cubans don't really have a firm grasp of this capitalism thing. Moreover, given the huge gap between the peso and hard currency economies, Cubans often have a hard time understanding the true value of the convertible peso or dollar. Prices are often grossly inflated for tourists, on the principle that they "must all be rich." Bargaining is possible at street markets, but it's not necessarily a fluid and enjoyable process. Still, if you think something is overpriced, definitely feel free to offer whatever you believe to be fair, or whatever you are prepared to pay.

## 8 Havana After Dark

Some would say Havana only really gets going after dark, when the slow pace and heat-induced stupor of the day finally wears off. This is a vibrant and truly cosmopolitan city with scores of bars, dance clubs, and theaters to choose from.

## THE PERFORMING ARTS

Cuba has a strong tradition in the performing arts. Cuban musicians, playing in a range of styles, are world-renowned. The **Cuban National Ballet** (© 7/855-3084; www. balletcuba.cu) has been garnering international accolades for decades, under the seemingly eternal direction of Alicia Alonso. And there's an active theater scene (and plenty of movie theaters), both of which are popular with locals, given the scant offerings of Cuban television. The major venues for the classical performing arts are the **Teatro Nacional de Cuba,** Paseo and Calle 39, Vedado (© 7/879-6011), which specializes in live theater performances by local and visiting companies; the **Gran Teatro de La Habana,** Paseo de Martí and Calle San Rafael, Centro Habana (© 7/862-9473), which is home to the Cuban National Ballet, as well as a prime venue for concerts and

---

*Moments*  **Feel the Beat**

The **Conjunto Folklórico Nacional de Cuba (Cuban National Folklore Group)** hosts the weekly **Sábado de la Rumba,** a mesmerizing show of Afro-Cuban religious and secular dance and drumming. The 2-hour shows are presented every Saturday at 3pm, at **El Gran Palenque,** Calle 4, between Calzada and Avenida 5 in Vedado. Call © **7/830-3060** or 7/830-3939 for more information or to make a reservation.

Similar shows are offered Thursday through Sunday at 10pm by the group **Obbara** at the Palacio de la Artesanía, Calle Cuba 64, between Calles Peña Pobre and Cuarteles, la Habana Vieja.

> **Tips**   **A Way In**
>
> Cuban women (and to a lesser extent Cuban men) tend to hang out at the entrance to popular clubs looking for an unattached foreigner to pay their admission. Their pleadings can be quite earnest. You are by no means obligated, but they really have no other means of being able to enter.

dance performances; and the **Teatro Amadeo Roldán,** Calle Calzada, between Calles D and E, Vedado (© 7/832-1168), which is home to the National Symphony Orchestra. Other important and working theaters include the **Teatro Mella, Teatro Karl Marx,** and the **Café Teatro Brecht.**

You can call any of the theaters listed above directly for performance schedules and ticket information, but your best bet is to ask at your hotel or pick up a copy of *Cartelera,* a free periodic bilingual magazine with listings for movies, theaters, bars, and live music that is available at the front desk of most hotels in Havana. Another good option is to contact **Paradiso** (© 7/832-9538), the tourism arm of the Ministry of Culture charged with organizing culturally themed travel to Cuba.

## THE CABARET, CLUB & DANCE SCENE

I'll bet Havana has more floor shows per capita than Las Vegas. In addition to the clubs and cabarets listed below, there are nightly and entirely respectable cabaret shows at the Habana Riviera's **Copa Room,** Paseo and Malecón, Vedado (© 7/834-4228); ARTex's **Patio de la Casa 18,** Calle 18, between Avenidas 5 and 7, Miramar (© 7/204-1212); and the **Cabaret Nacional,** Calle San Rafael and Paseo de Martí, la Habana Vieja (© 7/863-2361).

*Habaneros* love to dance and party, and you'll find a wild dance and club scene here. In fact, dance aficionados come to Havana from all over to learn the basic steps, fine-tune their moves, and watch the locals strut their stuff. Most clubs don't get going until after 10pm, and most stay pretty vibrant until the wee hours of the morning. While salsa is king in Cuba, most of the popular dance clubs catering to travelers have been putting some house, techno, reggaetón, and other modern dance tunes into the mix. Dress codes are somewhat casual, but locals still like to put on the ritz as much as possible before a night of dancing, so bring some finery if you plan to hit any of the more popular clubs.

**Cabaret Parisien**   Located at the Hotel Nacional, this venerable cabaret show is a vibrant and extravagant spectacle. Still, it will always play second fiddle to the Tropicana, which trumps it in terms of size and setting. Nevertheless, the show here is less expensive, and certainly more convenient, if you're staying at the hotel or in Vedado. Calle O (corner of Calle 21). © 7/873-3564. Show CUC$35; dinner packages start at CUC$55.

**Café Cantante Mi Habana**   Top acts often perform at this popular club. They also have a much more informal dance scene happening every afternoon between 4 and 7pm. This is a place where locals come to mix it up with foreigners who are in town specifically to learn how to salsa. Teatro Nacional, Paseo and Calle 39, Plaza de la Revolución. © 7/879-0710. Cover CUC$5–CUC$10.

**Casa de la Música Centro Habana** ★★   This place, with its massive dance floor and concert space in the heart of Centro Habana, is currently considered the best salsa dancing venue in town. The crowd is predominantly Cuban, and most can really dance. About half of the cover is usually applied to your food and drink tab. Calle Galianao 225, between Neptuno and Concordia. © 7/862-4165. Cover CUC$10–CUC$20.

**Casa de la Música Miramar** ✿✿   Housed in a beautiful former Masonic Lodge Hall, this place is associated with the national recording label Egrem. They have nightly concerts that range from bolero to salsa to jazz in their in-house club *Diablo Tun Tun*. Still, for me, the real treat here is the afternoon jam sessions, which take place daily from 4 to 7pm. Calle 20 (corner of Calle 35), Miramar. © 7/204-0447.

**El Rincón del Bolero** ✿   If you're looking for a slightly mellower scene, this is your spot. One of several bars and restaurants at the Dos Gardenias complex, this place specializes in the sad and sultry songs of bolero, and usually features some fine performers. Dos Gardenias, Av. 7 and Calle 26, Miramar, Playa. © 7/204-9662.

**Habana Café** ✿   This place is loosely modeled after the Hard Rock Cafe chain. There's an old propeller fighter dangling overhead and a vintage 1957 Chevy in the middle of the joint. There's a good-size dance floor, and the evening's entertainment is part cabaret, part revue show, and part dance party. The atmosphere is far less formal and far livelier than you'll find at most other cabarets. In the Meliá Cohiba, Paseo, between Avs. 1 and 3, Vedado. © 7/833-3636, ext 2630. CUC$10 minimum.

**Salón Turquino**   Located on the top floor of the Tryp Habana Libre, this dance club is one of the hotter and more popular dance spots in Havana. The views are great, there's a nightly cabaret show at 10:30pm, and they periodically feature top-billed live bands. Tryp Habana Libre, 25th floor, Calles L and 23, Vedado. © 7/834-6100. Cover CUC$10–CUC$20.

**Tropicana** ✿✿✿   Accept no substitutes. This is the real deal. It's expensive—in fact, overpriced—but if you're going to see a cabaret show in Havana, it might as well be at the Tropicana. First opened in 1939, this open-air dinner theater is still the defining cabaret show in Cuba, if not the world. You enter the lush garden theater after passing the club's signature sculpted "Fountain of the Muses." Dinner service starts around 8pm and is an uninspired but acceptable affair. The show itself begins around 10:30pm. Once the show begins, the stage and verdant surroundings become an orgy of light, color, costumes, and pulsating movement. Scores of scantily clad showgirls and dancers seamlessly weave together a series of different numbers. The 2-hour-long spectacle covers most of the bases of popular Cuban show and dance music, from *son* to bolero to *danzón* to salsa, with a bit of Afro-Cuban religious music thrown into the mix. After the show, you can continue the celebration by dancing the night away at the adjoining Salón Arcos de Cristal.

Virtually every hotel and tour agency in Havana can book you a night at the Tropicana; some include dinner and a bottle of rum at the nightclub, others are just for the show (including a complimentary cuba libre), or include dinner first at El Ajibe or another Miramar restaurant. Packages with transportation and dinner are only slightly more than for the show alone, and are therefore a decent deal. Since it's open-air, rain cancels the function. You'll get your money back on a rainout, but they offer no guaranteed reservations for a makeup show. Calle 72 (between Calles 41 and 45), Marianao. © 7/267-1010. reserves@tropicana.gca.tur.cu. Show CUC$50–CUC$60; packages with transportation and dinner CUC$70.

## THE BAR SCENE
In addition to the bars listed below, **La Bodeguita del Medio** (p. 99) and **El Floridita** (p. 98) are two famous watering holes. I also enjoy the rooftop bar at the **Hotel Ambos Mundos** (p. 88).

**Bar Dos Hermanos**   This is a slightly seedy port bar, but well within the safety net of restored Habana Vieja. A few *jineteras* and a *conjunto* (small musical band) are usually in attendance. There are tables scattered across two rooms, and a long, wooden bar with a good selection of call liquors. This place is open 24 hours. Av. del Puerto 304 (corner of Calle Santa Clara), la Habana Vieja. ℰ 7/861-3514.

**Café Monserrate**   I like the relaxed vibe at this popular bar, which attracts a mix of travelers and Cubans. The club's signature drink, the *coctel Monserrate* is a tasty blend of rum, grapefruit juice, mint, sugar, and grenadine that gives the mojito a run for its money. There's usually live music here, as well as *jineteros* and *jineteras*. Calles Monserrate and Obrapía, la Habana Vieja. ℰ 7/860-9751.

**Café O'Reilly**   While this bar and restaurant combo occupies two floors of this decaying building in Old Habana, all the action happens on the second floor. French doors open onto a small veranda, giving a good view of the folks strutting by on the street below. The food is mediocre, but the ambience is energetic, without feeling forced. Calle O'Reilly 203 (corner of Calle San Ignacio), la Habana Vieja. No phone.

**Café París**   This place is almost always crowded and rowdy. The *conjunto* plays loud, and the patrons try to top them. Known as a *jinetera* hangout, this is still a good place to go for a good time. Open 24 hours. At the corner of Calle San Ignacio and Calle Obispo, la Habana Vieja. ℰ 7/862-0466.

**Club Imágenes**   This place is done up like an upscale piano bar. The lighting is dark and the mood more subdued than you'll find at other joints. Still, they put on a nightly show, and even get things pumped up with karaoke every now and again. The small menu here includes a selection of tapas, making it a good choice when you want a snack. Calzada 602 (corner of Calle C), Vedado. ℰ 7/33-3606. CUC$5 minimum.

**El Gato Tuerto** ✦   This hyper-hip little club attracts a good mix of travelers and Cuban intelligentsia. The mood is dark, with walls of mirrors behind the tiny stage, and a long bar running the length of the longest wall. The club is small, so either reserve a table in advance, or get here early. The entertainment runs the gamut from old-style bolero to *nueva trova* and modern jazz. Performers range from mediocre to top-notch. Most evenings Alden Night, a melodramatic storyteller and poet, serves as master of ceremonies. The admission is applied to your first drink, so ask for the call liquor first. Calle O (between Calles 17 and 19), Vedado. ℰ 7/55-2696 or 7/833-2224. Cover CUC$5.

**Jazz Café** ✦   This place feels a little too slick and modern to be a jazz club, with chrome-trimmed tables and chairs, a curving wall of windows, and fairly bright lighting. But a jazz club it is, and next to La Zorra y El Cuervo (see below), this is the top spot to search out Cuba's best and brightest jazz talents. Third level of the Galerías Paseo mall, Avs. Paseo and 3, Vedado. ℰ 7/55-3302. CUC$10 minimum.

**La Zorra y El Cuervo** ✦✦   This is the premier jazz club in Havana and the first place to check if you want to catch any of the A-list jazz performers while you're in town. Modeled after an English pub, the basement-level bar space is small and cozy and relatively plain. The standard cover might double if someone like Chucho Valdés is playing. La Rampa, Calle 23 no. 155 (between Calles N and O), Vedado. ℰ 7/833-2402. Cover CUC$10.

**Lluvia de Oro** ✦   Open 24 hours, this is a raucous and rowdy bar in the heart of Old Havana. There's often live music and a lively mix of tourists, locals, *jineteros,* and *jineteras.* Calle Obispo no. 316 (corner of Habana), la Habana Vieja. ℰ 7/862-9870.

**Piano Bar Delirio Habanero**  This subdued and low-lighted club is a good place for a quiet and romantic evening. Located on the fourth floor of the Teatro Nacional, the walls of glass windows offer great nighttime views of Havana. The *criolla* cuisine is decent here. You can either come here to enjoy the joint's singular charms, or duck in for a break after dancing your butt off next door at the Café Cantante Mi Habana. Teatro Nacional, Paseo and Calle 39, Plaza de la Revolución. © 7/873-5713.

## CINEMA

Like its old cars, Havana's movie theaters are big, old classics. You won't find any multiplexes here. The films shown run the gamut from subtitled Hollywood blockbusters to local productions. Cuba actually has a very sophisticated film culture, and it's not uncommon to find mini-festivals and film series of classic foreign and independent cinema. The principal movie theaters are the **Cine Yara,** Calles 23 and L, Vedado (© 7/832-9430); **Cine Chaplin,** Calle 23, between Calles 10 and 12, Vedado (© 7/831-1101); **Cine La Rampa,** Calles 23 and O, Vedado (© 7/878-6146); and **Cine Payret,** Paseo de Martí and Calle San José, la Habana Vieja (© 7/863-3163). Admission is usually around 3 to 5 Cuban pesos, and you should be able to pay in pesos, not a dollar equivalent.

## GAY & LESBIAN NIGHTLIFE

Given Cuba's grudging acceptance of homosexuality, and tight state control over all official bars, restaurants, and nightclubs, there's no official gay or lesbian scene. Nor are there any official or unofficial gay or lesbian newspapers or weeklies. That said, the most sensual and sexually open nation in the Caribbean certainly has its gay and lesbian side. Currently, the 24-hour **Fiat Café,** Malecón between Calles Marina and Principe (© 7/873-5827), the area in front of the **Cine Yara,** Calles 23 and L, Vedado, and the corner of La Rampa and the Malecón are the de facto gathering spots for local and visiting gays and lesbians. Clubs and bars that do cater to gay and lesbian clientele prefer not to advertise the fact too openly. Your best bet for finding out the current gay and lesbian friendly spots, or getting invited to a *fiesta de diez pesos* (10¢ party)—a private party—is to head to either one of the spots mentioned above and ask around.

## 9 Side Trips from Havana

All the major tour operators in Havana offer a wide range of tours. Popular organized day-trip destinations include the beaches of **Varadero** and **Cayo Largo,** the natural wonders of **Soroa, Las Terrazas,** and **Viñales,** and the colonial gem of **Trinidad.** Themed tours might focus on the tobacco growing and cigar production of Pinar del Río and the Vuelta Abajo region, or a Hemingway circuit stopping at his old home in La Vigia, Las Terrazas in Cojimar, and one or two of his favorite haunts in Old Havana. Overnight excursions are also available to **Santiago de Cuba, Cayo Coco** and **Cayo Guillermo, Varadero,** and **Cayo Largo.**

If you have more time and a sense of adventure, you're best off reading about the destinations mentioned above in this book and doing it on your own. However, if time is tight or you'd rather leave the planning, driving, and decision-making to others, **Havanatur** (© 7/204-8409; www.havanatur.cu), **Cubanacán** (© 7/208-6044; www.cubanacan.cu), and **Cubatur** (© 7/833-3142; www.cubatur.cu) are your best bets for information and tour bookings around the country.

# 5

# Viñales & Western Cuba

*by Eliot Greenspan*

**W**estern Cuba is a pastoral and under-developed region, with some stunning scenery. When folks talk about western Cuba they mean **Pinar del Río** province, the third-largest province in Cuba. The area has been inhabited continuously for over 4,000 years beginning with the Guanahatabey, Ciboney, and Taíno indigenous tribes that settled this section of the island prior to the Spanish arrival. In addition to the province of Pinar del Río, the general geographic area of western Cuba also includes the Archipiélago de los Canarreos (the Canary Archipelago), considered a "special municipality." The two largest islands of the chain, **Isla de la Juventud** and **Cayo Largo,** are developed for tourism.

Pinar del Río is Cuba's prime eco-tourism destination. Rock climbing, caving, mountain-biking, hiking, and bird-watching are all excellent in this area. **La Güira National Park,** the **Guanacahabibes Peninsula,** and the **Sierra del Rosario Biosphere Reserve** make this one of Cuba's richest and wildest areas. The small hamlet of **Viñales** is widely considered one of the most beautiful in the country, and it is rapidly becoming the region's center for nature and adventure tourism. At the far western tip of the island, **María la Gorda** is one of Cuba's signature scuba diving destinations. And the diving at **Cayo Levisa,** Isla de la Juventud, and Cayo Largo isn't too shabby either. To top it all off, Cayo Largo has some of the nicest and least crowded beaches in Cuba.

Pinar del Río is also Cuba's most heralded tobacco-growing region. Cigars made from tobacco grown in the **Vuelta Abajo** area, just west of the city of Pinar del Río, are coveted the world over.

## 1 Pinar del Río

174km (108 miles) SW of Havana

Pinar del Río, the provincial capital, is named for the pine trees that grow along the banks of the Río Guamá, where the city is set. Originally founded as Nueva Filipina (New Philippine), it was re-christened Pinar del Río in 1774 and is one of the last major cities founded by the Spanish in Cuba. Pinar del Río is an animated little city of around 150,000, with a university, several hospitals, and some industry. The city's architecture features a mix of colonial and neoclassical in states ranging from finely restored to post-revolutionary decay. The city's major attractions can easily be visited in a day, and you would probably be better off giving more time and attention to the province's less urban destinations.

*Tips*  **Watch Out**

If you're driving a rental car, you will be swarmed by bicycle-riding *jineteros* (hustlers) offering you *casas particulares* and *paladares* (private-home rooms and restaurants) as soon as you enter town. They will latch on to your car at any traffic light, stop sign, or slow section and follow alongside if their pedaling can keep pace as you drive through town. For some reason they are particularly aggressive in Pinar del Río. If you want to lessen the attention, you might have to roll up your windows and shake your head a lot. Ambulatory *jineteros* and *jineteras* will also try to attach themselves to you as you walk around town.

## ESSENTIALS
### GETTING THERE
**BY BUS**   The **bus station** (© 82/75-5255) is located at Calle Adela Azcuy, between Avenidas Colón and Comandante Pinares. **Víazul** (© 7/881-1413 in Havana, or 82/75-2571 in Pinar del Río; www.viazul.com) has two daily buses at 9am and 2pm from Havana to Pinar del Río. The trip takes 2½ hours and costs CUC$12 each way. This bus continues on to Viñales. If you pick the bus up here, it costs CUC$6.50 to Viñales, although it's only CUC$13 direct, one-way from Havana to Viñales. Víazul buses to Havana leave Pinar del Río at 8:50am and 2:50pm daily.

**BY CAR**   Take the Autopista Nacional (A4) west to Pinar del Río. It's a straight shot, and the Autopista actually ends as it enters Pinar del Río. Two alternative routes are the old Carretera Central, which runs roughly parallel to the newer Autopista, and connects Havana with Pinar del Río, and the Circuito Norte or "northern circuit," a road that runs from Havana to Mariel to Bahía Honda. At La Palma, you'll want to head south on the Viñales highway and then on to Pinar del Río. Both of these routes are two-lane affairs that are slower and more picturesque than the Autopista. On either of these, slow moving ox-carts and heavy trucks combine with bicycle traffic, pedestrians, and potholes to slow you down—not necessarily a bad thing if you want to take in some of the scenery. I recommend integrating the Circuito Norte route into an itinerary that encompasses Pinar del Río, Viñales, and either Cayo Levisa or Cayo Jutías.

### GETTING AROUND
You can easily walk to most places in Pinar del Río. Taxis are also readily available all around town, and are either at hand, or can be called, at most hotels and casas particulares. **Havanautos** (© 82/77-8015) has an office at the Islazul Hotel Pinar del Río.

### ORIENTATION
The Autopista Nacional ends and turns into Calle Martí as it enters Pinar del Río from the east. As you enter town, you'll see the Hotel Pinar del Río on your right. The heart of downtown is straight ahead. At the western end of downtown you'll find the small, triangular-shaped Plaza de la Independencia. The main north-south byway, Calle Isabel Rubio, is also the old Carretera Central, and bisects Calle Martí by the post office.

    **Cubatur, Havanatur,** and **Islazul** all have offices downtown; they're your best sources of information. For currency exchange, there's a **CADECA** on Calle Gerardo Medina, next to the local Coppelia ice-cream outlet. On the same street, 2 blocks east of Coppelia, there's an **Etecsa** phone office where you can make local, national, and international calls and connect to the Internet. The main **post office** is located at the corner of Calle Martí and Calle Isabel Rubio (℄ 82/5442); it's open Monday through Saturday from 8am to 8pm. The **León Cuervo Rubio hospital** (℄ 82/2010) is at the junction of the Carretera Central and the Viñales highway.

## WHAT TO SEE & DO

The principal attraction in town is **Fábrica de Tabacos Francisco Donatién** ⚓ (℄ 82/75-3424), Calle Antonio Maceo, just off the Plaza de la Independencia. Several fine brands are rolled at this renowned cigar factory. You can walk through the timeless rolling station, where a caller reads news and short stories to keep the rollers interested. You'll also visit rooms where the final selection and grading, labeling, and boxing take place. You can buy some of the wares here, or at the well-stocked **Casa del Habano** across the street. The factory is open Monday through Friday from 9am to noon and 1 to 4pm, Saturday from 9am to noon. Admission is CUC$5, and includes a guided tour that lasts around 15 to 20 minutes.

The other main attraction in Pinar del Río is the **Casa Garay Fábrica de Guayabitas del Pinar** (℄ 82/75-2966), Calle Isabel Rubio, 3½ blocks south of Calle Martí. This little factory produces the town's signature Guayabita del Pinar liquor. They produce two types, *dulce* (sweet) and *seco* (dry). Both are cane liquors distilled with the fruit berries of a local bush. I like the *seco* quite a bit. It's a good quality sipping liquor that, if you stretch your imagination, is almost brandy-like. The factory is open during the same hours as Fábrica de Tabacos Francisco Donatién. Admission is CUC$1, and usually includes a quick guided tour and a stop at the tasting room. Bottles of Guayabita are on sale for around CUC$4.

Aside from the city's two main draws, you can easily spend a few hours walking around town, and perhaps stopping in at either the **Museo Provincial de Historia (Museum of Province History)** at Calle Martí 58 (℄ 82/75-4300), or the **Museo de Ciencias Naturales (Museum of Natural Sciences)** at Calle Martí and Avenida Pinares (℄ 82/75-3087). Neither contains exhibits or collections of great interest, although the latter is housed in a wonderful old building with ornate Moorish architecture. You could also check out the **Teatro Milanés** (℄ 82/75-3871), Calles Martí and Colón, a striking 19th-century theater that is open for visits during the day, and sometimes hosts evening concerts and performances. Admission to each of the above attractions is CUC$1.

## WHERE TO STAY

I personally recommend staying in Viñales (see below) and visiting the attractions in Pinar del Río on a day trip.

There is a host of casas particulares in Pinar del Río. You'll find them both congregated around the busy downtown area, as well as in the more typically residential neighborhoods on the outskirts of the city. Most charge between CUC$10 and CUC$15 per person and usually offer reasonably priced meal options.

### MODERATE

**Hotel Vuelta Abajo** ⚓   This is by far the best option in downtown Pinar del Río. This recently opened hotel occupies a large and meticulously restored old mansion in the heart of the city. The rooms are simply furnished and there is little in the way of decor. Still, the rooms are very spacious, and all have immensely high ceilings. It's worth the very slight splurge for the rooms with views and small balconies. Only four rooms here have a king-size bed; the rest come with two twins.

## Smoke 'Em If You Got 'Em

When Christopher Columbus first visited Cuba, he found the local population smoking a local herb, *cohiba*, through a pipe, or *tobago*. They called the act of smoking *sikar*. He brought back some samples, and it wasn't long before millions of Europeans were smoking tobacco rolled into cigars and cigarettes. Tobacco was grown commercially in Cuba as early as the 16th century, and by the late 17th century, it was the country's most important export crop. By all accounts, the finest cigars in the world come from Cuba. And of the Cuban cigars available, the crème de la crème are made with tobacco grown in the **Vuelta Abajo,** the low plains spreading west from the city of Pinar del Río.

Most of the tobacco grown in Cuba is grown on small farms. Seeds are planted each year beginning in late October and throughout November to stagger the harvest. In a little over a month, seedlings are transplanted to the fields or *vegas*. Plants are carefully tended and regularly topped to stimulate leaf growth lower down. The highest quality wrapper leaves, *capa*, are grown in semi-shade under protective mesh. Harvesting takes place January through April. Leaves are classified by plant type, growing region, growing condition (sun or shade), and where they grow on an individual plant. All go through an intensive and carefully monitored process of drying, sorting, preparing, fermenting, aging, and finally, rolling. Real care is taken in handling the prized *capas*. Lesser quality leaves end up as *capote* (binders) and *tripa* (filler).

Throughout Vuelta Abajo you'll pass field after field planted with tobacco and see the traditional high-peaked thatch-roofed drying sheds. Tobacco from the Vuelta Abajo region is shipped to various factories in the region and around Cuba. The finest brands—Cohibas, Partagas, Romeo y Julieta, Montecristo, Robaina, H. Upmann, Corona, and Hoyo de Monterey—are all made with tobacco from Vuelta Abajo.

Calle Martí 102, Pinar del Río. (℃ **82/75-9381.** www.islazul.cu. 39 units. CUC$52–CUC$65 double. Rates include breakfast buffet. MC, V. **Amenities:** Restaurant; bar; tour and activities desk; car-rental desk; laundry service. *In room:* A/C, TV, fridge, safe.

### INEXPENSIVE

**Hotel Pinar del Río**    Serving both Cuban and international guests in equal measure, this is by far the largest hotel in town. It's uninspired and largely unappealing. It is perennially run-down, and I'm not sure it's ever seen much better days. Still, the rooms are adequate, they offer a broad range of facilities and services, and it's an acceptable option if you're staying in Pinar del Río for 1 or 2 nights. The several bars and in-house dance club make it a lively joint. In fact, be sure you get a room as far from the club as possible, or you might not sleep much.

Calle Martí, Pinar del Río. (℃ **82/75-5070.** www.islazul.cu. 149 units. CUC$34–CUC$38 double. Rates include breakfast buffet. MC, V. **Amenities:** 2 restaurants; 3 bars; dance club; outdoor pool; tour and activities desk; car-rental desk; laundry service. *In room:* A/C, TV.

# WHERE TO DINE

## MODERATE

**Rumayor** ☆ CRIOLLA    This is probably the best dining option in Pinar del Río. Run by the Islazul chain, it's both a restaurant and nightly cabaret. The specialty here is slow-smoked chicken, and it's excellent. There are also several fish and meat dishes. Of these, the *chirna frita,* a fried fish in a garlic sauce, is good. The main dining room is indoors in a dark room decorated with Afro-Cuban motifs. Service is quick and attentive, a relative rarity in Cuba.

On the Viñales highway, 1km (½ mile) north of town. ☎ 82/76-3051. Reservations not required. Main courses CUC$6–CUC$26. MC, V. Daily noon–3pm and 6–10pm.

## INEXPENSIVE

**La Casona** *Value* CRIOLLA    This is certainly the most atmospheric place to eat in Pinar del Río proper. About eight heavy wooden tables with bench seating fill up the main dining room in this old colonial building. High ceilings, modern sculpted wall hangings, and long French doors that open on to the street give this place its character. The food is mediocre and simple. Avoid the pastas and stick to the roasted chicken or sandwiches. In the evenings, they open up a little patio beer garden, with live music and an informal feel.

Calles Martí and Colón. ☎ 82/77-8263. Main courses CUC$1–CUC$5. No credit cards. Daily 11:30am–11:30pm.

## PINAR DEL RIO AFTER DARK

**Rumayor** ☆ (see above) offers up a nightly cabaret-style show in its large outdoor amphitheater space. The show here leans heavier on Afro-Cuban dances and traditions, and is less ornate than those in Havana, but it's still a pretty good spectacle. The show starts at around 11pm and admission is CUC$5, which includes one drink.

Alternately, you could see what's happening at **La Casona** (see above), the dance club at Hotel Pinar del Río, or **Café Pinar,** Calle Vélez Caviedes 34 (☎ 82/77-**8199**). You can also see what's playing at the old **Cine Praga,** Calle Gerardo Medina, next to the Coppelia ice-cream parlor. Admission is just a couple of pesos, and you should be able to pay with Cuban pesos.

## 2 Viñales ☆☆

200km (124 miles) SW of Havana; 26km (16 miles) N of Pinar del Río

Viñales is an extremely picturesque town in the heart of Cuba's prime tobacco-growing region. The town itself sits in the center of a flat valley surrounded by stunning karst hill formations known locally as *mogotes.* The *mogotes* are irregularly shaped steep-sided geological formations that can rise as high as 300m (985 ft.) and have bases ranging from just a few hundred yards in diameter to as much as a couple of kilometers in length. The *mogotes* are part of the Sierra de los Organos mountain chain, and were formed by eons of erosion. Many consider this the most naturally beautiful spot in Cuba. To be sure, the view of the Viñales Valley from any of the surrounding hillsides is stunning, particularly at sunrise or sunset. The Viñales Valley is a great spot to bicycle around, and there are good options for bird-watching, hiking, and in particular, rock climbing and spelunking.

# The Viñales Valley

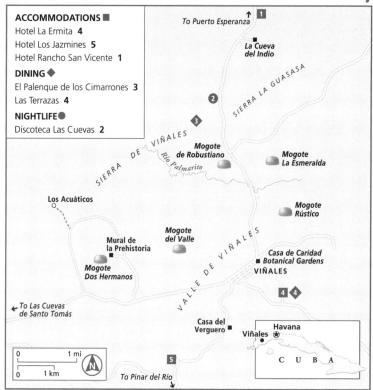

**ACCOMMODATIONS** ■
Hotel La Ermita **4**
Hotel Los Jazmines **5**
Hotel Rancho San Vicente **1**

**DINING** ◆
El Palenque de los Cimarrones **3**
Las Terrazas **4**

**NIGHTLIFE** ●
Discoteca Las Cuevas **2**

To Puerto Esperanza **1**

La Cueva
del Indio

SIERRA LA GUASASA

SIERRA DE VIÑALES

Río Palmarito

Mogote
de Robustiano

Mogote
La Esmeralda

Los Acuáticos

Mogote
Rústico

Mogote
del Valle

VALLE DE VIÑALES

Mural de
la Prehistoria

Casa de Caridad
Botanical Gardens
VIÑALES

Mogote
Dos Hermanos

←To Las Cuevas
de Santo Tomás

**4**  **4**

Casa del
Verguero

Havana
Viñales ✷

0        1 mi

0    1 km        **N**

**5**

C  U  B  A

To Pinar del Río

## ESSENTIALS

**GETTING THERE**   **Víazul** (📞 **7/881-1413** in Havana; www.viazul.com) has two daily buses at 9am and 2pm from Havana to Viñales, via Pinar del Río. The trip takes 3 hours 15 minutes and costs CUC$13 each way.

The **bus station** (📞 **8/79-3195**) is located at Salvador Cisnero 63, just across the street from the town's main plaza. Víazul buses for Havana depart Viñales daily at 8am and 2pm, passing through Pinar del Río about 40 minutes later, before continuing on to the capital. You can hire a taxi to Havana for CUC$50 to CUC$70 for up to four people.

To get here **by car,** take the Autopista Nacional (A4) west to Pinar del Río. From Pinar del Río, it's another 26km (16 miles) north on the well-marked Carretera Viñales. Entering Pinar del Río from the Autopista, you'll want to turn right at the post office, on Calle Isabel Rubio, and follow signs for Viñales.

**GETTING AROUND**   Taxis can be hired in Viñales, or called by your hotel. They tend to congregate around the central plaza. A cab to any of the local attractions should cost between CUC$2 and CUC$6. You can hire a cab for a full-day trip to anywhere around the region for around CUC$40 or CUC$60. If you'd rather rent a car, **Transtur** (📞 **8/79-6060**) has an office downtown just off the central park, as well as a desk at Hotel Los Jazmines, and **Havanautos** (✆ **8/79-6390**) has an office at the Viñales Cupet gas station.

This is a good region to bicycle around. The valley itself is almost perfectly flat and most of the major attractions can be reached along well-paved roads. You can rent late model mountain bikes in pretty good shape for around CUC$5 to CUC$10 per day. There's a stand renting them on a corner just across from the main plaza, or ask at your hotel.

## WHAT TO SEE & DO
### OUTDOOR ADVENTURES

Caves abound in this area and are one of the major attractions in and around Viñales. **La Cueva del Indio (The Indian's Cave;** ✆ **8/79-3202)** is the most popular cave and it's become a real tourist trap. Located about 5km (3 miles) north of Viñales at Km 33 on the Carretera de Puerto Esperanza, this cave gets its name from the fact that indigenous remains were found here. Only 1km (½ mile) or so of the extensive cave system here is open to travelers. A well-lit path leads from the entrance through a few small and narrow galleries to a tiny dock on an underground river. Here you board a small rowboat powered by an outboard engine for a quick trip of about 180m (600 ft.) up and down this river before exiting the cave at a dock area crowded with souvenir stands and a little snack bar. The entrance fee is CUC$5, and I don't think it's justified. Moreover, when the buses arrive in force, the line to get in is long and slow moving.

Those with an interest in more serious spelunking should head to **Las Cuevas de Santo Tomás** ✿. With over 45km (28 miles) of connected tunnels, chambers, and galleries, it's the largest explored cave system in Cuba. Some of these chambers and galleries are quite massive, with impressive stalagmite and stalactite formations. Unlike La Cueva del Indio, this cave system has been left in its natural state and you must visit it with headlamps and flashlights. So far, a relatively simple 1km (½ mile) section has been opened for guided tours, although more adventurous spelunking tours are in the works. Visits here, including a guide and equipment, run around CUC$15, and are best booked in advance with one of the tour agencies in town.

In addition to caving, the limestone mountains and karst formations of Viñales make for excellent **rock climbing.** Although climbing is still in its infancy as a sport in Cuba, the Viñales Valley is rapidly becoming a mecca for local and visiting climbers. So far, over 140 routes have been identified and climbed in the area. Some carry colorful names, such as "Razor's Edge" and "Friday 13th." A few attest to some of the hazards of the area, such as "Feeding Mosquitoes" and "Poison Oak, Guano, and Spines." For more information, check out **www.cubaclimbing.com**.

Unless you plan on scaling several *mogotes,* most of the **hiking** here is gentle and well groomed. There are several popular trails and routes, although you must hire an official guide to hike most of these. One of the most popular hikes is a simple walk through the farms and fincas of the valley just outside of town. This provides wonderful views of the surrounding *mogotes,* as well as encounters with the local farmers and a firsthand view of the tobacco-growing process. More athletic forays into the nearby forests and hills include hikes to and around the isolated little communities of **Los Acuáticos** and **Ancón,** as well as climbs to the summits of several *mogotes.* Guided hikes should run you between CUC$6 and CUC$20 per person, depending on the route and length of the hike. Do-it-yourselfers can wander the dirt roads and byways of the Viñales Valley, but must stay off the marked trails of **Viñales National Park.** For more information on guides and organized hikes, ask at your hotel, or check with

---

*Tips*  **Avoid the Crowds**

This area is an extremely popular destination for day trips out of Havana. If you're staying in Viñales, try to visit the various attractions here early, before the buses arrive, and then spend the afternoon walking around town, hiking a more remote trail, or lazing around your hotel.

---

the local office of the **Ministerio de Ciencia, Tecnologia y Ambiente (Ministry of Science, Technology, and Environment),** which, at press time, was building its new headquarters on the highway into Viñales, just beyond the Hotel Los Jazmines.

There are few well-defined trails for serious **mountain biking,** although there are plenty of dirt roads you can explore all around. You can rent late model mountain bikes in pretty good shape for around CUC$5 to CUC$10 per day. Ask at your hotel, or check the stand on the corner across from the main plaza.

## ATTRACTIONS & ORGANIZED TOURS

The Viñales Valley is part of the heart of Cuba's tobacco-growing region and a great place to take a tobacco tour. Typical tours start at the **Casa del Verguero,** a small farm that grows and dries the primary material, followed by a visit to the nearby de-veining station, or *despalilladora.* Here you'll see workers handle and sort the prized leaves for *capas,* or outer layers. You might also be given a quick tour of a final curing station, where the leaves emit an ammonia gas that will make your eyes tear. Finally, you'll visit a local cigar shop, **El Estanco.** However, you'll have to go into Pinar del Río (see above) if you want to visit an actual cigar factory.

Feel free to take a pass on the **Mural de la Prehistoria (Prehistoric Mural;** ✆ **8/ 79-3205).** Sure it's big, but this over-hyped attraction can't quite cut it as kitsch, is decidedly uninteresting as art, woefully inadequate as narrative, and just not impressive enough in execution to merit all the attention. Despite some fresh paint, which restored—and even improved on—the vibrant colors of artist Leovigildo González Morillo's original work, this massive mural lacks the style and weight of the works of his mentor, Diego Rivera. The mural is located 4km (2½ miles) west of Viñales and is open daily from 8am to 5pm. The CUC$1 admission is waived if you eat at the on-site restaurant.

One of the nicer attractions in Viñales is the little **Casa de Caridad Botanical Gardens** 🎄 located at the northeastern end of town. The lush gardens feature a mix of ornamental and medicinal plants and flowers, as well as orchids, bromeliads, palms, and fruit trees. If you're really lucky, you'll be able to munch on some freshly harvested fruit. No admission is charged, but donations are warmly accepted.

**Cubanacán, Cubatur,** and **Havanatur** all have offices right off the town's main square and offer a variety of tour options. Organized tours of the Viñales Valley can be booked with any of these operators and at all the hotels in town. These jampacked full-day tours run between CUC$25 and CUC$40 per person and usually include a visit to the Casa del Verguero, El Estanco, the Mural de la Prehistoria, the Cueva del Indio, and El Palenque de los Cimarrones, with lunch at one of the latter three, as well as a sunset cocktail at Hotel Los Jazmines. Other tour options include day trips to Pinar del Río, Cayo Levisa, Cayo Jutías, and María la Gorda, and cost between CUC$20 and CUC$70 per person.

# WHERE TO STAY
## MODERATE

The two hotels below do a brisk business with tour groups. It is basically essential that you have a reservation in advance.

**Hotel La Ermita**   Similar in style and setting to Los Jazmines (see below), this is a lovely and modest hotel set on the hillside just above the town of Viñales. There are excellent views from the grounds and restaurant here, although only a small percentage of the rooms offer the area's signature view. Those that do, such as second-floor corner room no. 64, are real steals. The rooms themselves are a little more spacious than those at Los Jazmines, and regular and recent upgrades have greatly improved them in terms of decor and comfort. Those in the newer buildings feature a private porch or balcony, with a couple of heavy Adirondack chairs. There's a popular kidney-shaped pool at the center of this compound and a poolside barbecue restaurant that I prefer to the hotel's principal buffet option. Even if you don't stay here, I recommend coming for sunset and perhaps staying for dinner at their Las Terrazas restaurant (see below).

Carretera de La Ermita Km 1.5, Viñales, Pinar del Río. ✆ 8/79-6071. Fax 8/79-6069. www.hotelescubanacan.com. 62 units. CUC$72 double. Rates include breakfast buffet. Rates lower in off season. MC, V. **Amenities:** 2 restaurants; 2 bars; outdoor pool; tennis court; tour and activities desk; massage; laundry service. *In room:* A/C, TV, safe.

**Hotel Los Jazmines** ✿   I give this hotel the nod over its nearby sister La Ermita, if only for the fact that you have much better odds of landing a room with a view. Most of the rooms are housed in two three-story buildings set on a hillside overlooking the Viñales Valley. All are clean and comfortable, if a tad on the small side, and feature French doors opening on to a little balcony from where you can soak in the sights. Touches of gingerbread wrought-iron work and stained glass give the place a sense of elegance. If possible, request one of the third-floor rooms in the newer block, nos. 301 to 316. Sixteen duplex *cabañitas* are located in a row heading downhill from the pool. These are a little bit smaller than the standard rooms, but are charming nonetheless.

Carretera de Viñales Km 25, Viñales, Pinar del Río. ✆ 8/79-6205. Fax 08/79-6215. www.hotelescubanacan.com. 78 units. CUC$72 double. Rates include breakfast buffet. Rates lower in off season. MC, V. **Amenities:** 2 restaurants; 2 bars; dance club; outdoor pool; tour and activities desk; car-rental desk; massage; laundry service. *In room:* A/C, TV, safe.

**Hotel Rancho San Vicente**   Located about 270m (900 ft.) north of the Cueva del Indio, this quiet nature hotel can almost be considered a spa. A half-dozen or so semi-private soaking pools (CUC$5) are fed by tepid mineral springs, and massage and mud treatments are available at very reasonable prices. Most of the clean and comfortable rooms are actually individual little bungalows, with two twin beds and a tiny front porch; those housed in triplex little ranches are slightly bigger inside, although less atmospheric. By far, the best rooms are the 20 new units housed in a series of two-story wooden buildings spread around the grounds. The whole complex is set amid a shady grove of pine, palm, and fruit trees. There's good bird-watching here, although the hotel doesn't offer any of the classic views Viñales is so famous for.

Carretera de Puerto Esperanza Km 33, Viñales, Pinar del Río. ✆ 8/79-6201. Fax 8/79-6265. www.hotelescubanacan. com. 53 units. CUC$58 double. Rates include breakfast. Rates lower in off season. MC, V. **Amenities:** Restaurant; bar; outdoor pool; tour and activities desk; massage; laundry service. *In room:* A/C, TV, safe.

## INEXPENSIVE

There is a host of casas particulares in Viñales, which for some reason call themselves *villas* here. Most are on either the main street through town or on the street 1 block southeast and parallel to it. All charge between CUC$8 and CUC$15 per person and usually offer reasonably priced meal options. I recommend **Casa Oscar Jaime Rodríguez,** Adela Azcuy 43 (© **8/79-3381**); **El Pelotero,** Calle Adela Azcuy 29 (© **8/79-3366**); or **El Relojera,** on the road to the Hotel La Ermita (© **8/79-3375;** eliosuares1960@yahoo.es).

## WHERE TO DINE

In addition to the places listed below, there are official—and uninspired—restaurants at most of the major tourist attractions, including the Mural de la Prehistoria and the Cueva del Indio. If you're staying at either Los Jazmines or La Ermita, you'd probably do well to venture away from their buffets and try one of the a la carte options. All paladares in Viñales have been closed by the government, although casas particulares are permitted to serve meals to their guests, and most will accept other diners with a certain amount of discretion.

**Casa de Don Tomás** CRIOLLA/SPANISH    This is probably the most popular restaurant in Viñales, and it's touted in most guidebooks as well as by tour and hotel operators throughout the region. The atmosphere in this restored 1879 colonial mansion is wonderful, and the building itself has been declared a national monument. You'll want to choose a table on either the small front patio or the more spacious back patio. The restaurant's signature dish, *Las Delicias de Don Tomás,* is a paella-like dish of Spanish rice cooked and served in an earthenware bowl and featuring bits of chicken, pork, fish, ham, and even lobster. It's usually slightly overcooked and under-seasoned. You'd definitely be better off opting for a simpler pork steak in *criolla* sauce, or the hefty portion of fried chicken. The house drink is called a "Trapiche," and it's made of rum, pineapple juice, and honey, and served with a sliver of sugar cane as the swizzle stick.

Calle Salvador Cisnero 140 (the main street in Viñales). © **8/79-3114**. Reservations recommended. Main courses CUC$5–CUC$14. MC, V. Daily 10am–10pm.

**El Palenque de los Cimarrones** ✦ CRIOLLA    I was prepared to hate this place. It's definitely a tourist trap catering to tour groups. Yet, the food was surprisingly good, and the show and setting were interesting and informative, without being too kitschy or corny. You reach the restaurant after paying a CUC$1 entrance fee and walking about 270m (600 ft.) through a narrow cave that bisects one of the area's signature *mogotes.* At the end of the path you come to a re-creation of one of the nomadic homes set up by runaway slaves who lived and hid in these caves. After a brief bit of Afro-Cuban music and dance, you reach the restaurant, which is a series of interconnected ranchos, each decorated and representing a different *orishá,* or Afro-Cuban deity. The main dish here is a slow-roasted chicken seasoned with oregano, cumin, garlic, and lime juice—it's excellent. And, the yellow rice with bits of ham, bacon, sausage, and peas puts Casa de Don Tomás's version to shame. The restaurant is only open for lunch, but the bar and snack bar located in the cave at the joint's entrance are open 24 hours. This spot also serves as a popular dance club on most nights (see below).

Km 36 on the highway to Puerto Esperanza, north of Viñales. © **8/79-6290**. Reservations not required. Main courses CUC$4–CUC$10. No credit cards. Daily 11am–4pm.

**Las Terrazas** *Value* CRIOLLA    This hotel restaurant has a wonderful perch above and view over the Viñales valley. The view itself is worth the price of admission, and the food is pretty good, as well. Standard Cuban cuisine is featured here, but there are a few twists. You can get Turkey Fricassee, which is turkey meat stewed in a tomato and white-wine sauce. I like the chicken Viñales, which is a boneless breast served au gratin. I recommend coming in time for sunset over the valley.

At the hotel La Ermita, carretera de La Ermita Km 1.5. ✆ 8/79-6071. Reservations recommended. Main courses CUC$5–CUC$7. MC, V. Daily 7am–10pm.

## VIÑALES AFTER DARK

Viñales has a couple of low-key little bars on the main road through town and if you're lucky, there might be a concert taking place at the local **Casa de la Cultura,** or the **Patio de Polo Montañez** ✦, both of which are located right on the central plaza, just off the church, or at the nearby ARTex shop, **Patio del Decimista.** The scene at either Los Jazmines or La Ermita is dependent upon the type of groups and guests in residence. When it's happening, my favorite spot is the **Discoteca Las Cuevas** ✦✦, which is located at the entrance to El Palenque de los Cimarrones (see above). Flashing lights and loud music get an atmospheric boost from the hanging stalactites. There's a cabaret-style show here most evenings beginning around 11pm; admission is CUC$5. However, most of the tour agencies in town offer a nightly package to the bar for around CUC$8 to CUC$10 per person, including round-trip transportation, admission, a half-bottle of rum, and a couple of soft drinks.

## 3 Sierra del Rosario Biosphere Reserve & San Diego de los Baños ✦

Soroa: 87km (54 miles) W of Havana; San Diego de los Baños: 120km (75 miles) W of Havana

The mountainous region between Havana and Pinar del Río is another prime destination in the country's budding eco-tourism industry. With both the **Sierra del Rosario Biosphere Reserve** and **La Güira National Park,** as well as eco-tourism projects in **Soroa** and at **Las Terrazas,** the area offers a wealth of opportunities to explore the flora and fauna of Cuba's inland mountain forests. Add the sulfurous mineral springs of **San Diego de los Baños** into the mix, and you've got the perfect recipe for some nature-based rest and relaxation.

## SIERRA DEL ROSARIO BIOSPHERE RESERVE

Declared a UNESCO biosphere reserve in 1985, the 25,000-hectare (nearly 62,000-acre) **Sierra del Rosario** encompasses a mountainous area of rapidly recovering secondary tropical deciduous forests, cut with numerous rivers and waterfalls. Nearly 100 species of birds can be spotted here, including over half of Cuba's 22 endemic species. Currently there are relatively few trails and facilities in the reserve, which is not open to individual exploration and trekking. Most activity is confined to two tourism developments, **Las Terrazas** and **Soroa,** which are connected by a loop of paved roads that begins and ends on the Autopista Nacional.

### ESSENTIALS

**GETTING THERE & AROUND**  There is no regular or reliable public transportation to this area. You will either have to rent a car, hire a taxi, or come with an organized tour (which can be booked at any major tour operator or hotel tour desk). Las Terrazas is located about 75km (47 miles) west of Havana. Take the Autopista Nacional (A4) west to Km 51. Here you'll see the sign and turnoff for Las Terrazas on your right. The heart of the complex is about 8km (5 miles) from the turnoff. About halfway there you'll hit the entrance, where you have to sign in and pay an entrance fee (CUC$3 per person; although this is waived for guests at the hotel here).

To get to Soroa, continue on the Autopista until the town of Candelaria at Km 62. The turnoff here is marked and it's another 8km (5 miles) to Soroa.

**ORIENTATION** The main offices at Las Terrazas are at Rancho Curujey; the community and Hotel Moka are a couple of kilometers away. Everything is well marked and connected by paved roads. If you don't have a reservation at Hotel Moka, you'll have to check in at Rancho Curujey before undertaking any tours or explorations of the reserve. The reserve gets busy in the high season and on weekends, and reservations, even for day visits, are recommended.

## WHAT TO SEE & DO

**Las Terrazas** ⊛ (ℂ 7/204-3739 in Havana, or 82/77-8555 on-site; www.lasterrazas.cu) is a neat and organized project designed around a working community. The community and Hotel Moka are set just above the shores of the diminutive **Lago San Juan.** There are a half-dozen or so trails and swimming holes, along with a smattering of other attractions, including the **Cafetal Buenavista,** an abandoned coffee plantation, and a few artists' and artisans' studios. If you're lucky you might spot one of the area's endemic lizards or amphibians, including the world's second-smallest frog.

Officially you must have a guide to hike any of the trails here. Guides can be provided either by Hotel Moka or by the administrative offices at Rancho Curujey. The trails around the **Cafetal Buenavista** make for a good couple hours of gentle hiking, and the restaurant here makes the whole thing rather convenient. Another popular hike is the slightly more rugged **La Cañada del Infierno (The Gorge Of Hell),** which follows a mountain river down beyond the ruins of yet another coffee plantation, ending a couple of kilometers later at the Santa Catalina sulfur springs. A guide will cost between CUC$5 and CUC$15 per person, depending on group size and length of your hike.

The newest attraction and adventure here is a zip-line and harness style **Canopy Tour.** The tour features five platforms connected by long steel cables, which you traverse with a climbing-style harness and pulley setup. The cables crisscross the little lake here two times. The tour takes about 50 minutes and costs CUC$30 per person.

**Soroa** is a small community with one basic miniresort (see below). The area's claims to fame are a lovely 22m (72-ft.) waterfall and a wonderful little botanical garden. You reach the base of **Salto de Soroa** after a gentle hike of around 450m (1500 ft.). There's a small pool here fit for wading. If you're more adventurous, you can hike the steep 2.5km (1.5-mile) trail to the natural lookout above and behind the falls. The rainbow that sometimes forms in the mist of this waterfall has earned the whole town the moniker "El Arcoiris de Cuba" (The Rainbow of Cuba). The entrance to the trails is located just a few hundred yards from the hotel, on the road to Havana; admission costs CUC$2 per person for those not staying at the hotel. Another nearby road leads up to a hill-top lookout called **El Castillo de las Nubes,** where you'll find a basic restaurant in a building built to resemble a small fortress.

With over 7,000 species of tropical plants and flowers from around the world, including 750 species of orchids, the **Jardín Botánico Orquideario Soroa** ⊛ is a must-visit for anyone passing through Soroa. The compact grounds are well tended and pleasant and there are usually at least 20 or so species of orchids in bloom. Admission costs CUC$3 and includes a 15- to 20-minute guided tour.

## WHERE TO STAY
### Expensive
**Hotel Moka** ⚘  This is the principal hotel in Las Terrazas and probably the nicest ecolodge in Cuba. The first-floor rooms have vaulted red brick ceilings, while those on the second floor have high-pitched ceilings. Each of the well-lit and spacious rooms has colorfully tiled floors and a small balcony; however, there are no queen- or king-size beds. The marble bathrooms come with a tub/shower combination and a bidet. The restaurant serves unspectacular and unimaginative food, and I recommend you try to take some of your meals at the nearby La Fonda de Mercedes, Hacienda Union, and Buena Vista restaurants. You can also rent a two-bedroom villa on the little lake below the hotel.

Autopista Nacional Km 51, Las Terrazas. ✆ **82/77-8600** at the hotel, or 7/204-3739 in Havana. Fax 7/204-5305. www.lasterrazas.cu. 25 units, 1 villa. CUC$100–CUC$135 double; CUC$145–CUC$160 villa. Rates include breakfast. MC, V. **Amenities:** Restaurant; bar; small outdoor pool; tennis court; mountain-bike and horse rental; activity desk; car-rental desk; laundry service. In room: A/C, TV, minibar, safe.

### Moderate
**Hotel & Villas Soroa**  The clean and compact rooms at this miniresort are not nearly as nice as those at Hotel Moka. Most have either two or three full-size beds, although a few have queen-size beds. The furnishings are simple and spartan. Somewhat nicer are the separate one- and two-bedroom *casitas*, some of which even come with private pools. This place does a fair amount of group traffic and is also popular with Cubans, especially on weekends. This is a good base for exploring Soroa, but I wouldn't recommend more than 1 or 2 nights here.

Carretera de Soroa Km 8, Pinar del Río. ✆ **8/5-3534.** Fax 8/5-3861. www.hotelescubanacan.com. 49 units. CUC$58 double. Rates include breakfast buffet. Rates lower in off season. MC, V. **Amenities:** 2 restaurants; 3 bars; outdoor pool; activities desk; massage; laundry service. In room: A/C, TV, safe.

## WHERE TO DINE
**La Fonda de Mercedes** (Finds) CRIOLLA  This is clearly the top dining option in Las Terrazas, even though there are only three or four items on the menu. The best dish is the Camagüey-style lamb, which is served shredded and cooked in wine, although the grilled chicken a la Pinareña, which is seasoned with orange juice, garlic, and cumin, is also good. There are only five large wooden tables on the open-air patio of Doña Mercedes Dache's apartment in this residential block of housing just below Hotel Moka, so reservations are a good idea. The wine list features the moderately priced and almost drinkable Soroa-brand red and white.

Edificio 9, Apto. 2, Las Terrazas. ✆ **8/77-8647.** Reservations recommended. Main courses CUC$5–CUC$9. No credit cards. Daily 9am–9pm.

## SAN DIEGO DE LOS BAÑOS & LA GÜIRA NATIONAL PARK
Just west of the Sierra de los Rosario, in the foothills of the Sierra de los Organos, you'll find La Güira National Park and San Diego de los Baños. **La Güira** is a small park that is nonetheless a favorite stop for bird-watching tours and general sightseers. **San Diego de los Baños** is a tiny town built on the edge of a lovely river and some natural mineral springs. The springs have been famed for their medicinal properties for centuries, and the local baths are a very popular destination for Cubans looking for a relaxing getaway, basic spa treatments, and physical therapy.

## GETTING THERE & AROUND

There is no regular or reliable public transportation to San Diego de los Baños. You will either have to rent a car, hire a taxi, or come with an organized tour. San Diego de los Baños is located about 133km (82 miles) southwest of Havana. Take the Autopista Nacional (A4) west to Km 102. You should see the sign and turnoff to your right. From here it's another 21km (13 miles) to town. A taxi from Havana to San Diego de los Baños should cost between CUC$40 and CUC$50 one-way. A few taxis are available in town. They should charge around CUC$3 to CUC$5 one-way to La Güira.

## WHAT TO SEE & DO

San Diego de los Baños is a tiny town built on the edge of a lovely river and some natural mineral springs. The **San Diego de los Baños Spa** (✆ 82/73-7880) is a relatively desultory facility that shows the wear and tear that it has borne over the years. This place does a heavy business in therapeutic and vacation care for Cubans. A host of physical and occupational therapists, and doctors, are on staff here. This is no Canyon Ranch; in fact, you'll feel as if you're heading down to a dungeon as you descend the two stories to the ground-level baths. Still, if you're staying at El Mirador next door (see below), you'd do well to stop in for a mud wrap (CUC$15), massage (CUC$20–CUC$30), or a soak in the tepid mineral pools (CUC$4 public pool, CUC$8 private pool). I'd advise against opting for the private pools. The public mineral baths are actually the best-maintained areas of this entire facility, with high ceilings and decent ventilation; the private baths, on the other hand, feel dark, slightly dirty, and claustrophobic.

La Güira National Park is located 5km (3 miles) west of San Diego de los Baños. You enter the park through the grand gates of the former Hacienda Cortina. There are some ruins and tended gardens near the entrance, as well as a restaurant and cabaret. There are no marked trails per se, but beat-up roads lead through the park and up to **Las Cabañas de los Pinos (Cabins in the Pines),** an abandoned mountain retreat where Fidel Castro's secretary and revolutionary hero Cecilia Sánchez liked to unwind, and on to the **Cueva de Los Portales** ✵, a small cave complex from where Che Guevara coordinated the Cuban defense forces during the Cuban missile crisis. The latter is probably the most interesting site in the area, and a must-see for anyone on the Che Trail. Inside, you can tour the compound and see where Che hung his hammock for afternoon siestas, where he and the men took target practice, where they cooked and ate, and where they played chess. You can even peek into the tiny room where the revolutionary icon slept during those troubled times. Admission is CUC$1.

## WHERE TO STAY & DINE

**Hotel El Mirador**   This little hotel is a surprisingly neat and well-run option in this neck of the woods. The rooms are all set in a two-story building above and behind the pool and reception. All of the rooms are clean and comfortable, with good light and well-kept rattan furnishings, though the bathrooms are a tad small and the beds a bit soft. There are well-tended gardens and grounds and a midsize pool. The main restaurant is actually pretty good for a Cuban chain hotel in the middle of nowhere. El Mirador does a mixed business of tourists and Cubans, and the pool and poolside bar are both usually lively. The restaurant here serves unimpressive, but acceptable, international fare.

San Diego de los Baños, Los Palacios, Pinar del Río. ✆ 82/77-8338. www.islazul.cu. 32 units. CUC$37–CUC$41 double. MC, V. **Amenities:** Restaurant; poolside grill; 2 bars; outdoor pool; activities desk; laundry service. *In room:* A/C, TV, safe.

## 4 Cayo Levisa ⓐ

113km (70 miles) W of Havana; 53km (33 miles) N of Viñales

Cayo Levisa is an isolated little island accessible only by boat. The island is around 3km (1¾ miles) long and just several hundred yards wide at most points. The entire northern shore of Cayo Levisa is one long stretch of white sand fronting a calm and startlingly turquoise blue sea. The beach is backed alternately by small stands of pine trees and stretches of thick mangrove. There's excellent bird-watching and scuba diving here. Cayo Levisa is part of the Archipiélago de los Colorados, which includes Cayo Paraíso, an even smaller little island reputed to be a favorite fishing haunt of Ernest Hemingway.

Several Havana tour agencies run day tours to Cayo Levisa, so the island's resort and beaches can fill up with anywhere from 50 to 100 extra visitors for the hours between 11:30am and 5pm. Still, there's enough beach to go around, and if you spend the night, you'll really feel like you've got the island to yourself and a few good friends.

### GETTING THERE

Hotel Cayo Levisa (see "Where to Stay & Dine," below) runs two **boats** daily to Cayo Levisa leaving from Palma Rubia at 10:30am and 5:30pm. The trip takes around 30 minutes. It may be possible to hire a boat to take you out if you miss the morning trip, but don't count on it. Return boats from Cayo Levisa leave for Palma Rubia at 10am and 5pm. If you don't have a pre-arranged tour to the island, the boat ride should run you CUC$25 per person round-trip, including lunch on the island.

To get to Palma Rubia from Havana by **car,** drive the northern highway from Mariel to Bahía Honda and continue on for another 40km (25 miles) west to Palma Rubia. If you're coming from Viñales, drive north to La Palma and then another 21km (13 miles) northeast to the embarkation point.

There is no regular or reliable **bus service** to Palma Rubia or Cayo Levisa. You could hire a **taxi** from either Havana (CUC$45–CUC$55 each way) or Viñales (CUC$25–CUC$35), but make sure you pre-arrange a pickup for your return trip, or you could have trouble getting out of Palma Rubia.

### FUN ON & OFF THE BEACH

The beach around 450m (1500 ft.) on either side of the main lodge is excellent for **sunbathing** and **swimming,** with broad stretches of soft sand and a gentle entry into the sea that allows you to walk out literally hundreds of yards before it gets too deep. The water can get a little rough and the weather cool when cold fronts blow through in the winter months, but this is the exception rather than the rule.

Cayo Levisa is an excellent destination for **diving** and **snorkeling.** There's a good dive operation on-site and some 23 identified dive sites within a 45-minute boat ride of the island. Most of the sites are less than 15 minutes away, and some are excellent for snorkeling. Rest stops often include a packed lunch at some deserted little island. Two tank dives per day will run you CUC$65, including equipment, with multiday packages available. Rental of snorkeling equipment costs CUC$5 per day.

If you're looking to follow in Papa Hemingway's footsteps, take a day trip to **Cayo Paraíso.** This small island is located about 10km (6 miles) east of Cayo Levisa. There's a small bust of Papa and a little shack that functions as a bar and grill, where you can buy lunch and drinks. The trip costs CUC$25, including transportation, snorkeling, and a refreshment. Snorkel gear will run you an extra CUC$5.

## WHERE TO STAY & DINE

**Hotel Cayo Levisa** ⭐ *(Finds)*    If you land one of the oceanfront bungalows here, you may never want to leave this idyllic little resort. I prefer the older rooms, which are individual bungalows, built in two rows parallel to the shore and staggered so they all get an ocean view. The rooms themselves are rather spartan, although they are relatively spacious with two twin beds, and perhaps their best feature, an ample front porch with a couple of sitting chairs. The newer rooms are slightly plusher, but you sacrifice a bit of privacy and isolation in these more modern wooden units. Scuba diving and snorkeling are the prime activities here, although you might be able to organize a game of beach volleyball, or get an open-air massage under the shade of palm trees at the water's edge from the resident massage therapist. Dining here is a la carte and the little restaurant serves good fresh seafood and *criolla* cuisine at reasonable prices.

Cayo Levisa, Pinar del Río. ✆ 82/75-6501. Fax 82/75-6506. www.hotelescubanacan.com. 33 units. CUC$72 double. Rates include breakfast and round-trip transportation from Palma Rubia. Rates lower in off season. MC, V. **Amenities:** Restaurant; bar; massage. *In room:* A/C, TV, safe.

## ANOTHER NEARBY ISLAND: CAYO JUTÍAS

A little bit west of Cayo Levisa, you can find similar attractions and isolated wonder at **Cayo Jutías** ⭐. Unlike its nearby sister, Cayo Jutías is connected to the mainland by a 3km (2-mile) *pedraplén*, or low-lying causeway. There's no hotel, but you can camp here, and the island is a popular destination for day trips out of Pinar del Río and Viñales. Aside from the nearly 7km (4 miles) of deserted white-sand beach, there's an open-air beachside restaurant serving standard *criolla* fare at reasonable prices. You can rent a large four-person tent and campsite for CUC$15. You can also rent Hobie Cats, windsurfers, and pedal boats.

To get to Cayo Jutías from Havana, drive the northern highway from Mariel to Bahía Honda and continue west to Santa Lucía. If you're coming from Viñales, drive north to San Vincente, then continue to San Caetano and Santa Lucía. The *pedraplén* to Cayo Jutías begins about 5km (3 miles) northwest of Santa Lucía. The toll for the *pedraplén* is CUC$5 per person. All of the major tour agencies offer day trips to Cayo Jutías from Viñales and Pinar del Río for between CUC$25 and CUC$30 per person, including lunch.

## 5 María la Gorda ⭐

306km (190 miles) SW of Havana

María la Gorda is a tiny beach and dive resort on the eastern end of the Bahía de Corrientes (Current Bay), which is formed by the long, curving Peninsula de Guanacahabibes. If you want to get away from it all, this is a good choice. The one hotel here caters almost exclusively to divers and dive groups, although it's also a good base for naturalists looking to explore the flora and fauna of the Guanacahabibes Peninsula, which UNESCO has declared an International Biosphere Reserve. The beach and hotel are named for a legendary Venezuelan beauty who was marooned here by pirates. María allegedly gained quite a reputation for her fleshy charms. She's long gone, but if you're looking to admire raw physical beauty, the sunsets here are some of the best in Cuba.

*Note:* The María la Gorda area sustained some hurricane damage during the active seasons of 2004 and 2006. Roofs were blown off and trees were downed at Villa María La Gorda. Everything should be up and running again by the time you read this.

## ESSENTIALS

**GETTING THERE**    There is no regular **bus service** to María la Gorda. If you are coming, check with the Gaviota hotel chain, which runs the only hotel here (see below)—they can arrange transportation to and from Havana with one of the tour agencies that use the hotel.

To get here by **car,** take the Autopista Nacional (A4) west to Pinar del Río. From Pinar del Río, it's another 94km (58 miles) to María la Gorda on the old Carretera Central passing through the prime tobacco-growing towns of San Juan y Martinez and Isabel Rubio, and then continuing on to Sandino and La Fe. You'll hit the water at Bahía de Corrientes at La Bahada. The road to the left leads 14km (8¾ miles) to María la Gorda. The road to the right heads out the peninsula another 54km (34 miles) to Cabo de San Antonio.

The **Marina María la Gorda** (© 82/77-1306) is an official entry and exit port for yachts. When arriving by sea, contact the marina before entering Cuban waters (19km/12 miles offshore) on VHF channels 16 or 19, or HF channel 2760. There's theoretically a Customs and Immigration officer on duty 24 hours, and water, electricity, and fuel can be had while tying up to the small pier here.

**GETTING AROUND**    **Transtur** (©/fax 82/77-8131) has a car- and scooter-rental desk here. A four-door compact car with air-conditioning will run you between CUC$55 and CUC$80 dollars daily, including insurance and unlimited mileage, while scooters go for around CUC$25 to CUC$35 per day.

## FUN ON & OFF THE BEACH

The beach right in front of the hotel quickly hits coral and rock outcroppings as soon as it meets the water. In fact, sand is at a premium here. You'd definitely be wise to bring along a pair of waterproof aquatic shoes or sandals. The best beach for sunbathing and swimming is about 1km (½ mile) southwest of the hotel near an abandoned marina. There are also some excellent beaches out toward Cabo San Antonio on the Guanacahabibes Peninsula.

**Scuba diving** ✿✿✿ is the principal activity here, and this is one of the top dive destinations in Cuba. Over 50 dive sites are located within a 1-hour boat ride of the resort, and many are much, much closer. Visibility is excellent and the waters of the bay here stay calm year-round, making entry and exit a breeze. The place has a bit of a reputation for whale sharks, which apparently congregate near here in October and November. However, my dive master had been working here for almost 2 years and had yet to see a whale shark. What you will see are fabulous coral and sponge formations, colorful tropical fish, turtles, eels, barracuda, and rays. It costs CUC$43 per dive, including a complete equipment package. There are also nightly scuba dives. Multiday dive packages and off-season rates are available. Snorkelers can reach some decent coral outcroppings in around 3 to 7.5m (10–25 ft.) of water within 90 to 180m (300–600 ft.) of the coast. Mask, fins, and snorkel will run you CUC$8 per day.

Depending on boat availability, half-day **fishing** trips can also be arranged for between CUC$150 and CUC$250 for up to four persons. Possible game ranges from tarpon to bonefish to a variety of deepwater fish.

Aside from the watersports mentioned above, the other main attraction here is exploring the nearby **Guanacahabibes National Park** ✿. There are three trails in the park, and you must have a guide to hike any of them. The land here is flat and you'll find a mix of lowland scrub, pine forests, and mangrove, dotted with numerous little lakes and lagoons. There are quite a few endemic bird, lizard, and mammal species. This was also the last refuge of Cuba's indigenous tribes as the Spaniards completed their conquest, and several small archaeological sites have been uncovered. There's a little lighthouse, Faro Roncali, at the point at Cabo San Antonio, and a park ranger station (Estación Ecológica; © **82/75-1007**) at La Bajada. It costs CUC$6 to CUC$10 per person to visit the park, including the guide, depending upon which trail you hike. If you just plan on driving your car or scooters out the road to Cabo San Antonio and visiting some of the beaches here, you may be able to get away without a guide, although as a rule they are averse to foreigners roaming around the park unaccompanied. Villa María La Gorda (see below) offers a guided tour of the park for CUC$25 per person, including a bag lunch and soft drink.

## WHERE TO STAY & DINE

**Villa María La Gorda**    Also known as the International Diving Center, this place is run by the Cuban Gaviota chain, and exists somewhere in that gray area between a no-frills dive camp and a modern resort. The rooms are adequate and fairly spacious, if nothing fancy. You'll definitely want to land one of the older oceanfront units, if possible. The older rooms that face the scrub forest backing the resort are much less appealing. A series of newer units are set back from the beach, and are pleasant individual and two-story wooden bungalows. The resort's restaurants are uninspired, although there are really no other options around. I actually spied quite a few guests buying cookies and crackers at the little gift shop here and calling it a meal. Still, the main restaurant does have a great setting, just steps from the water.

Península de Guanacahabibes, Pinar del Río. ©/fax **82/77-8131** or 82/77-8077. www.gaviota-grupo.com. 55 units. CUC$66 double. Rates include breakfast buffet. Lower rates in off season; higher during peak periods. MC, V. **Amenities:** 2 restaurants; bar; car- and scooter-rental desk; gift shop; laundry service; full-service dive shop. *In room:* A/C, TV, fridge, safe.

## 6  Isla de la Juventud

162km (100 miles) S of Havana

Isla de la Juventud hangs like an apostrophe off the southern coast of Cuba and is the largest and westernmost island in the Archipiélago de los Canarreos. Sometimes referred to as the Island of a Thousand Names, it was called variously Siguanea, Guanaja, and Camarco by the early indigenous populations. The island was later christened El Evangelista by Columbus, Parrot Island by pirates, and Isla de Pinos (Isle of Pines) throughout most of the 19th and 20th centuries. Some even call it Treasure Island, claiming Robert Louis Stevenson used it as a model for his book of the same name. Following the Cuban Revolution it was renamed Isla de la Juventud, or Isle of Youth, after a slew of secondary schools and colleges were built here to educate both Cuban and foreign students.

For travelers, Isla de la Juventud's primary attraction is its stellar scuba diving. The one working hotel serving foreigners here caters almost entirely to divers. Other attractions include some of the most elaborate and best-preserved indigenous cave paintings in the entire Caribbean basin.

## ESSENTIALS
### GETTING THERE
**BY PLANE**    **Cubana, AeroCaribbean,** and **Aerotaxi** have several daily flights to **Rafael Cabrera Mustelier Airport** (© **46/32-2300;** airport code GER) on Isla de la

Juventud from José Martí International airport in Havana. Fares cost between CUC$25 and CUC$50 each way, depending on the season. Demand is often very high, so be sure to make your reservation as far in advance as possible.

Regular public buses connect the airport and Nueva Gerona, 6.5km (4 miles) away. These are marked SERVICIO AEREO. The official fare is 1 peso, but foreigners are usually charged CUC$1. A taxi between the airport and downtown costs around CUC$5 or CUC$7.

**BY BUS & FERRY**    Isla de la Juventud is connected to the mainland by regular ferry service between Nueva Gerona, on the island, and the town of Batabanó, on the coast 71km (44 miles) south of Havana. Several types of ferries make the trip. You'll definitely want to book one of the two high-speed modern ferries. Either of these will make the trip in between 2 and 3 hours, and costs CUC$12 each way. These ferries depart Batabanó daily at 10am and 4pm, with return trips leaving Nueva Gerona at 7:30am and 3pm. The ferries often have varying schedules, according to demand. The ferry company, **Naviera Cubana Caribeña,** which books all of the vessels, has a desk in the main Astro bus terminal in Havana (📞 7/860-0330). Look for the ticket window marked NCC. Here you can buy a bus-ferry combination ticket, which I highly recommend. In Nueva Gerona, the ferry terminal and dock are approximately 4 blocks east of Calle José Martí (📞 46/32-4436). The reserved bus connection will run an extra CUC$4 each way. Buses are supposed to meet an awaiting ferry, but due to varying schedules, the connections sometimes do not work like a fine Swiss watch. In each direction, it is recommended you buy your ticket 1 or 2 days in advance.

## GETTING AROUND

Taxis are plentiful on Isla de la Juventud and around Nueva Gerona. Rides around town, out to the airport, or to one of the nearby beaches should cost between CUC$2 and CUC$7. A trip down to the Hotel El Colony will cost CUC$18 to CUC$22. There are three or four daily buses between Nueva Gerona and the Hotel El Colony. A full day with a driver should cost around CUC$60. If you want to rent a car, **Havanautos,** Calles 32 and 39 (📞 46/32-4432); **Micar,** Calles 39 and 30 (📞 46/32-6185); and **Transtur,** at the ferry terminal and Hotel El Colony (📞/fax 46/32-6666), have offices on the island.

There are also numerous horse-drawn taxis, which generally charge around CUC$1 to CUC$2 for short rides, or between CUC$4 and CUC$6 per hour.

## ORIENTATION

The main city, **Nueva Gerona,** sits near the northern tip of the island on the banks of the Río Las Casas, while the better beaches and scuba diving locations are on the southwest and southeastern shores. The **Hotel El Colony** (see below) is located on the shores of Siguanea Bay, on the central western coast of the island. The southern third of the island is an almost entirely uninhabited area of swamp and mangrove.

There are several banks and a **CADECA** office in Nueva Gerona. There's a **post office** at Calle José Martí 1810, a 24-hour **Farmacia José Martí** (📞 46/32-2484) on Calle José Martí and Calle 24, and an **Etecsa** phone center at Calles 41 and 28. All of the above are located either on or within a 1- or 2-block radius of the Calle José Martí pedestrian mall.

The downtown offices of **Cubanacán** (📞 46/32-6369) and **Ecotur** (📞 46/32-7101) are your best sources of local information, and where you should head to book a tour to any of the attractions listed below.

## WHAT TO SEE & DO

The island's most publicized attraction is the **Presidio Modelo (Model Prison; ℭ 46/32-5112)**, located about 5km (3 miles) east of Nueva Gerona. The massive five-story circular prison blocks are dire and imposing, and even brief visits give you an idea of how uncomfortable they must have been. This is the prison where Fidel Castro and other surviving conspirators were sent following the failed Moncada raid. There's a small museum in the block where Fidel and his compadres did time, and you can even visit the Comandante's former cell, no. 3859. The museum is open Monday through Saturday from 8am to 4pm, and Sunday from 8am to noon; admission is CUC$2. There's an extra CUC$3 charge for taking photos, and a CUC$15 fee for taking video.

If you're spending much time in downtown Nueva Gerona, you might want to stop in at the **Museo Provisional (ℭ 46/32-3791)**. Housed in an old building dating from the 1830s, this museum features a wide range of exhibits illustrating the island's history from pre-Columbian times to the modern era. Admission is CUC$1.

Nueva Gerona's **downtown park** is a great place to hang out, with some strategically placed benches for sitting and watching the townsfolk stroll on by. There's a pretty little colonial mission-style church, **Nuestra Señora de los Dolores,** on the northern edge of the park, and the snazzy looking Art Deco **Cine Caribe** on the eastern edge. Two blocks to the east, on the way to the ferry docks, you'll find **El Pinero,** at Calle 24 and the riverbank, the old working ferry that carried Fidel Castro and other Moncada rebels back to freedom following their release from the Presidio Modelo in 1955. The big black-and-white ferry is a local monument and interesting historical curiosity, but you can't board or tour it. Beginning at the park's western edge and running north for 5 blocks, Calle 39, also known as **Calle José Martí,** is a pedestrian-only street. This is where most of the town's shops, restaurants, and bars are located, and it's the site of the town's nightlife.

About 27km (17 miles) south of Nueva Gerona is an interesting botanical garden dubbed **La Jungla de Jones,** or the Jungle of Jones (ℭ 46/39-6246). A rather unkempt attraction, the gardens nonetheless have a broad and varied collection of tropical flora. Admission is CUC$3. Farther south, beyond the town of La Fe, you'll find the **Criadero de Cocodrilos,** a crocodile breeding project. The facilities are basic, but there are hundreds of these impressive reptiles here, ranging in size from little tots to monstrous adults. The facility is open daily from 8am to 5pm, and the CUC$3 entrance fee will get you a brief guided tour.

On the southeastern coast of Isla de la Juventud, 59km (37 miles) from Nueva Gerona is the **Cueva de Punta del Este** ⭐, a small complex of caves with over 200 ancient pictographs well preserved on its walls. This cave system has been called the "Sistine Chapel" of Caribbean indigenous art. The paintings are of abstract and geometric patterns and are thought to have both religious and celestial significance. There's a pretty white-sand beach here as well, so you can combine a visit to the caves with some beach time. There's no entrance fee to the caves, but you'll need a special permit and guide to enter this area, and your best bet is to visit as part of an organized tour, which can be arranged at your hotel or with **Cubanacán (ℭ 46/32-6369)** or **Ecotur (ℭ 46/32-7101)** in town.

## ON THE BEACH & UNDER THE SEA

Isla de la Juventud is one of Cuba's premier **dive destinations** ⭐⭐⭐, and the diving here is wonderful. The waters are crystal clear, there are walls and coral and caves, and there are even a few wrecks. The **Centro Internacional de Buceo (ℭ 46/39-8181)** is the main dive operator on the island, with their dive center at the small marina a few kilometers beyond the Hotel El Colony (see below). Most trips head to **Punta Francés** 🐾🐾, a national maritime park, with a beautiful stretch of white-sand beach fronting a calm and protected sea on the southwestern tip of the island. From here, many of the island's best dive sites are easily accessible. There are a couple of long piers out into the calm waters here. One has a buffet restaurant and bar at the end of it. On shore, there's a small park station, with bathroom facilities and some picnic tables. The park station also has several hundred chaise longues, which are broken out and spread along the beach whenever a cruise ship pulls in for a day tour. When this happens—once or twice a week—this quiet, isolated beach becomes a swarming mass of up to 1,500 sun worshipers. When the cruise ships aren't around, you'll have the joint almost to yourself. Dive trips cost between CUC$50 and CUC$80 for two-tank dives depending on the season, including a full equipment package. However, if you stay here for any length of time, you are best off buying a multiday, multidive package. Day-trippers can take the boat ride out to Punta Francés for CUC$10. If you go, the buffet lunch will run you CUC$12, with drinks sold separately.

The most popular beaches close to Nueva Gerona are the white-sand **Playa Paraíso** and the dark-sand **Playa Bibijagua.** These beaches are 5km (3 miles) and 8km (5 miles) east of town, respectively, and both are served by regular bus service from town. Oddly, the dark-sand Playa Bibijagua is actually the more popular spot, although neither is a prime beach destination by any standard.

## WHERE TO STAY & DINE

In addition to the hotel listed below there are many casas particulares in Nueva Gerona. You'll definitely be offered a couple as soon as you set foot on the island, whether you arrive by sea or by air. Check out the offering of whomever you feel gives you the best vibe, or head to either **Casa Rafael Céspedes Medina,** Calle 32 no. 4701 between Calles 47 and 49, Nueva Gerona (© **46/32-3167**), or **Villa Peña,** Calle 10 no. 3710, between Calles 37 and 39, Nueva Gerona (© **46/32-2345**). Both offer clean air-conditioned rooms with meals for between CUC$20 and CUC$25 per person, as well as reasonably priced rides around the island.

**Hotel El Colony**    This is primarily a dive resort, and I only recommend it for hardcore divers. The hotel itself was built in two stages. The original horseshoe-shaped two-story main building feels perpetually run-down. The newer "bungalows" are in better shape. These rooms are in one- and two-story blocks, and are spacious and modern, with two firm double beds, wicker furniture, and a small private terrace or balcony. The buffet restaurant is mediocre and overpriced. The nicest feature is the long pier and the Mojito Bar & Grill that sits at the end of it. This is a great place for sunsets, and when the wind is right, a good place to escape the fierce swarms of mosquitoes and sand fleas that often plague the nights here.

Carretera Siguanea Km 42 (49km/30 miles southwest of Nueva Gerona), Isla de la Juventud. © **46/39-8282.** Fax 46/39-8420. 77 units. CUC$45–CUC$70 double. Rates include breakfast buffet. MC, V. Taxis to or from Nueva Gerona or the airport cost CUC$18–CUC$22; public buses make the run 3 times daily for 2 Cuban pesos. **Amenities:** 2 restaurants; 2 bars; outdoor pool; watersports equipment/rentals; tour desk; car- and scooter-rental desk; laundry service. *In room:* A/C, TV, safe.

## ISLA DE LA JUVENTUD AFTER DARK

Start your evening with a stroll and mingle on Calle José Martí. If you get tired of that you can check out what's playing at the **Cine Caribe,** Calle 37 and Calle 28, or stop in at the **Caberet El Patio,** Calle 24 between Calle Martí and 37, which offers up this island's somewhat anemic version of a traditional cabaret show (admission CUC$3), and then becomes a dance club. Other spots right on Calle Martí include the neighboring **Casa de las Mieles** and **Nuevo Café Virginia,** which offer good options for a few drinks. The latter sometimes has live music and dancing. Or you can see if there's any live music or performance at the **Casa de la Cultura,** on Calle 24 at the corner of 37.

## 7 Cayo Largo del Sur ★★★

177km (110 miles) S of Havana; 120km (74 miles) E of Isla de la Juventud

Cayo Largo del Sur—or more simply, Cayo Largo—is the second-largest island in the Archipiélago de los Canarreos, and the only other island in the chain to support any population or tourism activity. The island's primary attraction is its uninterrupted kilometers of pristine white-sand beach, perhaps the best in Cuba. The island also offers fabulous scuba diving and snorkel opportunities, excellent wildlife viewing, and great bonefish, tarpon, and deep-sea fishing.

Cayo Largo has a long and rich history as a stomping and fishing ground for nomadic Caribe and Siboney indigenous populations. It was also visited by Christopher Columbus on his second voyage in 1494, and used as a base and stopover point by pirates and corsairs, including Sir Francis Drake, Henry Morgan, and Jean Lafitte.

Over three-quarters of all visitors to Cayo Largo come direct on charter packages to the island, never even setting foot on mainland Cuba.

## ESSENTIALS

**GETTING THERE**   The modern **Juan Vitalio Acuña Airport** (© **45/24-8141;** airport code CYO) accepts international traffic. Charter flights arrive here from Canada and Europe regularly throughout the year, with greater frequency during the high season. There are also daily flights here from Havana and Varadero by **Aerogaviota, Aerotaxi,** and **AeroCaribbean.** These are best booked in Havana with any of the many tour agencies (or for contact information see "Getting Around," in chapter 2). Fares run between CUC$120 and CUC$170 for the day tour. A taxi from the airport to any hotel on the island should cost between CUC$3 and CUC$6.

The **Marina Cayo Largo del Sur** (© **45/24-8212**) is an official port of entry to Cuba. If you're arriving by sea, contact the marina before entering Cuban waters (19km/12 miles offshore) on VHF channels 16 or 19, or HF channel 2760.

**GETTING AROUND**   There's a shuttle that periodically runs a route connecting the marina and all the major resort hotels here; fare is CUC$1. Taxis are also readily available on Cayo Largo. A ride anywhere on the island should cost between CUC$2 and CUC$10. You can also rent a car or scooter from **Transtur** (© **45/24-8245**), which has desks at most of the hotels on the island, as well as at the airport. Rates run around CUC$8 per hour for the first hour on a scooter, and about CUC$3 per hour for each additional hour; it's CUC$60 per day for a small jeep, including your first tank of gas and insurance.

## FUN ON & OFF THE BEACH

Most visitors to Cayo Largo spend most of their time sprawled out on the 24km (15 miles) of uninterrupted white-sand beach. While the beaches fronting most of the hotels here are some of the finest to be found in the Caribbean, both **Playa Paraíso** ★★★ and **Playa Sirena** ★★★ on the western end of the island deserve s pecial mention. Protected from the prevailing southeasterly trade winds, these beaches are broad expanses of some of the finest white sand to be found, and they are fronted by calm, clear Caribbean waters of postcard-perfect blue hues. Most of the beaches here are "clothing optional," and the large number of European and Canadian visitors to Cayo Largo make topless and nude sunbathing quite common. Shade can be at a premium here, so you'll want to park your towel or beach mat close to a coconut palm, or under a beach umbrella or one of the thatch roof *palapas* that are spread around. Be forewarned, demand usually far exceeds supply. If you have a portable beach umbrella or shade device, I highly recommend you bring it to Cayo Largo. The marina runs a basic restaurant and grill on Playa Sirena, and you can also rent Hobie Cats, windsurfers, and jet skis from them. Playa Paraíso is almost entirely undeveloped, with a few thatch roofed A-frame structures on the sand for shade.

Full- and half-day **boat trips,** either on large sailing catamarans or converted fishing boats, are a popular activity here. The trips usually include a stop at Cayo Iguana, a small island with a large population of endemic iguanas, as well as some snorkeling on the barrier reef. These trips also often stop at a spot called the *piscina natural* (natural pool). This slightly submerged sand bar is a beautiful and protected spot for a refreshing swim. These trips cost around CUC$60 to CUC$80 per person, including lunch. Most of the all-inclusive resorts on the island allow guests unlimited use of small sailboats, catamarans, and windsurfers. You can rent a larger cruising sailboat for the day, or even overnight, from the marina. Boats go for between CUC$250 and CUC$600 per day, with a skipper and crew.

Right beside the marina is a small turtle breeding and protection project **La Granja de las Tortugas.** You can visit the facility and usually see various young turtles in holding tanks or protected nests. The farm is open daily from 9am to 5pm; admission is CUC$1. Between April and September, the folks here occasionally offer nighttime trips to see the nesting turtles lay eggs. Inquire at your hotel or at the farm for details.

There's great **bonefishing** on the shallow flats and mangroves all around Cayo Largo. Tarpon and permit are also plentiful. Serious fishermen should contact **Casa Batida** (©/fax **5/24-8324;** www.fishingtime.it).

With rich coral reefs, steep walls, and numerous wrecks, Cayo Largo has excellent **scuba diving** and **snorkeling,** and unlike two of the island's nearby celebrated dive spots, María la Gorda and Isla de la Juventud, you can actually stay in a very comfortable hotel here. Dive and snorkel trips are run by the International Dive Center at the marina here, but can be booked by any hotel on the island. A two-tank dive trip costs CUC$60, with a full equipment package costing an additional CUC$15.

**Nightlife** on Cayo Largo is pretty much limited to the bars, dance clubs, and revue shows at its all-inclusive hotels.

## WHERE TO STAY & DINE

I find the hotel listed below to be by far the best choice on Cayo Largo, but the Sol Meliá company has another property just next door, the **Sol Pelícano** (© **45/24-8333;** www.solmeliacuba.com), which is another good option geared more toward families. In addition, the **Barceló Cayo Largo** (© **800/227-2356** in the U.S. and Canada, or 45/24-8080 on Cayo Largo; www.barcelo.com) is yet another luxury resort, while **Gran Caribe** (© **7/204-0575** in Havana, or 45/24-81111 on Cayo Largo; www.gran-caribe.com) runs several more rustic options here, including the **Club Lindamar, Club Coral,** and **Club Soledad.** Of these, Club Coral, with a lively small village feel, and Club Lindamar, with its spacious A-frame bungalows, are the best.

**Sol Cayo Largo** ★★ *Finds*     This is an animated and, at the same time, romantic all-inclusive resort set amid rolling dunes and limestone outcroppings bordering a stretch of Cayo Largo's fabulous Lindamar beach. The two-story blocks of rooms are done in a Cape Cod styling, with faux stressed paint that gives the place a worn and lived-in feel. The rooms are quite spacious and comfortable, with either one king- or two queen-size beds and a private balcony or terrace. I think it's worth the CUC$20 supplement for 1 of the 60 oceanview standard rooms. All of these are located on the second floor and come with some added amenities, including a little nightstand CD player, stocked minibar, and—my favorite feature—an inviting siesta-inducing Yucatán hammock strung on the balcony. The junior suites come with a connecting sitting room and an extra TV. They are making progress toward converting the health club into a full-fledged spa.

Cayo Largo del Sur, Archipiélago de los Canarreos (6km/3¾ miles from the airport). ℂ **45/24-8260.** Fax 45/24-8265. www.solmeliacuba.com. 296 units. CUC$270–CUC$310 double; CUC$400 junior suite. Rates are all-inclusive. Rates lower in off season; higher during peak periods. Children under 3 stay free in parent's room; children 3–12 stay for half off. MC, V. **Amenities:** 5 restaurants; 4 bars; dance club; large free-form outdoor pool; 2 lit outdoor tennis courts; well-equipped health club; nonmotorized watersports equipment; children's programs; game room; concierge; tour and activities desk; car- and scooter-rental desk; salon; massage; babysitting; laundry service. *In room:* A/C, TV, fridge, hair dryer, safe.

# 6

# Varadero & Matanzas Province

*by Eliot Greenspan*

An easy ride from Havana, Matanzas is Cuba's second-largest province, and the site of its principal beach destination: **Varadero.** In addition to Varadero, the province is home to the lovely colonial-era cities of **Matanzas** and **Cárdenas,** as well as the **Ciénaga de Zapata,** a vast wetlands area of mangrove and swamp taking up most of the southern half of the province. The southern section of Matanzas province also holds great historical and sentimental value to modern Cubans, as it was here, in the Bahía de Cochinos (Bay of Pigs), that the nascent Cuban revolutionary state defeated an invasion force trained, supplied, and abetted by the United States. Matanzas remains an important agricultural region with huge sugar plantations, as well as citrus groves and cattle ranches.

## 1 Matanzas

98km (61 miles) E of Havana; 40km (25 miles) SW of Varadero

Matanzas is a city of many names. "City of Bridges," "City of Rivers," and the "Venice of Cuba," all reference the fact that the city is divided by two major rivers, and connected back together by a series of pedestrian, auto, and rail bridges. Due to its slow pace and laid-back nature, it is also sometimes called Cuba's "Sleeping Beauty." However, the city is probably most proud of its moniker as the "Athens of Cuba," a name reflecting Matanzas's important cultural tradition and history. The first *danzón,* a languid and lyrical original dance and musical form, was originally composed and played in Matanzas in 1879 by native son Miguel Faílde, and Matanzas has a rich legacy of prominent poets, writers, painters, and musicians. Still, today's reality is that aside from its beautiful old city center, Matanzas is a relatively unappealing industrial port city of only passing interest to travelers. While it is a popular destination for day trips out of Havana and Varadero, there are no notable hotels or restaurants in Matanzas.

### ESSENTIALS
#### GETTING THERE

**BY PLANE**   The nearest airport is Varadero's **Juan Gualberto Gómez International Airport** (© **45/61-3036;** airport code VRA), located more or less midway between Varadero and Matanzas. See "Varadero," below, for more information.

**BY BUS**   The **bus station** is located at Calzada de Esteban and the corner of Calle Terry. **Víazul** (© **7/881-1413** in Havana, or 45/29-2943 in Matanzas; www.viazul. com) has three buses daily for Varadero, stopping in Matanzas to drop off and pick up passengers. The buses depart Havana daily at 8am, noon, and 6pm. The trip takes about 2 hours to Matanzas, and the one-way fare is CUC$8. The return bus for Havana leaves Matanzas at 8:55am, 12:35pm, and 6:55pm.

**BY TRAIN**    The main **train station** (© **45/29-2409**) is located on the southern outskirts of town on Calle 181. There are a half-dozen or so trains departing daily from Havana's Central Station to Matanzas. Matanzas is on the main train line to eastern Cuba, and most trains bound for Holguín, Santiago de Cuba, and other points east stop in Matanzas. The 90-minute ride costs CUC$3 to CUC$5.

One interesting alternative means of reaching Matanzas is the **Hershey Train** ✦, a legacy of the famous chocolate company's formerly vast network of sugar plantations in Cuba. This slow-moving electric train leaves from Havana's **Casablanca Station** (© **7/862-4888**). The Hershey Train station in Matanzas is located at Calle 67, in Reparto Versalles, just north of the Río Yumurí (© **45/24-7254**). This scenic trip takes between 3 and 4 hours, making numerous stops, and costs CUC$3. There are five departures daily in each direction, leaving more or less simultaneously from each terminal station at roughly 4:30am, 8:30am, 12:30pm, 4:10pm, and 9pm.

**BY CAR**    Matanzas is connected to Havana by a modern coastal highway, the Vía Blanca, which begins as you exit the tunnel connecting Habana Vieja with Habana del Este. It's a straight shot and scenic drive that generally takes around 90 minutes.

## GETTING AROUND

You can easily visit all the principal sites in downtown Matanzas by foot. **Taxis** are readily available in Matanzas, and tend to gather around the Plaza de la Vigía and Plaza de la Libertad. A taxi out to the Castillo de San Severino from downtown should cost around CUC$2 each way.

## ORIENTATION

Matanzas is divided into three distinct sections by the Yumurí and San Juan rivers. All let out on to the broad bay, Bahía de Matanzas. The northern section and the first you'll reach coming in on the Vía Blanca from Havana is **Reparto Versalles.** The central section, **Reparto Matanzas,** is where you'll find the city center and most of the local attractions. Heading south and out of town toward Varadero is **Pueblo Nuevo.**

There are currently no tour agencies with offices in Matanzas, but that is expected to change soon. The main **post office** is located at the corner on Calle 85 between Calles 288 and 290. There's an **Etecsa** center at Calles 288 and 83 (© **45/24-3123**). There's a **CADECA** branch behind the cathedral on Calle 282 between Calles 83 and 85 (© **45/25-3558**).

## WHAT TO SEE & DO

Matanzas has a very compact city center, and a few hours walking around are generally enough to get a good feel for things. There are two small plazas that anchor the social and cultural life of Matanzas, the **Plaza de la Vigía** and the **Plaza de la Libertad.** Both are within 5 blocks of each other in Reparto Matanzas, the central section of the city.

Probably the most visited site in Matanzas is the stunning neoclassical **Teatro Sauto** ✦✦, on the Plaza de la Vigía (© **45/204-2721**). The theater, which was finished in 1863, is the design of Italian architect and artist Daniel Dal'Aglio, who also painted the beautiful frescoes that adorn the ceiling. Dance, theater, and classical music performances are still regularly held here, and it's worth checking to see if there's anything playing while you're in town. Otherwise, you can take a guided tour of the theater for CUC$2. It's open Tuesday through Saturday from 9am to 8:30pm, Sunday from 10am to 4pm.

The other main attraction in town is the **Museo Farmacéutico** ⓕ, Calle 83 no. 4951, Plaza de la Libertad (ⓒ **45/204-3179**). Seemingly little has changed here since its founding in 1882 by the French pharmacist Ernesto Troilet. Porcelain jars of potions and elixirs are stacked high in beautiful floor-to-ceiling wood cabinets. The museum is open daily from 10am to 5pm; admission is CUC$2.

At the head of the harbor, close to the downtown center, you'll find a couple of small stretches of beach, where there will almost always be a few locals swimming, fishing, and sunbathing. However, the harbor is quite industrial and I'd highly recommend you head over to Varadero for some much more inviting beaches.

Out on the northern edge of the bay is the **Castillo de San Severino,** Avenida del Muelle. Built in 1734, this small fort served as a line of defense, slave trading post, and long-standing prison. It's been recently restored and is definitely worth a visit, if for nothing other than the great view it offers of Matanzas Bay. The Castillo is open daily from 9am to 5pm; admission is CUC$2.

On the outskirts of the city you'll find the **Cuevas de Bellamar** ⓕ, Finca La Alcancia (ⓒ **45/25-3538**), a cave complex of nearly 3km (1¾ miles) of galleries and passageways, with intricate stalactite and stalagmite formations, indigenous pictographs, and several underground streams and rivers. You can tour the first kilometer or so of caves for CUC$3 per person, including a guide. This section is lit, so no equipment or flashlights are needed. The caves are located 5km (3 miles) southeast of Matanzas, off a well-marked access road. They are open daily from 9am to 6pm.

## WHERE TO STAY & DINE

There are currently no hotels catering to travelers in Matanzas, and no restaurants worthy of a hearty recommendation. Most folks—and I recommend this—come here on day trips from either Havana or Varadero. In a pinch, there's the rather run-down **Hotel Louvre,** located right on the Parque de la Libertad (ⓒ **45/24-4074**), which will accept foreigners, as well as a handful of *casas particulares* congregated around the downtown center. The most happening spot in town is the **Café Atenas,** Calle Magdalena and Calle Milanés, Plaza de la Vigía (ⓒ **45/25-3493**), a simple 24-hour cafe and snack bar, with an easygoing ambience and comfortable seating both indoors and on a cool outdoor patio.

## MATANZAS AFTER DARK

Matanzas is a quiet city without much nightlife, with one notable exception. The younger sister to the venerable Tropicana in Havana, **Tropicana Matanzas** ⓕⓕ, Autopista del Sur Km 4.5 (ⓒ **45/26-5380** or 45/26-5555), seeks to provide the classic Tropicana cabaret experience to the thousands of tourists who come to Cuba and never venture far from Varadero. I don't exactly know why they didn't just build it in Varadero, but whatever the reason, it is located on the outskirts of Matanzas, about a 20-minute drive from Varadero. Like its famous sibling, this is a large open-air theater offering extravagant nightly performances. The artistic direction is shared between the two venues, and the show here is quite up to snuff. Scores of scantily clad showgirls and dancers seamlessly weave together a series of different numbers. Costumes are tight fitting, garish, and often feature gravity-defying headgear. The spectacle covers most of the bases of popular Cuban show and dance music, from *son* to bolero to *danzón* to salsa, with a bit of Afro-Cuban religious music thrown into the mix. The 90-minute show starts around 10:30pm each night. After the show, you can continue the celebration by dancing the night away at the adjoining dance club.

Virtually every hotel and tour agency in Varadero can book you a night at the Tropicana Matanzas; some packages include dinner and a bottle of rum at the cabaret, others are just for the show (including a complimentary cuba libre). Almost all include round-trip transportation. Tickets for the show should cost CUC$35. Packages with transportation and dinner cost around CUC$80. Since it's open-air, rain cancels the function. You'll get your money back on a rainout, but there are no guaranteed reservations for a makeup show.

## 2 Varadero ✶✶

140km (87 miles) E of Havana; 40km (25 miles) NE of Matanzas

Varadero is Cuba's most renowned and popular beach destination. Varadero is the common name for the entire length of the Hicacos Peninsula. The peninsula, which takes its name from a local spiny cactus, is 21km (13 miles) long, with a nearly continuous broad band of fine white sand fronting a clear blue sea. Backed by mangroves and the calm waters of Cárdenas Bay, it is less than a mile wide at its widest point. Large resort hotels line a large percentage of the entire length of this peninsula.

Home to indigenous populations and a base camp for itinerant Taíno and Carib fishermen, Varadero was largely ignored throughout the Spanish colonial period. While it was first developed as a summer retreat by some 10 families from Cárdenas in 1887, its real potential as a tourist destination was realized relatively late. The first hotel was built here in 1910, and U.S. industrial magnate Irénée Dupont built his Xanadú Mansion here in 1926. A small cadre of celebrities and gangsters followed, including Al Capone. Still, at the time of the Revolution, there were only three hotels in Varadero. Today, there are over 55, with more than 15,000 rooms . . . and construction continues.

## ESSENTIALS
### GETTING THERE

**BY PLANE** The **Juan Gualberto Gómez International Airport** (© **45/61-3036;** airport code VRA) is located 18km (11 miles) west of Varadero, roughly midway between Matanzas and Varadero. Direct charter and scheduled commercial flights arrive in Varadero from Montreal, Toronto, Vancouver, Cancún, Nassau, Montego Bay, and most major European hubs. The major international carriers servicing Varadero include **Air Canada, Air Transat, British Airways, Condor, Martinair, Mexicana, KLM,** and **LTU.** A taxi between the airport and Varadero should cost CUC$20 to CUC$30.

**Cubana, Aerogaviota,** and **AeroCaribbean** have regularly scheduled commuter flights between Varadero and most other major tourist destinations in Cuba. Fares range between CUC$40 and CUC$100 each way. While there is regular commuter service between Havana and Varadero and it's only a 30-minute flight, I still don't think it's a smart option. Once you add up the time and cost involved in getting to the airport, checking in, flying, claiming baggage, and grabbing a taxi to your hotel, it hardly seems worthwhile, given that it's an easy and enjoyable 2-hour drive.

**BY BUS** **Víazul** (© **7/881-1413** in Havana, or 45/61-4886 in Varadero; www.viazul.com) has three buses daily for Varadero, leaving Havana at 8am, noon, and 6pm. The trip takes 3 hours to Varadero. The return buses for Havana leave Varadero at 8am, 11:40am, and 6pm. The fare is CUC$11 each way. Víazul also has a daily bus from Varadero to Trinidad leaving at 7:30am. The trip takes around 6 hours and costs

# Varadero

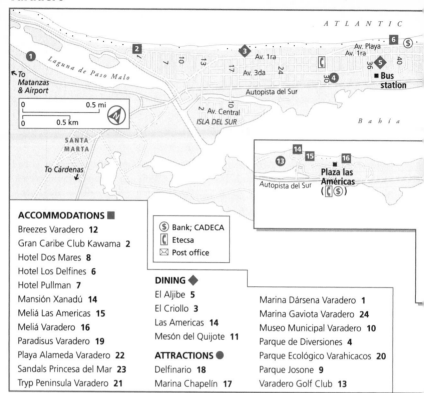

ATLANTIC

Av. Playa
Av. 1ra
Av. 1ra
Av. 3da
To
Matanzas
& Airport
Laguna de Paso Malo
Autopista del Sur
Bus
station

0   0.5 mi
0   0.5 km

SANTA
MARTA

Av. Central
ISLA DEL SUR

Bahía

To Cárdenas

Plaza las
Américas
Autopista del Sur

**ACCOMMODATIONS** ■
Breezes Varadero **12**
Gran Caribe Club Kawama **2**
Hotel Dos Mares **8**
Hotel Los Delfines **6**
Hotel Pullman **7**
Mansión Xanadú **14**
Meliá Las Americas **15**
Meliá Varadero **16**
Paradisus Varadero **19**
Playa Alameda Varadero **22**
Sandals Princesa del Mar **23**
Tryp Peninsula Varadero **21**

$ Bank; CADECA
Etecsa
✉ Post office

**DINING** ◆
El Aljibe **5**
El Criollo **3**
Las Americas **14**
Mesón del Quijote **11**

**ATTRACTIONS** ●
Delfinario **18**
Marina Chapelín **17**

Marina Dársena Varadero **1**
Marina Gaviota Varadero **24**
Museo Municipal Varadero **10**
Parque de Diversiones **4**
Parque Ecológico Varahicacos **20**
Parque Josone **9**
Varadero Golf Club **13**

CUC$22 each way. The return bus leaves Trinidad at 2:30pm. The **bus station** is located at Calle 36 and the Autopista del Sur. The ticket booth here also can book onward travel to Trinidad and various destinations to the east.

In addition, most of the hotels and tour agencies in Havana can arrange transportation on periodic transfer buses to Varadero, including a pickup at your hotel. In a similar vein, all of the hotels and tour agencies in Varadero can book you on similar buses heading back to the hotels and airport in Havana. The fare is around CUC$25 to CUC$35 each way.

**BY CAR**   Varadero is connected to Havana by a modern four-lane coastal highway, the Vía Blanca, that begins as you exit the tunnel connecting Habana Vieja with Habana del Este. It's a straightforward, scenic drive to Matanzas. The highway then threads its way through Matanzas, generally hugging close to the coast, and continues on the final 40km (25 miles) to Varadero. About 13km (8 miles) outside of Varadero there's a tollbooth (CUC$2 per vehicle each way). The trip generally takes around 2 hours.

## GETTING AROUND

Taxis are plentiful and relatively inexpensive in Varadero. A trip from one end of the peninsula to the other shouldn't cost more than CUC$8 to CUC$12, and most trips are just CUC$4 to CUC$6. If by some chance you can't flag one down, or there's

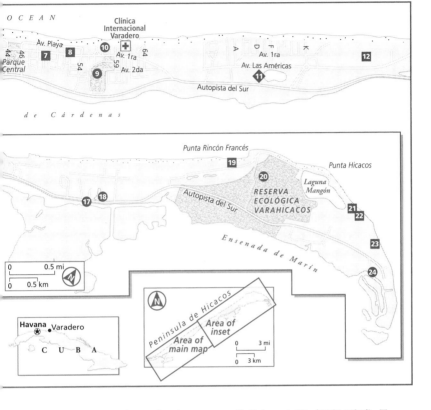

none hanging around your hotel, you can call **Cubataxi** (© 45/61-3674), **Transgaviota** (© 45/61-2620), or **Transtur** (© 45/61-2133). As in Havana, open-air **Coco Taxis** are also available for between CUC$8 and CUC$12 per hour.

A couple of separate companies have **open-air tourist trains** and **buses** that ply a loop from one end of Varadero to the other. You will see them circulating nearly constantly. It generally costs between CUC$2 and CUC$4 to hop on one of these for any distance. A day pass, with unlimited use of a specific line, costs between CUC$8 and CUC$15.

One of the best ways to get around Varadero is on a **scooter.** Rental agencies abound. Most rent modern, easy-to-use Vespa-style scooters for around CUC$10 to CUC$15 per hour, and CUC$30 to CUC$45 per day.

There are a host of **car-rental agencies** at the airport and around town. Virtually every hotel either has a car-rental desk, or can easily facilitate renting a car. The official contacts for the various agencies are **Cubacar** (© 45/66-7326), **Havanautos** (© 45/61-3733), **Transtur** (© 45/66-7715), and **Vía Rent A Car** (© 45/61-9001).

## ORIENTATION
**Cubatur, Cubanacán,** and **Havanatur** have offices all over Varadero and in the hotels. **CADECA** (© 45/66-7870) and **Banco Financiero Internacional** (© 45/66-7002)

> *Moments*  **Take a Detour**
>
> At 110m (361 ft.), the **Bacuanayagua Bridge** ⚓ is the highest in Cuba. It spans the beautiful Yumurí Valley. Most tourist buses will stop here for a quick break and photo opportunity, and if you are driving, you'll probably want to do so as well. A rugged side road leads off the highway if you want to explore this largely undeveloped valley. The bridge is located 7km (4¼ miles) west of Matanzas, right on the Vía Blanca en route from Havana to Matanzas and Varadero.

both have a handful of branches around Varadero, including at the airport and the Plaza las Américas mall. The **Clínica Internacional Varadero,** Avenida 1 and Calle 61 (© **45/66-8611**), is open 24 hours for emergency and routine medical care. They also have a 24-hour pharmacy.

## WHAT TO SEE & DO

This is a beach destination and, aside from lying on the beach and swimming in the clear waters of the Straits of Florida, most of the attractions and activities here are either found or conducted on or under the water. The nicest spot to visit in "downtown" Varadero is the **Parque Josone** ⚓, Avenida 1 between Calles 55 and 58 (© **45/66-7228**), a beautifully maintained little city park with cool shady grounds and gardens. There are paths winding around and over little lakes with fountains, several restaurants and food stands, and the park is dotted with gazebos and park benches. The park is open daily from 8am to midnight, and admission is CUC$2.

If it's raining, or you just can't take any more sunbathing, active adventures, or shopping, you could take a quick visit to the **Museo Municipal Varadero,** Calle 57 and Avenida de la Playa (© **45/61-3189**). Open daily from 10am to 4pm (CUC$1), the exhibits inside are of less interest and appeal than the beautiful old building that houses the collection. The perfectly maintained blue-and-white, two-story wooden building, with its gingerbread trim and red-tile roof, is a tribute to colonial Caribbean architecture and design.

If you've got kids, you might want to head to the **Parque de Diversiones,** Avenida 1 and Calle 30 (© **45/61-2431**), a small amusement park that has the types of rides and booths you might find at a county fair.

Near the Marina Chapelín, on the ocean side of the road, you'll find the **Delfinario,** Autopista Sur Km 12 (© **45/66-8031**). Open daily from 8am to 5pm, this attraction offers a 40-minute show by trained dolphins about four times daily. Admission is CUC$12 per person; it's CUC$5 extra to take photos, and CUC$55 for a 15-minute swimming session with the dolphins. While this place is highly touted by agencies and hotel tour desks, I personally find this type of attraction—and this one in particular—to be depressing and on the cruel side.

If you want a bird's-eye view of things, the **Centro Internacional de Deportes Aéreos,** Vía Blanca Km 15, off a little side road across from the Marina Dársena (© **45/66-7256**), offers parachute jumps and ultralight flights. Tandem parachuting costs CUC$150 per person. Ultralight flights run CUC$30 to CUC$300, depending on the length of time. You can also usually find ultralight flights leaving from different spots up and down the beach.

The **Varadero Golf Club** ⚓ (© **45/66-8442;** www.varaderogolfclub.com) features a lovely little resort course, with plenty of water, few trees, and almost no rough. There are beautiful views of Cárdenas Bay from most holes. Greens fees run CUC$77 for a round, plus an extra CUC$33 for a cart. Club rental will cost you CUC$15. You can play a twilight round of 9 holes for just CUC$30 after 5:30pm.

A large swath of the eastern end of the peninsula is protected as the **Parque Ecológico Varahicacos (Varadero Ecological Park;** C **45/61-3594)**. There are some gentle paths through the scrub forests here, and you can visit a series of small caves, some of which contain ancient indigenous pictographs. The park is actually broken up into two sections, with a small area close to the major hotel district, and the larger section farther east. Both are open daily from 9am to 5pm; admission is CUC$2.

## FUN ON & UNDER THE WATER

If you want to take out a Hobie Cat, windsurfer, paddle boat, or sea kayak, chances are your hotel will have them, either as part of your all-inclusive package or for hire. If not, simply hit the beach and walk a bit until you find some for rent.

There are three main marinas on Varadero: **Marina Gaviota Varadero,** at the far eastern end of the Autopista del Sur (C **45/66-7755**); **Marina Dársena Varadero,** at the western end of the Autopista del Sur (C **45/66-8060**); and Cubanacán's **Marina Chapelín,** Autopista del Sur Km 12.5 (C **45/66-7550;** www.cubanacan.cu). At any of these you can charter a sailboat, organize a fishing excursion, or arrange to go scuba diving. Moreover, the tour agencies and hotel activities desks can book any of these activities.

**FISHING**    The waters off of Varadero offer the opportunity to go deep-sea fishing for marlin, sailfish, tuna, snapper, dolphin, and more. Rates run between CUC$100 and CUC$400 for a half-day or CUC$400 and CUC$1,600 for a full day, depending on the size of the boat and the number of fishermen.

Fishing trips can also be arranged to the **Ciénaga de Zapata** area in southern Matanzas province. See "The Zapata Peninsula & Playa Girón," later in this chapter, for more details.

**SAILING**    There are many charter sailboat options available at each of the marinas mentioned above. The most popular outfit, **Jolly Roger** ⚓, Marina Chapelín (C **45/ 66-8444**), has a fleet of broad and comfortable catamarans. A range of cruise options is available, from half-day and full-day cruises to simple sunset sails. Many of the sailing adventures make stops at the small, uninhabited cays off the eastern coast of the peninsula; these trips can include lunch on one of the cays, as well as snorkel adventures on close-in coral reefs. Rates are CUC$30 to CUC$40 for a half-day, CUC$65 to CUC$90 for a full day.

There's a host of other boating options. Each of the marinas offers **converted fishing boats** and **barges** that take folks on tours ranging from snorkel trips to nearby cays and tours of Cárdenas Bay. Many of these boats are outfitted with a bar or two and carry either a live band or loud, recorded dance music. Some boats head out for a floating sunset party or a raging dance party under the moonlight.

If you feel like playing pirate, take a cruise on **El Galeón** (C **45/66-8886**), a modern re-creation of a square-rigger. The crew dresses in pirate garb, and the cruises range from 3-hour daytime sails to quick sunset cruises to all-night open-bar bashes. Prices range from CUC$25 to CUC$55 per person.

**Varasub,** Avenida de la Playa between Calles 36 and 37 (C **45/66-7027**), is an interesting take on the traditional glass-bottom boat. With view ports all along the steep side of its hull, it creates the impression of being in a submarine, although there's no diving. The 1½-hour tour leaves six times daily and takes you over areas of sandy sea bottom and some coral reef. The trip costs CUC$25 per person.

The popular **Jungle Tour** ✯, Marina Chapelín (✆ **45/66-8440**), is a 2-hour tour on small sit-on-top motorized watercraft, or Aqua-Rays, through the canals and mangroves backing the peninsula. A guide leads a caravan of the small craft, which can hold up to two adults. This tour leaves roughly every hour, with a total of eight departures daily; it's CUC$39 per person. You can book this trip at any hotel or tour agency in town.

**SCUBA DIVING & SNORKELING**   Most of the large hotels on Varadero either have their own dive operation or can arrange scuba and snorkel trips around the area. Scuba diving and snorkeling off of Varadero is generally pretty good, although rarely spectacular. There's an assortment of sites, including a black coral bed, various coral reefs, and an old wreck. True aficionados prefer the diving found in southern Matanzas province off the coasts of Playa Larga and Playa Girón. It's about a 90-minute drive from Varadero, and all of the dive operations here offer trips to these dive spots, an especially good choice if a norther is blowing and the waters are rough off of Varadero. If your hotel can't arrange this for you, contact **Scuba Cuba Barracuda,** Calle 59 and Avenida 1 (✆ **45/61-3481**).

One popular scuba and snorkel site worth mentioning is the **Cueva de Saturno,** located outside of Matanzas, on the road to the airport. This large cave houses a large deep *cenote* (pool) that can be explored with a mask and snorkel, or with full tank gear. The cave is open daily from 9am to 6pm; admission is CUC$3, plus CUC$5 for snorkeling. Most agencies and hotels can arrange a half-day trip for CUC$25 to CUC$30 per person, or CUC$45 to CUC$60 for a one-tank dive. There's even a 24-hour cafeteria on-site.

## ORGANIZED TOURS

All of the tour agencies in town offer a host of guided excursions to the principal cities and attractions within striking distance of Varadero. Options include half-day tours to Matanzas or Cárdenas, day tours to Havana or Trinidad, and overnight excursions to Cayo Largo, Cayo Coco, or Santiago de Cuba. Rates run around CUC$25 to CUC$40 for half-day tours and CUC$45 to CUC$90 for full-day excursions. Overnight trips vary widely depending on the means of travel (air or bus) and the type of accommodations. Your best bet to book any of these is to check at your hotel, or contact **Cubanacán,** Calle 24, between Avenida 1 and Avenida de la Playa (✆ **45/66-7835;** www.cubanacan.cu); **Gaviota Tours,** Calle 56 and Avenida de la Playa (✆ **45/61-1844**); or **Havanatur,** Av. de la Playa 3606, between Calles 36 and 37 (✆ **45/66-7589**).

**Gran Car,** Calle 26, between Avenidas 1 and 2 (✆ **45/61-4759**), offers a day trip spent tooling around Havana in classic cars. The trip includes a tour of Habana Vieja, with stops at the four major plazas, as well as a visit to a cigar factory, the Plaza de la Revolución, and a stop at the Hotel Nacional. This tour leaves Varadero daily at 8am and costs CUC$80, including lunch.

## SHOPPING

You'll not want for souvenir stands, T-shirt outlets, and overpriced hotel gift shops here, but good shopping options are limited. There are several outdoor arts and crafts markets around Varadero; the best, **Artesanía,** is at Avenida 1 and Calle 12. The **Plaza de los Artesanos** at Avenida 1 between Calles 44 and 46 is also good. **ARTex** has stores at each of these sites, as well as at Avenida 1 and Calle 35. At each you will find a broad (and standard) collection of trinkets, T-shirts, musical instruments, posters, and CDs.

**Taller de Cerámica Artística,** Avenida 1 between Calles 59 and 60 (© **45/66-2703**), is a working pottery studio and factory with a broad selection of finished goods for sale. Some are quite good and quite expensive. The work ranges from abstract and artistic to purely functional. You can usually watch a potter at work while shopping. In addition to a good selection of Cuban paintings and sculpture, **Galería de Arte Sol y Mar,** Avenida 1 between Calles 34 and 35 (© **45/61-3153**), carries some musical instruments and a decent selection of CDs.

For a dense collection and variety of shops, a decent destination is **Plaza las Américas,** Autopista Sur Km 11 (© **45/66-8181**). Options at this modern minimall and convention center range from high-end clothing boutiques to T-shirt shops, with everything from an art gallery to a music shop thrown in. There's even a small supermarket here, and several restaurants.

If you want cigars, the best-stocked shop in Varadero is **Casa de los Tabacos,** Avenida 1 and Calle 38 (© **45/61-4719**). They usually have one or two rollers making fresh stogies here, and there's a comfortable bar for enjoying their wares, while sipping a glass of rum or a strong espresso.

## WHERE TO STAY
### HOTELS

Most of the hotels on Varadero operate as all-inclusive resorts. Still, there are a few options for those who just want a room and breakfast, and the ability to pick and choose where they eat the rest of their meals. You can also purchase a day pass at many of the local all-inclusive options for between CUC$30 and CUC$80, which will allow you access to the resort's facilities, including their buffet meals and endless drinks.

### Expensive

**Mansión Xanadú** 🏌  The former mansion of Irénée DuPont de Nemours is now a high-end boutique hotel. While this is certainly the most distinctive boutique hotel in Varadero, its 1930s grandeur feels a little dated, and almost dingy in some instances. Moreover, the fact that it is such a tourist attraction takes away any real sense of intimacy and isolation. Still, you will be staying in what was once, and in some respects still is, the most luxurious address in town. The rooms are all spacious and meticulously maintained, with sparkling marble floors, Persian rugs, and antique furnishings. Most have narrow, intricately carved wooden balconies overlooking the ocean. However, be careful, a couple of the rooms only come with narrow full-size beds. All of the rooms are on the second floor, and on the third floor there's a lively bar with good views all around. The hotel is right on the Varadero golf course and guests enjoy unlimited privileges at the course. The hotel sits on a rocky outcropping a hundred or so yards from the beach, and while there's no pool or beach right here, guests can use both at the neighboring Meliá Las Américas.

Carretera Las Américas Km 8.5, Varadero. © **45/66-8482.** Fax 45/66-8481. www.varaderogolfclub.com. 6 units. CUC$150 double. Rates include full breakfast and unlimited greens fees. MC, V. **Amenities:** Restaurant; 2 bars; concierge; tour and activities desk; salon; 24-hr. room service; massage; babysitting; laundry service; dry cleaning. *In room:* A/C, TV, minibar, safe.

### Inexpensive

In 1998 the Cuban government outlawed casas particulares in Varadero, wanting to steer all business to the official state-owned hotels and resorts. The ban is still in effect, although there are folks who will rent out rooms in private houses. Still, since it's not legal, they don't like to advertise or call attention to themselves. If you really want to find a casa particular, ask a taxi driver or tour guide, or walk around the area between Calle 13 and Calle 64 in the heart of Varadero's downtown, and you should be able to find something.

**Hotel Dos Mares**   Run as a training school, this little hotel is housed in an old, three-story Spanish-style stucco building. The rooms here are a tad dark, but they are clean and comfortable. However, they come with big wall-mounted air-conditioning units that can be a bit loud. The good news is that you're centrally located and the beach is less than 90m (300 ft.) away. Moreover, since it's a training hotel, the service is usually pretty good.

Calle 53, between Avs. 1 and Playa, Varadero. Ⓒ/fax **45/61-2702**. www.islazul.cu. 34 units. CUC$47–CUC$60 double. Rates include breakfast. MC, V. **Amenities:** Restaurant; bar; tour desk; laundry service. *In room:* A/C, TV, safe.

**Hotel Pullman** *Value*   This old hotel probably has the most personality of any budget hotel in Varadero. It's located across the street from the beach, in a three-story stone building, with some pretty decorative masonry work crowning it. The compact rooms are all clean and well maintained, and the hotel is well located in the heart of Varadero's little town. There's a charming patio restaurant here, and a couple of the rooms even share a nice veranda.

Av. 1, between Calles 49 and 50, Varadero. Ⓒ/fax **45/61-2702**. www.islazul.cu. 15 units. CUC$47–CUC$60 double. Rates include breakfast. MC, V. **Amenities:** Restaurant; bar; tour desk; laundry service. *In room:* A/C, TV, safe.

## ALL-INCLUSIVE RESORTS

There are literally scores of large, all-inclusive resorts in Varadero. I've listed my top choices. In addition to the places listed below, good options include the **Barceló Marina Palace** (Ⓒ 45/61-1086; www.barcelo.com), **Brisas del Caribe** (Ⓒ 45/66-8030; www.hotelescubanacan.com), **Coralia Club Playa de Oro** (Ⓒ 45/66-8566; www.accor.com), **Iberostar Varadero** (Ⓒ 45/66-9999; www.iberostar.com), **Royal Sandals Hicacos Resort & Spa** (Ⓒ 800/545-8283 in the U.S. or Canada, or 45/66-8844; www.sandalshicacos.com), and **Sol Palmeras** (Ⓒ 45/66-7009; www.solmelia cuba.com).

The rack rates listed below are the utter high end of what you might pay. In fact, you should expect to pay much less. Most of these hotels sell the bulk of their rooms to wholesalers and package tour operators, who in turn sell quite attractive all-inclusive packages. Competition is fierce, and it pays to shop around. However, as this is a segment of the industry that depends on volume, some resorts try to make up for the low prices by skimping on food and drink quality, and upkeep. So be careful: If you come across a resort not listed here at a deal that seems too good to be true . . . it just might be.

*Note:* Since so much of the market here is European, many of the large resort hotels operate either exclusively on 220-volt electricity or a combination of 110-volt and 220-volt electricity. Although most hotels will lend you an adapter and converter, it's best to check beforehand and come with the proper adapters, if necessary.

### Very Expensive

**Meliá Las Américas** *✷✷*   Located just off the clubhouse and first tee of Cuba's only 18-hole golf course, this upscale hotel should be a golfer's top choice, although guests at any hotel in town can play the course. The Meliá Las Americas is a large resort hotel, with the bulk of its rooms in the five-story main building, as well as one-and two-bedroom bungalows in a series of smaller buildings spread around some lush gardens amid a maze of swimming pools and ponds. Still, the rooms in the main building are all large, spacious, and well maintained, and I'd choose them over the bungalows, if nothing else for their comfortable balconies with views over either the Caribbean Sea or the golf course and bay. The hotel sits right on a small section of beautiful beach, smack-dab between the golf course and the Plaza las Américas mall and convention center, making it one of the more strategically located hotels in Varadero. This hotel was recently reserved for adults only, and converted to an all-inclusive. They've also recently inaugurated two new dining options—a sushi restaurant and high-end steakhouse.

Autopista del Sur, Carretera Las Morlas, Varadero. ✆ **45/66-7600.** Fax 45/66-7625. www.solmeliacuba.com. 290 units. CUC$340–CUC$365 double; CUC$480 suite; CUC$530 Grand or Presidential suite. Rates are all-inclusive. Rates lower in off season; higher during peak periods. MC, V. Children under 18 not allowed. **Amenities:** 7 restaurants; snack bar; 4 bars; lounge; dance club; 4 outdoor pools; 18-hole golf course; small, well-equipped health club and spa; nonmotorized watersports equipment; concierge; tour and activities desk; car-rental desk; salon; 24-hr. room service; massage; laundry service; dry cleaning. *In room:* A/C, TV, minibar, hair dryer, safe.

**Meliá Varadero** ✿✿    This large hotel sits on a rocky outcrop with small sections of fine beach on either side. Seven pyramid-like spokes extend off a massive and lush central atrium lobby. Rooms are large, contemporary, and comfortable. All come with either a king-size or two twin beds and a private balcony with a couple of sitting chairs. While the bathrooms aren't exactly small, some are a bit narrow, with the toilet and bidet a bit close to the tub and shower. Almost all of the rooms have some view of the water; the further out on each spoke you go, the better the view. The hotel is located just off the Plaza las Américas complex, so between the in-house arcade and the neighboring mall, you'll have a wealth of shopping and dining options.

Autopista del Sur Km 7, Carretera Las Morlas, Varadero. ✆ **45/66-7013.** Fax 45/66-7012. www.solmeliacuba.com. 462 units. CUC$305–CUC$340 double; CUC$445 suite. Rates are all-inclusive. Children under 3 stay free in parent's room; children 3–12 stay for half off. Rates lower in off season; higher during peak periods. MC, V. **Amenities:** 5 restaurants; snack bar; 3 bars; lounge; outdoor nightly show; large outdoor pool; 2 lit outdoor tennis courts; small gym; watersports equipment; bikes; children's center and programs; game room; concierge; tour and activities desk; car-rental desk; shopping arcade; salon; 24-hr. room service; massage; babysitting; laundry service; dry cleaning. *In room:* A/C, TV, minibar, coffeemaker, hair dryer, safe.

**Paradisus Varadero** ✿✿✿    Located at the eastern end of the peninsula on a gorgeous and remote section of beach, this is the Sol Meliá chain's fanciest hotel in Varadero and part of its top-end brand Paradisus. Most rooms here are large junior suites with sunken sitting rooms that let out onto either a private terrace or balcony. The walls are done in a light pastel faux-faded wash, with hand-painted murals. Only a small percentage of the rooms here has an ocean view. A few suites have separate sitting areas and extra half-bathrooms. About half the units come with king-size beds, and the rest come with two twins. The one Garden Villa, however, is almost a world to itself, set on a point of land just above the ocean, with separate dining and sitting rooms, a full kitchen, a private lap pool and Jacuzzi, and a private three-story tower with a fabulous lookout. Service is attentive and friendly.

Autopista del Sur Km 15, Rincón Francés, Varadero. ✆ **45/66-8700.** Fax 45/66-8706. www.solmeliacuba.com. 422 units. CUC$450–CUC$575 double; CUC$610 suite; CUC$1,500 Garden Villa. Rates are all-inclusive. Children under 3 stay free in parent's room; children 3–12 stay for half off. Rates lower in off season; higher during peak periods. MC, V. **Amenities:** 4 restaurants; snack bar; 4 bars; lounge; cabaret; large outdoor free-form pool; 3 lit outdoor tennis courts; small, well-equipped health club and spa; extensive watersports equipment; children's center and programs;

game room; bikes; concierge; tour and activities desk; car-rental desk; 24-hr. room service; massage; babysitting; laundry service; dry cleaning; nonsmoking rooms. *In room:* A/C, TV, fridge, coffeemaker, hair dryer, safe.

**Sandals Princesa del Mar** ⭐⭐   This impressive resort property went a couple of years looking for a steady management contract, but they seem to have found that with the excellent and experienced Sandals chain. The rooms, facilities, and grounds here are all quite grand. There's a sort of modern plantation styling throughout. The best rooms here are the Concierge and Presidential suites, which almost qualify as a hotel within the hotel. All of these come with ocean or lagoon views, private Jacuzzis, and a host of other perks, including full room service 24 hours per day. The rest of the rooms are very nice as well, and can all be considered junior suites, at the very least. The decor is subdued and elegant. The resort has a wide range of dining options, activities, facilities, and entertainment programs.

Autopista del Sur, Carretera Las Morlas, Varadero. © **45/66-7200.** Fax 45/66-7201. www.sandalsprincesadelmar. com. 434 units. CUC$330–CUC$370 double; CUC$400–CUC$600 Concierge or Presidential suite. Rates are all-inclusive. Rates lower in off season; higher during peak periods. MC, V. Couples only; children under 18 not allowed. **Amenities:** 7 restaurants; snack bar; 5 bars; lounge; dance club; 2 large outdoor pools; 4 lit outdoor tennis courts; well-equipped health club and spa; watersports equipment; tour and activities desk; car-rental desk; salon; massage; laundry service; dry cleaning. *In room:* A/C, TV, minibar, hair dryer, coffeemaker, safe.

### Expensive

**Breezes Varadero** ⭐   This adults-only resort is part of the Superclubs chain, and sits on a beautiful section of beach near the western edge of the Varadero Golf Club. All rooms are either junior suites or suites; my favorites are the juniors housed in a separate three-story building on the eastern edge of the property. Some of the third-floor units here have excellent ocean views, but others are a bit too close to the popular dance club. I'd avoid the Tropical Suites, which have relatively uninviting separate sitting rooms. Overall there's an exuberant party vibe here. The expansive grounds are filled with tropical trees and flowers, most of which are marked. All watersports, including one daily scuba dive, are included.

Carretera Las Américas Km 3, Varadero. © **45/66-7030.** Fax 45/66-7005. www.superclubs.com. 270 units. CUC$238–CUC$568 double. Rates are all-inclusive. MC, V. Children under 14 not allowed. **Amenities:** 4 restaurants; snack bar; 8 bars; lounge; dance club; outdoor nightly show; large outdoor pool; 2 lit outdoor tennis courts; small gym; watersports equipment; bikes; tour and activities desk; car-rental desk; massage; laundry service; dry cleaning. *In room:* A/C, TV, fridge, coffeemaker, hair dryer, safe.

**Playa Alameda Varadero** ⭐⭐⭐   Located on the eastern edge of the peninsula, this is one of the newer and more upscale resorts in Varadero. The rooms here are housed in a series of three-story units spread around the resort's expansive grounds. The rooms are all junior suites, with two twin beds or one king-size bed, separate sitting areas, separate tub and shower units, walk-in closets, and either a balcony or terrace. Thick iron headboards, marble-topped tables, and large Italian tiles lend the rooms a fair amount of class. A broad pedestrian-only avenue leads from the reception and restaurant area to the large complex of pools, which includes a well-designed children's pool and play area. The resort's dance club and nightly cabaret theater are well removed from the rooms, so noise isn't a problem at night. There's an inviting bar down by the beach with a lookout tower.

Autopista del Sur Km 18, Punta Hicacos, Varadero. © **45/66-8822.** Fax 45/66-8833. www.gaviota-grupo.com. 391 units. CUC$260–CUC$440 double. Rates are all-inclusive. MC, V. **Amenities:** 4 restaurants; snack bar; 3 bars; lounge; dance club; large outdoor pool; 2 lit outdoor tennis courts; small, well-equipped health club; Jacuzzi; sauna; nonmotorized watersports equipment; bikes; children's programs; game room; concierge; tour and activities desk; car-rental

> **Tips** **Stake Your Claim**
>
> At some resorts, finding a chaise longue under a shady palapa is cutthroat. You will either have to stake out your turf early, or find a local worker who, for a small gratuity, will save you a prime spot.

desk; salon; massage; babysitting; laundry service; dry cleaning; 4 nonsmoking rooms. *In room:* A/C, TV, minibar, hair dryer, safe.

**Tryp Península Varadero** ★★★ (Kids)    This is my first choice for a family resort in Varadero. The facilities are top-notch, and the children's area is a standout, with a large children's pool area that's a virtual amusement park, with several fountains, an island castle, a crocodile slide, and a spouting whale. There's a separate area for toddlers, a large game room, and a beached galleon that serves as the jungle gym playground area. The rooms, housed in a series of three-story Key West–style buildings, are all junior suites, with rattan furniture and a host of amenities. Most have two twin beds, although a small percentage have king-size beds, and there are five suites. The whole complex is tied together by a series of wooden decks and bridges and concrete walkways passing over ponds and skirting a large lagoon. Located toward the far eastern end of the peninsula, the hotel is on a beautiful stretch of beach.

Autopista del Sur Km 17.5, Punta Hicacos, Varadero. (✆ **45/66-8800.** Fax 45/66-8805. www.solmeliacuba.com. 591 units. CUC$325 double; CUC$450 suite. Rates are all-inclusive. Children under 3 stay free in parent's room; children 3–12 stay for half off. Rates lower in off season; higher during peak periods. MC, V. **Amenities:** 4 restaurants; snack bar; 3 bars; lounge; cabaret; 3 outdoor pools; 2 lit outdoor tennis courts; small, well-equipped health club and spa; extensive watersports equipment; bikes; children's center and programs; game room; concierge; tour and activities desk; car-rental desk; small business center; salon; massage; babysitting; laundry service; dry cleaning. *In room:* A/C, TV, fridge, coffeemaker, hair dryer, safe.

## Moderate

**Gran Caribe Club Kawama** (Value    One of the oldest resort hotels in Varadero has, over time, become one of the best midrange all-inclusive options in the area. Built between 1930 and 1947, the original resort still stands as a series of two-story stone buildings built around a central courtyard. Inside, the rooms are totally modern, with attractive furnishings and good-size balconies, although no ocean views. The massive limestone blocks used to construct the buildings are polished and buffed on the inside, giving the interiors a cool and comforting feel. A host of newer units have less character, but are equally comfortable, and most are either right on or just off, the beach; some of these do have an ocean view. Part of the price savings here are reflected in the tiny 13-inch television sets and the rather insipid buffet meals. The resort is located on a nice stretch of beach toward the western end of the peninsula.

Calle O, Reparto Kawama, Varadero. (✆ **45/61-4416.** Fax 45/66-7334. www.grancaribe.cu. 235 units. CUC$90–CUC$220 double. Rates are all-inclusive. MC, V. **Amenities:** 3 restaurants; snack bar; 2 bars; lounge; dance club; nightly show; outdoor pool; small exercise room; sauna; nonmotorized watersports equipment; bike rental; tour and activities desk; car-rental desk; massage; laundry service; dry cleaning. *In room:* A/C, TV, fridge, safe.

**Hotel Los Delfines** (Value    This is a pretty little hotel complex and a pretty decent value. The beachfront resort was built in several stages, with a midsize swimming pool at its center. Rooms are standard issue, but they're clean, spacious, and comfortable, and everything is well maintained. For some reason, this 100-plus-room resort almost feels intimate, especially when compared to all the monster all-inclusives that are the rule of the roost here. The restaurant and buffet meals are unspectacular, but the hotel is in the heart of Varadero's downtown, close to plenty of dining and entertainment options, and since the rates are so low, you may not mind splurging for a meal out.

Av. de la Playa and Calle 39, Varadero. ℰ 45/66-7720. Fax 45/66-7727. www.islazul.cu. 103 units. CUC$100–CUC$120 double. Rates are all-inclusive. MC, V. **Amenities:** 2 restaurants; 2 bars; outdoor pool and children's pool; tour and activities desk; laundry service; dry cleaning. *In room:* A/C, TV, safe.

## WHERE TO DINE

Since most hotels in Varadero are all-inclusive, most folks take the majority of their meals at their hotel. However, it's natural to want some variety when faced with a week or more at one resort, even if it features several dining options.

There are a few restaurants in the **Camino del Mar** complex at Avenida Camino del Mar, between Calles 10 and 15. Of these, I recommend **Mi Casita** (ℰ 45/61-3783). The restaurants inside of **Parque Josone** are also dependable if unspectacular options; of these, the little lakeside Italian restaurant **Dante** (ℰ 45/66-7738) is my top choice. Finally, another long-standing and popular local restaurant, with wonderfully eclectic decor and decent *criolla* cooking is **Antiguedades** (ℰ 45/66-7329) at Avenida 1 and Calle 59.

### EXPENSIVE

**Las Americas** ℱ INTERNATIONAL    Arguably the most elegant restaurant in town is found, without any doubt, at the most exclusive address in town, occupying a couple of ground floor rooms and the oceanfront veranda of the Mansión Xanadú. The best seats are those on this veranda, at heavy wooden tables set with heavy china. The food is old school French and Continental fare, adequately done, but no more. Service is semiformal and surprisingly inattentive at times. There's a good, fairly priced wine list. Several hotels offer discount coupons here, so be sure to ask your concierge.

At the Mansión Xanadú, Carretera Las Américas Km 8.5. ℰ 45/66-7388. Reservations required. Main courses CUC$15–CUC$45. MC, V. Daily noon–10:30pm.

### MODERATE

**El Aljibe** ℱ CRIOLLA    While it lacks some of the charm and all of the history of its more famous sibling in Havana, this is still a dependable spot to dine when you tire of the limited options at your all-inclusive resort. The options here are actually limited as well, but the signature slow-roasted chicken is the way to go. As at the original El Aljibe, it is served all-you-can-eat family-style with white rice, black beans, fried plantain, French fries, and salad, accompanied by a delicious sweet-and-sour garlic *mojo* (gravy).

Av. 1 and Calle 36. ℰ 45/61-4019. Reservations recommended. Main courses CUC$9–CUC$28. MC, V. Daily noon–midnight.

**Mesón del Quijote** (Value SPANISH/SEAFOOD    Located on a small hillside between the Autopista and the beach resorts, the dining room of this popular restaurant is in a small building set beside the turret of a three-story imitation medieval castle. There are plenty of windows to enjoy the limited views afforded from its modest perch. I found the paella a bit of a disappointment, but the seafood and lobster are fresh and simply but well prepared. You can opt for the buffet (CUC$7) or order a la carte—I'd go for the latter. If you don't order one of the many lobster entrees, try the fresh fish filet in a caper sauce.

Carretera Las Américas, Reparto La Torre. © 45/66-7796. Reservations recommended. Main courses CUC$5–CUC$26. MC, V. Daily noon–midnight.

## INEXPENSIVE

In addition to the place listed below, **La Vicaria,** Avenida 1 and Calle 38 (© **45/61-4721**), is a good and very popular spot for light, inexpensive bites, in a pleasant open-air setting.

**El Criollo** ✸ CRIOLLA   This popular place is probably your best bet for straight-ahead Cuban cuisine in Varadero. The restaurant is housed in an atmospheric old building that re-creates the vibe of a typical Cuban country home. You'll definitely want a table on the large, open-air veranda under a gently sloping red-tile roof. Simple roast chicken and pork dishes are reasonably priced and well prepared. Even the lobster dishes are a good value here. This restaurant is not to be confused with El Bodegon Criolla, a weak imitation of Havana's signature La Bodeguita del Medio.

Av. 1 and Calle 18. © 45/61-4794. Reservations recommended. Main courses CUC$5–CUC$26. MC, V. Daily noon–midnight.

## VARADERO AFTER DARK

Almost every hotel here has some form of nightly entertainment, usually a Broadway theater review or local cabaret-style show. These can vary from sadly comic to totally professional. Most give way to a dance party. By far the biggest and best cabaret show, the **Tropicana Matanzas** ✸✸, is located about 20 minutes away on the outskirts of Matanzas; see p. 152 for details. Other cabaret options include the **Cabaret Continental** at Varadero Internacional (© **45/66-7038;** cover CUC$25); **The Mambo Club** at Gran Hotel, Carretera Las Morlas Km 14 (© **45/66-8565;** CUC$5); and the **Palacio de La Rumba** at the Hotel Bella Costa, Avenida Las Américas (© **45/66-8210;** CUC$10).

**Habana Café** ✸ in the Sol Club Las Sirenas, Avenida Las Américas and Calle K (© **45/66-8070**), is very similar to the Habana Café in Havana's Meliá Cohiba. The nightly cabaret and review show is top-notch, with a crack band laying down smooth Cuban rhythms. When the show ends, the circular, sunken floor is one of the more happening dance clubs in town. Admission is CUC$12, including your first drink; reservations are recommended.

Perhaps my favorite place for a show is the new **La Comparsita** ✸✸, Calle 60 and Avenida 3 (© **45/66-7415**), which is a lovely open-air space built to re-create the feel of a colonial-era courtyard. There are good sightlines from all the tables here and an excellent nightly show highlighting a wide-range of Cuban music and dance styles. Admission is CUC$5. They also have a happening bar upstairs.

**Cueva del Pirata,** Autopista Sur Km 11 (© **45/66-7751**), is a midsize cave that has been converted into a popular cabaret and dance club. Lights create eerie shadows among the stalactites. The nightly cabaret show begins around 10:30pm and has a pronounced Afro-Cuban emphasis. It's followed by dancing to either a live band or a DJ. Admission is CUC$5.

The **Casa Blanca Mirador,** atop the Mansión Xanadú (© **45/66-8482**), is a good spot for a quiet drink with a nice view. **Club La Pachanga** in the Hotel Acuazul, Avenida 1 and Calle 13 (© **45/66-7132**), is the most happening spot in the "downtown" area of Varadero, and a good option for getting away from the all-inclusive crowds. Here you're more likely to find independent travelers, and even some Cubans, although the latter will include a fair share of *jineteros* (hustlers). Admission is CUC$2.

## A SIDE TRIP TO CARDENAS

Located 18km (11 miles) southeast of Varadero, Cárdenas is a small, quiet city with beautiful colonial-era architecture and a timeless quality. Horse-drawn carriages and bicycles far outnumber cars on the streets here. Cárdenas is known as Cuba's "Ciudad Bandera" (Flag City), as it was here, in 1850, that the national flag was first flown. Because it's so close to Varadero, Cárdenas is popular—we'd say almost overrun—with day tours.

The city center is quite compact, and you can easily see most of the sights in a couple of hours strolling around. There are several small squares and parks in Cárdenas. The diminutive **Parque Colón,** Avenida Céspedes, between Calles 8 and 9, features an important statue of Christopher Columbus dating from 1862. Fronting it is the beautiful **Catedral de la Concepción Inmaculada** ✪, which is famous for its stained glass. In another main park, **Parque Echeverría,** sits the **Museo Casa Natal José Antonio Echeverría,** Calle Jenes 560, between Calzada and Coronel Verdugo (✆ 45/52-4145; admission CUC$1). This beautiful old home features tributes to various independence fighters and revolutionary heroes, including the museum's namesake, a murdered revolutionary student hero who was born here in 1932. The town's main market, **Plaza Molokoff,** Calle 12 and Avenida 3, is housed in an interesting two-story L-shaped iron building, topped with a large and high ornate dome. Out by the water's edge is the **Arrechabala Rum Factory,** where the brand Havana Club was born and where present-day Varadero and Buccanero rums are made. Tours of the factory are given daily between 9am and 4pm; admission is CUC$2.

Cárdenas is the birthplace and home of Elián Gonzalez, the little boy who became the center of an international custody dispute in late 1999 when he washed up on the shores off Miami after his mother died at sea. While you're unlikely to see Elián, almost anyone in town will gladly point out his humble home on one of the main avenues. There's always at least one guard out front. The **Museo a la Batalla de Ideas (Museum of the Ideological Battle),** Calle Vives 523 at the corner of Coronel Verdugo (✆ 45/52-3990), is housed in a beautifully restored old building, and features exhibits honoring the tragic child celebrity, alongside numerous other displays documenting Cuba's revolutionary battles. The centerpiece here is a statue of a young Cuban boy, dressed in the uniform of the Young Pioneers, tossing away a Superman doll. The museum is housed in a beautifully restored old firehouse. Admission is CUC$2, and another CUC$2 for a guided tour. It will cost you an additional CUC$5 to take photos and CUC$15 to take videos.

Very few travelers stay in Cárdenas, and there are currently no hotels or official casas particulares accepting foreign tourists in the city, although that may change. There's regular public bus service between Varadero and Cárdenas, but it's geared primarily to commuting Cuban workers. A taxi from Varadero to Cárdenas should cost around CUC$15.

## 3 The Zapata Peninsula & Playa Girón ✪

202km (125 miles) SE of Havana; 194km (120 miles) S of Varadero

The Zapata Peninsula juts off the southern coast of Matanzas province. The peninsula itself is almost entirely uninhabited; most of it is protected as part of the **Parque Nacional Ciénaga de Zapata (Zapata Swamp National Park)** ✪, a haven for birdwatchers and naturalists. The eastern edge of the peninsula is defined by the Bahía de

---

## *Moments*  Battle Marks

As you walk along the beaches of Playa Girón and Playa Larga, and drive the coastal road connecting them, you will notice tall concrete monuments marking the spots where a Cuban soldier died in the fighting. You will also notice many low-lying concrete machine gun nests, with their open rears for easy entry and thin front slits for wide-angle aiming. Feel free to try one on for size and a unique photo opportunity.

---

Cochinos (Bay of Pigs), the site of the failed 1961 U.S.-backed invasion of Cuba. The Bay of Pigs, and Playa Girón in particular, is a sort of national shrine to this stunning David-over-Goliath victory. Just off the shore, all along the Bay of Pigs and toward the east, the coast drops off steeply for a thousand feet or more, making this a true haven for scuba divers.

*Note:* Bring plenty of mosquito repellent. Since this is an area of vast swampland, mosquitoes can be fierce, particularly if there's no wind. I personally also pack lightweight long-sleeved shirts and pants.

## ESSENTIALS

**GETTING THERE**    The nearest **airport** is in Varadero; see "Varadero," earlier in this chapter, for complete details. There is no dependable **public transportation** to this area, although most tour agencies in Havana and Varadero offer trips here.

The Zapata Peninsula and the beaches of Playa Larga and Playa Girón are connected to the Autopista Nacional—and each other—by a well-maintained two-lane highway. If you're coming **by car,** get off the highway at the exit for Australia and Jagüey Grande, and head south for 17km (11 miles) to Boca de Guamá. From there it's another 13km (8 miles) to Playa Larga, and 34km (27 miles) to Playa Girón.

**GETTING AROUND**    Public transportation is very sporadic and unreliable in this area. Most visitors either have their own rental car or come on a guided tour. Both of the hotels listed below have car- and scooter-rental desks, so if you somehow end up here without wheels, you can easily rent some to get around. Local taxis also can be hired at either of the hotels listed below.

**ORIENTATION**    Heading south from the highway, you come first to Boca de Guamá. Continuing on, the road hits the head of the bay at Playa Larga and then follows the coast, in a southeasterly direction to Playa Girón. There are small communities in both Playa Larga and Playa Girón, but aside from the resorts, restaurants, and attractions, there's little of interest to travelers.

## WHAT TO SEE & DO

Most organized tours and independent travelers make a stop at **Boca de Guamá** (© **45/91-3224**), a contrived tourist attraction, built as a re-creation of a Native American village on a series of small islands at the center of the large **Laguna del Tesoro (Treasure Lake).** Boca de Guamá was severely affected by Hurricane Michelle, although it has been almost entirely rebuilt by now. Boat tours of the lake and canals (CUC$10) are available. On one small island in the middle of the lake, you'll be able to walk among 32 life-size figures of Taíno Indians sculpted by the late Cuban artist Rita Longa. You can also lunch or dine on crocodile meat at **La Boca,** a decent little tourist restaurant here. You can even stay at the **Guamá Hotel** (℅ **45/91-5515;** www.hotelescubanacan.com; CUC$47 double) here. The hotel features a series of individual circular bungalows built on stilts over the lagoons. The rooms themselves are decidedly spartan, but the setting is pleasant. At the entrance to Boca de Guamá, you'll find a roadside minimall of shops and restaurants (which also serve crocodile steaks), and the **Criadero de Cocodrilos (Crocodile Farm; ℅ 45/91-5562).** If you've never seen a crocodile up close, you will be awed by the size, power, and prehistoric aspect of these impressive reptiles. Admission is CUC$5 and includes a brief guided tour, with explanations of the crocodile's natural history and habits. A series of walkways and wooden bridges will carry you past numerous pens and cages of crocs of all ages and sizes. You can't exactly pick out your dinner, but it doesn't take much imagination to figure out where all the crocodile meat is coming from—at least you know it's fresh.

If you go to Playa Girón, it's worth taking a quick tour of the little **Museo Playa Girón.** Two rooms inside this simple building contain a series of photos, relics, and a written history detailing the Bay of Pigs invasion and battles, as well as some local history. A 15-minute documentary video (in Spanish) is shown throughout the day, and outside you can see the wreckage of tanks, heavy artillery, and a downed U.S. plane. The museum is open daily from 8am to 5pm; admission is CUC$2 for adults, free for children and students. Unfortunately, the written explanations are in Spanish only.

## OUTDOOR ACTIVITIES

You'll need a permit to enter the national park. The park station and entrance (℅ **45/ 98-7249**) is located 2km (1½ miles) west of Playa Larga. The permit costs CUC$10 per person, and includes a local guide. The state-run tour center located near the entrance has naturalist and fishing guides familiar with this area. In addition, all of the hotels and tour agencies in the area can arrange bird-watching excursions and fishing trips with local guides, and help you with arranging visits and permits to the national park.

### The Bay of Pigs

On April 16, 1961, an invasion force of 1,400 Cuban exiles, trained and backed by the United States, landed at several beach points along the Bay of Pigs in an ill-fated attempt to overthrow the Castro regime. They were quickly met by Cuban forces, led by Fidel Castro himself, and soon defeated. Fighting lasted less than 72 hours. Though they were entirely trained and supported—and even escorted—by the U.S. military and CIA, the invaders were left to fight on their own. President Kennedy was reluctant to commit any direct U.S. forces to the fight. The lack of air support and several serious tactical blunders contributed to the rout. The battle took the lives of some 160 Cubans and around 120 mercenary fighters. Some 1,195 of the invading troops were captured, and most of them were released 20 months later in a bartered exchange with the U.S. government for food, medical supplies, and hospital equipment. Today, the Bay of Pigs continues to be a source of great pride to Cuba's communist government and supporters, and an equally bitter pill for anti-Castro exiles and opponents.

**BIRD-WATCHING** ✦✦✦   The Zapata Peninsula is probably Cuba's richest bird-watching destination. Some 18 of Cuba's 24 endemic bird species can be spotted here, as well as large flocks of resident waterfowl and seasonal migrants. The Zapata Wren, Zapata Sparrow, and Zapata Rail are just some of the endemic species. Hurricane Michelle flattened much of the forest here, and it's currently much harder to spot some species, including the Bee Hummingbird, which in the past were quite common. Several trails through and around the national park, as well as outings in small boats, are available to birders.

**FISHING** ✦✦✦   Fishing for bass, trout, tilapia, tarpon, permit, bonefish, and the bizarre looking *manjaurí* (alligator gar) is excellent in this area. Prime fishing sites include the saltwater flats and mangroves of **Las Salinas de Brito** on the eastern edge of the peninsula, the **Hatiguanico River** deep within the national park, and the lagoons of **Boca de Guamá**. Rates range from CUC$25 to CUC$50 per person for a simple outing, and from CUC$200 to CUC$500 per day for a boat, guide, tackle, and lunch for up to three people. Ask at your hotel or any tour agency for details.

**SCUBA DIVING** ✦✦   The waters off the coast between Playa Larga and Playa Girón offer some of Cuba's best scuba diving. A steep wall, rich in coral and sponges, plunges to depths of over 300m (980 ft.). There are numerous caves to explore and visibility is typically excellent. In many cases, the drop-off is within 90 to 180m (300–600 ft.) of shore. The dive shops at both of the hotels here typically load people and gear into small buses or trucks and drive to one of numerous put-in points all along the shoreline. Both of the resorts listed below have full-service dive facilities on-site and offer a full menu of multiday dive packages. If you just want to try a dive or two, it should cost you around CUC$30 to CUC$40 for a one-tank dive, and around CUC$45 to CUC$65 for a two-tank dive, including equipment.

## WHERE TO STAY & DINE

Most visitors to this area take all their meals at their hotels. The few available alternatives include the restaurants at Boca de Guamá, and a couple of simple state-run roadside restaurants geared to tourists between Playa Larga and Playa Girón. The best of these is the **Cueva de los Peces,** Carretera Playa Larga a Girón Km 18 (✆ **45/98-4183**), with good seafood and *criolla* cuisine.

**Hotel Playa Girón**   Originally designed and built as a residential community, this place is now a midsize all-inclusive resort. The rooms are housed in a series of one-, two-, and three-bedroom ranch bungalows and duplexes. Most have a separate sitting area, although sometimes the unit's only television is in the sitting room, so you can write off watching TV in bed. Most have a fridge and sink in a sort of kitchenette area. Recent remodeling has greatly improved the furnishings and decor here. Still, this place is really only for hard-core divers or bird-watchers, because if you're looking for a week of sun and fun at an all-inclusive, Cuba has many much more appealing options.

The best feature is the resort's **Caleta Buena** ✦, a recreation area based around a series of natural pools in the coral and rock, located about 8km (5 miles) from the hotel. There's a grill restaurant, some sailboats, paddle boats, and windsurfers, as well as hammocks and shady palapas for kicking back, and use of the facilities here is part of the package.

Playa Girón, Montemar Natural Park, Matanzas province. ✆ 45/98-4110. Fax 45/98-4117. 287 units. www.hotelescubanacan.com. CUC$45–CUC$70 double. Rates include breakfast buffet. MC, V. **Amenities:** 4 restaurants; 6 bars;

dance club; 2 outdoor pools; nonmotorized watersports equipment; bikes; moped rental; game room; tour desk; car-rental desk; laundry service. *In room:* A/C, TV, safe.

**Hotel Playa Larga** The entire complex here feels rather depressing, despite ongoing efforts to spruce things up. The problem, as far as I'm concerned is the inherently desultory Soviet-era architecture. Some of the rooms are quite cramped, with worn, soft beds and noisy air-conditioning units. Other rooms are more spacious, although very precious few have queen-size beds (most just have two full beds). The small patch of beach here is acceptable, but it doesn't compare to the premier beaches found elsewhere in Cuba. This place is best for serious divers and bird-watchers, and even they would probably do better at the Hotel Playa Girón.

Playa Larga, Montemar Natural Park, Matanzas province. ✆/fax **45/98-7294**. www.hotelescubanacan.com. 68 units. CUC$45–CUC$60 double. Rates include breakfast. MC, V. **Amenities:** 2 restaurants; 2 bars; outdoor pool; 2 outdoor tennis courts; limited watersports equipment rental; moped rental; game room; tour desk; car-rental desk; laundry service. *In room:* A/C, TV, safe.

# 7

# Trinidad & Central Cuba

*by Eliot Greenspan & Neil E. Schlecht*

Central Cuba is an area rich in both historical and natural attractions. It is home to several wonderful colonial-era cities, as well as isolated and pristine beaches. Heading east from Matanzas into Cuba's central heartland you first hit Villa Clara province, which is devoted largely to sugar cane, citrus, and tobacco farming and cattle ranching. The provincial capital, **Santa Clara,** a lively university town, is often called "Che Guevara's City" and features an impressive monument and plaza dedicated to the fallen revolutionary. To the north of Santa Clara lie the tiny and well-preserved colonial-era city of **Remedios,** and the jaw-droppingly beautiful beach resort destination of **la Cayería del Norte.**

Abutting Villa Clara to the south is Cienfuegos province. The city of **Cienfuegos** is affectionately known as *La Perla del Sur* (The Southern Pearl). Cienfuegos is a busy port city with a pretty, colonial-era center and the country's second-longest seaside promenade, or *Malecón.* Cienfuegos is connected to Trinidad by a pretty coastal highway, and is definitely worth a visit on a loop trip around the region.

The province of Sancti Spíritus is the only one in Cuba to count two of the original seven *villas* (towns) in Cuba among its offerings. The colonial gem **Trinidad,** tucked in the southwest corner of the province, is the highlight of a visit to the central section of the country, or all of Cuba for that matter. The provincial capital, **Sancti Spíritus,** isn't a great deal larger than Trinidad, and though it is more ramshackle and rough around the edges, lacking Trinidad's remarkable collection of perfectly preserved architecture, it is still worth a visit to see its couple of colonial highlights.

## 1 Santa Clara ⊛

270km (168 miles) E of Havana

Santa Clara was founded in 1689 by settlers from Remedios looking for a site inland that would be less vulnerable to pirate attack. Heading east from Havana, Santa Clara marks the start of Cuba's central region. The city is strategically located on the island's spine, right on the main highway and train lines, and is the capital of Villa Clara province. Santa Clara is home to one of Cuba's principal colleges, la Universidad Central de las Villas (Las Villas Central University), and played an important role in both the independence and revolutionary wars. Thanks to the latter, Santa Clara is known as Che Guevara's city. Today, it is also home to several industrial factories, the legacy of Guevara's tenure as Minister of Industry and his special relation with this city. In addition to being an interesting destination in its own right, Santa Clara serves as the gateway to the colonial treasure of **Remedios** ⊛⊛⊛ and the up-and-coming beaches of **la Cayería del Norte (the Northern Cays)** ⊛⊛⊛.

## ESSENTIALS
### GETTING THERE
**BY PLANE**    Santa Clara's **Abel Santamaría Airport** (℗ 42/20-9138; airport code SNU) accepts both national and international flights. The latter are predominantly international charter flights bringing tourists on package tours to la Cayería del Norte.

**BY BUS**    Víazul (℗ 7/881-1413 in Havana, or 42/29-2114 in Santa Clara; www. viazul.com) travels daily to Santa Clara on the Havana–Santiago de Cuba and Varadero-Trinidad lines. From Havana, the bus departs at 9:30am, 3pm, and 10pm, arriving at 1:10pm, 6:45pm, and 1:45am, respectively (CUC$20); from Santiago, departure times are 9am, 3:15pm, and 10pm, arriving at 10pm, 3:35am, and 8:10am (CUC$36); and from Varadero, the bus leaves at 7:30am and arrives at 10:45pm (CUC$12). The main **bus station** is located on the western edge of town, on the Carretera Central, between Independencia and Oquindo.

**BY CAR**    Santa Clara sits right on the Carretera Central, and just off the Autopista Nacional, 270km (168 miles) east of Havana. It's a straight shot on the highway and generally takes about 3 hours.

**BY TRAIN**    Santa Clara is on Cuba's main train line. It is serviced several times a day on commuter lines connecting Havana with Holguín and Santiago de Cuba. Schedules change, so your best bet is to check at the station (℗ 7/862-1920 or 7/861-4259 in Havana). Rates run CUC$8 to CUC$15, depending on the train and class you choose. The Santa Clara **train station** (℗ 42/20-2895) is located on the northern end of town, at the end of Calle Luis Esteves.

### GETTING AROUND
Taxis are plentiful and inexpensive in Santa Clara. If you can't find one on the street or if your hotel can't hook you up, call **Cubataxi** (℗ 42/22-2555) or **Taxi OK** (℗ 42/20-2186).

Car-rental agencies in Santa Clara include **Havanautos** (℗ 42/20-8928), **Transtur** (℗ 42/21-8177), and **Micar** (℗ 42/20-4570).

### ORIENTATION
**Parque Vidal,** also called Plaza Mayor, is Santa Clara's center. In addition to having the greatest concentration of colonial-era buildings, most of the city's banks, businesses, and tourism operators are based within a 2-block radius of the park. The city is ringed by a beltway, or *Circunvalación.*

**Cubanacán,** Maceo 453, between Central and Caridad (℗ 42/22-6169), **Cubatur,** Marta Abreu 10, between Máximo Gómez y Villuendas (℗ 42/20-8980), and **Havantur,** Máximo Gómez, between Independencia and Alfredo Barreras (℗ 42/20-4001), can supply you with information and arrange a wide range of tour and onward travel options. There are a couple of banks and a **CADECA** branch near the Parque Vidal.

For medical emergencies, head to the **Policlínico** (℗ 42/20-2244) on Serafín García Oeste, between Alemán and the Carretera Central. There's a 24-hour **pharmacy** in the Hotel Santa Clara Libre at Parque Vidal 6.

## WHAT TO SEE & DO
Santa Clara is a great town to walk around. Thanks to the university here, the city's got a little bit of a typical college-town vibe. The heart of the city is the central **Parque Vidal.** The double-wide streets ringing the park are pedestrian-only and often

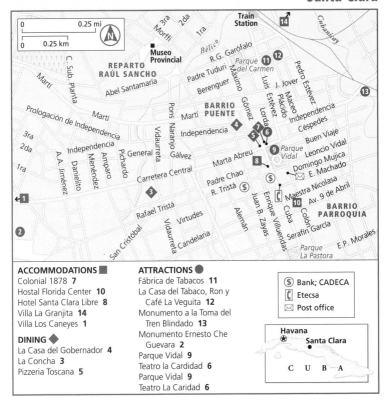

crowded with locals and lovers strolling in leisurely circles. There's a separate 5-block-long pedestrian-only mall (the Bulevar), a block behind the **Teatro La Caridad** (Ⓒ **42/20-5548**), where you'll find a series of shops and restaurants aimed at travelers and dollar-spending Cubans. The active and ornate 19th-century theater, modeled after the Paris Opera, often features concerts and shows, and is worth a quick tour (CUC$1) during the day.

The biggest attraction in town is the **Monumento Ernesto Che Guevara** ☆, Plaza de la Revolución Che Guevara (Ⓒ **42/20-5878**), which features a huge sculpture of the revolutionary hero, overlooking a vast plaza where massive demonstrations are often held. Underneath the statue is a museum with exhibits detailing the life and exploits of "El Che" and a separate mausoleum holding Guevara's remains, as well as tombstones (and some of the remains) of 37 other revolutionary fighters killed alongside Guevara in Bolivia. This place is deeply revered by most Cubans, so don't joke or take it lightly. The monument is located on the western outskirts of the city and is open Tuesday through Sunday from 9am to 4pm. Admission is CUC$3; no cameras or video cameras are allowed.

Another popular revolutionary landmark is the **Monumento a la Toma del Tren Blindado (Armored Train Monument)** at Carretera Camajuani and the train line. It's a small park built around the spot where Che Guevara and his soldiers derailed an

## Che Guevara

Perhaps no one person, not even Fidel Castro, is so clearly representative of the Latin American revolutionary movement in both image and deed as Ernesto "Che" Guevara. In broad terms, Cubans respect and fear Castro, but they love Che Guevara. Fidel gave the Revolution its brains and brawn, but Che gave it sex appeal.

Born June 14, 1928, in Rosario, Argentina, to a middle-class family, he set off on a motorcycle trip through the Americas in 1953, having just graduated with a medical degree. (For a good glimpse into this period of his life, see the 2004 film *The Motorcycle Diaries*). In 1954, he got caught in the crossfire of the CIA-supported overthrow of Guatemala's democratically elected leftist president Jacobo Arbénz. Exiled to Mexico in the aftermath of the coup, he met fellow exile Fidel Alejandro Castro Ruiz. The two hit it off immediately, and soon, Guevara was a principal figure in the Cuban revolutionary struggle.

Despite chronic asthma and an overall weak constitution, Guevara was famous for his gritty work ethic and dogged determination. Guevara led the decisive December 1958 battles to seize Santa Clara, and was later rewarded with several high posts in the new revolutionary government, including Minister of Industry and president of the National Bank. As the story goes, Fidel Castro, in need of someone to head up the National Bank said, "We need a good economist." Hearing him incorrectly, Guevara said, "I'm a good communist." Despite the misunderstanding, he was given the post. However, Guevara soon tired of the bureaucratic life of politics and government, and embarked on a crusade to spread the Revolution and liberate the rest of the world. A falling-out with Castro, never fully clarified, may have also been behind his renewed revolutionary wanderings.

In 1966, after a brief foray in the Congo, Guevara went to Bolivia—namesake of Simón Bolívar, an early Latin American freedom fighter and Pan-American nationalist—and began organizing a guerilla army. However, the United States military and CIA were already on his trail, and on October 8, 1967, Guevara was caught by a unit of the Bolivian army, aided by U.S. "advisors." After consultations with Washington, the injured Guevara was summarily executed in the remote highlands of Bolivia.

armored train during the critical battles for control of Santa Clara in 1958. In addition to the five cars and some sculptures, there's a tiny museum in this pleasant open-air park (CUC$1).

Santa Clara has an excellent **Fábrica de Tabacos** ❦ at Calle Maceo 181 (© **42/20-2211**). The factory occupies a full city block and produces high-quality Montecristo, Partagas, Romeo y Julieta, Punch, and Robaina cigars. It's open Monday through Friday from 7am to noon and 1 to 4pm. A 45-minute guided tour costs CUC$3 per person. Across the street, there's a well-stocked shop, **La Casa del Tabaco, Ron y Café La Veguita** ❦, Maceo 176-A (© **42/20-8952**). The cigar sommelier here, Marilín Morales Bauta, is quite charming and one of the premier experts in the field.

## WHERE TO STAY

In addition to the hotels listed below, Cubanacán's **Villa La Granjita,** Carretera de Maleza Km 2.5 (© **42/21-8190;** www.hotelescubanacan.com), is very similar to Hotel Los Caneyes, and in fact, tour operators use them interchangeably. Still, we find Los Caneyes to be slightly more comfortable and inviting.

There are scores of *casas particulares* (private rooms for rent) in Santa Clara. Most are within a block or two of either the Parque Vidal or the Plaza del Carmen. Recommended casas particulares in Santa Clara include **Casa Saramiento,** Calle Lorda 61, between Calles Independencia and Martí (© **42/20-3510;** www.geocities.com/paseovedado/sarmiento.html); **Casa Noelia Monteagudo,** Calle Síndico 2-A, between Calles Cuba and Colón (© **42/20-2784**); **Casa Laura Gómez,** Calle Bonifacio Martínez 4, between Calles Síndico and Nazareno (© **42/20-3481**); **Casa Orlando García Rodríguez,** Calle Rolando Pardo 7, between Parque Vidal and Maceo (© **42/20-6761**); **Casa Jorge Rodríguez,** Calle Cuba 209, between Calles Serafín García and Morales (© **42/20-2329;** garcrodz@yahoo.com); and **Hostal Florida Center,** Calle Candelaria 56, between Colón and Maceo (© **42/20-8161**).

### MODERATE

**Villa Los Caneyes** ⚓  Built to resemble a Taíno Indian village, this miniresort is the most comfortable option in Santa Clara. Most of the rooms are housed either in large, round six-unit structures or in individual bungalows. All are clean and roomy enough, although some have pretty low ceilings. The nicest rooms by far are in a new two-story "H" block; two of these are actually two-room suites. The grounds are planted with tall trees and flowering plants, and there's good bird-watching all around. The buffet meals are unspectacular, to say the least. This place does a brisk business in tours, so don't be surprised if you're sharing it with a large group or two. Like the Villa La Granjita (see above), it's located about 2km (3 miles) from downtown, so if you're staying here, you can't just wander around Santa Clara at will—you'll either be taking taxis or you'll need your own wheels.

Av. de los Eucaliptos and Circunvalación, Santa Clara. ©/fax **42/21-8140.** www.hotelescubanacan.com. 96 units. CUC$60–CUC$70 double; CUC$90–CUC$120 suite. Rates include buffet breakfast. MC, V. **Amenities:** Restaurant; snack bar; 2 bars; outdoor pool; small health club; game room; tour desk; car-rental desk; salon; massage; laundry service. *In room:* A/C, TV, fridge, safe.

### INEXPENSIVE

**Hotel Santa Clara Libre**  This 10-story hotel fronting Parque Vidal is currently the only true hotel option right in Santa Clara. It's definitely seen better days. Despite its rather desultory condition, it's almost always full. Perhaps that's because the rates are so reasonable. The lone, manually operated elevator is insufficient for demand. The rooms are acceptable, and anything above the fourth floor should give you a good view. The SCL, as it's popularly known, houses the run-down Cine Santa Clara. There's a rooftop bar here that affords good views of Santa Clara, although the high half-walls and grating put in for safety purposes block a good deal of the sightline.

Parque Vidal 6, Santa Clara. © **42/20-7548.** Fax 42/20-2771. www.islazul.cu. 166 units. CUC$29–CUC$36 double. Rates include buffet breakfast. MC, V. **Amenities:** 2 restaurants; 2 bars; dance club; tour desk; car-rental desk; laundry service. *In room:* A/C, TV.

## WHERE TO DINE

Dining options are rather scant and uninteresting in Santa Clara. Most folks end up eating at their hotel, particularly those staying at either Villa Los Canayes or Villa La

Granjita. There's little to recommend right around Parque Vidal, although for a quick and inexpensive bite, the **Pizzería Toscana** and **Colonial 1878,** both on the park, would do in a pinch. In addition to the place listed below, the Palmares-run **La Concha,** on Carretera Central at the corner of Calle Danielito (© **42/21-8124**), is a dependable though unexciting option near the Che Guevara Monument. You might check to see if they're serving dinner at **Hostal Florida Center** (© **42/20-8161**), a popular casa particular that sometimes also functions as a *paladar.*

**La Casa del Gobernador** CRIOLLA    This is probably the best and certainly the most atmospheric restaurant in Santa Clara. Tables are spread around a couple of rooms and an open-air interior courtyard of this old colonial home. The front room lets out on to the street through a series of saloon-style swinging half-doors. The food is standard *criolla* (Creole) fare. Most evenings there's some sort of entertainment, which might range from a small combo or comedian to a full-fledged cabaret-style show.

Calles Zayas and Independencia. © 42/20-2273. Reservations recommended. Main courses CUC$5–CUC$15; lobster CUC$26. MC, V. Daily noon–midnight.

## SANTA CLARA AFTER DARK

The **Bar La Marquesina** ⚡, just off the Teatro La Caridad, is a good bar, and it's open 24-hours daily. It usually draws a mix of college students, locals, and tourists. There's often a small group playing, and if you're lucky, you'll be able to pay in Cuban pesos. With an artsy bohemian vibe, **Club Mejunje** ⚡⚡, Calle Marta Abreu 12, is probably my favorite spot, featuring regular concerts, poetry readings, and theater pieces put on in their brick-walled open-air courtyard.

　　**Bar Club Boulevard,** Independencia 225, between Maceo and Unión (© **42/21-6236**), is the most upscale joint in Santa Clara. This Cubanacán property features live music, the occasional cabaret show, and a popular dance club. **El Sótano** (© **42/20-7548**), in the basement of the Santa Clara Libre, is the other hot dance club in town.

## A SIDE TRIP TO REMEDIOS

The tiny old city of **Remedios** ⚡⚡⚡ is considered one of Cuba's colonial gems. It's located 45km (28 miles) northeast of Santa Clara on a direct two-lane highway. There's not a whole lot to see in Remedios, but that's part of its charm. The small Plaza Martí sits at the colonial center of Remedios, watched over by the beautiful **Iglesia de San Juan Bautista** ⚡⚡, with its stunning baroque altar and celebrated pregnant Madonna.

　　For several weeks at the end of each year, the quiet town of Remedios becomes the site of one of Cuba's great street parties and religious carnivals, **Las Parrandas.** The infectious revelry keeps things lively throughout the holiday season. Things culminate on Christmas Eve in an orgy of drums, floats, and fireworks. The whole thing allegedly began in 1820, when the local priest sent some altar boys out to bang on pots and pans and scare some parishioners into the midnight Advent Masses. It later evolved into a sort of battle of the bands and fireworks between two sections of the small town. Today, the festivities drag out over the weeks leading up to Christmas Eve, and have even spread into neighboring hamlets. Still, Plaza Martí in Remedios is the place to be, and the night to be there is December 24. Be prepared to stay up late, and bring some ear protection. If you're not here near year's end, pop in at the **Museo de las Parrandas,** Calle Máximo Gómez 71, where you can get an idea of the pageantry by examining the small display of photos, costumes, and floats. No visit to Remedios would be complete without at stop at the atmospheric **Café El Louvre** ✻ (© 42/ 39-5639), which is set on a corner facing the town's central plaza and church.

Currently the only hotel option in Remedios is the quaint and modest **Hotel Mascotte**, Máximo Gómez 114, between Calle Margal and Avenida del Río (© 42/39-5144; CUC$43 double), which faces the small central park here. However, there are also various casas particulares located within a few blocks of the central park. Of these, head first to **Casa Angel Matamoros Santos,** Calle Hermanos García 116-A (© 42/ 395-0046); **Casa Rivero Méndez,** Calle Brigadier González 29, between Independencia and José Antonio Peña (© 42/39-5331); or **Hostal el Patio** ✻, Calle José Antonio Peña 72, between Antonio Romero and Hermanos García (© 42/39-5220).

## LA CAYERIA DEL NORTE

About 8km (5 miles) east of Remedios, you'll hit the small coastal town of Caibarién. Just outside of Caibarién you'll come to the toll (CUC$2 each way) for the 45km (28-mile) *pedraplén,* or causeway, that leads out to **la Cayería del Norte** ✻✻✻, a small string of tiny islands, mangrove swamps, and coral reefs with some of the nicest beaches in Cuba.

While the beaches on both Cayo Las Brujas and Cayo Santa María are spectacular, perhaps the premier beaches in this area are **Playa Ensenachos** ✻✻✻ and **Playa Megano** ✻✻✻, both on Cayo Ensenachos. The protected waters here are as crystal clear as you can imagine, and you can usually wade out a couple hundred yards without the water getting much above your waist. However, these once public beaches are now the exclusive domain of guests at the new **Royal Hideaway Ensenachos** (see below). If you want to enjoy them it will cost you CUC$80 for a day pass, which includes lunch and drinks at the resort's restaurants.

Aside from lying on the beach, the hotels listed below offer a wide range of watersports activities, as well as nature tours and bird-watching outings into the mangroves here, and organized tours to Remedios, Santa Clara, and beyond.

In addition to the two resorts listed below, the Spanish chain Meliá was well underway in the construction of it's newest and largest property on these cays, the **Meliá Las Dunas** ✻✻ (© 42/35-0100; www.solmeliacuba.com). This massive mega-resort will open in 2007 and have over 900 rooms. All three of the Meliá properties share the delightful and luxurious new **Aguas Claras Spa.**

### WHERE TO STAY & DINE
#### Expensive
**Meliá Cayo Santa María** ✻✻    This resort is a slight step up from its sister Sol property next door—the whole operation is slightly larger, slightly more luxurious, and slightly more elegant. The rooms, facilities, and setting are wonderful. The rooms themselves are quite spacious, with large wrought-iron furnishings, large, checkerboard tile floors, and private balconies. There is a variety of dining options, of which we recommend the Mediterranean option, and a stream of activities and entertainment options throughout the day and night. The beach in front of the hotel is a long beautiful stretch of soft white sand fronting a turquoise sea. The guests at this hotel can use the facilities at the Sol resort, but not vice versa.

Cayo Santa María, Villa Clara province. © **42/35-0500.** Fax 42/35-0205. www.solmeliacuba.com. 358 units. CUC$260–CUC$280 double; CUC$400 suite. Rates are all-inclusive. Children 3–12 stay for half off; children under 3 stay free in parent's room. Rates lower in off season; higher during peak weeks. MC, V. **Amenities:** 6 restaurants; 4 bars; cabaret; 3 outdoor pools; 2 outdoor tennis courts; well-equipped health club and spa; extensive free watersports equipment; bike rental; children's program; game room; concierge; tour desk; car-rental desk; salon; 24-hr. room service; massage; babysitting; laundry service; nonsmoking rooms. *In room:* A/C, TV, minibar, hair dryer, safe.

**Occidental Royal Hideaway Ensenachos** ★★   This massive new resort has top-notch facilities and virtually total dominion over two of the best beaches on the entire island, the namesake Playa Ensenachos and neighboring Playa Megano. The resort is divided into three sections: the Royal Hideaway, Royal Spa, and Royal Suites. All the rooms are large, modern, and luxurious, with marble floors and a private balcony or porch. Every block of rooms at the resort has its own private concierge. Guests at the Hideaway and Spa areas get to share all the common facilities, restaurants, pools, shops, and spa, whereas those in the Royal Suites section have their own private grounds and some separate facilities. The suites are massive, with kitchen facilities, large living rooms, private outdoor Jacuzzis, and private butlers. The resort's spa facilities are lovely. The elegance and luxury here may just border on being stuffy. The resort only opened in June of 2006, so it's a little early to tell if the food, service, and ambience will live up to its potential.

Cayo Ensenachos, Villa Clara province. ① **7/204-3584** in Havana. Fax 7/204-9227. www.occidental-hoteles.com. 506 units. CUC$250–CUC$370 double; CUC$350–CUC$450 suite. Rates are all-inclusive. Children 3–12 stay for half off; children under 3 stay free in parent's room. MC, V. **Amenities:** 6 restaurants; 4 bars; cabaret; 3 outdoor pools; 2 outdoor tennis courts; well-equipped health club and spa; extensive free watersports equipment; bike rental; children's programs; game room; concierge; tour desk; car-rental desk; salon; 24-hr. room service; massage; babysitting; laundry service; nonsmoking rooms. *In room:* A/C, TV, minibar, hair dryer, safe.

**Sol Cayo Santa María** ★★   Although neighboring resorts have upped the ante some, this is still one of my favorite all-inclusive options in Cuba. The facilities and service are excellent, the location is spectacular, and the place manages to provide a sense of isolation and escape, despite the fact that there are some 300 rooms here. The rooms themselves are quite comfortable, with plenty of space, large windows, modern furnishings, and private balconies. Only a handful of the second-floor units have ocean views, and these are the choice rooms here, obviously. The entire complex is relatively compact and easy to navigate. The beach in front of the hotel is long and almost immediately deserted, just 91m (300 ft.) or so away from the hotel. The large percentage of European and Canadian tourists here has made it a comfortable place for topless and nude bathing.

Cayo Santa María, Villa Clara province. ① **42/35-0200.** Fax 42/35-0505. www.solmeliacuba.com. 300 units. CUC$220–CUC$265 double; CUC$320 suite. Rates are all-inclusive. Children 3–12 stay for half off; children under 3 stay free in parent's room. Rates lower in off season; higher during peak weeks. MC, V. **Amenities:** 4 restaurants; 3 bars; dance club; cabaret; large free-form outdoor pool; 2 outdoor tennis courts; small, well-equipped health club and spa; extensive free watersports equipment; bike rental; children's program; game room; concierge; tour desk; car-rental desk; salon; massage; babysitting; laundry service; nonsmoking rooms. *In room:* A/C, TV, fridge, hair dryer, safe.

### Moderate

**Villa Las Brujas** ★ *Finds*   Perched on a rocky outcrop over the turquoise Caribbean, the individual and duplex villas here are connected by a raised, rugged wooden walkway through scrub and mangrove. At the end of the row of buildings, there's a long stretch of beautiful white-sand beach, which is seldom crowded, as there are so few rooms here. The rooms themselves are spacious and well appointed, with marble bathrooms, and separate sitting areas—making them all like minisuites. All but five have ocean views. Of these, the second-floor units have the best views. The restaurant, El Farallón, serves respectable *criolla* fare and fresh seafood, and there's a fun second-floor lookout above the restaurant. This is one of the few beach resorts in Cuba that has the feel of a boutique hotel.

Cayo Las Brujas, Villa Clara province. © **42/35-0199.** Fax 42/35-0599. brujagav@enet.cu. 25 units. CUC$65–CUC$95 double. MC, V. **Amenities:** Restaurant; bar; limited watersports equipment rental; tour desk; laundry service. *In room:* A/C, TV, stocked minibar, coffeemaker, hair dryer, safe.

## 2 Cienfuegos ✫

256km (159 miles) SE of Havana; 67km (42 miles) S of Santa Clara

Known as *La Perla del Sur* (The Southern Pearl), Cienfuegos is an uncharacteristically calm and inviting port city. Although Columbus visited the deep and protected harbor here on his second voyage, and the Spanish built the Castillo de Jagua in 1745, it wasn't until 1819, when a group of French colonists settled here, that Cienfuegos began to grow and develop. The French influence continued through most of the city's history, particularly throughout the 19th century, when Cienfuegos became a major shipping point for sugar, tobacco, and coffee. As trade with the United States increased, Cienfuegos lost some of its strategic importance to the northern ports of Havana and Matanzas.

Nevertheless, today Cienfuegos is still a busy port, with an assortment of heavy industry and important sugar-producing plantations surrounding it. In fact, the industrial smokestacks, high-tension electrical towers, and an abandoned nuclear plant significantly mar the landscape. However, the historic center and the beautiful bay and harborfront buildings and Malecón make it a wonderful city to explore and enjoy.

## ESSENTIALS
### GETTING THERE

**BY PLANE**    **Aerotaxi, Aerogaviota,** and **AeroCaribbean** all have regular commuter service to the small **Jaime González International Airport** (© **432/55-1328;** airport code CFG) located 5km (3 miles) northeast of downtown. The fare is CUC$42 to CUC$55 one-way from Havana. During the high season, charter flights from Canada and Europe also fly direct to Cienfuegos. A taxi from the airport to downtown should cost between CUC$4 and CUC$6.

**BY BUS**    **Víazul** (© **7/81-1413** in Havana, or 432/51-8114 in Cienfuegos; www.viazul.com) has two daily buses to Cienfuegos (actually an intermediate stop on the Trinidad route) leaving Havana at 8:15am and 1pm, and returning at 9:20am and 4:50pm. Fare is CUC$22 each way. The trip takes about 4 hours. From Cienfuegos to Trinidad, the fare is just CUC$6.50, and the ride around 2½ hours. The **bus station** is located at Calle 49, between Avenidas 56 and 58 (© **432/51-5720**).

**BY CAR**    From Havana, take the Autopista Nacional east. There are several possible turnoffs for Cienfuegos. The first and most popular is at Aguada de Pasajeros. This is marked and will bring you through the towns of Rodas and Abreus, before leading you into Cienfuegos. If you continue farther on the Autopista Nacional, your next turnoff will be at Cartagena. If you are coming from Santa Clara, you can take the turnoff at Ranchuelo, which is a straight shot into Cienfuegos. The trip should take 3½ to 4 hours from Havana.

### GETTING AROUND

**Taxis** are readily available around Cienfuegos. Most rides will cost between CUC$1 and CUC$3. If you can't find one, call **Taxi OK** (© **432/55-1600**). Tourists are technically not supposed to use the common horse-drawn taxis, as they are deemed too rustic and backward for the sophisticated foreigners, but some of the drivers will let you ride. You can either pay them in pesos, or give them a dollar or two. There are also plenty of bicycle-powered cabs and Coco Taxis around town.

Car-rental agencies in Cienfuegos include **Havanautos,** Calle 37 at the corner of Avenida 18, Punta Gorda (© 432/55-1211), and **Transtur** at the Hotel Jagua (© 432/55-1030).

## ORIENTATION

There are two main areas you should be concerned with in Cienfuegos: **Reparto Pueblo Nuevo,** which is the historic center of town and contains the city's central park, Parque José Martí, and other historic buildings; and **Reparto Punta Gorda,** a slightly newer section which heads out on a narrow strip to the southern point of the city, where you'll find the Hotel Jagua and the Palacio del Valle. Calle 37, or Prado, is the main north-south street and runs all the way to the tip of Punta Gorda. For a significant section it runs along the seafront, earning it the moniker the "Malecón" (boardwalk). It is bisected by Avenida 54, an east-west street, also called the "Bulevar," which is pedestrian-only for several blocks between the Parque José Martí and Prado.

The principal tour agencies in town are **Cubanacán,** Av. 54 no. 2903, between Calles 29 and 31, with a desk in the Hotel Unión (© 432/55-1680); and **Havanatur,** Avenida 54 between Calles 29 and 31 (© 432/55-1639). In addition to their main offices listed above, they are represented at or can be booked by most hotels in town.

There's a **Banco Financiero Internacional** at the corner of the Bulevar and Calle 29 (© 432/55-1625), and a **CADECA** branch on Avenida 56 between Calles 33 and 35 (© 432/55-2164). The **Clínica Internacional,** Calle 37 no. 202, between Avenidas 2 and 4, Punta Gorda (© 432/55-1623), is a small modern facility that can handle most emergencies and medical needs, and has a 24-hour pharmacy. The **post office** is located at Avenida 54 between Calles 37 and 35 (© 432/55-1686). There's an **Etecsa** (© 432/51-3046) office at Calle 31 between the Bulevar and Avenida 56, and another at Calle 37 and Avenida 2; both have Internet access and are open 24 hours.

## WHAT TO SEE & DO
### IN TOWN

The **Parque José Martí,** formerly the Plaza de Armas, is the city's hub. It's a broad city park with a gazebo/bandstand at its center and a little Arco de Triunfo (Arc of Triumph) dating from 1902 at its western end. Surrounding the park, you'll find Cienfuegos' most interesting historical buildings. The **Palacio Ferrer** (© 432/51-9722), on one corner here, is the city's Casa de la Cultura. This is a good place to find out if there are any interesting art exhibits or concerts going on while you're in town. You should also check out the view from the rooftop cupola here. On the eastern end of the park you'll find the **Catedral de la Purísima Concepción,** a beautiful neoclassical church finished in 1870. The church features wonderful stained-glass work imported from France. On the north side of the park is the **Teatro Tomás Terry** ✷ (© 432/51-3661). Inaugurated in 1890, the theater has been wonderfully maintained. It has been declared a national monument, and stars such as Enrico Caruso, Sarah Bernhardt, and Ana Pavlova performed here. Check to see if there will be any performances while you're in town; if not, you can tour the facility during the day. Admission is CUC$1 and includes a quick, guided tour. Across the park, on its south side, is the small **Museo Provincial,** which is only of interest to die-hard museum and local-history buffs.

Out on the end of Punta Gorda is the historic old **Palacio del Valle** ✷✷ (© 432/55-1226), an eclectic architectural masterpiece, which covers vast stylistic ground in

# Cienfuegos

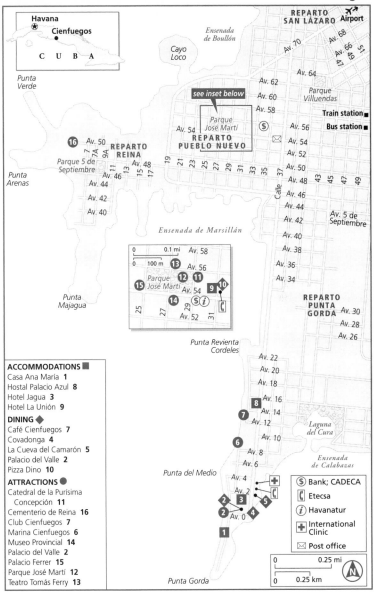

**Havana**
⊛  **Cienfuegos**
●
C U B A

Punta Verde
Punta Arenas
Punta Majagua
Punta del Medio
Punta Gorda

Cayo Loco
Ensenada de Boullón

REPARTO SAN LÁZARO    Airport ✈

Av. 70
Av. 68
Av. 66
Av. 64
Av. 62
Av. 60
Av. 58
Av. 56
Av. 54
Av. 52
Av. 50
Av. 48
Av. 46
Av. 44
Av. 42
Av. 40
Av. 38
Av. 36
Av. 34

Parque Villuendas

Train station ■
Bus station ■

*see inset below*

Parque José Martí

$ 

REPARTO PUEBLO NUEVO

✉

Av. 54

⑯  Av. 50

REPARTO REINA

Parque 5 de Septiembre

7  7A  9A  11  13  15  17  19  21  23  25  27  29  31  33  35  37  43  45  47  49

Calle

Av. 5 de Septiembre

Ensenada de Marsillán

0        0.1 mi
0    100 m
⑬  Av. 58
⑫  ⑪  Av. 56
⑮  Parque José Martí  Av. 54
⑨ ⑩
⑭  $ⓘ  🅲
25  27  29  31
Av. 52

REPARTO PUNTA GORDA  Av. 30
Av. 28
Av. 26

Punta Revienta Cordeles

Av. 22
Av. 20
Av. 18
Av. 16
Av. 14
Av. 12
Av. 10
Av. 8
Av. 6
Av. 4
Av. 2
Av. 0

⑧
⑦
⑥

Laguna del Cura

Ensenada de Calabazas

② ③ ⑤
② ④
①

**ACCOMMODATIONS ■**
Casa Ana María **1**
Hostal Palacio Azul **8**
Hotel Jagua **3**
Hotel La Unión **9**

**DINING ◆**
Café Cienfuegos **7**
Covadonga **4**
La Cueva del Camarón **5**
Palacio del Valle **2**
Pizza Dino **10**

**ATTRACTIONS ●**
Catedral de la Purísima Concepción **11**
Cementerio de Reina **16**
Club Cienfuegos **7**
Marina Cienfuegos **6**
Museo Provincial **14**
Palacio del Valle **2**
Palacio Ferrer **15**
Parque José Martí **12**
Teatro Tomás Ferry **13**

$ Bank; CADECA
🅲 Etecsa
ⓘ Havanatur
✚ International Clinic
✉ Post office

0        0.25 mi
0        0.25 km

its compact floor plan. The centerpiece here is the Salón Comedor (dining room), which dates to 1913 and tries to imitate the intricate Moorish stucco and tile work of Spain's Alhambra. Other rooms are done variously in baroque, neoclassical, and Gothic styling. The whole thing operates as a restaurant (see below), and there's also a wonderful third-floor rooftop balcony bar and lookout.

Cienfuegos has two picturesque cemeteries, featuring elaborate marble headstones, mausoleums, and aboveground burial crypts. The **Cementerio de Reina** ✦ is the older of the two and located on the western extreme of the city beyond the downtown center. The **Cementerio Tomás Acea** is in an eastern suburb of the city and features an elaborate entrance modeled after the Parthenon in Greece.

## ON THE OUTSKIRTS OF TOWN

Popular tours from Cienfuegos include visits to the **Castillo de Jagua** (© **432/9-6402;** admission CUC$1), which is located on the western flank of the narrow entrance to the harbor. Built between 1738 and 1745, the little fort sits on a hill above the quaint fishing village of Perché. Although the moat is dry, you still enter the castle by crossing the wooden drawbridge. Inside there are some basic museum-like exhibits and a mediocre state-run restaurant. You reach the castle either by driving to the Hotel Pasacaballos and taking the constant little ferry across (CUC$1), or via an organized tour out of Cienfuegos.

The **Jardín Botánico Soledad** ✦, Calle Central 136, Pepito Tey, Cienfuegos (© **432/54-5334**), was begun by U.S. sugar magnate Edwin Atkins in 1900, and taken over by Harvard University in 1919. With over 2,000 species of plants covering some 90 hectares (222 acres), it is the largest and most extensive botanical garden in Cuba. The grounds are beautiful to walk around, and there's usually good bird-watching here, although everything tends to be overgrown and unkempt, and markings are sorely lacking. The gardens are located 17km (11 miles) east of downtown, via the road to Trinidad. The garden is open daily from 8am to 4pm; admission costs CUC$3 for adults, CUC$1 for children.

Near Playa Rancho Luna is the new **Delfinario (Dolphin Show;** © **432/54-8120**). Captive trained dolphins and sea lions perform several times daily here. Although the amphitheater around a penned-in saltwater lagoon is spiffy, we find these types of shows and facilities depressing. The main pool and side pens here are particularly small and shallow. This place is open Tuesday through Sunday from 9am to 5:30pm, and has a reasonably priced little restaurant. Admission is CUC$5 for adults, CUC$3 for children. It will cost you an extra CUC$1 to take photos, CUC$2 to shoot video, and CUC$3 to get a kiss with a dolphin. A 15- to 20-minute swimming session with a dolphin costs CUC$50.

## ON & BELOW THE WATER

While Cienfuegos sits on a large and beautiful protected bay, the best (and really the only) beach is located 17km (11 miles) away at **Playa Rancho Luna.** The beach here is a long expanse of white sand, although the sand isn't quite as fine and silky as that found at some of Cuba's more famous beaches.

**Marina Cienfuegos,** Calle 35 between Avenidas 6 and 8, Punta Gorda (© **432/51-5230** or 432/55-1241), is your one-stop shop for all nautical needs. Here you can charter a sailboat or sport-fishing excursion; book a cruise around the harbor; or rent a jet ski, Hobie Cat, or windsurfer. Similar services are offered at the neighboring **Cienfuegos Yacht Club,** Calle 35 between Avenidas 8 and 12 (© **432/55-1275**), which is part of the **Club Cienfuegos** entertainment complex. This place even has a small patch of

## Beny Moré

Maximiliano Bartolomé Moré, better known as Beny Moré and perhaps most descriptively dubbed "El Bárbaro del Ritmo" (The Rhythm Barbarian), is Cienfuegos' pride and joy. Born in the nearby hamlet of Santa Isabel de las Lajas on August 24, 1919, Moré was probably the greatest Cuban singer and bandleader of his time. He sang and composed in a variety of genres, from mambo to *son* to cha-cha-chá. Tall and thin, with a velvet-smooth voice, Moré was the epitome of the debonair Cuban bandleader of the '40s and '50s. Although he never enjoyed the overseas success of Xavier Cugat or Pérez Prado, in Cuba, Beny Moré is considered the king.

sand with a little swimming area in front of it; some locals and tourists use it as a place to sunbathe and cool off. Several international regattas, fishing tournaments, and speedboat races are held in Cienfuegos each year. Check with the marinas or your hotel for details. You can book scuba-diving trips out of the **Faro Luna Diving Center** (© 432/54-8040) out at Hotel Faro Luna (see below). Between December and February, this is actually a pretty decent place to spot a giant whale shark.

## SHOPPING

The best shop in town is the **Galería Maroya,** Av. 54 no. 2506, between Calles 25 and 27, located on the southern flank of the Parque José Martí, next to the Palatino Bar. This place features a broad selection of Cuban arts and crafts, with a decent representation of local works. There's an excellent cigar shop, **Casa del Habano El Embajador,** at Avenida 37 between 33 and 35. Aside from this, there's an **ARTex** shop on Calle 35 between Avenidas 16 and 18 in Punta Gorda, and another right on the Bulevar (Av. 54 between 37 and 27). Each stocks a selection of typical souvenirs, and they usually have a good selection of CDs, including some by Beny Moré.

## WHERE TO STAY
### IN CIENFUEGOS
#### Expensive
**Hotel La Unión** ★★ (Finds)    This hotel, housed in a marvelously restored colonial mansion right on the Bulevar a block off of the Parque José Martí, is one of the nicest boutique hotels in the country. The standard rooms could use a little more elbowroom, so you might consider an upgrade to one of the 10 junior suites, which are quite spacious. The neoclassical furnishings are elegant, and the service is attentive. The inviting pool here is located in an interior courtyard, with a fragment of an old arched brick wall and a couple of sculpted lions standing guard over it. The open-air central courtyard bar is another great space to hang out and relax, as is their beautiful rooftop bar. The main restaurant, 1849, is merely acceptable, with uninspired buffets and a limited a la carte menu.

Av. 54 (corner of Calle 31), Cienfuegos. © 432/55-1020. Fax 432/55-1685. www.hotelescubanacan.com. 49 units. CUC$90 double; CUC$100–CUC$110 junior suite; CUC$170 suite. MC, V. **Amenities:** Restaurant; snack bar; 2 bars; outdoor pool; small exercise room; sauna; Jacuzzi; concierge; tour desk; car-rental desk; limited room service; in-room massage; laundry service. *In room:* A/C, TV, fridge, hair dryer, safe.

## Moderate

**Hotel Jagua** *Finds* *Value*   Following a complete remodeling, this hotel has fully recovered from the effects of Hurricane Michelle and is quite comfortable. The seven-story hotel is located out on the end of Punta Gorda, just across from the Palacio del Valle. The modern rooms are spacious, comfortable, cool, and bright, with a large sliding-glass door to let in light, white tile floors, and plenty of amenities. Those on the higher floors of the main building offer wonderful views over the city and harbor from private balconies. Only 12 of the rooms come with king-size beds; the rest have two twin beds. There's a large rectangular pool at the center of this complex, and a popular bar located on a small floating dock in the bay.

Calle 37 no. 1, Prado, Punta Gorda. ⓒ 432/55-1003. Fax 432/55-1245. www.grancaribe.cu. 149 units. CUC$55–CUC$75 double. MC, V. **Amenities:** 2 restaurants; 2 bars; cabaret; outdoor pool and children's pool; watersports equipment rental; tour desk; car-rental desk; in-room massage; laundry service. *In room:* A/C, TV, fridge, hair dryer, safe.

## Inexpensive

Cienfuegos has scores of good casa particular options. You'll find no shortage of *jineteros* (hustlers) offering to show you a room. You'll find the greatest concentration of casas particulares all along the Prado (Av. 37), as well as surrounding the Parque José Martí and on Punta Gorda. In addition to the place listed below, dependable and clean choices include **Casa Amistad,** Av. 56 no. 2927, between Calles 29 and 31 (ⓒ **432/51-6143**); **Casa Mercy,** Av. 50 no. 3911, between Calles 39 and 41 (ⓒ **432/51-8320**); **Casa Piñeiro,** Calle 41 no. 1402, between Avenidas 14 and 16, Punta Gorda (ⓒ **432/51-3808**); **Casa Aida & Ulises,** Av. 14 no. 4308A, between Calles 41 and 43, Punta Gorda (ⓒ **432/51-8116**); and **Vista al Mar,** Calle 37 no. 210, between Avenidas 2 and 4, Punta Gorda (ⓒ **432/51-8378;** gertrudis_fernandez@yahoo.es).

**Casa Ana María** *Finds*   This old colonial home is located right on the water, out on Punta Gorda near the Hotel Jagua. You get ocean views from each of the two rooms here, and there's a wonderful shared courtyard which also opens on out to the bay. Host Ana María Font D'Escoubet will prepare filling meals for reasonable rates, and can help arrange tours and activities around Cienfuegos.

Calle 35 no. 20, Punta Gorda. ⓒ 432/51-3269. 2 units. CUC$20–CUC$30 double. Rate includes breakfast. No credit cards. *In room:* No phone.

**Hostal Palacio Azul** *Finds* *Value*   This newly restored waterfront building is an excellent value, offering clean and comfortable rooms just off the *Malecón,* out near the tip of Punta Gorda. Rooms have high ceilings, antique-style tiled floors, and large bathrooms. A grand marble staircase leads up to the second floor, where you'll find my favorite room, "Dalia," a corner unit with a view of the Club Cienfuegos, the harbor, and the nightly sunset. All but one room, "Mariposa," comes with a private little balcony. When we last visited, there were plans of opening up a rooftop bar.

Calle 37 no. 1201, between Avs. 12 and 14, Prado, Punta Gorda. ⓒ 432/55-5828. Fax 432/55-1245. www.hotelescubanacan.com. 7 units. CUC$45–CUC$55 double. Rate includes breakfast. MC, V. **Amenities:** Restaurants; bar; tour desk; 24-hr. room service; laundry service. *In room:* A/C, TV, fridge, safe.

## NEAR CIENFUEGOS

In addition to the moderately priced hotel listed below, **Hotel Pasacaballos,** Carretera de Rancho Luna Km 22 (ⓒ **43/54-8013**), is a dour option catering to both Cubans and foreign budget travelers. The only true beach hotel close to Cienfuegos is **Hotel Rancho Luna** (ⓒ **43/54-8012;** www.hotelescubanacan.com); however, this is a rather mediocre option catering to package tour groups of folks who must be unaware that they have scores of better options all over Cuba. Still, if you want to go swimming for a few hours or the day, the beach here will certainly do.

**Hotel Faro Luna** ✦   This small hotel appeals primarily to scuba divers on multiday dive packages. There's a well-equipped dive center here, and scores of great dive sites offshore. The rooms are fairly comfortable, albeit spartan, and most even have an ocean view. Room nos. 209 and 210 have spacious private terraces overlooking the sea. A nice stretch of white-sand beach is about 180m (600 ft.) away. It's a little bit removed from downtown to serve as a base for exploring Cienfuegos, although if you've got a rental car and you want to mix some beach time with your city fun, this is an option.

Carretera Pasacaballo Km 18, Cienfuegos. ✆ **432/54-8034.** Fax 432/54-8062. 41 units. CUC$55–CUC$70 double. MC, V. **Amenities:** Restaurant; 2 bars; outdoor pool; watersports equipment rental; tour desk; car-rental desk; in-room massage; laundry service. *In room:* A/C, TV, fridge, safe.

## WHERE TO DINE

In addition to the places listed below, you can get good pizza and pastas at **Pizza Dino,** Calle 29 between Avenidas 54 and 56 (✆ **432/51-2020**). You could also try **Covadonga** (✆ **432/51-6949**), which is located out on Punta Gorda, next to La Cueva del Camarón. This place is sometimes referred to as "La Paella," after its signature dish.

**Café Cienfuegos** ✦ *Finds* CONTINENTAL/SEAFOOD   This is the most refined dining to be had in Cienfuegos. The elegant, second-floor dining room is part of the Club Cienfuegos complex. While not as ornate or elaborate as the Palacio del Valle, the ambience here is still very pleasant, and the food is a bit better to boot. While there is an assortment of steak, pork, and poultry dishes, we recommend you stick to the fresh fish and seafood. We particularly like the lobster chunks in a Frangelica sauce. The large, first-floor open-air bar area is set underneath a modern tent structure, with soaring spires. This is a great place to catch the sunset before heading in for dinner.

Calle 37 (Prado) between Avs. 8 and 10, Punta Gorda. ✆ **432/51-2891.** Reservations recommended. Main courses CUC$6–CUC$25. MC, V. Daily noon–11pm.

**La Cueva del Camarón** SEAFOOD   While nowhere near as elaborate as the Palacio del Valle (see below), this popular restaurant is also housed in a beautifully restored old mansion. Ornate Moorish-style tiled wainscoting greets you in the entryway, and works its way around the first floor and up the stairway. The high arched interior doorways feature intricate woodcarvings. Most of the seating and the joint's popular bar are located on an open-air patio right on the water, although there's a separate rooftop terrace that serves as a second bar, where you can also dine with an elevated view of the harbor. Stick with the seafood here. They've got fresh fish, shrimp, and lobster prepared however you like it, and they even have a decent selection of reasonably priced imported wines.

Calle 37 (Prado) no. 4 (at Av. 2), Punta Gorda. ✆ **432/55-1128.** Reservations recommended. Main courses CUC$5–CUC$24. MC, V. Daily noon–11pm.

**Palacio del Valle** ✦ CONTINENTAL/SEAFOOD   The food's not nearly as spectacular as the setting, but the luxurious and ornate surroundings just about make up for it. Music and entertainment in the main dining room is provided by the charismatic María del Carmen Iznaga Guillén, who claims to be the niece of the great Cuban poet Nicolás Guillén. Whether that's true or not, she is a genuine character, and worth a visit just to see and hear her play. The cuisine here is uninspired, but certainly acceptable.

This place is the de rigueur stop in town and there's a cattle-car feel to the operation at times. My favorite draw here is the rooftop bar, with its fabulous views over the harbor.

Calle 37 (Prado) and Av. 0, Punta Gorda. (C) **432/55-1226.** Reservations recommended. Main courses CUC$7–CUC$17; lobster CUC$28. MC, V. Daily noon–midnight.

## CIENFUEGOS AFTER DARK

The biggest draw in town is the **Club Beny Moré,** Av. 54 no. 2907 (the Bulevar) between Calles 29 and 31. There's a nightly cabaret show here (CUC$5) that features the classic sounds and songs of the club's namesake. The place also serves as one of the city's most lively dance clubs. The other popular spot to dance the night away is the **Guanaroca Disco** at the Hotel Jagua. There's also music nightly at the large, open-air bar at the **Club Cienfuegos.** For big concerts and special live music events, check out the **Casa de la Musica** at Calle 37 between avenidas 4 and 6. There's also a local **Casa de la Trova** at Avenida 16 and Calle 35, with nightly concerts (admission CUC$3).

For a quieter time, pick out a sidewalk table at the **Palatino Bar,** overlooking the Parque José Martí, or saddle up to a seat at the little hole-in-the-wall local hangout **Don Luis** on Calle 31, across from the Hotel La Union.

In addition to the places listed above, Cubanacán's floating dance club **La Niña** (CUC$2) heads out into the harbor most nights with music blaring. A similar option is offered up at the **Marina Cienfuegos.** Ask at your hotel, or check down at the docks to see what's happening.

## 3 Trinidad ⟨★⟨★⟨★

334km (207 miles) SE of Havana; 261km (162 miles) S of Varadero; 649km (402 miles) W of Santiago de Cuba

Tiny Trinidad is, quite simply, one of the finest colonial towns in all of the Americas. Wholly disproportionate to its diminutive size, Trinidad ranks as one of Cuba's greatest attractions. A few square blocks of cobblestone streets, pretty pastel-colored 18th-and 19th-century houses, palaces, and plazas, Trinidad's colonial-era core can be toured in just a few hours. But its serenity is so soothing that many visitors are easily coaxed into much longer stays. Magically frozen in time and tastefully scruffy where it needs to be, the streets tend to be more populated by horse-drawn carts than automobile traffic, and old folks still crouch by windows, behind fancy wrought-iron grilles, to peer out at passersby.

Founded in 1514 on the site of a native Taíno settlement, Villa de la Santísima Trinidad was the fourth of Diego Velázquez's original seven *villas.* Trinidad quickly grew and later prospered in princely fashion from the sugar-cane industry concentrated in the outlying Valle de los Ingenios. The sugar boom that took root by the mid-1700s created a coterie of wealthy local sugar barons, who built magnificent estates in the valley and manor houses in town and imported thousands of African slaves to work the fields. Trinidad's golden age, though, proved to be short-lived. Slave uprisings on plantations, intense European competition, and, finally, independence struggles throughout the Caribbean all took their toll on the Cuban sugar industry.

When the bottom dropped out of sugar by the 1860s, Trinidad's economy collapsed and the town drifted into obscurity. Its economic failure in the late 19th century is a true blessing in the 21st: Trinidad escaped further economic development and modernization that surely would have obscured the colonial nucleus that UNESCO honored as a World Heritage Site in 1988. Even in the 1950s, in pre-revolutionary,

# Trinidad

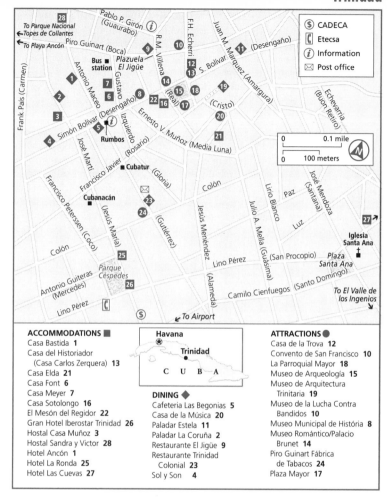

**ACCOMMODATIONS** ■
Casa Bastida **1**
Casa del Historiador
(Casa Carlos Zerquera) **13**
Casa Elda **21**
Casa Font **6**
Casa Meyer **7**
Casa Sotolongo **16**
El Mesón del Regidor **22**
Gran Hotel Iberostar Trinidad **26**
Hostal Casa Muñoz **3**
Hostal Sandra y Victor **28**
Hotel Ancón **1**
Hotel La Ronda **25**
Hotel Las Cuevas **27**

**DINING** ◆
Cafeteria Las Begonias **5**
Casa de la Música **20**
Paladar Estela **11**
Paladar La Coruña **2**
Restaurante El Jigüe **9**
Restaurante Trinidad
Colonial **23**
Sol y Son **4**

**ATTRACTIONS** ●
Casa de la Trova **12**
Convento de San Francisco **10**
La Parroquial Mayor **18**
Museo de Arqueología **15**
Museo de Arquitectura
Trinitaria **19**
Museo de la Lucha Contra
Bandidos **10**
Museo Municipal de História **8**
Museo Romántico/Palacio
Brunet **14**
Piro Guinart Fábrica
de Tabacos **24**
Plaza Mayor **17**

capitalist Cuba, the beauty and historical value of Trinidad prompted the government to declare it off-limits to further development.

## ESSENTIALS
### GETTING THERE
**BY PLANE**   Regularly scheduled and chartered **AeroCaribbean** and **Aerogaviota** light-aircraft flights from Havana and Varadero arrive in Trinidad at the little **Aeropuerto Alberto Delgado,** Carretera Casilda Km 1.5 (© **419/6393;** airport code TND), a couple of kilometers beyond the historic center of Trinidad. A taxi from the airport to Trinidad costs around CUC$5.

**BY BUS**   The quickest and best bus service to Trinidad is **Víazul** (© **419/4448** in Trinidad; www.viazul.com), which operates from Havana (© **7/881-1143**), Varadero (© **45/61-4886**), and Santiago de Cuba (© **22/62-8484**). From Havana (CUC$27 one-way), buses depart twice daily, at 8:15am and 1pm, arriving at 1:40pm and 6:30pm, respectively. From Varadero (CUC$22 one-way), buses leave at 7:30am and arrive at 1:25pm. From Santiago de Cuba (CUC$36 one-way), buses leave at 7:30pm, arriving at 7am the following day. Return buses leave Trinidad for Havana at 7:45am and 3:15pm; for Varadero at 2:30pm; and for Santiago at 8am.

The bus terminal, or **Terminal de Omnibuses** (✆ **419/4448**), in Trinidad is on Gustavo Izquierdo between Piro Guinart and Simón Bolívar, 2 blocks from the Plaza Mayor.

**BY CAR**   From Havana, the fastest route is to drive along the Autopista Nacional to Santa Clara (about 4 hr.), and then drop down through Jibacoa to Trinidad along the local road south. Another option is to continue on the Autopista Nacional to Sancti Spíritus (perhaps stopping for a look if you're not planning an overnight visit there), and circle back southwest to Trinidad for a scenic drive through the Valley of the Sugar Mills (see "Side Trips from Trinidad," later in this chapter). If you're driving in from Cienfuegos, there are actually two routes. We prefer the coastal road, which gives you some good sea views as you get close to Trinidad. From Santiago de Cuba, start out northwest on the unfinished Autopista Nacional and then take the Carretera Central through Bayamo, Camagüey, Ciego de Avila, and Sancti Spíritus. The journey from Santiago to Trinidad should take about 8 hours.

### GETTING AROUND
Getting around Trinidad is a simple affair. Almost everything of interest in town is clustered around the Plaza Mayor in the historic center. The streets of old Trinidad were made for exploring on foot, and you can easily get around the whole of the old city, and most of the newer parts just beyond the colonial core, very easily by foot.

**BY TAXI**   State-owned, registered taxis are available for travel back and forth between Playa Ancón and Trinidad, up the hill to Hotel Las Cuevas, or private hire for excursions. Call **Cubataxi** (✆ **419/2214**), **Taxi OK** (✆ **419/6317**), or **Transtur** (✆ **419/6417**). Taxis charge CUC$6 to CUC$8 to Playa Ancón. Little yellow Coco Taxis, slightly slower, non-air-conditioned three-wheel vehicles, charge CUC$5.

**BY CAR**   Though it is far easier to sign on for an organized tour to visit the surrounding area, including Topes de Collantes in the Sierra del Escambray, you might choose to rent a car to explore central Cuba or travel to more distant destinations. The drive northeast to Sancti Spíritus through the Valle de los Ingenios is particularly alluring. The major car-rental companies are **Cubacar** (✆ **419/6110**), **Havanautos** (✆ **419/6301**), **Vía Rent a Car** (✆ **419/6388**), and **Transtur** (✆ **419/6417**). Rates range from CUC$45 to CUC$75 per day for a standard four-door to CUC$80 and up per day for a 4WD vehicle.

**BY BICYCLE**   Locals sometimes rent out bikes (usually functional cruisers for CUC$2–CUC$4 per day) that you can use to get back and forth to the beach. However, be forewarned, it's downhill, then flat on your way to the beach, but the final few kilometers coming home will be uphill. The best place to ask is at your casa particular.

### ORIENTATION
The streets of Trinidad go by both original colonial and newer, post-Revolution names. Locals usually don't know both; what one person may call Boca another calls Piro Guinart. Streets are haphazardly labeled. Many longtime residents use the old names, but most businesses and institutions adopt the newer names, which are used

in this section. Be prepared to encounter some confusion if asking for an address—though Trinidad is so small that it's nearly impossible to be lost for long.

Your best bets for information about Trinidad and nearby excursions are any of the major state-run travel agencies. **Cubatur** (© **419/6314**), is at Antonio Maceo at the corner of Francisco Javier Zerquera (© **419/6314**), as well as in the Hotel Ancón (p. 193); **Cubanacán** is located on José Martí between Francisco Javier Zerquera and Colón (© **419/6302**); and **Havanatur** is on Lino Pérez 336 between Francisco Cadenea and Antonio Maceo (© **419/6183**), as well as in the Hotel Ancón.

**Banco de Crédito y Comercio** is located at José Martí 264 between Colón and Francisco Javier Sequera (© **419/2405**). It's open Monday through Friday from 8am to 6pm. A **CADECA** is at José Martí 166 (© **419/6262**); its hours are Monday through Saturday from 8:30am to 6pm, Sunday from 8:30am to 12:30pm.

For medical attention, go to the 24-hour **Clínica Internacional** located at Lino Pérez 103, at the corner of Reforma (© **419/6492**). There's a pharmacy on the Plaza Mayor, at Rubén Martínez 15 (© **419/3180**).

There are a handful of cybercafes around Trinidad, including **Etecsa Internet terminals** at the Etecsa office on Lino Pérez (on the east side of Parque Céspedes, between José Martí and Miguel Calzada); and within the Casa del Tabaco, at Francisco Javier Zerquera (at the corner of Maceo). But perhaps the best place to use your Etecsa card is in the lobby of the **Casa de la Música,** at the top of the stairs off of Fernando H. Echerri, just east of the Plaza Mayor. All are open daily from 9am to 6pm; rates are CUC$6 per hour with the Etecsa card. There are also Internet terminals inside the Cafetería Las Begonias and the Mesón del Regidor.

A small branch of the **post office** is housed within the Infotur office Simón Bolívar at the corner of Antonio Maceo; the main post office is located at Antonio Maceo 418, between Colón and Francisco Javier Zerquera. Both are open Monday through Saturday from 9am to 6pm.

## WHAT TO SEE & DO

Unquestionably, the greatest attraction in Trinidad is the town itself, which constitutes one of the finest colonial nuclei in the Americas and, justifiably, has been designated a UNESCO World Heritage Site in its entirety. The town's cobblestone streets contain a treasure-trove of small and grand colonial homes, churches, and quiet squares. Walking aimlessly about the curving streets of the old town is unmatched in Cuba for tranquillity and charm. About the only feature not authentically colonial about it is the neon cross that crowns the church on Plaza Mayor. Remarkably, as quaint as it is, Trinidad feels like a real town where Cubans live and work, rather than the film set it first appears to be.

A good way to get your bearings in Trinidad is to trace a path from the **Plaza Mayor,** the heart of the old town, heading west on Echerri and then down Piro Guinart to **Plazuela El Jigüe,** a quiet and pretty little square. Then head down Peña to Simón Bolívar and east on Antonio Maceo, the closest thing there is to a main drag in Trinidad.

At the corner of Antonio Maceo and Colón is a tiny **Piro Guinart Fábrica de Tabacos** (tobacco factory), where visitors can peek in on a couple dozen workers hand-rolling cigars. A couple blocks southwest of here, along Lino Pérez, is **Parque Céspedes,** the focal point of the "new" town (though newer than the colonial core of Trinidad, it remains anything but shiny and modern).

Northeast of old town, following Fernando H. Echerri to José Mendoza for several blocks, you'll reach **Plaza Santa Ana** and the ruins of **Iglesia Santa Ana,** which looks ancient but dates only to 1812. On the square is a former 19th-century prison, **Real Cárcel,** which today houses a touristy restaurant and souvenir shop.

## AROUND THE PLAZA MAYOR ✿✿

The neo-baroque, 19th-century Plaza Mayor, elaborately adorned with serene sitting areas, statuary, towering palm trees, and gardens enclosed by white wrought-iron fences, is one of Cuba's most beautiful. It's ringed by magnificent palaces and pastel-colored houses with red-tile roofs and wood shutters. On the northwest corner is the cathedral, Iglesia de la Santísima Trinidad, which most locals refer to as **La Parroquial Mayor.** The cathedral, completed in 1892, replaced the original 17th-century church that was destroyed in 1812 by a hurricane. The new construction, completed at the end of the 19th century, is rather simple on the outside, but the restored interior reveals a Gothic vaulted ceiling and nearly a dozen attractive carved altars. The cathedral can be visited Tuesday through Sunday from 11am to 3pm.

The highlight of the Plaza Mayor, and the most evocative reminder of Trinidad's glory days, is the lovingly restored **Palacio Brunet,** Fernando H. Echerri 52 at the corner of Simón Bolívar. The colonial mansion dates to 1704 (the second floor was built in 1808) and houses the **Museo Romántico** ✿✿ (© 419/4363). Its splendid collection of period antiques culled from a number of old Trinitario families convincingly summons a picture of the life of a local sugar baron in the 1800s. Don't miss the enormous *azulejo*-encrusted kitchen with a wood-burning stove. The views from upstairs are marvelous. The museum is open Tuesday through Sunday from 9am to 4:45pm. Admission is CUC$2; allow about 45 minutes for your visit.

In a pale yellow colonial building on the west side of the main square, **Museo de Arqueología** (© 419/3420) features a collection that encompasses natural sciences and pre-Columbian Cuba. It's mostly an uninspired hodgepodge of exhibits, though; you'll find bones of Indian natives and slaves, glass-enclosed stuffed animals, and a 19th-century kitchen, which, though interesting, is hard to classify as either archaeology or natural science. It's open Tuesday through Saturday from 9am to 5pm. Admission is CUC$1; budget only about a half-hour for a visit.

On the east side of the Plaza Mayor, in a squat, sky-blue mansion once belonging to the Sánchez Iznaga family, the **Museo de Arquitectura Trinitaria** (© 419/3208) features moderately interesting exhibits that trace the development of Trinidad, including examples of woodwork and ironwork, maps, models, and photographs. What is on display, though, can hardly compare to the real-life exhibits beyond the museum's doors. It's open Saturday through Thursday from 9am to 5pm. Admission is CUC$1.

The former Palacio Cantero, an 1830 palatial residence built by a noted sugar baron, houses **Museo Municipal de Historia** ✿, Simón Bolívar 423 between Peña and Gustavo Izquierdo (© 419/4460). In addition to antiques and 19th-century furnishings, there are bits and pieces of slave history, old bank notes, and exhibits of revolutionary Cuba. For many visitors, though, the highlight is the climb up narrow and rickety wooden stairs to the tower, which provides terrific bird's-eye views of Trinidad and the surrounding area. The museum is open Saturday through Thursday from 9am to 5pm; admission is CUC$2. Allow about an hour for your visit, a bit longer if you want to linger over the views.

The second of Trinidad's two major towers is the picturesque yellow-and-white domed bell tower belonging to the former 18th-century **Convento de San Francisco (Convent of Saint Francis of Assisi),** Fernando H. Echerri at Piro Guinart. Today the building hosts the dogmatic but rather fascinating **Museo de la Lucha Contra**

**Bandidos** (© **419/4121**), which focuses on revolutionary Cuba and the continuing "struggle against bandits." Exhibits document Fidel's battles against counterrevolutionaries—the *bandidos* in question—who sought to overturn the regime's ideals by winning support among *guajiros* (poor rural farmers) and fighting in the Sierra del Escambray in the 1960s. In addition to newspaper reports, you'll find machine guns, military maps, a CIA radio, and photos of the ragtag principals who finally, and quite extraordinarily, overthrew the Batista government in 1959. As is the case with the Museo Municipal de Historia, though, the biggest draw may be the panoramic views from atop the bell tower. The museum is open Tuesday through Sunday from 9am to 5pm; admission is CUC$1. Allow 45 minutes or so, including the visit to the tower.

## WHERE TO STAY

Trinidad has an abundance of casas particulares—nearly 350 at last count, including several in fine colonial homes that rank as excellent bargains and are particularly appropriate accommodations in this beautifully preserved old town. Visitors who arrive on the Víazul bus are met by dozens of card- and placard-waving folks hoping to get you to follow them to their homestays. They are perfectly innocuous and, for the most part, honest folks just trying to make a buck. Not all the casas are officially registered, however, and many are not as close in to the colonial center as you might wish to be. Have a map ready so they can show you clearly where their house is located. If you already have the name of a casa, don't mention that you are looking for "José" or "María" (for example); the homeowner you're talking to will morph into that person in no time. Houses in the old center of town generally charge CUC$25 to CUC$35 double; those a bit farther out (usually no more than a 15-min. walk from the Plaza Mayor) charge CUC$10 to CUC$20 double. Alternatively, you could stay at one of the large resorts on Playa Ancón, 12km (7 miles) away.

### IN TRINIDAD

When we last visited, the venerable old **Hotel La Ronda** (© **419/2248;** José Martí no. 239) was closed for extensive remodeling. It is expected to open some time in 2007, as an elegant little downtown boutique hotel.

#### Very Expensive

**Gran Hotel Iberostar Trinidad** 🏵🏵🏵   Facing the quiet Parque Céspedes, this restored and remodeled old building is now a beautiful and refined hotel in the heart of colonial Trinidad. Opened in February of 2006, this is by far the most luxurious and opulent hotel in the area. A stately air pervades this place, from the large lobby area, with its soaring atrium ceiling and central fountain and broad marble staircase,

---

**⟨Tips  Know Where You're Going**

Be careful. I've received reports of *jineteros* meeting incoming buses and taxis with the names of tourists they've gleaned from friends inside the bus or taxi company. They then proceed to tell them either that their reservation at a specific casa particular has been canceled, or that they are taking them to that casa, when in fact they are bringing them to a different casa altogether. If you have and trust your confirmed reservation at a casa particular, make sure you know the exact address and location of the house, and distrust touts who take you elsewhere.

---

to the rooms, restaurant, and all the rest. All the rooms are very spacious and tastefully done, with a broad range of amenities, including a phone in the bathroom. The junior suites are somewhat bigger, with a separate tub and shower, and walk-in closet. My favorite rooms are the second-floor standard units, nos. 106 through 111, with balconies facing the park. No children under 15 are allowed.

Calle José Martí and Calle Lino Perez, Trinidad. ✆ **419/6073**. Fax 419/6077. www.iberostar.com. 40 units. CUC$190 double; CUC$250 suite. Rates include breakfast. Rates lower in off season, slightly higher during peak weeks. MC, V. Children under 15 not allowed. **Amenities:** Restaurant; bar; tour desk; arcade; room service 7am–11pm; laundry service. *In room:* A/C, TV, minibar, dataport, hair dryer, iron, safe.

## Moderate

**Hotel Las Cuevas** ✿    Perched on a hill about a mile north of (and up above) the old colonial core of Trinidad, this hotel is named for the caves that dot the hillside. Built in the 1950s, the hotel is surprisingly large, featuring rows of concrete bungalow-style rooms, a round pool, and a fantastic underground cave dance club (a short distance from the property). The remodeled rooms are very comfortable, with exposed stone walls and good bathrooms. While it's a little inconveniently located up a steep hill (a quiet setting many will appreciate), you can easily walk (downhill) to the restaurants and nightlife of Trinidad, and then take a taxi home. The hotel is popular with tour groups.

Finca Santa Ana, Trinidad. ✆ **419/6133**. Fax 419/6161. www.hotelescubanacan.com. 109 units. CUC$70–CUC$90 double; CUC$100–CUC$120 suite. Rates include breakfast. MC, V. **Amenities:** 2 restaurants; bar; dance club; nightly show; outdoor pool; outdoor tennis court; scooter and bike rental; laundry service. *In room:* A/C, TV, safe.

## Inexpensive

In addition to the casas reviewed below, other recommended options include **Casa Elda** ✿, Jesús Menéndez 166, between Fernando Hernández and Ernesto Valdés (✆ **419/3283**), run by a sweet and extremely friendly couple; **Casa del Historiador** (Casa Carlos Zerquera), Fernando Hernández 54 (✆ **419/3634**), the lovely colonial home of Trinidad's official historian; **Casa Bastida** ✿ Maceo 539, between Simón Bolívar and Piro Guinart (✆ **419/6686**); **Hostal Sandra y Victor,** Maceo 613, between Piro Guinart and Pablo Pichs (✆ **419/6444;** hostalsandra@yahoo.com); and **Casa Sotolongo,** Real 33, between Rosario and Simón Bolívar (✆ **419/4169**).

**Casa Font** ✿✿    A gorgeous late-18th-century colonial house with a green facade, just a few steps from the bus station and in the heart of the old center, this family home has a great collection of antiques and a light, airy feel. For a casa particular, this is about as grand as it gets: chandeliers of Baccarat crystal, thick wood doors, colonial- and republican-era oil paintings, and mediapunto windows. Out back is a pretty courtyard with a well. The one room has a stunning *modernista* door and is large and very comfortable.

Gustavo Izquierdo 105 (between Piro Guinart and Simón Bolívar), Trinidad. ✆ **419/3683**. 1 unit. CUC$25 double. No credit cards. *In room:* A/C, no phone.

**Casa Meyer** ✿    A few paces from Casa Font, this is another spectacular 200-year-old colonial home, with a garden courtyard. The house has very high, wood-beamed ceilings and very nice antiques, though it is a bit darker than Casa Font. One bedroom is huge, with antique beds, while the new room set back in the garden is just as nice and perhaps even more tranquil.

Gustavo Izquierdo 111 (between Piro Guinart and Simón Bolívar), Trinidad. ✆ **419/3444**. 2 units. CUC$20–CUC$25 double. No credit cards. *In room:* A/C, no phone.

**Tips   Check In Before You Check In**

In Trinidad, if you make a reservation with one of the more popular casas particulares, it's a very good idea—if not essential—to reconfirm your reservation a couple of days in advance. Casas often let out rooms that haven't been reconfirmed.

**El Mesón del Regidor** ✿   This small, state-run inn is atmospheric. The four rooms here are simple, but recently renovated, with red brick floors and exposed beam and tile ceilings. Each has a private staircase leading up to it from the central courtyard and restaurant area. A couple of these staircases are steep and narrow. This hotel is just a few steps away from the Plaza Mayor.

Simón Bolívar 242 (between Muñoz and Rubén Martínez Villena), Trinidad. ✆ **419/6572**. 4 units. CUC$38–CUC$48 double. Rates include breakfast. No credit cards. *In room:* A/C, no phone.

**Hostal Casa Muñoz** ✿✿   A charming house run by an enterprising, English-speaking young man named Julio and his wife, Rosa, this is one of the best-run and friendliest casas in Cuba. In a breezy and centrally located colonial home built in 1800, it has one spectacular bedroom (featured in *National Geographic*), as well as another perfectly acceptable room, a great new kitchen, and several terraces, including one with fantastic rooftop views. Julio is a photographer and bon vivant with considerable advice on Trinidad's cultural scene; check out his collection of slides and pictures adorning the house. This place is popular and advance reservations are a must.

José Martí 401 (corner of Santiago Escobar), Trinidad. ✆/fax **419/3673**. www.casa.trinidadphoto.com. 2 units. CUC$20–CUC$30 double. No credit cards. *In room:* A/C, no phone.

### IN PLAYA ANCON

**Brisas Trinidad del Mar** ✿   The fanciest beach hotel in the general area of Trinidad, this place is semi-luxurious and easygoing. For those looking to combine beach time, great sea and mountain views, and easy access to Cuba's finest colonial city, this is without doubt the best option. The all-inclusive hotel apes the famed colonial architecture of nearby Trinidad, with pastel colors and pastel-colored imitations of the town's more famous landmarks, including the San Francisco tower and the Plaza Mayor. The hotel is on one of the best sections of Playa Ancón, and it has a great pool and all the services one could want, including language and dance classes and diving. Rooms are handsomely outfitted, nicely decorated with pale yellow walls and blue accents. If there's a drawback, it's that the food can be pretty average and bland.

Península Ancón, Trinidad. ✆ **419/6500**. Fax 419/6565. www.hotelescubanacan.com. 241 units. CUC$130–CUC$200 double. Rates are all-inclusive. Discounts available for longer stays. MC, V. **Amenities:** 2 restaurants; 2 bars; 24-hr. snack bar; outdoor pool; 2 outdoor tennis courts; gym; Jacuzzi; sauna; scooter and bike rental; children's center and programs; massage; laundry service. *In room:* A/C, TV, safe.

**Hotel Ancón**   While this place definitely plays second fiddle to the neighboring Brisas Trinidad del Mar, the Hotel Ancón is nonetheless a good option for travelers looking for plenty of services and amenities on the beach at a reasonable price. The older-style hotel—a large Soviet block plunked down on the sand—is pretty uninspiring, and rooms are moderate in size and rather simply decorated (bare-bones, even). About half of the rooms have oceanview balconies, and these are a definite plus. Still, we recommend you ask for a room in the newer wing, although these are in no way new, having been built in 1995. Rooms here have either mountain or sea views, and slightly more space and more modern decor. Activities include salsa and language classes, volleyball, aerobics, and more.

Carretera María Aguilar, Playa Ancón, Trinidad. ☎ **419/6123.** Fax 419/6121. www.hotelescubanacan.com. 279 units. CUC$100–CUC$140 double. Rates are all-inclusive. MC, V. **Amenities:** 2 restaurants; 4 bars; 24-hr. cafeteria; nightly show; outdoor pool; 2 outdoor tennis courts; laundry service. *In room:* A/C, TV, safe.

## WHERE TO DINE

The dining scene in Trinidad is one of the more enjoyable in the country—which, admittedly, is not saying much—not so much for the excellence of its restaurants but for the low-key atmosphere and a mix of both pretty good state-run establishments and *paladares* (private restaurants). Plenty of self-appointed guides will make their presence known, trying to lead you to an unofficial paladar; these are safe and often quite good, even if illegal (though that status has no consequence for you—feel free to dine wherever you like).

In addition to the restaurants listed below, the state-run **Plaza Mayor** is an acceptable option serving a decent buffet, in a beautifully restored old home and an even more beautiful courtyard.

### MODERATE

**Casa de la Música** CRIOLLA    It's not an obvious place to eat, perhaps, but one of Trinidad's best spots for live music also has a restaurant attached, and if you're lucky enough to score one of the tables on the terrace, you'll be within earshot of the band playing on the platform on the steps below. The restaurant is, on the whole, no better or worse than other state-run places in town. It serves the standard main courses—grilled chicken, pork, and fish, as well as lobster and a couple of inexpensive sandwiches and omelets. We also like this spot for lunch.

Fernando H. Echerri 3. ☎ **419/6622.** Reservations not accepted. Sandwiches CUC$1.50–CUC$3; main courses CUC$3.50–CUC$9; lobster CUC$26. MC, V. Daily 10am–10pm.

**Paladar Estela** ★★ *Finds* CRIOLLA    Enter through an elaborately decorated colonial house, 2 blocks north of the cathedral, into this private restaurant, which has a handful of tables set in an exuberant backyard garden setting, with tons of flowering plants, including red *estrella de navidad,* and a wall festooned with vines. Portions are nearly as voluminous as the flora, and light eaters can share one dish between two. Offerings include roast pork *a la cubana,* fried chicken, grilled fish, and ham omelet. However, my favorite is the perfectly spiced *ropa vieja* made with shredded lamb. All are served with *moros y cristianos* (black beans and rice), salad, fried banana, crackers, and fruit. The owner also has one room for rent (CUC$20 double).

Simón Bolívar 557. ☎ **419/4329.** Reservations not accepted. Meals CUC$6–CUC$8. No credit cards. Mon–Sat 7–11pm.

**Paladar La Coruña** ★ CRIOLLA    A pleasant private home restaurant with just three tables on the patio just beyond the living room, under a welcome ceiling fan, and a couple more under a bright bulb in the garden, this is another of Trinidad's excellent paladares. It has an oral menu only, but you can already guess what's served: chicken, pork, grilled fish. Meals begin with a salad and veggie plate, and the main course is served with a heaping mound of rice and beans, followed by a small plate of bananas and mango. Tables are very informal, with plasticized tablecloths, wood chairs upfront, and iron garden chairs in the garden. One wall of the paladar is decorated with souvenir money from customers around the world.

José Martí 430. No phone. Reservations not accepted. Meals CUC$7–CUC$12. No credit cards. Daily 7am–11pm.

**Restaurant El Jigüe** CRIOLLA   El Jigüe (*hee*-gweh) is a brightly lit, nearly formal dining room in a handsome, airy colonial house. It sits on one of the old town's prettiest and tiniest squares, next to a massive shade tree. Just a block from the Plaza Mayor, the restaurant has high-backed chairs, white tablecloths, and prominent chandeliers, which lend it an elegance not often seen in official restaurants in Cuba. Its specialty is *pollo El Jigüe,* which comes in a clay pot with pasta and cheese and is served with salad and coffee. Other dishes worth checking out are grilled fish, standard chicken, and lobster—the latter is, if not cheap, a better value here at CUC$20 than at many government-owned restaurants.

Rubén Martínez Villena 69 (corner of Piro Guinart), Plazuela El Jigüe. ☏ **419/6476.** Reservations not required. Main courses CUC$5–CUC$24. MC, V. Daily noon–3pm and 7–10pm.

**Restaurante Trinidad Colonial** CRIOLLA   This state-owned restaurant is more notable for its setting—in a pretty mauve-colored house set back from the street, with a couple of tables in a sunny courtyard—than its menu. The standard dishes of grilled fish, pork filet, grilled shrimp, and lobster feature decent-size portions but are a little unexciting, and service can be spectacularly inattentive. Better values are the set-price menus, which come with rice, vegetables, bread, and dessert.

Antonio Maceo 55. ☏ **419/6473.** Reservations not required. Main courses CUC$6–CUC$18. MC, V. Mon–Sat 9am–10pm.

**Sol y Son** ☆☆ CRIOLLA   One of Trinidad's long-standing paladares, this place is housed in an art- and furniture-bedecked 19th-century house that could double for an antiques dealer. Out back, on the porch of a very attractive, verdant courtyard, the restaurant features one of the more extensive menus among private restaurants. Choose from soups, spaghetti, a long list of fish (including a breaded filet stuffed with cheese), and grilled and roasted chicken and pork dishes. Check out the *cerdo borracho* (drunk pork), which is grilled and doused with rum. The patio has mounted ceiling fans, and during the day you should do your level best to sit beneath one, as it can get bloody hot.

Simón Bolívar 283 (between José Martí and Frank País). No phone. Reservations not accepted. Main courses CUC$6–CUC$9. No credit cards. Daily noon–3pm; Sun–Fri 6:30–11pm.

### INEXPENSIVE

**Cafetería Las Begonias** SANDWICHES/SNACKS   Once one of Trinidad's better restaurants, Las Begonias is now not much more than a snackateria, with 10 glass-topped tables on a red-tile floor, open to the street. Still, it's good enough for breakfast or a cheap light lunch. It serves mostly *emparedados* (sandwiches) and hamburgers, as well as the ubiquitous fried chicken. The house specialty is a sandwich, the *super rumbos* that is ham, cheese, and peppers on thick bread. This place has an Internet cafe attached.

Corner of Simón Bolívar and Maceo. No phone. Reservations not accepted. Main courses CUC$1.50–CUC$3.50. No credit cards. Daily 9am–10pm.

## SHOPPING

Trinidad, given its starring role on the tourist circuit, is one of the better shopping towns in central and eastern Cuba (though far from a shopper's paradise). In addition to the requisite cigar and music shops, several of Trinidad's atmospheric, cobblestone streets are converted daily into **street markets** featuring handicrafts, lace, and clothing items. While lace and clothing are the main attraction, you can also find interesting woodcarvings, musical instruments, masks, and a host of ceramic works. The street with the most variety tends to be Peña, near the Museo Municipal de Historia tower, while most of the lace and textile merchants, who occasionally have good guayabera shirts, tend to cluster on the small streets just east of the Plaza Mayor.

The art gallery on the south side of the Plaza Mayor, **Galería de Arte ARTex,** has two floors of contemporary art, much of it very accessible, and the traditional souvenir renderings of Trinidad.

The place for cigars and tobacco paraphernalia in town, **La Casa del Tabaco,** has two branches and carries all the finest Cuban cigars, carefully stored. The shop at San Proscopio 296 (at the corner of José Martí) is open daily from 9am to 8pm; the branch on Francisco Javier Zerquera (at the corner of Maceo), is open daily from 9am to 6pm. The latter location even has an Internet connection, in case you want to write home to take cigar orders.

Much of the ceramic wares you'll see for sale around Trinidad are produced by the Santander family, whose history in this art goes back generations. You can visit their small factory, **El Alfarero Casa Chichi** (© **419/3146;** Andrés Berro 51, between Abel Santamaria and Pepito Tey), although it's best to call in advance and tell them you're coming.

The most complete Cuban CD store in town, **ARTex,** is annexed to the Casa de Música on Fernando H. Echerri, where you'll find nightly performances of live music. The clerks will usually play just about anything you want to hear.

## TRINIDAD AFTER DARK

While most of Trinidad's old-town streets are coffin-quiet after dark, several joints bop with live Cuban music nightly. One of the best spots to sit outside, have a mojito or beer, and hear good traditional bands is the small plaza midway up the steps leading to the **Casa de la Música** ✷. The dance floor is usually a good mix of polished, semi-professional locals and foreigners whose hips are somewhat less smoothly oiled. The steps are often overflowing with people checking out some free music under the stars. Inside the Casa de la Música, a more raucous environment prevails until the wee hours (CUC$2 cover). Just around the corner on Fernando H. Echerri, **Palenque de los Congos Reales** has an open-air stage where you can sometimes catch Grupo Folclórico performing Afro-Cuban music and dance (performances aren't regularly scheduled). At other times there may be a standard *trova* or *son* group playing. The **Casa de la Trova,** Fernando H. Echerri 29, a block east of the Plaza Mayor, is the traditional spot to listen to Cuban bands and try out a few dance steps; it's open daily from 11am to 2pm and 10pm to 2am, and there's a CUC$1 cover charge during the day, CUC$2 at night. A similar spot is **Casa Fisher** (ARTex), on Lino Pérez between José Martí and Francisco Codatia, but the scene here can be pretty hit-or-miss.

The **Ruinas del Teatro Brunet** ✷, Maceo, between Zerquera and Simón Bolívar, puts on a nightly Afro-Cuban cabaret-style show in the spacious courtyard of the ruins of the city's first theater; admission is CUC$3. Another bar set in a delightful open-air courtyard in the ostensible ruins of a colonial home, the **Ruinas de Segarte** ✷, Jesús Menéndez between Echerri and Valdés, is an intimate affair which is open 24 hours, and also has live music most nights. Finally, **Las Parrandas,** Rubén Martínez Villena 59, between Símon Bolívar and Piro Guinart, is the home base for a venerable band of elder musicians, who play in a funky, open-air space amid the carcasses of old cars and other detritus.

**La Canchánchara,** Rubén Martínez Villena at Pablo P. Girón, sometimes has a few musicians assembled, but it's mostly just a little open-air courtyard bar in an atmospheric colonial house, a good place to kick back in old wooden chairs and have a mojito or the eponymous house drink, made with aguardiente, lime, and honey. It's open daily from 10am to 9pm (but no food is served).

One of the most unusual nightspots in Cuba has to be the dance club carved out of a deep two-level cave, **Discoteca Ayala** (also called "La Cueva"; ℂ **419/6133**). Though it can be deadly hot, and the kitsch factor is undeniable, it's still pretty cool to dance to blasting disco-salsa tunes as colored lights bounce off stalactites. The crowd on weekends is largely Cuban. Now if they could only install air-conditioning to go with the lights and sound system, nocturnal spelunking would be even more appetizing. To get there, you can either walk up a path leading directly behind the cathedral, off Juan Manuel Márquez, or take the longer route from Hotel Las Cuevas (it's not actually on the premises of the hotel, though it's under the same management). Open nightly until 3am (later Fri–Sat); admission CUC$3.

## SIDE TRIPS FROM TRINIDAD

Though the colonial streets of Trinidad are the main draw, the town is perfectly situated for quick trips to the beach (one of the best on the southern coast) and gorgeous surrounding countryside, which includes the Sierra del Escambray mountains and picturesque valley that was once home to the sugar plantations that made Trinidad wealthy in the 18th and 19th centuries.

**PLAYA ANCON** ⚑   Though it can't quite compare with Cayo Largo, Varadero, Cayos Coco and Guillermo, Cayos Santa Maria and Ensenacho, or Guardalavaca—Cuba's prettiest and most prestigious beaches—Playa Ancón is still a very beautiful beach and it has one distinct advantage those other, isolated stretches of sand don't: the proximity of Trinidad. At just 13km (8 miles) from town, Ancón, a 3km (2-mile) strip at the end of a peninsula, is a quick and easy ride to and from Trinidad, so beach lovers can stay here and visit the colonial wonder of Trinidad at their will. The beach is made up of wonderful white sand, and there's good snorkeling and diving at some 30 offshore dive sites (both the Brisas de Mar Trinidad and Playa Ancón hotels, as well as the major travel agencies in town, offer diving and snorkeling excursions beginning at CUC$30 a head, as well as watersports). **Cayo Blanco** is a tiny offshore island reputed to be one of the best dive spots, with a huge variety of coral. Local operators also offer "seafari" expeditions to Cayo Blanco, with boat trips to the island, lunch, and snorkeling.

Northwest of Playa Ancón, about 8km (5 miles) from Trinidad, is **La Boca,** a small fishing village that's the popular beach spot among locals. Few tourists make it to La Boca, though there are a couple of casas particulares that rent rooms.

To get to Playa Ancón, take a taxi or Coco Taxi. Alternatively, the energetic can rent a bike; see "Getting Around," earlier in this section.

**EL VALLE DE LOS INGENIOS** ⚑⚑   Trinidad got rich off the sugar trade back in the 18th and 19th centuries, and the Valle de los Ingenios (Valley of the Sugar Mills) was one of the most productive sugar-cane growing areas in all of Cuba. The gorgeous, verdant valley is no longer king of the sugar trade, which once supported 60 mills, but for visitors, it makes a wonderful day trip. The zone has been declared a UNESCO

Cultural Heritage Site. A 1907 American steam train, especially for tourists, departs daily for the valley, making the journey out to one of the old sugar estates, **Manaca-Iznaga,** in just over 30 minutes from Trinidad. The old manor house (Casa Hacienda) remains and is now a pretty good tourist restaurant; but the main attraction is the fantastic, 45m-high (150-ft.) pointed tower, built in 1845, which visitors can ascend (CUC$1 fee) for spectacular views of the surrounding area. A huge bell once hung here and tolled for the toiling slaves in the fields, signaling the beginning and end of their working days. There's a surprisingly good little restaurant in a hacienda-style home here, that offers up a filling lunch for between CUC$4 and CUC$8.

A steam train departs Trinidad daily at 9:30am and returns around 3pm. Tickets (CUC$10 round-trip) can be purchased from any tour operator around town, or directly at the **train station** 1km (½ mile) from the center of Trinidad on Calle Antonio Guiteras Final (✆ **419/3348**).

**PARQUE NACIONAL TOPES DE COLLANTES (SIERRA DEL ESCAMBRAY)** 👁👁 Northwest of Trinidad, along dangerously curving roads, are the thickly pine-covered mountains of the Sierra del Escambray, a beautiful range that cuts across central Cuba. From Trinidad, the Topes de Collantes National Park, which covers 175 sq. km (70 sq. miles), is the main draw, a cool refuge from the heat that usually bakes the stone streets of Trinidad. It's a splendid area for hiking, though a sad and lifeless resort village of Soviet-style hotels also offers therapeutic spa treatments.

Of the several well-established trails, the most popular route is **Salto de Caburní,** a hike that begins near a graffiti-covered house, the Casa de la Gallega (where simple lunches are served), and terminates in a great 75m (250-ft.) waterfall and swimming hole. The clearly marked trail, through dense forests of palm, pine, and eucalyptus trees, is fairly challenging, with several steep descents, often along a muddy, narrow path. The water in the deep green pool makes for a brisk swim. Another popular hike, which also has a waterfall as its reward at the end, is **Salto Vega Grande.** Each of these trails is a 4km (2-mile) hike each way.

The Topes de Collantes resort, about 20km (12 miles) from Trinidad, welcomes mostly Cubans; but several of its hotels accept foreign guests. Of these, the top choice is **Villa Caburní** (✆ **42/54-0231;** www.gaviota-grupo.com). The massive and rather unattractive **Kurhotel** (✆ **42/54-0180;** www.gaviota-grupo.com) is most notable as a sort of lakeside spa offering a variety of therapies, including hydrotherapy. Still, it's hard to recommend this place, when most visitors have access to such vastly better services at home.

Though it's possible to rent a car and explore the region on your own, paying a CUC$4 entrance fee at the Topes de Collantes resort, hikers are advised to sign on for organized bookings, since many trails are not well indicated. The Trinidad travel agencies, such as Havanatur and Cubatur, offer Sierra del Escambray jeep excursions for between CUC$30 and CUC$40 per person. The **Complejo Turístico Topes de Collantes** (✆ **42/54-0193** or 42/54-0297) may be able to assist independent hikers.

## 4 Sancti Spíritus

70km (43 miles) NE of Trinidad; 386km (239 miles) E of Havana

Sancti Spíritus lies smack-dab in the middle of the island and is the capital of the province of the same name. Perched on the banks of the Río Yayabo, the old town is a warren of corkscrew streets, many lined with fine, if weathered, colonial homes. Like

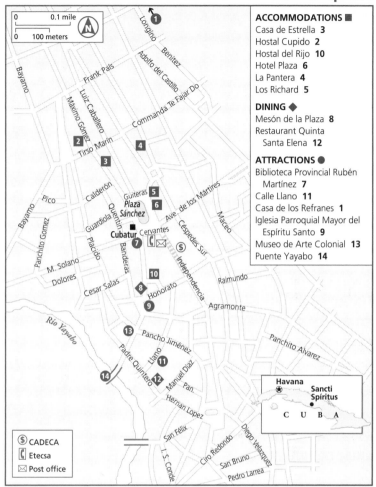

**ACCOMMODATIONS** ■
Casa de Estrella **3**
Hostal Cupido **2**
Hostal del Rijo **10**
Hotel Plaza **6**
La Pantera **4**
Los Richard **5**

**DINING** ◆
Mesón de la Plaza **8**
Restaurant Quinta
  Santa Elena **12**

**ATTRACTIONS** ●
Biblioteca Provincial Rubén
  Martínez **7**
Calle Llano **11**
Casa de los Refranes **1**
Iglesia Parroquial Mayor del
  Espíritu Santo **9**
Museo de Arte Colonial **13**
Puente Yayabo **14**

Trinidad, the town was one of the original seven *villas* founded by Velázquez in the early 16th century. Today, Sancti Spíritus is a small and not greatly significant, mostly modern provincial capital with an unassuming, lived-in feel. Though much of the city is run-down, it is beginning to renovate some of its more important colonial buildings, including one of the finest house-museums and one of the best-preserved colonial churches in the country, with the hopes of attracting a greater percentage of the travelers that stop off in nearby Trinidad.

For most visitors, a day or even a half-day in Sancti Spíritus should do the trick. Sancti Spíritus is unlikely to blow your socks off, and it's certainly not an essential stop in Cuba, but it's one of those places that will help complete the picture of contemporary Cuban life.

## ESSENTIALS
### GETTING THERE
**BY BUS**   Víazul (© 7/881-1143 in Havana; www.viazul.com) has three daily buses to Sancti Spíritus on the Havana–Santiago de Cuba line leaving at 9:30am, 3pm, and 10pm. From Havana, it's just over 5 hours (CUC$25). Víazul also makes the 1-hour trip to Sancti Spíritus directly from Trinidad (© 419/4448) daily at 8:15am on the Trinidad–Santiago de Cuba route (CUC$6.50). From Santiago, buses leave at 9am, 3:15pm, 7:30pm, and 10pm, and the trip takes around 10 hours (CUC$30).

   The bus terminal in Sancti Spíritus (© 41/2-4142) is located at Carretera Central Km 388, between Circunvalación and the Carretera de Jíbaro. Taxis charge about CUC$2 or CUC$3 for a ride to the center of town.

**BY TRAIN**   The no. 17 train travels daily from Havana's Estación Central to Sancti Spíritus, departing at 9:45pm and arriving at 6am; the fare is CUC$15 for adults, CUC$7 for children under 12. For more information, call © 7/862-1920 or 7/861-4259. The **Estación de Tren** (© 41/2-4228) in Sancti Spíritus is located at the end of Avenida Jesús Menéndez, southwest of the Puente Yayabo.

**BY CAR**   Driving from Havana, the fastest route is along the Autopista Nacional (A1) to Santa Clara, and then continuing along the Carretera Central to Sancti Spíritus (about 5 hr.). The short drive from Trinidad, along the Circuito Sur, is one of the prettiest in Cuba, as the road rolls through fields of sugar cane with the Sierra del Escambray looming in the background. From Santiago de Cuba, start out northwest on the unfinished A1 and then take the Carretera Central through Bayamo, Camagüey, and Ciego de Avila (about 6 hr.).

### GETTING AROUND
Call **Cubataxi** (© 41/2-2133), **Taxi OK** (© 41/2-6015), or **Transtur** (© 41/2-8533) for a taxi, or hop aboard one of the horse-drawn *coches* (which officially only accept pesos, but most will accept a CUC$1–CUC$2 offering for the fare). Unlicensed taxis also circulate on the streets of Sancti Spíritus. To rent a car, call **Transtur** (© 41/2-8544) or **Micar** (© 41/2-5168). Rates are about CUC$45 to CUC$75 per day for a standard four-door car.

### ORIENTATION
For a relatively small town, Sancti Spíritus is rather spread out. However, you're unlikely to spend much time beyond the old town, where you can easily walk everywhere. You'll only need a taxi (or horse-drawn *coche*) for getting to the bus terminal, train station, or your hotel, if you choose to stay at one of the inconveniently located large hotels on the outskirts of town.

   The closest Sancti Spíritus comes to having a tourist information office is the travel agency **Cubatur** (© 41/2-8518), Máximo Gómez 7 on the west side of Plaza Sánchez. Cubatur also offers hotel discounts and discounted set meals at various restaurants in the city, including Quinta Santa Elena and Restaurant Mesón de la Plaza; ask for details.

   The **Banco Financiero Internacional,** on Independencia between Plaza Sánchez and Honorato, is open Monday through Saturday from 8am to 6pm. The **CADECA** branch at Independencia 31 is open Monday through Saturday from 8:30am to 6pm, Sunday from 8:30am to noon.

   If you need medical attention, **Hospital Provincial Camilo Cienfuegos** is located on Carretera Central at Bartolomé Masó (© 41/2-4017).

You can make long-distance or international phone calls or log on (CUC$6/hr. with the Etecsa card) at the **Etecsa** booth on the south side of Plaza Sánchez; it's open daily from 8am to 9pm. The main **post office** is located at Independencia 8, between Plaza Sánchez and Honorato. It's open Monday through Saturday from 8am to 6pm, Sunday from 8am to noon.

## WHAT TO SEE & DO

It won't take much more than a morning or afternoon to check off Sancti Spíritus's principal attractions. The old town is very untouristy and unassuming, and perfect for an easygoing stroll.

**Calle Llano** ✦ is the most atmospheric street in Sancti Spíritus, a bent-elbow cobblestone alleyway (one of the only remaining stone streets in town) of pastel-colored and tiled-roof houses. It's often very still, except for a few kids playing stickball. **Puente Yayabo,** the bridge over the river at the southern edge of old town, is a 19th-century take on a European Romanesque stone bridge. Locals don't pause long enough to wonder whether a medieval-style bridge built in 1825, in a town not founded until well into the 16th century, looks odd or not; they bound over it at great speed, on bicycles, in horse-drawn wagons, and in 1950s Chevys on their way to and from the Colón residential district.

The main hub of life in Sancti Spíritus is **Plaza Serafín Sánchez,** a large public square that has a handful of fine colonial buildings in various states of disrepair mixed in with bland modern constructions. It certainly doesn't qualify as one of Cuba's most attractive plazas, but it is perennially busy with cars buzzing around and people meeting up. One of the most notable edifices on the square, on the corner of Solano and Máximo Gómez, is the **Biblioteca Provincial Rubén Martínez,** an early-20th-century library that looks more like the local opera house. The main sights in town are a short walk south of here.

Perhaps Sancti Spíritus's most splendid colonial home, **Museo de Arte Colonial** ✦✦, Plácido 74 at Jesús Menéndez (© **41/2-5455**), is the city's standout attraction. The opulent former palatial mansion of one of Cuba's most elite families, the Valle-Iznaga clan, who fled Cuba after the Revolution, it became the property of the state in 1961. Ninety percent of what you see inside, from furniture to paintings, is original. Though the family obviously kept an impressive collection of Limoges porcelain, French gilded mirrors, Italian marble tables, and Baccarat crystal chandeliers here, it wasn't their primary residence; the house was used mostly to host family members in transit, so the furnishings were rather eclectic. The three bedrooms are decorated in grand style, though, with handmade lace, embroidered sheets, and hand-painted glass. Note the gorgeous and very Cuban leather *sillón fumador* (smoking chair) and, in the music room, the mid-18th-century American piano, one of only two of its type in Cuba. In the tearoom is the family seal, which says a lot about the arrogance of the rich and powerful: *"El que más vale no vale tanto como Valle vale"* ("He who has the greatest worth isn't worth as much as a Valle is worth"—playing off the Spanish word for "worth" with the family surname). The museum is open Tuesday through Friday from 9:30am to 5pm, Saturday from 2 to 10pm, and Sunday from 8am to noon. Admission is CUC$2; a guided tour in English, Spanish, or French is CUC$3, photos CUC$1, and video CUC$5.

**Iglesia Parroquial Mayor del Espíritu Santo** ✦, Jesús Menéndez between Honorato and Agramonte, is one of the best-preserved colonial churches in Cuba and the oldest building in Sancti Spíritus. A small, faded blue church with a tall bell tower, the austere construction dates to 1680. The church's massive ceiling beams are impressive, as is the blue-and-yellow painted nave. Though the church is unlikely to wow most visitors, it is a quietly evocative, authentic colonial sight that recalls a day when Sancti Spíritus may have looked more like Trinidad. It's open Tuesday through Saturday from 9 to 11am and 2 to 5pm; admission is free.

If you're in town in spring (Feb–May), you can catch a game of *béisbol* (or as it's known colloquially, *pelota*), played by the local professional baseball team at the **Estadio José Antonio Huelgas,** Circunvalación Olivos 2 (© **41/2-4168**).

If you have occasion to be north of downtown, take a peek at the curiosity that is the so-called **Casa de los Refranes (House of Aphorisms).** The bricks that make up the exterior of Tomás Alvarez's modest roadside house are covered with many hundreds of sayings and slogans, some banal and others philosophical (they look like graffiti, but they're actually baked in a ceramic-like process). The house is on Carretera Central, just past the bus stop, up the road from Villa Los Laureles hotel.

## WHERE TO STAY

Sancti Spíritus has one of the best new boutique hotels in Cuba, as well as an excellent collection of casas particulares clustered within easy walking distance of the old town's main attractions. In addition to La Pantera (see below), three recommended casas are **Casa de Estrella,** Máximo Gómez 26 (© **41/2-7927**), a comfortable and friendly bargain option with two rooms; **Los Richard,** Calle Independencia 28 (© **41/2-6805**), a great spot just off Plaza Sanchéz, with two good rooms; and **Hostal Cupido (Casa José Luis Díaz)** ✪, Máximo Gómez 51 between Tirso Marín and Calderón (no phone), a very clean and private one-bedroom apartment that sleeps three quite comfortably.

**Hostal del Rijo** ✪✪ *Value*    This handsomely restored, light-blue colonial mansion on Plaza Honorato del Castillo is part of a growing trend in elegant boutique hotels, and best of all, it's a steal. The house was in complete ruins just several years ago, but it has been completely redone and now exudes colonial character and charm. The rooms are huge, especially room nos. 5, 6, 7, and 8, which look out onto the plaza and have balconies with views of the tower of La Parroquial church. If at all possible, reserve one of these second-floor rooms, as they have much more style than those on the ground floor. The accommodations have restrained decor, with sedate colors and old photos of Sancti Spíritus. Ceilings are so high that chirping birds often flutter in and fly around in the public rooms in the morning. The two-story structure is built around a lovely patio with a fountain, where you'll find the hotel's excellent little restaurant. There's also a nice bar and large TV lounge that opens onto the plaza.

Honorato del Castillo 12, Sancti Spíritus. © **41/2-8588.** Fax 41/2-8577. www.hotelescubanacan.com. 16 units, 1 suite. CUC$40–CUC$50 double; CUC$65 suite. MC, V. **Amenities:** Bar; limited room service. *In room:* A/C, TV, fridge, safe.

**Hotel Plaza**    A cute and comfortable small hotel right off Plaza Sánchez, this remodeled place has a rooftop terrace and mirador with long views of Sancti Spíritus. The decor features clay murals and swinging cocoon-like chairs on the floor above the bar. Rooms have high ceilings and feature similar motifs upstairs. The best, largest rooms face the plaza and the street; these rooms are quite expansive, with blue-and-white tile floors. Bathrooms, though, are disappointingly small. The bar has a two-story *barro* (clay) mural of a colonial town set in relief against a tall brick and stone atrium-like wall; it's a very good spot for a drink, as a band is often playing. A lobby computer with Internet access is available to both guests and nonguests.

Independencia 1 (Plaza Sánchez), Sancti Spíritus. (℃ **41/2-7102.** Fax 41/2-8577. www.hotelescubanacan.com. 27 units. CUC$35–CUC$45 double. Rates include breakfast. MC, V. **Amenities:** Bar; car-rental desk; limited room service. *In room:* A/C, TV.

**La Pantera** (★ *Value*    This elaborately decorated, beautiful 1806 house, a former paladar now converted into a casa particular, is one of the nicest you'll find in Cuba. It has marble pillars, high ceilings, handsome original floors, and elegant dining and sitting rooms. The bedrooms have private bathrooms, and each sleeps three people, with a double bed and twin. The family that runs La Pantera is very friendly and efficient, and good, plentiful meals are served to guests. The only thing out of place in this classy house are the cheesy posters and black light–like pictures of naked and scantily clad babes in the rooms—which would seem more appropriate in an auto garage.

Independencia 50 (between Comandante Fajardo and Hernán Laborí), Sancti Spíritus. (℃ **41/2-5435.** 2 units. CUC$20–CUC$25 double. No credit cards. *In room:* A/C, fridge, no phone.

## WHERE TO DINE

**Mesón de la Plaza** (★ CRIOLLA    Set on one of Sancti Spíritus's most attractive plazas, this handsome 1850s house is open to the street and features two rooms with high ceilings and picnic-style tables with benches. The restaurant is very clean, well managed, and popular, especially with a lunchtime tourist crowd. It breaks out of the Cuban restaurant doldrums with a couple of house specialties: garbanzo soup with bacon, pork, and sausage; and *ropa vieja* (shredded beef), served here in an earthenware pot. Those two dishes plus a glass of sangria make for a very good meal, but you might also opt for grilled shrimp or fish filet with tamarind sauce. *Note:* The restaurant is apt to close early at night, around 9pm, if there are no customers.

Máximo Gómez 34, Plaza Honorato. (℃ **41/2-8546.** Reservations recommended for lunch. Main courses CUC$4–CUC$10. MC, V. Daily 11am–11pm.

**Restaurant Hostal del Rijo** (★★ CRIOLLA    Set in an airy central courtyard beside a stone fountain and surrounded by an abundance of potted plants, this restaurant features fancy wrought-iron furniture and an overall elegant ambience. Aside from the wonderful environs, this place also has a creative and deft young chef, who takes chances with local ingredients and dishes—an uncommon occurrence at most state-run restaurants. We recommend the roast pork in a fruit glaze, or the *camarones silver dry,* which are shrimp cooked in a dry rum sauce. You'll even find a fairly decent and reasonably priced wine list here.

Honorato del Castillo 12, Sancti Spíritus. (℃ **41/2-8588.** Reservations recommended. Main courses CUC$6–CUC$17. MC, V. Daily 7am–11pm.

**Restaurant Quinta Santa Elena** (★ CRIOLLA    This restaurant near the river and Puente Yayabo occupies a lovely colonial home with handsome rooms and a relaxing grand terrace that opens onto the garden backyard, with river views. Popular with groups, especially at lunch, it features traditional Cuban music and good meals and service. Standard dishes like fried fish filet and pork and beef steaks are enlivened by a couple of twists, including *ropa vieja,* the classic Cuban dish of tangy shredded beef, and *vaca frita,* a traditional dish of roast beef.

Padre Quintero (between Llano and Manolico Díaz). (℃ **41/2-9167.** Reservations recommended for lunch. Main courses CUC$3–CUC$12. MC, V. Daily 9am–midnight.

## SANCTI SPIRITUS AFTER DARK

Sancti Spíritus is rather obviously not much of a party town, but it has a couple of spots to hear live Cuban music. Probably the best bar in town is in the **Hotel Plaza** on Plaza Sánchez. For a drink or live music, **Casa de la Trova,** Máximo Gomez between Plaza Honorato and Solano, is a hopping place with an open-air patio; it's popular with a 30- to 60-something crowd. The **Casa de la Música,** Padre Quintero 32, is a good-looking place with an open-air sitting area and stage, and a terrace that overlooks the Río Yayabo. The stage area has been embellished by a fancy neo-baroque mural/relief, which sports Carnival costumes and Sancti Spíritus personalities and literary figures. The place has a pretty good light and sound system and has shows Friday through Sunday (groups can arrange for music Tues–Thurs by speaking with the Cubatur agency); the cover charge is CUC$1. If you're feeling in the mood to join the show, head to **Café ARTex,** on Plaza Sanchéz, where the locals get down to some serious karaoke almost every night.

If you're interested in an *espectáculo* (Cuban music and dance show), head out to the cabaret show at the **Villa Los Laureles** (© **41/2-7345**), which is followed with salsa dancing at the hotel's dance club. Theater and dance performances, rather inconsistently scheduled (children's programs seem more popular), are held at the **Teatro Principal** (© **41/2-5755**) on Jesús Menéndez, near the Puente Yayabo.

For Cuban and Latin American (and occasional subtitled American and European) films, there are two **movie houses** on Plaza Sánchez.

# 8

# Camagüey & the Northeastern Coast

*by Eliot Greenspan & Neil E. Schlecht*

The extraordinary, powdery beaches of **Cayo Coco** and **Cayo Guillermo,** the cays that lie off the mainland and jut into the deep blue of the Atlantic Ocean, are the primary attractions of Ciego de Avila province. It is a remote area, but one with the infrastructure and natural gifts that make it perfect for idyllic sun, sand, and sea holidays. The namesake provincial capital Ciego de Avila and other towns and cities in this province hold few attractions for visitors.

A little farther east, predominantly flat low-lying Camagüey province, southeast of Ciego de Avila, is the largest in the country, though it is also the least densely populated. It occupies the widest swath on the island, 120km (75 miles) from the Atlantic coast to the Caribbean coast. **Camagüey,** the provincial capital, is Cuba's third-largest city, after Havana and Santiago de Cuba, and is a relatively undiscovered colonial gem of a city that is worth exploring.

## 1 Cayo Coco & Cayo Guillermo ★★

98km (61 miles) N of Ciego de Avila; 550km (341 miles) E of Havana; 270km (167 miles) NE of Trinidad; 202km (125 miles) NW of Camagüey

One of Cuba's premier beach destinations, distinguished by some of the most pristine sands and water on the island, Cayo Coco and Cayo Guillermo are cousin cays reached by crossing a 27km (17-mile) *pedraplén,* or man-made causeway, that extends from the mainland over the shimmering, shallow waters of the Atlantic. The cays share some of the same attributes as Varadero, but with a more isolated and natural feel, and without the interminable string of hotels.

Though these cays were explored way back in 1514, when Diego Velázquez named the stretch of islands and cays along the north coast **Jardines del Rey (The King's Gardens),** Cayo Coco was only developed for tourism in the early 1990s. The development on its neighboring cay, Guillermo, is newer still. Until construction of the causeway in 1988, the Cayos remained completely isolated, exclusively known to local fishermen and adventurous sailors like Ernest Hemingway.

The cays are part of the Archipélago de Camagüey, which extends 300km (185 miles) along the north coast and consists of some 400 large islands and small cays. Cayos Coco and Guillermo, the most developed of the entire stretch, are populated by just a handful of resort hotels—although more are planned. The unspoiled beaches have spectacular white and powdery sand and the waters are a classic Caribbean-style crystalline turquoise. The area's natural gifts are some of the best in Cuba: nearly 400km (250 miles) of coral reef, plus an eco-tourist's bundle of lagoons, marshes, and

## A Bridge So Far

To declare that Cayo Coco and Guillermo are only nominally connected to the rest of Cuba is no exaggeration. One has to pass a guarded checkpoint (CUC$2 toll each way) to access the *pedraplén* that bridges the distance between the mainland and the cays. The only Cubans allowed to pass the checkpoint are the 3,500 employees of the resort hotels or others with official work business there. If you are driving a rental vehicle, your car may be inspected to insure that you are not transporting any Cuban interlopers. A few Cubans who are the lucky beneficiaries of special vacations from the state are also allowed access. When people talk about Cuba's penchant for creating apartheid-like tourist sites, the northern cays are often cited as a prime example.

Though having exclusive rights to enjoy the cays may not sit well with some foreign travelers, the prohibition on Cubans has been successful in nipping *jineterismo* in the bud. The ubiquitous escorts you find in many other parts of the island are nonexistent here. It's pretty simple: If they can't get here, they can't do much to drum up business.

one of the island's most abundant populations of birds, with more than 150 species. The latter include the Americas' largest native colony of pink flamingos, estimated at upwards of 10,000 birds, which often appear as a gauzy pink haze shimmering on the horizon (except in May, when they venture close to the causeway), as well as herons, pelicans, black and white egrets, the white ibis, and other tropical species. The waters off the cays are flush with grouper, snapper, and mackerel, while deeper off the coast fishermen find marlin and swordfish.

A third cay east of Cayo Coco, Cayo Romano, and the beaches out on Cayo Paredón Grande (tiny despite its name), are the next bull's-eye targeted for Cuban hotel development in the archipelago, although no construction has yet begun. For now, the main resorts are Cayo Coco and Cayo Guillermo, and they're quite popular with Canadian and British travelers, as well as a good number of Germans and French. The focus for most guests is trained squarely on the beaches, swimming pools, watersports, dining and drinking, in-house activities, and nightly entertainment; rare is the traveler who comes seeking something else. If you have other activities in mind, your sense of isolation could be significant, although for those who get antsy, all the hotels offer local excursions as well as day trips and overnights to Trinidad, Camagüey, and Havana.

## ESSENTIALS
### GETTING THERE
**BY PLANE**   The **Aeropuerto Internacional Jardines del Rey,** Carretera a Cayo Coco (℅ **33/30-9165;** airport code CCC), accepts international flights from Canada, Mexico, Germany, the U.K., and Spain. There are daily domestic flights on **Cubana** and **AeroCaribbean** from Havana and Santiago.

The hotels all have airport pickup services for clients. If you have not prearranged transportation to your hotel, there are usually a couple of state-owned taxis hanging

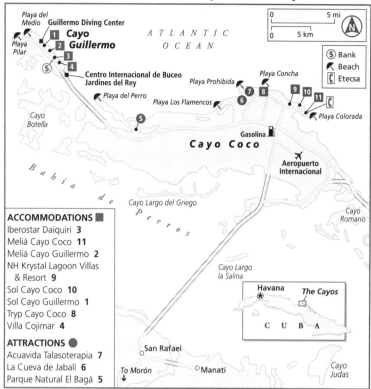

ATLANTIC OCEAN

Playa del Medio
Guillermo Diving Center
**1** Cayo
**2** Guillermo
Playa Pilar
**3**
$
**4**
Centro Internacional de Buceo
Jardines del Rey
Playa del Perro
Playa Prohibida
Playa Los Flamencos
Playa Concha
**7** **8**
**6**
**9** **10** **11**
Playa Colorada
**5**

$ Bank
Beach
Etecsa

0    5 mi
0    5 km
N

Cayo Botella

Cayo Coco

Gasolina

Aeropuerto Internacional

Bahía de Perros

Cayo Largo del Griego

Cayo Romano

Cayo Largo la Salina

Havana    The Cayos

C U B A

San Rafael

To Morón
Manatí

Cayo Judas

**ACCOMMODATIONS** ■
Iberostar Daiquiri **3**
Meliá Cayo Coco **11**
Meliá Cayo Guillermo **2**
NH Krystal Lagoon Villas
  & Resort **9**
Sol Cayo Coco **10**
Sol Cayo Guillermo **1**
Tryp Cayo Coco **8**
Villa Cojimar **4**

**ATTRACTIONS** ●
Acuavida Talasoterapia **7**
La Cueva de Jabalí **6**
Parque Natural El Bagá **5**

about. The fare from Aeropuerto Internacional Jardines del Rey is about CUC$8 to Cayo Coco and CUC$14 to Cayo Guillermo.

**BY BUS** If you're traveling independently to the cays from within Cuba, getting there on your own without a rental car is complicated. The only bus services that travel across the checkpoint are those belonging to official tour operators, such as **Cubanacán, Cubatur,** and **Havanatur.** All of these operators offer package deals and transportation options to the cays from all of their major operational points, including Havana, Santiago, Varadero, Trinidad, and Ciego de Avila.

A more complicated way to the cays is to take a **Víazul** (✆ 7/881-1413; www.viazul.com) bus to Ciego de Avila, and then hire a taxi all the way to the cays (CUC$40–CUC$50). All Víazul buses on the Havana-Santiago route stop in Ciego de Avila. Fare is CUC$30 from Havana, and CUC$26 from Santiago. Since it is illegal to transport foreigners and Cubans without permission to the cays, when you hire a cab, be sure your driver has permission; otherwise, he would have to drop you off about a half-mile from the checkpoint, where you would then need to hitchhike a ride either from a Cuban worker or foreigner in a rental car, in addition to explaining to the suspicious checkpoint guards how you got there without onward transportation.

**BY CAR/TAXI** Only tourists in rental cars and officially registered, state-owned taxis are allowed to cross to the cays. To drive to the cays, head north out of Ciego de

Avila toward the city of Morón, and follow the signs out to the cays. You can pick up a taxi in either Ciego de Avila or Morón, the two nearest cities of note. Call **Turistaxi** (© **335/22-9997** in Ciego de Avila) or **Cubataxi** (© **33/3290** in Morón).

## GETTING AROUND

You won't get very far on foot. The cayos are deceptively large, and there's no place to go on foot anyway, unless you want to visit an adjacent hotel. The best way to get around the cays is by **moped,** or **bicycle** if you're feeling especially fit. Most of the hotels have mountain bikes (free for guests) and mopeds that rent for CUC$25 to CUC$35 a day.

There is a tourist bus that makes the entire circuit from one end of Playa Coco to the far end of Playa Guillermo. The bus runs around every 1½ hours, and costs CUC$5.

All of the hotels can call you a cab, or you can try **Taxi OK** (© **33/30-8197**). If you prefer to drive yourself, there are car-rental companies located on both Cayo Coco and Cayo Guillermo, and the majority of the hotels have agencies on the premises. **Havanautos** has an office at Hotel Ciego de Avila (© **33/26-6345**) and in Morón (© **33/5-2114**); **Micar** has agencies in Ciego de Avila (© **33/26-6157**) and Morón (© **33/5-2152**); and **Transtur** has an office in Ciego de Avila (© **33/26-6229**) and in Morón (© **33/5-2222**). All have operational centers on Jardines del Rey, with desks at most of the major hotels. Due to high demand and isolation, rates are relatively expensive on the cays, about CUC$60 to CUC$100 per day for a standard four-door. You're sometimes better off renting a car in Ciego de Avila or another city before traveling to the cays.

All the hotels offer a variety of **organized excursions,** either directly or through tour representatives, which transport guests by bus or minibus from one cay to the other, or to other destinations, such as Playa Pilar on Cayo Guillermo. You're probably just as well using whatever operator is working out of your hotel, or you can call **Cubanacán** (© **33/30-1225**), **Cubatur** (© **33/30-1029**), or **Havanatur** (© **33/30-1371**) to set something up.

## ORIENTATION

**Banco Financiero Internacional** (© **33/30-1252**) has several branches on the cays. For medical attention, go to **Clínica Internacional Cayo Coco** (© **33/30-1202**), next to the Villa Gaviota on Cayo Coco.

Several of the hotels have Internet access for their guests. In addition, there is an **Etecsa** booth next to the Sol Cayo Coco hotel; it's open daily from 8am to 9pm. You can also make long-distance and international calls from here or at the banks of pay phones outside of several hotels. International and domestic mail can be handled at any of the hotels.

## WHAT TO SEE & DO

Cayo Coco is the better known of the two cays, probably due to its earlier development. The best-known **Cayo Coco beaches** ★★ are **Playa Larga** and **Playa Colorada; Playa Los Flamencos,** a few kilometers west, is a slightly more isolated and quieter beach, and beyond this is **Playa Prohibida.** Together they're among the most stellar beaches to be found in all of Cuba. In the interior of the cay are lagoons and marshlands, havens for the local bird and animal populations.

Cayo Guillermo is connected to Cayo Coco by a 15km (9-mile) *pedraplén.* **Cayo Guillermo beaches** ★★ (**Playa El Paso, Playa del Medio,** and **Playa Larga**) are every bit as spectacular as those on Cayo Coco; in fact, at low tide, the crystal-clear

## Papa & the Cayos

Ernest Hemingway's love of sailing and deep-sea fishing is well documented, a great source of his love affair with Cuba. The novelist was one of the first to explore Cayo Guillermo; in the '30s and '40s, Hemingway used to set sail off the coasts of the northern cays in dogged pursuit of marlin and swordfish in the Atlantic. The celebrated beach on Cayo Guillermo, Playa Pilar, is even named for the author's beloved fishing boat, *The Pilar*. In an episode befitting his he-man, roguish character, Hemingway enlisted his crew and boat to hunt for Nazi submarines off Cuba's northern cays at the height of World War II (according to some, the island was awash with Nazi sympathizers and agents). Papa's companion was, as ever, Gregorio Fuentes, the model for the aged fisherman in *The Old Man and the Sea*.

In Hemingway's novel *Islands in the Stream*, the main character looks longingly across the bay at Cayo Guillermo, asking rhetorically, "See how green she is and full of promise?" Evidently the Cuban authorities, intent on developing the cays a half-century after Hemingway first explored them, feel the same way.

waters are so shallow that you can comfortably wade out several hundred meters, making them preferable to the beaches on Cayo Coco for many guests. The landscape is very similar to Cayo Coco, but Guillermo boasts the most spectacular beach of either cay, and perhaps the entire northern coastline: **Playa Pilar** ✿✿✿, long ago explored by Ernest Hemingway and today a popular day trip for hotel guests on both cays. When we last visited, rumors were rampant that one or more large hotels were slated to be built on Playa Pilar. This would be a shame in my opinion.

### DIVING & OTHER WATERSPORTS

With long, pristine stretches of coral reef, and warm, crystal-clear waters, the cays are one of the best diving spots on the planet. There are a couple dozen dive sites, including five superior sites easily accessible from the cays, which range in depth from 5 to 40m (15–130 ft.). All the hotels on Cayo Coco and Cayo Guillermo can organize diving excursions, but you may wish to directly consult one of the main outfits, like **Blue Diving** (✆ **33/30-8180** or 33/30-8179; www.bluediving.com), which has a dive center at the Meliá Cayo Coco, right on the beach. They offer certified programs, with several dive packages to choose from, international licensing courses, and diving excursions to Playa Santa Lucía and Trinidad. A two-tank dive is CUC$80, including equipment.

Most of the hotels have their own catamarans, sailboards, and other vehicles and facilities for watersports. **Tropicat** (✆ **33/30-1324**) operates catamaran cruises around the coral reef beyond the cays for either a half or full day. **Cubanacán Náutica Aguas Tranquilas** on Cayo Coco (✆ **33/30-1221**) has a wide range of watersports programs, including "seafari" catamaran trips to Paredón Grande, east of Cayo Coco; glass-bottomed boat trips out to the coral reef with opportunities for snorkeling; and a whole complement of water skis, kayaks, and windsurfing boards. The **Puertosol Marina** on Cayo Guillermo (✆ **33/30-1637**) has a six-vessel pier and similar capabilities and facilities, including diving and sport-fishing trips. Full-day catamaran trips run about CUC$70 per person, half-day trips, CUC$40. An hour-long glass bottom boat trip is just CUC$20,

**Jungle Tour** ⟨ (✆ **33/30-1515**) offers small speedboat trips (self-driven, with a guide) through a maze of mangrove canals, marshes, and wetlands of Cayo Guillermo, a scenic trip with stops for snorkeling. There are four departures daily (CUC$39 per person).

### ORGANIZED TOURS

All the hotels offer day trips to remote beaches, including the finest in the cays, **Playa Pilar,** and **city tours** by minibus to Morón, Trinidad, and Camagüey, or to Havana and Santiago, by plane. Other options include Sugar Cane Tours and visits to **Sitio Lagüira** (a purpose-built dude ranch). Horseback treks and jeep safaris through the interior of the cays and to Morón are also available. A popular trip is to **Laguna de la Leche** ⟨, a massive lake on the outskirts of Morón with plenty of pelicans, flamingos, and other native birds. The lake's name comes from the water's murky, milky appearance (caused by limestone deposits). Another, much smaller lake that's worth a visit is **Lago La Redonda,** where you'll find thick mangroves, swamps, and funky woodlands growing out of the still waters. It's best seen by *lancha* (motorboat) tour leaving from the little restaurant at its entry. On a cruise through, you'll see huge spider webs, massive mounds of termites in trees, and thick Spanish moss. Both lakes are most often visited in combination with a city tour of Morón. Consult a tour operator representative from **Havanatur, Cubatur,** or **Cubanacán** in the lobby of any of the hotels for information and current prices.

One of the only true attractions here, aside from the beaches and nature, is the **Parque Natural El Bagá** (✆ **33/30-1063**), an interesting little complex that features a series of nature trails and lookouts through mangroves, litoral forest, and on raised platforms over lagoons. They also have a small reconstruction of an ancient indigenous village, with periodic live shows of local actors engaged in re-creations of Taíno dances. (Parents, be forewarned: The women in the shows are topless.) They even have a wonderful stretch of beach right here. Admission is CUC$15, but most tour agencies offer tours to the park with transportation and lunch included for around CUC$25.

### TIME FOR SOME PAMPERING

Although nowhere near as opulent as many modern spas, the new **Acuavida Talasoterapia** (✆ **33/30-2157**) offers a wide range of massage and spa treatments. Options range from mud baths and seaweed scrubs, to full-body massages, and a host of water-based treatments. The large facility has five pools in a range of sizes and temperatures. Some are freshwater pools, while others take advantage of the neighboring seawater. There's a salon on premises, as well as a small medical facility.

## WHERE TO STAY & DINE ON CAYO COCO

Almost all visitors to Jardines del Rey come as part of an all-inclusive package and take all their meals at their hotels. If you want to take a break from your hotel fare, check out the simple shack, **Ranchón Playa Prohibida,** located out on Playa Prohibida, where a full lobster meal, with rice and beans and two good-size tails, will run you around CUC$15. If you're out at Playa Pilar, there's the similar **Ranchón El Pilar** offering similar fare at similar prices.

## A Stopover in Morón

Located 37km (23 miles) north of Ciego de Avila, Morón (moh-*rohn*) is the small gateway city to the cays, and home to most of the 3,500 Cubans who work at the resort hotels. With just a few dusty streets traveled by bicycles, horse-drawn carriages, and antique American autos, charmingly low-key Morón is most notable for its splendid but dilapidated collection of colonial buildings that line the main street, **Calle Martí.** Most visitors arrive by bus or taxi from Ciego de Avila or Camagüey or on an organized tour from one of the hotels on the Cayos. Though Morón possesses a **Municipal Museum,** Calle Martí 374 (✆ **33/5-4501;** admission CUC$1) with pre-Columbian arti- facts and idols, and an evocative **1920s railway station,** most travelers are content to stroll up and down Martí, absorbing the relaxed local flavor. The town mascot is the cock of Morón, a bronze statue placed at the foot of a clock tower near the Hotel Morón (the cock crows twice daily).

Some visitors decamp in Morón as a less-expensive alternative to the all- inclusive luxury hotels on the cays. By far the best place to stay in town is **La Casona,** Cristóbal Colón 41-C (✆ **33/5-2236;** fax 33/5-2128), an elegant and beautiful, if simple, small hotel in a yellow colonial manor house. It has seven enormous but sparsely furnished rooms with extremely high ceilings, marble floors, private bathrooms, and air-conditioning, and the hotel has a family-style restaurant, small pool, and an open-air bar out back. Though rooms could perhaps be a bit better cared for, the hotel is an atmospheric place to crash for CUC$36 (double occupancy). The large, unattractive, and uninviting **Hotel Morón,** Av. Tarafa (✆ **33/5-2230;** www.islazul.cu), run by Islazul, is a distant second choice. It does have a pool, however. Double rooms cost just CUC$28.

Easily the best spot for a meal in Morón is **Restaurante-Bar La Fuente,** Calle Martí 169 between Libertad and Ignacio Agramonte (✆ **33/5-5758).** The upscale and very cute restaurant has original art on the walls and an open central patio and fountain. Focusing on the tourist trade, it serves lots of salads, omelets, and main courses (CUC$5–CUC$20) like grilled fish and lobster. At night the essential visit is to the **Casa de la Trova,** Calle Libertad between Narciso López and Martí, for a dose of traditional Cuban tunes.

### VERY EXPENSIVE

**Meliá Cayo Coco** ✦✦✦   This elegant flagship of the Meliá chain is the top hotel on Cayo Coco and one of the finest hotels in Cuba. Popular with wedding parties and honeymooners, it was recently converted into an adults-only resort. The property is hip and stylish throughout, chic for an all-inclusive beach hotel. The resort has 76 fan- tastic bungalow rooms built out over a natural lagoon, separate from the other facili- ties and very private. Suites and junior suites are huge, with dining tables, inviting screened balconies, and very nice bathrooms. Superior standard doubles on the lagoon have refined decor and unscreened balconies. In this case, we actually prefer the first floor units, as they feature fabulous private balconies close to the lapping water. The rest of the grounds away from the lagoon are nicely landscaped; and rooms in the main part of the hotel are arranged like a tropical village. The hotel's excellent stretch of beach, Playa Las Coloradas, fronts a pretty, protected bay. The hotel's Las Caletas restaurant is a beautiful open-air tent-like affair built on a dock over the lagoon. An interesting feature on the premises is the Club Cubano, an information center that offers Spanish classes, seminars, dance lessons, and information on Cuban culture. Guests are free to patronize the dance club and other facilities at the Sol Meliá hotel next door. There's also an open-air theater with nightly entertainment.

Cayo Coco, Jardines del Rey. © **33/30-1180.** Fax 33/30-1195. www.solmeliacuba.com. 250 units. CUC$260–CUC$315 double; CUC$325–CUC$400 suite. Rates are all-inclusive. Rates lower in off season; higher during peak periods. MC, V. Children under 18 not allowed. **Amenities:** 4 restaurants; snack bar; 5 bars; outdoor pool; 2 lit outdoor tennis courts; fitness center; Jacuzzi; sauna; full-service dive shop; watersports equipment; free bikes; scooter rental; game room; concierge; tour desk; car-rental desk; salon; massage; laundry service. *In room:* A/C, TV, minibar, hair dryer, safe.

## EXPENSIVE

### NH Krystal Laguna Villas & Resort ☆☆
One of the newer hotels on the cays and one of the largest in Cuba, this resort is made up of two conjoined complexes, connected by a system of asphalt walkways. The grounds are extensive and chock-full of facilities, including three amphitheaters and a host of restaurants and bars. Half of the rooms are corporate-style blocks, while the others are very attractive wooden cabin-like casitas built over a natural lagoon. The latter, considered the "villas" here, are the best feature of the hotel, and have living rooms with a sofa bed, two-room bathrooms, high ceilings, and open balconies overlooking the lagoon. The standard rooms are housed in large blocks with an apartment-complex feel, and all are junior suites with a connected sitting room. The beach, hidden behind the lagoon, isn't visible from the property; to get to the sands on Playa Larga, you've got to walk about 5 minutes. The impressive resort was recently taken over by the NH hotel group, and is currently receiving over $8 million dollars in renovations and improvements.

Cayo Coco, Jardines del Rey. © **33/30-1470.** Fax 33/30-1498. www.nh-hotels.com. 690 units. CUC$170–CUC$250 double; CUC$250–CUC$330 villa. Rates are all-inclusive. Children 2–12 stay for CUC$35 per day; children under 2 stay for free. MC, V. **Amenities:** 8 restaurants; 2 bars; dance club; 4 outdoor pools; 3 lit outdoor tennis courts; gym; Jacuzzi; dry sauna; free bikes; scooter rental; children's center and programs; game room; concierge; tour desk; car-rental desk; babysitting; laundry service. *In room:* A/C, TV, fridge, hair dryer, safe.

### Sol Cayo Coco ☆ *Kids*
Yet another of Sol Meliá's hotels on Cayo Coco, this is probably the best-suited hotel on the cay for families. Constructed in 1997, the large hotel has a very relaxed feel. Families make up a great percentage of clients, and the kids' club, minigolf, soccer field, and kid's corner restaurant are tailored to youngsters. It's the only hotel on the cays with two beaches—it sits on a nice expanse of Playa Las Coloradas and also offers guests access to a sensational secluded section of Playa Larga reached by crossing a bridge over a river, to spectacularly limpid, shallow waters. Rooms are a good size, with an airy, beachy feel, and light blue walls, and almost all of them have sea views. The hotel's Club Nautico is one of the largest in Cuba, with over 10 catamarans and other watersports facilities. The hotel offers all kinds of special packages.

Cayo Coco, Jardines del Rey. © **33/30-1280.** Fax 33/30-1285. www.solmeliacuba.com. 268 units. CUC$215–CUC$245 double; CUC$285 suite. Rates are all-inclusive. Children 3–12 stay for half off; children under 3 stay free in parent's room. Rates lower in off season; higher during peak periods. MC, V. **Amenities:** 4 restaurants; 4 bars; dance club; 2 outdoor pools; 2 lit outdoor tennis courts; gym; Jacuzzi; sauna; watersports equipment; free bikes; scooter rental; children's center and programs; game room; concierge; tour desk; car-rental desk; salon; massage; babysitting; laundry service. *In room:* A/C, TV, minibar, hair dryer, safe.

**Tryp Cayo Coco** ★★    The granddaddy of all the Cayo hotels is the Tryp Cayo Coco, built in 1996 and recently restructured and remodeled. Half of the hotel was taken over by the Spanish Blau chain a few years ago. The remaining section has standard but cheery double rooms, with red-tile floors and green rattan chairs, headboards, and mirrors. The rooms are adorned with big, colorful pillows, and vibrant tropical paintings above the beds, and all have open-air balconies. Many of the rooms have sea views. The buildings and restaurants are spread out across the still extensive, village-like property. The pool areas are ample, with lots of greenery. They even have a small pond area with some resident flamingos.

Cayo Coco, Jardines del Rey. © **33/30-1300.** Fax 33/30-1386. www.solmeliacuba.com. 508 units. CUC$215–CUC$265 double; CUC$320 suite. Rates are all-inclusive. Children 3–12 stay for half off; children under 3 stay free in parent's room. Rates lower in off season; higher during peak periods. MC, V. **Amenities:** 5 restaurants; coffee shop; 6 bars; dance club; 2 outdoor pools; 3 lit outdoor tennis courts; gym; Jacuzzi; sauna; watersports equipment; free bikes; scooter rental; children's center and programs; concierge; tour desk; car-rental desk; massage; babysitting; laundry service. *In room:* A/C, TV, fridge, hair dryer, safe.

# WHERE TO STAY & DINE ON CAYO GUILLERMO
## VERY EXPENSIVE
**Meliá Cayo Guillermo** ★★    The fanciest property on Cayo Guillermo, this imposing luxury hotel wraps around the extensive pool area, with several restaurants and bars scattered about the property, including a breezy open-air grill restaurant down by the beach. The section of beach the hotel fronts is one of the finest on the cays, with thick palm trees sprouting out of pristine white sand. The hotel has a beautiful, long wooden pier that extends out into the surf, where you can venture for total privacy, as well as a couple of shaded hammocks set out in the sea grazing the shallow waters. Rooms are second in elegance only to the Meliá Cayo Coco, and a recent remodeling has really spruced them up substantially. Suites are very large bungalows with a sitting area, backyard, and Jacuzzi, while junior suites have two rooms and two bathrooms. Rooms sport a beachy decor that is surprisingly informal for a luxury hotel, though it doesn't take away from its abundant comforts. The grounds are lush and luxurious, and feature several lotus gardens.

Cayo Guillermo, Jardines del Rey. © **33/30-1680.** Fax 33/30-1684. www.solmeliacuba.com. 291 units. CUC$295–CUC$320 double; CUC$400 suite. Rates are all-inclusive. Children 3–12 stay for half off; children under 3 stay free in parent's room. Rates lower in off season; higher during peak periods. MC, V. **Amenities:** 4 restaurants; snack bar; pub; dance club; outdoor pool; 2 lit outdoor tennis courts; fitness center; Jacuzzi; watersports equipment; free bikes; scooter rentals; children's center and programs; game room; concierge; tour desk; car-rental desk; salon; massage; babysitting; laundry service. *In room:* A/C, TV, stocked minibar, coffeemaker, hair dryer, safe.

## EXPENSIVE
**Iberostar Daiquirí** ★★    This large resort hotel sits on a beautiful section of beach. Run by a Spanish chain, the hotel has several long, three-story blocks constructed around a large pool surrounded by gardens, as well as a host of smaller three-story buildings spread around their ample grounds. The rooms are good-size with modern and tasteful decor, tile floors, and multicolored bedspreads. Every room has either a balcony or terrace. The better rooms have views of the ocean. All the rooms have two full beds, though the suites have queen-size beds and a separate sitting room. The Iberostar has an excellent children's program, and a host of available activity and tour options.

Cayo Guillermo, Jardines del Rey. © **33/30-1650.** Fax 33/30-1641. www.iberostar.com. 312 units. CUC$200–CUC$280 double. Rates are all-inclusive. MC, V. **Amenities:** 3 restaurants; 4 bars; dance club; outdoor pool; 2 outdoor tennis courts; gym; sauna; watersports equipment; bike and scooter rental; children's center and programs; game center; concierge; tour desk; car-rental desk; babysitting; laundry service. *In room:* A/C, TV, minibar, hair dryer, safe (extra charge).

**Sol Cayo Guillermo** 🌟🌟 Although its nearby sister the Meliá Cayo Guillermo may be a bit swankier, this is still my favorite place to stay on Cayo Guillermo. This well-designed hotel has plenty of personality and a relaxed vibe. All the accommodations are loosely described as bungalows, although there are a few two-story blocks and duplex units here. The rooms are bright and cheery, decorated in sunny yellow and blue beach tones. They have beamed, peaked wooden ceilings, and nice tile and marble bathrooms (all with showers only). We especially like the built-in luggage racks made from drift-wood. The best rooms are the individual bungalows set close to the beach, although the second floor superior rooms are also a good bet, with large private balconies equipped with hammocks. The grounds are very nicely designed and maintained, and the beach is a wonderful long stretch of white sand. The hotel is popular with a broad range of travelers, from honeymooners and families, to singles and retirees.

Cayo Guillermo, Jardines del Rey. 📞 **33/30-1760.** Fax 33/30-1748. www.solmeliacuba.com. 268 units. CUC$230–CUC$255 double. Rates are all-inclusive. Children 3–12 stay for half off; children under 3 stay free in parent's room. Rates lower in off season. MC, V. **Amenities:** 4 restaurants; snack bar; 24-hr. bar; dance club; outdoor pool; 2 lit outdoor tennis courts; fitness center; Jacuzzi; steam room; watersports equipment; free bikes; scooter rental; children's center and programs; game room; concierge; tour desk; car-rental desk; salon; massage; babysitting; laundry service. *In room:* A/C, TV, minibar, coffeemaker, hair dryer, safe.

### MODERATE

**Villa Cojimar** The oldest of the four Cayo Guillermo hotels (built in 1992), this Gran Caribe hotel has received some long overdue upgrading in recent years. The rooms are now quite modern and attractive, although overall this hotel still lags far behind the competition in terms of style, facilities, and amenities. That said, it's one of the cheapest options on the cays, it's right on the beach, and the rooms are certainly acceptable. It has rather skimpily manicured grounds, a large central pool area, and a meager open-air theater where dance classes and the nightly show are staged.

Cayo Guillermo, Jardines del Rey. 📞 **33/30-1712.** Fax 33/30-1725. www.grancaribe.cu. 212 units. CUC$85–CUC$140 double; CUC$150–CUC$200 suite. Rates are all-inclusive. MC, V. **Amenities:** 3 restaurants; snack bar; 3 bars; dance club; nightly show; outdoor pool; 2 outdoor tennis courts; fitness center; watersports equipment; bike and scooter rental; game room; concierge; tour desk; car-rental desk; massage; babysitting; laundry service. *In room:* A/C, TV, fridge, hair dryer, safe.

## JARDINES DEL REY AFTER DARK

Most folks simply take advantage of the bars and nightly shows at their all-inclusive resort. The Sol Cayo Coco has one of the largest, most atmospheric, and liveliest dance clubs of the large resorts. Another alternative is the nightly cabaret show at **La Cueva de Jabalí** 🌟 (📞 **33/30-1206**). The show is rather simple and pedestrian, but the setting is quite interesting in the belly of a small underground cave. Admission is CUC$5. The show starts at 10pm and dancing follows. Mosquitoes are sometimes a problem inside the cave, so wear some repellent, or long-sleeved clothing.

Another alternative is **La Bolera,** a four-lane bowling alley/bar/cabaret near the Meliá Playa Guillermo.

## 2 Camagüey 🌟🌟

553km (343 miles) E of Havana; 110km (68 miles) E of Ciego de Avila; 328km (203 miles) W of Santiago de Cuba

One of Cuba's most historic and important cities, Camagüey is an excellent place to visit to get a feel for Cuba's colonial-era grandeur. Founded as the sixth of Cuba's original seven *villas* in 1514—as a port town originally named Santa María del Puerto del

# Camagüey

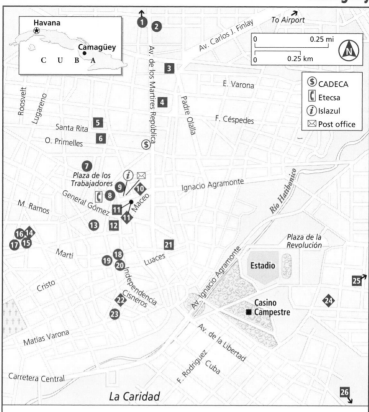

**ACCOMMODATIONS** ■
Casa Los Vitrales **21**
Casa Manolo **5**
Casa Manolo Banegas **12**
Casa Xiomara & Rodolfo **6**
Gran Hotel **11**
Hotel Colón **4**
Hotel Camagüey **26**
Hotel Plaza **3**
Villa Teresita **25**

**DINING** ◆
Don Ronquillo Restaurant **10**
El Ovejito **14**
La Campana de Toledo **22**
Restaurant El Retorno **24**
Salón Caribe **11**

**ATTRACTIONS** ●
Casa de la Trova **19**
Casa Natal del Mayor
  (Ignacio Agramonte) **9**
Casa Natal Nicolás Guillén **13**
Hospital de San Juan de Díos **23**
Iglesia de Nuestra Señora de la Merced **8**
Iglesia de Nuestra Señora del Carmen **16**
Iglesia San Juan de Díos **23**
La Catedral **20**
Monasterio de las Ursulinas **17**
Museo Provincial General Ignacio Agramonte **2**
Parque Agramonte **18**
Plaza del Carmen **15**
Plaza San Juan de Díos **23**
Teatro Principal **7**
Tifereht Israel Synagogue **1**

Príncipe—the city was later moved to a different spot by Diego Velázquez himself in 1516 and transplanted again to its present, inland location in 1528. The town didn't receive its final name, which means "Son of the Tree" in the Taíno language, until after the conclusion of the Spanish-American War in 1898.

Camagüey retains a strong colonial imprint, with a highly irregular layout and warren of narrow, bending streets and alleyways, handsome colonial houses, two of the most dignified colonial plazas in Cuba, and an unequaled collection of impressive if evocatively dilapidated 16th-, 17th-, and 18th-century churches. In fact, Camagüey is often called *la ciudad del Barroco* (city of baroque) or *la ciudad de las iglesias* (city of churches). Another symbol of the city is the *tinajón,* a massive terra-cotta water jug used in the 18th and 19th centuries to collect rainwater. These now largely decorative items can still be seen in the serene gardens and courtyards of the city's colonial houses.

Travelers intent on experiencing the cultural offerings of urban, interior Cuba should not skip Camagüey. The birthplace of Cuba's national poet, Nicolás Guillén, Camagüey claims some of the strongest artistic and literary traditions in Cuba and one of the country's most vital cultural scenes, with an active community of plastic artists and the internationally renowned Camagüey Ballet. Camagüey is also recuperating its distinguished historical character, plowing ahead with invaluable restoration work of the city's classic colonial structures. The 1998 visit of Pope John Paul II gave the city added impetus to refurbish its crumbling set of colonial churches. Yet, it is not just a museum set piece—it's a lively city that explodes with a weekly Saturday night street festival. Travelers could conceivably blow through and see the principal attractions in a day, but Camagüey requires at least 2 or 3 days to unfurl its significant charms.

## ESSENTIALS
### GETTING THERE
**BY PLANE**   You can fly from Havana and Santiago de Cuba to Camagüey on **Cubana;** there are also international charter flights from Canada and Great Britain. Flights arrive at **Aeropuerto Internacional Ignacio Agramonte,** Carretera Central Nuevitas Km 8 (✆ **32/26-1862** or 32/26-1525; airport code CMW), 9km (6 miles) west of the city. A local bus runs from the airport to Parque Finlay and back, but a taxi is probably your best bet.

**BY BUS**   Víazul (✆ **7/881-1413** in Havana, or **32/27-1668** in Camagüey; www. viazul.com) travels daily to Camagüey on the Trinidad–Santiago de Cuba and Havana–Santiago de Cuba lines. From Havana, the bus departs at 9:30am, 3pm, and 10pm, arriving at 6:05pm, 11:55pm, and 6:15am, respectively (CUC$36); from Santiago, departure times are 9am, 3:15pm, and 10pm, arriving at 4:35pm, 10:55pm, and 3:30am (CUC$20); and from Trinidad the bus leaves at 8am and arrives at 1:20pm (CUC$16).

The main bus terminal for long-distance buses, the **Terminal de Omnibuses** (✆ **32/27-3463**) is located 2km (1¼ miles) southeast of the city, at Carretera Central 180 at the corner of Calle Perú. For buses to locations within Camagüey province, there is a separate **Terminal Municipal,** several blocks north of the old center, near the intersection of Padre Olalla and Avenida Carlos J. Finlay (just north of the railway station).

**BY TRAIN**   Camagüey is on the main Havana–Santiago de Cuba railway line, with nearly a half-dozen daily trains originating in Havana and Santiago de Cuba. Train schedules change frequently, and depending on the season, many trains don't operate on a daily basis; verify the current schedule by calling © 7/862-1920 or 7/861-4259, though it's often better to go in person to the train station and purchase tickets at least a day in advance. Trains arrive in Camagüey from Morón, Santa Clara, and Ciego de Avila as well. The large and busy local train station (© 32/29-2633) is on Avenida Carlos J. Finlay, across from the Hotel Plaza.

## GETTING AROUND

The labyrinthine layout of Camagüey's old town is extremely complicated, though it is pretty compact. The best way to get to know the historic center is by foot. In fact, in and around Camagüey, you will mostly depend on leg power, though taxis may be necessary to get back and forth between a couple of the hotels.

**BY TAXI**    Taxis are plentiful around town, and a few are usually stationed in front of any hotel. Alternatively, you can call **Cubataxi** (© 32/28-1247) **Transtur** (© 32/28-2413), or **Turistaxi** (© 32/27-1208) for local and long-distance hire. Horse-drawn carriages and bicycle-powered rickshaws also function as taxis around the historic center.

**BY TRAIN**    Not a traditional train, but a *trencito*—a green and yellow tractor with cars and operated by Cubanacán—runs from Hotel Camagüey on Carretera Central to downtown Camagüey, bypassing the major arteries and major attractions of the historic center. Tickets (CUC$2) can be purchased at any tour agency at any hotel.

**BY CAR**    A car isn't necessary if you are planning to stay put in Camagüey, but if you're looking to go beyond the city, the major car-rental companies are **Havanautos** (© 32/29-1535) and **Transtur** (© 32/27-1015), both of which have offices in most of the major hotels in town. Rates are about CUC$50 to CUC$80 per day for a standard four-door car.

## ORIENTATION

You'll find a **Banco Financiero Internacional** (© 32/29-4846) at Independencia 221, at Plaza de Maceo. It's open Monday through Friday from 8am to 4pm. There is a **CADECA** (© 32/29-5220) at República 353. The above are two of the most centrally located branches, but you'll find several other banks and money exchange houses around the city.

If you need medical attention, **Policlínica Centro** is located at República 211, at the corner of Reforma (© 32/29-7810).

An **Etecsa** telephone and Internet kiosk is on Calle Independencia at Ignacio Agramonte, across from La Merced church and the Islazul office; it's open daily from 9am to 9pm. The main branch of **Correos** is at Ignacio Agramonte 461; it's open Monday through Saturday from 9am to 5pm.

Most of the major Cuban tour agencies operate several tour desks around Camagüey, and at all the major hotels. **Islazul** operates a booth with tourist information, maps, and Internet service at Ignacio Agramonte 448, on Plaza de los Trabajadores (© 32/29-2550). **Cubanacán** has offices at the Galería Colonial, Ignacio Agramonte 406 (© 32/29-4905), as well as at the Hotel Colón, Gran Hotel, and Hotel Camagüey. **Havanatur,** Calle Monteagudo between Cuba and Carretera Central (© 32/28-1564), is well equipped to arrange all sorts of excursions, local guides, and tour programs.

# WHAT TO SEE & DO

Camagüey's *casco histórico* (old quarter) is the primary draw, and most sights of interest are within easy walking distance of its epicenter, just north and west of the Hatibonico River. The historic zone represents one of the largest colonial sectors in Cuba, spread over 300 hectares (740 acres), and Camagüey boasts more than a dozen colonial churches. As in Havana, the office of the City Historian is actively engaged in restoring as many of the city's historic buildings as it can manage, and by law, all businesses in the district contribute 2% of their revenues toward the restoration cause.

**Parque Agramonte,** which occupies the spot where the old Plaza de Armas existed in 1528, shortly after the transfer of the city to its present location, is the best place to get your bearings. In its center is a bronze and pink granite equestrian statue of the most famous citizen of Camagüey, Ignacio Agramonte. Each corner of the park is marked by a tall royal palm, planted to pay tribute to four local martyrs of the struggle for independence, executed in the square by Spanish forces for treason. The park is an agreeable spot, with elegant street lamps and marble benches popular with locals. It is flanked by attractive colonial houses, including the **Casa de la Trova** (where live traditional Cuban music can be heard daily), and the early-18th-century **Catedral** on the south side. The church is a good example of the city's ongoing efforts to resurrect neglected historic buildings. Dedicated to Nuestra Señora de la Candelaria, patron saint of Camagüey, the cathedral has been transformed, in the span of less than 3 years, from a dull and uninspiring church to an attractively austere house of worship, showing off beautiful *vigas* (wood ceiling beams).

**Calle Maceo,** just north of Parque Agramonte, is the city's principal shopping avenue, a busy pedestrian artery stuffed with shops and bars. The other principal reference point of downtown Camagüey is the much-trafficked but disappointingly pedestrian **Plaza de los Trabajadores (Workers' Square).** On it are two of the city's more important sights: the birth house of Ignacio Agramonte, and the church of La Merced.

Southeast of the historic core, across the unspectacular Hatibonico River, lies **Casino Campestre,** the largest natural city park in Cuba. Inaugurated in 1860, it was transformed into a public park at the beginning of the 20th century. Its tall, shady royal palms, public monuments, and children's attractions make it a favorite with Camagüeyanos. Nearby, on the other side of the Cándido González baseball stadium, is the **Plaza de la Revolución,** a massive but cold square honoring Cuba's revolutionary legends past and present: Agramonte, Che, and Fidel. Pope John Paul II said Mass at this spot in 1998.

## THE TOP ATTRACTIONS

**Casa Natal del Mayor (Ignacio Agramonte)**   Ignacio Agramonte y Loynaz, Camagüey's favorite son and the national hero of the independence struggle—known to all as "El Mayor"—was born December 23, 1841, in this pale yellow 18th-century house. Agramonte's birthplace displays classical colonial elements, both baroque and Hispanic-*mudéjar*. The house, now a National Monument, may interest those with a thirst for Cuban history; others may simply be interested in viewing the lovely carved wooden ceilings upstairs and smattering of period furnishings (only some are original to the house) of an authentic colonial house. A number of artifacts aim to reveal Agramonte's boyhood life here and his later achievements, with documents including love letters to Amalia Simoni (who would later become his bride), photographs, newspaper accounts of battles, and Agramonte's pistol.

Ignacio Agramonte 459, Plaza de los Trabajadores. *C* **32/29-7116.** Admission CUC$2. Tues–Sat 10am–5pm; Sun 8am–noon.

**Casa Natal Nicolás Guillén** Camagüey's most important literary figure, considered Cuba's national poet, was born in this house, which stands as a simple tribute to his life and enduring work. Guillén, an Afro-Cuban born here in 1902, only lived in the house for 2 years, though he returned to Camagüey after studying law in Havana and worked as a journalist for a local paper. The house now functions primarily as a research and cultural center, with occasional poetry readings and concerts. A smattering of photographs, personal memorabilia, and copies of a handful of poems connect the house to the life and work of Guillén.

Calle Hermanos Agüero 58 (between Cisneros and Príncipe). *C* **32/29-3706.** Free admission. Mon–Fri 8am–5pm.

**Iglesia de Nuestra Señora de La Merced** ★ The most significant structure on the rather plain Plaza de los Trabajadores is this massive 18th-century brick church, Camagüey's most distinguished and, in its day, the largest in Cuba. A chapel existed on this spot in 1601; the present structure dates to 1748 (it was reconstructed in 1848 and again in 1909 after a fire). To one side of a lush cloister is the old convent, which still houses a rapidly decreasing number of nuns. The church is an eclectic architectural mix. Adorning the ceiling are surprising Art Nouveau murals, added in the 20th century. Also of note are the painted wood, neo-Gothic altar and the **Santo Sepulcro,** a 1762 casket elaborately fashioned from 25,000 silver coins and carried high by eight men during Easter processionals. Down narrow stairs behind the principal altar is a mysterious crypt, the remains of an extensive underground cemetery. Most of it was closed off after fire damage, but six macabre tombs with skeletons remain and are on creepy view alongside a small museum of 18th- and 19th-century objects uncovered at the church.

Av. Agramonte 4 (Plaza de los Trabajadores). *C* **32/9-2740.** Free admission. Daily guided tours (in Spanish) available 9am–4pm.

**Museo Provincial General Ignacio Agramonte** Several blocks north of the historic center of the city, Camagüey's largest and most important museum houses the second-largest collection of paintings in Cuba, bested only by the Museo de Bellas Artes in Havana. The museum concentrates on Cuban fine arts (from the early 19th c. to contemporary works), but also packs in moderately interesting collections of natural history and archaeology. There is also a selection of decorative arts, including furnishings and porcelain from the colonial and Republican periods. The natural history rooms display native Cuban species, such as sharks, fish, and exotic fauna. These exhibits may be interesting for kids bored with Cuban history and fine art, but you've

---

*Tips* **Camagüey's Synagogue**

Camagüey has one of the more active, if still tiny, Jewish communities in Cuba, and many Jewish visitors from overseas pay a visit to the city's small synagogue, **Tifereth Israel,** Calle Andrés Sánchez 365, between Capdevila and J. Agüero, La Vigía (*C* **32/28-4639**). Inaugurated in 1998, the synagogue serves just a handful of families, and the community is in the process of restoring the small Jewish cemetery in the city, which had suffered from neglect.

surely seen better. The building itself is worth a look around, as it features a handsome patio with a wealth of indigenous trees and *tinajones* (large ceramic pots).

Av. de los Mártires 2 (between Ignacio Sánchez and Rotario). (C) **32/28-2425**. Admission CUC$2 adults, free for children under 12. Mon 1–5pm; Tues–Thurs and Sat 10am–5pm; Fri noon–7pm; Sun 10am–2pm.

**Plaza del Carmen** ☆☆ *Finds*   A narrow pedestrian-only street of pastel-colored colonial row houses opens on to an irregularly shaped square. Renovations have revamped the 18th-century square with street lamps, huge *tinajeros* (clay pots used for storing water), and slightly larger-than-life sculptures of locals in various poses of daily work and pleasure. The restored spot has done much to uncover a classic Camagüey colonial plaza.

Not long ago, the church and convent at the end of the open square stood roofless, in utter ruins. The baroque-style **Iglesia de Nuestra Señora del Carmen,** which dates to 1825, is now immaculately restored. It is the only church in Camagüey, and indeed in the whole eastern half of Cuba, topped by two towers. The early-19th-century **Monasterio de las Ursalinas (Ursuline Convent)** next door is now an architectural showpiece distinguished by handsome arches framing the expansive patio. Built in 1829, the convent later became a refuge for hurricane victims and a school for the poor after the sisters transferred their headquarters to Havana. In the years subsequent to the Revolution, it served several purposes; most recently it was a nondescript warehouse. The building was taken over in 1999 by the City Historian's office, and today the convent is an eye-pleasing beauty, well worth a peek inside.

Plaza del Carmen. (C) **32/29-6901**. Free admission. Monastery daily 8am–5pm; plaza daily 24 hr.

**Plaza San Juan de Dios** ☆☆☆   A National Monument and one of the most remarkable colonial relics in Cuba, this elegant and serene square looks like a meticulously designed movie set. Its charms are subtle but undeniable. The colonial arches, cobblestones, and houses with red-tile roofs and window grilles speak volumes about Camagüey's colonial past. The square, whose present design dates to 1732, holds great significance for Cubans: The body of the national independence war hero Ignacio Agramonte was brought here, after being burned by the Spaniards, for identification in 1873.

On one side of the square are the 17th-century church and hospital of the order of San Juan de Dios. **La Iglesia San Juan de Dios** features a baroque colonial interior with dark-toned woods and the original brick floor. The bell tower, from which there is a splendid view of all the church belfries spread across the skyline of the *centro histórico,* is open to the public and worth the rickety climb up. The church adjoins the handsome **Hospital de San Juan de Dios,** established to serve the poor. Padre José Olallo Valdés (1815–89), who furthered that mission, has been beatified by the Catholic Church and is on his way to being made a saint. Off one side of the cloisters are the remains of Agramonte, making the church even more of a sacred place for Camagüeyanos. The city now puts on art exhibits, concerts, and historical displays, such as old pharmaceutical objects or women's fashions, in one corner of the hospital. The understated but noble colonial structure contains a notable courtyard, thick doors, and an elegant wood staircase.

Plaza San Juan de Dios. (C) **32/29-1318**. Admission CUC$1. Mon and Wed–Sat 9am–7pm; Sun 9am–1pm.

## SHOPPING

You'll find *artesanía* (handicrafts) stands set up on **Plaza San Juan de Dios** Friday through Sunday. Another spot for handicrafts is **Centro/Galería ACAA** (Asociación Cubana de Artesanos Artistas), just off the Plaza de los Trabajadores at Calle Padre

Valencia 2 (© **32/28-6834**), which features exhibits and sales, including clay and ceramics, with artisans working out back.

If you want to visit an **artist's studio,** we highly recommend the work of the amiable husband-wife team Joel Jover and Iliana Sánchez. Their home studio is Calle Martí 154, on the north side of Parque Agramonte (© **32/29-2305**). Another well-known and very welcoming artist is Oscar Rodríguez Lasseria, a talented **ceramicist** whose studio is on Calle Tomás Betancourt 307, between Joaquín de Agüero and Benavides (© **32/28-1400**), a bit removed from the *centro* in La Vigía district. Oscar conducts invitational seminars with ceramics artists from around the world. *Note:* If you purchase any artworks in Camagüey, you'll need to take them to the **Institute of National Culture (INC)** (© **32/29-7556**) to get official permission and documentation to export them from Cuba. The local office is located on the second floor of the old hospital on Plaza San Juan de Dios; it's open Monday through Friday from 8am to noon, and the fee is CUC$10.

Check out the **Casa del Tabaco** in the Galería Colonial, Ignacio Agramonte 406 (© **32/28-3944**), for a fine selection of Cuban cigars. The gentleman in the shop is very willing to educate customers about the fine art of Cuban tobacco. He'll tell you that Fidel used to smoke a Cohiba Lancero (which goes for about CUC$350 a box).

Pick up CDs and tapes of Cuban music at any **ARTex** shop. Perhaps the best one is within the Casa de la Trova, on Calle Cisneros (© **32/29-1357**). Other branches are on República 38 and Ignacio Agramonte 109.

## WHERE TO STAY

Camagüey has an appealing supply of attractive and affordable hotels—most owned and operated by the Cuban Islazul chain—and several have undergone extensive restorations that have brought back their old-world charm. For visitors interested in home stays, the city also offers a host of excellent private accommodations.

### MODERATE

**Gran Hotel** ★★ Camagüey's most classic hotel dates from 1939. Its clubby, old-world feel is accentuated by an abundance of watering holes—this midsize hotel has four bars, including the Piano Bar, a great dark place that's one of the best cocktail lounges in Cuba. Another good bar is the spot on the rooftop, which is shaded by palm trees. There's more to the Gran Hotel than places to wet your whistle, though. It has a medium-size terrace pool that features a nightly show that is part water ballet, a pretty triangular patio with a fountain, an elegant top-floor restaurant with panoramic views, and a handsome, breezy lobby with an old elevator of beautiful wood, and displays of local art and handicrafts. The rooms are nicely appointed and have high ceilings and small TVs. A handful of corner "special" rooms (nos. 1 and 7 on each floor) are the prize, though; they are larger, with separate, but small, sitting rooms and handsome dressers. A few interior rooms on each floor have no windows to speak of.

Maceo 64 (between General Gómez and Ignacio Agramonte), Camagüey. © **32/29-2093** or 32/29-2094. Fax 32/29-3933. www.islazul.cu. 72 units. CUC$52–CUC$58 double. Rates include buffet breakfast. MC, V. **Amenities:** Restaurant; cafeteria; 4 bars; nightly show; small outdoor pool. *In room:* A/C, TV, safe.

### INEXPENSIVE

Recommended *casas particulares* are **Casa Xiomara & Rodolfo** ★, Oscar Primelles 615, between Lugareño and San Ramón (© **32/28-1948**), an amazingly large and well-equipped apartment that's a very nice option for two couples or a family traveling together; **Casa Manolo Banegas,** Calle Independencia 251, between Hermanos Agüero and General Gómez (© **32/29-4606**); **Casa Manolo,** Santa Rita 18, between República and Santa Rosa (© **32/29-4403**); **Casa Los Vitrales,** Calle Avellaneda 3, between General Gómez and Martí (© **32/29-5866**); and **Villa Teresita,** Av. de la Victoria 12, between Padre Carmelo y Freyre (© **32/29-7108**).

**Hotel Camagüey**    This large hotel, set on the outskirts of Camagüey, isn't particularly convenient, or attractive—its 1960s block exterior is rather undistinguished. But, as the largest hotel in town, it has all the services one could require, and is a friendly, well-run option. Rooms are average-size and somewhat plainly decorated, but perfectly comfortable for a short stay. Other hotels located in the old center have more character and represent better values, but for large groups that need facilities and services, the Hotel Camagüey may be the best option in the city. It's also got a nice, mid-size pool, which nonguests can use for a CUC$3 fee.

Carretera Central Este Km 4.5, Jayamá, Camagüey. © **32/28-7267.** Fax 32/28-7181. 142 units. CUC$40–CUC$45 double. MC, V. **Amenities:** 2 restaurants; cafeteria; bar; dance club; cabaret; outdoor pool; tour desk; car-rental desk; small shopping arcade; limited room service; laundry service. *In room:* A/C, TV, safe.

**Hotel Colón** ★ *Value*    Having undergone a massive face-lift, this midsize hotel is now one of the best options in Camagüey. Opened in 1927 by Catalan owners, the lobby—a feast of colorful glazed tiles, columns, and a marble staircase—features a handsomely restored, antique dark-wood bar. The rooms, many of which are set around a pretty open-air colonial patio, have also been redone. Though the rooms are considerably smaller than those at the Hotel Plaza (see below), they are very clean and have high ceilings, colorful tile floors, fairly elegant appointments, and nice bathrooms decorated with tile motifs. The five "matrimonial" rooms at the back off the patio on the second floor are the largest and feature queen-size beds, though they are the same price as all other rooms. Other rooms off the long, airy hallway that leads to the street are less appealing and only have either two or three twin beds. The rooms at the end of the hallway—nos. 201 and 235—do have small balconies overlooking the street, though, and they're larger than others along the hall. However, with these two, street noise from Camagüey's main artery below could be an issue. The open-air grill restaurant in the patio is a good place for a bite to eat. The lobby bar, though, should be your last stop of the evening; it's a splendid spot for a mojito.

Calle República 472, Camagüey. © **32/28-3346.** www.islazul.cu. 48 units. CUC$38–CUC$44 double. Rates include continental breakfast. MC, V. **Amenities:** Restaurant; bar. *In room:* A/C, TV, safe.

**Hotel Plaza** *Value*    This character-filled place is directly across from the train station. Built in 1907, it's a little funky but oddly cool for the right kind of traveler—one who values uniqueness over strict adherence to hotel standards. The lobby has two welcoming bars; one is chilly with air-conditioning, while funky Bar Pergola has high ceilings, glowing green light from skylights, and slow-moving ceiling fans. The main restaurant, El Dorado, is, surprisingly, almost elegant. Each of the 67 large rooms is different, with sizes and shapes determined by the structure of the building. Most are newly refurbished, with new furniture, tile floors, and new but tiny TVs. Try to get a room with a private balcony on the north- or west-facing side of the building, although rooms on the interior, with views of the patio, are quieter than those facing the street.

Van Horne 1 (between República and Avellaneda), Camagüey. © **32/28-2457.** www.islazul.cu. 67 units. CUC$32–CUC$38 double. Rates include continental breakfast. MC, V. **Amenities:** Restaurant; 24-hr. cafeteria; 2 bars; car-rental desk. *In room:* A/C, TV, safe.

## WHERE TO DINE

In addition to the places listed below, **Café Callejón de la Soledad** (© **32/29-1961**) is an atmospheric outdoor cafe on a cobblestone alley, just beside the 18th-century Iglesia de Nuestra Señora de la Soledad.

**Don Ronquillo Restaurant** ⚑ CRIOLLA   Tucked back in the Galería Colonial, this upscale colonial-style restaurant is one of the best in town. While its prices are somewhat higher than other restaurants, for the most part it's worth it. The restaurant has a breezy feel, lemon-yellow walls, and mural paintings at either end. The menu offers a nice assortment of well-prepared dishes, including breaded shrimp and snapper, chicken *cordon bleu,* and a juicy steak "Mayoral" in a red-wine sauce. Unusual for a Cuban restaurant outside of Havana or the beach resorts, it has a pretty decent wine selection.

In Galería Colonial, Calle Ignacio Agramonte 406 (between República and Lopez Recio). © **32/28-4262**. Reservations recommended. Main courses CUC$7–CUC$15. MC, V. Daily 11am–10pm.

**El Ovejito** ⚑ *Finds* CRIOLLA   Set just off the quaint little Plaza del Carmen, this restaurant specializes in lamb dishes, hence the name "little lamb." Heavy wooden tables and wood and rough cowhide chairs are spread through several rooms of this lovingly restored home dating to 1827. There are huge, soaring arched wooden doorways and several ceramic murals by Oscar Lasseria on the walls. When the weather permits, grab one of the several tables under large canvas umbrellas on the cobblestone plaza in front of the restaurant. The house special is a roasted leg of lamb, stuffed with bacon and carrots and served with a thick and tasty red sauce. There are several other lamb dishes on the menu, as well as a smaller selection of chicken and beef entrees.

Plaza del Carmen, Calle Hermanos Agüero, between Onda and Carmen. © **32/29-2524**. Reservations recommended. Main courses CUC$4–CUC$8. MC, V. Wed–Mon noon–9:30pm.

**La Campana de Toledo** ⚑⚑ CRIOLLA   Although it's a tad touristy, this elegantly rustic restaurant still ranks as the city's most enjoyable dining experience. The gorgeously restored 18th-century house has a lovely patio with great shade trees and several tables out by the aged bell (which gives the restaurant its name). The well-prepared dishes go beyond the standard offerings: Try *picadillo a la Habanera* (beef hash), the house specialty; *boliche mechado,* beef stuffed with bacon and served with French fries; rice and beans; or choose from among a number of salads and grilled fish. Service is excellent. The restaurant is most popular for lunch, but at night, the patio is illuminated and the square is wonderfully quiet.

San Juan de Dios 18 (between Ramón Pinto and Padre Olallo), Plaza San Juan de Dios. © **32/29-5888**. Reservations recommended. Main courses CUC$5–CUC$11; lobster CUC$25. MC, V. Daily 11am–10pm.

**Restaurante El Retorno** *Value* CRIOLLA   This surprising *paladar* is more professionally managed and outfitted than many state-run restaurants. The dining room (you enter through the living room and head up a flight of stairs) is nicely decorated in cabin-style wood paneling, with hanging plants, a wood bar, and air-conditioning that is a savior to the sweaty. The owner does everything, imparting a very family-like atmosphere to the place. Though it's a peso restaurant, foreigners are welcome, and the extensive menu is a bargain. Dishes include the requisite chicken of all stripes, pork steak, pork chops, beef, spaghetti, salads, and *asado en cazuela* (a stew of barbecued meats).

Calle Bella Vista 115 (between Andrés Sánchez and Tomás Betancourt), La Vigía district. No phone. Reservations not accepted. Main courses CUC$7–CUC$10. No credit cards. Daily noon–midnight.

**Salón Caribe** ⭐ *(Value)* INTERNATIONAL/CRIOLLA    This sophisticated, top-floor restaurant of Camagüey's coolest hotel has panoramic views of the city. Surprisingly elegant, it has large, faux-crystal chandeliers, large mirrors, cool breezes, and black-and-white tile floors. During the day, there's a good-value buffet lunch for CUC$8, with a variety of soups and salads, *pescado a la catalana* (Catalan-style fish filet), fish enchiladas, hamburgers, Creole fried chicken, and the house specialty, *ropa vieja* (tangy shredded beef).

In the Gran Hotel, Maceo 64 (between General Gómez and Ignacio Agramonte). ℭ 32/29-2314. Reservations recommended for dinner. Main courses CUC$3–CUC$8. MC, V. Daily noon–3pm and 7–10pm.

## CAMAGÜEY AFTER DARK

Built in 1850, the neoclassical **Teatro Principal,** Padre Valencia 64, between Tatán Mendéz and Lugareño (ℭ **32/29-3048**), is an elegant showpiece with a grand marble staircase and chandeliers. The theater is home to the distinguished **Ballet de Camagüey** ⭐⭐, known for its international tours and second only to Havana's ballet company. The company is well worth seeing if you are lucky enough to be in town when a performance is scheduled; we recently caught an excellent performance of *Giselle.* Paradiso/ARTex, a cultural tour promoter, offers group visits to the ballet company, with backstage tours of the theater, interviews with choreographers and dancers, and the opportunity to sit in on a rehearsal. Tours are CUC$5 per person. Call **ARTex** at ℭ **32/28-5242** for more information. Other performances scheduled at the Teatro include those of the local Orchesta Sinfónica.

Camagüey's **Casa de la Trova** ⭐⭐, Salvador Cisneros 171 (ℭ **32/29-1357**), is one of the liveliest in Cuba, with good bands and great local crowds. The handsome colonial structure facing the newly renovated Parque Agramonte has a large, open-air patio under tall palm trees and an elegant but relaxed atmosphere. It's open Tuesday through Sunday from 9am to 7pm, Tuesday through Thursday from 8:30pm to midnight, and Friday and Saturday from 8:30pm to 2am; admission is CUC$2 to CUC$3 and includes your first drink.

**Galería Colonial,** Calle Ignacio Agramonte 406, between República and Lopez Recio (ℭ **32/28-5459**), is a complex of shops and restaurants, with a couple of bars and occasional cabaret shows and live bands in a large, open-air courtyard.

Tucked behind a door at the back of the lobby of the Gran Hotel is **Piano Bar Marquesina,** Maceo 64, between General Gómez and Ignacio Agramonte (ℭ **32/29-2550**). This sumptuously atmospheric cocktail lounge serves classic bar drinks. A sexy side room, where couples tend to canoodle, turns into a small dance club late in the evening; occasionally there's live music. The Hotel Colón has the city's other great hotel bar: the elegant, old-world **Lobby Bar,** República 472 (ℭ **32/28-3346**). Open since 1927 but newly and splendidly restored, you should come here for a cocktail to start or finish off the evening.

---

### *Moments* Dancing in the Streets

**La Noche Camagüeyana** is a traditional Saturday night street party that gets the townsfolk going with dancing, live music, flowing booze, and local eats on pedestrian-only Calle Maceo and Calle República. Tourists are welcome, and we encourage you to join the fun, but keep an eye on your belongings.

El Cambio, Calle Martín 152 (© 32/29-7170), is a cool, slightly bedraggled little drinking hole on the northeast corner of Parque Agramonte and open to the street. Open since 1909, it has a thick patina of graffiti on its walls and a ceramic mural over the bar by a well-known local artist, Oscar Lasseria. And best of all, it never closes.

The Gran Hotel features a *ballet acuático* (aquatic ballet show) at its pool bar nightly at 9:30pm. The **Panorama Cabaret** (© 32/28-3636) is an open-air bar and dance club with panoramic views in the Hotel Puerto Príncipe. **Copacabana,** Carretera Central Este, near the Casino Campestre (© 32/25-3858), is an entertainment complex with a *centro nocturno* (nightclubs and bars) set amid gardens, with music and dance shows and an open bar daily from 9:30pm to 4am.

## FARTHER EAST: CAYO SABINAL & & SANTA LUCIA &

Guarding the entrance to the Bay of Nuevitas, Cayo Sabinal is the easternmost of the cays belonging to the Archipiélago Sabana-Camagüey (Jardines del Rey). Boasting about 30km (20 miles) of beaches on its north side and protected by stunning coral reefs offshore, it's one of the prettiest and most remote spots along the coast. Still a place of modest fishermen, marshlands, and wild animals, Cayo Sabinal—extremely rich in native flora and fauna—is of growing interest to eco-tourism groups. The cay is perfect for those wanting to escape the all-inclusive tourist resorts that dominate much of Cuba's coastline, but woefully under-equipped for those looking for some semblance of facilities.

Cayo Sabinal is sometimes called the *isla de los corsarios,* an allusion to its vast pirate history. At the eastern extreme of the cay, out on Punto Maternillos, is the 1848 **Faro de Colón (Columbus Lighthouse)** and the ruins of a fortress, **Torreón de San Hilario** (1831), which guarded the entrance to the Bahia de Nuevitas and stands as a relic of 19th-century pirate wars. The central, almost virgin **Playa de Los Pinos,** the longest beach on the cay, is the perfect place for those travelers searching for solitude where it's usually very difficult to find: on one of Cuba's pristine northern beaches. It fits most anyone's definition of a perfect beach—bone-white sands, warm turquoise waters, and virtually no people. For anyone looking to spend the night, there is a series of rustic cabanas (and attendant restaurant/snack bar) right on the beach.

Cayo Sabinal's isolation is its greatest charm, something easily retained given how complicated it remains to get there. Many roads remain unpaved and rocky, and there is no public transportation. **Cubanacán** (© 32/33-6449) occasionally offers group excursions to Sabinal if there's enough interest. The Cuban eco-travel tour agency **EcoTur** (© 32/22-5844 or 7/204-7520) runs jeep safari eco-tourism excursions to Cayo Sabinal and other places in Camagüey.

Farther east from Cayo Sabinal, and actually part of the mainland, Santa Lucia is another stretch of amazingly white, soft sand with a handful of all-inclusive hotels catering to a mix of Canadian and Italian charter groups and local Cubans enjoying merit vacations. The best of these are the **Brisas Santa Lucía** & (© 32/33-6317; www.hotelescubanacan.com) and the **Club Amigo Caracol** & (© 32/33-5158; www. hotelescubanacan.com), although, for my money, there are plenty of better options at other beach resort destinations around the country. This is a very isolated little area, and aside from a handful of organized tours and hotel activities, there is little else to see or do in Santa Lucia.

# 9

# El Oriente

*by Eliot Greenspan & Neil E. Schlecht*

Prior to the 1959 Revolution, the eastern half of Cuba was a single province, straightforwardly called "El Oriente," or the East. Most Cubans still refer to everything east of Camagüey—a region much more scenically and historically interesting than most of central Cuba—as El Oriente, even though it is now composed of the distinct provinces of Holguín, Granma, Santiago de Cuba, and Guantánamo. The region is less known and visited than the west, but every bit as rewarding for travelers (and perhaps more so). The farther east you go, the more emphatically Caribbean it feels. The region's remarkable landscapes include the north coast's exuberant banana and coconut groves, densely wooded peaks of the Sierra Maestra, and tropical rainforest on the east coast.

The wars of independence began in El Oriente in the 1860s, and nearly a century later Castro concentrated his power base in the inaccessible **Sierra Maestra.** Quiet but dignified **Bayamo,** which played a pivotal role in Cuba's revolutionary struggles, is the capital of Granma province. The gorgeous beaches of **Guardalavaca,** part of Holguín province, make it the fastest-growing resort in Cuba, while tiny, remote **Baracoa,** where Columbus first dropped anchor at the extreme northeastern edge of Guantánamo, is one of the most beautiful, rugged spots on the island. The former capital city of the Spanish colony, **Santiago de Cuba,** is not only known as a vibrant musical center, but also the cradle of the Revolution; see chapter 10 for full coverage of Cuba's "Second City."

## 1 Guardalavaca ★★

56km (35 miles) N of Holguín; 190km (118 miles) NW of Santiago de Cuba; 258km (160 miles) NE of Camagüey

Guardalavaca's rural and somnolent past is reflected in the resort's poetic name, which literally means "watch the cow." Though today the moniker evokes a pastoral setting that hardly seems consistent with the coterie of full-fledged, all-inclusive resort hotels that gaze out over some of the finest beaches in Cuba, Guardalavaca remains charmingly low-key. But it is one of the hottest destinations on the island.

Guardalavaca is both a bucket-term for a series of neighboring beaches north of Holguín and the namesake for one small town and specific beach. For my money, Guardalavaca is the finest resort area in the eastern half of the island; though considerably smaller, it is poised to pose a stiff challenge to Varadero as the nation's premier vacation destination. Not (yet) nearly as massively commercialized, Guardalavaca is perhaps even more beautiful, a stunning three-stripe canvas of intensely green tropical vegetation, stone-white sand, and pristine turquoise seas well protected by coral reefs.

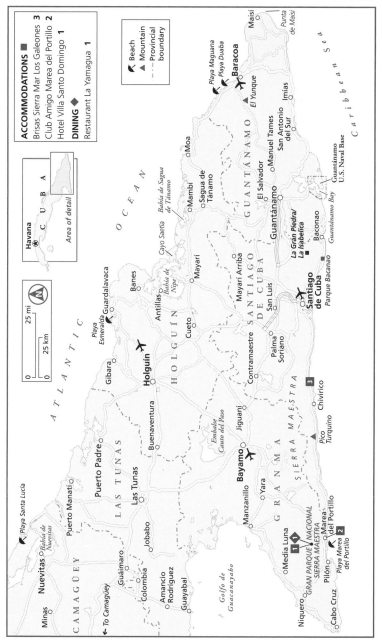

*Tips*    **When Not to Come to Guardalavaca**

The month of May in Guardalavaca is heavy with tropical rains, as is the early part of June. August is sweltering and too humid for all but the most committed sun worshipers.

Christopher Columbus first sailed around the coast at Guardalavaca, landing just to the west at the Bay of Bariay in late 1492. He declared it "the most beautiful land that human eyes have ever seen." Columbus may have been given to hyperbole, repeatedly touting the unrivaled virtues of the places where he dropped anchor, but his assessment of Guardalavaca remains pretty accurate. The area was originally home to several indigenous groups, and today it is recognized as Cuba's archaeological capital, primarily for the discovery of the 15th-century Arawakan Indian village and burial site near Guardalavaca, one of the most important pre-Columbian sites in the Caribbean. The *bohíos* (thatched-roof huts) that dot the thickly wooded hills still evoke a sense of Caribbean discovery more than 500 years later.

The town of Guardalavaca remains a dusty country backdrop to the resort hotels that now dwarf it. The foundations of Guardalavaca's resort development were laid in the late 1970s: Fidel Castro himself inaugurated the first hotel here, swimming laps in its large square pool. "Guardalavaca" now denotes not only the eponymous town and beach, but is also used to refer to the entire resort, strung along several nearby beaches and continuing to expand. Playa Esmeralda and Playa Pesquero (also known as Costa Verde) are the two newest and most exclusive beaches to be developed.

The backdrop to the beaches is a bucolic region thick with sugar-cane fields, grazing cattle, and luxuriant, rolling hills sprinkled with royal palms. The zone is being touted as an eco-tourist paradise; in addition to scuba diving at a dozen dive sites, hiking, biking, and horseback-riding trips are primed to take off in the near future. A dozen nature preserves, including one declared a UNESCO World Biosphere Reserve, dot the region. Side trips from Guardalavaca are easy to arrange.

## ESSENTIALS
### GETTING THERE
**BY PLANE**    The gleaming **Aeropuerto Internacional Frank País,** Carretera Central Vía Bayamo Km 11.5 (© **24/46-2512;** airport code HOG), is about 70km (43 miles) south of Guardalavaca, and 14km (8¾ miles) south of Holguín, the provincial capital. The airport is about an hour from hotels in and around Guardalavaca. Both national and direct international flights from Canada and Germany (via **Air Canada, Air Transat, Iberia, LTU,** and various package charters) arrive at the airport here. The main domestic carriers are **Cubana** (© **24/46-8148** in Holguín, or 7/834-4446 in Havana; www.cubana.cu) and **AeroCaribbean** (© **24/46-8556** in Holguín, or 7/879-7524 in Havana; www.aero-caribbean.com), which offer daily flights from Havana and Varadero. Flights between Holguín and either Havana or Varadero run around CUC$90 to CUC$110 each way.

The hotels all have airport pickup services (buses and minibuses) for clients. If you have not prearranged transportation to your hotel, there are usually a couple of state-owned taxis hanging about. Rates run between CUC$25 and CUC$35.

**BY BUS**   Víazul (© **24/46-1036** in Holguín, or 7/881-1413 in Havana; www. viazul.com) travels to Holguín on its Havana–Santiago and Trinidad–Santiago (three times daily) lines. From Havana, the buses depart at 9:30am, and 3pm, and arrive at 10pm, and 3:20am, respectively (CUC$48). From Trinidad (© **419/2404**), the bus leaves at 8am and arrives in Holguín at 4:45pm (CUC$26). From Santiago, departures are at 9am and 3:15pm, arriving at 1:20pm and 6:40pm, respectively (CUC$12). The main bus station in Holguín is located on Carretera Central between 20 de Mayo and Independencia (© **24/42-2111**), just west of downtown.

There are several daily buses from the main bus station in Holguín to Guardalavaca. However, these are heavily used by workers, and demand far outstrips supply. For travelers, the best way to travel between Holguín and Guardalavaca is by taxi or rental car.

**BY CAR/TAXI**   The easiest way to get to Guardalavaca, if you don't have a prearranged bus service to take you from the airport, is by rental car or state-owned taxis. Getting from the airport, through the city of Holguín, and out onto the highway to Guardalavaca is quite confusing. One of the best ways to navigate it is to hire a local tout for a few dollars to ride with you until you're on your way.

Guardalavaca's beauty and proximity to areas of interest, including Baracoa, make it one of the better areas in Cuba to rent a car for some regional sightseeing. Car-rental agencies in Holguín include **Cubacar** (© **24/42-4187**), **Havanautos** (© **24/46-8412**), and **Vía** (© **24/3-0996**). Almost all of these have desks at the airport, as well as at one or more of the beach resorts. Car rentals average about CUC$45 to CUC$80 per day for a standard economy car.

## GETTING AROUND

Playa Guardalavaca is small enough that you can easily walk from any of the hotels here to the La Roca dance club and the restaurants in town. Playa Esmeralda is about 3km (1¾ miles) from Guardalavaca, a manageable walk. The rest of the beaches and attractions are quite far.

The best way to get around the beaches of Guardalavaca is by **bicycle** (if you're feeling fit) or **moped** *(moto)*. Most of the hotels have mountain bikes (free for guests) and mopeds that rent for CUC$25 to CUC$35 a day.

Any of the hotels can arrange a taxi for side trips in the area. You can also call directly **Cubataxi** (© **24/46-8294**) or **Taxis OK** (© **24/3-0243**) on Playa Guardalavaca. All the hotels also offer excursions either directly or through tour operator representatives.

---

### *Tips* Day Trips to Guardalavaca

The relatively expensive all-inclusive hotels pretty much have a lock on the splendid beaches around Guardalavaca. If you would like to visit the beaches and spend the day there without paying for the privilege of sleeping at one of the hotels, you can design a day trip from Holguín if you have a rental car. (Note that if you don't have your own wheels and have to take a taxi, the cost will equal or surpass the cost of staying in one of the less-expensive all-inclusive hotels, and you'd have to travel 1½ hr. back to your hotel in Holguín, making it hardly worth the effort.) The major hotels sell day passes (generally CUC$40–CUC$70) that allow you to use the facilities, including pool and beaches, and eat and drink all you wish.

---

Each of the major hotels has representatives of one or more car-rental agencies on the premises. You could also contact **Cubacar** (✆ **24/42-4187** in Holguín; or 24/3-0389 on Playa Guardalavaca), or **Havanautos** (✆ **24/3-0468** in Guardalavaca, or 24/46-8412 at the Frank País airport).

One interesting alternative for touring the area is a tourist train that runs twice daily between Guardalavaca and the Aldea Taína, with intermediary stops at all the major resorts, beaches, and tourist attractions in between. Cost is CUC$3 for the entire circuit.

## ORIENTATION

The best sources of visitor information are the hotels themselves and the representatives of the major tour operators (Havanatur, Cubatur, and Cubanacán) who operate out of the hotels.

**Currency exchange** and **postal service** is available at any of Guardalavaca's hotels. Most of the large resort hotels have **Internet access** for their guests.

For medical assistance, contact **Clínica Internacional,** Calle 2 s/n, Playa Guardalavaca (✆ **24/3-0291**). It has a pharmacy on the premises; another pharmacy is within the **Paradisus Río de Oro** (p. 233).

## WHAT TO SEE & DO

Most folks come here on all-inclusive packages, and many are content to spend their entire time in a chaise longue on the beach or beside the pool. However, there are a wide range of tours and activities available for the less lazy.

### BEACHES, DIVING & OTHER WATERSPORTS

The spectacular beaches around Guardalavaca are this resort area's main attraction. Tracing the coast are more than 1,200km (740 miles) of snowy white beaches lined by royal palm trees, framed by exuberant vegetation, and gazing out to some of the clearest, most inviting waters Cuba has to offer. The best beaches are **Guardalavaca, Esmeralda, Pesquero, and Yuraguanal**—all of which have major hotels lining them—and small **Don Lino.** Many of the beaches are long and wide expanses of sand, but the jagged coastline is also peppered with tiny coves that are nearly private. Near the gentle arc of Esmeralda is a series of tiny cove beaches that in practice are almost exclusively for the guests of the Paradisus Río de Oro hotel (p. 233).

Guardalavaca has a dozen excellent dive sites, including Boca de las Esponjas (Mouth of Sponges), El Salto (the Waterfall), and El Cañón de los Aguajíes (Grouper Canyon), and is well known for its abundant and vibrant sponges. Near Guardalavaca is a group of submerged caves, Los Tanques Azules, which are popular with experienced divers. **Eagle Ray and Coral Reef Scuba Diving Center** (✆ **24/3-0316**) is on Playa Guardalavaca, and **Sea Lovers Scuba Diving Center** (✆ **24/3-0030**) is on Playa Esmeralda. They offer dive packages, underwater camera rental, and diving gear rental. Certification programs are also offered, with several dive packages; a single dive costs CUC$40 to CUC$55.

The most popular watersports are sailing, kayaking, wind surfing, canoeing, and pedal boating. Most of the hotels have their own catamarans and other vehicles and facilities for watersports. **Marina Internacional Puerto de Vita** (✆ **24/3-0446**) operates catamaran cruises around the coral reef beyond the cays for either a half or full day. **Cubanacán Náutica** (✆ **24/3-0491**) has a wide range of watersports programs, including "seafaris" with snorkeling to Playa Pesquero, and yacht rentals for sport fishing.

## PARQUE NACIONAL BAHIA DE NARANJO

The **Bahía de Naranjo,** about 5km (3 miles) west of Guardalavaca (℅ **24/3-0439**), is a 1,000-hectare (2,470-acre) nature park of mangrove swamps and thickly wooded wilderness. Within the park, visitors can hike along trails and take boat rides. There are plenty of man-made attractions to round out the more ecologically oriented offerings. The **aquarium** at Cayo Naranjo, a sliver of an island reached by boat, isn't really a large-scale aquarium in the traditional sense; it's part of a *parque recreativo* (tourist complex), but it does feature tropical fish as well as a daily marine show at noon (CUC$25) and, best of all, an opportunity to swim with dolphins (CUC$50). While we are normally fairly appalled by the conditions of most dolphin attractions, including others around Cuba, this place has some of the largest natural ocean pens you will find anywhere, and allegedly the dolphins are allowed to swim in the open ocean regularly. You'll also find rodeo, watersports, horseback riding, and a seafood restaurant that features an Afro-Cuban show. The park is open daily from 7am to 4pm. The best way to visit is by organized excursion, offered by all the beach hotels (most packages are about CUC$60 per person, including transportation, admission, and a dolphin swim).

### ON DRY LAND

One of the most popular activities on dry land here is **horseback riding.** There's plenty of wide-open terrain and wonderful sea views to be enjoyed. However, be sure to bring plenty of protection from the often-brutal sun here. Most hotels can arrange a riding excursion for you. There are stables in front of Hotel Club Amigo Guardalavaca, or you can contact Gaviota's **Rancho Naranjo** equestrian center at ℅ **24/3-0433** and sign up for an organized horseback excursion.

### BANES

A slow-moving, dusty little town about 30km (20 miles) southeast of Guardalavaca, Banes is best known for its unlikely association with the towering figures of 20th-century Cuba. Fulgencio Batista, whose government the rebels deposed in 1959, was born here in 1901. Fidel Castro and his brother, Raúl, were born nearby in Birán. The hotels and tour operators in Guardalavaca arrange guided excursions to Banes, though if you wish to go independently, you could easily do so by rented moped or taxi.

Fidel married the daughter of the conservative mayor of Banes in 1948 at the small **Iglesia de Nuestra Señora de la Caridad,** on a plaza at the edge of the park. (They divorced 6 years later.) Of perhaps greater significance in town is the **Museo Indocubano** ☞, Av. General Marreo 305 (℅ **24/8-2487**), specializing exclusively in Cuba's pre-Columbian history. Its collection is among the best in Cuba; among the 20,000 items or so, exhibits include fragments of ceramics, jewelry, tools, and a valuable 13th-century gold "idol of Banesa," just 4 centimeters high. The museum is open Tuesday through Saturday from 9am to 5pm, and Sunday from 8am to noon; admission is CUC$1.

Tucked into the hills of the Banes zone are 96 archaeological sites from the Native American groups that once populated the area. **Museo El Chorro de Maíta (Maíta's Stream Museum)** ☞, Cerro de Yaguajay (℅ **24/3-0421**), represents the largest and most important discovery of a Native American cemetery in Cuba. The community dates from 1490 to 1540. The burial ground contains the remarkably well-preserved remains of 108 Taíno men, women, and children (62 are on display), including a single Spaniard, most likely a friar, whose body is marked by a cross. A *cacique* (tribal chief), lying in a fetal position, is distinguished by a copper medal placed on his shin.

Several skulls are deformed, a beautification practice that involved applying two pieces of wood to the head with ropes. Found among the remains were Spanish ceramics and jewelry and objects crafted from gold, copper, coral, and quartz; many are displayed in cases. The museum is open Tuesday through Saturday from 9am to 5pm, Sunday and Monday from 9am to 1pm. Admission is CUC$2; it's CUC$1 extra to take photographs, CUC$5 for video.

Across the street from the Museo El Chorro de Maíta is **Aldea Taína** (© **24/3-0422**), a re-creation of a native Arawakan Indian village that features models of native dwellings and life-size, clay-figure Native Americans performing quotidian tasks. It manages to summon the cultural practices of a long-extinct culture. The highlight for most visitors is the live show, organized through any of the local tour operators, of Native American dances and rituals, performed by "native" women going, well, native. On the village premises is a restaurant featuring some items that were staples of the Taíno diet. The village is open daily from 9am to 5pm; the live show is Tuesday, Thursday, and Sunday at 8:30pm. Admission to the village is CUC$3 (CUC$1 extra for photos, CUC$5 for video).

## WHERE TO STAY

The entire area is developed around the all-inclusive resort concept, and visitors have no other options. Playa Guardalavaca was the original beach resort developed in the late 1970s, but today, resort hotels are distributed on several beaches along the coast. Principal among them are Playa Esmeralda, Playa Turquesa, and Playa Pesquero, where the hotels are more upscale than Guardalavaca, and the beaches even finer. Guardalavaca is dominated by Cubanacán properties, for the most part older and more affordable than newer hotels in other parts. The Spanish chain Sol Meliá has concentrated its hotels in a row along Playa Esmeralda.

### PLAYA GUARDALAVACA

**Club Amigo Atlantico-Guardalavaca**   Over the years, several neighboring projects here have been fused into one massive all-inclusive resort. The oldest hotel at this resort, the Atlántico, was built in 1976 and its age shows in its basic structure. Three large '70s Soviet-style blocks are built around a square old-style pool. However, the newer section of villas is considerably nicer and closer to the beach, and really should be your first and only choice here. These large, tastefully decorated villas are much more modern, with marble bathrooms and small terraces; some have good sea views. The pool is much better as well. But the rooms and the grounds still can't compare with nicer properties in the area. The hotel has only a tiny cove beach; you have to walk along a boardwalk to get to the real beach, a not inconsiderable jaunt. On the whole, it's a decent if unexciting option that clings to its glory days as the first property on the beach, when Fidel himself swam in the pool.

Playa Guardalavaca, Banes, Holguín. © 24/3-0180. Fax 24/3-0200. www.hotelescubanacan.com. 603 rooms, 144 villas. CUC$100–CUC$150 double. Rates are all-inclusive. MC, V. **Amenities:** 4 restaurants; 2 snack bars; 4 bars; dance club; nightly show; 4 outdoor pools; outdoor tennis court; children's programs; concierge; tour desk; car- and scooter-rental desk; massage; babysitting; laundry service. *In room:* A/C, TV, safe.

**Hotel Brisas Guardalavaca** ✪   Like a couple of other all-inclusive beach hotels in the area that have upgraded their facilities, this hotel is a hybrid: part standard resort hotel with a big and rather uninteresting block structure, and part more intimate villa-style accommodations. The two sections are connected and considered one property, but guests would be wise to draw a firm distinction; the star above applies only to the villas, which are much more striking. Mediterranean in style and set amid pleasant gardens, the pastel-colored, red-tile–roofed villas are large and luxurious, with balconies. The atmosphere is one of tranquillity, with easy access to an attractive stretch of beach. The standard hotel next door, built in 1994, doesn't fare well in comparison. Rooms aren't very inspiring for the price, but many of them have good sea views.

Calle 2, Playa Guardalavaca, Banes, Holguín. © 24/3-0218. Fax 24/3-0162. www.hotelescubanacan.com. 231 rooms, 206 villas. CUC$140–CUC$180 double; CUC$160–CUC$220 villa. Rates are all-inclusive. MC, V. **Amenities:** 4 restaurants; snack bar; 8 bars; dance club; nightly show; 2 outdoor pools; 2 lit outdoor tennis courts; watersports equipment; bikes; children's programs; Jacuzzi; sauna; concierge; tour desk; car- and scooter-rental desk; massage; babysitting; laundry service. In room: A/C, TV, minibar, hair dryer, safe.

## PLAYA ESMERALDA

**Paradisus Río de Oro** 🏨🏨🏨    One of the finest and most luxurious all-inclusive resort hotels in Cuba, this Sol Meliá flagship hotel is perched above a low, rocky cliff overlooking Playa Esmeralda. Set amid lush, meticulously landscaped gardens are handsome two-story blocks of rooms and slightly more exclusive casitas, consisting of two apartments with separate terraces and outdoor showers. The rooms are very large and well appointed, with separate sitting areas, balconies, and large bathrooms. Of these, those on the second floor have higher ceilings than those below, and those on the corners have larger balconies. There are also two massive private oceanview villas, with private swimming pools, that are easily the top accommodations in Guardalavaca. Walkways wend through lush vegetation and around ponds; scattered about the grounds are private sitting areas and hammocks strewn lazily between trees. A couple of the specialized restaurants are in high demand, so it's a good idea to make reservations for the duration of your stay upon arrival. The restaurants' selections are considerably better than most other all-inclusives. The superb main beach is a short walk down some stairs built into the cliff, but the hotel also features three nearly private, tiny cove beaches accessed through the gardens (few guests seem to know about them). A serene, blue, wood bridge over a large pond leads to the other two Meliá hotels on Esmeralda. At night the bridge is illuminated and is a particularly good spot if you're in the mood for a romantic walk after dinner. This hotel was recently reserved for adults only, and there are plans to greatly improve and expand their spa facilities, including some open-air massage gazebos built out over the ocean.

Carretera a Guardalavaca, Playa Esmeralda, Holguín. © 24/3-0090. Fax 24/3-0095. www.solmeliacuba.com. 300 units. CUC$390 double; CUC$460 superior suite; CUC$1,500 villa. Rates are all-inclusive. Rates lower in off season; higher during peak weeks. MC, V. **Amenities:** 5 restaurants; 4 bars; nightly show; 2 outdoor pools; 3 lit outdoor tennis courts; gym; Jacuzzi; sauna; watersports equipment; bikes; game room; concierge; tour desk; car- and scooter-rental desk; salon; massage; babysitting; 24-hr. room service; laundry service. In room: A/C, TV, minibar, coffeemaker, hair dryer, iron, safe.

**Sol Río Luna y Mares Resort** 🏨🏨 *Kids*    This complex consists of two formerly separate Sol Meliá properties on Playa Esmeralda joined at the hip. Formerly the Río de Luna and Río de Mares, they've merged—and guests at either one are free to use the facilities at both—but the two hotels deserve to be thought of separately, since they're slightly different in character and design. We prefer the Río de Luna, which was built in 1992 but more recently remodeled. It has a sedate, open-air lobby and medium-size pool, and the overall design of the hotel is more intimate. Suites have two rooms, with two bathrooms and a large balcony or small terrace. The Río de Mares, while somewhat newer, has a slightly more impersonal feel, with rooms built in large wings in a U-shape around the pools. However, the rooms on the third and fourth floors here have excellent views, and the junior suites are immense, with massive terraces. The rooms are all very cute and playfully rustic, with amenities that include a large TV and CD player. The long stretch of beach fronting the two hotels is superb. The wide range of activities, facilities, and a well-run children's program make this an excellent option for families.

Carretera a Guardalavaca, Playa Esmeralda, Holguín. (✆ 24/3-0030. Fax 24/3-0065. www.solmeliacuba.com. 464 units. CUC$210–CUC$230 double; CUC$245–CUC$305 suite. Rates are all-inclusive. Children 3–12 stay for half off; children under 3 stay free in parent's room. MC, V. **Amenities:** 4 restaurants; 2 snack bars; 4 bars; dance club; nightly show; 2 outdoor pools; 2 lit outdoor tennis courts; gym; Jacuzzi; sauna; watersports equipment; bikes; children's center and programs; concierge; tour desk; car- and scooter-rental desk; salon; massage; babysitting; laundry service. *In room:* A/C, TV, minibar, coffeemaker, hair dryer, iron, safe.

## PLAYA PESQUERO & PLAYA YURAGUANAL

**Blau Costa Verde Beach Resort** ★★ *(Kids)*   This resort has a decidedly tropical feel, with light pastel colors. The huge concrete structure you drive up to, though, is not the most attractive. It consists of six big building blocks, with three open-air restaurants built around the large figure-eight pool. Rooms are cheery, done in light colors with an ocean theme, but not overly large and TVs are rather small. The bathrooms, however, are surprisingly large and nicely designed in tile and marble. Some rooms have distant beach views. The sands are a 50m (165-ft.) walk away, but the beach is lovely, and the water has amazing crystal-clear turquoise tones. A kids' club, kiddie pool, childcare, playground, and shallow "children's beach" will appeal to families. The food here is actually pretty good for a large-scale all-inclusive.

Playa Pesquero, Rafael Freyre, Holguín. (✆ 24/3-0510. Fax 24/3-0515. www.blau-hotels.com. 309 units. CUC$110–CUC$180 double; CUC$200–CUC$350 suite. Rates are all-inclusive. Children 2–12 stay for half off; children under 2 stay free in parent's room. MC, V. **Amenities:** 3 restaurants; snack bar; 2 bars; dance club; nightly show; 2 outdoor pools; 3 lit outdoor tennis courts; gym; Jacuzzi; sauna; watersports equipment; children's center and programs; concierge; tour desk; car- and scooter-rental desk; salon; massage; babysitting; laundry service; nonsmoking rooms. *In room:* A/C, TV, minibar, hair dryer, safe (w/extra fee).

**Occidental Grand Playa Turquesa** ★★ *(Kids)*   This large resort is set above a beautiful broad beach and next to some lovely natural forests. Perhaps the most distinctive feature here is the seven swimming pools, several of which are connected in cascading fashion by waterfalls. Rooms are large, modern, and well-kept. They feature large, cool ceramic tile floors in a checkerboard pattern, and stylish wrought-iron headboards over the beds. All have a private balcony, although many of these are quite compact. The grounds here are lush and shady. There a several good a la carte dining options, as well as the ubiquitous large buffets. The pizza and ice-cream stand on the beach is a big hit here. This hotel has an extensive array of watersports and activities available, and an excellent children's program.

Playa Yuraguanal, Rafael Freyre, Holguín. (✆ 800/858-2258 in the U.S. and Canada, or 24/3-0540. Fax 24/3-0545. www.occidental-hoteles.com. 531 units. CUC$200–CUC$300 double; CUC$300–CUC$500 suite. Rates are all-inclusive. Children 2–12 stay for half off; children under 2 stay free in parent's room. MC, V. **Amenities:** 5 restaurants; 2 snack bars; 6 bars; dance club; nightly show; 7 outdoor pools; lit outdoor tennis court; gym; Jacuzzi; sauna; watersports equipment; children's center and programs; concierge; tour desk; car- and scooter-rental desk; massage; babysitting; laundry service; nonsmoking rooms. *In room:* A/C, TV, minibar, hair dryer, safe.

**Playa Costa Verde** ★★ *(Kids) (Value)*   Originally built for and run by the Jamaican Superclubs chain, this attractively designed property is now under management by the Cuban Gaviota company. The resort offers an excellent value for families, with whom it is extremely popular. Although rooms do not have sea or beach views, they are quite large, with very nice decor in bright greens and deep blues, tile floors, and balconies or terraces. They represent some of the best-equipped and -designed rooms I've seen among high-end beach hotels in Cuba. In addition to the beautiful rooms, this hotel has a wide range of activities and an excellent children's program. A spectacular section of Playa Pesquero is a 5-minute walk from the pool over a bridge and wetlands. One of the specialized restaurants here is especially worthy of mention: It's Japanese.

Playa Pesquero, Rafael Freyre, Holguín. © 24/3-0520. Fax 24/3-0525. www.gaviota-grupo.com. 480 units. CUC$300–CUC$336 double; CUC$460 suite. Rates are all-inclusive. Children 2–12 stay for half off; children under 2 stay free in parent's room. MC, V. **Amenities:** 4 restaurants; snack bar; 4 bars; dance club; nightly show; 2 outdoor pools; 4 lit outdoor tennis courts; fitness center; Jacuzzi; sauna; watersports equipment; children's center and programs; game room; concierge; tour desk; car- and scooter-rental desk; salon; massage; babysitting; laundry service. In room: A/C, TV, minibar, coffeemaker, hair dryer, safe.

**Playa Pesquera** ☆☆ (Kids   This massive hotel is the largest in Cuba (although a Meliá property currently under construction elsewhere in Cuba is using the same blueprint). Your experience here begins with a fabulous open-air lobby with lily-pools, large sculptures, and several romantic sitting areas. The rooms are all in two-story blocks spread around the massive grounds ringing the large free-form pool, spa, and entertainment area. Rooms are all spacious and cheery, and all have a private balcony or porch. The superior rooms are really junior suites, and the extra space and sitting area is quite nice. This resort has a whole host of organized activities and entertainment options, as well as a broad selection of restaurants and bars. Of the a la carte restaurant options here, La Trattoria is particularly appealing, with a series of private dining gazebos spread around a small re-creation of Venice's canal system, replete with a real gondola. Be sure to reserve one of these in advance if you're looking for a romantic dinner.

Playa Pesquero, Rafael Freyre, Holguín. © 24/3-0530. Fax 24/3-0535. www.gaviota-grupo.com. 944 units. CUC$350–CUC$450 double; CUC$450–CUC$600 suite. Rates are all-inclusive. Children 2–12 stay for half off; children under 2 stay free in parent's room. MC, V. **Amenities:** 6 restaurants; 2 snack bars; 6 bars; dance club; nightly show; massive outdoor pool; 3 lit outdoor tennis courts; fitness center; 4 Jacuzzis; sauna; watersports equipment; children's center and programs; game room; concierge; tour desk; car- and scooter-rental desk; salon; shopping arcade; massage; babysitting; laundry service. In room: A/C, TV, dataport, coffeemaker, safe.

## WHERE TO DINE

Few visitors eat anywhere besides their all-inclusive hotels, of course. However, if you're just day-tripping to Guardalavaca, or you can't take another hotel buffet, check out **El Cayuelo,** near the Las Brisas hotel on Playa de Guardalavaca (© 24/3-0737), which serves decent *comida criolla* and seafood; **El Ancla,** Playa de Guardalavaca (© 24/3-0381), for seafood; and **Pizza Nova,** Playa de Guardalavaca (© 24/03-0137), for excellent thin-crust pizzas and basic Italian fare. Other tourist restaurants in the zone include **El Conuco de Mongo Viña,** Playa Esmeralda (© 24/3-0915), as well as **Restaurante Cayo Naranjo** (© 24/3-0132) and **Yaguajay Restaurant** (© 24/3-0422), both within the tourist complex of Parque Natural Bahía de Naranjo.

## GUARDALAVACA AFTER DARK

All of the all-inclusive hotels offer free nightly entertainment of varying quality; as a general rule, the stages, dancers, and musicians increase in quality along with the price, so expect the nightly cabaret at the Río de Oro to far outclass what Club Amigo puts on. Some are well-produced, professional, lively affairs and a pretty good time. Others are, well, cheesy and embarrassing. Most hotels change the program every night over a 1- or 2-week schedule, so if you want to drop in every night, you'll at least see a new presentation (the musicians and dancers, though, may very well be the same).

When the tourist-targeted entertainment gets to be too much, head for the one place you can be assured of spotting (and maybe even interacting with!) locals. For those who need a break from packaged entertainment, the **Disco La Roca** (© **24/3-0167;** CUC$5 cover) in Guardalavaca is the place to be outside of the hotels. It is partly open-air and has good beach views.

## SIDE TRIPS FROM GUARDALAVACA

The following are the most common and easily accessible side trips from Guardalavaca. Though it may seem unfair to characterize the largest city and provincial capital, Holguín, as a day trip from the beach, the fact of the matter is that the overwhelming majority of visitors to this section of northeastern Cuba have sun and surf on their minds.

### HOLGUIN
56km (35 miles) SW of Guardalavaca; 734km (455 miles) E of Havana; 134km (83 miles) NW of Santiago de Cuba

The provincial capital, officially called San Isidoro de Holguín, may be known across Cuba as the "city of parks," but it doesn't get a whole lot of tourist traffic. Holguín is a pleasant but unremarkable city with only a modicum of attractions. Still, it makes a good day trip for resort visitors who would otherwise see nothing of Cuba save Guardalavaca's all-inclusive hotels and brilliant beaches.

Holguín, the fourth-largest city in Cuba, has a compact center that's easy enough to get around; visitors can manage the highlights in an unhurried day. The city's few elegant plazas, colonial buildings, and small dose of museums do not rival the highlights of Trinidad or Camagüey, and much of the city's historical character has been subsumed by industrial expansion. The great majority of the city's buildings date from the 19th and 20th centuries.

Pleasant **Parque Calixto García** (also called Parque Central), named for a 19th-century patriot, represents the heart of the city. The hero of the wars of independence is paid tribute with a large marble statue in the park's center. Benches are usually occupied by locals watching the town and time pass by. Two nearby churches of note are the handsome domed **Iglesia de San José** (on Plaza Carlos Manuel de Céspedes), which has an unusual baroque interior to go with its remade neoclassical facade, and the imposing 18th-century **La Catedral de San Isidro de Holguín** (Calle Mandulay, on Parque de las Flores), which features *mudéjar* (Moorish-style) carved wooden ceilings.

Of special note in Holguín is the unusual **Familia Cuayo Fábrica de Organos,** a studio that still produces handmade *órganos pneumáticos* (air-compression organs) with hand-cut music sheets, and restores musical instruments—perhaps the very last of a breed. Eighteen workers make only four organs per year. A large organ, for which there is today a very limited market, costs about CUC$23,148. You can drop in during business hours at Carretera a Gibara 301 (© **24/42-4162**), and someone is sure to give you a look around.

**La Loma de Cruz (Hill of the Cross),** 3km (1¾ miles) north of the city, can be climbed by ascending the nearly 500 steps to the top, where there's a wooden cross that was placed there in 1790. Though the often-windy hill offers excellent views of Holguín in the flat valley and the surrounding countryside, the hilltop is a little forlorn. The **Mirador de Mayabe** is the other acclaimed viewpoint, about 10km (6¼ miles) from the city center. On the hill, **Cerro de Mayabe,** are a hotel and restaurant, and the locally famous sideshow of Panchito, the beer-guzzling donkey (he stands next to Bar del Burro, the pool bar at the Mirador de Mayabe hotel, and chugs beers for customers who buy him one). However, Panchito is not the first trained donkey to work this sideshow, and it's rumored that more than one of his predecessors has died of alcohol-related causes.

Holguín's **Cabaret Nocturno** ★ (✆ **24/42-5185**) is an open-air cabaret show. Its "Corazón Caribeño" show (Wed–Mon 10pm–2am) is very professional and entertaining, considerably better than the ones put on nightly by the all-inclusive hotels in Guardalavaca. Afterward, the stage becomes a hopping dance club. Admission is CUC$10, or you can buy a package at any of the hotel tour desks for around CUC$30, which includes transportation from your hotel and a cocktail.

For details on getting to Holguín, see "Getting There," earlier in this section.

## GIBARA
35km (22 miles) N of Holguín

A sleepy, charming early-19th-century provincial port, Gibara—sometimes referred to as *La Villa Blanca*, or the White Village, due to its one-time whitewashed appearance—is home to a number of fine colonial-style buildings. The town, today a modest fishing village, has great scenery overlooking a wide natural bay, and a very tranquil atmosphere. Two pretty little beaches and a *Malecón* (promenade) line the picturesque bay, and inland is the **Silla de Gibara,** a flat-topped mountain that locals claim is the hill described by Columbus when he first happened upon Cuba (it is much more probable that he landed in Baracoa, much farther east of here, and that the mountain described in his journal is El Yunque).

On the top of Los Caneyes hill are the ruins of an old **fortress,** which protected merchants involved in trade with Europe and the U.S. (a 30-min. walk up the hill rewards hikers with excellent views of the town and bay). Trade soon diminished with the introduction of the railroad, and the fortunes of Gibara suffered, leading to an exodus of a significant portion of its population. Gibara's moment in the sun is still reflected in the handful of grand mansions and public buildings.

The main plaza is marked by an attractive yellow church with red-tiled cupolas and African oak trees. Of greatest interest is the **Museo del Arte Colonial Cubano,** Independencia 19 (✆ **24/3-4687**), housed in an impressive neoclassical house constructed in 1872. The sumptuous mansion, which once belonged to an elite merchant, features huge *mediopunto* stained-glass windows, yellow and blue tiles, and quality period furnishings. Another attraction in Gibara is the **Museo de Historia Natural,** Independencia, between Luz y Caballero and Peralta, which contains a collection of diurnal and twilight butterflies and a smattering of natural oddities. Both museums are open Tuesday through Saturday from 9am to 5pm, Sunday from 8am to noon; admission is CUC$1.

In 2003, Cuban filmmaker Humberto Solas chose Gibara as the site for his first **Festival de Cine Pobre (Poor Film Festival;** ✆ **7/55-3657** in Havana; www.cuba cine.cu/cinepobre), a film festival dedicated to independent and low-budget filmmaking. The festival is held each year in late April.

For all intents and purposes there's no public transportation available to tourists connecting either Holguín or Guardalavaca to Gibara. This is just as well, since it is quick and convenient to take a taxi there and back for around CUC$30 to CUC$40. Gibara is also featured as a day trip by most of the tour operators in Guardalavaca.

## CAYO SAETIA
130km (81 miles) SE of Guadalavaca

This pristine cay, on the eastern side of the Bahía de Nipes, isn't terribly easy to get to, but if isolated and totally unpopulated sugar-white cove beaches and wild game are of interest to you, it might be worth the effort. This erstwhile exclusive game resort was once the private stomping and hunting grounds of Cuba's military and political brass. The cay has an exceptional roster of flora and fauna, which includes not only deer and wild boar, but also a wild collection of exotics such as antelopes, ostrich, water buffalo, and zebras. Most excursions include snorkeling, boat rides, jeep safaris, horseback riding, and lunch on the beach. While this place is billed as an eco-tourist get-away, this seems to include stalking semi-captive and imported game under the rubric of "eco-tourism." There's only one hotel on the cay, **Villa Cayo Saetía** ✵ (© **24/9-6900; www.gaviota-grupo.com**), with just a dozen simple, yet tasteful rooms and cabanas. Cayo Saetía is about 90 minutes from Guadalavaca by jeep and just 20 minutes by helicopter (the preferred method of transport). Contact **Gaviota Tours** (© **24/42-5350**), which runs the place, or any of the hotels or travel agencies in Guadalavaca.

## 2 Bayamo & the Sierra Maestra ✶
757km (469 miles) E of Havana; 201km (125 miles) E of Camagüey; 127km (79 miles) W of Santiago de Cuba; 73km (45 miles) S of Holguín

Granma province is unusually easygoing and lethargic, even by the standards of stifling hot and dry eastern Cuba, but its retiring pace and unassuming nature belie a turbulent, indelible role in modern Cuban history. Bayamo, the capital of the province, and the densely forested, impenetrable mountains of the Sierra Maestra at the extreme southwest corner of the Oriente region have long been at the forefront of political turmoil and rebellion. The otherwise unassuming region may just be the place where Cuba's independent streak runs deepest.

Bayamo, one of Cuba's original seven *villas* and today a midsize city and the capital of Granma province, is considered the birthplace of Cuban independence. The *himno nacional,* or national anthem, was first sung here after the city was seized by the Liberating Army and became the capital of the Republic at Arms in 1869. South of Bayamo, the Sierra Maestra, a national park comprising a spectacularly verdant and rugged range that reaches right down to the Caribbean coast, is where Fidel Castro and his band of rebels sneaked back into Cuba after a period of exile in Mexico in 1956. The rebels hid in the mountains, depending upon the assistance of sympathetic *guajiros* (peasants), and based their long-shot revolution there, covertly raising the antenna of Radio Rebelde and scoring decisive victories on the road to eventual triumph. How influential was the province as a turning point in 20th-century Cuban politics and society? Important enough that after the Revolution it received the name of the yacht Fidel and his brothers in arms sailed in from Mexico, and the government-owned and operated national daily newspaper is now named for the province: Read all about it in *Granma.*

Today Bayamo and the Sierra Maestra are considerably better known for their historical associations than they are as a traveler's destination. Bayamo is pleasant and peaceful, but its citizens and well-maintained colonial structures don't really try too hard to impress visitors. Meanwhile, much of the Sierra Maestra remains difficult to penetrate for all but the most intrepid hikers. However, it is relatively simple and rewarding to trace the revolutionary steps of Fidel and Che Guevara, visiting the fascinating installations of the rebel group—preserved as they were in the tense days of the late 1950s—tucked high in the mountains. The dramatic coastline that bends around the southeastern base of the Oriente, where the mountains scrape the edge of the sparkling Caribbean, makes an excellent, if time-consuming, ground approach to Santiago de Cuba, and is worth the trip for the scenic value alone. A handful of package tourism hotels are perched on the rocky coast, where the sands aren't much to speak of, but the incomparable sea and mountain views, and diving and hiking opportunities, not to mention very favorable package prices, more than compensate for that.

## ESSENTIALS
### GETTING THERE
**BY PLANE**   You can fly from Havana to Bayamo on **Cubana** (© **23/42-3916** in Bayamo, or 7/33-4446 in Havana; www.cubana.cu) three times a week. Flights arrive at **Aeropuerto Carlos Manuel de Céspedes,** Carretera a Holguín (© **23/42-3695;** airport code BYM), 10km (6¼ miles) north of the city. Fares are CUC$90 to CUC$100 one-way. By registered taxi, the trip to town is about CUC$4.

**BY BUS**   Víazul (© **23/42-4036** in Bayamo, or 7/881-1413 in Havana; www.viazul.com) is the most convenient mode of transportation for traveling to Bayamo from Havana and Santiago, and major cities in between. On the Trinidad–Santiago de Cuba line, the bus departs Trinidad at 8am and arrives in Bayamo at 6:15pm (CUC$28). Buses from Santiago bound for points west leave at 9am, 3:15pm, and 10pm and stop in Bayamo 2 hours and 5 minutes later (CUC$8). On the Havana–Santiago line, there are three daily departures at 9:30am, 3pm, and 10pm; the trip from Havana is roughly 14 hours and costs CUC$48.

The main bus terminal for long-distance buses, the **Terminal de Omnibuses**, is located on the outskirts of downtown, on Carretera Central near Avenida Jesús Rabi, on the road to Holguín. Horse-drawn carriages and unregistered taxis await passengers to ferry them downtown for a dollar or two.

**BY TRAIN**   Though traveling by train is probably not the most comfortable or efficient way to get to Bayamo, train no. 13 departs Havana's Estación Central at 8:15pm and arrives the next morning at 10:30am (CUC$26). Not all Havana–Santiago trains stop in Bayamo, so check before boarding one. Train schedules change frequently, and depending on the season, many trains don't operate on a daily basis; verify the current schedule by calling © **7/862-1920** or 7/861-4259, though it's often better to go in person to the train station and purchase tickets at least a day in advance. The Bayamo train station is on Calle Línea between José Antonio Saco and Parada (© **23/42-4955**), 1km (½ mile) from the center.

### GETTING AROUND
The compact old town of Bayamo is very simple to get around on foot. You're only likely to need a taxi to get back and forth to your hotel, if you stay out at the large Hotel Sierra Maestra, or to get to the airport or bus or train station to move on. Contact **Turistaxi** (© **23/42-4187**), or **Cubataxi** (© **23/42-4513**) for local and long-distance taxis. Alternatively, you can take a horse-drawn or bicycle taxi anywhere in town for CUC$1 to CUC$2.

Getting to the Sierra Maestra mountains is rather more complicated, necessitating a rental car, hired taxi, organized excursion, or some adventurous hitchhiking. If you wish to explore the Sierra with any degree of independence, or make the coastal drive to Santiago de Cuba, your own wheels are virtually indispensable. There's a **Havanautos** office within the Servi-Cupet gas station on Carretera Central (*☎* **23/42-7375**). Rates are about CUC$45 to CUC$80 per day for a standard four-door compact car.

## ORIENTATION

Bayamo's historic center sits on a high bluff overlooking the Bayamo River. For information about excursions in the province, visit one of the major tour operators. **Cubatur** has an office inside the Hotel Royalton, and **Havanatur** has an office on the western side of Parque Céspedes. The tour desk at the Hotel Sierra Maestra is also a good place to get information and arrange tours and excursions.

A **Banco de Crédito y Comercio** branch is on General García between Saco and Perucho Figueredo. It's open Monday through Friday from 8am to 8pm. There is a **CADECA** on Saco between Donato Mármol and General García; it's open Monday through Friday from 8am to 6pm, and most hotels will also have an exchange desk.

For medical attention, go to **Hospital General Carlos Manuel de Céspedes,** Carretera Central on the way to Santiago de Cuba (*☎* **23/42-2144**). A 24-hour pharmacy can be found on the south side of Parque Céspedes.

The main **post office** is on the west side of Parque Céspedes. It's open Monday through Saturday from 9am to 6pm. An **Etecsa** telephone and Internet kiosk is across from the Hotel Royalton, on Calle Maceo at the edge of Parque Céspedes; it's open daily from 9am to 10pm.

## BAYAMO

The second Spanish city founded in Cuba in 1513, as Villa de San Salvador de Bayamo, is small and quiet for a provincial capital. The laid-back town welcomes relatively few visitors except for day-trippers, and locals refrain from hassling foreign visitors—unless it is to offer to sing the Cuban national anthem for you, the city's pride and joy.

Bayamo grew wealthy in the 17th and 18th centuries from contraband and later sugar and cattle. Many of the local elite were privileged enough to send young men off to Spain and France to study, and a number of them returned with enlightened ideals about colonialism, with a strong desire for Cuban independence. Carlos Manuel de Céspedes (1819–74) was a wealthy businessman who, in 1868, freed his slaves and formed a small army that set about achieving that goal. The movement was known as the *Grito de Yara,* a call for independence or death. His forces succeeded in capturing Bayamo and giving life to the War of Independence against Spain. The rebels held Bayamo for 3 months until it was evident that the superior numbers of Spanish troops would soon defeat them. Rather than surrender, the rebel army audaciously chose to burn the city, in the ultimate act of sedition. Most of the city was wiped out by this act of self-immolation in 1869.

## WHAT TO SEE & DO

**Parque Céspedes** *★★* is the focal point of downtown Bayamo. It's an exquisite, peaceful square flanked by tall royal palm trees. The light blue and pink building at one end of the square, which today houses a pharmacy, is where the great blaze began. At one end of the plaza is a marble bust of the independence fighter Perucho Figueredo that carries the words and music to *La Bayamesa* (later the national anthem), which implores followers not to fear "a glorious death" and encourages Cubans that to "die for the homeland is to live." On the other side is a stately granite and bronze statue of Carlos Manuel de Céspedes. Ringing the square are handsome, pastel-colored, arcaded

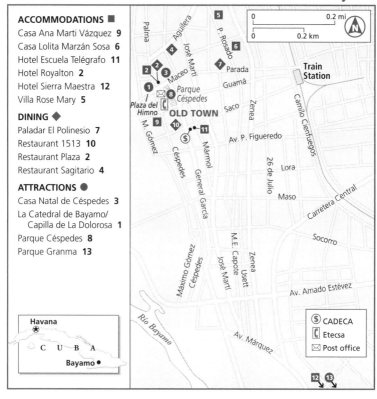

**ACCOMMODATIONS** ■
Casa Ana Marti Vázquez **9**
Casa Lolita Marzán Sosa **6**
Hotel Escuela Telégrafo **11**
Hotel Royalton **2**
Hotel Sierra Maestra **12**
Villa Rose Mary **5**

**DINING** ◆
Paladar El Polinesio **7**
Restaurant 1513 **10**
Restaurant Plaza **2**
Restaurant Sagitario **4**

**ATTRACTIONS** ●
Casa Natal de Céspedes **3**
La Catedral de Bayamo/
   Capilla de La Dolorosa **1**
Parque Céspedes **8**
Parque Granma **13**

$ CADECA
C Etecsa
✉ Post office

colonial-style (post-1869) buildings. Had the city not been consumed by fire, in all likelihood it would resemble the remarkable colonial core of Trinidad.

Next to the Hotel Royalton on the north side of the plaza, the **Casa Natal de Céspedes** 𝒞, Calle Francisco Maceo 57 (𝒞 **23/42-3864**), the birthplace of the "father of the Cuban nation," is the only house on the square that escaped destruction from the fire. The significance of it alone being saved is not lost on Cubans. Today it is a museum, open Tuesday through Friday from 9am to 5pm, Saturday from 9am to 2pm and 8 to 10pm, and Sunday from 10am to 1pm; admission is CUC$1. The house has been lovingly restored; the two-story building holds a chronological exhibit about the Céspedes family, elegant 19th-century colonial furnishings, objects belonging to Céspedes (such as his ceremonial saber), and a few odds and ends that help piece together the story of Bayamo's independent streak (including the original printing press that produced the first newspaper of free Cuba, *El Cubano Libre,* in 1868). Céspedes is remembered for refusing to trade his surrender for the life of his son, who was captured by the Spanish army; the Cuban patriot replied in writing that all Cubans were his sons and he could not be expected to trade their independence for the life of one man. The Spaniards promptly shot his son Oscar.

Just west of the museum and Parque Céspedes, dominating a small open square called **Plaza del Himno,** is **La Catedral de Bayamo** (or La Catedral del Santísimo

Salvador), an immense, ocher-colored, 16th-century church that succumbed to the 1869 fire. Rebuilt several times over the course of its life, the church was recently magnificently restored. It features a high peaked wood-beam ceiling, and above the altar, an attention-getting battle mural commemorating a pivotal local episode when the parish priest blessed the rebel army flag. This blurring of the lines between church and state was not the only overtly political statement to take place in the cathedral; the first singing of the revolutionary anthem was staged here in 1869. The cathedral is open to visitors daily from 9am to 1pm and 3 to 5pm. To one side of the cathedral, the small chapel **Capilla de La Dolorosa (Chapel of the Lady of Sorrows),** which dates to 1630, is distinguished by a lovely Moorish-style carved wooden ceiling and fine baroque altarpiece.

Heading south from Parque Céspedes, Calle General García has been turned into a pleasant pedestrian mall, with several shops, simple restaurants, and tour agency offices.

## WHERE TO STAY

Quite a few *casas particulares* can be found in the old center of Bayamo. **Villa Rose Mary,** Pío Rosado 22 between Ramírez and Avenida F.V. Aguilera (© **23/42-3984;** varezsanchez@yahoo.es), is an attractive house with two comfortable, clean, air-conditioned rooms. Each room (CUC$20 double) has its own private entrance. **Casa Lolita Marzán Sosa,** Pío Rosado 171 between Capote and Parada (© **23/42-2974**), offers two upstairs rooms (CUC$20 double), each with air-conditioning and a bathroom within, plus independent entrance, and a shared kitchen, and dining room. **Casa Ana Martí Vázquez,** Céspedes 4 between Maceo and Canducha (© **23/42-5323;** lmartivazquez@yahoo.es), has two nicely furnished rooms with extremely high ceilings. The rooms (CUC$15 double) share a bathroom; one has air-conditioning and the other a fan.

### Inexpensive

In addition to the hotels listed below, another good option and excellent value is the training school **Hotel Escuela Telégrafo,** Calle José Antonio Saco 108 (© **23/42-5510;** www.ehtgr.co.cu), which is in the heart of downtown and charges just CUC$20 to CUC$30 double for a room with air-conditioning, television, and a small refrigerator.

**Hotel Royalton** ⭐  Set facing Parque Céspedes, this charming, boutique hotel is the top choice in town. Dating to the 1940s, this place features tastefully decorated rooms with air-conditioning, TVs, and small but immaculate bathrooms with showers only. Four rooms have small balconies with great plaza views. Off to one side of the lobby is the dependable and brightly lit **Restaurant Plaza,** which features a nice sidewalk terrace and a generous plate of fried chicken with excellent French fries, as well as chicken fricassee and beef with garlic sauce.

Calle Maceo 53, Bayamo. © **23/42-2290.** Fax 23/42-4792. www.islazul.cu. 33 units. CUC$27–CUC$33 double. MC, V. **Amenities:** Restaurant; bar. *In room:* A/C, TV, fridge.

**Hotel Sierra Maestra**  Located 2km (1¼ miles) from Parque Céspedes, this large and friendly hotel has an excellent outdoor swimming pool and a quiet relaxed feel. Rooms are smallish but well appointed with air-conditioning and TV. Most have a balcony of some sort. Most rooms are in a large, nondescript three-story block of a building backing the pool. My favorite rooms are in the separate *cabaña* section of two-story units. At night, this place has a decent bar scene and probably the liveliest dance club in town.

## Dear Granma

In early December, 1956, Fidel Castro, his brother Raúl, Ernesto (Che) Guevara, and a group of idealist revolutionaries, including some who had previously stormed the barracks in Santiago de Cuba and Bayamo, sailed back from exile in Mexico with weapons and an audacious plan: to overthrow, once and for all, the Batista government. They set sail aboard a yacht christened the *Granma,* purchased from a couple of Americans in Veracruz. The stealth journey was beset by all manner of hitches, including bad weather and scarce provisions. Just 82 men disembarked at Las Coloradas beach 2 days later than planned, with few weapons and virtually no supplies.

Batista forces had been tipped off to the operation, and prompt aerial bombing killed about half the rebels; the others fled for the mountains in small groups. After suffering an ambush, only 16 men remained, and when the survivors eventually met up at Cinco Palmas in the Sierra Maestra, only a dozen men remained. They had but eight rifles to their names. Against monumental odds, they nonetheless began to plan their offensive. Batista, no doubt convinced that the attempted sedition had been effectively quashed, announced to the world that Castro and the other leaders had been killed and withdrew government forces from the area—a fatal mistake.

Crafty Castro began slowly but surely to gain adherents and advance the rebel cause of the 26th of July Movement. Astonishingly, a band of just over a dozen fighters at the campaign's inception—propped up by a growing network of *guajiros* and vast, inaccessible terrain—somehow ended up toppling the Batista regime just 2 years later.

Today the spot where the rebels landed ashore, at the southwestern tip of Cuba near Cabo Cruz, is a national park, **Parque Nacional del Desembarco del Granma.** A monument features a replica of the Granma; the real vessel is in the Museo de la Revolución in Havana.

Carretera Central Km 1.5 on the way to Santiago de Cuba. © **23/42-7974.** www.cubanacan.cu. 114 units. CUC$35–CUC$44 double. MC, V. **Amenities:** Restaurant; bar; large outdoor pool. *In room:* A/C, TV, safe.

### WHERE TO DINE

Only a few *paladares* remain in Bayamo. Aside from the place listed below, **Paladar El Polinesio,** Parada 125 between Pío Rosado and Capotico Bayamo (© **23/42-3860**) is the second-best restaurant in town. Another good option is **Restaurante 1513,** Calle General García between Saco and Guamá (© **23/42-2939**), which only accepts Cuban pesos, allowing you to enjoy a fulfilling meal for under CUC$2.

For dessert, stand in line with locals at the ice-cream parlor **Tropicrema,** located just off the southwest corner of Parque Céspedes.

**Restaurant Sagitario** ⚐ CRIOLLA    This place serves large and well-prepared meals in a very pleasant backyard patio with weathered brick walls. The house specialty is pork steak cooked with ham and cheese; the *pargo* (red snapper) is also quite good. Service here is friendly and downright efficient.

Calle Mármol 107 between Maceo and Francisco Vicente Aguilera. ℂ **23/42-2449**. Reservations recommended. Main courses CUC$6–CUC$9. No credit cards. Daily noon–11pm.

## BAYAMO AFTER DARK

Bayamo is an extremely quiet and laid-back town. Still, after dark, there are a couple of happening nightspots where locals and visitors alike gather. Bayamo has the requisite **Casa de la Trova,** which is a good place to catch live music. But my favorite haunt here is **La Bodega** ⍟, which has a large open-air patio overlooking the river, and often features live music as well.

## SIERRA MAESTRA ⍟⍟

Cuba's highest and longest mountain range stretches about 140km (90 miles) west to east, across three provinces: Granma, Santiago de Cuba, and Guantánamo. Its highest peaks are only several kilometers from the coastline, making for some exciting visuals whether you're perched up in the mountains or cruising along the coast. The entire range forms part of the **Gran Parque Nacional Sierra Maestra,** and its thickly forested, rugged nature, with steep, deep green mountains swathed in wispy clouds, are impenetrable for most traffic, though the area is splendid for hikers. While there are many trails just begging to be explored, until recently most remained closed to the public; hard-core hikers should perhaps anticipate encountering some closed trail heads. The heart of the Gran Parque is a park-within-a-park, the **Parque Nacional de Turquino** ⍟, which includes Turquino, the nation's highest summit at just under 2,000m (6,560 ft.).

Deep folds and craggy ravines make these mountains very inaccessible, and they are, not surprisingly, very sparsely populated, with only small numbers of *guajiros*—many of whose families once gave shelter and support to the rebels in their midst—living very simply in thatched-roof *bohíos* with no electricity or running water. Tucked away in the mountain range are dozens of endemic species of birds and plants.

Unless you're a physically prepared hiker with all your own equipment and several days or more for hikes, your best bet is to head to the Turquino Park, where there is, at least, minimal infrastructure and the lasting legacy of Fidel Castro and his committed band of rebels, which formed the **Comandancia de La Plata,** a base command for their guerrilla war in 1956 after return from exile in Mexico (see "Dear Granma," above). The two main trails into the mountains are the **Pico Turquino Trail** and the **La Plata Trail;** the latter visits the rebels' base camp.

The road south from Bayamo is a long, lush tropical adventure; it cuts through beautiful sugar-cane fields where pigs, peacocks, and machete-wielding farmers roam, with the rounded, green peaks of the Sierra Maestra looming in the background. **Villa Santo Domingo,** 65km (40 miles) south of Bayamo by good road, is where you'll find the entrance to the national park as well as a rustic hotel and restaurant that serves as a perfect base camp for those who want to trace the trail of Fidel and Che, ascend Pico Turquino, or just explore the rugged beauty of the national park. The **Hotel Villa Santo Domingo** (ℂ **23/59-5302;** www.islazul.cu; CUC$34–CUC$37 double, including breakfast), where Fidel and his brother Raúl have been frequent guests in the past (Fidel favors cabin no. 6), sits down a bit on the left side of the road, on the banks of the Yara River. The 20 attractive little cabins have twin beds, private bathrooms, air-conditioning, TVs, solar-powered hot water, and fridges. Also on the grounds are a good restaurant and outdoor grill, as well as a bar, video and game room, and hammocks. Even for those not staying at the hotel, the rustic, open-air **Restaurant La Yamagua** is the best place to eat in the area if you didn't bring your own provisions. For groups, the restaurant does a good *parrilla* (barbecue) of *cerdo asado* (roast pork), salad, rice, dessert, and coffee for CUC$14 a head. The menu includes standards of *comida criolla,* several different preparations of chicken, and pork steak.

## HIKING IN THE SIERRA

Hiking deep into the Sierra Maestra is a superbly rewarding experience for any hiker, but—given the mountains' historic role in the success of the Revolution and the fact that much of the Sierra remains a military zone—the Cuban government zealously protects access to it. By law you need permission and a guide to explore the national park. Remember, Fidel's cronies hid from Batista's forces and the CIA for more than 2 years in the dense forest of the Sierra, so finding your way around is a complicated task. Park authorities don't look kindly upon foreigners seeking to explore the park on their own.

Guides can be contracted at the official entrance to the national park, the **Centro de Información de Flora y Fauna,** about 200m (650 ft.) along the road beyond the Hotel Villa Santo Domingo. Visitors pay a CUC$10 fee to enter the park and, if they have come independently, contract a guide for hikes into the Sierra. This also is the spot to arrange treks and bird-watching. You will need to arrive with all necessary gear, as no one in the area rents equipment. The center offers a number of different hikes and prices. All prices are per person and include a guide:

- Comandancia La Plata del Ejército Rebelde (see below), CUC$10
- Alto de Naranjo, the shortest hike possible and the actual starting point for the Pico Turquino and La Plata trails, CUC$5
- Palma Mocha, a 1-day trek toward Pico Turquino, CUC$10
- Aguada de Santo Domingo to Pico Turquino, CUC$35 including 1 night in the Aguada refuge (for which you'll need a sleeping bag)
- Santo Domingo–Aguada–Pico Turquino–La Majagua–Las Cuevas, CUC$40 (includes 2 nights of camping)
- Local walks along the river and bird-watching (5–10am and 4pm–dusk), CUC$5

To gain access to the Pico Turquino or La Plata trail, hikers must either climb or take a tough-as-nails flat-bed truck (CUC$5 and 45 min. one-way) up a treacherously steep paved road, with thrilling hairpin turns, to **Alto de Naranjo.** A minimum number of 10 to 12 hikers is usually required for the truck service.

Places to get more information about trekking in the Sierra Maestra are **Agencia de Reservaciones del Campismo,** General García 456, Bayamo (② **23/42-4200**), and **Islazul,** General García 207, Bayamo (②/fax **23/42-3273**), which runs the Villa Santo Domingo hotel at the entrance to the park.

### Pico Turquino ✿✿

The hike to Pico Turquino, the highest summit in Cuba, requires a minimum of 2 nights in the area (1 night camping). The trek from Alto de Naranjo is about 15km (9 miles). Experienced, fast hikers can do the ascent and descent in a day, but most people choose to camp overnight at the *refugio,* several kilometers below the summit. The trek through an amazing array of tropical ferns, vines, and dense cloud forest, punctuated by the sharp calls of unseen birds, is terrific, with stunning panoramic views all around, and is only really difficult at the steep end. It gets quite cold at night, so make sure you're prepared with proper clothing and equipment.

## Comandancia de la Plata 🏛🏛

Though not nearly as challenging a hike—you can do the 6km (4 miles) up and back in about 2 hours—the trail to La Plata perched on a mountain ridge reverberates with thrilling history, no matter on which side of the political fence you fall. Visiting the rudimentary installations of Fidel Castro's rebel base camp is a remarkable experience. When you learn the story of the rebellion and visit the crude installations from which Fidel directed his offensive, it's hard not to have at least some appreciation for why this man clings so tenaciously to power and the ideals of the Revolution: Look what he did to get there.

After about 20 minutes on the trail, about 800m (2,600 ft.) above sea level, hikers come to the **Alto de Medina,** a small wooden house with old photos of Fidel and his comrades in the Sierra campaign. It functions as a checkpoint, and trekkers must leave their cameras behind (no photographs are permitted of the Comandancia La Plata). Farther up along the trail, you come to a **small museum** about the revolutionary guerrilla warfare waged in these mountains. You'll see what, at one time, was a small hospital, and eventually, you'll arrive at the huts where Che and Fidel (with his *compañera* Celia Sánchez) lived. Fidel never allowed anyone but Celia inside the shack; the bench where he conducted interviews at the door is still there. Ingeniously constructed under the cover of thick forest, the installations make it quite apparent how the rebels eluded capture and assassination. The hilltop rising above the camp is where the guerrillas covertly erected the antenna to broadcast their rebel message on the nascent Radio Rebelde.

## THE COASTAL ROAD TO SANTIAGO DE CUBA

The Sierra Maestra crashing down to the rocky beaches and black sands of the south coast, against the sparkling blue waters of the Caribbean, is one of the most dramatic sights in Cuba. To trace the coast to get to Santiago de Cuba is to take the scenic route; it is a roundabout way to get to your destination, to be sure, but well worth it if you're a fan of rugged, bravura landscapes. If you're pressed for time and headed to Santiago, the inland route from Bayamo is much more direct.

The coastline is remarkably absent of any sort of villages or installations for long stretches at a time: just you, the open road, and the sea to your right and Sierra Maestra to the left. The road is pretty good for most of the trajectory, although rockslides aren't uncommon. While you can usually make the trip in any normal sedan, a four-wheel-drive vehicle is recommended for the added clearance, if nothing else. The beaches, such as they are, range from passable soft gray stone to forbidding big black rock.

A smattering of large resort hotels is located at certain points along the coast, and while it's a stretch to describe them as beach resorts, they do offer splendid sea views, a host of watersports, and plenty of trekking opportunities. Most are package tourism confines, aimed largely at seniors. Canadian charter planes fly direct to Manzanillo, and the hotels then bus in groups of 100 vacationers or more for an inexpensive weeklong coastal Cuban vacation. Whether those guests arrive expecting fine, white, powdery Caribbean sand we don't know (we certainly hope not). Although we were initially turned off by the notion of an all-inclusive hotel hovering illogically on "beaches" that suffer so in comparison with those along the north coast, we have to admit that there are a couple of hotels that wouldn't be awful places to vacation, as long as your expectations are simple. They include the **Club Amigo Marea del Portillo,** Carretera Granma Km 12.5, Pilón (② **23/59-7081;** www.hotelescubanacan.com).

## Goin' (or Not) to Gitmo

On the radio in Guantánamo city and along the road to Baracoa, the unmistakable sounds of English-speaking DJs and American pop music appear out of nowhere. That radio is courtesy of the U.S. government, emerging from behind barbed-wire fences at the base at Guantánamo Bay, known to American military personnel as "Gitmo." The base is an eyebrow-raising anomaly in revolutionary Cuba, as it's probably the least likely spot in the world for the U.S. to have a naval base. Washington continues to hold an indefinite lease on the base, which was established in 1903 as a reward for the U.S. role in the Spanish-American War—making it the oldest overseas American naval base.

Pursuant to the original agreement, signed by President Theodore Roosevelt, which called for an annual payment of 2,000 gold coins ($4,085), the U.S. government continues to send its rent checks, even though Fidel Castro hasn't cashed a single one since he came to power in 1959. Castro understandably would rather forgo the paltry sum than lend legitimacy to the American presence in Cuba. A 1934 treaty that reaffirmed the lease of the base stipulated that both the U.S. and Cuba must mutually agree to terminate the lease—and when was the last time Washington, D.C., and Havana agreed on anything?

Though it has official missions (refueling and reconnaissance), in peace times the Guantánamo base has existed primarily to continue to poke thorns in Castro's side. That was, until 2001, when the U.S. military decided to send Al Qaeda prisoners captured in the wars in Afghanistan and Iraq to Guantánamo. Since then, the base has been a source of international news and controversy. Most of the detainees continue to be held and interrogated without access to lawyers or the filing of any formal charges.

Cubans have grudgingly learned to live with the base. They no longer expect a U.S. invasion at any moment, and the U.S. now returns those Cubans who, rather than attempt to cross the Atlantic, try to escape Cuba by crossing over to the American base. Only a small handful of Cuban workers still cross military checkpoints every day to get to their jobs on the base.

Gitmo has about 3,000 full-time residents who, though surrounded on three sides by Cuba, live as if in American suburbotopia, with typical suburban homes, U.S. products, American cars, cable TV, a golf course, and, of course, a McDonald's. However, this gated community has a sign (on the Cuban side) that reads REPUBLICA DE CUBA, TERRITORIO LIBRE DE AMERICA (Republic of Cuba, Free Territory of America).

From Marea del Portillo, the road continues another 40km (25 miles) or so to Santiago de Cuba province. The views take in desert-like landscapes, massive dry mountains of the Sierra Maestra, black rocky beaches, and large waves crashing ashore, a highly scenic drive. The only village of any real size is **Chivirico,** a small fishing settlement about 75km (45 miles) outside of Santiago de Cuba. The best hotel en route to Santiago de Cuba is the all-inclusive **Brisas Sierra Mar Los Galeones** ⚓ (℃ **22/ 29-110;** www.hotelescubanacan.com), a massive, multitiered hotel overlooking a sandy brown beach. Though the overall facilities are fairly impressive—there are four restaurants, five bars, two tennis courts, a fitness room, and a large swimming pool—the rooms are standard and uninspiring with ugly flowered curtains and tiny TVs. There are plenty of better all-inclusive hotels in other parts of Cuba, but this place does combine well with a visit to Santiago. Rates are CUC$110 to CUC$145 double, all-inclusive. From here it's another hour or so to Santiago; see chapter 10 for full coverage.

## THE ROAD TO BARACOA

**Guantánamo province,** by virtue of a Cuban song seemingly known the world over ("Guantanamera") and an attention-getting, anachronistic U.S. military base, gets more ink and initial interest than it probably deserves. The easternmost province on the island only has one true draw, but it's one of the highlights of Cuba: the tiny tropical gem Baracoa. The only real reason to stop over in the sweltering and unappealing city of Guantánamo is to visit the distant lookout trained at the contentious **American naval base** isolated on Cuban soil. That's as close as you'll get—and honestly, outside of the novelty factor, there's nothing much to see.

The parched landscape of the southern coast begins to change gradually in color along the spectacular 40km (25-mile) road **La Farola,** which courses southeast of Santiago and wends its way through the mountains along the route to Baracoa. Things get more and more lush, with thick tropical vegetation and beautiful views at every turn. Be forewarned, in addition to its beauty, this is a tight and winding road with a seemingly endless series of white-knuckle hairpin turns. Baracoa, isolated from the rest of Cuba before the building of the road, is a beguiling little town, known for its chocolate and coconut and connections to Columbus. It's been known to bewitch more than a few travelers into staying much longer than they'd planned.

## 3 Baracoa ⚓⚓⚓

236km (146 miles) NE of Santiago de Cuba; 150km (93 miles) NE of Guantánamo; 332km (206 miles) E of Holguín

Swathed in generous tropical vegetation and refreshed by 10 rivers, Baracoa is perhaps the most picturesque spot in all of Cuba. The historic town sits on a lovely oyster-shaped bay, **Bahía de Miel (Honey Bay),** and the landmark flat-topped mountain known as **El Yunque (The Anvil)** looms in the background.

Not only is Baracoa, for my pesos, the most beautiful place on the island, it's also the oldest. That Baracoa was the first settlement established by Diego Velázquez in 1511—making it the oldest colonial city in the Americas—is not in doubt. Christopher Columbus is thought to have first landed at this spot in late November 1492, and locals claim that he planted a wooden cross here to mark his arrival (the cross, carbon-tested for age, is on display in the Asunción church in town).

After its founding, Nuestra Señora de la Asunción de Baracoa remained the capital of the new Spanish colony for just 4 years; when Velázquez moved the capital west to Santiago, on a bigger and deeper bay, Baracoa's isolation had already begun. The small fishing and farming village remained virtually cut off from the rest of Cuba, with no true road in until the 1960s, when a scenic roller coaster of a highway was cut through the mountains.

For such a small, isolated settlement, Baracoa is loaded with things to do and see. It swims with possibilities for hiking, white-water rafting, and boating. Baracoa really

# Baracoa

shines the first week of April, when heady street parties (part of a *semana de cultura,* or cultural week) commemorate the date General Antonio Maceo disembarked at nearby Playa Duaba in 1895, marking the beginning of Cuba's War of Independence. The greatest pleasure Baracoa offers, though, is just being here. Most people make the trek just to take in its extraordinary beauty, tranquillity, and abundant charms. A UNESCO Biosphere Reserve, the tropical seaside town is tucked into green hillsides covered with cocoa and coconut groves, and surrounded by beaches lined by royal palms. As the abundant greenery attests, Baracoa is huddled in the midst of the wettest region in Cuba.

## ESSENTIALS
### GETTING THERE
**BY PLANE**   There are flights three times a week on **AeroCaribbean** and **Cubana** from Havana to Baracoa; however, flight schedules are notorious for frequent changes and cancellations. Fares run between CUC$95 and CUC$120 one-way. Flights arrive at the small **Aeropuerto Gustavo Rizo** (© **21/4-5376;** airport code BCA), west of the bay near the Hotel Porto Santo and about 4km (2½ miles) west of downtown. Although flights are infrequent, **Cubana** flies here occasionally from Santiago de Cuba, and the fare is a very reasonable CUC$40 one-way. By taxi, the trip to town costs about CUC$3 to CUC$4.

**BY BUS** Most visitors arrive overland; the ride from Santiago de Cuba is especially spectacular, if lengthy. A **Víazul** bus (℡ **22/62-8484** in Santiago, or 21/4-2239 in Baracoa; www.viazul.com) departs Santiago daily at 7:45am and arrives in Baracoa at 12:30pm (CUC$17). The trip makes stops in Guantánamo and four other small towns. The same bus departs Baracoa at 2:15pm and arrives in Santiago at 7pm. The route is very popular, especially in high season; make reservations for the trip at least a day in advance, as these buses sell out frequently and fast.

The Baracoa **Terminal de Omnibuses** (℡ **21/4-2239**) is located at the end of José Martí near Avenida de los Mártires.

**BY CAR** You can drive to Baracoa from either Santiago de Cuba, along the scenic La Farola highway (see "The Road to Baracoa," above), or from Guardalavaca/Holguín along the northern coastal road through Moa. Allow between 3½ to 4 hours for either route.

### GETTING AROUND

You can easily get around most of Baracoa on foot or *bicitaxi*. To reach the beaches, rivers, and mountains around Baracoa, you'll either need to contract a taxi, rent a car, or sign on for an organized excursion. **Turistaxi** (℡ **21/4-3581**) and **Cubataxi** (℡ **21/4-3737**) make local and long-distance runs.

A car is a good idea if you really want to do some independent exploration of the surrounding area, or travel to, say, Santiago de Cuba or Guardalavaca. There's a **Havanautos** office at the Baracoa airport (℡ **21/4-5343**); **Cubacar** (℡ **21/4-5212**) and **Vía Rent-a-Car** (℡ **21/4-5137**) also have agencies in Baracoa. Rates are about CUC$50 to CUC$80 per day for a standard four-door compact car.

### ORIENTATION

The **Havanatur** office at Antonio Maceo 120 (℡ **21/4-5358**) can provide travel information, as can the personnel of the tour desks at the Hotel El Castillo and Hotel Porto Santo. Other tour agencies include **Gaviota** in the Hotel El Castillo (℡ **21/4-5165**); **Cubatur,** Martí 181 (℡ **21/4-5306**); and **Archipiélago,** Coronel Cardoso 24 (℡ **21/4-3665**), which specializes in outdoor trips in the area.

A **Banco de Crédito y Comercio** branch is on Calle Antonio Maceo. Traveler's checks can be cashed at the Hotel El Castillo and Hotel Porto Santo.

For medical attention, go to **Hospital Octavio de la Concepción,** Carretera a Guantánamo (℡ **21/4-3014**). There's a small *policlínico* (**medical clinic**) on José Martí 427, and a **pharmacy** on Antonio Maceo 132.

The main **post office** is on Calle Antonio Maceo 136, near Plaza Independencia; it's open Monday through Saturday from 9am to 6pm. You can make local, long-distance, and international phone calls or use one of the two computer terminals at the **Etecsa** office on Calle Antonio Maceo, just past Plaza Independencia; it's open daily from 8am to 8pm.

### WHAT TO SEE & DO

Baracoa is its own greatest attraction. Its bustling streets are lined with gaily painted clapboard houses, and the rivers, beaches, and mountains beyond the city are perfect for outdoor exploration.

In the 18th and 19th centuries, Baracoan settlers built three fortresses to protect the town from pirate attacks. **El Castillo de Santa Bárbara,** the oldest of the bunch, sits high above town, with splendid views of the bay and surrounding countryside; it has

> ⌒ *Fun Fact* **Sweet Tears**
>
> One of the more fanciful legends in Baracoa surrounds the Río Miel, or Honey
> River. It is said that a local Taíno Indian girl fell in love with a visiting sailor and,
> as his departure date neared, cried such tears that the river overflowed and her
> sailor couldn't bear to leave. Locals say that if you wash your hands in the Río
> Miel, you'll return; if you swim in it, you'll stay.

now been converted into a hotel. **Fuerte de la Punta,** facing the seaside promenade,
is now a restaurant. The third, **Fuerte Matachín,** near the entrance to town, houses
the municipal museum, **Museo Matachín,** Calle Martí s/n at the *Malecón* (✆ 21/
4-2122). It holds a number of interesting historical exhibits related to the history of
Baracoa and its legends and myths. The museum also has a collection of extraordinary,
vividly colored and striped *polimitas* (snail shells), which locals used to make into
necklaces and sell to tourists before the supply dried up. The museum is open Tuesday through Sunday from 8am to 4pm; admission is CUC$1 with a guide, and photo
and video privileges cost an extra CUC$2.

**Nuestra Señora de la Asunción,** Maceo 152 (✆ 21/4-3352), the rather austere
cathedral, was constructed in 1512, though it was burned by the French in 1652. The
current structure was rebuilt at the beginning of the 19th century. It is most notable
for the **Cruz de la Parra,** a small wooden cross on display inside a glass case. Locals
insist that Columbus himself planted the cross on the banks of the bay in 1492,
shortly after disembarking on Cuban soil for the first time. Whether or not there's any
truth to that claim, carbon dating has in fact established that the cross is more than
500 years old (making it one of the oldest Christian relics in the Americas, if not the
oldest). The hardwood is native to Cuba, though, so if Columbus did leave it, he must
have fashioned it *in situ* rather than having brought it with him, as was originally
believed. The cross has greatly dwindled in size, due to the faithful over the years who
thought nothing of slicing off a memento for themselves.

Next to the church is **Parque de la Independencia** (also called Parque Central), a
popular gathering spot for locals and tourists enjoying a few lazy days in Baracoa. A
bust of the rebel Taíno Indian leader Hatuey (whose countenance today appears on
beer bottles) adorns the square. Hatuey took up arms against the early *conquistadores*
until he was caught by the Spanish and burned at the stake.

In the area around Baracoa are as many as 50 **pre-Columbian archaeological sites**
related to the major Native American groups that inhabited the area (Siboney, Taíno,
and Guanturabey). The only native group to survive is the Yateras, a small community that has succeeded in preserving their traditions, marrying only among each other
and living along the Río Toa.

## OUTDOOR EXCURSIONS AROUND BARACOA

Baracoa's potential as an eco-tourism destination has just begun to be exploited. The
spectacular area around Baracoa offers excellent opportunities for treks and white-
water rafting. The region features patches of secondary rainforest, and abounds in
banana, yucca, mango, coconut, and tall royal palm trees, and at least 10 flowing
rivers. The earth here is rich in iron, which gives it a red tone.

Distinctive **El Yunque** 🏵🏵, described in Spanish chronicles as an anvil-shaped,
high and square mountain, dominates the landscape; Columbus wrote of seeing it on

his approach to the bay. Frequently bathed in mist, the flat-topped limestone mountain (575m/1,886 ft.) is about 10km (6¼ miles) west of Baracoa, and its slopes can be climbed in 4 hours round-trip. The slopes have been declared a UNESCO Biosphere Reserve. El Yunque is part of the Parque Natural Duaba and is home to scores of bird species and unique plants. In fact, 16 of Cuba's 24 endemic bird species can be found in this area. You can also spot the endemic *coco thrinas* palms, which look like tall dandelions. The trek through tropical forest, with views of rare ferns and orchids, is beautiful, but it can be intensely humid. Those who aren't up for the hike can always drive, though it's rough going along the unpaved road. Adventurers in search of white-water rafting possibilities should check out **Río Toa,** the widest river in Cuba and part of a national park.

Javier Rabazza at **Archipiélago/Ecotur,** Coronel Cardoso 24 (© **21/4-3665**), organizes a variety of nature outings with transportation and guides, including tube rafting on the Río Duaba, white-water rafting on the Río Toa, various treks, visits to caves with ancient petroglyphs, and boating excursions along rivers (one of the best trips is along the gorgeous Río Yumurí, 30km/19 miles east of Baracoa, where there's a charming little fishing village). **Havanatur** (© **21/4-5358**), **Cubatur,** Martí 181 (© **21/4-5306**), and the **Gaviota** office at the Hotel El Castillo (© **21/4-2125**) also offer organized excursions.

Baracoa is blessed with a few superb beaches, which, due to the town's isolation, haven't yet been built up with huge all-inclusive hotels (this will certainly change in the coming years). **Playa Maguana** ✦ is about 22km (14 miles) from town on the road to Moa. It's a peaceful place with picture-perfect golden sands and is popular with local families and fishermen. There's a small hotel here (see "Where to Stay," below). A smaller and more isolated beach, **Playa Nava,** is another 6km (3¾ miles) west. It's not as pretty as Maguana, but you're likely to have it to yourself. Nearer to Baracoa, **Playa Duaba** isn't much of a beach at all; it's where the river of the same name meets the sea, but it's a good spot for lunch and is the staging point for easygoing boat trips along the river. ***Note:*** Baracoa, the rainiest spot on the island, gets downfalls in heavy bunches during the months of May, June, December, and January—something to consider if you're looking for beach time.

## WHERE TO STAY

There's nothing fancy or especially luxurious in easygoing Baracoa—except the spectacular views of the bay and surrounding mountains—but one of the main hotels, in the oldest fortress in town, is a charmer. The little town is populated by more than 150 casas particulares, most right within the old town; several are excellent and among the best deals of their kind in Cuba.

### MODERATE

**Hotel El Castillo** ✦✦ *Finds*    Perched up on a hill with the best views of Baracoa and the bay, and a picture-perfect pool, this easygoing Gaviota hotel—the lower part of which inhabits an old fort—is the top place in town to stay. Its simple rooms don't quite measure up to the privileged location and general ambience, though they're pretty good size, have colonial-style furnishings, and are set around the pool. If you can get room no. 201 do so, as it's a large corner room with a queen-size bed, and one of only two rooms with a bed big enough for a couple. All the rest have two or three twin beds. If we owned the place, we'd restyle it as a swank hotel. Advance reservations are essential.

Calle Calixto García, Loma el Paraíso, Baracoa. (© **21/4-5195.** Fax 21/35-5223. www.gaviota-grupo.com. 34 units. CUC$50–CUC$62 double. Rates include breakfast. MC, V. **Amenities:** Restaurant; snack bar; 2 bars; outdoor pool; car- and scooter-rental desk; laundry service. In room: A/C, TV, safe.

**Hotel Porto Santo**   Gaviota runs this hotel right on the bay near the spot where Columbus supposedly deposited the cross marking his arrival in the Americas. Slightly larger than the El Castillo (see above), this one gets more tour groups. Its best feature is a large pool with a deck and thatched-roof bar overlooking the bay and cute private cove beach. In fact, the view here may be even better than that from El Castillo, because from here you are looking at Baracoa. In truth, rooms aren't very large or nicely decorated, and all have rather small bathrooms, but those in the last wing have the best bay views (something I'd request). All come with a small balcony or private patio. The location is somewhat isolated, though, and can be a pain if you're looking to make frequent trips into town.

Carretera del Aeropuerto, Baracoa. (© **21/4-5103.** Fax 21/4-5135. www.gaviota-grupo.com. 60 units. CUC$58–CUC$68 double. Rates include breakfast. MC, V. **Amenities:** Restaurant; grill; 2 bars; nightly show; outdoor pool; car- and scooter-rental desk; laundry service. In room: A/C, TV, minibar, safe.

**Villa Maguana** ★★   This little place, 21km (13 miles) from Baracoa, doesn't look like much from the outside. But the secluded and peaceful inn fronts a totally private, pretty cove next to a 2km (1¼-mile) white-sand beach. The four rooms are large and charmingly rustic, like private cabins, with dark wood furniture and red and yellow decor; two have great terraces with rocking chairs overlooking the transparent water. Note that room nos. 1 and 2 face the beach. The villa would be a great place for a large family or four couples to rent and just hang out here on the beautiful outskirts of Baracoa.

Carretera Moa a Baracoa, Baracoa. (© **21/4-5165.** Fax 21/4-5223. www.gaviota-grupo.com. 4 units. CUC$55–CUC$65 double. Rates include breakfast. MC, V. **Amenities:** Restaurant; bar. In room: A/C, TV, minibar, safe.

## INEXPENSIVE

There are over 150 casas particulares in Baracoa. Recommended casas include **Casa Brisas del Atlántico** ★, Calle Frank País 3, between Avenida Malecón and Máximo Gómez (© **21/4-3457** or 21/4-5147), which has two rooms with a separate entrance and a huge rooftop terrace with sea views; **Casa La Colina** ★, Calle Calixto García 158 altos, between Céspedes and Coroneles Gulano (© **21/4-3477**), which also has a superb terrace; **Casa Isabel Garrido** ★, Calle Calixto García 164A (© **21/4-3515**), which has a large terrace and a small balcony overlooking the street; **Casa Daniel Salomón Paján,** Calle Céspedes 28, between Rupert López and Maceo (© **21/4-2122**); **Casa Walter,** Calle Rupert López 47, between Céspedes and Coroneles Galano (© **21/4-3380**), a central option whose third-floor terrace has a high-pitched red-tile roof; **Casa Miguelin,** Calle Maceo 168 (© **21/4-3569**), whose owner is a professional and excellent chef; and **Casa Tropical,** Calle Martí 175 (© **21/4-3437**).

**Hostal La Habanera** ★ _Value_   Fronting the Plaza de la Independencia, this recently renovated downtown colonial structure is an atmospheric, affordable, and perfectly located option. The rooms are all spacious, with high ceilings, bright patterned bed linens, rattan headboards, and sparkling tile floors. All come with two twin beds, and unfortunately they weren't planning on adding any larger beds anytime soon. However, for a budget option, you'll be surprised to find a large television, with four international cable channels. My favorite rooms are the four that share a long broad veranda overlooking Calle Maceo.

Calle Maceo 68, at the corner of Calle Frank País. © 21/4-5273. Fax 21/4-5274. 10 units. CUC$40–CUC$55 double. Rates include breakfast. MC, V. **Amenities:** Restaurant; snack bar; bar; tour desk; massage; laundry service. *In room:* A/C, TV.

**Hotel La Rusa** *Overrated*   This legendary little hotel was established by a Russian émigré (and princess) and former dancer ("La Rusa de Baracoa"), who, over the years, became active in Cuban revolutionary politics and later played host to Fidel, Che, and the poet Nicolás Guillén. Today, this big yellow house right by the sea doesn't really live up to its storied past. In fact, it is very run-down and seedy. The brightly colored but mediocre rooms are small and have tiny bathrooms (showers only). The biggest plus here is that the hotel fronts the sea, across the street from Baracoa's *Malecón.*

Carretera del Aeropuerto, Baracoa. © 21/4-3011. Fax 21/4-2337. 12 units. CUC$24–CUC$30 double. Rates include breakfast. MC, V. *In room:* A/C, TV, minibar.

## WHERE TO DINE

Diners resigned to the plain, unimaginative food in the rest of Cuba are in for a treat in Baracoa. The town and region revel in a unique cuisine found nowhere else in Cuba, one that makes ample use of local coconut and chocolate. The region produces about three-fourths of Cuba's coconuts, so logically it plays a strong part in the local diet. Try *cucurucho,* a coconut pudding with fruit (orange and papaya) and honey wrapped in palm leaves; fresh fish embellished with coconut sauce; and the drinks *sacoco,* rum and coconut milk drunk from green coconuts, and *chorote,* chocolate with cornstarch. **Casa de Chocolate,** Maceo 121, is the place to get thick hot chocolate and locally made candies.

**La Colonial** *☞* BARACOAN/CRIOLLA   The only officially sanctioned *paladar* left in Baracoa, this well-run place in a lovely colonial home is quite good, and deserves to be supported by travelers. There's no fixed menu; ask about fresh dishes and catches from the daily roster of seven to eight main courses, including fish and shrimp cooked in *leche de coco* (coconut milk). Once you get beyond the tacky floral plastic tablecloths, the decor and ambience here are actually somewhat romantic.

Martí 123. © 21/4-5391. Reservations recommended. Main courses CUC$7–CUC$9. No credit cards. Daily 10am–11pm.

**La Punta** BARACOAN/CRIOLLA   On a covered terrace within the walls of one of the original three forts in Baracoa, this state-run restaurant is an elegant, tranquil spot, perfect for lunch. It has good service and well-prepared dishes such as dorado and *pargo* (grilled fish), and stuffed *jaiba* (sea crab). Typical Cuban dishes such as beefsteak, pork, and fried chicken are also available. Although the walls of the fort block most of the views, especially from the tables, if you walk around the grounds, you can peek through the canon slots at the Atlantic Ocean, Baracoa bay, and some stunning scenery. The bar here is open 24 hours.

Fuerte de la Punta. © 21/4-5224. Reservations not accepted. Main courses CUC$6–CUC$11. No credit cards. Daily 7am–10:30pm.

**Restaurante Duaba** BARACOAN/CRIOLLA   The restaurant within the Hotel El Castillo does big business serving Baracoa specialties to its guests but it's a good option for anyone in Baracoa. Try any of the locally flavored dishes, such as Creole soup, calalú, Santa Bárbara fish filet, *jaiba* (sea crab), or *cobo enchilado,* a huge shellfish. There are also some good options for vegetarians, including stuffed eggplant and a vegetable plate. The daily set menu is a little pricey at CUC$14; you'll do better order-ing a la carte.

In Hotel El Castillo, Calle Calixto García, Loma el Paraíso. (℃ **21/4-2125.** Reservations recommended. Main courses CUC$4–CUC$12. MC, V. Daily 7–10pm.

## BARACOA AFTER DARK

Baracoa has an amazingly lively after-dark scene for a town so small. In fact, its nightlife ranks among the best in Cuba. Virtually all the clubs and live-music venues are conveniently located on a single street, **Calle Antonio Maceo,** making Baracoa throb most nights like a tiny, tropical New Orleans, with traditional Cuban and con-temporary dance music and revelers spilling out into the street until the wee hours. The scene is especially buoyant on Saturday nights (*El Sabado Baracoese*), when Bara-coans host a massive street party along Maceo. Unique to Baracoa are the enthusiastic *animadores,* or emcees, who introduce songs and bands and entertain audiences with florid language, poetry, and humor. Club cover charges are generally CUC$1 to CUC$3.

The first spot to stop is the local **Casa de la Trova** ☞☞, Maceo 149, a comfortable, well-lighted place loaded with locals and featuring good bands and a gregarious emcee. If you're lucky, you'll get to hear **Maravilla Yuqueña,** a wonderful group, with a venerable old lead singer who should be far more famous than he is. Down the street, **485,** Maceo 485, has a Trova-like covered patio and the livelier **485 Disco** next door. Across the street, **La Terraza** is a huge open-air terrace on top of a building. It has a nightly show and full-throttle, decibel-busting music under the stars, with dancers and occasional dance contests (where, if you can shake it like the locals, you might win a fried chicken!). A more sedate spot, within shouting distance of the sound system of La Terraza, is **El Patio ARTex,** a cute, brightly colored cafe with red lamps and a slanted corrugated tin roof. The live music is pure Cuban *son.*

Finally, for a raging dance spot outside of downtown, head up the steep steps that run up beside the Hotel El Castillo to **El Ranchón.** This place is inconsistent, but when it goes off, it draws a lot of locals for some serious salsa dancing.

# 10

# Santiago de Cuba

*by Eliot Greenspan & Neil E. Schlecht*

Set on the seaside, near the island's eastern tip, **Santiago de Cuba** 🎖🎖🎖 is the country's second-largest city. Vibrant, tropical, and often sweltering, Santiago is the country's liveliest cultural showpiece, outside of Havana. With a population just under a half-million people, Santiago is a world apart, with a unique history and rhythms all its own. The city has produced some of Cuba's greatest contemporary musicians as well as several of its most stalwart revolutionaries, and it has served as the stage for some of the most storied events in Cuba's modern history. The capital of the old Oriente province, it has the largest Afro-Cuban population in Cuba and a resolutely Afro-Caribbean feel that distinguishes it from the rest of Cuba.

Founded in 1515, Santiago was one of the first of seven towns in Cuba and the Spanish colony's capital until 1553. Diego Velázquez, the founder of the original seven *villas,* built his mansion here, and the house still stands in the heart of the historic quarter. The Spanish character of the city would soon be supplemented by other influences. After the 1791 revolution in Haiti, a large number of French coffee plantation owners fled with their African slaves and made their way to Santiago. Black Haitian workers followed, as did large contingencies of West African slaves, sold to work on the plantations.

While downtown Santiago has the requisite noise, traffic, and urban chaos of a large city, it retains the intimate, friendly feel of a provincial capital, with counterbalancing peaceful neighborhoods where men play dominoes outdoors on hilly streets.

Santiago continues to earn its reputation as one of the liveliest and most individualistic cities in Cuba. The city's annual Carnival celebrations in July are famous throughout Cuba. Afro-Cuban religious traditions, including Santería and other forms of worship, have their strongest hold here. And Santiagueros are also recognized for their take on Cuban Spanish, with a unique vocabulary and singsong rhythm.

Santiago fans out from a large, deep natural bay—guarded by the 16th-century El Morro fortress—and sits at the base of low mountains. Fine excursions await visitors with time to explore outside the city: **El Cobre** 🎖🎖 is a sacred shrine set in the beautiful foothills of the Sierra Maestra, while **Gran Piedra** is a great rocky area just outside the city that invites hiking and relaxation in its cool environs.

## 1 Orientation

### ARRIVING & DEPARTING

**BY PLANE**   Direct international scheduled and charter flights arrive at the **Aeropuerto Internacional Antonio Maceo** (✆ **22/69-1053;** airport code SCU). Airlines regularly servicing Santiago include **Air Jamaica, Air Transat, Condor Airways,**

**Copa,** and **Cubana.** Charter flights run between Miami and Santiago several times each week.

Daily flights connect Santiago with Havana and other Cuban cities via **Aero-Caribbean** (© **22/68-7255** in Santiago, or 7/33-4543 in Havana) and **Cubana** (© **22/65-1578** in Santiago, or 7/33-4446 in Havana; www.cubana.cu). A one-way fare between Havana and Santiago runs between CUC$100 and CUC$120. Flight duration is roughly 2 hours.

The airport is 8km (5 miles) south of the city. There are several car-rental agencies at the airport. The quickest and safest way to the city is by registered taxi; the trip into town is CUC$7 to CUC$10.

**BY BUS    Víazul's** (© **22/62-8484** in Santiago, or 7/881-1413 in Havana; www.viazul.com) Havana–Santiago de Cuba line, with stops in Santa Clara, Sancti Spíritus, Ciego de Avila, Camagüey, Bayamo, and Holguín, is the best way to get to Santiago by bus, especially if you're planning to see any points of interest between Cuba's two main cities. For the 16-hour trip from Havana, buses depart at 9:30am, 3pm, and 10pm, arriving at 1:35am, 6:50am, and 11:30am, respectively (CUC$55 one-way). From Trinidad (© **419/2404**), a bus leaves daily at 8am and arrives at 8:15pm (CUC$36 one-way). From Camagüey (© **32/27-0194**), the trip is about 7 hours; buses leave at 12:10am and 6:30am, and 1:30pm and 4:20pm (CUC$20 one-way). Buses depart Santiago for Havana at 9am, 3:15pm, and 10pm.

Víazul also has once daily service between Santiago and Baracoa, leaving Santiago at 7:45am and returning from Baracoa at 2:15pm. Duration is 4 hours and 50 minutes; fare is CUC$17 one-way.

The **Terminal de Omnibuses** (© **22/62-8484**) for Víazul and less-comfortable Astro buses (the offices are next door to each other) is located on Avenida de los Libertadores at the corner of Avenida Yarayó, about 2km (1¼ miles) from Parque Céspedes. A taxi to downtown costs about CUC$3.

**BY TRAIN**    The Cuban *ferrocarril* (railway) is relatively dependable, but delays, mid-run breakdowns, and other problems are still quite common. Taking the train is a potentially adventurous experience for those who wish to see the "real Cuba," but can be frustrating for those who need to adhere to a schedule.

A special fast train, also known as the "French Train" or "Tren Francés," travels from Havana to Santiago (12 hr. with stops in Santa Clara and Camagüey). It offers *primera especial* (CUC$62) and *primera clase* (CUC$50) service, featuring reclining seats, air-conditioning, and cafeteria services. Prices are discounted by 50% for children under 7 years old, and **Ferrotur** claims it will refund the fare if arrival is more than 1 hour late. Daily departure from Havana in the high season is at 6:05pm, arriving at 6:30am in Santiago.

Other services include the following regular trains (also with air-conditioning and food services on board): no. 11, departing Central Station in Havana at 3:15pm and arriving at 5:15am, and no. 43, leaving La Coubre Station in Havana at 6:20am and arriving at 11pm (both CUC$32). Train schedules change frequently, and depending on the season, many trains don't operate on a daily basis; verify the current schedule by calling © **7/862-1920** or 7/861-4259, though it's often better to go in person to the train station and purchase tickets at least a day in advance.

In Santiago, the large, modern **Terminal Central de Ferrocarriles** is located on Avenida Jesús Menéndez at Paseo de Martí (© **22/62-2836**), across from the Caney rum factory.

# Santiago de Cuba

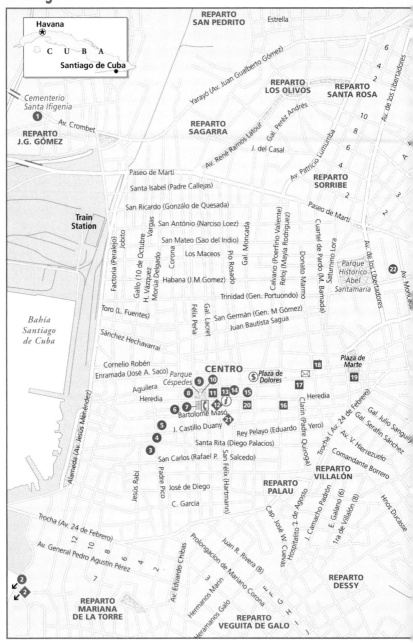

Havana

C U B A

Santiago de Cuba

REPARTO
SAN PEDRITO

Estrella

Cementerio
Santa Ifigenia

Av. Crombet

REPARTO
J.G. GÓMEZ

Yarayó (Av. Juan Gualberto Gómez)

REPARTO
LOS OLIVOS

REPARTO
SANTA ROSA

Av. René Ramos Latour

REPARTO
SAGARRA

Gal. Peréz Andrés

J. del Casal

Av. Patricio Lumumba

REPARTO
SORRIBE

Paseo de Martí

Santa Isabel (Padre Callejas)

San Ricardo (Gonzalo de Quesada)

Paseo de Martí

Train
Station

Vargas

San António (Narciso Loez)

San Mateo (Sao del Indio)

Los Maceos

Gal. Moncada

Pío Rosado

Calvario (Poerfino Valiente)

Reloj (Mayía Rodríguez)

Cuartel de Pardo (M. Barrada)

Donato Marmo

Saturnino Lora

Parque
Histórico
Abel
Santamaría

Av. de los Libertadores

Factoria (Peralejo)

Jobito

Gallo (10 de Octubre)

H. Vázquez

Morúa Delgado

Corona

Habana (J.M.Gomez)

Trinidad (Gen. Portuondo)

Toro (L. Fuentes)

Félix Peña

Gal. Lacret

San Germán (Gen. M Gómez)

Juan Bautista Sagua

Bahía
Santiago
de Cuba

Sánchez Hechavarrai

Cornelio Robén

Enramada (José A. Saco)

Aguilera

Heredia

Parque
Céspedes

CENTRO

Plaza de
Dolores

Plaza de
Marte

Bartolomé Masó

J. Castillo Duany

Rey Pelayo (Eduardo

Santa Rita (Diego Palacios)

Clarín (Padre Quiroga)

Trocha (Av. 24 de Febrero)

Av. V. Hierrezuelo

Gal. Julio Sanguil

Gal. Serafín Sánchez

Comandante Borrero

San Carlos (Rafael P.

San Félix (Hartmann)

San Félix P. Salcedo)

REPARTO
VILLALÓN

Jesús Rabí

padre Pico

José de Diego

C. García

REPARTO
PALAU

Cap. José W. Cuevas

Hospitalito 2 de Agosto

J. Camacho Padrón

E. Galano (6)

1ra de Villalón (8)

Hnos Ducasse

Trocha (Av. 24 de Febrero)

Av. General Pedro Agustín Pérez

Juan R. Rivera (8)

Prolongación de Mariano Corona

REPARTO
DESSY

REPARTO
MARIANA
DE LA TORRE

Av. Eduardo Chibás

Hermanos Marín

Hermanos Galo

REPARTO
VEGUITA DE GALO

Alameda (Av. Jesús Menéndez)

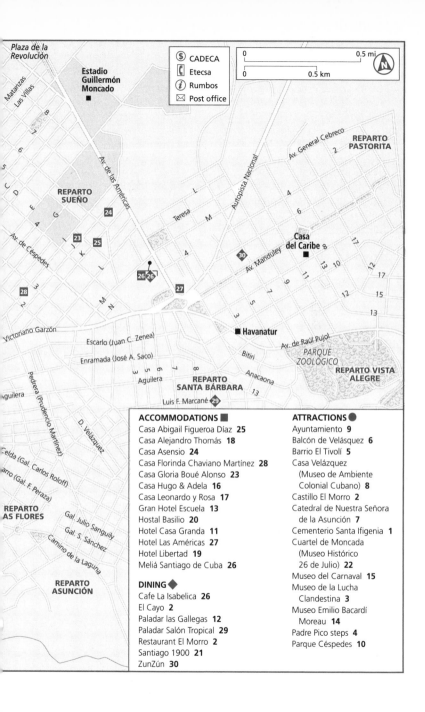

Plaza de la Revolución

Estadio Guillermón Moncado

$ CADECA
Etecsa
(i) Rumbos
Post office

0                    0.5 mi
0            0.5 km

Matanzas
Las Villas

REPARTO PASTORITA
Av. General Cebreco

REPARTO SUEÑO

Av. de las Américas

Autopista Nacional

Teresa

Casa del Caribe

Av. Manduley

Av. de Céspedes

Victoriano Garzón

Escarlo (Juan C. Zenea)

Enramada (José A. Saco)

Havanatur

Av. de Raúl Pujol

PARQUE ZOOLÓGICO

REPARTO VISTA ALEGRE

Aguilera

Bitiri

Anacaona

REPARTO SANTA BÁRBARA

Luis F. Marcané

Pedrera (Prudencio Martínez)

aguilera

D. Velázquez

Celda (Gal. Carlos Roloff)

arro (Gal. F. Peraza)

REPARTO AS FLORES

Gal. Julio Sanguily

Gal. S. Sánchez

Camino de la Laguna

REPARTO ASUNCIÓN

ACCOMMODATIONS ■
Casa Abigail Figueroa Díaz 25
Casa Alejandro Thomás 18
Casa Asensio 24
Casa Florinda Chaviano Martínez 28
Casa Gloria Boué Alonso 23
Casa Hugo & Adela 16
Casa Leonardo y Rosa 17
Gran Hotel Escuela 13
Hostal Basilio 20
Hotel Casa Granda 11
Hotel Las Américas 27
Hotel Libertad 19
Meliá Santiago de Cuba 26

DINING ◆
Cafe La Isabelica 26
El Cayo 2
Paladar las Gallegas 12
Paladar Salón Tropical 29
Restaurant El Morro 2
Santiago 1900 21
ZunZún 30

ATTRACTIONS ●
Ayuntamiento 9
Balcón de Velásquez 6
Barrio El Tivolí 5
Casa Velázquez
  (Museo de Ambiente
  Colonial Cubano) 8
Castillo El Morro 2
Catedral de Nuestra Señora
  de la Asunción 7
Cementerio Santa Ifigenia 1
Cuartel de Moncada
  (Museo Histórico
  26 de Julio) 22
Museo del Carnaval 15
Museo de la Lucha
  Clandestina 3
Museo Emilio Bacardí
  Moreau 14
Padre Pico steps 4
Parque Céspedes 10

## Santiago, City of Struggle & Rebellion

Santiago has long demonstrated a fiercely independent streak. Among Cubans the city is known affectionately as the *cuna de la Revolución,* or the cradle of the Revolution. The first slave uprisings in Cuba occurred in Santiago, and the city had prominent roles in the wars of independence against the Spanish in 1868 and 1895. Antonio Maceo rejected a pact with the colonial power, laying the foundation for continued resistance, and became one of the leaders of the rebel army. Each of the 29 generals during the 30-year war against the Spanish came from the city, and the Bay of Santiago was the site of the 1898 naval battles between the U.S. and Spain. Teddy Roosevelt and his Rough Riders stormed the Loma de San Juan, a low hill just east of the city, in battles against the Spanish that led to Spain's imminent defeat and withdrawal from Cuba (though Cuba's independence was effectively usurped by the Americans in the years after the Spanish-American War).

In 1953, the young firebrand Fidel Castro and a band of insurgents attacked the Moncada military barracks in Santiago (the failed but famous 26th of July episode). After many of his rebels were tortured and killed by the army, Castro was captured and he issued his famous declaration, "History will absolve me," in defense of his seditious actions. A local Santiago schoolteacher, Frank País, sparked an uprising of university students in 1957, attacking police headquarters. Assassinated by the Batista army in the streets of Santiago, he became a martyr of the Revolution. Castro returned from exile in Mexico to wage war from the cover of the Sierra Maestra, west of Santiago, and 2 years later the rebel leader ultimately announced victory, on January 1, 1959, from the balcony of the governor's mansion (today Town Hall) in Parque Céspedes. Castro rewarded the city that supported him with the title "Heroic City of the Revolution."

**BY CAR**   Driving to Santiago is a good way to see the breadth of the country. The six-lane, toll-free Autopista Nacional (A1) and the Carretera Central run the length of Cuba, straight down the spine of the country from Pinar del Río to Santiago. However, east from Sancti Spíritus it is just two lanes just about the entire way to Santiago, and the going can be slow at times, since there are equal numbers of cars, trucks, horse-drawn carriages, bicycles, and pedestrians making use of the Carretera Central. Santiago is 860km (533 miles) east of Havana, 127km (79 miles) east of Bayamo, and 134km (83 miles) southeast of Holguín.

### VISITOR INFORMATION
Most of the major tour agencies, including **Cubanacán** (© 22/64-3445), **Cubatur** (© 22/64-1181), and **Havanatur** (© 22/62-4823), have offices in the airport and at several hotels in town. They all offer guided city tours, excursions to El Cobre, Sierra Maestra, and La Gran Piedra, and group trips to Baracoa and more far-flung destinations.

### CITY LAYOUT
The historic center of the city rolls across low hills to the east of the **Bahía de Santiago.** The focal point of colonial Santiago is **Parque Céspedes.** This historic square

boasts perhaps the oldest house in the Americas. **Calle Heredia,** which leads east from the square, is a popular street with plenty of foot traffic, and it is lined with live music venues, colonial houses and museums, and artisans selling their crafts. South of Parque Céspedes is the charming, hilly **El Tivolí** district and its emblematic Padre Pico steps. **Plaza de Dolores** is an attractive and shady little square heading east, a popular and easygoing hangout ringed by a handful of restaurants, bars, and cafes. **Plaza de Marte** marks the divide between old Santiago and the newer section, leading along the long and wide avenue Victoriano Garzón out toward the nicest suburbs in Santiago and districts of several hotels and *casas particulares* (private-home accommodations), **Reparto Sueño, Reparto Vista Alegre,** and **Reparto Santa Bárbara.**

Old and new street names (pre- and post-Revolution) are still sometimes used interchangeably in Santiago. The most common pre-Revolution street names used in the old colonial center are: Enramada (for José Antonio Saco); San Basilio (Bartolomé Masó); San Pedro (General Lacret); Santo Tomás (Félix Peña); Marina (Aguilera); and Carnicería (Pío Rosado).

## 2 Getting Around

**BY TAXI**   Among the many taxi companies available for local and long-distance hire are **Taxis OK** (© 22/65-4568), **Transtur** (© 22/63-2195), **Turistaxi** (© 22/68-7000), and the least expensive, **Cubataxi** (© 22/65-3777). Taxis of many different stripes and comfort, all varying small degrees in price, congregate near the cathedral on Parque Céspedes and at the major tourist hotels. Be sure to ask prices before contracting one, as tourist gouging is a favorite local pastime (from the Meliá Santiago to Parque Céspedes, the fare is CUC$3 to CUC$4; from downtown to El Morro should run CUC$8 to CUC$12). Cheaper taxis, both registered and unregistered, can be found parked around Plaza Marte. With the latter, negotiate a price but understand that the driver may be uncomfortable taking you directly to the door of your hotel if he's not officially licensed to carry foreigners.

Coco Taxis are also common around Santiago. Coco Taxis should be a bit less expensive than regular taxis, although the drivers will usually first quote you the going cab rate, so try to negotiate. There are also *bici* (bicycle) and *moto* (motorcycle) taxis, both of which are convenient and inexpensive (usually CUC$1) but occasionally hairraising for many passengers given the volume and often-chaotic nature of car traffic in Santiago.

**BY CAR**   The major car-rental companies, which all have offices at the airport, are **Havanautos** (© 22/68-6161), with outlets at the Cupet gas station on Carretera Central, Hotel Casa Granda, and Hotel Las Américas; **Micar** (© 22/69-2791); **Cubacar** (© 22/69-4195), also at Meliá Santiago; and **Transtur** (© 22/68-7000), with branches at Hotel Las Américas, Hotel Villa San Juan, and Hotel Casa Granda. Rates are about CUC$45 to CUC$80 per day for a standard four-door compact car.

**BY FOOT**   The area of greatest activity and cultural interest to many visitors in the historic center—the few streets around Parque Céspedes—is easy to get around on foot, though some areas, such as the Tivolí district, are extremely hilly. However, many hotels are at least a couple of kilometers from the city center, and a good number of the city's foremost attractions, such as El Morro, are beyond the city and require transportation.

## FAST FACTS: Santiago de Cuba

*Airport* See "Arriving & Departing," above.

*Car Rentals* See "Getting Around," above.

*Currency Exchange* A **CADECA** (© 22/65-1383) can be found on Calle Aguilera 508. The local branch of **Banco Financiero Internacional** (© 22/42-7361), where you can exchange traveler's checks and get cash advances, is on Félix Peña 565. **Banco de Crédito y Comercio** (© 22/62-3316), with similar services, is on Félix Peña between Aguilera and Heredia. Both are open Monday through Saturday from 8am to 3pm. A rare ATM can be found at the **Banco Popular de Ahoro** (© 22/64-2454) on Plaza Dolores. You can also change money at the Meliá Santiago, and most other hotels in the city.

*Emergency* Dial © **116** for any emergency.

*Hospitals & Medical Assistance* **Clínica Internacional**, Avenida Raúl Pujol at Calle 10 in Reparto Vista Alegre (© 22/64-2589), has 24-hour emergency services, a dentist, and English-speaking doctors. There are **pharmacies** at the clinic and along Calle José Antonio Saco. For an ambulance, dial © **22/62-3300**.

*Internet Access* An **Etecsa** Internet kiosk (© 22/62-4784) with two terminals is on Heredia 156, on the south side of Parque Céspedes. It's open daily from 7am to 10pm. You can also find cybercafes at the Meliá Santiago and Hotel Casa Granda.

*Police* The police station is located at Mariano and San Gerónimo (© **116**). However, the probability of finding an English speaker is remote. In case of an emergency, one of the better hotels (such as the Casa Granda or Meliá Santiago) should be able to help or at least interpret with the police.

*Post Office* The main post office is on Calle Aguilera 517 at Padre Quiroga (© 22/65-2397); it's open Monday through Saturday from 8am to 8pm. There are basic postal facilities in all the major hotels. A **DHL** office can be found at Calle Aguilera 310 at the corner of San Félix (© 22/68-6323).

*Safety* Santiago is one of Cuba's more unsafe cities, if only because the local *jineteros* are relentless in accosting foreigners. They are, for the most part, innocuous. Still, if you're attending a street festival, concert, or Carnival, put your money in a money belt and leave your watch, jewelry, and knapsack behind (these items will be safer in your hotel or casa particular). Also, be careful and keep an eye on your bags at the Santiago bus and train stations. All that said, Santiago, as with the rest of Cuba, is still relatively safe for a large city.

*Taxis* See "Getting Around," earlier in this chapter.

*Telephone* Santiago's area or city code is **22**, but many numbers are still published under the old system and area code 226. The "6" is now placed before the number.

You can make local, long-distance, and international phone calls with a phone card from the **Etecsa** telephone and Internet kiosk on Heredia 156 (Parque Céspedes, on the street level of the cathedral). It's open daily from 7am to 11pm.

## 3 What to See & Do

Many visitors in search of what makes Cuba unique actually prefer the country's second city to the capital, even though Santiago is unpolished and has few grand examples of colonial architecture.

## THE TOP ATTRACTIONS

A major gathering spot day and night for Santiagueros, aggressive jineteros, and travelers alike, **Parque Céspedes** ✿ is a menagerie of eclectic architecture, to put it mildly. Its benches, tall shade trees, and gas lamps are ringed by colonial, 19th-century, and modern structures, including the ancient mansion of Diego Velázquez (see below), as well as the handsome colonial governor's mansion (Town Hall), the baroque cathedral, and the city's oldest hotel, Casa Granda.

The **Ayuntamiento,** or Town Hall (also called the Palacio Municipal), a huge white building on the north side of the square with blue wooden grilles, was originally built in 1515. It was greatly renovated in the 1950s after an earthquake, but it has retained its elegant colonial lines, balcony, and patio. Fidel Castro addressed the adoring masses here on January 1, 1959, after the Rebel Army had taken the city and announced the triumph of *La Revolución.*

Across the park, the early-19th-century **Catedral de Nuestra Señora de la Asunción** is a massive, ornate, pale yellow and white basilica with twin towers—one of several churches to occupy the site since the 16th century after its antecedents were destroyed by pirates, earthquakes, and other natural disasters. The frescoes on the arches and dome of the interior have been magnificently restored. Inside is a massive pipe organ, and in the crypt are the remains of the Spanish conquistador Diego Velázquez.

**Casa Velázquez (Museo de Ambiente Colonial Cubano)** ✿✿   The 1515 mansion that once belonged to Diego Velázquez, founder of the original seven *villas* in Cuba, still stands despite the unrepentant fumes of tour buses and recent fires that have threatened it. The house has a notable Moorish influence, with a wonderful carved cedar ceiling (most of which had to be reconstructed after a fire). The top floor was the living quarters; the ground floor was the commercial part of the house, where Velázquez maintained offices and horse carriages were kept. The house's elaborate frescoes have been supplemented by very amateurish reproductions, a real sin against the authenticity that is elsewhere so apparent. The museum aims to depict the varied styles and epochs of colonial life, seen through period furnishings from the 16th to the 19th century. You'll find some splendid pieces of French, British, Spanish, and Cuban furniture; Spanish ceramics; carved chests; and French porcelain. Several dressers have extraordinary inlaid designs, proof of the wealth of the bourgeoisie in colonial Cuba. A second house in back, blue and white with an attractive courtyard, is not part of the original Velázquez house. Allow an hour for your visit.

Félix Peña 612 (corner of Aguilera), Parque Céspedes. © **22/65-2652.** Admission CUC$2 (plus CUC$1 for guided tour in Spanish or English). Daily 9am–1pm and 2–5pm.

**Castillo El Morro** ✿✿   Guarding the entrance to the Bahía de Santiago, this seemingly impregnable fortress is built atop a rocky promontory and entered across a formidable drawbridge. The medieval and Renaissance-style structure, a UNESCO World Heritage Site, is a warren of platforms, passageways, and cells spread across five levels and protected by 1.5m-thick (5-ft.) walls. It was engineered in 1638 by the Italian architect who built similar fortresses in Havana as well as Cartagena, Colombia, and San Juan, Puerto Rico, to protect against pirate attacks. (This it didn't do so well, as pirates including Henry Morgan succeeded in ransacking the place.)

The site, where the sun beats down unrelentingly, offers magnificent views of the bay and the Caribbean coastline stretching all the way to the Sierra Maestra. Inside the fortress, built above a dry moat, is a sparse museum (with display explanations in Spanish only) detailing the history of piracy, El Morro, and Santiago de Cuba. One room contains artifacts related to the 1898 Spanish-American War, principal naval battles of which were fought right in the Bay of Santiago. Nineteen modern American ships sunk all seven Spanish ships; ironically, the Spanish ship Cristóbal Colón was the last to sink, thus closing the door on the history of Spanish colonialism in the Americas.

A daily ceremony, called the "Puesta del Sol," takes place at sunset, recalling the 19th-century importance of the fortress. Youngsters dressed as *mambises,* or members of the Cuban rebel army, lower the flag and shoot off the ancient 1805 Spanish cannon to cries of "¡Viva Cuba Libre!" Visiting El Morro for the day-ending ceremony, when it has cooled off some, is an excellent idea. You'll need about an hour to tour the complex. Avoid the hours of 11am to 4pm at all costs; if you do come in the middle of the day, two great spots for lunch—and cooling off—are the nearby Restaurant El Morro and El Cayo (see later in this chapter for both).

To get there, an organized excursion or a car or taxi is required. The fortress is about 15km (10 miles) south of the center of Santiago along the Carretera del Morro.

Bahía de Santiago. ✆ **22/69-1569.** Admission CUC$4 (photos CUC$1, video CUC$5); free guided tours are available in English, French, and Italian. Daily 9am–8pm.

### Cuartel de Moncada (Museo Histórico 26 de Julio) ✟   The yellow barracks of the Spanish army, east of downtown, represent a pivotal episode in modern Cuban history. The ocher-colored exterior is still pockmarked with bullet holes, a reminder of the July day in 1953 when Fidel Castro and a band of ragtag but idealistic rebels launched an assault on the barracks, with the intention of stealing arms and jump-starting a revolution. First built by the Spanish in 1859, the barracks were burned down and then rebuilt in the late 1930s. Today, the Art Deco–style barracks house a museum focused on that day and the revolutionary struggle. For anyone interested in Cuban history, regardless of ideology, a visit to the museum is a must.

Fidel and his poorly funded troops, including his brother Raúl and Abel Santamaría, arrived at daybreak dressed like army soldiers (though the street shoes they wore, rather than military boots, would give them away). Some 120 men attacked the barracks, but the plan failed miserably and 61 were killed. The others escaped but were soon captured; many were tortured to death by Batista's army (a torture cell is on view). Batista announced to the press that 500 well-funded militiamen had attacked the barracks and had been killed in a gun battle. A young journalist succeeded in getting photographs of the tortured and murdered young revolutionaries out of Santiago and to Havana, where the pictures were published, galvanizing many Cubans against the Batista regime.

The museum exhibits the rebels' small rifles and pistols, bloodstained uniforms, photographs, letters, and other documents that tell the amazing story of the subsequent exile of the surviving rebels and guerrilla warfare in the Sierra Maestra. Exhibits are labeled in Spanish only, so a guide might be a good idea.

Calle Trinidad (corner of Moncada). $©$ **22/62-0157**. Admission CUC$2 (photos CUC$1, video CUC$5); free guided tours are available in English, French, and Italian. Tues–Sat 9am–7pm; Sun 9am–1pm.

**Museo Emilio Bacardí Moreau** ★ Begun by Emilio Bacardí, the founder of the political and rum dynasty in 1899, this highly personal collection constituted one of the first museums in Cuba. Now a provincial museum, it remains an eclectic art and historical assembly. The grand, gleaming white neoclassical building was erected in 1928 to house the idiosyncratic collection. On the first floor is a wide variety of artifacts documenting indigenous peoples, slavery, and the wars of independence, including an extensive array of armaments. Bacardí also collected personal items belonging to Cuban national heroes, including those of Antonio Maceo and Carlos Manuel Céspedes. Don't miss the tiny stage set of a colonial Santiago street (through a door on the south side of the first floor). The second floor is an art museum exhibiting national and international paintings. There are several contemporary pieces, including a larger-than-life sculpture of Che Guevara in heroic pose. In an annex, which must be entered from a side door on Calle Aguilera, is an archaeology room holding an Egyptian mummy (smuggled out of Egypt in 1913), a pair of Peruvian mummies belonging to the Paracas (pre-Inca) culture, various ceremonial objects, pre-Columbian ceramics, and a shrunken head from the Amazon. Allow an hour or so to see it all. All of the display information here is in Spanish, but English-speaking guides are available.

Calle Pío Rosado (at Aguilera). $©$ **22/62-8402**. Admission CUC$2 (photos CUC$1, video CUC$5); free guided tours are available in English. Mon 2–8pm; Tues–Sat 10am–8pm; Sun 9am–noon.

## OTHER ATTRACTIONS

**Barrio El Tivolí** (Finds) A charming, hilly neighborhood just south of Parque Céspedes (loosely bordered by Av. Trocha and Calle Padre Pico), El Tivolí was once the most fashionable place to live in Santiago. Today it's a relaxed place of steep streets, weathered and decrepit wooden houses, and a couple of attractions, but mostly it's a good place to wander.

The famous **Padre Pico steps** are named for a Santiaguero priest who aided the city's poor. Castro once roared fire and brimstone down on the Batista government here, but today you'll find more pacifistic chess and dominoes players who've set up all-hours tables on the steps. Take the steps up to the **Museo de la Lucha Clandestina (Museum of the Underground Struggle),** General Rabí 1 between Santa Rita and San Carlos ($©$ **22/62-4689**), which is housed in a handsome 18th-century mansion on a hill, Loma del Intendente. Inside are exhibits related to the November 1956 attack on this former police headquarters, led by rebel leader and schoolteacher Frank País and his

---

( *Tips* **Terrace with a View**

The **Balcón de Velázquez,** at the corner of Heredia and Mariano at the edge of El Tivolí district, is a marvelous lookout over red-tile rooftops of the city as it slopes down to the Bay of Santiago. Named for the Spanish conquistador who founded the city, the terrace was reconstructed in the 1950s and now is a site of cultural goings-on; it has been said that the original terrace in this very spot was used by Velázquez himself to observe incoming ships in the bay. An escape tunnel once ran from the spot, protected by cannons, all the way to the bay. Admission is free, but you'll have to pay CUC$1 if you want to take photographs.

brother Josué, both executed by the army. Frank País's funeral was massively attended by Santiagueros, a signal that the Revolution would have significant local support. Other photos and documents attest to the phenomenal years of tension, rumors, and conflict that led to the rebels' triumph. The museum is open Tuesday through Saturday from 9am to 5pm, and Sunday from 9am to 1pm; admission is CUC$1.

Barrio El Tivolí, just south and west of Parque Céspedes.

## Cementerio Santa Ifigenia ✦

Northwest of the city center, this sprawling cemetery, dating to 1868, is a small city of the dead, populated by elaborate marble tombs and sarcophagi, including several spectacular mausoleums (many of which are pre-1868, having been moved here from other cemeteries). By far the most famous is that of José Martí, a massive stone and marble circular structure built in 1951 (Martí died in 1895). The Lincolnesque mausoleum is near the entrance to the museum, at the end of a private path. Martí once wrote that he wished to die, "without a homeland but without a master" and to be buried with "a bouquet of flowers and a flag." In addition to Martí, the remains of Emilio Bacardí, Carlos Manuel de Céspedes, Pedro (Perucho) Figueredo (author of the Cuban national anthem), and heroes of the Moncada 26th of July rebel attack are interred here. The newest addition to the celebrated figures buried here is the great musician and native-son, Compay Segundo. In addition, the cemetery's palm-lined paths abound with a wealth of other fascinating tombs for families famous and unknown.

Calzada Crombet. ☎ 22/63-2723. Admission CUC$1. Daily 7am–6pm.

## Loma de San Juan

This low-rise hill in the center of Reparto Vista Alegre, a leafy, upscale neighborhood, is where the decisive last battle of the Spanish-Cuban-American War was fought. Teddy Roosevelt and his army of an estimated 6,000 Rough Riders stormed the hill and defeated the Spanish troops. At the entrance to the park is the Arbol de la Rendención (Tree of Surrender), where the Spanish forces capitulated to the Americans. Something that still irks Cubans today, besides the commonly used name of the war that leaves them out, is that the Cubans were not even signatories to the surrender. While there are several plaques and monuments in the neatly manicured park that pay tribute to the North Americans who participated and died in the war, there are few dedicated to the Cuban fighters (though the Tomb of the Unknown Mambí, or independence fighter, can be found there).

Reparto Santa Bárbara, at the intersection of Av. de Raúl Pujol and Carretera de Siboney Km 1.5 (next to the Hotel San Juan).

## Museo del Carnaval (Kids)

Santiago's Carnival is the most famous in Cuba, and this small museum, in one of the oldest houses on Calle Heredia, aims to give visitors some historical perspective. Carnival counts centuries of tradition; the first published reference to the celebration was in 1669. It displays old costumes, black-and-white photographs, huge papier-mâché masks, and hand-painted and embroidered *mamarrachos* (capes). Percussion instruments show how popular the celebration is: They include old car parts and simple wood instruments. The final room displays a couple of the most recent winners of the costume contests—elaborate and huge affairs. **Folklore and music and dance events** ✦ are held at the museum Tuesday through Saturday at 4pm, with *rumba* performances on Sunday. Plan to spend about half an hour viewing the displays. All the printed display information here is in Spanish.

Calle Heredia 303 (corner of Pío Rosado). ☎ 22/62-6955. Admission CUC$1 (CUC$3 with guide, CUC$1 for photos). Tues–Sat 9am–8pm; Sun 9am–5pm.

*Tips* **Bay of Santiago**

Santiago's deep natural bay is one of the city's defining characteristics. The narrow entrance to the Bahía de Santiago, past the Castillo El Morro, stretches 8km (5 miles). During the Spanish-American War, the contingency of Spanish ships was huddled within the bay, and the Americans were perched on the coast waiting to ambush them.

Today, Santiago's marina is popular with European and (believe it or not) U.S. yachts. Visitors can book a 1-hour trip around the entire bay for CUC$12 per person. If you just want to cross over to the fishing village on the tiny island of Cayo Granma for lunch, the ferry is CUC$3 round-trip. For more information, contact the **Santiago Marina,** Calle 1 no. 4, Punta Gorda (© **22/69-1446;** marlin@ stgocub.scu.cyt.cu).

**Plaza de la Revolución**   This massive, raised platform monument to Antonio Maceo features a startling equestrian statue of the great patriot surrounded by 23 enormous iron machetes slicing toward the sky, like daggers in the sides of the colonial power. Maceo, a Cuban of mixed blood, was called the "Bronze Titan" of the Cuban independence wars. Beneath the work is an eternal flame. The monument's an emphatic statement, to be sure. An underground room houses a small and rather uninspiring museum dedicated to the man.

Av. de las Américas (at Los Desfiles and Carretera Central). © 22/64-3053. Admission to museum CUC$1. Daily 8am–10pm; museum Mon–Sat 9am–5pm; Sun 9am–1pm.

## 4 Where to Stay

Santiago may not be blessed with the range of hotel offerings Havana has—in fact, it has less than a half-dozen hotels within easy reach of downtown—but it has enough variety among its few hotels that most guests shouldn't have trouble finding a decent place to stay at any price level. Only one of Santiago's major hotels is within the historic district, which is lively and fun but too noisy and chaotic for many visitors. Most of the tourist hotels are on the outskirts of the city, an easy and inexpensive cab ride away.

Especially popular in Santiago are casas particulares; the city has hundreds of state-sanctioned private homestays, including some of the coolest casas in Cuba, several in historic homes in the heart of the old district and others in tranquil, leafy suburbs. Reparto Sueño alone has dozens of casas.

For those who might prefer to stay outside the city as an overnight excursion or even with plans to make a day trip out of Santiago, there are a couple of hotels along the coast and near some of the outlying attractions. Those hotels are listed in section 8, "Side Trips from Santiago de Cuba."

### CENTRO HISTORICO
#### MODERATE
**Hostal Basilio** ★ *Value*   This new little hotel is in a beautifully restored old home in the heart of downtown. The good-size rooms have very high ceilings with ornate crown molding. Throughout the hotel you'll find attractive tile work on the floors and wainscoting. Only two rooms here have anything besides two twin beds, and of these,

room no. 5 is the better bet, with a king-size bed. Still, my favorite room may just be no. 1, which has a lovely window overlooking the street—so this is not the room to choose for those easily bothered by street noise. The hotel has a small in-house restaurant serving reasonable local and international fare.

Calle Basilio 403 (between Calvario and Carnicería). (℃ **22/65-1702.** Fax 22/68-7069. www.hotelescubanacan.com. 8 units. CUC$54 double. Rates include breakfast. Rates lower in off season; higher during peak weeks. MC, V. **Amenities:** Restaurant; bar; tour desk; laundry service. *In room:* A/C, TV, minibar, safe.

**Hotel Casa Granda** 🏨🏨   A large, elegant building right on Parque Céspedes, this classic Santiago hotel is a landmark in the city. Graham Greene's character Wormold, from *Our Man in Havana,* stayed in the 1914 hotel, which underwent a full-scale renovation in 1995. Best known perhaps for its terrace bar with live music and roof garden with great views over the cathedral and Santiago, the Casa Granda is one of the best places to stay in the city. Its location is superb, as long as you don't mind the hustle and bustle of travelers and *jineteros* in the square. The hotel features large rooms with high ceilings and restrained decor. As with most state-run hotels in Cuba, double beds are at a premium here, in fact just 15 rooms come with a queen-size bed, and the rest have two twins. Rooms either have views of the park, Calle Heredia, or the interior—the noise-sensitive should opt for the latter. If you want a view of the park, room nos. 403 through 407 are your best bets. The tile and marble bathrooms are quite nice, with good tubs. The elegant a la carte restaurant on the first floor is handsome, with good food and service, but it's not cheap.

Heredia 201 (between San Félix and General Lacret), Santiago de Cuba. (℃ **22/65-3021** or 7/204-6366. Fax 22/ 68-6035. www.grancaribe.cu. 58 units. CUC$60–CUC$110 double; CUC$95–CUC$120 junior suite. Rates include breakfast. MC, V. **Amenities:** 2 restaurants; 2 bars; car-rental desk; tour desk; limited room service; laundry service. *In room:* A/C, TV, fridge, hair dryer, safe.

### INEXPENSIVE

There are scores of casas particulares in downtown Santiago; I've listed my favorites below. If these are full, you can also try **Casa Berta Peña,** Calle Heredia 308 ((℃ **22/ 62-4097**); **Casa Pedro Guillermo,** Calle Corona 805 ((℃ **22/62-0101**); **Casa Maria de la Cruz Figueroa,** Calle Rey Palayo 83 ((℃ **22/62-8778**); and **Casa Mosqueda y Prada,** San Basilio 502 ((℃ **22/62-5953**).

**Casa Alejandro Thomás**   A nicely furnished and airy colonial-style home, this conveniently located place is just a 5-minute walk from Parque Céspedes. It has two small but well-equipped rooms upstairs off a terrace. Each has its own bathroom, and one has its own independent terrace. The rooms share a small kitchen facility upstairs. Guests are welcome to lounge in the handsome family sitting room with leather club chairs, sofa, and TV.

Calle Aguilera 682 (corner of Barnada), Santiago de Cuba. (℃ **22/62-0844.** 2 units. CUC$25 double. No credit cards. *In room:* A/C, no phone.

**Casa Hugo & Adela** 🏨 *Finds*   High above the hubbub below, featuring an expansive, private corner terrace with views of Santiago all the way to the bay, this place rents one large third-floor room with an independent entrance. The owners are very friendly and speak English. If this room is not available, there are about four other options on the same corner.

San Basilio 501 (corner of Reloj), Santiago de Cuba. (℃ **22/62-6359.** 1 unit. CUC$25–CUC$30 double. No credit cards. *In room:* A/C, TV, fridge, no phone.

**Casa Leonardo y Rosa** ⭐ Very centrally located, just a couple of blocks from Parque Céspedes on a relatively quiet, short street, this large and gorgeous colonial house has an ornate blue and white facade. The house has extraordinarily high ceilings, chandeliers, and wainscoting on the walls. One room (featuring a great marble bathroom) is in the main house; the other room, which we prefer, is on the second-floor of a cheery-colored addition out back. The private bathroom is downstairs, off the spacious open-air courtyard, with a huge fish tank built into the wall.

Calle Clarín 9 (between Aguilera and Heredia), Santiago de Cuba. ℭ 22/62-3574. 2 units. CUC$20–CUC$30 double. No credit cards. *In room:* A/C, no phone.

**Gran Hotel Escuela** *(Value)* This hotel-school offers good value and excellent location in the heart of Santiago's historic center. The rooms themselves are rather uninspired and spartan, but they are clean and spacious, with firm beds—although only two rooms here come with a double bed. A few rooms have tiny balconies overlooking bustling Calle Enramada. This hotel has historically been favored by local and visiting artists and musicians. Be forewarned, there's no elevator here, and all the rooms are on the second and third floors.

Calle Enramada (corner of Calle San Félix), Santiago de Cuba. ℭ 22/65-3020. www.granhotelstgo.cu. 15 units. CUC$30–CUC$40 double. MC, V. **Amenities:** Restaurant; bar; laundry service. *In room:* A/C, TV, fridge, safe.

**Hotel Libertad** Fronting the busy Plaza de Marte, this hotel is another good budget option, run by the Islazul chain. Only half of the rooms here have windows, and you will definitely want a room with a window. Room no. 214 is the hotel's largest and best offering. All have simple furnishings, and small, but functional bathrooms. About half the rooms here have double beds, a high percentage for a state-run hotel chain. Aside from its central location, the best feature here is the third-floor rooftop bar. This hotel caters to both Cubans and foreigners.

Calle Aguilera (across from Plaza de Marte), Santiago de Cuba. ℭ 22/62-3080. Fax 22/62-8394. www.islazul.cu. 16 units. CUC$38 double. Rates include breakfast. Rates slightly lower in off season. MC, V. **Amenities:** Restaurant; 2 bars; laundry service. *In room:* A/C, TV.

## THE OUTSKIRTS
### EXPENSIVE

**Meliá Santiago de Cuba** ⭐⭐ *(Kids)* This unique, postmodern high-rise, a mass of blue, red, and gray steel girders and glass, is the largest hotel in Santiago and easily its most luxurious. It's in a peaceful area about 2km (1¼ miles) from the historic core, which is perfect for guests who need a little bit more tranquillity and space. It has facilities and services in spades, including the best outdoor pool in the city—the cost of the hotel is nearly worth it for the pool alone. Rooms are attractive and large, with huge windows offering up excellent views, particularly from the higher floors. The hotel has an excellent nightly cabaret show in its atmospheric **Santiago Café,** which is an indoor reconstruction of a miniature colonial city.

Av. de las Américas (at Calle M), Reparto Sueño, Santiago de Cuba. ℭ 22/68-7070. Fax 22/68-7170. www.solmelia cuba.com. 302 units. CUC$115 double; CUC$145–CUC$165 suite. MC, V. **Amenities:** 4 restaurants; 3 bars; nightly show; 3 outdoor pools; 2 lit outdoor tennis courts; small gym; sauna; tour desk; car-rental desk; business center; small shopping arcade; salon; 24-hr. room service; laundry service. *In room:* A/C, TV, minibar, hair dryer, safe.

### MODERATE

**Hotel Las Américas** *(Value)* A comfortable and friendly older-style hotel just down the street from the Meliá Santiago, Las Américas isn't fancy, but it's a good place to stay, with plenty of services, attractive gardens, and a midsize pool. The rooms seem to always feel in need of an update in decor and some maintenance, but they are good sized and have nice gray-marble bathrooms and cable television. The hotel dance club is quite popular with young Santiagueros. Nonguests here can use the pool facilities for a CUC$5 fee.

Av. de las Américas (at General Cebreco), Reparto Sueño, Santiago de Cuba. © **22/64-2011**. Fax 22/68-7075. www. islazul.cu. 70 units. CUC$58–CUC$69 double. Rates include breakfast. MC, V. **Amenities:** 2 restaurants; 2 bars; dance club; outdoor pool; tour desk; car-rental desk; laundry service. *In room:* A/C, TV, fridge, hair dryer, safe.

### INEXPENSIVE

**Casa Abigail Figueroa Díaz** ✦   A corner house in a tranquil neighborhood in the shadow of the towering Meliá Santiago, this casa offers an independent entrance for guests. Its one bedroom is actually an apartment with a large sitting room; it's nicely equipped and has a large, clean bathroom. The huge upstairs terrace is totally independent, entered through a separate door and courtyard.

Calle 5 no. 601 (corner of Calle K), Reparto Sueño, Santiago de Cuba. © **22/64-5823**. 1 unit. CUC$20–CUC$25 double. No credit cards. *In room:* A/C, fridge, no phone.

**Casa Asensio** ✦ *Value*   This fine house with an upstairs apartment is run by a friendly woman, Isabel. The huge apartment has an even larger private rooftop terrace. There's an independent entrance and a separate kitchen, a large, comfortable bed, and good-size bathroom. Abstract art is painted on the walls, and you have access to the home's little garden.

Calle J no. 306 (between Calle 6 and Av. de las Américas), Reparto Sueño, Santiago de Cuba. © **22/62-4600**. reinaldo.asensio@tin.it. 1 unit. CUC$25 double. No credit cards. *In room:* A/C, kitchenette, fridge, no phone.

**Casa Florinda Chaviano Martínez**   This large and well-furnished house is impeccable. The lone bedroom for rent here is big and meticulously maintained. It features a great rooftop terrace and breezy patio covered with vines.

Calle I no. 58 (between Calles 2 and 3), Reparto Sueño, Santiago de Cuba. © **22/65-3660**. 1 unit. CUC$25 double. No credit cards. *In room:* A/C, TV, fridge, no phone.

**Casa Gloria Boué Alonso**   There is no shortage of nicely furnished 1950s-style houses in the Sueño district; this one has funky, overstuffed furniture and two rooms, one of which is upstairs with its own massive terrace. The other room is downstairs, and is very spacious with the largest private bathroom you're likely to find in Cuba. There's a common sitting room with a television showing only local channels.

Calle J no. 212 (between Calles 4 and 5), Reparto Sueño, Santiago de Cuba. © **22/64-4969**. 2 units. CUC$20–CUC$25 double. No credit cards. *In room:* A/C, fridge, no phone.

## 5 Where to Dine

Santiago has a unique take on Cuban and Caribbean cuisine, but it isn't an especially great place for dining; there are few really good restaurants, and even fewer *paladares*. A couple of the better restaurants are outside of downtown, and it's best if you plan ahead to combine them with sightseeing. Just a couple of officially sanctioned paladares and the state-run restaurants (many of which are concentrated around Plaza Dolores) are nothing to look forward to. Understandably, many visitors tend to eat at their hotel restaurants—as good an option as any. The Meliá Santiago de Cuba and Hotel Casa Granda have elegant restaurants that are worth a splurge even for nonguests; Hotel Las Américas also has a dependable, low-key restaurant out back by the pool. Although you can only get sandwiches and simple dishes there, one of my favorite lunch spots is the open-air terrace bar at the Hotel Casa Granda. On a hot afternoon, this is the coolest place in town—in both senses of the word. A couple of appealing options are on the outskirts of the city—good ideas when organizing day trips to El Cobre or La Gran Piedra.

## CENTRO HISTORICO
### MODERATE

**Paladar Las Gallegas** *Value* CRIOLLA   Four sisters run this friendly, down-home place just a couple blocks from Parque Céspedes. Portions are large, the food is pretty good, and the spacious dining room—a cross between a living room and a salon—has a peaked beam ceiling, four tables (including two on narrow balconies overlooking the street), an ornate chandelier, and red satin curtains. The house specialty is lamb; there's also smoked pork and the predictable chicken. All dishes come with rice and salad. Go early or late; many nights the tiny place is full, though the wait usually isn't long.

San Basilio 305 altos (between General Lacret and San Félix). © **22/62-4700**. Reservations not accepted. Main courses CUC$8–CUC$10. No credit cards. Daily 1–11:30pm.

**Santiago 1900** ★ *Value* CRIOLLA   Beyond the doorman controlling access with antique red-leather ropes on brass stanchions lies an elegant and reasonably priced restaurant. There are several interior dining rooms as well as a wonderful open-air ground floor patio with a stone fountain in its center, and two open-air spaces on the second floor balcony. Some of the tables up here have a good view of the city's church steeples. The menu is pretty standard Cuban fair, but it is very well-prepared, and the ambience is wonderful. This place attracts a mixed Cuban and foreign clientele.

Calle Basilio 354 (between Carnicería and San Félix). © **22/62-3507**. Reservations not required. Main courses CUC$6–CUC$10. No credit cards. Daily noon–10pm.

## THE OUTSKIRTS
### EXPENSIVE

**La Isabelica** ★★ INTERNATIONAL   This small, romantic restaurant serves up French-influenced cuisine in a tranquil and elegant setting. We recommend the fresh grouper in a saffron sauce, served over a bed of spinach. You also can't go wrong with the roasted duck breast with caramelized papaya. There's a decent and reasonably priced wine list, and the service is attentive and efficient. Dinner here gets you a free entrance into the hotel's nightly cabaret show.

In the Meliá Santiago, Av. de las Américas (at Calle M), Reparto Sueño. © **22/68-7070**. Reservations recommended. Main courses CUC$11–CUC$18. MC, V. Daily 7–11pm.

**ZunZún** ★★ CRIOLLA   This elegant and upscale restaurant occupies a handsome 1940s house in the Vista Alegre neighborhood. It has five private salons for intimate dining, and a couple of tables on a broad front veranda, which are my favorites. With relatively soft lighting, marble floors, and period furnishings—some original to the house—ZunZún (formerly Tocororo) is the place in town to splurge. Everything is very well prepared and nicely presented. It's especially good for seafood, such as a mixed grill of fish and shellfish; medallions of lobster, shellfish, and shrimp; garlic shrimp; and lobster with cilantro sauce. Carnivores can opt for a beef filet in red-wine sauce or a spicy lamb stew. The tables here have white tablecloths and candles—rarities in Cuba.

Av. Manduley 159, Reparto Vista Alegre. © **22/64-1528**. Reservations recommended. Main courses CUC$8–CUC$24. MC, V. Daily noon–10pm.

*Finds* **A Boho Coffeehouse**

Not to be confused with the elegant restaurant at the Meliá Santiago, **Café La Isabelica** is a lively 24-hour joint on the edge of Plaza Dolores, at the corner of Aguilera and Porfirio Valiente (© **22/64-2634**). Thick with an Afro-Cuban vibe and just the right quotient of dive-bar aesthetics, it's virtually an institution among budget travelers and visitors hanging out in Santiago for extended periods—the kind who may or may not be studying percussion or dance. The coffee's good, strong, and cheap. If you're looking to meet Santiagueros (with honorable and occasionally less honorable intentions) or other travelers, La Isabelica is the place.

## MODERATE

**Paladar Salón Tropical** *⚜* CRIOLLA    One of the most elegant paladares in Cuba—in fact, it's swankier than most state-owned and hotel restaurants—this attractively decorated place, with stained-glass windows, lace tablecloths, and high-backed chairs, also has a terrific, breezy, plant-covered terrace. The views are excellent; it's a marvelous environment for having a couple of beers . . . and waiting interminably for your dinner. It's own popularity has overwhelmed this place, and service can be glacially slow at times. Depending upon what is available, the menu might offer a smorgasbord of choices including chickpea stew, pork *cordon bleu,* shish kabobs, liver, and barbecued chicken. The paladar is quite popular with smooching Cubans as well as bored *jineteras* with their romantic "dates." Reservations are highly recommended, and the operating hours listed below are not strictly enforced—this place often closes early or unexpectedly.

Fernández Marcané 310 Altos (between Calles 9 and 10), Reparto Santa Bárbara. © **22/64-1161**. Reservations recommended. Main courses CUC$7–CUC$10. No credit cards. Mon–Sat noon–11pm.

## BAHIA DE SANTIAGO

### EXPENSIVE

**Restaurant El Morro** *⚜* CRIOLLA    A hugely popular and pleasant open-air place, perched on the coast near the fortress of the same name and boasting spectacular views of the sparkling blue Caribbean Sea, this restaurant, happily, isn't a tourist trap. Putting El Morro into the "expensive" category is a bit misleading; it offers a good-value CUC$12 lunch for groups and a series of CUC$10 *platos fuertes* (main courses with accompaniments). Try the lobster if you're in a mood to splurge; otherwise, there's a fish filet stuffed with cheese, spicy shrimp, and chicken with pineapple. The long black tables are under a wood-beamed canopy thick with vines and hanging plants and white *tumbergia* flowers, a most welcome refuge from the scorching sun that makes midday at El Morro fortress a daunting proposition.

Carretera del Morro Km 8.5, Bahía de Santiago. © **22/68-7151**. Reservations recommended for lunch. Main courses CUC$8–CUC$25. MC, V. Daily 9am–11pm.

### MODERATE

**El Cayo** *Finds* CRIOLLA    This relaxing spot for lunch is a boating excursion and dining outing rolled into one. In a pretty blue-and-white clapboard waterfront house on a tiny island in the middle of the Bay of Santiago—you have to take a CUC$3 round-trip ferryboat from the **Santiago Marina** (© **22/9-1446**) to get there—is this breezy, tranquil restaurant that's popular with organized groups but is perfect for independent travelers, too. Sit on the covered wraparound balcony overlooking the water and try any of the specialties, which quite logically are seafood dishes: Spanish mackerel, lobster, red snapper, marlin, or fish soup.

Cayo Granma, Bahía de Santiago. © 22/69-0109. Reservations recommended for lunch. Main courses CUC$6–CUC$25. MC, V. Daily 11am–7pm.

## 6 Shopping

Opportunities for shopping in Santiago, despite the city's cultural traditions, aren't that much better than many smaller cities in Cuba. Your best bets, as elsewhere in Cuba, are handicrafts, music and musical instruments, and the always-dependable rum and cigars.

### ART & HANDICRAFTS

Sellers and craftspeople line both sides of **Calle Heredia** from Parque Céspedes on up to Calle Porfirio Valiente. The informal daily market features a range of handicrafts and souvenirs, including sculptures of shapely (as well as rail-thin) women carved from ebony and other precious woods, paintings, masks, papier-mâché dolls, musical instruments, and jewelry. The **Fondo Cubano de Bienes Culturales,** Calle Heredia at General Lacret (© **22/65-2358**), also handles a fair selection of handicrafts and musical instruments. A number of state-owned crafts and souvenir shops with similar merchandise but inflexible pricing occupy the storefronts at the base of the cathedral on **Parque Céspedes.** New and orderly free-standing crafts and souvenir stalls line the road leading to the **El Morro** fortress (across from the El Morro restaurant). The area used to be a good spot to pick up informal paintings from local artists, but everything is now all cleaned up and moved inside.

Locally produced abstract and figurative art is available at a handful of galleries, including the one within the lobby of the **Hotel Casa Granda** and **Galería de Arte Oriente** on Calle General Lacret 653, between Aguilera and Heredia.

### CIGARS & RUM

The **Barra de Ron Caney,** at the rum factory that used to be the original Bacardi plant before the Revolution (when the owners fled to The Bahamas and the U.S.), is a gift shop selling an array of types and vintages of Cuban-produced rum, as well as cigars, nice silver jewelry, and other souvenirs. You can taste before you buy. The factory and shop are on Av. Jesús Menéndez 703 between San Antonio and San Ricardo (© **22/62-5576**), across from the train station. The shop is open daily from 9am to 5:30pm. Alternately, you can check out the **Museo de Ron** (© **22/62-3080**), at San Basilio

---

*Tips* **Bring on the *Béisbol***

Santiago is yet another baseball-mad Cuban city, and the local professional team is usually among the best in the national league. The *pelota* (as it's popularly known) season begins in late winter and continues through the spring. Games are held at the **Estadio Guillermo Moncada** on Avenida de las Américas (© **22/64-1209**). Ask your hotel about getting tickets (it's usually possible to purchase them right before game time at the stadium ticket booth).

358, which offers a brief illustrated guide to the history and process of rum production, with a shop attached and pleasant bar next door.

Cigars can be purchased at hotel shops or **Casa del Habano,** next door to the Caney rum factory (✆ **22/62-2366**), which even has a smokers' lounge and bar. *Note:* I'd be especially wary of the quality of cigars you are offered by *jineteros* on the street.

## MUSIC

Santiago is the capital of *son* and other indigenous forms of Cuban music, and there are a few good spots to pick up CDs and tapes of Santiaguero musicians (though overall, Havana has a much better selection of music stores). The **EGREM** music label has shops at the Antonio Maceo airport, Fondo Cubano de Bienes Culturales, and the Hotel Las Américas. The **Casa de la Trova** (p. 276) has an **ARTex** store, and there's a small record shop attached to the **Casa de la Música,** Mariano 564, between Aguilera and José Antonio Saco. Most of the artists you may have an opportunity to see live sell CDs at their performances.

## 7 Santiago de Cuba After Dark

### THE PERFORMING ARTS

The biggest draw in town for travelers, besides the locally grown Cuban music scene, is the **Cabaret Tropicana Santiago** ✫✫✫, Autopista Nacional Km 1.5, north of Santiago (✆ **22/68-7020** or 22/64-2579). It's second in size and fame only to Havana's internationally regarded Tropicana, but Santiago's show is no second banana. It's a slickly produced cabaret show—different from the one in Havana—with excellent singers and dancers and extraordinarily elaborate costumes. Dinner is available, and drinks aren't cheap, but the Tropicana is a must-see, especially if you don't have an opportunity to catch the program in the capital. The show begins at 9pm daily; there's also a dance club on the premises, open until 3am. The show without dinner and including one drink is CUC$35. There's an additional CUC$5 charge for taking pictures during the show, and CUC$15 if you want to shoot video. Packaged excursions with dinner and transportation can be purchased at the larger hotels and all tour operators.

You'll find a much more scaled down, much less expensive cabaret show at the **Santiago Café** ✫ (✆ **22/68-7070**), in the Meliá Santiago. The cover here is just CUC$5, which includes two drinks. While nowhere near as elaborate or intense as the Tropicana, this is still a very good night out and respectable little cabaret show.

The top spots for cultural events such as dance and theater (which inevitably take a back seat to live music) are the sleek **Teatro Heredia,** Avenida de los Desfiles, across from the Plaza de la Revolución (✆ **22/64-3178**); **Teatro Oriente,** Calle José Antonio Saco 115 (✆ **22/62-2441**); **El Quitrín,** San Gerónimo 463 (✆ **22/62-2528**); and **Ateneo Cultural** (✆ **22/62-3635**), in an old Law School building on Félix Peña. Performances to keep an eye out for are those by **Ballet Folclórico Cutatumba,** an extraordinary Afro-Cuban outfit that has toured in North America and Europe, and **Conjunto Folklórico de Oriente,** which often performs at Hotel Casa Granda. You may not catch all the spiritual and cultural elements embedded into their show, but the music and dance are infectious nonetheless. Teatro Heredia is headquarters for the **Feria del Caribe** in June. The **Museo del Carnaval,** Heredia 303 (✆ **22/62-6955**), has folklore programs most days of the week, and a Sunday *rumba* show at 6pm. For other dance programs, see the **Casa del Caribe,** below.

## Carnival & Other Santiago Festivals

Santiago is well known among Cuban cities for its sparkling music festivals, which thrust Afro-Caribbean culture and the local musical genius to the forefront of urban life. If you can stand the stultifying heat in late July, Carnival is the most exciting time to visit the city.

In Santiago, *Carnaval* is not a pre-Lenten celebration as it is in other Latin American countries. In the 17th century, slaves reshaped the traditional (and much more solemn) Catholic veneration of the city's patron saint, Santiago Apóstolo, and the attendant religious processions, into a festive celebration. The slaves' revelry was much more raucous than that of the white Christians, who began to refer to the slaves' participation as the *Fiesta de Los Mamarrachos* (party of the Crazies). Gradually, the rest of Santiaguero society began to appreciate and even participate in Carnival. French and Haitian elements were incorporated after the 18th-century influx of those populations. By the 20th century, Santiago's Carnival had gone the way of samba and Carnaval in Brazil, which was appropriated from marginal black communities and transformed into a mainstream cultural affair.

Today, unsurprisingly, even Carnival is linked to politics. The 3-day celebration also serves to commemorate the 26th of July Movement that was the foundation for the Revolution. Yet politics seem light-years away from the popular explosion that erupts on Santiago's sweltering streets. Queen-topped, garish floats glide through the streets, frenetic drum-beating conga parades rock the neighborhoods (the biggest are the barrio congas of day 1), and masked *diablitos* (devils) dart daringly through the throngs. African elements, including representations of *orishás* (Yoruba gods), are omnipresent. *Comparsas,* the Carnival band processions, don papier-mâché masks and brightly colored costumes.

Today, Carnival manages still to be exuberant, even though funds for fancy costumes are tough to come by and homemade instruments predominate (during the years of the so-called Special Period in the mid-1990s, economic conditions were so tough that Carnival had to be canceled for a couple of years). Some conga ensembles, such as Los Hoyos, trace their origins back to the 19th century. Dance troupes to be on the lookout for include Cabildos, La Placita, and Izuama y Olugo. The focal points of Carnival activities are along Avenida Jesús Menéndez and Victoriano Garzón, where the parade and float judging takes place.

Preceding Carnival is the **Fiesta del Fuego,** or **Festival del Caribe,** in the first week of July, which brings a cornucopia of cultural workshops, theater, and artistic performances to Santiago. Also worth catching, although not nearly as frenzied as Carnival, is the **Festival de Rumba** in mid-January, which is also celebrated with street dancing and music.

## LIVE MUSIC

Santiago is all about the music. Some of the biggest personalities on the Cuban music scene, such as **Compay Segundo, Eliades Ochoa,** and **La Vieja Trova Santiaguera,** hail from Santiago. Although Compay died at 95 in 2003, Ochoa and La Vieja Trova Santiaguera are still active, touring both in Cuba and internationally. Calle Heredia, just off Parque Céspedes, is Cuba's version of Bourbon Street, but much less commercialized. Four or five places burst with addictive live traditional Cuban music on any given night, and several have bands during the day, too. Personal local favorites we can't recommend highly enough include **Los Jubilados,** a band of gregarious septuagenarians that often plays at the Casa de la Trova; **Kokoyé,** a folkloric band playing traditional Afro-Cuban and Afro-Haitian music; and the **Vocal Divas,** a talented women's a cappella group.

Several of the spots below are not only great for hearing live music, but also for watching local patrons who make dancing to Cuban music a sultry art form all their own. Give it a try yourself and don't worry about looking foolish; unless you've had professional training, you simply can't compete with Cubans on the dance floor, so don't even try. If you're without a partner, there's usually no shortage of Cuban men and women (some of whom will invariably be *jineteros* and *jineteras*) willing to give you a whirl. At places like the Casa de la Trova and other spots around town, you're likely to find music throughout the day, beginning around noon, and well into the night. At most clubs, the music starts around 9pm and really heats up from around 10pm until 2am.

**Casa de las Tradiciones** 𝕱𝕱   More cramped and heaps more intimate than the more touristy Casa de la Trova, this old house (called "La Casona" by locals) in the Tívoli section of town is loaded with character and decorated with dozens of paintings and photos on the walls. For me, the place just screams "Santiago de Cuba." It gets perfectly steamy when there's a tight band playing and any more than two couples working the dance floor. Calle Rabi 154. ☏ **22/65-3892.** Cover CUC$1.

**Casa de la Trova** 𝕱𝕱𝕱   Decades of raw and infectious Cuban music seep from the walls of this legendary live music venue, the greatest of the country's Casas de la Trova. Old-timers may complain that it doesn't have the character it once did, due to makeovers, but its long front room and back patio and the grand upstairs salon still outclass most any other Cuban music joint. All the greats have played here; you may catch an up-and-coming star, or a band of octogenarians that rightly should be every bit as famous as the guys in Buena Vista. They aren't, but you'll enjoy their music all the more for their relative obscurity and chance to see them in such a welcoming environment. Heredia 304 (between Pío Rosado and Porfirio Valiente). ☏ **22/62-3943.** Cover CUC$1 daytime, CUC$2–CUC$3 at night.

**Casa del Caribe** 𝕱   This cultural center has a full schedule of music events and other goings-on starting at 8pm every night of the week. The program starts slow, early in the week, with boleros and *música feelin'* and usually builds to Afro-Cuban music and dance on Thursday, Caribbean and Latin American folk dance on Friday, and a happening Haitian or Afro-Cuban program on Saturday beginning at 6pm. Concerts are held on two leafy outdoor patios. There are also cultural conferences and workshops. Calle 13 no. 154 (corner of Calle 8), Vista Alegre. ☏ **22/64-2285.** Cover CUC$1–CUC$2.

**Patio de ARTex**   If there's not much happening at the Casa de la Trova, peek in here ⸢or live Cuban music almost every night of the week. Heredia 304 (between Pío Rosado and ⸀firio Valiente). ☏ **22/65-4814.** Cover CUC$2.

**ʼo de los Dos Abuelos**   This place on the Plaza de Marte is a good spot to lis-ᵇ*boleros* and *feelin'.* The scene is a little older and more sedate than most of the places listed above, but folks still get up and dance. Moreover, the patrons and players show real love for the romantic ballads and tragic love songs that are the staples here. Calle Pérez Carbó 5 (across from the Plaza de Marte). © 22/62-3302. Cover CUC$2.

## BARS & CLUBS

In addition to the places listed below, it's worth checking to see if they've reopened the **Bello Bar,** which has been closed for over a year for "remodeling." This bar occupies the entire 15th floor of the Meliá Santiago hotel and offers stunning 360-degree views of Santiago. In general, bars open around noon and stay open as long as there are patrons, usually between midnight and 2am. Dance clubs and music joints tend to get going around 10pm and stay open until at least 2am.

**Club 300**    This is a dark, enveloping nightclub with occasional live music and a fair share of *jineteras* "jes dying to meetchu," as Mick Jagger used to sing. Open daily until 4am. Calle Aguilera (between General Lacret and San Félix). © 22/65-3532. Cover CUC$2.

**Discoteca La Iris**    This sweaty dance club, extremely popular with young locals, seems to be pumping at all hours of the day, with ear-shattering disco, salsa, merengue, and Latin rock. Calle Aguilera 617 (between Bamada and Plácido). © 22/65-4910. Cover CUC$2.

**Hotel Casa Granda Terrace Bar**    A great spot for people-watching over the Parque Céspedes, this convivial terrace/balcony bar is always hopping, with a good mix of foreigners and Cubans hoping to meet foreigners. The hotel also has a **Rooftop Garden** bar on the top floor with excellent views of the cathedral and Santiago Bay, although this pleasant open-air space almost always feels underused. Calle Heredia 201 (between General Lacret and San Félix). © 22/65-3021.

**La Taberna de Dolores** *Finds*    This local hangout, and my favorite low-rent watering hole in Santiago, is in the pretty, leafy patio of an old colonial house. This joint usually has live music or karaoke and always has cheap draft beer in plastic mugs. The crowd is mostly Cuban with a few backpacker sorts. With a minimal bit of Spanish (like *cerveza*) you should be able to pay in Cuban pesos—be sure to ask about paying in *moneda nacional,* although be sure you have some *moneda nacional* in your pocket when they give you the bill. Calle Aguilera (at Reloj), Plaza Dolores. © 22/62-3913.

## 8 Side Trips from Santiago de Cuba

Excursions to all the places listed below, as well as to Guantánamo and Baracoa (see chapter 9), can be arranged at the tour desks found in most hotels, or with **Cubanacán** (© **22/64-3445**), **Cubatur** (© **22/64-1181**), and **Havanatur** (© **22/62-4823**) in Santiago.

## BASILICA DEL COBRE

18km (11 miles) W of Santiago de Cuba

The most important shrine for Cubans and the most famous church in the country is lodged in the foothills of the Sierra Maestra near the old copper mines that give it its name. The triple-domed church with the mouthful name of **El Sanctuario de Nuestra Señora de la Caridad del Cobre,** built in 1927, rises on Maboa hill and is photogenically framed by green forest. The faithful come from across Cuba on pilgrimages to pay their respects to (and ask for protection from) a black Madonna, the *Virgen de la Caridad* (Virgin of Charity). She is nothing less than the protectress of Cuba, and her image, cloaked in a glittering gold robe can be seen throughout the country. Her parallel figure in Afro-Cuban worship is Ochún, goddess of love and femininity, who is also dark-skinned and dressed in bright yellow garments. In 1998 the Pope visited and blessed the shrine, calling the Virgin "La Reina de los Cubanos" (Queen of Cubans), and donated a rosary and crown.

According to legend, Cuba's patron saint was rescued bobbing in the Bay of Nipe in 1611 by three young fishermen (or miners, depending on who's telling the story) about to capsize in a storm. The Madonna wore a sign that read YO SOY LA VIRGEN DE LA CARIDAD (I am the Virgin of Charity). With the wooden statue in their grasp, they miraculously made it to shore. Pilgrims, who often make the last section of the trek on their knees, pray to her image and place *votos* (mementos) and offerings of thanks for her miracles; among them are small boats and prayers for those who have tried to make it to Florida on rafts. Ernest Hemingway—whose fisherman in *The Old Man and the Sea* made a promise to visit the shrine if he could only land his marlin— donated his Nobel prize for literature to the shrine, but it was stolen (and later recovered, but never again to be exhibited here). The Virgin sits on the second floor, up the back stairs, encased in glass. When Mass is being said, the push of a button turns the Virgin around to face the congregation. The annual pilgrimage is September 12, and the patron saint's feast day is July 25. The Basílica is open daily from 6am to 6:30pm; admission is free.

You can take a taxi to El Cobre for CUC$20 to CUC$30 round-trip. The no. 2 bus runs between Santiago and El Cobre four times daily, leaving from the main bus station in Santiago. To enhance the spiritual experience, or to merely have a serene and incredibly cheap overnight stay, there's an inn behind the church, **Hospedería de la Caridad,** which welcomes foreigners who abide by the strict rules (10pm curfew and repeated requests for quiet); a stay costs a mere 15 pesos a night. If you can pay in *moneda nacional* this only comes out to about 58¢, although they generally charge foreigners a few CUCs. There are only 15 austere but well-kept rooms; it's necessary to reserve by phone (© **22/3-6246**) at least 15 days in advance.

## LA GRAN PIEDRA & LA ISABELICA
27km (17 miles) E of Santiago de Cuba

A tortuous coastal road east of Santiago ascends the mountains to **La Gran Piedra (The Big Rock),** an enormous 25m-high (80-ft.) rock perched 1,200m (3,900 ft.) above sea level. You can climb a half-hour or so on foot to the top of the rock for a panoramic bird's-eye view of thickly wooded eastern Cuba and the majestic Sierra Maestra that extends to the Caribbean and as far as the eye can see. The air is much sweeter and cooler than in Santiago. Admission is CUC$2. Near the foot of the trail is the modest **Gran Piedra** (© **22/68-6147;** www.islazul.cu), a rustic little hotel with a restaurant, as well as the **Jardín Ave de Paraíso,** a small botanical garden with birds of paradise and other flowers. The garden is open daily 8am to 5pm, and admission is CUC$1.

About 2km (1¼ miles) beyond Gran Piedra, a passable dirt track leads to **Museo La Isabelica,** Carretera de la Gran Piedra Km 14, an early-19th-century coffee plantation *finca* (country house) that once was the property of newly arrived French immigrants who fled Haiti after the slave revolt there in 1791. The owner named La Isabelica for his mistress (and later wife), a beautiful slave. The house was a stone mansion built in the style of rural French manor houses in Haiti. It was one of about 60 coffee plantations in the area, which proved very hospitable for planting coffee beans. The 200 Arabica

> ### *Tips*  El Dye-kee-*ree*
>
> The daiquiri (in English, *dak*-ur-ee), the famous rum cocktail that was a favorite of both JFK and Hemingway, was first concocted in Cuba at the end of the 19th century. If you're the kind of barfly who makes pilgrimages to the birthplaces of alcoholic libations, then walk a straight line to **Playa Daiquirí,** within the Baconao Park Reserve. It's tough to speak easy of the beach's attributes, which are marred further by a massive hotel, but if you make it there, you'll forever have cocktail fodder: You can say you were knocking back "dye-kee-*reez*" in the spot where Teddy Roosevelt and the Rough Riders stumbled upon *tierra firma* during the Spanish-American War of 1898.

coffee plantations in the region helped Cuba become the number-one coffee producer in the world until 1850, when it was surpassed by Brazil. These Franco-Haitian plantations were recently declared UNESCO World Heritage Sites. On the premises of La Isabelica are a workshop, original furniture, and slave instruments. The house has recently been renovated and provides a glimpse into the life of the period. It's open Tuesday to Sunday 9am to 5pm (closed Monday), and admission is CUC$2.

## GRAN PARQUE NATURAL BACONAO
25km (16 miles) SE of Santiago de Cuba

A UNESCO biosphere reserve, **Parque Baconao** is spread over some 40km (25 miles). The local dark-sand beaches are scruffy and the hotels are isolated, but the park hides a number of attractions, several of them man-made, for visitors with a couple of extra days in Santiago.

The road leading southeast out of Santiago is lined with 26 monuments to revolutionary heroes who died in the attack on the Moncada barracks. About 10km (6 miles) east is the **Valle de la Prehistoria,** Carretera Bacanao Km 6.5 (© **22/63-9039**), Cuba's very own Jurassic Park—a lifeless and cheesy attraction. Lodged on farmlands are 250 massive life-size statues of dinosaurs and a giant, club-wielding Stone Age man. The park is open daily from 8am to 5pm; admission is CUC$1. Nearby, in a nod to more recent history, the **Museo Nacional del Transporte (Automobile Museum),** Carretera Bacanao Km 8.5 (© **22/63-9197**), has a decent number of old cars, some more valuable and in better shape than others. One vehicle, a 1951 Chevrolet, was driven by Fidel's brother Raúl to the Moncada attack (he got lost); a Cadillac on view belonged to the legendary singer Beny Moré. The museum's collection of vintage American cars has been built by the novel practice of offering Cubans new Russian-built Ladas for their old Cadillacs and Chevys. Next door is a collection of several thousand model and Matchbox cars. The museum is open daily from 8am to 5pm; admission is CUC$1; an extra CUC$1 is charged to take photos.

On the coast, at Km 27.5, is the **Acuario Baconao** (© **22/35-0005**), a rather sad little aquarium that runs daily dolphin and sea lion shows. Admission is CUC$5. You can also swim with the dolphins for around 15 minutes for CUC$40.

### WHERE TO STAY ALONG THE COAST
The best place to stay outside of Santiago, if you really want to explore Parque Baconao and the southeast coast, is **Gran Caribe Club Bucanero** 𝒦, Carretera de

Baconao Km 4, Arroyo de la Costa (© **22/68-6363;** www.hotelbucanero.com). A large, comfortable hotel clinging to the coast, this all-inclusive has a very Mediterranean feel. It has a small, private cove beach with fine sand, deep blue waters, and a backdrop of tall cliffs. Rooms all have exposed stone walls and are nice if not especially luxurious; bathrooms, though, are small. While this place is under 30 minutes from Santiago, many visitors are more than content to stay put, enjoying the beach, volleyball, watersports, the great little bar perched up above the sand, and the open-air dance club tucked into the canyon. The hotel has a dive center, and rock climbers can tackle the cliffs behind the hotel. Rooms cost CUC$90 to CUC$145 double all-inclusive; the hotel offers day passes, good for all facilities, for CUC$30.

# Appendix A:
# Cuba in Depth

*by Eliot Greenspan & Neil E. Schlecht*

Cuba is an ongoing and enduring enigma. By any conventional measure, this Caribbean island should be a speck in the global geopolitical ocean. Yet for nearly half a century, this complicated nation of 11.4 million people has commanded the world stage in a manner wholly incommensurate with its small size and economic insignificance. A former colony of Spain and playground of American high rollers, Cuba struck out on its own in the late 1950s, and the nation remains a hot topic in the corridors of the world's power brokers. Fiercely independent but rarely free, and the unlikeliest of major players, Cuba arouses passions like perhaps no other nation.

For decades, those inflamed feelings have focused on the Communist regime that one man, Fidel Castro, brazenly engineered. Hated and worshiped in almost equal measure, Castro—the longest-surviving head of state in the world—has defied critics, confounded pundits, and frustrated his own followers. Slowly, though, the world is learning that Cuba is more than a coveted property in a high stakes game of Risk. Wider exposure to Cuban culture (especially its music), the island's colonial treasures, and the Cuban people has given rise to a love affair that transcends international politics.

## 1 History 101

### PRE-COLUMBIAN SOCIETY & THE SPANISH CONQUEST

Cuba was not populated by overachieving civilizations in the days before the arrival of the Spanish, as, for example, Mexico, Guatemala, and Peru were. However, Native American tribes that included the Siboney, Taíno, and Guanajatabey (the group that would come to be known as the Arawaks), numbered about 100,000 and had lived on the island since at least 1000 B.C. Hunters, gatherers, and farmers, these native Cubans cultivated *cohiba* (tobacco), a crop upon which the island's economy would one day depend. The island's relatively peaceful and isolated existence was shattered by the arrival of Christopher Columbus, who dropped anchor along the northeast coast of Cuba on October 27, 1492, and quickly scribbled a notation in his journal exclaiming

that the land he'd discovered was "the most beautiful that human eyes have ever seen."

The Spanish conquest of the island began just a few years later. In 1511, Don Diego Velázquez de Cuellar sailed from neighboring Hispaniola with a band of about 300 *conquistadores*. Velázquez sailed to Baracoa and made that settlement the first of the famous original seven *villas* on the island (the others were Bayamo, Havana, Sancti Spíritus, Trinidad, Camagüey, and Santiago de Cuba). The Spanish process of colonization was identical across the Caribbean and Central and South America: Velázquez and his fellow Spaniards extracted quick riches from the land and people, and made slaves of the native tribes. American Indian resistance led by the Taíno chief Hatuey failed after he was captured and burned at the stake by the Spanish. Thousands of Native Americans soon died from exposure to European viruses the Spaniards brought with them, and entire villages, reduced to forced labor, committed suicide. By the mid-1500s the native population on the island had declined from more than 100,000 to a mere 3,000. Spanish rule would continue for almost 400 years.

## LIFE AS A COLONY: EXPANDING TRADE & PIRACY

Having largely depleted the island of its native peoples (and, of greatest importance to the colonizers, its labor pool), the Spanish brought African slaves to Cuba in the first quarter of the 16th century. Sugar was being produced, but it had not yet become an important commodity, and until the end of the 1500s, Cuba did not count among Spain's most important colonies—though it was strategically significant as a Caribbean base. French and British pirates coveted the island enough, however, to conduct repeated raids on it; in 1555 Havana was sacked and decimated by the French pirate Jacques de Sores, and later Francis Drake and Henry Morgan would follow similar paths. The Spanish empire hastened to fortify the port cities of Havana (which became the capital in 1607) and Santiago de Cuba for defensive purposes. The Caribbean was rife with contraband trade.

In 1762, British forces captured Havana, holding it for only a year before trading it back to Spain in exchange for Florida. Cuban trade expanded to countries other than Spain, most notably the American colonies. A strong tobacco industry had been planted in Cuba; after 1763 sugar-cane exports took off. Hundreds of thousands of African laborers were imported at the end of the 18th century to meet the demands of the sugar industry.

By the middle of the 19th century, Cuba was actively producing one-third of the world's sugar. Half a million slaves—nearly half the population of Cuba—worked the plantations, and at least 3,500 trading ships visited Cuba annually. Cuba, by the late 1800s, had become one of the most valuable colonies in the world. However, a series of violent slave uprisings presaged the more organized efforts at revolt on the horizon.

## TOWARD INDEPENDENCE

Residents of Spanish descent who were born and raised in Cuba, known as *criollos* (Creoles), held managerial positions on sugar-cane plantations. However, they were excluded from governing the prosperous colony. During the 19th century growing numbers of *criollos,* particularly in El Oriente, the island's poorer eastern half, began to agitate for greater participation and autonomy.

Carlos Manuel de Céspedes, a *criollo* plantation owner who had been involved in uprisings in Spain, led the call for Cuban independence on October 10, 1868. He liberated slaves from his estate, La Demajagua, and issued the rebel rallying cry that would unite independence-minded *criollos,* known as *El Grito de Yara.* During the Ten Years' War (1868–78), which saw a short-lived Republic based in Bayamo and produced the first Constitution, 50,000 Cubans, including Céspedes himself, and more than 200,000 Spanish perished in the revolt. Although Cuba remained a colony of Spain, the war precipitated the abolition of slavery on the island in 1886—making Cuba the last of the American colonies to do so—and established the foundations of a national identity.

In large part, though, that national consciousness came from voices beyond Cuba's borders. Cuba's most esteemed patriot, José Martí, led the next and most important uprising against Spain in 1895. Exiled at the age of 18 for his strident political views, Martí became a journalist and poet. From exile in the United

States, he argued for Cuban freedom and formed the Cuban Revolutionary Party. Martí, today revered as the spiritual father of the Cuban nation, was killed during the Second War of Independence.

The United States was not a disinterested observer of the political upheaval taking place in Cuba in the 19th century. The United States had trained its sights on Cuban sugar production and its global market, as well as the island's strategic significance. The United States was hoping to purchase the island from Spain, but Martí warned of the dangers of a Cuba transformed from a colony of Spain into a satellite of the United States ("I know the Monster, because I have lived in its lair," he wrote).

In February 1898, the USS *Maine,* hovering off the coast of Cuba in a show of protection for U.S. interests on the island, sunk in Havana's harbor, killing the entire crew of 260. Spanish responsibility was never proved, but the United States seized upon the disaster as a pretext to declare war on Spain. The Spanish-American War—known in Cuba quite logically as the "Spanish-Cuban-American War," in recognition of the role played by Cuban patriots—lasted only a few months. The United States defeated the Spanish troops, and Spain surrendered its claim to the island by the end of the same year. A provisional military government took over until Cuba became an independent republic in 1902.

## U.S. INVOLVEMENT: NOT THE REPUBLIC CUBANS ENVISIONED

The United States, the primary purchaser of Cuba's sugar, dominated the island's economy and to a considerable extent controlled its political processes. Until the 1950s, Cuba was besieged by political corruption and violence. Fulgencio Batista, though only a sergeant in the army, managed to dictate Cuba's internal affairs through a series of puppet presidents for

nearly a decade before winning the presidency outright in 1940. Though Batista retired in 1944, he staged a military coup and returned to power in 1952. Batista's corrupt dictatorship, supported by the United States, overlooked growing poverty across the country while Batista himself fattened his overseas bank accounts.

Havana was effectively ruled by a group of millionaires more powerful than anywhere else in Latin America, a distortion that allowed Cuban officials to claim that Cuba had the second-highest per capita income in the region. The capital was overrun by brothels, casinos, and gangsters, with high rollers in zoot suits transforming the city into their personal playground. Meanwhile, most of the country was mired in poverty, and more than half of all Cubans were undernourished in 1950. The nascent republic's unequivocal dependence on the United States, corruption, and absence of social equality reinforced the seeds of discontent that had been planted as far back as the 1920s.

## GUERRILLA WARFARE & REVOLUTION

By the 1950s, the climate was ripe for revolution, though it would come in fits and starts. A band of young rebels attacked the Moncada Barracks, the country's second-most-important military base, in Santiago de Cuba on July 26, 1953 (the rebels would later take the date of the attack as the name for their movement, calling it the *Movimiento 26 de Julio*). The effort failed miserably, and many of the rebels were killed or later captured and tortured by the military. But the attack gave its young leader, a lawyer named Fidel Castro Ruz, the bully pulpit he needed. Jailed and tried for offenses against the nation, Castro's legendary 2-hour defense—presaging an uncanny ability to speak for hours at length about Cuba and the Revolution—included the now-famous words, "History will absolve me" (the title of Castro's revolutionary manifesto). Castro was imprisoned offshore on the Isla de la Juventud until May 1955, when Batista granted an amnesty to political prisoners.

Castro fled to Mexico, where he spent a year in exile planning his return to Cuba and the resumption of his plans to overthrow the government. The following year Castro sneaked back to the southeastern coast of Cuba, along with a force of 81 guerrillas, including Ernesto "Che" Guevara and Castro's brother Raúl, aboard a small yacht, the *Granma*. The journey was beset by myriad problems and delays, including unfortunate weather, and Batista's forces were tipped off to the rebels' imminent arrival. Only 15 rebels reached their planned destination, the Sierra Maestra mountains. From such unlikely beginnings, the rebel forces evolved into a formidable guerrilla army, largely through the assistance of peasants who were promised land reform in exchange for their support.

Following 2 years of dramatic fighting in the mountains and strategic points, Castro's insurrection gained strength and legitimacy among a broad swath of the Cuban population. Batista saw the end in sight and on January 1, 1959, he fled the country for the Dominican Republic. The combat-weary but triumphant rebels, known as the *barbudos* (the bearded ones), declared victory in Santiago de Cuba and then entered Havana a week later.

## CUBA UNDER CASTRO

The new government immediately set about restructuring Cuban society: It reduced rents, instituted agrarian reform, and limited estates to 400 hectares (1,000 acres). As part of a comprehensive nationalization program, the government expropriated utilities, factories, and private lands. The fledgling government also embarked upon wide-ranging programs designed to eradicate illiteracy and provide universal healthcare and free schooling.

The Revolution's lofty aims were mitigated by cruder attempts to consolidate state power. The transition to a centralized, all-powerful state antagonized many Cubans, mostly elites. Castro placed the media under state control, as it remains today, and promised elections were never held. Local Committees for the Defense of the Revolution (CDRs) kept tabs on dissenters. In the early years of Castro's reign, many thousands of people suspected of opposing the Revolution were interrogated, imprisoned, or sent to labor camps, along with other social "undesirables," such as homosexuals and priests.

In just 3 years after the triumph of the Revolution, nearly a quarter of a million Cubans—mostly professionals and wealthy landowners—fled the country. They settled in nearby Florida and established a colony of conservative Cuban-Americans that in the coming decades achieved not only economic success but also a level of political clout that was disproportionate to its size.

Washington, opposed to Cuba's political evolution and spurred on by politically active Cubans living in Miami, continued to try to isolate Castro in Latin America. Just 1 year after Castro took power, in 1960, the U.S. government launched a trade embargo against Cuba in retaliation for Cuba's state appropriations and seizures of the assets of U.S. businesses. The trade embargo, which Cuba terms a blockade, and travel restrictions later imposed on most U.S. citizens, continue to this day. In 1961 the United States broke diplomatic relations with Cuba, and CIA-trained Cuban exiles launched an attempted overthrow of the Castro government. The Bay of Pigs mission was an utter fiasco and a severe black mark against the Kennedy administration. Cuba's resistance strengthened Castro's resolve to stand up to the United States.

Castro had not revealed any Communist leanings in the decade since coming to power, but soon after the Bay of Pigs, Castro declared himself a Marxist-Leninist. Some historians have argued that the aggressive ploys of the U.S. government were fundamental in pushing the Cuban government into the arms of the American enemy in the Cold War, the Soviet Union and its Eastern bloc of potential trading partners. The USSR was only too eager to develop a strategic relationship with an ideological opponent of Washington in the backyard of the United States. By the end of the 1980s, the USSR dominated Cuban trade and provided Cuba with subsidies worth an estimated annual $5 billion.

In the fall of 1962, the Soviet Union under Nikita Khrushchev installed 42 medium-range nuclear missiles in Cuba. A tense standoff ensued when Kennedy ordered a naval blockade on the island and demanded that the existing missiles be dismantled. The world waited anxiously for 6 days until Khrushchev finally caved to U.S. demands to turn back his ships. The possibility of a nuclear war was averted in return for a U.S. promise never to invade Cuba.

Another 200,000 people abandoned Cuba as part of the Freedom Flights Program between 1965 and 1971. In 1980, Castro lifted travel restrictions and opened the port of Mariel (west of Havana); during the Mariel Boatlift, at least 125,000 Cubans—many of whom Washington charged were criminals and drug addicts—made it to U.S. shores before President Carter forced Castro to close the floodgates.

## THE SPECIAL PERIOD

Soviet trade and subsidies propped up Cuba's heavily centralized and poorly performing economy until the end of the 1980s. But the fall of the Berlin Wall and dismantling of the Soviet Union suddenly left Cuba in an untenable position, as supplies of food, oil, and hard currency were cut off while the U.S. trade embargo continued.

The Cuban government initiated a "Special Period" in 1990—a euphemism for harsh new austerity measures and hardship to be borne by the large majority of Cubans. Rationing of basic goods had existed for most of Castro's years in power, but limited government distribution now included many more necessities. During the Special Period and years since, most Cubans found it virtually impossible to subsist on rations alone.

Complicating the delicate situation was the 1992 Cuba Democracy Act, which broadened the U.S. embargo to cover a ban on trade with Cuba for foreign subsidiaries of U.S. companies. Though the U.S. government denies that its trade embargo can be blamed for the shortcomings in the Cuban economy and resulting shortages of food and medicine, many analysts believe that the embargo has greatly exacerbated the difficulties experienced by ordinary Cubans. Meanwhile, Castro has held on to power and made few concessions, even using the U.S. trade restrictions to his advantage: They have given him something and someone to blame for Cuba's grinding poverty and lack of goods.

With the economy in shambles, the Cuban government has been forced to introduce a limited number of capitalist measures. Foreign investment, which has taken the form of joint ventures primarily in the fields of tourism and mineral and oil exploration, has been openly encouraged. Castro, with inescapable irony, legalized the American dollar in 1993—even establishing state-owned, dollar-only stores, small-scale private enterprises like *casas particulares* and *paladares* (private homestays and restaurants), and the introduction of private farmers' markets. While these capitalist initiatives have benefited some Cubans, giving them access to dollars (through jobs in tourism or relatives sending remittances from abroad), the dual economy has ultimately turned many other Cubans into have-nots, unequal in a socialist society.

In August 1994, in a frantic safety-valve measure designed to alleviate some of the economic pressure on the state, Castro lifted restrictions on those wishing to leave. More than 30,000 Cubans accepted the invitation and set out across dangerous waters to Florida on *balseros* (homemade rafts). Faced with the political embarrassment of an influx of poor Cubans, President Clinton abolished the standing U.S. policy granting automatic asylum to Cuban refugees. Instead, they were returned to the Guantánamo Bay Naval Base to await repatriation.

After Castro visited the Vatican in 1996, Pope John Paul II returned the favor. His visit to Cuba in 1998 prompted a relaxation of the government's harsh views of the Catholic Church in Cuba. In late 1999, 6-year-old Elián González became the latest face of political animosity between the United States and Cuba. González survived for 2 days alone on a raft after his mother and other escapees had perished, only to become the object of an international tug-of-war. Castro and most Cubans, in huge demonstrations, demanded the boy's return to be with his father in northern Cuba. Castro's opponents in the United States sought to allow the boy to stay with distant relatives in Miami. After weeks of wrangling, the Immigration and Naturalization Service returned Elián to his father and Cuba, where he received a hero's welcome.

The normally quiet U.S. naval base at Guantánamo Bay has been in the news in recent years after Al Qaeda prisoners from the wars in Afghanistan and Iraq were taken to the base for interrogation and detention. Former President Jimmy Carter made a historic visit to Cuba in spring 2002, voicing support for Castro's call for an end to the trade embargo and travel restrictions while also criticizing the Cuban government's lack of democracy. Carter met with dissidents and gave an uncensored and at times harshly critical speech in front of Castro that was broadcast on Cuban television.

However, Carter's visit had little lasting effect. In 2003, Castro jailed some 75 prominent dissidents and government critics, imposing stiff sentences following abbreviated trials. In early 2004 and again in 2006, the Bush administration tightened the screws on U.S. citizens' right to travel to Cuba, virtually eliminating all educational and humanitarian licenses and severely reducing the amount of time and money that Cuban-Americans can spend in Cuba.

## 2 Cuba Today

From the stunning overthrow of the dictator Fulgencio Batista in 1959 by a ragtag revolutionary army to Castro's tenacious hold on power, Cuba was one of the major stories of the 20th century. And although virtually everything about Cuba is filtered through an ideological lens, Cuba is a fascinating living laboratory of social and political experimentation, and a test case for a people's perseverance. A defiant Castro has weathered the fierce opposition of the U.S. government and the hostility of Cuban exiles in Miami, just 145km (90 miles) to the north. While some of his radical reform goals have been achieved, Cubans have also been greatly disheartened by the regime's abject failures. The Cuban people have been forced to make unfathomable sacrifices in the face of a poorly planned (and worse performing) economy and the ongoing American trade embargo.

Cuba was once the dazzling iconoclast, held in awe by much of Latin America for its willingness to stand up to the United States. Lately, though, Castro finds himself increasingly isolated, and few are those who don't believe that Cuba is a Communist dinosaur. Castro has promoted foreign investment and joint ventures in oil, mining, and tourism, but Cuba remains willfully individualistic.

The country's uniqueness is also the source of its phenomenal appeal. Cuba is a puzzling anachronism, a creaky and sputtering country caught in a tortuous time warp. Many of Havana's crumbling colonial buildings are little more than facades, propped up like a movie set. While most of the planet plunges ahead at a dizzying digital pace, Cuba crawls along in slow motion. Homes, which Cubans do not actually own but are instead given title to by the state, have only the most rudimentary appliances— if they have any at all. Vintage Chevy and Cadillac jalopies from the '40s and '50s, their chrome fenders pock-marked and their engines patched together with a hodgepodge of parts, lumber down the streets of dimly lit cities. In rural areas, even antique cars are a luxury; transportation is more commonly by oxen-led cart and rickety iron bicycle.

To many visitors, Cuba offers a mystifying but welcome retreat from the whiz-bang of technology and convenience most of us have become accustomed to. Groups of underemployed men while away the hours playing dominoes on card tables set up in the street. Septets of octogenarian musicians play traditional Cuban *son,* music with roots in the 1920s and whose rhythms are largely unaffected by outside influence and changing global tastes. Neighbors gather on door stoops in the wilting heat of the late afternoon to chat and fan themselves, and they form friendly networks working together to solve problems of accommodation, transportation, plumbing, and electricity.

Many travelers, convinced that Cuba cannot forever remain a land of time travel, hasten to experience the country before it gets reeled in by a ravenous Western world. Cuba's tourist potential is almost unlimited, and the government has embraced tourism as its best and perhaps only hope to bring in hard currency and employ large numbers of people. The largest island in the Caribbean, Cuba is abundantly blessed with palm trees, sultry temperatures, hip-swiveling rhythms, stunning beaches, warm people, and a surfeit of rum and the world's finest hand-rolled cigars. In the mid-1980s, only about 250,000 annual visitors traveled to Cuba; in 2007, nearly 3 million visitors are expected. Tourism has now surpassed the source of Cuba's original wealth, the sugar industry, to become the country's top revenue earner. If all Americans were allowed to travel legally, politicians and hoteliers reason, Cuba might receive as many as 10 million visitors annually. Yet massive tourism is still a dream in Cuba. Most travelers still cling to package tours and tourist resorts clustered on beaches.

Modern Cuba is a tangled mass of contradictions. The socialist regime, ostensibly founded upon an egalitarian revolution, doesn't allow its own citizens to step foot into certain tourist enclaves, including many resorts, hotels, and restaurants. The centralized economy is dependent upon capitalistic joint ventures with foreign investors from Canada, Great Britain, Germany, Italy, and Spain. A long list of goods and services are readily available to foreigners but cannot be enjoyed by nationals. Plenty of Cubans survive only with the assistance of political and religious opponents of the regime who've fled the country and send hundreds of millions of dollars in hard currency each year to relatives.

Cubans often fall back on an all-purpose national refrain to describe what their lives are like: *No es fácil.* It isn't easy. Cubans are specialists in what might be called the *arte de inventar*, the art of inventing solutions where there are none. That means fighting to make ends meet through odd jobs and hustling. Setting up neighborhood networks that distribute contraband goods, such as cigars nicked from the tobacco factory. Running illicit *paladares* in living rooms and backyards, serving black market lobster or beef. Driving unlicensed taxis fueled by pilfered gasoline. Cuba is an entire nation jimmy-rigged and bandaged with duct tape.

Unless you're ensconced in a gleaming, all-inclusive beach resort, where the realities of Cuban life are whitewashed for the benefit of tourists, the grinding deficiencies of the Cuban economy and bottomless needs of the Cuban people are hard to ignore. Talk to almost any Cuban and he'll tell you about appallingly overcrowded conditions, state rations that don't cover basic needs, the scarcity of basic commodities, and the $10-to-$20 monthly salaries paid in the almost worthless Cuban currency, the peso. Workers trained by the state as engineers and doctors instead scramble for more lucrative positions as bellboys, while others cobble together a few dollars worth of hard currency from occasional, often extralegal, odd jobs. Ration booklets allow Cuban citizens to buy a certain amount of basic goods at highly subsidized prices in Cuban pesos. However, the rations allotted do not suffice: just 6 pounds of rice and sugar, 20 ounces of beans, 2 pounds of sugar, 1 pound of chicken, two bottles of cooking oil, some bread, plus some cigarettes, coffee, and a few other goods. Anything beyond those miserly provisions—the odd piece of beef, a pair of decent shoes—must be purchased on the black market or in hard currency–only stores.

Yet Cuba is remarkably free of the execrable poverty sadly common in Africa, India, and even other parts of Latin America. Housing is provided by the state—homeless people sleeping on the streets are nowhere to be seen in Cuba—and all citizens receive regular food rations. Many appear surprisingly well dressed, no doubt a privilege of possessing a job that earns a few dollars or having family members outside of Cuba who send money that helps ease the pain.

Fidel Castro took power with a commitment to remake the nation by overhauling its economy, land ownership, education system, and healthcare. On a social agenda, Cuba has been remarkably successful. All Cubans receive free healthcare (though most hospitals and pharmacies are lacking in the most basic supplies, like aspirin and X-ray plates). Compulsory state education through high school is free, and the national university system has produced some extremely accomplished professionals in medicine and the sciences. Average life expectancy rose from 57 years in 1958 to 77 in 2006—the highest in Latin America. Infant mortality, just 6.22 per 1,000 births, is the lowest in the region and equal to or better than many developed countries. Literacy rates are above 95% (the government claims to have erased illiteracy entirely), violent crime is almost nonexistent, and the pervasive sexism and racism of prerevolutionary Cuba have given way to a more equitable landscape.

Those achievements receive less attention, though, than Cuba's strangled economy and continued political repression. Opponents of the socialist regime, both outside of Cuba and increasingly within the country, make the case that Cuba is a nation with no semblance of democracy. A single political party dominates all Cuban life. Cubans cannot speak freely, the media are state-owned and closely orchestrated by the Communist Party, and ordinary citizens have no rights to travel beyond Cuba.

Hundreds of thousands of Castro's early opponents fled Cuba in the early days of the Revolution, when the state was busy expropriating private property, land, and businesses. Since then thousands more have tried, only a few successfully, to make it to U.S. shores, often in rickety *balseros* (rafts). The less daring but equally hopeful form daily queues at the U.S. Interests Office in Havana and other foreign embassies desperately hoping for exit visas. On three major occasions, including the Mariel Boatlift in 1980, Castro has sought to relieve pressure by allowing large groups, many of them deemed "undesirables," to emigrate.

The U.S. trade embargo and travel restrictions are still firmly in place, and President George W. Bush has made them even more stringent. But the embargo has done nothing to bring down Castro and little to force him to adopt more inclusive, democratic policies. In fact, the U.S. stance has emboldened Fidel Castro, giving him a tangible enemy to rally his troops against, and may have even stifled change in Cuba. As one Cuban told me, "Fidel eats well every day. Don't worry about him. As for the rest of us, well, that's another question."

Despite years of difficulty and isolation, *La Revolución,* now nearly 50 years old, continues to be the nation's rallying cry and raison d'etre. Schoolchildren don't become Boy or Girl Scouts, but Young Communist Pioneers. Secretive local chapters of the Committee for the Defense of the Revolution (CDR) keep tabs on dissenters and those not upholding the party line. Throughout the country, giant billboards function like government pep talks to convince a population more worried about shoes and food than ideology to stay on the path. Billboards proclaim quaint notions like VICTORIA DE IDEAS (A Victory of Ideas), VIVIMOS EN UN PAIS LIBRE (We Live in a Free Country), LA REVOLUCION SOMOS NOSOTROS (We Are the Revolution), and even the melancholy rationalization SOMOS FELICES AQUI (We're Happy Here). Larger-than-life portraits of heroes and martyrs like Che Guevara (the roguish icon of revolution the world over), José Martí, Camilo Cienfuegos, and "Los Cinco" (five suspected spies convicted and imprisoned in the United States) guard the entrances to towns and are plastered on the walls of shops, offices, and homes. Perhaps fittingly, most of these billboards and portraits are now worn and faded.

Amid the extraordinary dilapidation of Havana and other decaying towns, it's near impossible for travelers not to wonder: What must this place once have looked like? Formerly grand, and now just badly faded and deteriorated buildings stand—if barely so—as harsh evidence of 4 decades of frustration, empty state coffers, and bankrupt promises of an idealistic, battle-hardened regime. Cubans are exhorted to fight on to bring the Revolution to fruition, but many Cubans, especially the young who've known nothing but Fidel, are weary of waiting. *Un año más*—one more year, they say.

Cuba, though, is as exhilarating as it is perplexing. One of the most exciting, mind-bending, and sensation-tingling countries one can visit, Cuba is a flood of indelible images. Many are inspiring, others heartbreaking. An open-air cafe with a smiling band of preternaturally cool musicians locked in a perfect groove. Huge crowds of hitchhiking Cubans gathered on the side of the road, desperate for a lift. Noisy Carnival *rumbas* and conga groups piercing the heat with Afro-Caribbean rhythms. Sexy couples with well-oiled hips gliding across dance floors. Those combative billboards forlornly pitched along the side of empty highways. Crowded *camellos,* crazy people-hauler flatbed trucks that look like urban transportation in a post-apocalyptic world. Mile-long lines for ice cream at

Coppelia shops. Kids playing *pelota,* the national pastime of baseball, with a stick in the hollows of a ruined building.

But perhaps the truest picture of Cuba comes from the people themselves. Resilient and eternally patient Cubans somehow find the will to rise above devastating poverty, shortages, dense bureaucracy, and political authoritarianism. Hospitable like few others, they invite visitors into their cramped homes even if they've nothing to offer them. Schoolchildren, like an ad for the UN in identical maroon and mustard-colored uniforms, smile sweetly for photographs.

Cuba remains a quandary and a country full of potential. Hope can be seen in the painstaking restoration of landmark colonial buildings in Habana Vieja, whose decrepitude only a few years ago was the perfect metaphor for Cuba. Who can predict what will become of Cuba after Castro? Hope grows on both sides of the political spectrum for greater engagement, but as always, intransigence lingers. And—as Castro prepares to turn 80—Cuba soldiers on.

## 3 Cuban Culture

### TOURIST APARTHEID & *JINETERISMO*

One of the most disconcerting aspects of contemporary Cuba is the government's creation of exclusive "foreigner-only" tourism zones where Cuban nationals aren't welcome. Effectively, there are two Cubas, a reality that reeks of something akin to tourism apartheid, as many observers have noted. One Cuba is the gritty and sometimes grim country where things don't always work and consumer goods are hard to come by. The other Cuba is tailor-made for tourists at beach resorts and tourist-friendly draws like Habana Vieja. There, in ultra-modern hotels and restaurants that feature imported products and English-speaking waiters, ordinary Cubans aren't allowed to set foot. At all-inclusive beach resort destinations like Cayo Santa Maria and Cayo Coco, the line drawn between the foreigners and nationals is a literal one: a guarded border checkpoint beyond which unauthorized Cubans cannot pass. Foreigners need nothing more than a passport for access to the finest beaches, the best coastal resort hotels, and a selection of restaurants and foods that are beyond the imagination of average Cubans. In resort areas like those, the only Cubans guests see are the ones wearing uniforms—the staff.

On rare occasions, Cubans are given merit vacations as part of a state incentive program and allowed to vacation for a very nominal rate at one of the lesser, Cuban-owned hotels in a beach resort such as Playa Santa Lucía or Cayo Coco. The irony—that achieving beyond your programmed goals and working hard to advance the socialist nation may win a Cuban worker the right to vacation on Cuban soil where only foreigners are permitted—can't be lost on anyone.

The unequal relationship between hosts and guests is present in other forms, too. A troubling divide has developed in Cuban society, between those who have legitimate access to hard currency, either through family members who send remittances from abroad, or jobs in foreign businesses or tourism that provide tips or wages in dollars, euros, or CUCs, and those have no way to earn them. Most Cubans have to invent ways to get their hands on hard currency. The presence of foreign tourists from Europe and North America and dependence on the hard currency they bring have produced an uncomfortable situation in which many Cubans are reduced to hustling for hard currency, since state salaries paid in pesos are woefully inadequate and dollars, euros, or CUCs are necessary for a wide spectrum of goods and services. The word for "hustler," *jinetero* (literally, jockey) is a ubiquitous noun in the Cuban vocabulary; female escorts, or hookers, are often called *jineteras* or, more prosaically, *chicas* (girls).

Hustling foreigners is merely an extension of the scrambling that for so long has been a way of life in Cuba. Improvising on a daily basis and depending upon the support networks of families and friends is largely the only way to get by, and Cubans gladly extend the practice to visitors. People everywhere are willing to help out in a pinch. If you need a place to stay, a place to eat, a ride somewhere—anything can be arranged at a moment's notice.

Hustling is most pervasive where tourists are most common: Havana (especially Habana Vieja) and Santiago de Cuba, which has some of the most persistent *jineteros* on the island. Tourists on the street are met with a barrage of friendly sounding but pestering questions, all delivered with the aim of selling something: "Hey man! Where you fron? You wan paladar? You wan cigar? Chica?" Most small-time hustlers on the streets are innocuous enough, but their constant mantras can become tiresome and, worse, prompt unfair suspicions of the motives of all Cubans. The good news is that most hustlers are rather easily waved off with either a well-directed glare or a simple, polite, "No, gracias." While it's easy to put your guard up, it would be unfortunate if visitors allowed some two-bit hustling to deflect all overtures from locals. The Cuban people are warm, naturally gregarious, and keenly interested in speaking with foreigners. To an uncommon degree, a highlight of visiting Cuba is interacting with Cubans and sharing the realities of your respective lives—the best way to penetrate decades of disinformation campaigns.

*Jineteras* are a regrettable constant of tourism in Cuba. Middle-aged men from Italy, Spain, Germany, and other countries are conspicuously accompanied by much younger, and much more attractive short-term girlfriends, usually mulattas and Afro-Cubans. Some are professional prostitutes, with *chulos* (pimps) and a simple work-for-hire approach. But many more are merely young women (many with dependent children) and, alarmingly, girls looking for temporary companionship with a foreign male as a way to get by, an admission ticket to the other Cuba they wouldn't ordinarily see: a chance to visit a decent restaurant or a nightclub.

Cuban society is marked by sexual permissiveness and, though prostitution is illegal, a relaxed, laissez-faire attitude toward *jineteras* and foreign tourists. Casas particulares in many provinces are legally permitted to register *chicas* as the guests of their foreign clients. In the few municipalities that have ordinances forbidding such intercultural dalliances, casa owners complain that they are unfairly singled out and losing money because they are unable to rent out rooms to their most habitual clients. The shameless selling of sex may very well shock and repulse some visitors to the island. For Cuban tourism, it's a large and ongoing problem, no matter how blasé Cubans may appear to be. Foreign men on the prowl are a dollar-earning component of tourism not just for the girls but for the state, and the Cuban government, which touts itself as an exceptional promoter of social justice, can be seen as complicit in the systematic abuse of its young women. Equally damaging for the state, the current situation harkens back to the rampant prostitution sex shows of pre-revolutionary days.

## CUBAN MUSIC

Perhaps no other nation—certainly no other nation of its size—is as spectacularly endowed musically as is Cuba. The seductive sounds of richly percussive

Cuban music are, in many people's minds, Cuba's greatest export. In the late 1990s, a series of records and a documentary film brought a group of aging Cuban musicians to the world's attention. The unexpected popularity abroad of the Buena Vista Social Club and its individual artists—Ibrahim Ferrer, Compay Segundo, Rubén González, Eliades Ochoa, and Omara Portuondo—made traditional Cuban sounds very much in demand throughout Cuba and internationally. Buena Vista and company, though, is only the latest round of Cuban music to circle the globe, echoing the earlier mambo and cha-cha-chá crazes that took the United States and Europe by storm in the 1950s.

Within Cuba, music is a daily presence across the island, from rural areas and dusty provincial towns to the capital. It seeps out of cafes and *casas de la trova* in the midafternoon and thunders out of dance halls as the sun rises over the *Malecón*. The musical diet is a dizzying menu of styles with uncommon appeal, so emphatically tropical that you can almost hear the humidity in the vocals, chords, and percussion.

Cuba's musical heritage, an onomatopoeic stew of salsa, *rumba,* mambo, *son, danzón,* and cha-cha-chá, stems from the country's rich mix of African, Spanish, French, and Haitian cultures. The roots of contemporary Cuban popular music lie in the 19th century's combination of African drums and rhythms along with Spanish guitar and melody. Most forms of Cuban music feature Latin stringed instruments, African bongos, congas, and *claves* (wooden percussion sticks), and auxiliary instruments such as maracas and *guiros.*

The heartbeat of Cuban music is the *clave,* which refers to a distinctive rhythm and the instrument used to play it. While the actual instrument is not necessarily played in every song, all Cuban rhythms are built up from the simple concept of the *clave.* There is an incredibly sophisticated theory surrounding this five-note beat—but in a nutshell, it's a repetitive, two-bar pattern with two slight variations: the *son clave,* which is the basis of folkloric and popular styles like *son, son montuno,* and mambo; and the *rumba clave,* which is the basis of folkloric and religious styles with a more distinctly syncopated and African flavor, especially the percussion-and-vocal music known as *rumba.*

The perennial form of Cuban traditional music is **son** (literally, "sound"; pronounced *sohn*), a style of popular dance music that originated in the eastern, poorer half of the country known as El Oriente in the early 1900s. Though it was born of miscegenation, *son's* development in the 20th century encountered very little of the cross-fertilization of genres that normally takes place. *Son* thus remains a profoundly traditional and pure indigenous style of music. African rhythm instruments (most notably the bongos and maracas) combine with the Cuban *tres,* a small, high-pitched guitar featuring three sets of double strings. Giants of *son* include Trio Matamoros, Ignacio Pineiro, and Sexteto Habanero, while current stars playing traditional *son* include La Vieja Trova Santiaguera and the individuals who formed the Buena Vista Social Club. The percussive swing of *son* can be heard in many newer forms of Cuban music; it forms one of the lynchpins of modern salsa.

**Son Montuno,** which is closely related to *son,* is important for its conscious fusion of several formerly unconnected elements. Developed by blind *tres*-player Arsenio Rodríguez, *son montuno* incorporated the conga drum into popular music for the first time, and assigned the repetitive *tres* arpeggios known as *montunos* to the piano. This style sounds a bit like a more relaxed version of cha-cha-chá.

**Rumba** is some of the most intensely African music in Cuba, an outgrowth of

Afro-Cuban religion and slave music. Based on percussion and voice, it features call-and-response in both African languages and Cuban Spanish. There are three primary variations: *yambú,* which is the slowest; *guaguancó,* with a relaxed mid-tempo feel; and *columbia,* which is the most frenetic. *Rumba* is prominently featured in *Carnaval* celebrations in Santiago de Cuba; perhaps the best-known *rumba* group in Cuba, now in its third generation, is the legendary Muñequitos de Matanzas.

**Danzón,** which evolved from the contradanza performed by Haitian and French immigrants in the late 19th century, is a European dance hall style played by *orquestas.* **Boleros** are slow-paced romantic ballads, while **trovas** are ballads that have been performed since colonial days. The **nueva trova** is a style of acoustic, politically motivated music that arose after the Revolution and coincident with *nueva canción* throughout Latin America. The biggest stars of nueva trova, still hugely popular throughout the Spanish-speaking world, are Silvio Rodríguez and Pablo Milanés. Newer proponents to look for include Santiago Feliú, Amaury Pérez, and Carlos Varela. **Cuban jazz,** incorporating sophisticated Afro-Cuban elements, is much prized in international jazz circles. Two of the genre's big names are the pianists Chucho Valdés and Gonzalo Rubalcaba.

The origins of **mambo** are hotly debated. Some argue that brothers Orestes and Israel "Cachao" Lopez invented the style when they incorporated African influences into the *danzón,* while others are convinced that flutist Arcaño pioneered the genre. Regardless, there is no question that bandleader Perez Prado first popularized mambo when he made it the focus of his sound.

*Songo* was created by members of Los Van Van, one of the most popular Cuban bands since the 1970s. The rhythm was largely the brainchild of drummer "Changuito" (José Luis Quintana) and bassist Juan Carlos Formell, who fused the funky grooves of Motown's James Jamerson with a traditional style known as **charanga.** The innovations of Los Van Van led directly to **timba,** the rowdiest style to date. This heavily amplified dance music displays a mature knowledge of jazz, hip hop and funk, and folkloric Afro-Cuban styles. Leading groups include NG La Banda, Bamboleo, Charanga Habanera, and Klimax.

Singer **Beny Moré** has to be mentioned as the most emblematic voice of Cuba. This beloved hero mastered practically every style Cuban music, but is perhaps best remembered for his treatments of *son, son montuno,* and boleros. Any CD collection of Moré provides a crash course on the music of Cuba.

You can and will hear live music anywhere you go in Cuba, but the best places for authentic traditional *son* and more modern styles are Havana, Trinidad, Camagüey, Santiago de Cuba, and Baracoa. The last three possess the best Casas de la Trova in the country, spots thick with sultry air, slowly rotating ceiling fans, and grinning octogenarians plunking away on weathered guitars and stand-up basses. Cubans seem only too happy to share the dance floor with tentative foreigners.

## CUBAN MUSIC IN THE UNITED STATES

Cuba's musical impact in America didn't begin with the Buena Vista Social Club. It seems that Cuban music is re-discovered by nearly every generation in the U.S. Afro-Cuban influences have been discerned by musicologists in the music of New Orleans (most notably in the "second line" parade beat), but it first swept the U.S. in 1931, when Don Azpiazu's version of "El Manicero" ("The Peanut Vendor") became a hit. This tune, which has been recorded countless times,

## Afro-Cuban Percussion Instruments

**Tumbadoras**   Generally known outside of Cuba as congas, these tall, conical drums are typically played by seated musicians. Three similar-looking *tumbadoras* are employed in *rumba* music: *tumba,* the largest and lowest in pitch; *quinto,* the smallest and highest in pitch, which solos and interacts with the dancers; and *conga* or *segundo,* which falls in the middle in terms of size and pitch. In a contemporary mambo or salsa group, two or three *tumbadoras* are simultaneously played by a single musician. By varying the shape and position of their hands, *congueros* (conga players) are able to elicit an impressive variety of sounds from each drum. Famous proponents include Chano Pozo, Mongo Santamaría, and Tata Güines.

**Timbales**   These two metal drums, about the size of snare drums and mounted on a single stand, are known as *macho* (smaller and higher in pitch) and *hembra* (larger and lower in pitch). The primary rhythms are most commonly played on the sides of the drums (in mambo, a syncopated pattern called *cáscara,* or "shell," is played) and various figures on cowbells mounted to the timbales. This instrument evolved from classical music's tympani, and was first used in *danzón.* Without doubt the most famous *timbalero* was actually the Harlem-born Puerto Rican, Tito Puente, although there are numerous Cubans with greater facility than "El Rey." Most Cuban *timbaleros* since Changuito have expanded their setups to include the typical components of the American drum set.

**Bongos**   Although associated with spaced-out beatnik poets, the bongos are a very serious instrument in Cuba, particularly in *son.* Bongos consist of two wooden drums—also known as *macho* and *hembra*—that are joined in the center of each shell. The basic rhythm is *martillo* ("hammer"), which places the heaviest accent on the fourth beat of each bar. This pattern is broken up by improvisational riffs known as *repiques.* The *bongocero* is responsible for

spawned a minor craze for the "exotic" rhythms of Cuba, and the percussive parade music of *Carnaval* soon led to the popularity of the *conga* rhythm (albeit in an extremely diluted form). But the next major impact of authentic Cuban music was largely the work of Mario Bauzá, a classically trained arranger and clarinetist. Bauzá arrived in New York in the 1930s and was soon in heavy demand as a sideman. So great were his musical gifts that when a Cuban group needed a trumpet player able to play authentic styles, Bauzá mastered the instrument in a matter of days. He served for many years as musical director for jazz drummer Chick Webb, and in that capacity helped discover Ella Fitzgerald. While working with Cab Calloway, Bauzá urged his boss to hire Dizzy Gillespie.

But the real impact of Mario Bauzá came when he was hired by brother-in-law Frank Grillo (better known as "Machito") as musical director for his new band. Bauzá insisted that their band be called the "Afro-Cubans," clearly stressing the roots of the music. He combined traditional Cuban rhythms with all the tricks of the trade he learned as a jazz musician, such as complicated chord progressions, playing a handheld cowbell called *campana;* this is employed during musical climaxes, such as the *coro,* in which vocalists sing repetitive backgrounds, and instrumental solos.

*Maracas* Typically made of rawhide cylinders filled with seeds or beads of some sort, and attached to short wooden handles, *maracas* are usually played by background singers. They are used in many styles of music, but are vital to *son.*

*Guiro* This handheld instrument is simply a hollowed-out gourd. A thin stick is dragged along grooves that have been carved into the side, yielding a distinctive tone. *Guiros* are also played by background singers. Although used in many folkloric and popular styles, its sound is most emblematic in cha-cha-chá.

*Chekeré* A large, circular gourd surrounded by beads fixed onto net-like strings, this simple instrument yields a surprising variety of sounds, which are produced by shaking and striking the *chekeré*. It is most often used in explicitly African folkloric and religious genres, but it has also made its way into popular styles.

*Claves* Comprised of two thick cylinders of wood, usually about 7" long, this instrument plays a relentlessly repetitive and syncopated pattern. More than an instrument, *la clave* is in a sense the paradigm behind all Afro-Cuban music. The particular variation (*rumba clave* or *son clave*) and the "direction" of the *clave* (meaning which bar of the two-bar pattern is played first) determine what the other instruments can and cannot do; it even determines what the more attuned dancers do. It's a fascinating topic that has yielded academic papers and years of intensive study by musicians. If you have an opportunity, ask a friendly *Cubano* or *Cubana* to try to explain it while music is being played.

dense harmonies, and daring solos. The success of this band quickly spawned a host of other mambo groups in New York, most notably those led by Puerto Ricans Tito Puente and Tito Rodríguez. Puente was not only a great showman and solid percussionist, but also a Juilliard-trained composer and pianist who demanded the highest musical standards in his band. His friendly rival, the golden-voiced Tito Rodríguez, also trained at Juilliard and held his groups to equally exacting standards.

Throughout the 1950s, mambo and its slower offshoot cha-cha-chá were inescapable. New York clubs like the Palladium were packed to the gills and populated with stars (Brando and Duvall were regulars, and became pro-caliber dancers along the way). "I Love Lucy" of course featured the exploits of fictional bandleader Ricky Ricardo; while Desi Arnaz always took a more sanitized approach to the music, songs such as "Babalu" hinted at the real roots (*Babalú-Ayé* is part of the Santería pantheon of *orishás*).

As mambo was gaining popularity in New York, a parallel trend was developing. **Latin Jazz** featured many of the elements of mambo, but with a firm focus on the incendiary solos of Be-Bop. Mario Bauzá instructed Dizzy Gillespie in the intricacies of Cuban rhythmic theory, and Dizzy became interested in combining this foundation with Be-Bop. When Bauzá introduced Dizzy to Cuban conga legend Chano Pozo, all the elements were in place. Pozo's tune "Manteca," co-penned by Gillespie and Gil Fuller, became a smash hit in 1947. Pozo, known for his fiery temper, was tragically gunned down in Harlem by another Cuban tough.

In a way, mambo is still popular today, though known as **salsa.** This genre, mainly developed in New York City by Puerto Rican immigrants, is explicitly premised upon the rhythms of Cuba. Pianos still play *tres*-inspired figures; the percussion section is comprised of three distinctly Cuban instruments (congas, bongos, and timbales); basses still play the syncopated *tumbao* pattern used in *son;* and the two-bar *clave* rhythm is the seed from which all these components grow. Salsa is, as Celia Cruz once said, all Cuban rhythms joined together.

## SANTERIA & AFRO-CUBAN CULTURE

Cuba's prominent African-influenced culture is one of the nation's defining characteristics. African culture brought by slaves and developed within the context of the Spanish colony has had a profound impact on religion, music, and indeed, virtually all of Cuban society.

One of the most salient aspects of Afro-Cuban culture is *Santería* (also called Regla de Ocha). Frequently misunderstood and misinterpreted as a religious cult or form of "voodoo," Santería is in fact a major syncretic and animistic religion that by most estimates has a greater following in Cuba than does Catholicism. Its practice is not restricted to Afro-Cubans or a certain socioeconomic class.

Santería has its roots in the Yoruba culture of West Africa and today is also practiced in varying forms and under various names in Puerto Rico, Haiti, Brazil, and other countries with large populations of descendants of African slaves. Practitioners of Santería worship a complex pantheon of deities, called *orishás,* each with a specific character as in classical Greek mythology. In Cuba, African slaves continued to practice their religion by melding it with the Catholicism of colonizers and slave owners: all the *orishás* had (and continue to have) a parallel Catholic saint, which allowed followers of Santería to mask their identity, and thus their true religion, from slave owners, who persecuted such native expressions of faith. The blurring of lines between Catholicism and Santería continues to this day, with many believers following a line of faith that essentially merges the two.

The *orishás,* believed to be the direct emissaries of God (Olofi), rule over every aspect of nature and life on earth. The faithful develop very personal relationships with individual *orishás* and look to them for both spiritual and material guidance. Followers use prayer, song, and ritualistic offerings (including occasional animal sacrifices) to communicate with *orishás,* though they most often need the assistance of a *santero,* or priest, to perform rituals that allow them to divine the *orishás'* instructions and plans for individuals. Altars or shrines are kept in many homes.

The different *orishás* are distinguished by colors and numbers; they also have distinct human characteristics, such as favorite foods and other items they prefer to receive as offerings. Across Cuba, one can see people wearing the colored beads of their chosen saint—red and white for Changó, blue and white for Yemayá. Those undergoing initiation rites to become *santeros* dress head-to-toe in white.

## The Major Orishás

Each *orishá* is associated with a range of attributes and characteristics, including Catholic saints, unique personalities, colors, numbers, days of the week, feast days, and even ceremonial rhythms. Each *orishá* has numerous manifestations that in turn have distinct characteristics. A sampling of the *orishás* and some of their attributes follows.

*Eleggúa* Represented by St. Antonio, Eleggúa is the keeper of all roads and doors. His colors are red and black, and his feast day is June 13. His day of the week is Monday, and his numbers are 3 and 21.

*Yemayá* The goddess of the sea is represented by la Virgen de Regla. The colors of Yemayá are blue and white. Her feast day is September 7. Her day is Saturday, and her number is 7.

*Changó* Represented by St. Bárbara, the god of war likes red and white. His feast is on December 4 (some followers of Santería find significance in the fact that legendary *conguero* Chano Pozo was murdered on the eve of St. Bárbara's feast, believing that he somehow provoked the displeasure of his *orishá*). Changó's day of the week is Friday. His numbers are 4 and 6.

*Ochún* The goddess of love and fertility is represented by la Virgen del Cobre. Her colors are green and yellow, and her feast is on September 8. Her day is Saturday, and her number is 5.

*Obatalá* Our Lady of Mercy represents the god of peace. His color is white, and his feast is September 24. Obatalá's day is Thursday, and his number is 8.

*Babalú-Ayé* Represented by St. Lazarus (the beggar mentioned in the Gospels, rather than the man Jesus raised from the dead), *Babalú-Ayé* is the god of illness and epidemics. His color is purple and his feast day is December 17. His days of the week are Friday and Wednesday, and his number is 17. The other *orishá's* hold him in such esteem that Babalú-Ayé is granted permission to possess any disciple, even if dedicated to a different *orishá*.

*Orúnla* St. Francis of Assissi represents the god of wisdom and divination. His colors are green and yellow, and his feast is on October 4. He is unique in that every day of the week is considered Orúnla's. His number is 16.

Havana's **Casa de Africa Museum,** Obrapía 157, between San Ignacio and Mercaderes in Habana Vieja (© **7/861-5798**), has exhibits on Santería for those interested in learning more. The museum is open Tuesday through Saturday from 9am to 5pm, Sunday from 9am to 1pm; admission is CUC$2. Through local contacts, Spanish-speaking visitors can sometimes arrange for a *santero* or *babalao* (high priest) to perform ritualistic divinations.

# Appendix B:
# Useful Spanish Terms & Phrases

Cubans speak fast and furiously. There's a very nasal and almost garbled quality to Cuban Spanish. Cubans tend to drop their final consonants, particularly the "s," and they don't roll their "rr"s particularly strongly, converting the "rr" into an almost "l" sound in words like *carro* or *perro*. Cubans seldom use the formal *usted* form, instead preferring to address almost everyone (except those much older or of particular social or political stature) as *tú*. Likewise, you'll almost never hear the terms *señor* or *señora* as forms of address—Cubans prefer *compañero* and *compañera*. Cubans are also direct. They will almost always answer the phone with a curt *"Diga,"* which translates roughly as a mix between "Tell me," "Say what?," and "Speak."

## 1 Basic Words & Phrases

| English | Spanish | Pronunciation |
|---|---|---|
| Good day | **Buenos días** | *bweh*-nohss *dee*-ahss |
| How are you? | **¿Cómo está?** | *koh*-moh ehss-*tah*? |
| Very well | **Muy bien** | mwee byehn |
| Thank you | **Gracias** | *grah*-syahss |
| You're welcome | **De nada** | day *nah*-dah |
| Goodbye | **Adiós** | ah-*dyohss* |
| Please | **Por favor** | pohr fah-*vor* |
| Yes | **Sí** | see |
| No | **No** | noh |
| Excuse me (to get by someone) | **Perdóneme** | pehr-*doh*-neh-meh |
| Excuse me (to begin a question) | **Disculpe** | dees-*kool*-peh |
| Give me | **Déme** | *deh*-meh |
| Where is . . . ? | **¿Dónde está . . . ?** | *dohn*-deh ehss-*tah* |
| the station | **la estación** | lah ehss-tah-*seown* |
| a hotel | **un hotel** | oon oh-*tel* |
| a gas station | **una estación de servicio** | *oo*-nah ehss-tah-*seown* deh sehr-*bee*-syoh |
| a restaurant | **un restaurante** | oon res-toh-*rahn*-teh |
| the toilet | **el baño** | el *bah*-nyoh |
| a good doctor | **un buen médico** | oon bwehn *meh*-thee-coh |
| the road to . . . | **el camino a/hacia . . .** | el cah-*mee*-noh ah/*ah*-syah |
| To the right | **A la derecha** | ah lah deh-*reh*-chah |

| To the left | **A la izquierda** | ah lah ees-*kyehr*-dah |
| Straight ahead | **Derecho** | deh-*reh*-choh |
| I would like . . . | **Quisiera . . .** | key-*syehr*-ah |
| to eat | **comer** | koh-*mehr* |
| a room | **una habitación** | *oon*-nah ah-bee-tah-*seown* |
| Do you have . . . ? | **¿Tiene usted . . . ?** | *tyeh*-neh oos-*ted* |
| How much is it? | **¿Cuánto cuesta?** | *kwahn*-toh *kwehss*-tah? |
| When? | **¿Cuándo?** | *kwahn*-doh? |
| What? | **¿Qué?** | kay? |
| There is | **(¿)Hay ( . . . ?)** | eye |
| (Is there . . . ?) | | |
| What is there? | **¿Qué hay?** | keh eye |
| Yesterday | **Ayer** | ah-*yer* |
| Today | **Hoy** | oy |
| Tomorrow | **Mañana** | mah-*nyah*-nah |
| Good | **Bueno** | *bweh*-noh |
| Bad | **Malo** | *mah*-loh |
| Better (best) | **(Lo) Mejor** | (loh) meh-*hor* |
| More | **Más** | mahs |
| Less | **Menos** | *meh*-nohss |
| No smoking | **Se prohibe fumar** | seh pro-*hee*-beh foo-*mahr* |

## NUMBERS

| | | | | | |
|---|---|---|---|---|---|
| 1 | **uno** | *ooh*-noh | 16 | **dieciseis** | dyess-ee-*sayss* |
| 2 | **dos** | dohss | 17 | **diecisiete** | dyess-ee-*syeh*-teh |
| 3 | **tres** | trehss | 18 | **dieciocho** | dyess-ee-*oh*-choh |
| 4 | **cuatro** | *kwah*-troh | 19 | **diecinueve** | dyess-ee-*nweh*-beh |
| 5 | **cinco** | *seen*-koh | 20 | **veinte** | *bayn*-teh |
| 6 | **seis** | sayss | 30 | **treinta** | *trayn*-tah |
| 7 | **siete** | *syeh*-teh | 40 | **cuarenta** | kwah-*ren*-tah |
| 8 | **ocho** | *oh*-choh | 50 | **cincuenta** | seen-*kwen*-tah |
| 9 | **nueve** | *nweh*-beh | 60 | **sesenta** | seh-*sehn*-tah |
| 10 | **diez** | dyess | 70 | **setenta** | seh-*ten*-tah |
| 11 | **once** | *ohn*-seh | 80 | **ochenta** | oh-*chen*-tah |
| 12 | **doce** | *doh*-seh | 90 | **noventa** | noh-*behn*-tah |
| 13 | **trece** | *treh*-seh | 100 | **cien** | *syehn* |
| 14 | **catorce** | kah-*tor*-seh | 200 | **doscientos** | doh-*syehn*-tohs |
| 15 | **quince** | *keen*-seh | 500 | **quinientos** | kee-*nyehn*-tohs |

1,000 **mil**    meel

## DAYS OF THE WEEK

| Monday | **lunes** | (*loo*-nehss) |
| Tuesday | **martes** | (*mahr*-tehss) |
| Wednesday | **miércoles** | (*myehr*-koh-lehs) |

| | | |
|---|---|---|
| Thursday | **jueves** | (*wheh*-behss) |
| Friday | **viernes** | (*byehr*-nehss) |
| Saturday | **sábado** | (*sah*-bah-doh) |
| Sunday | **domingo** | (doh-*meen*-goh) |

## 2 More Useful Phrases

| English | Spanish | Pronunciation |
|---|---|---|
| Do you speak English? | **¿Habla usted inglés?** | *ah*-blah oo-*sted* een-*glehss* |
| Is there anyone here who speaks English? | **¿Hay alguien aquí que hable inglés?** | eye *ahl*-gyehn ah-*key* keh *ah*-bleh een-*glehss* |
| I speak a little Spanish. | **Hablo un poco de español.** | *ah*-bloh oon *poh*-koh deh ehss-pah-*nyol* |
| I don't understand Spanish very well. | **No (lo) entiendo muy bien el español.** | noh (loh) ehn-*tyehn*-do mwee byehn el ehss-pah-*nyol* |
| The meal is good. | **Me gusta la comida.** | meh *goo*-stah lah koh-*mee*-dah |
| What time is it? | **¿Qué hora es?** | keh *oh*-rah ehss |
| May I see your menu? | **¿Puedo ver el menú (la carta)?** | *pweh*-doh vehr el meh-*noo* (lah *car*-tah) |
| The check, please. | **La cuenta, por favor.** | lah *kwehn*-tah, pohr fah-*vor* |
| What do I owe you? | **¿Cuánto le debo?** | *kwahn*-toh leh *deh*-boh |
| What did you say? | **¿Cómo? (colloquial expression for American "Eh?")** | *koh*-moh? |
| I want (to see) . . . | **Quiero (ver) . . .** | *kyehr*-oh (vehr) |
| a room | **un cuarto or una habitación** | oon *kwar*-toh, *oon*-nah ah-bee-tah-*seown* |
| for two persons | **para dos personas** | *pah*-rah dohss pehr-*soh*-nahs |
| with (without) bathroom | **con (sin) baño** | kohn (seen) *bah*-nyoh |
| We are staying here only . . . | **Nos quedamos aquí solamente . . .** | nohs keh-*dahm*-ohss ah-*key* sohl-ah-*mehn*-teh |
| one night | **una noche** | *oon*-ah *noh*-cheh |
| one week | **una semana** | *oon*-ah seh-*mahn*-ah |
| We are leaving . . . | **Partimos (Salimos) . . .** | pahr-*tee*-mohss (sah-*lee*-mohss) |
| tomorrow | **mañana** | mah-*nya*-nah |
| Do you accept . . . ? | **¿Acepta usted . . . ?** | ah-*sehp*-tah oo-*sted* |
| traveler's checks? | **cheques de viajero?** | *cheh*-kehs deh byah-*heh*-ro |

## 3 Some Typically Cuban Words & Phrases

**Ahí Namá**   There it is, that's it!

**Babalao**   Afro-Cuban religious priest

**Bachata**   Party, hanging out

**Bárbaro**   Great, fabulous

**Bodega**   Store

**Bohío**   Traditional, palm-thatched rural or indigenous dwelling

**CADECA**   Acronym for *casa de cambio* (currency exchange office)

**Camello**   Flatbed truck-bus hybrid

**Casa particular**   A private home with rooms for rent

**Chama**   Child

**Chévere**   Cool, excellent

**Cirilo**   Yes or yeah

**Coche**   Horse-drawn carriage

**Cola**   Line or queue

**Compañero/compañera**   Literally, "partner," most common form of an address, as opposed to *señor* or *señora,* which are almost never used

**Compay**   Friend

**Coppelia**   National ice-cream chain, almost synonymous with ice cream

**Diga**   Literally, "speak"; this is a very common phone greeting

**Divisa**   U.S. dollar

**Fanoso**   Cheapskate

**Fruta bomba**   Papaya

**Fula**   U.S. dollar (slang)

**Guagua**   Bus

**Guajiro/Guajira**   Peasant or farmer

**Guarachar**   To hang out or party

**Guayabera**   Loose embroidered-and-pleated men's shirt

**Hacer botella**   To hitchhike

**Jinetero/jinetera**   Literally, "jockey"; used to refer to anyone hustling a foreigner for money

**Orishá**   Santería deity

**Paladar**   Private home restaurant

**Paradero**   Train station

**Por nada**   You're welcome

**Puro**   Cuban cigar

**¿Qué bolá?**   "What's going on?" (slang)

**Santero**   Afro-Cuban Santería religious priests

**Yuma**   Street slang for the United States of America

**Zafra**   Sugar-cane harvest

# Index